Correction Symbols

W9-BYZ-958

Ab	Abbreviation, 530
Adj	Adjective Form, 497–498
Adv	Adverb Form, 501
Agr	Problem in Agreement, 520–526
Amb	Ambiguous Reference, 520–521
Aud	Audience Not Taken into Account, 9–12
Ap	Apostrophe Problem, 535–537
Art	Articles, 503–504
Awk	Awkward Construction
Cap	Use Capital Letter, 495; 530
Case	Error in Case, 494–497
Coh	Cohesion Problem, 416–426
Col	Colloquialism, 546–565
Conj	Conjunction, 392; 502–503
CS	Comma Splice, 517
D	Diction, Word Choice, 374–380
Det	Needs More Detail, 92–93; 119–121
Dev	No Clear Principle of Development, Chapters 4 and 5
DM	Dangling Modifier, 387–389; 527–529
Emph	Weak Sentence Emphasis, chapter 13
Exac	Exactness Problem, 374–380
Fig	Inappropriate Figure of Speech, Chapter 12
Frag	Sentence Fragment, 405–406
Gr	Grammar Error, 494–540
Hyph	Inappropriate Hyphenation, 538; 542
Ital	Italicize (Underline), 495
LC	Use Lower Case, 495
Log	Error in Logic, 167–193
MM	Misplaced Modifier, 526–529
Noun	Noun Forms, 494–497
Num	Wrong Form of Number
OM	Something Is Omitted
P	Punctuation Error, 530–538
¶	Need Paragraph Break, 413–438
no ¶	No Paragraph Break, 413–438

//	Error in Parallelism, 396–399
Pass	Weak Passive Voice, 510–512
Pl	Plural Needed or Inappropriate, 542–543
Prep	Preposition, 501–502
Pron	Inappropriate Pronoun Form, 496–497
Ref	No Referent for Pronoun, 520–521
Rep	Unnecessary Repetition, 467–477
Run	Run-on Sentence, 406–407; 517–518
Sp	Spelling Error, 540–546
Sub	Faulty Subordination, 386–387; 501; 505; 526–529
T	Tense Shift or Problem, 512
Tone	Inappropriate Tone, 348–353
TR	Need Transition, 429; 535
Use	Usage Problem, 546–565
Var	Need Sentence Variety, 408–412
Vb	Wrong Verb Form, 498–500; 510–515
Wdy	Wordy, 52–69; 355–358
WW	Wrong Word, 546–565
'	Apostrophe, 535–537
[ ]	Brackets, 537–538
⊄	Close Up Space,
:	Colon, 533–534
;	Semicolon, 533–534
,	Comma, 534; 535
no ,	Omit Comma, 534; 535
—	Dash, 538
. . .	Ellipsis, 539
( )	Parentheses, 537–538
.	Period, 530–531
#	Space Needed
୭	Delete
X	Obvious Mistake
∧	Obvious Omission
∩	Transpose
?	Unclear

Writing As Thinking

Writing As Thinking

Lee A. Jacobus

University of Connecticut

Macmillan Publishing Company

NEW YORK

Macmillan Publishing Company
866 Third Avenue, New York, New York 10022

Library of Congress Cataloging-in-Publication Data

Jacobus, Lee A.
  Writing as thinking.

  Includes index.
  1. English language—Rhetoric.   I. Title.
PE1408.J27   1989   808'.042   88-8860
ISBN 0-02-360160-4

Printing: 1 2 3 4 5 6 7   Year: 9 0 1 2 3 4 5

CREDITS

P. 9: Fred R. Pfister and Joanne F. Petrick, "A Heuristic Model for Creating a Writer's Audience," *College Composition and Communication*, May 1980, pp. 213–220. © 1980. Reprinted with permission of the publisher and the authors.

P. 30: Ruth Mertens Galvin, "Control of Dreams May Be Possible for a Resolute Few," *Smithsonian*, August 1982, p. 101. By permission of the publisher.

P. 38: Ray Bradbury, from Marilee Zdenek, *The Right Brain Experience*, New York: McGraw-Hill, 1983, pp. 76–77. By permission of the publisher.

P. 39: I. B. Melchior, from Marilee Zdenek, *The Right Brain Experience*, New York: McGraw-Hill, 1983, p. 94. By permission of the publisher.

P. 77: Frank Beaver, "Cinematic Time and Space," *Dictionary of Film Terms*, New York: McGraw-Hill, 1983, pp. 54–55. By permission of the publisher.

P. 86: D. H. Lawrence, excerpt from *Phoenix*, copyright 1936 by Frieda Lawrence, copyright renewed © 1964 by the Estate of the late Frieda Lawrence Ravagli. All rights reserved. Reprinted by permission of Viking Penguin, Inc.

P. 92: Edmund Wilson, "The Old Stone House," from *Upstate—Records and Recollections of Northern New York*, © 1971 by Edmund Wilson. Originally appeared in *The New Yorker*. Reprinted by permission of Farrar, Straus and Giroux, Inc.

P. 93: Edward Hoagland, excerpt from *The Edward Hoagland Reader*, New York: Random House, 1973. Reprinted by permission of the publisher.

Pp. 95–97: Russell Baker, "The Flag," from *Esquire Magazine*, December 1975. Reprinted by permission of Don Congdon. Copyright 1975 by Russell Baker.

Pp. 100–101: Nathan Glazer, "Compensating Groups for Past Wrongs," from *Affirmative Discrimination: Ethnic Inequality and Public Policy*, by Nathan Glazer, copyright © 1975 by Nathan Glazer. Reprinted by permission of Basic Books, Inc., Publishers.

P. 104: James Baldwin, "Fifth Avenue Uptown: A Letter from Harlem by James Baldwin," copyright © 1960 by James Baldwin. From *Nobody Knows My Name*. Reprinted by permission of Doubleday, a division of Bantam, Doubleday, Dell Publishing Group, Inc.

Pp. 116–117: Jane Kramer, from *The Last Cowboy*, Harper & Row Publishers, 1977. Reprinted by permission of the author.

Pp. 119–120: Selection from "Travels in Georgia," from *Pieces of the Frame* by John McPhee, copyright © 1973, 1975 by John McPhee. Originally appeared in *The New Yorker*. Reprinted by permission of Farrar, Straus and Giroux, Inc.

PREFACE

THEORY AND PRACTICE

This book has developed from thirty years of writing and teaching writing, and from a commitment to certain basic principles of classical rhetoric. Modern theories of discourse and composition process have helped us understand how to adapt these principles to contemporary purposes. My own teaching has ranged from junior high school to executives in modern industry, along with developmental writers, freshmen, upperclassmen, and doctoral students. That experience has helped me find ways in which rhetorical theories can not only help writers discover their subjects, but think, plan, revise, and present their work in a manner that will promote communication and acceptance.

PROCESS AND PRODUCT

Our contemporary shift in emphasis from the finished piece of work to an examination of the processes by which that work is realized has changed the way we teach writing. We have opened up the "game" so that people can examine and experiment with the principles of each stage of thought, planning, and execution.

Emphasis on process has not necessarily atomized instruction in writing: it has helped writers understand better what kinds of thought and inquiry will yield useful results at a given stage of the process. As this book insists, the processes of writing are constantly repeating themselves. Invention, planning, revision, and editing are taking place all the time, at virtually any stage of the act of writing. One thinks before writing, while writing, and afterward, while reading what has been written. Every review of each stage of a piece of writing implies the possibility of growth and change.

The product, the piece of writing that finally leaves the writer's hand and is given to a reader, is obviously of importance. Readers are more concerned with product than they are with the prewriting, the planning, and the strategies that go into an article, study, report, or essay. This book tries to be pragmatic about what people do when they write and what they produce from the act of writing.

Here the product is treated as dynamic, in motion, capable of improvement. As Paul Valéry said in a different context, a piece of writing is never finished—it is abandoned. Many students assume that minor tinkering constitutes revision, that typing a version that existed first in ballpoint pen or pencil means rewriting. The reluctance writers have about rewriting (when they understand what it is) stems from a product-bound view of writing. Revising, rewriting, and the final polish of editing are natural processes. Revision, for the writer, is a synonym for opportunity.

THE STRUCTURE OF THE BOOK

The five parts of this book correspond to the parts of classical rhetoric: invention, organization, style, memory, and presentation. The first two parts are interactive, and the book stresses this point by making constant use of the means of development not only to organize segments of a piece of writing, but also to develop ideas in the first place.

The interaction of the means of development with invention and organization reminds us that the act of writing, like that of thinking and reflecting, involves numerous recursive patterns and recursive moments. A writer can develop a thought by depending upon an analysis of circumstance or cause and effect. Likewise, a writer can devote a segment of an essay—a group of three or five paragraphs, possibly several pages, to a discussion of circumstance or cause and effect. Seeing the way in which invention can feed organization is central to what this book tries to achieve in developing the thinking of the writer.

Invention: Beginning the Processes of Writing _____

Chapter 1, "Prewriting: The Writer's Situation," establishes the writer's situation in terms of the audience, the writer, the subject, and the writer's purposes. The consideration given these fundamental elements is for some writers a measure of the kind of thought they are willing to give the process of writing. The problems of the writer's egocentricity and the writer's relationship to an audience that will respond to the written word are largely those of awareness and reflection. The subject of a piece of writing is qualified by many things. Among them is the question of whether the subject is chosen freely by the writer, or part of a work-related situation. The writer's purposes can be manifold, although they can usually be reduced to one overriding purpose. The clarity with which that is understood may qualify the success of the entire venture. The Writer's Workshops, which are common to every chapter in the book, encourage mastery of the concepts in each chapter.

Chapter 2, "Prewriting: First Stage of the Writing Process," focuses on the gathering of material for writing, with suggestions and examples for keeping a writer's journal. The role of the subconscious in composing is discussed and developed, drawing on the experience of working writers. All methods of free associating assume the subconscious is an essentially creative side of our nature. Brainstorming, clustering, free writing, and relaxation relate to the intervention of the subconscious in the writing processes. Based on my own experience, as well as the work of contemporary theorists, I have suggested a few methods that can help many apprentice writers develop ideas and possibly even encourage inspiration.

Chapter 3, "Writing and Rewriting: From Thesis to Draft," shows how treating a thesis as a dynamic, changing concept can help shape the earliest stages of writing. The concept of the dynamic thesis is especially aimed at avoiding the thesis-bound, product-centered approach that can sometimes develop when a writer is working with a limited understanding of how a thesis can be useful in the early stages of problem solving in writing. The chapter emphasizes revision, outlining, and re-outlining. It also encourages the shared experience of peer editing and collaborative discussions. Some novel suggestions for various forms of outlining and for avoiding tinkering in the revision stages are offered here, along with suggestions for outlining each draft. Some considerations of the advantages of writing on a word processor are taken into account, with a special consideration of the application of the computer to the structure of rhetoric. The concept of maintaining a dynamic of thinking and writing is the focus of this chapter.

Chapters 4 and 5, "Means of Development, Parts I and II," are central to the book. They treat eight means of development: definition, comparison and contrast, cause and effect, possibility and circumstance, description, illustration by example, classification, and analysis. These are illustrated from writings of students and professionals, and the emphasis of the chapters is on the ways in which these means of development aid in the early stages of invention. The means of development generate ideas and act as self-instructional tools for the writer. The principles in these chapters can be applied to organizational problems, but they are of first importance in the early stages of writing. They form the bridge that carries writers from invention to drafting and organization.

Organization

Part II, "Organizational Principles," focuses on the structural demands of specific forms of writing. The means of development figure in each chapter in this part, with an emphasis on those which have a special relevance for certain kinds of writing and certain organizational demands. Therefore, Chapter 6, "Narrative Writing," emphasizes journal keeping, the use of brainstorming and free writing to help sharpen a sense of detail and description. But it also shows how special considerations of chronology, anecdote, and attention to character, setting, point of view, and dramatic action contribute both to the problems of invention and organization of the narrative.

The use of the means of development in Chapter 7, "Informative Writing," is demonstrated to be of value for discovering ideas, developing them, and for organizing them. Definition, comparison, cause and effect, and possibility are all shown to be useful in the process of writing informative pieces. The chapter ends with a discussion of process analysis and the way in which it contributes to the structure of informative writing.

Chapter 8, "Argument," includes materials a thoughtful writer needs to analyze and construct a useful argument. Special problems of invention and organization are involved in writing an argumentative piece. Brainstorming, clustering, and free associating all have their role in the early stages of argument. Knowing one's audience is essential to the construction of a good argument. Certainly as important is the establishment of the writer's purpose, a point that is interpreted carefully in the early stages of the chapter. Analysis of the use of premises, induction and deduction, and the rebuttal of arguments all figure here. The analysis of arguments and the resultant use of hierarchic or Nestorian order naturally follows a discussion of the ways in which the writer evaluates the various separate arguments that constitute an argumentative piece.

This book treats the premise as the basis of argument and discusses the analysis of premises in considerable detail. The valuable methods of Stephen Toulmin, in the establishment of the moments of data, claim, and warrant, are also discussed thoroughly. These are as important for invention as for organization, as the chapter establishes. Not only are there many illustrations to analyze, but there are also many opportunities in the Writer's Workshops for the student to explore the principles developed in this chapter.

Chapter 9, "Literary Analysis," shows how to use annotating and careful reading as an aid to invention. The means of development are central to writing about literature, and the chapter reviews the usefulness of comparison, description, cause and effect, illustration by example, and analytic techniques. Establishing the relative value of one's arguments is important here. Special to the chapter are ideas developed as a result of considering questions of genre. The critical theories supporting this chapter are derived from a values-based aesthetic that regards familiar elements of form from a contemporary point of view. The methods of reader response criticism, which involve the reader in a very active fashion, are detailed in this chapter and can help form the basis of writing about literature.

Chapter 10, "The Research Paper," begins by encouraging the writer to choose a subject that is of personal importance, something that he or she has often wanted to know something about, but which has been elusive. Or, barring that possibility, it urges the writer to connect with studies in academic areas other than English. The subject of John Brown's raid on Harper's Ferry is reviewed in terms of several of the means of development to show how they function as instruments of invention. Various approaches to research are discussed, with some examples. Computer searches, computer online catalogs, and databases are also treated in enough detail as to be useful to the general researcher. Bibliography, with the latest MLA and APA styles, conventions of citation, and techniques of note-taking are all explained with illustrations. The use of the library, computer searches, keeping notes—all of these are treated in detail. Organizational questions follow a consideration of how the researcher establishes a thesis and follows that with subordinate theses. A sample student research paper on the Holy Shroud of Turin ends the chapter.

Chapter 11, "Writing for Business," reviews the role of a business audience for one's work, then concentrates on some of the special forms of business writing: the résumé, the letter of application, the interview, and specialized varieties of business letters, such as the cover letter, the letter of inquiry, and the letter of response. The question of boilerplating, especially in the age of computers, is also discussed with examples. Instruction in memo writing ends the chapter.

Style: The Art of Revision

The third part of the book is about style. This is traditionally an advanced consideration in rhetoric. These chapters may certainly be called into use in an earlier place in a study of writing, but they do imply some awareness of invention and organization.

Chapter 12, "Style: Words and Figures of Speech," focuses on diction: word choice and figures of speech. The way word choices affect tone, and the varieties of tone available in the plain style follows, with detailed discussions of the uses of imagery and metaphor. Metaphor is treated as a mode of thought, not as a decoration. This chapter establishes that tropes are not ornamental but that they involve a way of thinking and have a generative force of their own. The chapter ends with a discussion of denotation and the judgmental character of connotative prose.

Chapter 13, "Style: A Rhetoric of the Sentence," treats some of the problems of sentence grammar as a basis for a discussion of rhetorical choices of sentence structure. The parts of the sentence are illustrated. The uses of parallelism, accumulation, and periodicity are illustrated by numerous writers, including students. Revision and editing of sentences, with a focus on some recurring problems, show how the principles of the chapter can be put to use in various stages of writing.

The paragraph is the subject of Chapter 14, "Style: A Rhetoric of the Paragraph." After a review of the history and theory of the paragraph, I make a few commonsense suggestions, including the use of the topic sentence, some ideas on achieving coherence, and ways to put the means of development to work on the paragraph level. The paragraph zone is a concept that recognizes current practice: breaking one paragraph up into several sections that visually resemble numerous paragraphs. The topic sentence and its development may, for purposes of easing the look of a column or page, occupy several separable blocks.

And although many professional writers do not seem to use topic sentences in many of their paragraphs, the usefulness of this technique for the apprentice writer is illustrated in the work of a modern historian. In the case of Robert Gottfried, a succession of topic sentences constitutes a form of outline. Several methods of paragraph development are explored, including the use of the question/answer technique. The chapter ends with an examination of the special functions assigned to opening and concluding paragraphs.

The part on style ends with Chapter 15, "Style: Imitating Accomplished Writers." This is an advanced approach involving the close analysis of well-written passages. The analysis depends on an understanding of the structure of sentences, and it involves imitation at a level that lies below the surface. The imitation of the structure of paragraphs follows, and once the deeper structure can be imitated, I suggest an examination of the surface features of style of certain writers. This is a challenging series of exercises, but many student efforts have been startling—to them as well as to their peers. The origin of this chapter lies in work with developmental students in a special program at the University of Connecticut. Its effect on students at any level has been surprising.

Memory

For the ancients, memory was the section of rhetoric devoted to the skills needed to commit the main points of a speech to memory. Today these techniques are better suited for helping writers make their writing more memorable. Structures of repetition, methods of concatenation of thought and expression, as well as the use of aphorism help fix expressions and thoughts in our mind. The aphorism has traditionally been a very powerful device in writing, but its very power and convincing qualities have made it seem unachievable by the apprentice writer. Chapter 16, "Memory: Being Memorable," offers some techniques to help writers construct aphoristic statements and use them well.

Presentation: A Modern Writer's Stylebook

The last part of rhetoric concerns the final presentation of the written work. Chapter 17, "A Modern Writer's Stylebook," includes important information on grammar, including common writing problems, spelling, usage, and, finally, the presentation of the manuscript. These are all specific issues that relate to the appearance of the work, and although the section is meant to be consulted at any of the stages of writing, it contributes directly to the final stages of writing.

Ancillary Material

In addition to the book itself, several supplements are available. The Instructor's Manual contains suggestions for classroom assignments based upon my experience with using the text over a period of five semesters with various level students. Its intent is to convey some important pointers on what works well under what conditions. With the help of Mia Mussolino, I have also prepared brief selected bibliographies in each of the key areas covered by the text. Judith Davis Miller of Sacred Heart University, who also class-tested the text, prepared the test bank. It is available in two forms: printed and on computer disk (in a format made available by Microtext ©, which affords the instructor considerable flexibility in composing tests). The tests are entirely devoted to material covered in Part V, "Presentation." I have also prepared a set of overhead transparencies which will help illustrate certain important points of editing and revision as well as demonstrating some basic principles of organization. Finally, an online handbook is available for those whose students are composing on a computer. The handbook is memory-resident and can be used with any popular word processor. The material in it comes from "A Modern Writer's Stylebook," Chapter 17.

ACKNOWLEDGMENTS

A book of this kind is indebted to scholars, editors, and students. First, I owe everything to the giants of rhetoric, beginning with Plato, and including Aristotle, Cicero, Quintilian, and a number of anonymous authors. The Renaissance produced a number of skilled rhetoricians and some theorists. I learned greatly from Thomas Wilson, Peter Ramus, Abraham Fraunce, Henry Peacham, Sir Philip Sidney, John Donne, John Milton and their critics, such as Wilbur Samuel Howells, William Ong, P. Albert Duhamel, and Thomas Sloane. My own teachers, Israel J. Kapstein, Randall Stewart, A. D. Van Nostrand, and Edwin Honig were especially helpful in showing me what the art of writing could be. More recently, I have learned and continue to learn from contemporary teachers and scholars of rhetoric, such as Edward Corbett, James Kinneavy, E. D. Hirsh, Nancy Sommers, Linda Flower, Donald Murray, Maxine Hairston, Frank D'Angelo, W. Ross Winterowd, Richard Lanham, Ken Macrorie, James Moffett, Peter Elbow, Janet Emig, and many more whose work appears in the journals and conferences that keep us all alert and informed. My editor, Eben Ludlow, has been a steady, experienced guide. Aliza Greenblatt has patiently guided the manuscript through production and has been enormously helpful. My students have been unerring in their responses, both in terms of their critique of the text and in terms of their performance as writers. Those who have gone on to become professional writers and teachers have sent their books, essays, and other materials for me to enjoy. Sometimes I have chanced upon them, and I have been delighted to see what they have done.

Among those who reviewed the manuscript, I want to thank the following people: Lucien L. Agosta, California State University, Sacramento; Deborah C. Andrews, University of Delaware; Bruce Avery, University of California, Santa Clara; Bonnie Braendlin, Florida State University; Pauline Buss, William Rainey Harper College; Marilyn M. Cooper, Michigan Technological University; William Coyle, Florida Atlantic University; George Haich, Georgia State University; David A. Jolliffe, University of Illinois at Chicago; Eileen T. Lundy, The University of Texas at San Antonio; Mary E. McGann, Rhode Island College; Elizabeth Metzger, University of South Florida; Judith Davis Miller, Sacred Heart University; Ronald D. Morrison, University of Kansas; Patricia Y. Murray, De Paul University; John C. Shafer, Humboldt State University; David E. Stacey, University of Louisville; Linda Stanley, Queensborough Community College, CUNY; and Richard Young, Carnegie Mellon University. I would also like to thank Joseph Zwier and Jacqueline McCurry for their help with permissions. My colleagues William Sheidley, A. Harris Fairbanks, Michael Meyer, and Feenie Ziner were generous in their support of the book and helpful in discussing some of its details.

Finally, thanks to the students who graciously permitted me to include their work in this book. Their enthusiasm for this project was especially sustaining to me through every stage of writing and class-testing. *Writing As Thinking* is dedicated to them and to all of my writing students.

L.A.J.

CONTENTS

XV

11 Writing for Business   304

PART III
Style

PART IV

Memory

Writing As Thinking

PART I

Invention: Beginning the Process of Writing

Introduction _____

TRADITIONALLY, the first part of writing is called invention, a term that covers all the steps in the process of thinking up things that you will write about. Discovering what you already have within you to write about is a subtle, but fascinating process. The root of the word *education* means "to lead out from" because the theory was that students knew what was important, but had to have it drawn out by a teacher or a process. The processes that achieve this are called heuristics, another term for all those things you do that are self-educational. Mastering a few specific heuristics can make you a totally self-sufficient writer and end those periods in which you might sit staring at a blank page.

The value of thinking clearly about the four basic elements in the writer's rhetorical situation—audience, writer, subject, and purpose—is much greater than it may seem on the surface. A clear and exacting understanding of your audience will produce a thoughtful, concerned, and balanced approach to writing. It will help you sense more completely how you present yourself to your audience, and how, therefore, you appear as a writer. A good knowledge of your subject may or may not require some research. It definitely will require some reflection and consideration. The last element in the writer's rhetorical situation is the purpose for which you write. Establishing a clear sense of purpose in your writing and following through on it will make things easier for you and your audience.

Keeping a journal is among the more valuable aids to writing because it acts as a repository for ideas when they are fresh in your mind. One problem with good ideas is that they come and they go. If you do not write them down, you are almost certain to lose them. A journal, as it is kept by many writers, can also include meditations, reflections, sketches of things you might want to write, and any variety of prewriting exercises, from brainstorming to free writing. It is a storehouse of creativity.

The techniques of brainstorming, grouping into patterns, clustering, and other such approaches to stimulating the unconscious can be powerful tools for opening up unsuspected creative forces. They all aim to reach beneath the conscious mind so as to tap your deepest creative powers. Most writers report that the techniques work, and that they help them discover things they would never have otherwise observed or realized.

But as powerful as these techniques are, they can be supplemented by a method based on questioning, as for example we see in the well-known journalism questions who, when, where, why, and how. And then, we have one of the most powerful of all modern heuristics, Kenneth Burke's Pentad, which is a system of questions that centers on five key elements of any kind of event we can imagine: Act, Scene, Agent, Agency, and Purpose. Each of these elements, when thoroughly considered, can produce a great deal of useful information and ideas for examination and analysis.

The point of these techniques is that they provide you with new ideas, and offer avenues of investigation, directions for your thought, and considerations that may give you a sense of freshness and new awareness.

Once you have begun to draft your work, several new concerns begin to develop. For one thing, you will discover that your writing will eventually improve when you provide a clear statement about what you are doing. Such a statement is a thesis statement. It establishes your subject and your approach to your subject. It helps your reader understand you and focuses your thinking and your efforts.

Like many aspects of writing, thesis statements are not to be thought of as permanent. They evolve, just as your writing will evolve. You expect to write a draft that will then be developed into another version, which then may give way to a third and final version. Each draft represents an opportunity to improve your thinking and to clarify your understanding of your subject.

Outlines, which are the staple of most professional writers, should also change and evolve. It is wise to practice outlining before a first draft and after every subsequent draft to account for new ideas and thoughts. The way in which you can revise is one of the subjects of Chapter 3.

One very powerful tool of invention is the computer, whose advantages are discussed in some detail in Chapter 3. Writing on a computer helps in the act of revision probably more than any other method. It is a great help in all aspects of writing, but it is especially useful when you are thinking up ideas and want to begin outlining them.

All the ideas in Part I are designed to get you going. They represent a careful distillation of some of the most current and influential research in invention, which has been a very lively and fruitful area for some years. Some of the techniques will be more appealing to you than others. Use them and do not worry about the others. But be willing to experiment, to develop ideas, and to carry them out.

1

Prewriting: The Writer's Situation

Writing is as natural as speaking, making music, painting, sculpting, or acting. It is a personal creative expression with roots in our spontaneous needs for communicating with ourselves and others. Like other arts, there is sometimes a mystery implied in its practice, but also like other arts it is something anyone can take part in at some level. At its best, writing is the art of using language well, both in terms of thought and expression. Writers study the processes of writing in order to become more flexible, more thoughtful, more responsive to the needs of their readers, and to help ensure that they have expressed themselves well and communicated clearly.

To a large extent, the study of writing also helps demystify writing. Because writers are self-conscious and interested in talking about what they do, a great body of literature now exists about writing and its many processes. It is less concerned with the tricks of the trade than it is with maintaining the individual creativity of the writer, and therefore the best writing about writing does not set down rules. It points the way toward opportunities available to all writers and shows that some approaches to writing problems can produce solutions that respect the individuality of the writer.

Writers spend their apprenticeship studying other writers, absorbing advice about writing, and, most important of all, writing their own work. Other writers can provide inspiration and a mark of excellence. The best advice opens new avenues to the writer because it suggests approaches that are not immediately obvious, but which give the writer a direction that may be essential to writing efficiently. Many of the procedures and processes of writing, such as those that help produce good ideas, those that help develop and organize those ideas, and those that help express them in their best manner have been described and clarified in ways that help all writers. The study a writer does is rounded by the practice of writing itself. Writing makes writing easier and more satisfying.

This book provides many samples of writing from student writers and professionals, and it provides commentary on these samples to show what we can learn from them. Further, the various stages of writing are detailed and discussed in such a way as to help the apprentice writer master them by putting them to use immediately. The Writer's Workshops scattered through the book provide plenty of opportunity to experiment with the principles under discussion. The act of writing is central to the experience of learning to write well, so you will find that at every stage of the process, you will be given a chance to try out an approach to see how it works for you.

Language: Spoken and Written

Spoken and written language differ in ways that sometimes confound us. People who write very well sometimes have trouble speaking in public, and the opposite is true as well. Yet, writing developed after speaking and to some extent as a convenience to transmit the spoken word to others who had not heard it. For some time now, there has appeared to be a powerful distinction between the written and the spoken word, and its effect has been to make people uneasy when they begin to write.

Apart from the mechanical act of using a pen, typewriter, or computer to record thoughts, speech differs from writing in some subtle ways. First of all, the processes of speech are immediate, virtually unconscious. Because often no one is judging what you say, you feel freer and take more chances. You know you cannot go back to what you say early in a conversation, so you do not worry about it. You don't revise your speech except to make an instant correction or two. And, much more important, you have your audience right in front of you. If your audience starts to grow restless, you can touch a shoulder, ask what's wrong, and make important midcourse adjustments in what you are saying. You can't do that when you write.

Because your audience hears and sees you, you can modulate your voice to produce some satisfying irony, or you can imitate anger or amusement in the tone of your voice. Your hands can shape the things you describe. You can pause dramatically or you can smile in anticipation. You have a great many advantages when you are talking. One of the most important is that if your audience does not understand what you are saying, it can tell you. Then, you can try again. Have you ever noticed how often some people will say, "You understand what I mean?" Or, "Right? Am I right?" These expressions and others sometimes help speakers establish themselves in the mind of the listener. They reveal a self-consciousness in the speaker, a concern that the listener know who is talking.

SPEECH: IMMEDIATE RESPONSE

The fact that you get such immediate responses from your audience can make speaking feel very natural. But the word *immediate* has an important message. It means not only quick, but also close. Most of the time your audience is one person with whom you are close. Or it is a group—*your* group. You know them well. Knowing your audience makes the job of speaking or writing much easier. When you are asked to speak in front of a group of people whom you do not know, then your entire situation changes. You may lose some of your sense of ease.

However, even if you are nervous, you know that your audience will be there to respond almost instantly to what you say. If you amuse them, they will laugh. If you annoy them, they will show signs of hostility or restlessness. If they like what you say, they may applaud you. If you are boring them, they will fall asleep. If you watch your audience and listen for its responses, you will know how you are doing.

WRITING: DELAYED RESPONSE

One difference in writing is that you are not always sure who your audience is and whether or not it will be interested in what you write. Even worse, you won't know its response for a long time. Consider three common writing situations. First, you have to write a letter explaining that you feel you were misled by the advertising on a product, and even though it is well beyond the normal refund date, you want your money back. It will take quite a few days before you know whether your arguments were persuasive or not. Second, you are in a freshman English class and you have been asked to write a short essay on Machiavelli's "The Qualities of the Prince." You write what you think is a terrific essay, hand it in, and wait. Third, if you are very lucky when you graduate, you will have a job in which some writing is essential. You will write reports and hand them in. It may take weeks before you find out whether what you have written is useful or not. In any event, the delayed response can be annoying. It can hurt morale.

THE WRITER'S SITUATION

Like someone speaking, when you write you are in a situation that has certain demands that you can choose to respect or ignore. Many writers labor for a long time before they can see the value of observing their situation and its various aspects. The four aspects needing your greatest attention are

1. your audience
2. yourself as writer

3. your subject
4. your purpose

These are four cornerstones of writing. They represent important opportunities for you as a writer. To begin with, you address an audience of real people, readers who will respond to your work. At the same time, your writing presents to them a person—you—who has values, ideas, opinions, observations, and a personality that can please or displease them. The person you present in your writing is not always the person you want others to see. Therefore, you may have to examine what you write in order to present yourself at your best. Your subject can be something you feel passionate about, or it may be something assigned to you. Not everyone feels passionate about sales reports in a corporation, but those who write them recognize their value. Finally, you have a purpose for writing. You wish to inform, entertain, convince, or explain. Often, your purpose in writing will come first in the process (just as any one of these four aspects may come first in your mind). But first or last, each of these aspects of the writer's situation must be given full importance.

Your Audience

WRITING FOR A VISIBLE AUDIENCE

Probably the most normal situation for you is writing for a visible audience. That means it may be your peers, who might read your essay as a favor to you, hear part of it read in class, or be asked to act as peer editors to help you improve it. You may even talk to your peers in the act of reading and be able to respond with answers to their questions. Usually, their questions mean you have a writing problem that needs editing.

In addition to your peers, you will usually have a teacher whom you see in a classroom or conference. In either case, you will build up a sense of what your visible audience is like. You will learn its political leanings, what kinds of language can be offensive, possibly even what kinds might be impressive. Gradually, you will begin to develop a complex intuition about your audience. To a large extent, this will qualify everything you write.

Who Reads Your Writing?

Plato and other classical thinkers advised speakers to create a catalog of the qualities of their audiences. Are they young or old, rich or poor, well disposed toward the speaker or not, well educated or not, in high society or low? Some people still recommend this approach, but there are some serious problems with it. For example, you can only establish so many categories before such a catalog becomes unwieldy. And audiences are so complex—even an audience of one—that such a catalog is likely to do nothing but create a stereotype. That kind of stereotyping is usually called prejudice. So I cannot recommend that you follow such a procedure.

Some writers give no thought to their audience at all. Unfortunately, the common pattern among apprentice writers is to ignore the entire question. This is unfortunate because anyone who wishes to make a living from writing does so essentially by knowing precisely which audience to appeal to. Basically, all good writers develop a clear sense of audience. To a certain extent, it is a matter of good manners: think first of the needs of the other person, in this case your audience.

But apart from questions of commercial success, your first principle is to recognize that your audience deserves consideration. The most important consideration takes the form of clarity and the next takes the form of completeness. You have heard the expression, "Tell the truth, the whole truth, and nothing but the truth." That can mean telling things simply, directly, clearly, completely. Say what you mean, and provide all the detail and information necessary to understand what you say.

Peer Editing

One of the ways you learn quickly about audience needs is to listen to the questions of peer editors. One suggestion this book makes is to join with a group of two or three other people who are writing. Preferably you should be working with them in the same writing program. Your peer editors are readers whose job is to give you thoughtful responses to what you write.

Peer editors do not correct your spelling, your punctuation, or other mechanics. You need to do that in your revision phases. Peer editors ask

> *Tips: Peer Editing*
> - Peer editors provide a supportive atmosphere for discussing writing.
> - Peer editors provide positive response, not negative criticism.
> - Peer editors concentrate on making sure a piece is complete and that unnecessary material is omitted.
> - Peer editors do not worry about mechanical details of writing: those are the responsibility of the writer later on.
> - Peer editors ask helful questions and are honest about things that confuse them.
> - Peer editors can make suggestions for revision, but they never rewrite a piece.
> - Writers whose work undergoes peer editing keep track of the suggestions and questions of the peer editors.
> - Writers whose work undergoes peer editing are careful not to react defensively to questioning, but to concentrate on learning from it.

questions that relate to whether you have communicated enough to help them understand what you understand about the events you describe or the ideas you are examining. In a peer editing situation, you need to be ready to keep track of questions you have not dealt with completely. You also need to be ready to respond with questions that are useful, probing, and helpful. (See the box entitled "Tips: Peer Editing.")

Peer editing is perfect for getting you in immediate touch with your audience. You can listen carefully and learn how your writing affects someone else. Even if your peer editors are not your primary audience, you will be able to learn something from their reactions. Some possible general questions that peer editors may ask of your writing might be

Who is the most important person in your piece?
When or where does this take place?
What importance do you see in what you are writing about?
What am I supposed to take away from this piece? Why is it important to me?
What other important ideas or events should be included here for complete understanding?
What is included here that could be omitted or thinned out?

These questions are certainly very general, but they are a beginning. When you are in a peer editing situation, you will discover that your questions will be related to much more concrete details drawn from the pieces you read. But your purposes as a peer editor are to help writers be complete, communicate clearly, and avoid distracting themselves with unnecessary digressions.

What Do You Know About Your Readers?

Pfister-Petrick Audience Questionnaire
Recently, two researchers in writing developed an approach to help writers clarify their knowledge of their audience. Fred R. Pfister and Joanne F. Petrick set up a questionnaire for writers that focused on four important areas. What follows is an adaptation of their model, with questions to help guide the writer during the prewriting process.

Situation	*Questions*
Establishing the audience in its environment.	What is the audience's age, social, economic, and ethnic background?
	What is its cultural and educational background?
	What are its values? What is it most concerned with: learning, money, job, home, society, spirituality, materialism?

	What are its commonly held beliefs or prejudices?
The writer's subject in relation to the audience.	How much does the audience know about the subject?
	What is the audience's general opinion about the subject?
	If the opinion is strong, can it be changed?
	Is the opinion of the audience derived from reason, emotion, or prejudice?
	Is this the right subject for this audience?
The writer's relationship to the audience.	What is the audience's opinion of the writer? Is it positive, negative, or neutral?
	What does the writer share with the audience in terms of interests, beliefs, experiences, opinions, goals?
	What is the writer's purpose in addressing the audience?
	What is the audience's purpose in reading the writer's work? What does the audience expect?
The writer's product in relation to the audience.	Is the form of the essay (or other writing) appropriate for this audience?
	What tone should the writing take in order to communicate with the audience?
	Is the word choice and the level of formality or informality appropriate for the audience?
	Is the style at the right level of simplicity, complexity, or grace for the audience?

Many of these questions involve a simple yes/no answer, although even then some thought should go into a response. For example, determining whether or not the style is at the right level for a given audience may involve a reexamination of an essay to see whether the expectations of formality or simplicity are *really* being answered in the essay. So, coming up with a *yes* can involve plenty of rethinking and possibly some revision.

WRITING FOR AN UNSEEN AUDIENCE

When your audience is unseen, you must take the time to consider its possible qualities. What is the likelihood that your audience is of a given ethnic or social background? What is the likelihood of its having a specific level of education, or of its sharing the same background information? Is there a chance that your audience knows more about your subject than you do? Is there a chance that your audience is interested in your subject before you start? Consider each of the following categories:

- the audience in its environment
- the subject in relation to the audience
- your relation to the audience
- the form of the written word in relation to the audience and its expectations

Creating Your Audience

A common strategy for working with an unseen audience is to create it yourself. For instance, if you send a piece to your college newspaper, your beginning can establish exactly whom you wish to reach. Consider how these openings select the audience that will read each piece:

> Anyone who has a roommate who comes in at all hours, turns on the light while you're sleeping, and knocks things around while getting ready for bed will understand why I got mad as a hornet the other night.

> I couldn't even see what kind of pitch it was. The whole thing happened so fast, and I was absolutely overcome with baseball fever. My job, believe it or not, was to interview Pete Rose, Cincinnati's player-manager, the day he broke Ty Cobb's record for the most hits in a baseball career. People said it would never be done. But there it was, and I saw the bat as it swung, and watched the ball bounce into the field for a single.

> Experts in plasma physics will be excited to hear that there have been some new discoveries. Particles and quarks are on their way out.

> Have you ever wondered why some cakes rise and some fall?

> You prospective June brides will be excited to hear about the bridal fair we've got planned for the end of term in McBride Hall.

> I know you are a fictional character, and fictional characters don't really exist. But to me you are Holden Caulfield, and you will always be as real as anyone I have ever known. Holden, you are the kind of brother I always wanted to have.

These are very simple strategies to establish your audience. In the first example, you are speaking to current or past students living in a dormitory, or people who share a single-bedroom apartment. Other people may want to read what you say—you are not necessarily cutting them out. But if you know that what you describe will appeal to a specific kind of audience, then you have a very clear sense of what will work in your essay and what will not.

The second example speaks to baseball fans, and assumes that the reader will be familiar enough with the game and its record holders that the importance of Pete Rose's feat will be obvious. If this were aimed at an audience that was unsympathetic to baseball, or that did not understand the terminology, then everything would have to be expressed much differently. The third example appeals to people with some expertise in physics. The fourth assumes that the audience has had experience in baking cakes. The fifth is very explicit: it is addressed especially to women who expect to marry in June. The last is perhaps the most explicit of all: the writer has created an audience of one, Holden Caulfield from J. D. Salinger's famous novel *The Catcher in the Rye*. In that case, of course, the imagined audience will never read the essay, but those of us who do will sympathize by supplying a substitute audience. Anyone who knows Holden Caulfield will immediately become the audience that reads the piece. Those who do not know him will probably pass it by.

In every case the writer has specifically targeted an audience. After that, the job of writing is more natural, easier than it would be if no audience were imagined at all. When your audience is unseen, you can construct it. Experienced writers often invent their audience. By holding a clear imaginative construct in your mind, you transform your readers into the audience you wish them to be. You eliminate those who are not interested in your subject and instantly identify those who are. It gives your writing an edge.

Demographics and Media

Really advanced work on the writer/audience relationship has been done on a large scale in the last twenty-five years by magazines, which survive these days essentially by appealing to a specialized audience. For that reason, every magazine has done research on its readers. If you were an advertiser, *Ms. Magazine, Esquire, Atlantic, The New Yorker, Life, Time, Newsweek, Jet, Yachting, Guns and Ammo, Ski, Rolling Stone, Scientific American, Women's Day,*

Tips: Meeting Audience Needs
- Identify your audience.
- Imagine it as clearly as possible.
- Establish its environment.
- Decide how your subject relates to your audience.
- Ask whether the form you have chosen for your writing is appropriate for your audience.
- Decide whether you can create your audience with your opening passages.

Parade, National Enquirer, Playboy, Ebony, Byte, Tennis, and hundreds more could send you a report that would tell you their readers' average age, income, educational level, disposable spending money, the cars they drive, the clothes they wear, their preferred entertainment, and much more besides. They target their audience even more carefully than Pfister and Petrick recommend because it is the key to their survival. (See the box entitled "Tips: Meeting Audience Needs.")

Writer's Workshop: Your Audience

riter's orkshop

1. Select a subject of your own or choose one from the following brief list, and then write an introductory statement that will appeal to each of the kinds of audiences identified for you.

   Sample Subjects

   Hunger in Africa   Role of media in politics
   The nuclear freeze   International terrorism
   Interracial dating   Apartheid

   a. Your audience is one person whom you know and address by name.
   b. Your audience belongs to a different ethnic and cultural group from yours and may or may not be sympathetic to your views.
   c. Your audience is your teacher and your peers in your college writing course.
   d. Your audience is composed of people your age who agree with you and look to you for more information on your subject.
   e. Your audience is twenty-five years older than you on the average, and definitely disagrees with your views on your subject. But your argument might change their mind.
   f. Create your audience by your approach to the subject.

2. Select a subject from the list in Item 1, or choose a subject of your own. Your audience is your teacher and your peers. Answer all the relevant questions listed in the analysis of audience by Pfister and Petrick. After you have done so, write a first paragraph that demonstrates an understanding of your audience.

3. Assume that your audience for the paragraph you wrote in Item 2 is your classmates, but not your teacher. How would you alter it? After answering Pfister and Petrick's questions again, rewrite the paragraph.

4. Rewrite the paragraph in Item 3 for an audience of your peers that is not connected with your college, has not been to college, and does not have a background in your subject. You may want to go through Pfister and Petrick's questions again.

5. Peer editing: write an essay that will be examined by your peer group. Form small groups of three or four people. Then submit your essay to

your peers, and read their essays yourself. As a peer editor, ask the following questions:

Who is the intended audience for this piece?
As a prospective audience, am I given the intellectual respect I deserve?
Is the writer assuming too much background from me?
Has the writer satisfied my needs as the audience?
Has the writer established a clear relationship with the audience?

Yourself As Writer

Along with the job of imagining an audience comes the job of seeing yourself as others see you. When you are a writer, you present yourself to your audience. Sometimes you will disappear, as if into the wallpaper, when writing an essay for an academic class. Sometimes you will present yourself forcefully. You present yourself best when you are in control of your subject, when you recognize your audience and its interests, and when you feel you have something important to say. When you write, one of your aims is to present your confident, secure self, not your contentious, insecure, or frightened self.

THE EGOCENTERED WRITER

In the beginning, most writers are egocentric. They assume that their audience is an extension of themselves, that it knows what they know, that it thinks and speaks in the same professional jargon they use. The result is that their writing is limited to people exactly like them: it communicates to a very small audience. This form of egocentricity is caused by a failure to think of the audience and to recognize that its background and needs are different from yours. (See the box entitled "Tips: Detecting Signs of Egocentricity.")

The form it takes in apprentice writing is a little different. It is less a matter of using the jargon of a profession or trade, and more a matter of saying only part of what you mean and assuming that because you know what you mean your audience will automatically understand. Consider the following paragraph from a student essay describing an unpleasant part-time job:

The worst job I ever had was working for a supermarket. I had to get up early and be there when the first deliveries were made. Then I had to stay late and clean out the bins and put the bad food out in the dumpster in the back.

That was really awful. You could smell that dumpster for miles. It had fish and bad meat and stinky vegetables. And what was really bad was the bees that got in there in the summer because they would make it dangerous to toss something else in there. I never got stung, but a couple of the other guys did. Reshelving and bagging were other jobs I thought were pretty dumb. I used to save all my paycheck, though, and hoped that I wouldn't have to work in a supermarket later on.

James

In general, this is an adequate description of life in the bowels of a supermarket, but the writer has taken a great deal for granted. For one thing, the writer assumes we all know what a supermarket is and how it works. This is surely reasonable, but can you tell from what the writer says what his job was? Are you absolutely sure you know what a *dumpster* is? Do you have any idea how early or how late the writer had to be on the job? *Reshelving and bagging* are the only terms that give us a clear clue. However, the writer calls them *other jobs*, which makes us think at first that they are separate from his job in the supermarket. We sense they are semitechnical terms with special meaning to someone with experience working in a supermarket. The writer does not tell us where he was, how old he was, whether it was his first job or a recent job, whether he worked there for a week or for years. Of course, the writer himself knows all that information. He just forgot that we do not.

In conversation, James explained that he worked in a local supermarket in a big congested city, where the people were very demanding. Because of the problems of getting deliveries in the city, he often had to put in ten-hour days in the summer. During the school year, he worked from 6:30 A.M. to 8

Tips: Detecting Signs of Egocentricity
Being egocentered is quite normal for most of us. But in writing, it can be a problem. Some of the signs of egocentricity are

- using jargon or specialized terms.
- assuming that the writer's point of view is universally shared.
- ignoring the audience's point of view.
- assuming that the audience already knows what the writer is talking about—hence no elaboration is needed.
- not explaining things that only an audience with specialized experience could understand.
- assuming that processes appropriate to a specific situation are universally understood.
- withholding basic information that the writer takes for granted, but which could only be known by the writer or someone with the same background or experience.

TIP

o'clock, only minutes before school opened. After school, he was on the job from 3 P.M. to 6 P.M. He had this job all through middle school and high school, and he saved every one of his paychecks so that he could go to college. Finally, he mentioned that this was the only job he'd ever had, except for a few baby-sitting stints and some lawn mowing. All these were things he knew well enough, but he did not think to mention them.

BECOMING DECENTERED

In writing, you can treat egocentricity as a form of ignorance: ignoring the audience. The cure for it is to assume that you need to elaborate and explain things that you may understand well, but which an audience—who is not you—may need to know. As a writer, the path to decenteredness has as its first step the examination of assumptions. What do you assume as the writer? Are those assumptions shared by your audience?

An honest examination of assumptions is often the best means by which to increase communication with your audience. We often write with so many assumptions that we are unaware of them. Take James's experiences in the supermarket. He assumes you know that food is delivered early in the morning, but he never tells us what kind of food it is. He assumes you know that food spoils even in a supermarket, but he does not tell you how or why it does so. He even assumes you will understand that because he is male the job he does in a supermarket will probably be different from that of a female. Notice that he never mentions working the cash register or cashing checks. And these are only a few of the assumptions he thinks his audience instantly shares with him.

Writer's Workshop: Yourself As Writer

1. Experiment with some personal statements that are designed to reveal yourself to an audience. Choose one of the following writing assignments and write a paragraph about yourself:
   a. Describe a typical night out with friends in your hometown.
   b. Explain the most important elements of your favorite hobby.
   c. What was the most interesting job you have held?
   d. Which musician/performer excites you most?
   e. What do you imagine yourself doing ten years from now?
   f. Tell us about your closest friend.
   g. What values do you hold most dearly?
2. Explain one of the following procedures in a paragraph:
   a. How to read a book
   b. How to change a flat tire
   c. How to bake a cake
   d. How to give CPR (cardiopulmonary resuscitation)

    e. How to register for a new semester
    f. How to park a car
3. Peer editing: write a single paragraph, introducing yourself to your peer editing group. Respond to the following questions, which you may use yourself when you read similar paragraphs from your peers:

Is your environment clearly described?
Are your ambitions implied in the paragraph?
Are your values implied in the paragraph?
Have you assumed knowledge that your audience could not have?

4. Explain the current styles in dating in a letter to a relative. Keep track of the assumptions you make about your relative's understanding. Are they reasonable?

Your Subject

The third element in writing is your subject, loosely defined as what you are writing about. The best kind of subject is the one that forces itself upon you because you are fascinated with it. Another kind is the one that is provided for you by a class assignment or a work-related situation. Both can result in good writing, but each is different.

WHEN YOUR SUBJECT CHOOSES YOU

When you see a situation that you can no longer tolerate, and you know that a letter to the editor, a report to a supervisor, a complaint to a congressman, a plea to a judge, or an appeal to a dean or high official can make a difference, then you have a subject that has chosen you. This book is preparing you, among other things, for those moments in your life when a subject chooses you. Because when a subject chooses you it will be important, and you must be ready for it.

A letter to an editor is an example of a subject choosing itself for a writer. When you see a letter that decries terrorism and kidnapping, you see a writer who simply has had it with such goings on. Whether or not the letter can stop such behavior may not be the point. The writer may only wish to express anger and frustration. On the other hand, the writer may have conceived a plan or an approach to terrorism and kidnapping that should be given a wider audience and perhaps some consideration. This is why people write to major newspapers like the *New York Times* and the *Washington Post*. Such newspapers have the appropriate audience of high officials who can take such advice under consideration.

The same thing happens locally. In a recent issue of a university alumni magazine there was an interchange between current undergraduates. One, annoyed by the behavior of several members of a black fraternity, wrote a long letter essentially condemning the concept of a black fraternity. In response a member of that fraternity pointed out that the first writer condemned a group and a concept on the basis of very limited experience. He went on to defend the concept of a black fraternity on the basis of brotherhood, common interests, and successful sharing. The controversy raises very interesting issues. Among them is the question of whether any fraternity, which, by definition, must reject some applicants for membership, should be tolerated on a college campus. Then comes the question of whether a fraternity that selects only on racial grounds is appropriate.

Other kinds of situations provide subjects for writing. For example, if you are away from home when a relative or close friend dies or is seriously ill, you may not be able to pick up the phone and express your feelings. You may find that the only satisfactory way available to you is through a letter. If you have left a girlfriend or boyfriend behind when you went away to college, letters may be in order—many of them. This is especially true if your friend is on a junior year abroad. Likewise, if you find your funds running out faster than you expected, a carefully worded letter home may help save the day. In all these cases you will know your audience intimately and can present yourself in your best light as a writer.

Satisfying Your Needs As a Writer

When you feel moved enough to write, you want to be assured that you are up to the task. Therefore, it is important to consider the stance you take as a writer, the expectations your audience has of you, and the expectations you have of your audience. You have to decide whether or not you have decentered yourself enough so that you communicate fully and have considered your audience's needs. Then, you must go on to clarify your subject, to develop your points regarding it, and to draw whatever conclusions follow from your presentation. Your subject needs to be stated carefully and established in an appropriate context. Then, your views on it must be presented clearly. Most of this book is about that process.

WHEN YOUR SUBJECT IS CHOSEN FOR YOU

Of course, there is the alternate situation: you are busy doing your job when the boss comes in, spots you, and says, "Jones, I need a report on sales of the widget for the last quarter. Why don't you include your recommendations for how we can improve them." It is not likely that you've had this experience in your career as yet, but if you are very lucky you will. More likely you have seen a purple-inked syllabus that says something of this sort: "Read Robert Frost's 'Stopping by Woods on a Snowy Evening,' and write a short essay on Frost's use of metaphor."

This last example is an assignment. In this case, both the subject, a poem by Robert Frost, and the approach are assigned. It involves analysis and examination. Such assignments are common to most people's experience in college and secondary school.

Then, there is the more open assignment. You are given a range of choices. Write an essay on one of the following: conditions of life for the aristocrat in France before the 1789 French Revolution, conditions of life for the clergy at the same time, conditions of life for the common city dweller, or conditions of life for the rural peasant. Your approach is descriptive, explaining what the facts are, perhaps drawing a conclusion where appropriate.

Finally, you may have a totally open assignment—except for the subject. For example, it is conceivable to be asked to write on one of the following: table tennis, mass murder, modern prisons, capital punishment, blind dates. I have purposely mixed very serious and very trivial issues here because such ranges sometimes occur in an open assignment. Your job then is to find a fit between your interests and the assignment.

Satisfying Your Audience's Needs

When your subject is chosen for you, satisfying the audience's needs is of utmost importance. For example, if your assignment is to write about the use of metaphor in a poem by Robert Frost, then it is not appropriate to write about the time when you had a really neat experience on a sleigh ride through a lightly falling snow in Vermont. Nor would it be appropriate to concoct a fictional dialogue between the horse in Frost's poem and the lights in the village below. Both these approaches are useful in a creative writing course, but not in a study of literature.

Making Your Subject Appropriate

In the case in which you choose from a range of possible subjects—such as the range that included mass murder and blind dating as choices—your most important job is to choose the subject that best fits you. Aristotle once said that it is easy to be eloquent on a subject that you know a great deal about. And he is right. Chances are, you know much more about blind dating than mass murder. Unfortunately, you may be more interested in writing about mass murder because you think it is a more important subject. However, if you do, the only way you can treat the subject appropriately is to make yourself an expert in it.

Unfortunately, in a situation in which you are being given a range of subjects to choose from, all too often your writing may tend toward the trivial. This is not cause for alarm. Some trivial subjects yield fascinating, and by no means trivial, essays. Suppose you had recently been on a blind date that had ended miserably with a violent attack. In that case, the subject would

Tips: Choosing Subjects

Surveying a range of choice carefully before beginning to write will pay you rich dividends. You can simplify the process by noting the following suggestions:

- Scan the list of choices for one that has a connection with you. Have you had personal experience with the subject?
- Has a close friend or relative had experience with the subject?
- Can you describe in detail an experience related to the subject?
- Is there among the list of subjects one that you have previously studied?
- Is there among the list of subjects one that you can research conveniently?
- Do you have a friend who is expert on the subject?
- Is there a current resource in the library or at home that you can rely on?
- Is there a convenient institution (museum, collection, specialized library, or local authority) that you can visit?

truly have chosen you because of your special experience. You would have a great deal to say about it, and plenty of cause to say it. (See the box entitled "Tips: Choosing Subjects.")

Writer's Workshop: Your Subject

1. List three possible writing subjects related to your intended major in college. List two special activities you like to take part in. What possible subjects for writing are related to these activities? Use this information to list the titles of at least two possible pieces of writing that you could begin now.
2. Following is a list of assigned subjects for a one-paragraph essay. Choose one and explain how it is related to your major or your special interests.

mass transportation in the 1990s
the benefits of fast food
famine in Africa
advertising slogans
overseas trade
restrictions
the cost of health care
the interstate highway system
leisure time in the eighties

3. Write a paragraph on one of the subjects in Item 2, selected on the basis of its appropriateness to your intended major and/or your special interests.

Your Purpose

ALL WRITING HAS A PURPOSE

Writing can serve a wide variety of purposes:

persuasion
providing information
self-expression
analysis
entertainment
explaining a process
reporting the facts
interpreting the facts
demonstrating competence

Traditionally, one of the most common purposes is persuasion. You write a letter home to persuade your parents to send you some money. You write a letter to your senator to persuade him or her to vote a specific way on an important bill. You write an essay on blind dating to persuade people to look at it differently in light of your experience. Much of your writing is persuasive, which is why problems of persuasion are studied in considerable depth by writers.

Poetry satisfies the need for self-expression and artistic purpose, whereas literary criticism and other forms of detailed examination satisfy the needs of analysis. When you discuss metaphor in Robert Frost's "Stopping by Woods on a Snowy Evening," you are practicing analysis. You shape your essay by recognizing your purpose: self-expression produces a poem; analysis produces literary criticism.

When you start out to entertain a reader, you often construct a narrative with description, characterization, and chronological reporting. These are included in the overall purpose of entertaining your readers. We all know that the minute someone begins to tell a story, we become involved and interested. If we tell the story well, we achieve our purpose of entertaining our listener or reader.

Narratives can also begin with the purpose of self-expression. In a sense, you tell a story of your experience in order to express your feelings and reactions to what happened. Many autobiographies are written with the purpose of self-expression, narrating in an orderly way the events that were most important, then establishing why.

Informative writing can begin with one of several purposes: to explain a process, report the facts, interpret the facts, or even demonstrate competence. Informative writing includes gathering data, explaining its nature, and interpreting its significance so that your reader can appreciate its importance. Sometimes its most important purpose will simply be providing information.

What, for example, is the purpose of a résumé? Usually it is to provide information in the most readable, useful fashion. What is the purpose of a letter of application for a job? Usually, it is to demonstrate enough competence to land the job. A letter of inquiry may request information, inquire about certain facts, ask more information about some processes, or ask for a demonstration of competence.

Any long essay will have one major purpose guiding its design, but within the segments of the essay there may be any number of minor purposes. A section of a research paper may take as its purpose the job of providing information. Another section may describe a complex process, while yet another can gather important facts in preparation for interpreting them.

Good writing is always guided by its purpose. The clearer you are about your purpose for writing, the more likely you will be to find the right shape for it.

Purpose and Form

Most of the time the proper form for a piece of writing is obvious. If you are writing a letter to a friend, you do not turn it into an essay on methods of irrigation in Ethiopia unless you are in the Peace Corps. However, there are times when you might be tempted to turn a research paper into a personal letter, producing vague introductory comments that reveal only your opinions and impressions. Such things are more appropriate for a letter to a friend or for a page in your journal.

On the other hand, there is sometimes good reason to choose an unusual form for your writing. Martin Luther King, Jr., wrote "Letter from Birmingham Jail" as an open letter to clergymen, but he published it so that we could "read over his shoulder" and be moved by his arguments. His letter's purpose was to persuade the clergymen that he was correct and operating in the most reasonable Christian fashion. The letter, besides being persuasive, also connects with the great biblical letters of St. Paul, which therefore gives King's letter more power.

Keep in mind that one of your choices is the choice of form. In business, you find that a letter has a different form from a memo. A memo has a different form from a report, and certain reports have their own individual and distinct forms. Fortunately, businesses are set up in such a fashion that they provide models for their various forms of writing. Your purposes in

Tips: Clarifying Your Purpose
- Before you write, express your purpose in a simple statement.
- Establish your purpose for writing in the piece you write, even if you only imply your purpose.
- Review the following kinds of purposes:

  persuasion
  providing information
  self-expression
  analysis
  entertainment
  explaining a process
  reporting the facts
  interpreting the facts
  demonstrating competence
- Remember that subsections of what you write may serve subsidiary purposes.

writing will usually determine the form you choose. (See the box entitled "Tips: Clarifying Your Purpose.")

Writer's Workshop: Purpose and Form

1. Analyze a piece of prose writing. What is its subject? What is its purpose? What is its form? Answer these questions as simply as possible, using the simplest description of the subject and the best choice among possible purposes. Remember that a long piece may have one overall purpose, although its segments have distinctly different purposes.

2. Write down a subject that you feel has chosen you. Which of the following purposes would be most appropriate for this subject:

persuasion
information
entertainment
self-expression

Which of the following is the most appropriate form for a piece of writing using the subject and purpose you have chosen:

letter
essay
report
memo

poem
prose fiction

3. Write a paragraph using the decisions you made in Item 2.
4. Analyze a piece of writing you produced from another assignment in any of your courses. Establish its subject, its purpose, and its form. Is your purpose completely clear? Is your subject defined and clearly established? Is the formal nature of the piece appropriate to the audience? What revisions would you make now if you could write the piece again?
5. Which of the following purposes do you find serves most of your writing:

persuasion
information
entertainment
self-expression

6. Read the front page of your campus or local newspaper. Which purpose is most commonly served by the articles that receive most attention? Turn to the editorial page of your campus or local newspaper. Which purpose is most commonly served by the editorials? Turn to the comic pages of your campus or local newspaper. Again, which purpose is most commonly served in that section? How many purposes can you find in your newspaper? Identify each and establish what kind of subject each treats and which form the writing takes.

2

Prewriting: First Stage of the Writing Process

Prewriting concerns everything that the writer does before beginning a first draft. It includes the stages of selecting a topic, thinking about the form that might be appropriate for the writing, reflecting on the audience and yourself as a writer. But it also includes the processes of working up your material. In a sense, this part of prewriting is also writing: you jot ideas down, you keep track of their relationship, and you decide on ways you may use them.

Keeping a Journal

The first stages of writing usually begin with journal keeping. For those who write regularly, a journal keeps track of good material for later use. For the occasional writer, the journal provides inspiration and aids in recall. Some writers keep track of day-to-day events of interest, things people have said in conversation, summaries of newspaper items, notes about books and articles that will be of possible use. Often newspaper or magazine clippings and various jottings—TV programs, titles, ideas, observations, quotations—will find their way into a journal. One very powerful element in a journal can be a photograph or series of photographs, especially if you are traveling or keeping track of a specific environment or event.

If you decide to write a letter to an editor about the United Nations, your journal entries may well be focused on considerations regarding the UN. You might begin by writing down what you know about the UN, what your expectations and hopes for it are. You may want to jot down the reactions your friends had when they found out you were going to write on the UN. You may also have come across a comment on television about the UN, and jotting it down will help you later when you write. You may have come across an essay or an article in a newspaper relevant to what you want to say. In this way, the journal becomes an aid to memory and an aid to being complete.

In a journal you keep track not only of events, but of your feelings about events and their implications. Your journal is the place for your meditations on things that strike you as interesting. Suppose, for example, someone has inadvertently insulted you. What kinds of feelings did you have? If the person who did so realized his error and apologized, what kind of feelings did he seem to have? What thoughts do you have on the question of misunderstandings?

The writer never knows what is going to be important later, so the journal must include everything that has the kernel of a good idea. Personal experience, carefully detailed, is one of the most impressive resources of the writer. Personal experiences ring true and help us understand others. But for those who do not keep a journal, personal experience becomes something like a dream: it fades out of memory with hardly a trace.

When your journal is not intended to be read by anyone but you, you know who your audience is. You also know you can experiment and shape the journal any way you like. This kind of freedom is marvelous because you can try out all kinds of new ideas. Sometimes a journal is a shared piece of writing, and usually the entries are then a little more formal. That is the case in the following sample entry from a journal designed to be a record of an experience. This is from a student in a course called The Arts in England, taught in London between semesters.

A LONDON JOURNAL

Monday January 8. This morning we went to the Victoria and Albert Museum to see the Constables. First of all, I didn't know what they were, but now I am a Constable "fan." Mrs. Partridge, the docent lecturer, explained that Constable is the most widely recognized English landscape painter and that he painted many of his most famous scenes right near where he lived. His father owned a mill, so you could see why he included scenes of mills in some of his paintings. I didn't know it, but there were canals all through England then. They were like roads, and one of the paintings I liked best was "Boatbuilding at Flatford Mills." This is a large painting, probably 3 by 4 feet. It's in oils, like all his finished work. It shows a boat, in the process of being built, with a very interesting landscape, trees, bushes, and plains. This boat would have been made to be used in the canals, which is why its bottom is pretty flat, and why it is fairly long, almost cigar-shaped. We also saw "The Haywain." My sister has a big reproduction of it in her living room. It shows the white cottage that Willy Lott lived in. Apparently he knew Willy Lott when he was a child, and the story was that Willy Lott never spent more than 3 days away from home. I don't know why that's so important, but Mrs. Partridge made a point of mentioning it. I think I'll try to find out more about that. The painting has a cart—a haywain—in the middle, in a stream. Mrs. Partridge told us that the reason it's in the stream is that the iron "tire" on

the wooden wheel got very hot hitting stones in the road, and that they had to cool it down in a stream like that or it would burn the wood. One of the things I really found interesting was to see the full-size "sketches" for the finished paintings. I expected a sketch to be sketchy, but these are large, and in oil, and the surfaces are very rough in texture. I really liked them better than the finished paintings. One thing I plan to do is come back and study the small notebooks Constable used. He used to make watercolor sketches in the outdoors in his notebooks. Then he'd come into the studio and start on a full-size painting. His notebooks were like a journal, except they had pictures. I want to come back and study them some more.

Charlene

This is a special situation. The writer was learning a great deal in a very short time, and in an exotic, exciting place. As a result, her journal entry has a kind of breathlessness. Much has been left out. We do not know much about her emotional responses to the paintings, other than that she became a fan fairly quickly. But for Charlene, the details are here so that they can be developed later if she chooses to do so. If she does not choose to do so, this entry will serve to bring the experience back into her imagination.

The advantage Charlene had over most of us is that she was excited by a new experience. In your journals, you should try to learn how to treat all experience as if it were novel. And you should try to describe and bring to life the place, the people, the circumstances of all the experiences that interest you. (See the box entitled "Tips: Keeping a Journal.")

Tips: Keeping a Journal
Be sure when you begin your journal that you keep track of

- *Dates:* keep track of when you are writing, even to the point of writing the time of your entries or the time of any events you mention.
- *Places:* your home; your dorm room; houses or rooms of friends; places that were important to you in childhood; exotic places you have visited; important landscapes.
- *People:* those who are closest to you; new friends; friends from childhood; people in the news.
- *Events:* recent happenings: your personal experiences with people, such as dating, arguments, getting along with parents; experiences that have been narrated to you; events in the news; crises and your reaction to them.
- *Concepts:* ideas that strike you as significant; ideas you have trouble accepting; ideas others hold; new ideas you've encountered in college; social circumstances and the way they affect you.

Professional writers keep notebooks almost to excess. It is usually interesting to look into the journal of a good writer, such as the *Journal* of Henry David Thoreau, famous as the writer of *Walden*.

January 23, 1858. The wonderfully mild and pleasant weather continues. The ground has been bare since the 11th. . . .

A fine afternoon. There has been but little use for gloves this winter, though I have been surveying a great deal for three months. The sun, and cockcrowing, bare ground, etc., etc., remind me of March.

Standing on the bridge over the Mill Brook on the Turnpike, there being but little ice on the south side, I see several small waterbugs (*Gyrinus*) swimming about, as in the spring . . .

At Ditch Pond I hear what I suppose to be a fox barking, an exceeding husky, hoarse, and ragged note, prolonged perhaps by the echo, like a feeble puppy, or even a child endeavoring to scream, but choked with fear, yet it is on a high key. It sounds so through the wood, while I am in the hollow, that I cannot tell from which side it comes. I hear it bark forty or fifty times at least. It is a peculiar sound, quite unlike any other woodland sound that I know.

Walden, I think, begins to crack and boom first on the south side, which is first in the shade, for I hear it cracking there, though it is still in the sun around me. It is not so sonorous and like the jumping of frogs as I have heard it, but more like the cracking of crockery. It suggests the very brittlest material, as if the globe you stood on were a hollow sphere of glass and might fall to pieces on the slightest touch. Most shivering, splintery, screeching cracks these are, as if the ice were no thicker than a tumbler, though it is probably nine or ten inches. . . .

To insure health, a man's relation to Nature must come very near to a personal one; he must be conscious of a friendliness in her; when human friends fail or die, she must stand in the gap to him. I cannot conceive of any life which deserves the name, unless there is a certain tender relation to Nature. This it is which makes winter warm, and supplies society in the desert and wilderness. Unless Nature sympathizes with and speaks to us, as it were, the most fertile and blooming regions are barren and dreary. . . .

I do not see that I can live tolerably without affection for Nature. If I feel no softening toward the rocks, what do they signify?

I do not think much of that chemistry that can extract corn and potatoes out of a barren [soil], but rather of that chemistry that can extract thoughts and sentiments out of the life of a man on any soil. It is in vain to write on the seasons unless you have the seasons in you.

One delightful quality of this journal entry is its sensuousness. Thoreau sees things and reports on his sight. He sees waterbugs racing on the surface of the water. He reports on the way the sun moves around him. He hears

many sounds in the woods: the fox, the cracking of the ice, echoes. And once he has reported faithfully on his senses' observations, he then takes stock of things. At the end of the entry, he meditates on his observations and tells us that our relationship with nature must be a personal one and that he has a distinct affection for it. His final paragraph uses analogy, telling us that a landscape can not only yield a crop of corn and potatoes, but that it can yield a crop of thoughts and sentiments as well. His final observation reminds us that we must feel nature within us if we are to respond warmly to it.

Writer's Workshop: Maintaining a Journal

1. Select a notebook that is a convenient size—perhaps one you can carry with you. Date it and place your name and address in it, and begin to keep your journal. Date every entry, record where you are as you write, and begin with a careful observation of your physical circumstances and the important events of your day. Let your thoughts and your observations flow freely.

2. Once you have begun your journal, assign yourself a subject of importance to write on. Begin in your journal to meditate upon the subject. In each of your entries tell yourself something about the subject's value to you and to others. Then begin looking in newspapers and magazines for articles you can photocopy or clip out and attach to your journal pages. Be sure to consider editorial cartoons and newspaper comic strips. Watch TV for comments on your subject and jot them in your journal. Do the same for conversation. If someone is talking about your subject, jot down the basic gist of their conversation.

3. After you have kept your journal for a week or two, go back to it and write a short piece on your subject. Use as much detail from your journal as possible. Be sure to convert the material from your journal into an appropriate form for whatever purposes you have and relate it to the audience you feel is going to read the essay.

Discovering Ideas Through the Creative Unconscious

Everything discussed so far concerns your conscious mind and conscious activities. You consciously make notes as you read something interesting; you consciously write down observations, ideas, and reactions in your journal. When you sit down to write, whether with a pencil, typewriter, or word processor, you summon up conscious structures and observations. However,

writers, like all creative people, must spend a good deal of their time scouring the unconscious for ideas.

UNCONSCIOUS THOUGHT

The findings of Sigmund Freud and others have pointed toward a deep mental repository called the unconscious. It takes over when we sleep, and it controls our dreaming states. Research shows that those of us who are prevented from dreaming may go insane. Not all of us recall our dreams when we wake. In fact, relatively few persons do. The process of dreaming seems to include an amnesiac aspect that forces the dream memories to dim and fade quite rapidly. On the other hand, there is a group of people who are called lucid dreamers. They, unlike almost everyone else, can control their dreams. They learn to do so by writing down their dreams the instant they awake. Sometimes they force themselves out of deep sleep in order to do so. They report that they can actually decide how their dreams will turn out. Ruth Mehrtens Galvin writes:

Countless examples exist of scientists who made great breakthroughs during dreams and awoke with the solution to their problems. . . .

We usually forget our dreams as soon as we awaken. Even as we attempt to write down the details, they slip away. People who keep dream diaries, though, can cultivate the art of dream recall.

Probably no one spent more time recording his dreams than a 19th-century French aristocrat, Baron d'Hervey, the Marquis of Saint-Denys. Born in 1822 and educated at home, he began writing down every dream he could remember, when he was only 13 or 14. By 1841 he had filled 22 volumes. During the first month and a half of his journal, he recalled only fragments of dreams. In six months, he not only remembered dreams every night, but in about a third of them also recognized that he was dreaming and consciously directed what happened. Hervey de Saint-Denys had become a lucid dreamer.

Such intervention with unconscious processes is rare, but it shows that with practice, we can make use of our unconscious. Freud said that the unconscious is always with us, that it pops up when we least expect it. He felt that the lapses we make in everyday speech, when we say things that embarrass us, are controlled by the unconscious. We may unconsciously wish to offend someone, and despite our conscious control and conscious censorship, we blurt out a word or phrase that gives us away. Sometimes, according to Freud, we surprise ourself with such lapses because we have repressed our real feelings so deeply that we no longer know what they are. The unconscious suddenly reveals our genuine feelings to us.

Techniques for finding ideas that can go into your writing are often based on tapping the unconscious. These are techniques that help you relate one idea to another, uncovering associations and producing *leads* that push your thinking in any of several directions. Some of the methods mentioned here are systematic: you are given a procedure which, if followed, will produce results. In all cases some ideas will result, but as a writer you will always have a wide range of choice as to whether or not to use the results. In a way, these procedures represent a gathering of raw materials. Your job is to refine them and put them to use.

FREE ASSOCIATING

One way of tapping the rich creative sources of the unconscious is to say the first thing that comes into your head, then follow instantly (*without thinking about it*) with anything it relates to. What you say in reaction to the word *mother*, or *home*, or *brother* could give insight into what you really feel about what the word stands for. Free associating lulls the conscious guard of censorship. Because it gets you in touch with your deep feelings, it can provide material that really matters to you. When that happens, obviously your writing will be more important to you. It will also be more interesting to read.

Free associating stimulates creativity. Imagine for a moment that you have been asked for an editorial for your college paper and have been given three subjects to write about: drinking in your college, college housing, and food on campus. Your editor wants a brief article on one of those subjects. One student, Hector, facing this problem, chose drinking and began with a very fast period of free associating. His method was to write down a word, then add the first word that he associated with it. He worked for less than two minutes and his words looked like this:

Drinking: abuse, drunks, fights, damage, insults, dirt, cursing, parties, Saturday night, the dorm, falling down, getting sick, beer smells, kegs, tapping, froth, foam, ice, loud music, bottles, empties, cleanup, giggling, nonsense, regrets.

GROUPING INTO PATTERNS

Hector's words reveal some patterns. The patterns are words that relate to one another and create a subtopic. This method might produce many words that may be so distantly connected that they can't serve as material for the same piece. But usually patterns emerge, suggesting clearly related ideas that group together.

1	2	3	4
abuse	parties	falling down	beer smells
drunks	Saturday night	getting sick	kegs
fights	the dorm		tapping
damage			froth
insults	**5**	**6**	foam
dirt	bottles	giggling	ice
cursing	empties	nonsense	
	cleanup	regrets	

Hector has, in 120 seconds, developed an immense amount of material for the subject of drinking in college. He could see his purpose in writing as persuasive: he could be opposed to undergraduate drinking, he could favor or oppose it with reservations, or he could choose to be informative and simply be the observer of the scene. He could write an essay that takes into account each grouping of words above, beginning with a description of the Saturday night parties in the dorms, following with descriptions of tapping the kegs, serving the frothy brew, proceeding to the giggling, the nonsense, the regrets (if there are any to report), and possibly continuing with the rest of the list, all the way to the cleanup. Hector could make a powerful statement about the unpleasant aspects of drinking on his college campus just by relying on these patterns to guide him.

CLUSTERING

Gabriele Lusser Rico has pioneered a technique related to free associating and patterning. She has especially good results with it in producing poems

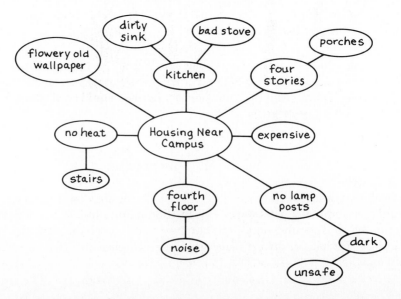

and expressive pieces. It is a visual technique that depends on beginning with a key word or statement and following the associative lines until a new line suggests itself. Its advantage is that it produces many lines of thought, most of which can be developed from the word, statement, or image that is included in each "balloon." The sample on page 32 is based upon an adaptation of her work in clustering.

One of the strengths of the clustering technique used in this fashion is that a great many concrete words show up, such as: *wallpaper, dirty sink, porches, fourth floor, no heat.* These lead you toward specific description or detailing. The more abstract terms, such as *expensive,* and *unsafe,* lead you toward making judgments. The clustering took only one minute; the following paragraph was developed in five minutes.

HOUSING NEAR CAMPUS

Our apartment is near campus, on the fourth floor of a gray building whose front seems to be entirely composed of porches, one piled on top of the other. The wallpaper is peeling in the bedrooms and even in the living room. Every room has different wallpaper, and it is all old and flowery. It crumples in your hand from age. The whole place is supposed to have heat supplied by the landlord, but in the wintertime it is cold. I don't think we got any heat at all last year. All we hear is the noise of the pipes rattling, but the heat never seems to get all the way up to our floor. My girlfriend says the kitchen is repulsive, and I suppose it is. The gas stove is mucky and looks dangerous to me. Lucy is also afraid to visit us at night because there are no streetlights. She says she feels scared having to walk home in the dark. When I told her what we are paying she complained that it was much too expensive for what we've got. She wants me to move.

Todd

Todd did not intend this paragraph to be an editorial in the paper, but simply to express some of his own feelings about a problem he faced. He did this very quickly, with a willingness to follow the ideas wherever they led him. He reported that he made a point of including all the items he had clustered just because he thought he should. But he also said he felt that he could have developed a number of ideas more fully than he did. If he had not been doing this as an exercise, he said he would have used only part of his clustering and developed it much further.

Todd also realized that he had worked up some important ideas that could have been clustered, too. For instance, he could have used the word *move* as the central word for a clustering. It would have produced interesting material for a further development of this idea. The same is true for other key words, such as *wallpaper, gas stove,* and even *girlfriend.*

This is the advantage of this method: the key word can suggest a wide range of ideas which, in some cases, can support their own clustering. It is a technique that guarantees you a rich support of ideas and suggestions. The fact that they are balanced between concrete and abstract words is very helpful for you as a writer.

BRAINSTORMING

Brainstorming was originally a cooperative venture that differs somewhat from free associating in that no effort is made to associate one word with another or one idea with another. Instead, the sky is the limit. You may introduce the craziest notion that comes into your mind. Anything goes. The point of it is to completely free up your imagination. You are invited to think up the wildest things you can. After you have a good sample then you can go back and see what looks to be of value to you. Brainstorming demands that you let everything flow because you never know in advance what can be useful to you.

Brainstorming was developed in industry to search for new solutions to a wide variety of problems. At first, it was used by a group, and people spoke in response to the suggestions of others around them. Now, however, it has proved valuable for individuals. First, you have to free yourself as much as possible. You need to avoid the internal censors that we all have, so the question of rapidity is very important. Don't stop and think. When brainstorming, simply turn thought into action. The action can be the spoken or the written word. Try both. Originally, brainstorming was spoken, but now more often it takes the form of a random list of words or phrases written down at breakneck speed.

If you find a list impractical, take a tape recorder and speak into it, then write down the words you produce. You will also find this a very exciting approach if you have formed into editorial groups, or if you have a friend who will work with you and respond to your ideas as you respond back. Brainstorming produces unexpected results, which is what makes it so valuable.

The following is a brainstorm session on the third of our subjects for an editorial, food on campus.

Food on campus
watery eggs for breakfast
they look like ostrich eggs
eggs and the physics class experiments
breaking eggs—a lot of omelets
the toast is burned almost every day
hot coffee and cold tea
dirty glasses
the food servers insult me because I complained
gleaming steel hot tables

the turtle soup, yuk!
vegetarian table, not bad stuff
burned hamburgers
spilled milk
whose cows are these?
high ceilings
spotless clean
why do we need chipped dishes?
why are the Coke machines locked on weekends?
move along, Sonny
the incredible food fight
a pea shot like a bullet into my eye
ketchup stains on my white shirt again
sugar crunching on the floor
no paper napkins
garbage and the flies outside

Some of these statements may have no place in a paragraph on the subject of the food on campus, while others can suggest interesting directions. The connection with the watery eggs for breakfast, the ostrich eggs—a wild idea here—and the experiments with dropping eggs in a physics class all developed simply because the writer let herself go and was willing to accept any idea that came to mind, however unusual. (See the box entitled "Tips: Brainstorming, Free Associating, and Clustering.")

Tips: Brainstorming, Free Associating, and Clustering
- Do not censor any ideas that occur to you.
- Write down the first thing that comes into your head.
- Follow your lines of thought as much as possible.
- Set an absolute time limit of two minutes or so, then stop.
- Review your lists of words or phrases.
- Add to them if you wish.
- Look for patterns and new ideas to work up through clustering or brainstorming.

TIP

Writer's Workshop: Free Associating, Clustering, and Brainstorming

1. Keep track of some of your dreams. Keep your journal by your bedside and write your dreams down as soon as you wake. This may take practice at first, because some people feel they cannot recall dreams. You may want to begin with memories of past dreams.
2. Practice clustering by choosing a subject you are currently working on, or choose from the following:

cigarette smoking
hunger
homeless city dwellers
the poor
the affluent
racial problems
your job plans
helping others
the U. S. president
women in politics
cancer
falling in love

3. Brainstorm a subject for an essay. Work with another person, developing words in response to each other as rapidly as possible. If you need to, keep a tape recorder going as you exchange terms. Otherwise, write the words down. Be sure to disable your internal censor by being as rapid as possible. Spend from three to five minutes in brainstorming.
4. Use the clustering technique beginning with any key word you choose. Pick one or two important words from your clustering and cluster again, using them as key words.
5. Examine your lists and write a paragraph or two based on your clustering or other associating work.

Free Writing: Talking to Yourself

Free writing, like free associating, is performed without a censor. You don't have to worry about grammar, spelling, or sentence fragments. All you need to do is get started, and then force yourself to keep going.

Write as fast as you can without lifting your pen or pencil from the page. There is no censorship, no attempt to be brilliant, no attempt to make everything accurate or right. With free writing there is no right way of doing things. Read the following brief example:

Okay. The assignment—my community—it's a funny place no, it's not really funny. it's just that what it looks like to me now and what it looked like to me when I was a kid is so different red brick railroad station. some kind of weird guys, drunks hanging out near the men's room taxis and the big round pillars. what color? I guess just concrete. the rumble of the trains overhead. How come I remember the trains? My father used to go on the trains. He took the train to work. I'd be there in the evening. Summer evenings The train would be late. Then the time I went in on a weekend. My father had to buy a commuter ticket. There was a man dying on the floor. Heart attack. What a scene. I was open-mouthed frightened. He was in so much pain. Couldn't breath. He should have relaxed. Someone should have helped him but everyone was scared. He gasped and gasped. I don't know what happened to him. Maybe I should write about that. What I did or didn't do when I had the chance. How old was I? Must have been eight. I think about eight or nine. I didn't know anything about how to help in case of emergency. Did anyone else? Life went on, though. Summer evenings, the train would be late. I'd go up on the platform, waiting, waiting. The commuters would pour off the train. My father would be there and we'd walk home, talking. It was always interesting. People coming off the train. All the fathers. Some mothers, too. Everybody looking very busy. I took the train, too   But only on vacations   Into the city   Always a new adventure. Now the place looks so small. It's rickety and old-fashioned. Not as many trains, I don't think. Buildings nearby have been leveled. Not as many people getting on and off the trains as used to. It looks scrawny. It used to have such power, such mystery. But it seems that time has taken some of it away. Or is it just me?

Tucker

In this sample, every statement is short. It is a collection of phrases, randomly produced. Nothing was held back, nothing censored. One thought helped create the next, which is the point of these kinds of exercises. Sensory memories center on the color of things, images that the writer saw, the noisy rumble of the train pulling in. Such sensory detail makes the image not only come alive for the reader, but for the writer as well. The writer is stimulated to remember more fully and more fruitfully. The place recalls the train station, which recalls evenings waiting for the father, which recalls a memorable scene of a possibly dying man, which recalls the writer's age at the time, and on and on. This might be a lively beginning for an essay, but before an essay could be constructed, the writer should look for the patterns of related ideas, then decide which are the most fruitful for development.

A number of possible essays could be developed from the following brief sample of ideas:

- What it was like to have a commuter for a father
- An eight-year-old's reaction to a heart attack
- The differences between a childhood recollection and the realities perceived a few years later
- Daily life in a busy train station
- Summer evenings at the train station

When you use the free-writing technique, be willing to follow your thoughts in any direction they seem to be going. Try to use specific sensory information: colors of things, sounds, smells, textures, any intense feelings you remember. They stimulate ideas and produce valuable associations.

1. Talk to yourself. Get several sheets of lined paper and begin by talking to yourself about the problem of writing. Tell yourself a story; recall an event in your past; express your concerns over what is on your mind at the moment. Don't worry about being accurate in your writing; let the thoughts flow. Be rapid, but don't rush too much if you find yourself developing some interesting ideas.

2. If you need a specific strategy to follow here, begin by reminding yourself of what you were thinking as you fell asleep last night. Then simply tell yourself the story of what you did during the day, beginning from the moment your feet hit the floor as you arose. Don't be afraid of digressing. Digressions are creative moments, and good writers usually allow themselves to digress in order to find out what they are really thinking about.

3. Once you are finished with your free writing, go back over it and jot down a list of ideas or recollections or events that you think might (a) make good subjects for writing or (b) be useful as elements within a piece of writing.

Putting Your Unconscious to Work

Creative people of all kinds—artists, scientists, thinkers—have long credited mysterious forces in the mind that aid them in creation. They may well be referring to the unconscious. Writers in particular have often reported that they left their work incomplete, put it in the back of their mind for incubation, and have found that when returning to work, solutions for seemingly insoluble problems have suddenly come to hand. (See the box entitled "Tips: Putting the Unconscious to Work.")

The science-fiction writer, Ray Bradbury, talks about how he engages the unconscious in his work:

I like that lovely period in the early morning when you're half-in and half-out of sleep and you're in a free-association state. Where a metaphor comes this way, and one comes that way, and they collide and make a new metaphor. And if you have enough energy, you get out of bed quickly and write it down. But that's not the regular dream state. It's the in-between, which to me is the most important. Because it's a relaxed state. And every afternoon since I was a child I take a nap. I never really go to sleep, but my mind is balanced like a feather in-between, which to me is the most important. Because it's a relaxed state. Then before I lie down I say to my subconscious, "Now, we have a little problem here, would you help me? And I'm

> *Tips: Putting the Unconscious to Work*
> Writers regularly use the approaches Bradbury and Melchior de-
> scribe. They may work for you.
>
> - Write your assignment in your journal and give it a title.
> - Consciously recite the title to yourself as you go through the day.
> - Jot notes for ideas—anything that strikes you as possibly useful.
>   Review them during breaks or while waiting for a friend.
> - Before going to bed, review your notes. Meditate on your title while
>   listening to instrumental music.
> - As you go to sleep, give yourself the task of working on your
>   assignment.
> - When you awake, review your notes and add to them. During the
>   day, start your writing. Repeat the process until you finish your
>   assignment.

going to lie down now and I'm going to turn my back and pretend you're not
even there.'' And quite often I solve problems and jump up from my nap
and run to the typewriter. And everything is answered. So that's a good
thing for people to play with.

Another writer, I. B. Melchior, uses the same system. He writes the following:

When I have no idea what to do, I "sleep" on it. If it's a tough problem, I'll
take a nap in the middle of the afternoon, but usually I do this before I go to
sleep at night. I'll think of the problem, and invariably the next day I'll realize
I dreamed the entire solution . . . many times I'll just lie down on a bed and
doze until I get the answer. I keep a pad and pen next to my bed and at night
I'll write on that without opening my eyes. . . . It's simply the fact that you
let your unconscious, or subconscious do the work.

Discovering Ideas Through Questioning

The free-associating methods described above are excellent for freeing up a
writer. They are quick, imaginative, and avoid all censorship or judgment
until later stages of writing. However, there are many other methods of
finding good ideas for writing that also work very well. They depend on a
system of questioning and usually have a set of questions established to help
as a guide. They work well because they encourage you to be interactive with
ideas. The questions act as one half of a dialogue. Your responses are the
second half.

THE JOURNALISM QUESTIONS

The most well-known group of questions that guide the writer is the one we associate with journalism:

Who?
What?
When?
Where?
Why?
How?

One virtue these questions have is that when they are answered you will have enough information to write something useful. Their original purposes are to guarantee completeness in reporting because they ask all the basic questions that a good newspaper article needs to include. But they are also valuable because they can provide any kind of writer with information that might not at the moment seem relevant, but which can be developed into something interesting.

Take as an example the usefulness of these questions when applied to one of the three subjects we have already discussed: drinking, housing, and food on campus. If after writing the paragraph he did, Todd were to consider his housing situation using these questions he would see that they expand his paragraph in interesting directions:

Who?   Todd, his roommates, and his girlfriend, Lucy
What?   An old fourth-floor apartment in a gray building.
When?   This school year.
Where?   On Elm Street in the Hill section of Providence.
Why?   Because Todd wanted to live off campus.
How?   Expensively, because he has no heat and there are no streetlamps.

In his original paragraph Todd concentrated on the second question and left most of the rest of them unanswered. If he wanted to develop his original paragraph he could easily do so by answering any of the other questions in detail.

Any one of the journalism questions could help Todd find direction, but not all of them will be of equal value. One problem with these questions is that they can be answered very quickly and very superficially, leaving the writer with the illusion that everything has been said. The best way to work with these questions is to treat them as spurs to thought. It would be good to use a clustering or free-writing approach to the simple answer you might give to one of these questions.

KENNETH BURKE'S PENTAD

In 1945, Kenneth Burke began a study of motive in literature which, as he indicates, began to get out of hand. It blossomed under his touch until it comprised the core of a theory that has now been credited with producing one of the most original of modern methods of working up ideas for writing. It is based on five terms, the Pentad, which are a shorthand for a complex pattern of questioning: Act, Scene, Agent, Agency, Purpose. These terms are as subtle and complex as the journalism questions are obvious and simple.

Here is how Burke introduces his Pentad:

What is involved, when we say what people are doing and why they are doing it? An answer to that question is the subject of this book. The book is concerned with the basic forms of thought which, in accordance with the nature of the world as all men necessarily experience it, are exemplified in the attributing of motives. These forms of thought can be embodied profoundly or trivially, truthfully or falsely. They are equally present in systematically elaborated metaphysical structures, in legal judgments, in poetry and fiction, in political and scientific works, in news and in bits of gossip offered at random.

We shall use five terms as generating principles of our investigation. They are: Act, Scene, Agent, Agency, Purpose. In a rounded statement about motives, you must have some word that names the *act* (names what took place in thought or deed), and another that names the *scene* (the background of the act, the situation in which it occurred); also, you must indicate what person or kind of person (*agent*) performed the act, what means or instruments he used (*agency*), and the *purpose*. Men may violently disagree about the purposes behind a given act, or about the character of the person who did it, or how he did it, or in what kind of situation he acted; or they may even insist upon totally different words to name the act itself. But be that as it may, any complete statement about motives will offer *some kind* of answers to these five questions: what was done (act), when or where it was done (scene), who did it (agent), how he did it (agency), and why (purpose).

When Burke says that the terms in his Pentad may be applied profoundly or trivially, he reminds us that all the methods of discovering ideas can be applied profoundly or trivially. But methods like Burke's Pentad can make an enormous difference in the writing of anyone who uses them carefully. Creative insights are what make the best writing valuable; and creative insights are produced by reflection and examination. They come from within the writer, not from without; they are the result of learning a process by which insights can be coaxed into your awareness and put to use.

Act

The world of experience exists in terms of acts and action. Burke reminds us that Act is not only colossal, like the eruption of a volcano such as Mt. Etna or Mt. St. Helens, but also more subtle, as, for instance, the conception of an idea silently within the mind of an individual. Thoughts, which to many people do not seem a form of action at all, have created more permanent change in world affairs than eruptions, floods, or other natural catastrophes.

Language itself is an act that is both a process and product of thought. When someone says something that hurts your feelings or makes you feel delighted, nothing outward seems to have happened; yet you have been seriously affected. When someone uses inflammatory language in the medium of radio, television, or the newspapers, you see the potential for language to produce action in others, but you must also see that it is an act in itself. Writing is this kind of act.

E. B. White once visited Walden Pond in Concord, Massachusetts. He had read Henry David Thoreau's *Walden*, in which the simple life, confronting basic needs, supporting spiritual values, and avoiding the complexities and distractions of modern materialism, were praised in language so eloquent it has become a model for such writing and such thought. When White visited the scene, he found that commercial enterprises had begun to cash in on Walden's fame, that the woods Thoreau had loved was now a mere park, that the tourists who threw trash in the area had either never read Thoreau or ignored the values he felt so passionate about. White wrote an essay in response to what he'd seen. It makes extraordinary use of the terms in Burke's Pentad.

He casts his piece in the form of a letter to Thoreau and begins

Miss Nims, take a letter to Henry David Thoreau. Dear Henry: I thought of you the other afternoon as I was approaching Concord doing fifty on Route 62. That is a high speed at which to hold a philosopher in one's mind, but in this century we are a nimble bunch ("Walden" in *One Man's Meat* [New York: Harper and Row, 1939].

White creates a special audience by addressing his letter to a dead author and national figure. His primary audience are those readers who know and admire Thoreau.

Burke refers to his five terms as questions, and although they are more than that, we will consider their value as part of a system of inquiry into a subject. See the box entitled "Tips: Questions for Using Act As a Means of Discovery" for some of the questions that would constitute an inquiry into Act.

After he visited Walden, E. B. White acted in language to complete the thoughts (also acts) that the visit generated. One possible result of his letter is that those people who are still living and who still care about Thoreau may become concerned enough over the desecration of a place sacred to America's spiritual development to take action to preserve it. To some extent that is exactly what happened, as visitors to Walden today can attest.

White's is an act of a literary person responding to another literary person in the form of writing. Can writing make things happen? Well, Thoreau's

Tips: Questions for Using Act As a Means of Discovery
- What action has occurred?
- What kind of act is it?
- Is it a simple or complex action?
- How many different actions can be identified?
- Which actions are most important?
- What actions are still ongoing?
- What past or future actions are relevant to the present action?
- What is the importance of the action?
- Was the action necessary?
- Was the action desirable?
- What was the result of the action? What might happen?

Walden made White go to Concord and see it in a way that he would not have seen other towns or other parks. Writing, like other acts, has consequences. It can make things happen, and the most obvious results are the growth of awareness and the capacity for change.

The acts implied in White's essay are

Thoreau visited Walden Pond in the past.

Thoreau wrote an important book about his experience.

In the present, or very recent past, E. B. White visited Walden.

E. B. White, like Thoreau, wrote about Walden; however, he included his reflections on Thoreau and his values.

E. B. White ironically compared modern styles and values with both the values Thoreau reacted against and those he held.

Among the ongoing acts observed by White were those of nature: activities of robins, flies, and frogs; activities of people: lawn mowers; trailer dwellers; litter-strewing tourists; stone-throwing, song-singing boys.

Scene

The second term in Burke's Pentad relates to the place in which the action occurs as well as the time in which it occurs. This means that Scene will include not just the physical locale, but the social circumstances, the historical circumstances, and the cultural background. The Scene, in other words, has the same potential complexity that Act has, which is why it is a key part of the Pentad. (See the box entitled "Tips: Questions for Using Scene As a Means of Discovery.")

In *Walden*, Scene is of first importance. Without the background of the physical place, with its important cultural history, its link to the New England past of transcendentalism, a quasi-religious philosophical belief in the capacity of the human soul to transcend materialism and material limitations, the essay would be of very little interest. A writer's visit to a tourist-trashed state park would not be unusual; whereas, a visit to a place, a Scene, which is

> *Tips: Questions for Using Scene As a Means of Discovery*
> - Where is the action set?
> - When is it set?
> - What are the important details of the Scene?
> - What influence has the Scene on the Action?
> - What relationship has the past of the Scene on the present of the Scene (or on its future)?

linked with the deepest spiritual aspirations of the most spiritual of Americans has profound implications for giving us insight into what America has become. The relative importance of the Scene in E. B. White's essay is clear from its very title: ''Walden,'' just as its importance was clear to Thoreau in the title of his book: *Walden.*

E. B. White's essay constantly shifts between past and present. He comments on houses that belonged to people Thoreau knew, just as he comments on details of the Scene (Thoreau's frog, his bluebottles) that he saw. But he also brings Thoreau up to date, by commenting on the route numbers that now bring the visitor to Walden, the landmarks the visitor would see, and the kinds of trash that now litter what was, in Thoreau's time, a woods. He describes a discarded popcorn wrapper, a floating shirt, a DuBarry pattern sheet, crusts in waxed paper. They all contribute toward clarifying how the present Scene differs from the past, while at the same time implying that the changes have been for the worse. The Scene literally stands for the values of the present age: garbage values.

Agent

The third term in Burke's Pentad refers to the person or persons in the Scene taking part in the Action. Traditionally, this would be the actor. The Agent is the character we watch in action. It can be an animal, a person, an insect, a natural force, such as a breeze, a tremor, a thunderclap, or any abstract doer. Fate is said to be an Agent; chance or luck might be an Agent; faith or despair can be an Agent. Yet, such Agents are abstract until identified or embodied.

All Agents, however, imply other Agents, such as those who are behind the scenes, those who might act against the primary Agent, or Agents who might be in supportive roles. Even one-actor plays imply many other Agents, some of whom are referred to, described, and qualified although they do not appear. Some Agents are apparent; others are not. (See the box entitled ''Tips: Questions for Using Agent As a Means of Discovery.'')

E. B. White is the primary Agent in his essay. Moreover, we know that he respects classic American literature and knows a good deal about what Thoreau wrote in *Walden,* so it is safe to assume that he is worthy to be reporting on the state of Walden Pond in his day, and that he is aware of what he is

> *Tips: Questions for Using Agent As a Means of Discovery*
> - Who is the primary Agent? (This question demands details of appearance, behavior, qualities.)
> - Is the primary Agent a person, animal, thing, force, or abstraction?
> - What secondary Agents are present or implied?
> - Is there a counter-Agent?
> - Are the Agents worthy, self-aware, competent?
> - Is the Agent responsible for its action?

doing and why. He constantly takes responsibility for his actions, so we are all the more convinced that he knows what his mission is.

Another Agent looms in the background of the piece: Henry David Thoreau. If you wished to, you could look him up in the *Dictionary of American Biography*, and you would learn that he was a man who grew tired of the modern world and its insistences on getting ahead, accumulating wealth, and possessing things. He was disturbed by waste and when he went to Walden Pond, he determined to live deliberately and simply, hoping that he would live life, not miss out on it by concentrating on the things that were not important. By invoking his "ghost," E. B. White was able to make some contrasts between the past and the present in terms of the changes in the American ideals.

The counter-Agents in this piece are the tourists who visit Walden Pond and the citizens who live near it. They throw stones at frogs and leave their beer bottles; they put up signs saying No Swimming, and then they swim anyway; they make state parks to commemorate important events, then they desecrate them. Finally, boys sing patriotic songs without being patriotic, or without understanding much of what America once stood for. Because they are boys, they stand for the future of America, just as Thoreau stands for the past.

Agency

An Agent must have the means to do something. Agency is the ways and means of action. Agency can be as simple as the reference to a tool: boys used a stone to silence a frog. It can be as complex as allusion to something not present: White comments on Walden Pond by alluding frequently (sometimes quoting or mimicking) Thoreau and *Walden*. Such allusions are useful for White's commentary on what he observes: they remind us of what the promise of Walden was; they help us perceive what the present reality is. (See the box entitled "Tips: Questions for Using Agency As a Means of Discovery.")

Every action must be accomplished by some means. Every Agent has an Agency, often an agency that is peculiar to the Agent. For example, writing is itself an agency for the act of expressing and communicating a sense of values. Writing is an agency that is peculiar to both Thoreau and White, and

> *Tips: Questions for Using Agency As a Means of Discovery*
> - What did the Agent use to complete his Act?
> - Was the Agency simple (one thing) or complex (several things interacting)?
> - Was the Agency concrete (a thing) or abstract (an idea or force)?
> - Was the Agency worthy of the Act or Agent?
> - Was the Agency peculiar to the Agent?

that fact helps further explain why they went to a specific place and then, in response to that act, wrote about it. Because both men were interested in some of the basic values of life and both saw themselves as contemporary Americans, both write about much the same things: living simply, facing reality, and searching for the spiritual life. They both used writing as an agency to comment critically on contemporary American life.

Purpose

The final item in Burke's Pentad is Purpose. Establishing Purpose is much like establishing the cause for something. Acts that are caused by people are the results of motive, whether of an individual or a group. Acts that are the result of natural forces, such as a tornado or a flood, are usually easy to discuss in terms of causes, but not easy to discuss in terms of purpose. Winds and waters ordinarily are not thought of as being purposive. Consequently, Purpose is most relevant to circumstances in which the Agent is a person or an animal whose motives can be interpreted. (See the box entitled "Tips: Questions for Using Purpose As a Means of Discovery.")

> *Tips: Questions for Using Purpose As a Means of Discovery*
> - Why was the Act done?
> - Is there one Purpose or several?
> - Is the Purpose expressed or implied?
> - Is the Purpose clear or confused?
> - Is the Purpose worthy?
> - Is the apparent Purpose the same as the achieved Purpose?
> - Was the Agent aware of Purpose?

E. B. White's Purpose is to tell Thoreau how things have changed at Walden Pond. However, because Thoreau is long dead, his Purpose extends to us, the readers who are living. He wants us to know that things are not good in Walden Pond, and that its present custodians are defiling it in ways that would have shocked the very person who made it important for American culture. Because it is abstract, establishing Purpose requires imaginative and perceptive analysis. Yet it is essential. Purpose will often completely qualify an act; we often talk about people who have done the right thing for the wrong reasons, or people who have done wrong things for right reasons. The way you finally understand an Act will depend upon your understanding of the Purpose that lies behind it.

USING THE PENTAD IN DISCOVERING IDEAS

The Pentad is useful when you want to tell a story about something you have done or when you want to accumulate material to use in a discussion of people, nature, or machines in action. It is a comprehensive means of producing information and making sure, as with the journalism questions, that you include all important information. It is especially good for uncovering details and guaranteeing yourself a thorough analysis of your subject.

The Pentad is more of a conscious process than those already discussed, but it can be used in conjunction with any of the techniques of association mentioned earlier. However, it is not completely limited to conscious experience. Using the Pentad begins in consciousness, but soon leads you into areas that are just as creative as those we have explored. The questions are subtle enough to open up avenues of thought you may not have realized were available to you. They actually reveal your innermost thoughts in ways that can surprise you.

Here is an example of how one person used the method to work up ideas for an essay. Jane decided she might write on the atomic bomb because there had just been a silent vigil around the lake on her campus. She began with a brainstorming session, then developed the following cluster:

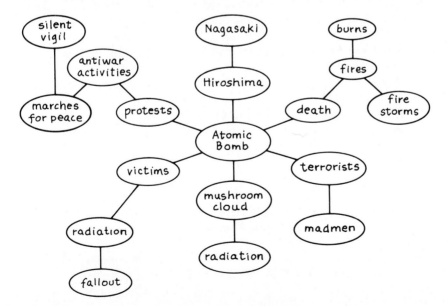

She felt that what she had so far was moving in many different directions, and she thought that she would have to choose one to help her focus her piece. She intended to write a short description of the silent vigil she took part in so that students who had not been there would know what effect it had on her. Using Burke's Pentad as her next step, she began to work up a great deal of material. Here are some samples from her responses to the questions on Act, Scene, Agent, Agency, and Purpose:

Act

- What action has occurred? A silent vigil to protest atomic bombs.
- What kind of act is it? It's a good act, an act that involves the best in people.
- Is it a simple or complex action? In some ways it is simple: we just stood around the lake with candles, but in other ways it's complex because a lot of people died and if we aren't careful many more will die as a result of atomic bombs.
- How many different actions can be identified? Basically one. We gathered at dusk and lighted our candles.
- Which actions are most important? The candles gave us a sense of warmth and belonging. I felt that I was part of something that was almost global.
- What actions are still ongoing? Peace vigils are going on all over the country. Other colleges are planning vigils.
- What past or future actions are relevant to the present action? In the past it is the use of the bomb on Japan. Who knows where it could be used in the future.
- What is the importance of the action? World survival depends on world peace. We were trying to promote world peace.
- Was the action necessary? Some people don't think so. I do.
- Was the action desirable? Of course. I don't think there is anything more desirable than world peace.
- What was the result of the action? What might happen? People became aware of their own responsibilities as citizens. If you let things go and don't take some action, then where will we end up? There have been a lot of protests, and I think leaders listen. Our leaders are talking about disarmament. That's good.

Scene

- Where is the action set? It was set on Mirror Lake, the most beautiful and probably the most public spot on campus.
- When is it set? It was set on August 6, the anniversary of the bombing of Japan.
- What are the important details of the Scene? There is an island with pine trees in the lake. There are lots of ducks that live on the lake. There

were cars passing on the road next to the lake, and they all slowed down to see what was happening. Some people who came late had their candles lighted to help them find their way.

- What influence has the Scene on the Action? The lake reflected the candles back to us so it made the whole area glow. The ducks sometimes flew over us then went off and away. It was very hot in the afternoon, but the air over the lake was cooling.
- What relationship has the past of the Scene on the present of the Scene (or on its future)? I don't know. I haven't been to any earlier vigils there. Maybe if I go again I can answer this.

Agent

- Who is the primary Agent? I suppose I am if I write about this as a personal experience.
- Is the primary Agent a person, animal, thing, force, or abstraction? A person, me.
- What secondary Agents are present or implied? Sure, there must have been two hundred other people there. Some were students, but most people were from the town, I think.
- Is there a counter-Agent? I suppose the only counter-Agent is the bomb itself. It's a pretty big counter-Agent.
- Are the Agents worthy, self-aware, competent? Very much so. There were professors there, and lots of older people as well as students.
- Is the Agent responsible for its action? I am. I think the others were, too.

Agency

- What did the Agent use to complete his Act? We used a candle and silence.
- Was the Agency simple (one thing) or complex (several things interacting)? In one sense simple—a one-candlepower light hoping to light up the world of peace. I guess the motives of some of the people would make the vigil complex. Some of the people may have been in a war, for instance. I even had a fantasy that one of the older men might even have been in the airplane that bombed Hiroshima.
- Was the Agency concrete (a thing) or abstract (an idea or force)? It was both. We were concrete, real people. But the spirit of peace is an idea. We want to make it a world force.
- Was the Agency worthy of the Act or Agent? Definitely. To burn down a building or cause damage of any kind would be like joining forces with war. A peaceful vigil for peace.
- Was the Agency peculiar to the Agent? No. I don't think so. After all, we could have had a cake sale or set up talks and workshops. We could have done lots of things. We chose to have a silent vigil.

Purpose
- Why was the Act done? To make the world know we want peace.
- Is there one Purpose or several? I guess you could say there were several. I heard one woman say she felt good being here because she thought that at least she had done one thing for peace today. Maybe there's a general purpose and a personal purpose.
- Is the Purpose expressed or implied? I don't know. Maybe implied?
- Is the Purpose clear or confused? I thought it was pretty clear.
- Is the Purpose worthy? Of course. Totally.
- Is the apparent Purpose the same as the achieved Purpose? I don't know how to answer this. I suppose yes.
- Was the Agent aware of Purpose? Yes, no question.

When Jane finished going through these questions, she had begun to reveal to herself a great deal about what she had seen and felt. She said, for instance, that after looking at her answers she realized that the visual experience of seeing all the candles ringing Mirror Lake had been, in a sense, almost religious. She realized that the other place she connected with candles was church, and she then realized that the silent vigil she took part in was like a prayer meeting.

When she wrote her piece, she focused on the religious feelings she had when she took part in the vigil. She also realized that she probably would never have gone if people had told her they were going to pray for peace down by the lake. The experience of using the Pentad and reviewing her answers altered and deepened her vision of what she was doing.

Writer's Workshop

Writer's Workshop: Burke's Pentad

1. Go through your journal to find an event that you recorded as being interesting. Be sure it is an event that you took part in. First, spend some time in brainstorming, free associating, or clustering. Then proceed question by question through the Pentad, dealing with Act, Scene, Agent, Agency, and Purpose. When you are finished, review your work and circle the answers you feel are most useful to you in a description or discussion of the event you chose. Write a piece of one or two paragraphs in length for the purpose of helping your readers (your peers) realize what importance the event had for you.

2. As an alternative to finding an event in your journal to write about, choose an event related to your studies in history, sociology, or science. Choose something that you are studying in enough depth, so that you have information and details at hand for use in an informative piece whose purpose is to let someone who has not studied this event understand its importance and scope. Use the questions designed for the Pentad. If you find that there are some important informational questions you cannot answer, be sure to review the material

you have on the event to fill in details. Write a brief discussion of two or three paragraphs.

3. Peer Editing: in an editorial group, read your piece to your peers. Set your group up so that you respond to what you have read by reviewing each member's answers to the questions for Act, Scene, Agent, Agency, and Purpose. Probe into the answers that each person gave and ask whether they are complete enough to be useful in writing. Aim to establish what kinds of answers produce the most useful material for writing. In your own use of the Pentad, keep track of how you approach each question and which questions give you the best chance to work up new material.

4. Creative Writing: use Burke's Pentad to guide you in writing a short story or a narrative poem. Use the questions for the Pentad to help you invent an Act, Scene, Agent, Agency, and Purpose. The questions should help you establish the primary action, where the action takes place, who does it, who the supporting actors are, the means they use to achieve the action, and what the purposes for the action were. If no action suggests itself to you, consider one of the following:

A young woman meets her boyfriend to tell him they are no longer going together.

Brothers return home to find that their parents are going to place their grandmother in a nursing home.

A young person finds that his or her roommate is moving out, and that there is no way he or she can pay all the rent alone.

Parents meet the new boyfriend (girlfriend).

A young man goes to his first job and finds out that his boss is an alcoholic.

Two people meet each other while working for the Red Cross Relief Agency.

5. Turn to the color plates in this book and analyze either Paul Delaroche's "Lady Jane Grey" or Berthe Morisot's "The Harbor at Lorient" in terms of the Burke Pentad. Use the questions for the Pentad to provide material for a short piece of writing, the purpose of which is to explain the action.

3
Writing and Rewriting: From Thesis to Draft

Writing is an act of discovery. Professionals often say that they would not write if they knew what they were going to say before they started. Even writers who have done brainstorming, free writing, and outlining find that writing itself produces new ideas and new insights. Sometimes it is comforting to think that many fine writers don't know quite what they are going to write until they write it.

Constant Revision and Multiple Drafts

Revision is a continuous process. It begins the minute you start writing because things rarely come out the way you want them to the first time. As you write you look back and strike a word or phrase or insert something you left out. When you reread a paragraph you find there are pieces of sentences you need to move. If you write on a computer, you find yourself making many changes, then reformatting to see what you have newly revised. Rereading almost always implies revision, particularly as you become a more experienced writer.

One aim of revision is accuracy. You want your prose to be accurate, to avoid the basic mistakes in grammar, syntax, or spelling that most of us commit at one stage or another of writing. But another aim of revision is to reflect on whether you have taken your audience carefully into your considerations. How do you present yourself? Is your subject clear? Have you remained steady in expressing your purposes as a writer? Probably the most important aim of revision is discovering the shape and form of what you want to say.

Revision is a process. It lasts as long as you write. When you give what you write to someone else, or put it away for the last time, then revision stops.

At least until you go back to the piece—if you do—another time. The revision process happens in stages, although some stages repeat themselves at several points, as follows:

During the act of writing:

1. As you think of what you are writing, and as you select and reject from among your possible choices of words and thoughts.
2. As you finish writing down a word or a phrase and go back to reconsider what you have said.

At this stage, you are mainly considering problems of wordiness, repetitiveness, and accuracy—in terms of both clear grammar and clear meaning.

After you have written a draft:

1. Immediately after you finish and have reread the entire piece: this is your first editing stage.
2. Several hours, or a day after your first re-edited draft, and as you revise in preparation for your second draft.

At this stage, you are revising for problems of spelling, punctuation, sentence accuracy (avoiding fragments and run-on sentences), and organization.

After your second draft:

1. Allow some time after you finish the draft, and possibly after having someone else read your work.

At this stage, you are revising for style, completeness, effectiveness, and clarity. You may go through several more drafts at this stage.

Unfortunately, most apprentice writers do not think this systematically about revision. Sometimes they write a draft in longhand, do some basic tinkering with the prose, then type it up for delivery. Or if they work on a computer, they tinker as they go along, changing a word here and there, a phrase here and there, tightening a sentence here or there. They almost instantly become better writers when they begin to practice the art of constant revision and multiple drafts.

Your Thesis: A Strong Beginning

Before reaching the stage of drafting and redrafting, however, you must approach the actual writing with some ideas in mind. First, you must know what it is you are writing about, and second, you must have given some thought to your audience's expectations, needs, and character. If you clearly understand your purposes for writing—persuasion, providing information, self-expression, or entertainment—you will be ready to begin to give shape and form to your writing.

One of the best ways to start is by creating a thesis statement that establishes your writing aims. The thesis statement controls the scope and focus of your writing. It tells your audience what to expect from the piece and it limits your scope, making it easier for you to know what you are doing and when you are finished. To an extent, the thesis statement is a general claim that will be made good by the specifics of the rest of your piece of writing.

Your thesis identifies your subject and what you want to say about it.

Put in a slightly different way: your thesis tells your audience what is to be argued, explained, or focused upon in your writing. It may tell your reader what your approach is, and give a hint of your conclusions. In a sense, it acts as a signpost for your writing, guiding your reader to the understanding that you provide.

FORMULATING A THESIS

Creating a strong, clear thesis before writing is not a luxury, it is a necessity. Some people can do it well, whereas others do it poorly. Those who do it well usually realize that a thesis statement is a dynamic concept, not carved in stone, not something static and forever. Just as every aspect of your writing is subject to review and revision, the thesis is capable of being redone again and again.

Many intuitive writers find a thesis to be confining and difficult. The fact is that such writers can benefit from establishing their thesis during the process of early drafting, so if you feel you are more intuitive than you are a careful planner, then look for chances to create a thesis that can guide you as you write. You may find that while you are in the act of writing, your thesis will come to you much more quickly, and more reliably, than it will before you begin.

However, no matter what kind of writer you are, discovering your thesis early in the process of writing will give you a strong beginning. Even if you end up by radically changing your thesis, you will find that having one to start with helps you get going and keeps you on the right track.

To some extent the choice of using a strong thesis statement depends on your purposes as a writer. A strong thesis statement that states the intention of a piece, qualifies its subject, and reveals your approach will produce logical and well-structured writing. Its goal is basic clarity. As a by-product it also helps you avoid dullness and meandering, qualities that are often a result of poor focus and bad planning.

A clearly formulated thesis statement is most useful when your purposes are to persuade or inform, when you will probably include your thesis statement early in whatever you write. But when your purposes are entertainment or self-expression, you have a wider latitude: you may include or not include a thesis statement as your intuition (or another reader) advises you.

You always have several choices regarding the thesis statement. For one thing, you may wish to break it into several sentences or have it self-contained in one. Further, you may chose to state your thesis plainly and openly —especially if your primary purpose is to be clear in what you are writing— or you may choose to imply it. An implied thesis is often common in an expressive piece of writing, because the end purpose of informing or persuading is often either secondary or omitted. The concept of the thesis statement should be regarded as dynamic. There is not just one kind of thesis any more than there is just one place to state it.

A Sample Thesis

A thesis usually needs defense, elaboration, example, or support and development. For that reason, the thesis is not a declarative factual statement. Rather, it is a statement that your audience might question or wonder about. It is not a self-evident truth. If it were, then there would be no need for your writing. The thesis statement not only establishes your subject, clarifies your intentions, and suggests the limits of your discussion, it also helps lead the reader into your work.

One student writing on the subject of nuclear energy had brainstormed the idea, coming up with a number of useful ideas for a beginning. She had then gone on to do some basic research. She read some current articles on the questions of safety and on the question of need for nuclear energy. Then she spoke with some people who worked in the nuclear energy plant near her hometown. Because her father worked in the plant, she had the chance to discuss certain issues over a period of several days. She saw her purpose as essentially informing her audience about the key points in the current debate about nuclear power. Her best early thesis statement was

> Although there have been some serious accidents in the nuclear industry in recent years, such as the Three-Mile Island shutdown in the U.S. and the Chernobyl meltdown in the U.S.S.R., nuclear energy is still basically safe and very necessary in order to support energy needs through the twenty-first century.

You can see that this writer devised herself certain tasks. For one thing, she wanted to talk about the recent accidents to clarify their nature and to explain their seriousness. She also went on in her essay to provide as much information as she could about the lessons that have been learned from these accidents. She wanted to clarify the risk that society takes in supporting nuclear reactors. In addition, she wanted to establish the need for nuclear power. The people she talked with were firm in their confidence in the safety of the reactors. And the reading she had done included statistics clarifying the need for a stable source of energy into the next century, when oil will become scarce.

The process this student used was to

- find her subject: nuclear energy
- decide on the basis of her research what aspects of the subject she would treat: safety and need
- establish her purpose in writing: to persuade and inform
- take a position regarding her subject: to defend nuclear energy as a safe industry

Not all thesis statements depend on research and interviews. In many cases you feel strongly enough about things so you can establish a thesis depending on your experience and your reasoning. However, the process is still the same: you find your subject, decide what is important about it and what your purpose is in view of your audience, and then establish your position.

Following are some sample thesis statements from relatively short student essays. They all have the potential of being developed into full-length pieces of writing.

Huge universities give students a poor and inadequate education.

Death is not a comfortable topic for anyone to discuss, but it is a tragic mistake to attempt to shield a child from anything, regardless of how upsetting or unpleasant the subject matter.

Children should be accurately informed of their sexuality and of the differences between the two sexes. If a child is old enough and curious enough to ask questions concerning birth, he or she is definitely old enough to receive truthful answers to the questions.

Sex role stereotypes will persist in American society despite efforts made in recent years to abolish them.

Each of these statements is flexible enough to appear at the beginning of an essay, somewhere in the first paragraph, or somewhere deeper in the piece. And each has the advantage of implying what is to follow. The first has the obligation of making a comparison between huge universities and smaller colleges. It also needs to define what *huge* means and what *getting an education* means. Then, it has the task of defending what is clearly a controversial view. The third has the obligation of establishing why it is healthy for children to face questions about sexuality at an early age.

USING THE THESIS

Linda, who provided the thesis statement about sex role stereotypes, developed her ideas in a short statement. She had had some personal experience—the "How fast do you type" kind of inquiry from a potential employer. Her aim was to investigate common kinds of stereotyping and to assess the chances of ending the practice. After doing some preliminary investigation, she felt that sex role stereotyping is here to stay—at least for a while.

Linda planned a short essay, and her audience was both teacher and classmates, because she knew her piece of writing would be distributed in class and discussed. (This is true of all the examples that follow.) The strength of her thesis statement is that, for a short essay, it focuses her attention exactly. She has the job of establishing what sex role stereotyping is, and explaining why it will survive. Here is her first paragraph:

Sex role stereotyping will persist in American society despite efforts made in recent years to abolish it. This is because the idea of correct and separate roles for males and females has been firmly built, not upon historical fact, but upon myth. And, it is characteristic of the myth that it is long-lived. This is due to the fact that myth is not based upon logic but upon desire and humans are prone to follow their desires. People believe in a myth because they want to believe in it. Thus those who believe that a woman's role is that of homemaker just as it always has been, when in fact that has never been woman's true role, are believing in a myth. They believe this because they want to believe it. The development of this myth can be seen by examining history, art, and religion. This examination will make it clear that the myth will survive and therefore so will sex role stereotypes.

Linda

Linda develops the thesis statement in several ways that give her a clear direction and a strategy for proving her thesis. Her second sentence introduces the reason for her assumption that stereotyping will survive: it is based on myth. Her next sentences explain why a basis in myth means survival. Finally, she points to the evidence of the myth in history, art, and religion. Later in the piece, Linda went on to give examples from history, art, and religion that she felt contributed to the myth of stereotyping, and she discussed the reasons why the myths are accepted.

WATCHING A THESIS GO WRONG

The previous examples are happy ones in that they help the writer shape the remainder of the piece of writing. However, a poor thesis statement can have devastating effects. When a writer is vague, unfocused, and unclear in intention, a piece of writing can appear muddled, inconclusive, and unconvincing. Take the following example. It is the beginning of an essay on schooling. Unfortunately, it confused the peer editing group that first heard it.

Children would do better in school if there were rewards for doing well. Children have no choice about school. They must go to school until they are

16. Some subjects must be taken. Whether you learn quickly or slowly, whether you try or not, all children spend the same amount of time in school.

I suggest proficiency exams for each grade in each subject. If students passed these exams early there would be substantial rewards tailored to the individual student.

Burt

This beginning has some problems. For one thing, we do not know enough specifics—we do not yet know that Burt's reaction was caused by his recent visit to his old high school. He had had a number of specific experiences, but instead of using them in the essay, he kept them in reserve—hidden. Then, there is the confusion between the first sentence of paragraph one and the first sentence of paragraph two. Burt's purpose is to persuade us that proficiency exams should be given in the school (now that he's safely out!). But he confuses this with the question of providing rewards so children would do better.

Burt's peer editors pointed out the confusion. They saw that proficiency exams would be thought of as punishments, not rewards. This surprised Burt, but he learned that his thesis did not clarify any connection between rewards and exams. All the details in the paragraphs had been omitted. In part this is because of Burt's inadequate preparation—he did no brainstorming, clustering, or free writing. He did no reading or interviewing, he had no journal entries, and he had therefore nothing concrete to say. In that condition, he was almost doomed to writing an unsatisfactory opening.

THE THESIS STATEMENT: RESTRICTING THE TOPIC

In the following example, Stanley began with what he thought was a good thesis statement: "Marriage is a difficult institution." He thought he was clear and direct. Well, in a sense he was. But he did not restrict his topic or point toward his approach. He was too broad in his claim. In a sense everything is a "difficult institution." School is a difficult institution. Divorce is a difficult institution. What Stanley did not do right away was to make his thesis statement work for him by establishing the limits of his topic or revealing his approach to the topic.

Marriage is a difficult institution. This difficulty becomes compounded when the partners are from different socioeconomic backgrounds. People who are raised to value different ideas toward economic and social matters will continue to view these things from their own standpoint once they have entered into marriage. Some kind of accordance on these issues is necessary unless one partner is to be totally subservient to the other. Although it may be possible to make adjustments, it is unlikely that one's values will change drastically. It can be shown, statistically, that marriages among people of different socioeconomic backgrounds have a higher failure rate than those from a similar one. People from different backgrounds have few things in common. Their preferences in social activity and literature might differ which would serve to create a gap in the relationship. Marriage consists of a series of shared goals which are influenced by the values that each person brings into the relationship. What becomes of these goals when the values they are derived from are incongruent?

Stanley

Stanley's failure to produce a good thesis statement has led to a classic writing error: the failure of the second sentence to have a clear reference for the pronoun *this*. You can see that Stanley thought the word *difficult* in the first sentence meant the same thing to his audience that it meant to him— clear evidence of his egocentricity. He did not think of his audience's preparation for his opening paragraph. Consequently, there is no difficulty identified or established in that first sentence for *This* to refer to. What difficulty does he mean? What has his thesis statement restricted?

Stanley's peer editors asked many questions: What is a socioeconomic group? How is it defined, and what are the chief elements that distinguish one from another? Some of his audience had personal examples of people from different socioeconomic groups who had married successfully. Some questions were raised about how and why people who are so distinct could have met and fallen in love if their values were so different. Virtually every question raised about the paragraph demonstrated the vagueness of the concept in Stanley's mind. And that vagueness began with the thesis statement. (See the box entitled "Tips: Writing a Thesis Statement.")

Tips: Writing a Thesis Statement
- Your thesis statement is dynamic: it can change.
- Your thesis statement restricts your topic.
- Your thesis statement reveals some of your conclusions and your approach to your topic.
- Your thesis statement reflects your analysis of your audience.
- Your thesis should be designed to give you a clear direction for your writing.
- Your thesis statement can be stated directly or implied.

TIP

Writer's Workshop: Thesis Statements
1. The following thesis statements fail either to restrict their subject, reveal the conclusions of the writer, or hint at the approach the writer will use. The first example shows such a thesis statement rewritten. Supply revised versions of the remaining thesis statements.

Writer's Workshop

    a. Roommates are a problem.

       Revised: Living with a stranger poses the first significant problem a college student is likely to have, particularly if his or her roommate is careless, noisy, or selfish.

    b. Conquering hunger should be our number one priority.

    c. Parents really do not know their children.

    d. The worst fear city dwellers have is crime.

    e. Atomic testing is undesirable.

    f. There are many problems with Darwin's theory of evolution.

2. The following paragraph comes from the beginning of a brief essay on the subject of career choices. The writer was doing her student teaching at a local high school and when she finished her stint, she began to worry about whether she had chosen the right career. Identify the thesis statement. Analyze it for its usefulness in this paragraph. Then comment below on the contribution the thesis statement seems to have made to each of the identified qualities of the paragraph.

> As a future teacher of English, I am worried. And scared. I've been teaching English at E. O. Smith High School this past semester, and have discovered that many of the students there are totally apathetic toward the teaching of English. I would estimate that approximately 70% of the students I worked with felt that English was useless and therefore a waste of time. They (the students) have no interest in grammar or composition, and think that much of literature is stupid and unnecessary. I have always wanted a challenging career, but the odds I am facing are overwhelming!
>
> **Stephanie**

What is the thesis statement?

How does the thesis statement restrict the topic?

Comment on the paragraph:

    What is the subject of the paragraph?

    What details support the thesis statement?

3. Create a thesis statement for each of the following subjects. You may substitute a subject of your own if some of these do not appeal to you. Try to bring genuine information to bear on these subjects. Use prewriting techniques before you write, and be sure to refer to the principles that should guide a good thesis statement.

macho behavior	labor unions
racial prejudice	intercollegiate sports
political pressure	majoring in English (or your choice of major)

[handwritten margin note:] Parents are concerned about their children's health effects heavy metal music has on think children's health and the messages the lyrics teach them.

Outlining

If you have mastered the traditional outline, then you should be grateful. It is a wonderful help in writing. But if you have resisted outlining in the past, try to be open minded. Outlining can take many forms. One of the simplest is just to make a list of the points you want to include in your writing.

Brainstorming, searching the unconscious, clustering, and free writing help you express yourself on a topic and result in a gathering of many ideas. Your thesis gathers and focuses these ideas. When you go over your prewriting you will find that some ideas are dispensable, some are of first importance, and some are of lesser importance. At this point, you can make a list of the most useful ideas.

If your purpose is persuasion, you would list the principal arguments or reasons for accepting your view. If your purpose is to inform, you might list the most important facts or separate pieces of information that you want to impart. If your purpose is to entertain, you would list the most important characters, events, or situations that must be included in what you write. If your purpose is self-expression, then you would list the concepts, problems, ideas, or topics that relate to your overall concern. When you have a list, you can flesh it out by seeing what related elements can be included under the headings of some of your main points.

THE CONCEPT OF DYNAMIC OUTLINING

The traditional outline that most of us learn in school looks like this:

I. Main subject
    A. A main idea relating to the subject
       1. A subcategory of the idea above
       2. Another subcategory of the idea above
          a. A point relating to I. A. 2.
    B. Another idea relating to the main subject
II. The second main subject

The items in each of these categories could be a single element in a list, a sentence that makes a clear statement, or a single word that implies an entire potential thought. It could come directly from the material you have gathered in your prewriting, or it could come from a reworking of that material. However, it must be thought of as a structure that can change.

OUTLINING FROM PREWRITING MATERIAL

Stu was concerned about date rape. First, he brainstormed the subject and followed up with clustering. Then he practiced free writing for three minutes, maintaining as much speed as possible in order to free his unconscious. He made a list of the material that resulted from his experiments, and from that list, he prepared an outline.

Date rape is the rape, usually of a woman, by a person known to her, usually her date or a friend. Until reading an article in the local newspaper, Stu had never heard of date rape. Soon he found out that it was much more common than he thought, but that the victims of date rape rarely came forth with complaints. What impelled him to write in the first place was a statement in the campus paper that suggested men are not concerned enough to care about date rape. Stu felt that the writer of the article, a woman, was being anti-male on an issue that he personally felt was reprehensible.

Prewriting: Brainstorming

Here is the first list of ideas he came up with when he began his prewriting:

Date rape: loss of trust; disappointment; betrayal; violence; shame; aloneness; feeling used; hating men; what's special about date rape; seeming coy; leading people on; sex without love; loss of freedom; counseling a good thing; men need counseling, just as do women; counseling means education; what does education mean?; would students accept counseling?; situations in which rape occur; is it frequent?; are women always victims; who is to blame; what can the university do?; do men really care?

Stu then went on to group his observations and see if there were any patterns, any additions that he needed:

1	2	4
loss of trust	violence	counseling a good thing
disappointment	hating men	men need counseling,
betrayal		just as do women
shame		counseling means education
aloneness	3	what does education mean?
feeling used	what's special	
loss of freedom	about date rape?	
	seeming coy	
	leading people on	
	sex without love	

<table>
<tr><td>5</td><td>6</td></tr>
</table>

5	6
situations in which	what can the university do?
rape occur	do men really care?
is it frequent?	
are women always	
victims?	
who is to blame?	

Stu realized that Group 1 described the results of a date rape. Group 2 concentrated on the effects of date rape, while Group 4 focused on counseling. Group 3 tried to deal with what makes date rape different from other kinds of rape, with an eye toward thinking about why it would happen. Group 5 really relates to Group 3, because it too concentrates on what is special about date rape. Finally, Group 6 concerns itself with what can be done in the university community.

With this kind of breakdown, Stu made the following list of primary subjects to handle in his own article in response to the one he had read:

1. Date rape causes a loss of trust in a person who may be otherwise close and likeable.
2. Because of the forcing involved in rape, women may end up hating men.
3. Date rape is special because sometimes a woman may seem coy to a man, and the man may misunderstand. It could be a communications problem.
4. What are the situations in which date rape can occur?
5. What the university can do.

Prewriting: Free Writing

After gathering these materials together, Stu felt the list he had made was a good start toward an outline. He had a sense that the issues he could deal with were implied in these five primary subjects, so he took them as a basis for his three minutes worth of free writing, which follows:

Date rape: the thing is that with a date you trust people. It's not like having someone jump out of an alley and hold a knife to your throat, but more like having someone you like suddenly turn mean or suddenly not listen to you when you say no. Or think maybe you don't mean it when you say no. That's what Laura said—it's not listening. You say no and you mean it but the person forces you to do something you don't want to do and the more he forces you the less you want to do it. And if you get raped you feel like the world has given way. You lose respect for yourself and especially for the person you thought might have become something special to you. Men say that girls say no just because they want to seem like nice girls, or they want to seem hard to get, but they really want to have sex all the time. They just want to let the boy think they are being proper. Maybe some girls are this way. There ought to be a way of telling. The newspaper said boys don't care about this, but the guys I talked to said date rape was rotten. I think guys care. I care. Laura said she knew guys who cared. The problem could be a communications problem and if that is true then the university could do something. There could be workshops, information bulletins, maybe something in the newspaper. The Rape Crisis Center could publish something on it. We could have a dorm meeting.

OUTLINING FOR A FIRST DRAFT

Stu began to see that he was developing some ideas for a possible thesis statement. Several points emerged: date rape was likely to shatter trust in a friend; date rape might involve a complex form of an inability to communicate; the university might be able to help by setting up informative workshops. Stu decided all these elements would find their way into his writing, but that probably the most important thing he had uncovered—the item that gave him the clearest opportunity for persuasion—was the last item: the question of workshops. So he set up a thesis statement to help him focus his thinking.

The university can make a good contribution to stopping date rape on this campus by holding workshops for both men and women.

Stu then went on to make the following outline, basically adapting his lists to the more formal structure of the traditional outline:

I. Date rape: What workshops can explain
  A. What is date rape
    1. A definition
    2. How it differs from ordinary rape
  B. The results of date rape
    1. Loss of trust in friends
    2. A sense of shame
    3. Disliking men
  C. Situations in which date rape occurs
    1. A failure to understand each other's feelings
    2. Misreading the meaning of "No."
II. Why workshops should be available to everyone
  A. Date rape is a problem for both men and women
    1. If there is a communications problem, workshops can bring issues into the open
    2. Men and women see certain sexual issues very differently
      a. A workshop can help women see how a man could think a woman was being coy when she wasn't

b. A workshop can give women a chance to express their feelings about sex

c. A workshop could give both sexes a chance to see how different or similar their interpretations of a situation can be

WRITING THE FIRST DRAFT

Stu decided to shape his article as an editorial, knowing that the campus paper might run it as a letter to the editor. An editorial would state a position and recommend a procedure—both of which were part of his purpose in writing. The opening of his first draft follows. His light editing is indicated and his thesis is underlined.

Date rape is quite different from other kinds of rape. For one thing, it occurs between people who are not strangers. They might even have been very good friends. Date rape [is often the result of] often happens during or after a date. In other words, when people are together for social reasons. It's [a bad kind] [particularly] special because before the rape, [people] the victim, usually a woman, had a sense of trust for the rapist. The awful thing about date rape is that this sense of trust is hurt. As a man, I think this is just as bad as any other kind of rape.

The university can make a good contribution to stopping date rape on this campus by holding workshops for both men and women. One of the possible causes of date rape may be lack of communication. That means lack of understanding between a couple. In a college environment, a series of workshops [on dating and] on date rape could do a lot of good. It could help [people] men understand what "No" means, and help women understand what men think is expected of them. Workshops won't end date rape. But they could make it less likely to happen.

First Light Revision

Stu took these paragraphs and tried to smooth them out, worrying mainly about wordiness, directness, and focus. He realized the paragraphs had two functions: to define date rape and to suggest what colleges could do to help stop it.

Date rape occurs between people who are friends, and therefore it is very different from other kinds of forcible rape. As its name implies, it occurs during a social situation, a date. [Because a date is a situation that involves trust between people, date rape] One of the worst aspects of date rape, in my mind, is the fact that it involves a loss of trust between a man and a woman. [As a man, I think date rape is awful.] Men have as much reason as women to complain about date rape, since having a date depends on trust.

One thing colleges can do is to set up workshops for men and women so that date rape won't happen as much as it does. A lack of communication may be at the core of some date rapes, and a series of workshops can do a lot of good. They could help men understand what "No" means, and help women understand what men think is expected of them. Workshops won't end date rape. But they could make it less likely to happen.

The thesis statement took a slightly different form in this revision. Again, like the outline, the thesis must be regarded as dynamic and changeable. When Stu had a reasonable draft, he examined it for several things:

Audience: Did I properly address my audience?

Writer: Did I present myself as sympathetic to victims of date rape? Would I offend my audience?

Subject: Is my subject clear? Did it need further definition? Do I have enough information?

Purpose: Is my purpose in writing—to recommend the establishment of workshops—clear? Is the beginning clearly persuasive?

How to Avoid Tinkering: Set Aside the First Draft

Stu left his editorial alone for an evening, and when he went back to it, he thought he should change the opening definition of date rape and focus instead on his suggestion that workshops be set up to discuss it. At this stage, he did what many writers do when writing short pieces: he put his first draft aside after a reading, and wrote his revision without referring to it.

This may sound a bit crazy to you, but in fact it is not. Too many people think of revision as changing some words, tightening some sentences, adding some material, taking out other material. And, yes, these are definitely stages of revision. But this kind of tinkering does not result in much more than superficial improvement. A first draft is like a demented, tyrannical Roman emperor. It holds sway over your imagination. Set your early draft aside, thus overthrowing the "tyrant," and revise from a new outline.

OUTLINING FROM THE FIRST DRAFT

In response to the examination of his beginning from the point of view of its serving his audience, subject, and purpose, Stu decided to refocus the beginning and to concentrate first on why the college should have workshops and what his recommendation is. Then, he decided he would define date rape as well as his reaction to it. He came up with this relatively sketchy outline:

1. Establish that workshops can help
   a. Refer to recent editorial
   b. Explain why workshops are needed
   c. Explain how they can help in communications
2. Explain what date rape is
   a. Dating is a situation of trust
   b. Men care about date rape too

With a completed first draft, Stu felt his outline did not have to be much more detailed. Some people actually become quite detailed at this point, and some do not. Because outlining is a dynamic process, there is no one way to approach it. Stu's next draft follows:

A recent editorial in the *Daily Campus* stated that date rape was relatively common on this campus and others. The author went on to suggest that the men on campus were not as concerned about this as the women. I would like to respond by saying that, as a man, I feel very concerned. I would like to propose that the Counseling Center set up Date Rape Workshops that would focus on what date rape is, and on the possible misunderstandings that cause it. Some men may not realize that "No" really means No, and some women may not realize that men can have a wrong idea of what is expected of them on a date. A workshop during Freshman Week could go a long way toward making date rape a thing of the past.

The worst thing about date rape is that it happens in a social situation that should be marked by trust. A date is a friend, not a rapist. When this is not true, everyone suffers because the trusting atmosphere that should mark a successful date is missing. Men feel this just as do women, although it is obvious that women are much more hurt as victims of rape. It is to everyone's benefit to hold workshops that will improve the dating atmosphere on this campus.

THE FINAL STAGE: POLISHING

Stu had come a long way from his first outline. But before he did the final typescript, he went back over his last draft in order to polish. Polishing involves looking for chances to improve the rhythms of sentences, the choice of words, the positioning of ideas. When you polish you do not set aside your early draft. You improve it directly. In his final polishing, Stu changed many details. The thesis is again underlined.

An editor of the *Daily Campus* recently pointed out that date rape was prevalent on this campus and others. She suggested that the men on campus were not as concerned about this as the women. As a man, I would like to reassure her by saying that I feel concerned enough to propose that the Counseling Center set up Date Rape Workshops to clarify what date rape is, and the possible failures of communications that cause it. Sometimes a man may not realize that "No" really means No. Sometimes a woman may not realize that men can misunderstand the signals they are getting on a date. <u>A workshop during Freshman Week could help toward making date rape a thing of the past.</u>

Date rape happens in a social situation that should be marked by trust. A date is a friend, not a rapist. When this is not true, everyone suffers because the trusting atmosphere that should mark a successful date is missing. Men feel this just as do women, although obviously women are much more hurt as victims of rape. Workshops on date rape can help improve the dating atmosphere on this campus, and that is to everyone's benefit.

Writer's **W**orkshop

Writer's Workshop: From Thesis to Draft

1. The best way to handle this assignment is to take a controversial issue from events in your immediate environment. If you cannot do that, survey your earlier Writer's Workshop efforts for a subject that you feel is significant enough to work on. If you need to, you may work with a recent assignment you have been given for writing. Or, finally, you may choose from the following list of possible topics:

   your intellectual environment
   the quality of your library
   student-teacher relationships
   the drug scene on your campus
   your obligation to people in the third world
   what we can do about highway safety
   how to improve TV news
   the general quality of TV
   welfare payments to the poor
   is unemployment inevitable
   how your campus compares with others

Follow this procedure:

- Brainstorm for three minutes on your subject; then group your words and phrases.
- Cluster, using a key word derived from your brainstorming.
- Make a list of the primary subtopics you have developed and organize them into a rough outline.
- Practice free writing for five minutes on your subject.
- Derive a thesis statement from a review of your brainstorming, grouping, and free writing.
- Make your first detailed outline.
- Write your first draft without worrying about being absolutely accurate in every detail.
- Perform your first light revision. Correct spelling, faulty sentences, wordiness, and other such problems.
- Examine your revised first draft for the following:
  a. *Audience:* Did you properly address your audience?
  b. *Writer:* Do you present yourself as you wish? Are you objective or have you taken sides?
  c. *Subject:* Is your subject clear? Does it need further definition? Do you have enough information?
  d. *Purpose:* Is your purpose in writing clear? Are you using the appropriate form for your purpose?
- Make a new outline from the first draft.
- Set your first draft aside and write a new draft using your new outline.

- After a reasonable time to gain some distance from what you have written, polish your new draft.

This is an elaborate procedure. Each stage of this procedure will teach you a great deal, and following the procedure will make your writing the best it can be.

Begin with one of your own pieces of writing. Treat it as if it were a first draft and apply the following procedure, derived from the more lengthy procedure described in Item 1.

- Perform light revision as necessary. Correct spelling, faulty sentences, repetitiousness, and other such problems.
- Examine your revised draft for the following:
  a. *Audience:* Did you properly address your audience?
  b. *Writer:* Is your position clear as the writer?
  c. *Subject:* Is your subject clear? Does it need further definition? Do you have enough information?
  d. *Purpose:* Is your purpose in writing clear? Are you using the appropriate form for your purpose?
- Make an outline from this draft.
- Set your draft aside and write a completely new revision from your outline.
- After a reasonable time to gain some distance from what you have written, polish your new draft.

Writing with a Computer

The computer has revolutionized the life of professional writers, and it offers immense opportunities for the apprentice writer. The sense of liberation from the tyranny of the typewritten page has been immense primarily because as you write on a computer, you know that you do not have to retype pages if you make a mistake. While you are actually writing, you can erase words, lines, and paragraphs at the stroke of a key, and after you have printed out a draft, you can correct it on paper, make your corrections in your file (the computer term for the piece you are working on), and print out a new version with a minimum of effort. If you need more copies, the computer is there to serve you.

WHAT WORD PROCESSING CAN DO FOR YOU

The advantages of writing on the computer are directly related to the organizational principles of this book: invention, organization, style, memory, and presentation. The computer is able to make extraordinary contributions to your writing in each and every one of these areas. The kinds of software (computer term for the program that runs the computer) available to use on computers will vary depending on computer type, but the function of the software is basically the same whether you are using Apple/Mackintosh machines or IBM and IBM-compatible machines. Some of the following references to specific software include so-called Freeware, software that is free to the user, and which the user pays for only after lengthy testing to his or her satisfaction.

Invention: The Computer Advantages

Working up ideas on the computer is simplified in part by the ease with which lists can be made and later printed out. The computer permits you to set up a list of terms, ideas, observations, or thoughts, and then—as you review the list and think of new possibilities—it permits you to add blank lines between items and put in your second thoughts. On a blank paper, this process begins to get messy and invites disorder. The computer, because of its capacity to simplify erasure and addition, keeps everything neat and organized.

One of the most interesting developments in computing involves a form of software sometimes described as *idea processors.* These are relatively sophisticated outline programs and their ease of use is one of their strengths. Some of these programs are Thinktank, produced by IBM, and rather expensive; Maxthink, produced by Neils Larsen, and relatively inexpensive; and PC-Outline, a free program, part of the Freeware experiment.

The outlining programs allow you to brainstorm a topic and then sort out related items, place them in a reasonable order, and set them up as an outline. These programs permit you to work without the roman numerals or the I.A.1.a. patterns you would use on paper, but they insert them for you at the stroke of a command key. The advantages of these outliners is evident early on. First, they provide you with a clear sense of order. But more important, they permit you to work intensely with a specific segment of your outline. For instance, if you have a major heading, I. The Causes of the Civil War, and you go to the next level, A. Economic Differences Between the North and the South, you will find that the program fills the screen only with that level of the outline, so you can work without distraction on building up detail on the differences between North and South. This focus is a powerful feature that leaves you completely free to elaborate your thinking. When you press the proper function key, you find that the entire outline returns and you are then able to reconsider some of the elements you have included. In many ways, the advantages and importance of outlining are made truly clear by these programs, which must be thought of as one of the best aids to prewriting available today.

Organization: The Computer Advantages

The outlining programs offer many advantages for the writer when it comes to organizing a piece of writing. Because the outline can be altered so readily, you can make major changes in the structure of your work before you begin writing. You can also experiment with several versions of a piece by restructuring your outline in any of several ways. This can be done on paper, of course, but not as readily as on the computer.

But the real advantage of the computer in terms of organization comes into play once you have a version of your piece of writing. In other times, many writers painstakingly scissored up their work and repasted it to new paper in an effort to reorganize and reposition important ideas. The time and labor involved in that procedure made it one that some writers simply skipped. They could not face it, and so sometimes permitted themselves to present work that was less than their best.

Now even the least expensive word processing programs, such as PC-Write (Freeware) and Textra (by Norton) permit cutting and pasting right on the screen. You can mark a paragraph and move it anywhere in your piece.

Tips: Writing on a Computer
- Use the tutorial that comes with your word processing program so that you understand its full features.
- Consider an outliner program to help in your prewriting stages.
- Be sure to purchase high quality disks on which to save your writing. Keep your disks in a plastic case where they cannot be bent or damaged.
- Treat your disks with special care: keep them away from metallic objects, such as paper clips, or anything that has a magnetic field (for example: telephones, tape recorders, speakers, and any motor-driven appliances).
- As you write, save your file as you go along, perhaps as often as once a screenful. Consider how much you could afford to lose at a time if the power failed. Save your final file twice, on two disks. Disks are cheap. Do not be stingy. Your time is too precious.
- Give your files logical names so you can find them later. If you are writing on the Civil War, store your files as CIVILW1; CIVILW2, etc., for the different drafts of your piece.
- Store one of your disks in a permanently safe place. Treat your working disk with respect—do not eat or drink near your computer or your disks.
- Do not work on the computer when you are tired or anxious. When you get impatient, turn to something else for a while.

You can do the same for a sentence or a phrase. And once the move is made, what you see is clean and neat in appearance.

In addition, if you make a change in your work that involves altering a word, name, phrase, or title that appears frequently, you can make a global change—a change of every mention of that word or phrase. Also, if you have a term, such as *World Bank*, which you repeat through the paper, you can write it using *wb* as a shorthand, then when you are finished you can make a global change so that *wb* becomes World Bank everywhere you use the combination. (See the Box entitled "Tips: Writing on a Computer.")

Style: The Computer Advantages

Some of the more elaborate word processing programs, such as Word Perfect, Word, Framework, Manuscript, and Symphony include some extraordinary options. One is a thesaurus that at a keystroke will suggest synonyms and antonyms for any word you specify. If you find a choice presented to you that you think is preferable to your own, a keystroke will then put it in your work.

These programs also include a style checker that will show you how often you use a specific word or phrase. If you are overusing it, the program alerts you. Some programs, such as Textra and the one available from Macmillan for this book, include a handbook of English usage that can be called up while you are writing, so if you are concerned about how to use a specific kind of punctuation, for instance, you can review the rules.

But beyond all the special advantages of these programs, the computer permits you to make stylistic changes very easily. When you reread and notice repetitious phrases or terms, you can easily change them to make them more graceful and effective. As most writers using computers admit, the greatest stylistic advantage is the ability to make a great many small changes very quickly. That advantage alone will improve your style immediately.

Memory: The Computer Advantages

The capacity of the computer to keep track of notes and information is unparalleled. Some of what the computer does can be done on paper, but not so efficiently. The advantage in notetaking is considerable because inexpensive programs, such as PC-File and File Express can search through the files you make (you should establish your notes on a subject as separate files and save them) and call up every reference to specific ideas, titles, or people. The brilliance of these programs makes them indispensable to the researcher and student.

For very elaborate record keeping, programs such as dBaseIII+ are useful because they can keep, sort, and search thousands of files and get information from any of them almost immediately. The more elaborate programs are impressive, but difficult to learn. They are very useful to the advanced researcher, but the least expensive of the programs will do very nicely for almost all your needs.

One extraordinary advantage of the computer entails the searches that can be carried out in databases. A database is a collection of information on a specific area of interest—art, law, education—and searching these for articles or books that might be important to your work is relatively easy with a computer. Information on how this is done is provided for you in Chapter 10: "The Research Paper." Although this feature does not make your writing especially easier, it relates to your gathering information and making yourself expert in an area of your special interest.

Presentation: The Computer Advantages

Among the extras sometimes provided with word processing programs is a spell-checker. One of the best is called Wordproof. It will check every word in your file and when it comes across one that is not in its dictionary, it will signal you, give you a range of choices including what it thinks is the word you are looking for, and at your command it will insert the properly spelled word.

The advantage of this is obvious. You will not hand in essays with avoidable typographical errors or need to caret in corrections with pen on a final draft. The spell-checker will not find certain errors. For example, if you wrote *two* when you meant *too*, the spell-checker will not notice. It will only notice words that are spelled incorrectly. Usually, that feature is more than enough.

The presentation of a piece of work is quite important. A reader responds much more favorably to work that is clean, clear, well formatted, and nicely presented. The computer's ability to provide copies makes your job of producing a clean, good-looking final draft much easier than by any other means. And you can do all this even in face of the kinds of deadlines that are common for the apprentice writer.

Using a word processor makes the job of writing faster and easier. It will not substitute for good ideas, for inspiration, for intuition, or for the hard work that is needed in making any writing interesting. Some critics suggest that the word processor has made writers more wordy and perhaps more glib. But that is not a necessary consequence of using a computer. It is something that need not be said of you. If you have access to a computer, by all means use it for your writing. It will liberate you and provide you with a powerful means of improving your work.

4

Means of Development—
Part I

Prewriting and the Means of Development _____

Brainstorming, grouping, clustering, journal keeping, and free writing are all designed to loosen you up and begin the process of finding good material to use in your writing. They help you think. The use of various strategies of questioning, such as the journalism questions and the Burkean Pentad give you a powerful method of producing original ideas that can make your writing vibrant and alive. Once you have gone through these steps, you have many options to help you develop the ideas these processes have found for you.

The most common and most important means of development are the subject of this chapter:

definition
comparison and contrast
cause and effect
possibility and circumstance

Each of these represents an intellectual process that guides your thinking in a specific direction. You may use the means of development to help you structure a single sentence. Or you may use it to help you structure a para-graph, section of a longer piece, or the entire piece. You may mix these means of development within paragraphs, sections, or entire written pieces. You may use them to produce new ideas or to develop ideas you already have.

Their flexibility can be demonstrated in a simple experiment. We will start with a single key word on which to begin the process of clustering.

Poverty is a major question in our society, and beginning any essay on it demands some research and reflection. In the early stages of thinking about

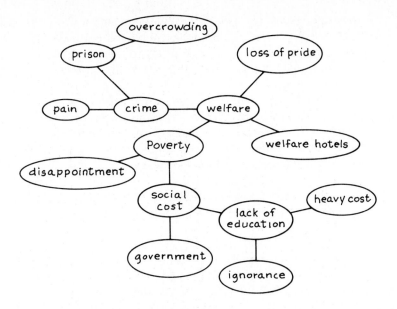

the subject, and after such a clustering has been done, there is plenty of room to begin to marshall the means of development. We will take each in turn and show, in miniature, how they can be brought to bear on such a topic.

Definition: A number of terms that have been developed need definition in any piece of writing that would grow from this beginning. For example, to be complete, you would need first to define "poverty." Do you define it in terms of annual income, the way the government does? Do you define it in terms of a psychological outlook, the way some sociologists do? Do you define it in terms of style, the way some pop sociologists do? What about the welfare system? It needs definition for anyone who has not been involved with it. What do the social agencies that administer the welfare program mean by the word "welfare"? Is anyone's welfare really being considered? What about society's welfare?

Comparison: Any number of comparisons suggest themselves here, but the most obvious is with countries that do not have welfare systems. What is their system? Does it work? Is it superior to ours, or is it inferior? What about the comparison right here between people who are on welfare and those who are not? What are their differing attitudes toward welfare? How valid are their respective views?

Cause and effect: The clustering already implies that there is a causal relationship between poverty and crime. Is crime the effect of poverty? Or is poverty the effect of crime? Or is it possible that there is no causal relationship between poverty and crime? Is the fact that most of the people in prison are poverty stricken a mere coincidence? What is the causal relationship between welfare and crime? Does a liberal welfare program retard crime, or does it make a difference at all? Think of the consequence of poverty on those who are poor—the clustering produced terms such as pain and disappointment. How do poor people express themselves?

Possibility and circumstance: Given the circumstances most of the poor live in, is there any hope that any welfare program could help them out of poverty? The Bible says the poor will always be with us. Does that mean there is no possibility of welfare helping eradicate poverty? The clustering produced observations about education and ignorance. Is it possible to make education attractive to the poor? Is it possible to make it available to them? If ignorance is a possible consequence of poverty, is it possible to make poverty obsolete? Is it possible for the poor ever to be anything but poor?

Each of the means of development represents an inquiry of the kind that you have already seen in the Burkean Pentad. The reason to conduct such an inquiry is to help you take a basic idea and develop it in directions that have a richness of possibilities. By using each of these means, you will find ways of expressing thoughts that you possessed, but which you may have been unaware of possessing. The means of development, like the techniques of prewriting, empower you as a writer.

Development by Definition

Definition invites you to define your subject or any key term you develop through clustering or brainstorming. It should be invoked in the earliest stages of prewriting. To an extent, the reluctance to provide adequate definitions can be a symptom of the ego-centered writer, and the very use of this means of development can function to help decenter yourself and begin forming an adequate relationship with your audience.

Definition constitutes a method of limiting something—your subject or a subtopic of your subject—from other things like it. Dictionary definitions give the shortest, most concise distinguishing features of something. However, the most fruitful application of the means of definition is not to construct a dictionary entry. After all, the dictionary contains many thousands of words and must be incredibly economical in order to avoid producing an unwieldy book. (See the box entitled "Tips: Using Definition.")

The example by Frank Beaver on page 77 ("Cinematic Time and Space") is a literal definition of a term used in the study of film. Because it comes from a handbook aimed at a general audience interested in film, it takes no sides in an argument, but rather seeks to clarify what might be otherwise obscure.

Tips: Using Definition
- Establish the qualities of something with enough detail to clarify your understanding of it.
- Limit the meaning of something so as to restrict its application to the present situation.
- Clarify the significance of a specific idea in relation to other ideas in your writing.
- Provide examples that make the abstract concept more reasonably concrete.

CINEMATIC TIME AND SPACE

A term which indicates the relationship of time and space in the motion picture. In a theatrical experience space remains static and constant. On the other hand, space in the cinema can be altered because the camera serves as a selective intermediary in the screen experience. Individual shots within a motion picture are capable of breaking up the rigid space-time continuum of the real-world experience.

In the real-world experience a man rises from his armchair where he has been reading the evening newspaper, crosses to the bar, and mixes a drink. His movements from the chair to the bar must be made through actual space and time. In the cinema experience the man can rise and start his movement to the bar. This initial movement can be followed by a brief two-second shot of a startling headline in the newspaper lying on the armchair, followed immediately by a close-up of the man sipping his drink at the bar and contemplating the impact of the headline.

Cinematic space is thus intimately woven with the unique temporal (time) possibilities of the motion picture. A character's movement, for example, can be made to appear unusually prolonged through the addition or repetition of visual space. In *Bonnie and Clyde* (1967), the moment of recognition by the two killers that they are about to be ambushed is extended with unusual effects by intercutting numerous close-ups of the gangsters as they glance at one another.

Through the elimination or addition of visual space in photographing and editing a film, time can be either expanded or contracted.

This example moves from a simple statement that could be a definition in a small dictionary to a more reasoned statement with examples and descriptions. The first sentence is abstract, with no specific references, whereas the next-to-last paragraph is made concrete by reference to events in the film *Bonnie and Clyde*. The second paragraph contrasts time and space in the real world with time and space as they can be treated in film. The discussion helps us appreciate film technique, the movement of the camera from object to object, each with its statement about time and space, and the omission of events which, in life, must be lived through.

The following examples by students show how development by definition works, how it clarifies the writer's thought, communicates clearly with the audience, and provides the writer with important material for writing. The act of working out these definitions actually made the authors more aware of what they meant. And that is exactly the point behind applying these means of development. They produce new understanding.

The first example, by a freshman named David, is an effort to search out meaning. David was wrestling with an idea concerning language. He was aware that communication often fails because people define words in different ways and do not recognize the differences. The first paragraph establishes the fact that there is a problem; the second paragraph establishes the definition of a term, *translation*.

There are major problems with language that hinder our ability to share emotions, exactly as they are, with others. The first is that there are too few words in languages to go into enough detail and transmit the exact emotion. To be able to know precisely how another person feels, we need to know everything that has ever happened to that other person that is related to the feeling being felt. Unless we have known and experienced all this, we cannot truly know the feelings through the use of language. A third problem of language is what I call the problem of translation.

The problem of translation happens when, in an interaction, a message is given by the first person to another and is changed from its original meaning because of the use of language, and because of the second person's translation and application of judgment to the message. For example, imagine that I am depressed because my birthday has been forgotten this year by friends and family, and in my childhood, my birthdays usually occurred either at a time of family crisis at a time when things were "cooling down" after a fight and the celebration was depressing or forgotten. If a friend were to ask me why I was so depressed, I would tell him that my birthday had been forgotten this year. In saying that, I would be omitting the past hurts I had suffered because I either repressed the feelings, or because it seemed a trivial point at the time. Now the message has been reduced to "I'm upset because I had been forgotten on my birthday," which could be translated by the listener as childishness, selfishness, self-pity, feelings of insecurity, or a number of other things that really have nothing to do with my actual feelings, or the idea that I was trying to get across.

David edited out the awkwardness in his writing later, but it is useful to observe how he moved directly from a situation in language to a term of his own construction, and then to a process of definition that made the term explicit within his intentions. He demonstrates his willingness to try to clarify what he means so that we can share his insight. The extract here was written in response to an assignment to experiment with definition, and it appeared in the context of a much longer discussion of the arts.

David establishes his subject: the understanding of emotions through descriptive language. Then he qualifies the limits of language and introduces the term *translation,* which is really quite limited in meaning at first. David realizes how limited it is, and sees that a definition in terms of simple language needs amplification: it needs an example. His example is unusually complex. At first the disappointment over a forgotten birthday seems simple enough, but as he unfolds the situation, with all its possibilities and the implication of family tensions, he demonstrates how an expression of disappointment can be mistranslated.

In the following example titled "Disorderly Eating," Christine soon realized that some of her terms were unknown to her audience. She uses two examples, one of which, by way of contrast, helps define her concept. Christine had explored her topic carefully and does not define her terms for her own use. The terms *bulimic* and *anorexia* are familiar to her, and they are not abstract concepts that she herself had to work out in her writing. Her intentions are strictly to clarify the concepts for any segment of her audience who might not know them.

Many people know that they must alter their eating habits, but do not realize that they have an eating disorder. From the person who cannot pass up a piece of chocolate cake to the bulimic who consumes literally pounds of food each day, eating disorders are not uncommon. The bulimic is a victim of a serious eating disorder; the chocolate cake eater of a minor eating disorder. People inflicted with a serious eating disorder are not stricken with a disease, but are victims of a psychological disorder that originated as a result of several complex forces.

Two extreme victims of eating disorders are the anorexic, who starves herself into excessive weight loss, and the previously mentioned bulimic, who gorges herself and then, to avoid weight gain, induces vomiting. More often than not, victims of serious eating disorders tend to be female and teenage, however eating disorders can occur in anyone. Usually the anorexics and bulimics are victims of society when the cultural ideal of being slender becomes a goal and then an obsession. Anorexics and bulimics no longer view food as a source of nourishment; for them, food is an enemy by being a cause of their disorder, and at the same time, food is a friend by being a means of control over their body.

Christine defines two kinds of eating disorders by contrasting one with the other. Generally, it is easier to understand one thing if it is related clearly to something which is its opposite. Often, for instance, we define a difficult word by citing its opposite, or antonym. The technique works for concepts, too.

Development by Comparison or Contrast _____

Because it is such a natural mode of thought, development by comparison feels like second nature to most of us. We compare almost everything we see and do with other things in order to make a choice of activities, to decide where to go, what to see, what to do. Comparison lies at the root of all value judgments, moral or aesthetic. As children, we learn about the world by making comparisons. As writers, we expand our understanding of whatever interests us by making careful comparisons. By applying the means of comparison carefully, we can also help our audience see the distinguishing and significant features of our subject. (See the box entitled "Tips: Using Comparison or Contrast.")

Tips: Using Comparison or Contrast
- Provide a clearer understanding of an unfamiliar thing by comparing it with something your audience already understands.
- Provide a better understanding of two related but distinct things by showing what qualities they share and what each possesses uniquely.
- Emphasize the similarities of two things when you wish to compare them.
- Emphasize the differences between two things when you wish to contrast them.
- Assess the relative merits of alternatives by comparing courses of action or benefits and limitations.

We can see one of the most fruitful uses of development by comparison by examining the way Christine continued developing her discussion of eating disorders. She had mentioned anorexics and bulimics—the undereaters and the overeaters—but she had not completely clarified their distinction. Christine took the opportunity to clarify the differences between the two groups by comparing them directly.

Ironically the cliché "having cake and eating it too" applies well when comparing the anorexic to the bulimic. Anorexics allow themselves to, in a sense, have cake, but not to eat it. As a cat enjoys catching a mouse, purely for sport, so an anorexic enjoys baking and decorating a cake. Playing with food but not consuming it is many anorexics' favorite pastime.

Bulimics, in contrast, allow themselves to have their cake and eat it too. But bulimics are not satisfied with only a piece of cake. When they want to have cake, they have a whole cake: about ten pieces.

Christine later realized this comparison could have been expanded profitably. But it already has some valuable features. For example, she compares the general situation of anorexics and bulimics with the familiar saying, "Having your cake and eating it too." Her illustration helps clarify the behavior of both groups, while clearly distinguishing between each. She is also able to use the familiar behavior of a cat playing with a mouse to illustrate the behavior of the anorexic. These comparisons illuminate the unfamiliar by reference to the familiar. In the process, she gives us useful information about both kinds of problem eaters.

The purpose of the comparison in the following example is quite different. John's essay, "About My Father," begins with some childhood memories. In referring to the Bible, John realizes his audience is not as familiar with it as he is, but all he needs is the sense of awe that most people already associate with the Bible. The details are less important than the feeling that will be imparted by them.

My memories of him remind me of a dream a king had. The king's name was Nebuchadnezzar. The book of Daniel in the Bible records his dream. "You looked, O king, and there, before you stood a large statue—an enormous, dazzling statue, awesome in appearance." This statue had a head of pure gold, silver arms and chest, bronze belly and thighs, iron legs, and partly iron, partly black clay feet. My first memory of my father was pure gold. These innocent and untrained eyes could find no flaw in him. He commanded my love, my adoration, my reverence, and my fear. I felt secure in his hands. He was God to my little eyes, but as I grew, silver memories were added to my golden memory of him.

This biblical statue produced the reminder that although someone may be very important, he may also have feet of clay. That means simply that with all the grandeur, such a person is still very ordinary. The allusion reminds us that most of us begin by revering our parents, and then little by little we realize that our parents have limitations—like everyone else. As we mature, we learn how to deal with those limitations and yet not lose respect for our parents.

The comparison is subtle, between the biblical symbol and the living man. In a sense the father is distanced in the child's imagination in the same way the Bible is distanced in the imagination of the adult.

Writer's Workshop: Definition and Comparison
1. In one sentence each, without going to the dictionary, and without repeating the word you are defining, offer your definition of four of the following terms:

idealism	a just war	insensitivity
academic excellence	→ putting humanity	local color
→ fidelity	first	stubbornness
thoughtfulness	competition	embarrassment
my country right or	excellence	moodiness
wrong	→ the American Way	self-confidence
wisdom	upward mobility	respect
miserliness	flag-wavers	prejudicial treatment

2. Choose the definition from Item 1 that you think is best. Rework it if you have some more ideas about it, and then extend the definition to one or two paragraphs in length. Remember, there are several effective ways of moving from a one-sentence definition to a fuller definition:

   • Find a contrasting situation, term, or concept, and offer a description of it in order to clarify your term.
   • Develop examples from your experience, the experience of others, or from your reading.
   • Offer an analysis of the way your term functions, who it affects or concerns, when and where it is appropriate or likely to be found, what its parts or elements are, and how they relate to the whole.
   • Restate your definition from another point of view, keeping in mind the needs of your audience.

3. Choose one of the following groups of terms (or one of your own) and write a single paragraph that depends upon comparison or contrast for its focus and development.

   science and humanities
   play and work
   rock music and easy-listening music
   yours and your parents' attitudes on social behavior
   sports on television and sports in a live setting
   listening to records and "listening" to MTV
   feminists and male chauvinists
   conservative and liberal
   moral behavior and immoral behavior
   education and training

4. Compare the portrait of M. Bertin by Ingres with the portrait of Mlle. Charlotte du Val-d'Ognes by Constance Marie Charpentier. Consider the personalities they project, the colors that dominate each composition, and the clues you have as to social status or occupation. Which person would you rather speak with? What would you talk about?

Development by Cause and Effect

It is always difficult to imagine something that has not been caused by some past situation or action. We think about anorexics and wonder what causes such a disorder. We think about poverty and wonder what causes it. Somehow our belief is that if we understand the cause, we can eradicate it, or at least alleviate it. Today, for example, sociologists and government officials are deeply in disagreement about the causes of crime. Some blame the environment; others blame the nature of the criminal. Causal analysis of criminal acts determines both the law and the terms of punishment.

Determining the cause of something such as crime demands an analytic skill because causes are not attached to actions. Instead, they remain invisible. They need to be figured out. For that reason, development by means of cause and effect is both interesting and challenging. Your reader has a basic interest in cause and effect, just as all people do. Therefore, your reader will respond with both concern and understanding when you develop an idea in this fashion. (See the box entitled "Tips: Using Cause and Effect.")

Tips: Using Cause and Effect
- Explain what your topic can cause or did cause.
- Explain what effect it can have or did have on something else.
- Explain what has caused your topic to be as it is, thus producing some insight into its nature.
- Establish the difference between any apparent causes and genuine causes, particularly if they are a source of confusion.

The following is the second paragraph of an essay on the effects of recreation on the average person. Sidney is writing in a hurry. He could benefit from further revision, because it is clear that many of his ideas could be developed further. Nonetheless, Sidney has opened a useful vein of thought which makes it easier for him to write.

Not taking enough time for play can be very damaging to your health. Stress is a very dangerous thing. It can lead to many ailments. Two of the most prevalent are ulcers and heart attacks. The daily stress builds up a lot of nervous energy inside that starts to eat away at us. If that energy isn't used by pleasant activities such as exercise, it will continue to build up inside until it causes serious damage. Many people are in too much of a hurry. They have to realize that they are losing a lot more time by trying to do too much at once. You can take years off your life by not giving your body time to relax. They are so concerned with getting ahead that they don't sit back and enjoy life. It is not until their later years when they realize what they have missed, but by then it is too late to do anything about it. When people look back at their life, it is the "useless activities" that create the fondest memories. The memories of the great business deals and late night meetings fade quickly and are a poor comfort for a lonely old man.

Sidney focuses only on cause and effect, reaching all the way from youth to old age. His first sentence is the topic sentence (or thesis statement) of the entire paragraph, and although it does not openly use the term *cause*, it explains what a lack of playtime can cause. The nice thing about a paragraph such as this is that anyone can do it. Everyone is curious about what things cause or what the effects of a given action might be. None of this process of thought is exotic.

The following sample is from a lengthy essay by a woman who plans to be a professional musician. The prospects for anyone studying to be a professional are not bright, if only because there are so many good musicians and so few possible jobs. Her first observations (beginning with the third paragraph in her essay) treat the effects of the oversupply of musicians. Literally, as Christine shows us, there is too much of everything in music—except opportunity.

The music industry is experiencing a tremendous glut, as aspiring young musicians continue to enter an already saturated market. The *Los Angeles Times* calls this the "golden age of violinism" because of a large number of superior violinists exhibiting an extraordinary range of style. The sale of instruments continues to rise. Our music schools turn out dozens of exceptional musical artists every year, but there are no jobs waiting for even the best of them. Our city symphonies have a hard time continuing operations, and rely largely on private donations and fund-raisers for their subsistence. Musicians who finally get jobs in symphonies are often forced to maintain other jobs simultaneously, jobs that do not interfere with the rehearsal and concert schedule. State funding for the arts, so common in Europe, is remarkably meager in the United States. Our cultural achievements do not match our technological advances. How then, did a country with so little support of classical music end up with such a group of superior musicians? The answer lies partly in the very nature of music.

Christine establishes the effects of a glut of musicians, and she goes on in the next paragraphs to a related question: how did a failure to support classical music have the effect of producing so many excellent and superior musicians? Christine found herself returning again and again to the question of cause and effect. In a sense, she was so deeply involved with the subject herself that she was using her writing to help her work out some personal issues. She was questioning the effect of her choosing a career in music.

Unfortunately, the act of writing reconfirmed an already depressing picture. More important, it made her reflect seriously and honestly about her future plans. She realized that her hopes had been, to an extent, supported by idealistic teachers who, she now felt, could have been harsher with her when she was younger. Christine was not bitter; she was simply becoming wiser.

_____ Development by Possibility and Circumstance

People naturally want to know about the circumstances related to any topic because such knowledge produces deeper understanding. The question of possibility relates to the knowledge of circumstance. For example, knowing that a poor young person from an ethnic neighborhood could become rich and famous demonstrates what is possible even for those in poverty in America. Such examples of the rise from poverty abound, and what makes them most interesting is the analysis of the circumstances that made it possible for the individuals to succeed.

Past circumstances—history—are related to possibility. In order to determine whether or not something is possible, one may look at the past. If something has been done by someone somewhere, then it is possible that it can be done again. An examination of the past, both custom and practice, is one avenue into establishing possibility.

Whenever you are considering a topic that involves change, such as eradicating poverty, the means of development by analysis of possibility and circumstance is very important. For instance, if you think that the government should reduce the poverty in the inner city, you must address the question of possibility and circumstance. First, is it possible for a government to reduce poverty? Second, what are the circumstances that support poverty in the inner city? Any intelligent discussion of the subject of poverty must treat these issues. (See the box entitled "Tips: Using Possibility and Circumstance.")

The example of an analysis of circumstances and what they have made possible (on page 86) is from the hand of a brilliant writer. D. H. Lawrence grew up in the environment that he describes: the coal mining community of Nottingham, England. In a sense, the question that underlies the passage is, "Why is it not possible for the coal miners to live well, to avoid being beaten down?" D. H. Lawrence sees the answer in the fact of the ugliness of the man-made environment of Nottingham in comparison with the natural beauty that surrounds the mines.

Lawrence mixes means of development here. He not only relies on possibility and circumstance, but adds comparison and causal analysis. One could say, for instance, that the ugliness of the environment causes the conditions

Lawrence describes. Mixing the means of development is common to most writers.

The real tragedy of England, as I see it, is the tragedy of ugliness. The country is so lovely: the man-made England is so vile. I know that the ordinary collier [coal miner], when I was a boy, had a peculiar sense of beauty, coming from his intuitive and instinctive consciousness, which was awakened down pit. And the fact that he met with just cold ugliness and raw materialism when he come up into daylight, and particularly when he came to the Square or the Breach, and to his own table, killed something in him, and in a sense spoiled him as a man. The woman almost invariably nagged about material things. She was taught to do it; she was encouraged to do it. It was a mother's business to see that her sons ''got on,'' and it was the man's business to provide the money. In my father's generation, with the old wild England behind them, and the lack of education, the man was not beaten down. But in my generation, the boys I went to school with, colliers now, have all been beaten down, what with the din-din-dinning of Board Schools, books, cinemas, clergymen, the whole national and human consciousness hammering on the fact of material prosperity above all things.

The men are beaten down, there is prosperity for a time, in their defeat —and then disaster looms ahead. The root of all disaster is disheartenment. And men are disheartened. The men of England, the colliers in particular, are disheartened. They have been betrayed and beaten.

Now though perhaps nobody knew it, it was ugliness which really betrayed the spirit of man, in the nineteenth century. The great crime which the moneyed classes and promoters of industry committed in the palmy Victorian days was the condemning of the workers to ugliness, ugliness, ugliness: meanness and formless and ugly surroundings, ugly ideals, ugly religion, ugly hope, ugly love, ugly clothes, ugly furniture, ugly houses, ugly relationship between workers and employers. The human soul needs actual beauty even more than bread. The middle classes jeer at the colliers for buying pianos—but what is a piano, often as not, but a blind reaching out for beauty. To the woman it is a possession and a piece of furniture and something to feel superior about. But see the elderly colliers trying to learn to play, see them listening with queer alert faces to their daughter's execution of *The Maiden's Prayer,* and you will see a blind, unsatisfied craving for beauty. It is far more deep in the men than the women. The women want show. The men want beauty, and still want it.

The most touching aspect of this passage is its confidence in the basic goodness of the men who worked the coal mines. Lawrence's confidence is in the workers, the laborers, none of whom created the ugliness that surrounded the mines: that was created by the wealthy mine owners and employers who, at some remove from the Square, the brick workers' tenements, lived in baronial splendor. You might ask whether Lawrence is being too harsh on the women in the community. He condemns their materialism but he sees them as a product of their environment just as he sees the men as beaten down by their circumstances. The ugliness of the man-made environment has been translated into an ugliness of spirit.

The following example is from a student, Paulette, who had been a lifeguard for several summers before coming to college. In her last year in high school, she had a terrible experience, which she describes. Her writing is naturally not as detailed and vivid as D. H. Lawrence's, but she makes an effort to bring us to the scene she witnessed and to understand the circumstances that made it possible for one of her friends, a fine athlete, to die prematurely.

The day it happened my friends and I went for our usual swim at Oswega Lake, seeking relief from the sweltering August heat. The clear water sparkled in the sunlight and reflected the oak trees which stood on the sloping bank. It was a fairly small lake in Connecticut but the bank sloped sharply to a depth of twenty feet. We were all good swimmers; Marty and Bob were on the high school swim team and I took swimming lessons for years. We were having a great time playing tag and searching the muddy bottom for interesting objects while Terry, another friend, scouted around the bank. Terry didn't know how to swim but we thought he was okay since he stayed on land. It's not that Terry was unathletic. After all, he was the captain of the basketball team. He just never learned to swim. We didn't even realize that Terry had drowned until it was time to go home and we couldn't find him. We figured that he went for a walk, but when we found him he was dead.

It happened when I was seventeen but I'll never forget how we dragged his limp body out of the water, how we ran as fast as we could to tell his parents, and how we all cried at the funeral. It's sad to think that his death was made possible just because he never learned to swim.

Paulette's writing sample came from a position paper that urged the university to make swimming lessons mandatory for those students who could not pass a swimming test. She was very passionate about this subject, and the sample is from her third draft—somewhat refined and polished from its original version. The fact that she truly cared about this matter helped her writing take on an extra vividness and vitality. Personal experience made this important to her.

Writer's Workshop: Cause and Effect and Possibility and Circumstance

1. Describe the circumstances in which you spent your early years. Consider the issues that interest D. H. Lawrence in his recollection of life in Nottingham among his parents and the coal miners. Consider the circumstances of your life in terms of the economic characteristics of your own family and the community; the atmosphere of your education; the physical setting of your community, including questions of beauty as well as of natural resources; and the historical patterns that have been established in the community and your own family.

2. Choose one of the following list of potential subjects for an editorial, essay, or meditative study. In one or two paragraphs establish its causes and effects.

   hard feelings in your best friend
   misunderstandings with parents
   distrust of North Americans in Central America
   fear of failure in a child
   uncertainty regarding the future among current college students

3. Examine the following list of controversial issues and write a short paragraph on two of them establishing whether or not there is a possibility of change for them.

   the generation gap as revealed in differing tastes in music between people
      in their twenties and people in their fifties
   the Cold War between the United States and Russia
   the stand on abortion taken by Right to Lifers
   equal pay for equal work
   racial prejudice in your section of the country
   stockpiling of nuclear weapons

4. From the color-plate section, choose a single painting and explain the circumstances that seem associated with its subject matter. What appears to be the limits of possibility as expressed in the painting? How important are questions of possibility or cause and effect in the painting? What effect does the painting have on you?

5

Means of Development— Part II

Another group of means of development is available to the writer. Like those in the previous chapter, they are not only a means for developing a topic, but also an instrument for developing new ideas. They produce new insights and help make your presentation of arguments and information fuller and more useful. They help you say things that probably would not otherwise have occurred to you.

The means of development I am referring to are:

description
illustration by example
classification
analysis

Using the Means of Development

We begin with the very same clustering on the word *poverty* used in the last chapter.

Using these next four means of development with this clustering produces good results:

Description: Anything you write about poverty will be much more force-ful if its circumstances are described in detail. The look, feel, and smell of welfare hotels, with their aura of disappointment and anticipation, make a fine candidate for description. The same is true for the jails the impoverished often end up in.

Illustration by example: Most popular magazine and newspaper articles on poverty begin with the example of a given person or a given family who suffers from poverty. The example of the individual is always much more impressive to a reader than any generalities about poverty. An example of a mother living in a welfare hotel with one son in prison, fearful that her other children may wind up there, is like a picture. It is worth a thousand words of generalization.

Classification: We classify people and things almost automatically. We see some people as yuppies, some as jocks, some as nerds. In the case of poverty, there are many possible classifications. Among them are the teenage mothers who have no husband, the middle-aged man with no home, the disappointed young alcoholic streetcorner man, the aged huddling in a rat-infested apartment in a dangerous neighborhood. We can classify the poor into further groups: those with education who could change their lives but won't, and those uneducated who can see no way to change their lives. John Kenneth Galbraith sees two classifications: case poverty and insular poverty. In the first, an individual family is poor because of sickness, alcoholism, or some disorder specific to that case. In the second, an entire group of people, such as a given neighborhood, is poor, and the causes are not clear.

Analysis: Finding the causes of poverty is one kind of analysis. But there are more. For example, the means of development by analysis asks the question, Why? Why does society bear the huge cost of poverty in its inner cities? The social cost itself bears analysis and explanation, which is at the heart of analysis.

Description

Description is basic in creative writing and in writing that attempts to describe a process, particularly when it involves physical machinery, objects, or locales. Description makes most forms of writing more vital, more effective, more moving. At times it is essential, as in a narrative of events; sometimes it may be ornamental, as in a letter home. In informative writing, it takes on a special quality because it is a principal instrument of conveying information.

Good description depends upon detail and judgment. Your judgment is needed to guarantee that not too much detail is offered, but that what is offered conveys a clear impression of your subject. The details should come from your own observation. In addition, good description involves the naming of specific items that conjure up imaginative visions in your audience. For example, you would find the invitation to "imagine a bright, new Swiss Army knife with all its blades open to view," a much better description than "imagine a penknife with its blades open." Another skill in description is the capacity to refer to objects and things that your audience is sure to know in order to clarify what you are describing.

The following is by a professional, Edmund Wilson, one of America's best writers of nonfiction, who tells us about a house that he inherited in upper New York State. It had been in his family for a long time, and it meant a great deal to him. His description begins with what sounds like the description of a process: its history and building. But that is only the beginning. He includes details of history as if that too were descriptive. He includes measurements, details of materials, details of construction, detailed observation of the parts of the house, such as its doors.

THE OLD STONE HOUSE

It was built at the end of the eighteenth century: the first event recorded in connection with it is a memorial service for General Washington. It took four or five years in the building. The stone had to be quarried and brought out of the river. The walls are a foot and a half thick, and the plaster was applied to the stone without any intervening lattice. The beams were secured by enormous nails, made by hand and some of them eighteen inches long. Solid and simple as a fortress, the place has also the charm of something which has been made to order. There is a front porch with white wooden columns which support a white wooden balcony that runs along the second floor. The roof comes down close over the balcony, and the balcony and the porch are draped with vines. Large ferns grow along the porch, and there are stone hitching posts and curious stone ornaments, cut out of the quarry like the house: on one side, a round bottomed bowl in which red geraniums bloom, and on the other, an unnamable object, crudely sculptured and vaguely pagoda-like. The front door is especially handsome: the door itself is dark green and equipped with a brass knocker, and the woodwork which frames it is white; it is crowned with a wide fanlight and flanked by two narrow panes of glass, in which a white filigree of ironwork makes a webbing like ice over winter ponds. On one of the broad sides of the building, where the mortar has come off the stone, there is a dappling of dark gray under pale gray like the dappling of light in shallow water, and the feathers of the elms make dapplings of sun among their shadows of large lace on the grass.

The lawn is ungraded and uneven like the pastures, and it merges eventually with the fields. Behind, there are great clotted masses of myrtle-beds, lilac-bushes, clumps of pink phlox and other things I cannot identify; pink and white hollyhocks, some of them leaning, fine blue and purple dye of larkspur; a considerable vegetable garden, with long rows of ripe goose-berries and currants, a patch of yellow pumpkin flowers, and bushes of raspberries, both white and red—among which are sprinkled like confetti the little flimsy Calfornia poppies, pink, orange, white and red. In an old dark red barn behind, where the hayloft is almost collapsing, I find spinning-wheels, a carder, candle-molds, a patent bootjack, obsolete implements of carpentry, little clusters of baskets for berry-picking and a gigantic pair of scales such as is nowadays only seen in the hands of allegorical figures.

THE APPEAL TO THE SENSES

The Wilson excerpt is impressive description. It is detailed, specific, concrete. Like all good description, it creates images in our minds through an appeal to the senses. Usually, we recognize a natural hierarchy: the sense of sight first, the sense of sound second, the sense of touch third, and the senses of taste and smell next. Most description, like that of Edmund Wilson, appeals to the sense of sight—and in his case centers on colors, including the imagined colors of flowers. He does not tell us how things sounded because most of them are inanimate.

Consequently, Wilson concentrates entirely on the look of things. He gives us sizes, materials, relationships between parts, colors, small objects in the barn. He gives us the names of flowers, which helps him avoid becoming cluttered with too much special description. Those of us who recognize the flowers will get a very particular image. Those of us who do not recognize each flower will get a more general picture of flowers. But everyone will be able to construct an image. Wilson refers to materials: stone, plaster, woodwork, brass, iron, and glass. This is what the house is made of, and not to mention these materials would have given a much less specific picture of the place.

The capacity to name items in the visual field is extremely important. He mentions myrtle, lilac, phlox, hollyhocks, larkspur, gooseberries, currants, pumpkin flowers, raspberries, and poppies. Then he mentions a spinning wheel, a carder, and other abandoned old machines. This capacity to be specific gives the description the sense of being there. Even if we do not know all the specific items, we know enough to make the description real to us.

Edward Hoagland, a nature writer, shows us one way of introducing more senses than just sight. His essay, "Hailing the Elusory Mountain Lion," is about his experiences in New England examining evidence to confirm the presence of mountain lions in that habitat. The following paragraph, however, is about another encounter—with a bear. Because it was near nightfall, the sense of sight is not as prominent as it is in Wilson's description.

Recently, walking at night on the woods road that passes my house in Vermont, I heard footsteps in the leaves and windfalls. I waited, listening— they sounded too heavy to be anything less than a man, a large deer or a bear. A man wouldn't have been in the woods so late, my dog stood respectfully silent and still, and they did seem to shuffle portentously. Sure enough, after pausing at the edge of the road, a fully grown bear appeared, visible only in dimmest outline, staring in my direction for four or five seconds. The darkness lent a faintly red tinge to his coat; he was well built. Then, turning, he ambled off, almost immediately lost to view, though I heard the noise of his passage, interrupted by several pauses. It was all as concise as a vision, and since I had wanted to see a bear close to my own house, being a person who likes to live in a melting pot, whether in the city or country, and since it was too dark to pick out his tracks, I was grateful when the dog inquisitively urinated along the bear's path, thereby confirming that at least I had witnessed *something*. The dog seemed unsurprised, however, as if the scent were not all that remarkable, and, sure enough, the next week in the car I encountered a yearling bear in daylight two miles downhill, and a cub a month later. My farmer neighbors were politely skeptical of my accounts, having themselves caught sight of only perhaps a couple of bears in all their lives.

A DIFFERENCE IN PURPOSE

Hoagland is using description differently from the way Wilson did. His purposes are to describe the circumstances surrounding an incident, and not to describe a specific locale as Wilson does. The purpose guiding Hoagland's writing includes telling us about what happened, and in a significant sense his paragraph involves not just description, but also narration. It is a natural thing to mix the means of development in this fashion, and the illustrations in this chapter are designed to reveal what happens when a specific means, such as description, is the primary mode in a given piece of writing. Keep in mind, though, that your immediate purpose in writing must always guide you when choosing a means or mixing it with another means. (See the box entitled "Tips: Creating Good Description.")

The following example is from a student essay. Joanne is struck by a photograph which is so powerful that it has involved her in a writing project on starvation in drought-sick Africa. This is the opening paragraph of her essay, and its purpose is to help put us in the frame of mind she was in when she began writing. It also serves the purpose of clarifying her own feelings.

I cannot stop staring at the picture. A middle-aged man, dressed in ragged and torn clothes, stands in the sand among the crowd. His eyes squint from the sun's glare, and reveal a strong worry. This Ethiopian adult has walked two hundred miles in ninety degree weather, merciless, searing heat, able to continue only because of dire need for his child and the prospect of something better waiting for them both. The boy hangs in his arms, a pitiful sight. Probably a mere six years old, he looks more like a skeleton wrapped in skin, muscles not evident and bones jutting out. Flies sit on his face and eyes. One hand hangs limply, unable to brush off the bugs; the other hand rests softly on his head. His face expresses suffering, yet he is too weak to cry. The shred of a shirt barely clothing his otherwise naked body looks like a cloth one would reject as unfit to dust a house with. A wearisome month having passed, they have arrived at their destination, a camp in Sudan with medical vaccinations for the child, as well as food, water, and clothes.

Joanne has presented us with what is, alas, an all too familiar picture. She has used Wilson's techniques and concentrated on the sense of sight because she is reacting to a picture, not to an event. However, she is able to see from the picture that the heat is overwhelming, and so she can also appeal to our sense of touch—we feel heat—as well as our sense of sight. She has been specific in naming things: dust, Ethiopia, flies, skeleton. But she does not deliver the proliferation of items in the way that attracted Wilson. She does not need to do so. Her description has done its job and it is highly effective. There is a narrative element in her description as well, and it shows up in her mentioning that the people in the photograph have been traveling, that it is exceptionally hot, and that they have reached their destination. These details are very important to the description.

TIP

Tips: Creating Good Description
- Appeal to the senses: sight, sound, touch, taste, and smell.
- Name things accurately: be specific and concrete.
- Respect physical locale where appropriate: consider space (left, right, up, down, far, distant) as an aid for being all-inclusive in your description.
- Be aware of the needs of your audience and make the description serve them, particularly if your audience is unfamiliar with what you describe.

Illustration by Example

Few processes of thought can be more natural than our urge to give an example of what we mean. Most writers begin with certain generalizations that eventually demand illustration if we are to follow what is being said. Often we find ourselves in conversation requesting an example in order to better understand what a speaker means. (See the box entitled "Tips: Using Illustration by Example.")

Tips: Using Illustration by Example
- When possible, begin with a general principle that needs illustration.
- Make your examples specific and concrete: where possible, draw from personal experience or rely on careful research.
- Examine your examples for their relevance to your generalization: do they illustrate your point?
- Be aware of the needs of your audience and make your examples clear and relevant to them.

Sometimes in writing it is possible to accumulate examples that demonstrate a point or establish a writer's position. It is possible to extend examples into a full-blown essay, making a general point and then illustrating its ramifications with a variety of examples. In the beginning of "The Flag," Russell Baker does just that. He also describes things, tells us a narrative, analyzes cause and effect, and more. But one of the most interesting things he does is to employ example after example. He is his own first example, explaining his own feelings about the flag. Then he ends with a spate of examples of improper uses of the flag.

THE FLAG

At various times when young, I was prepared to crack skulls, kill and die for Old Glory. I never wholly agreed with the LOVE IT OR LEAVE IT bumper stickers, which held that everybody who didn't love the flag ought to be thrown out of the country, but I wouldn't have minded seeing them beaten up. In fact, I saw a man come very close to being beaten up at a baseball park one day because he didn't stand when they raised the flag in the opening ceremonies, and I joined the mob screaming for him to get to his feet like an American if he didn't want lumps all over his noodle. He stood up, all right. I was then thirteen, and a Boy Scout, and I knew you never let the flag touch the ground, or threw it out with the trash when it got dirty (you burned it), or put up with disrespect for it at the baseball park.

At eighteen, I longed to die for it. When World War II ended in 1945 before I could reach the combat zone, I moped for months about being deprived of the chance to go down in flames under the guns of a Mitsubishi Zero. There was never much doubt that I would go down in flames if given the opportunity, for my competence as a pilot was such that I could barely remember to lower the plane's landing gear before trying to set it down on a runway.

I had even visualized my death. It was splendid. Dead, I would be standing perhaps 4,000 feet up in the sky. (Everybody knew that heroes floated in those days.) Erect and dashing, surrounded by beautiful cumulus clouds, I would look just as good as ever, except for being slightly transparent. And I would smile, devil-may-care, at the camera—oh, there would be cameras there—and the American flag would unfurl behind me across 500 miles of glorious American sky, and back behind the cumulus clouds the Marine Band would be playing "The Stars and Stripes Forever," but not too fast.

Then I would look down at June Allyson and the kids, who had a gold star in the window and brave smiles shining through their tears, and I would give them a salute and one of those brave, wistful Errol Flynn grins, then turn and mount to Paradise, becoming more transparent with each step so the audience could get a great view of the flag waving over the heavenly pasture.

Okay, so it owes a lot to Louis B. Mayer in his rococo period. I couldn't help that. At eighteen, a man's imagination is too busy with sex to have much energy left for fancy embellishments of patriotic ecstasy. In the words of a popular song of the period, there was a star-spangled banner waving somewhere in the Great Beyond, and only Uncle Sam's brave heroes got to go there. I was ready to make the trip.

All this was a long time ago, and asinine though it now may seem, I confess it here to illustrate the singularly masculine pleasures to be enjoyed in devoted service to the Stars and Stripes. Not long ago I felt a twinge of the old fire when I saw an unkempt lout on a ferryboat with a flag sewed in the crotch of his jeans. Something in me wanted to throw him overboard, but I didn't since he was a big muscular devil and the flag had already suffered so many worse indignities anyhow, having been pinned in politician's lapels, pasted on cars to promote gasoline sales and used to sanctify the professional sports industry as the soul of patriotism even while the team owners were instructing their athletes in how to dodge the draft.

Baker's imagination draws on himself at three points in his life: as a child at a sports event; as a young pilot, inspired by the example, in turn, of the way people behaved in wartime motion pictures; and then as a much older man tempered by the realization that the flag has been put to many ignoble purposes.

The final paragraph shows that Baker can still be stirred by the flag, but now his emotion is tempered by experience. That paragraph is loaded with examples: the unkempt lout first, but then politicians, cars, and the professional sports industry. All these have in some way dealt irreverently with the flag. This realization keeps his writing under control.

Professional writers naturally use description and illustration by example with greater complexity and subtlety than most of us. That is why they are professionals. Yet because these means of development are natural to our thinking, everyone can make use of them effectively. Edward, in the following excerpt from a student essay, attempts a relatively complex series of illustration by example. He begins with a statement from Machiavelli's *The Prince*, which he was reading in class. The question he poses is simply whether or not it is true that "being disarmed makes you despised," as Machiavelli says. He begins by referring to contemporary politics. Then he moves to the larger issues of the arms race between the United States and the Soviet Union, and finally uses his own experiences as examples of the way people behave.

MACHIAVELLI ON MILITARY MIGHT

In regard to the prince, Machiavelli asserted that "being disarmed makes you despised," a statement that seems to hold true today in a world of power struggles, coups, and political alliances. Weak and unstable countries often pledge allegiance to powerful nations in return for military assistance. Castro's takeover in Cuba and the Sandanistas' rule in Nicaragua illustrate the importance of military might in controlling a country. These and other power-hungry dictators warmly receive military aid from the Soviet Union and other advocates of communism.

Today's arms race clearly illustrates the importance of military strength as a "deterrent to war." Powerful nations such as the Soviet Union and the United States have controlled world politics for years mainly due to their military supremacy, but with the advent of crude, inexpensive nuclear weapons, developing countries may be able to gain substantial control through the threat of nuclear war. Might seems to indeed command respect.

This viewpoint need not apply to state affairs alone. Few, if any, of us like to be considered weak, whether it be physically, mentally, or spiritually. I myself often try to avoid anything I do not do well in, whether it be a weak subject in school or a weak backhand on the tennis court. Man seems to have a basic "need" to be strong, which may be a product of nature or of socialization.

Edward uses today's arms race as an example to illustrate Machiavelli's argument. He sees the effect of the arms race on the world. He sees its effects in smaller nations, its current evidence in the superpowers, and traces its origins to the individual. Essentially, he agrees with Machiavelli.

riter's Workshop

Writer's Workshop: Description and Illustration by Example

1. Describe one of the following places, events, or things to a person whom you think has never visited, witnessed, or seen it.

a pig roast
a traffic jam
a nuclear war protest
mountaineering
saturday morning television
sailboating
skydiving

bargaining in an antique shop [or other shop]
campaigning for an office
working in a _____
a computer
a bank

Read your description to your peer editing group and keep track of the questions they ask. How many of them relate to the adequacy or inadequacy of your description?

2. Describe the circumstances surrounding the most important historical event you remember living through. Be sure to give dates, historical background where necessary, a description of personages involved, scenes that were important, and a detailed accounting of the sequence of events.

3. Write a brief statement using illustration by example as your means of development. Illustrate one of the general principles that follow:

It's always best to think before you speak.
Money talks.
Haste makes waste.
You can never know too much.
It's not what you say, it's what you do that counts.
You never know who will be your friend.
He who lives on hope dies fasting.
It's not who you are, it's who you know.
Doing things the hard way is sometimes the best way.

4. Defend television against those who say it is mindless and idiotic in content. Use both description and illustration by example.

5. Describe one of the paintings in the color-plate section to someone who has not seen it. Choose from Richard Estes' "Diner," Paul Delaroche's "Execution of Lady Jane Grey," or Edgar Degas' "Self-Portrait."

Classification

At first glance, classification may not seem to imply a means of development at all. You might think of classification as something that simply is. For example, you naturally assume that people are classified into two types: male and female. Letters are classified into vowels and consonants. Nouns are classified as proper and common. And on and on. The world as we know it has been constantly classified by people who have a wide variety of backgrounds and motives. How often has society been classified into aristocrats and peasants, or upper class, middle class, and lower class? The instinct to classify is almost impossible to resist. We classify foods: meat, poultry, fish, and vegetables. We classify people as meat eaters or vegetarians. In the category of vegetarians, we have those who will eat fish, eggs, milk, and cheese; and then we have those who will eat nothing but vegetables.

Some writers act as if these classifications are given to us from on high. They seem to exist rather than to have been created. That is why classification has a powerful rhetorical force: it seems to have the strength of authority accompanying it. So the first thing to realize is that classification is something you can do yourself. It is based on the recognition of differences among things of the same kind. It requires imagination, observation, and a good basic knowledge of your subject.

Let us suppose as an example that you have read a nasty letter to the editor of your college newspaper attacking the student body for watching too much television. Suppose the writer of the letter had seen a group of students in a lounge watching soap operas and had based her letter on this experience. If you were to write a letter in response, one of the first things you might want to do is establish a classification of television programs into a pattern such as documentaries, news programs, movies, situation comedies, live sports, cartoons, and soap operas. You could establish that the letter writer had only considered one kind of television show and had based an opinion on a limited experience. If you wanted to defend watching soap operas, then you could classify them in ways that would establish a distinction of kind or of quality or both.

We can see the usefulness of classification in the following excerpt from an essay by Nathan Glazer, a sociologist who is a student of the contemporary changes in our society. He discusses whether or not it is appropriate for our society to compensate social groups—usually referred to somewhat inaccurately as minorities—for past wrongs. In order to argue the case, Glazer begins a system of classification, considering first those groups that would receive compensation and those that would not, and then examining some subgroups. Although he makes them seem totally natural and logical, his classifications are relatively arbitrary but powerful aids to his statement. Watch how his discussions of each classification affect your thinking on this issue.

COMPENSATING GROUPS FOR PAST WRONGS

The supporters of the new policy generally argue that it is a temporary one. They argue (or some do) that consideration of race, color, and national origin in determining employment and education is repugnant, but it is required for a brief time to overcome a heritage of discrimination. I have argued that the heritage of discrimination, as we could see from the occupational developments of the later 1960s, could be overcome by simply attacking discrimination. The statistical-pattern approach was instituted *after,* not before, the remarkably rapid improvement in the black economic and occupational position in the 1960s. I have argued that the claim that school assignment on the basis of race and ethnicity is only temporary is false, because the supporters of such an approach now demand it whatever the circumstances, and the Constitution is now so interpreted that it can be required permanently.

We have created two racial and ethnic classes in this country to replace the disgraceful pattern of the past in which some groups were subjected to an official and open discrimination. The two new classes are those groups that are entitled to statistical parity in certain key areas on the basis of race, color, and national origin, and those groups that are not. The consequences of such a development can be foreseen: They are already, in some measure, upon us. Those groups that are not considered eligible for special benefits become resentful. If one could draw a neat line between those who have suffered from discrimination and those who have not, the matter would be simpler. Most immigrant groups have had periods in which they were discriminated against. For the Irish and Jews, for example, these periods lasted a long time. Nor is it the case that all the groups that are now recorded as deserving official protection have suffered discrimination, or in the same way.

The Spanish-surnamed category is particularly confused. It is not at all clear which groups it covers, although presumably it was designed to cover the Mexican Americans and Puerto Ricans. But in San Francisco, Nicaraguans from Central America, who were neither conquered by the United States nor subjected to special legislation and who very likely have suffered only from the problems that all immigrants do, given their occupational and educational background, their economic situation, and their linguistic facility were willy-nilly swept up into one of the categories that had to be distributed evenly through the school system. The Cuban immigrants have done well and already have received special government aid owing to their status as refugees: Are they now to receive, too, the special benefit of being considered Spanish-surnamed, a group listed in the goals required in affirmative action programs?

The protected groups include variously the descendants of free immigrants, conquered peoples, and slaves, and a single group may include the descendants of all three categories (e.g., the Puerto Ricans). Do free immigrants who have come to this country voluntarily deserve the same protected treatment as the descendants of conquered people and slaves? The point is that racial and ethnic groups make poor categories for the design of public policy. They include a range of individuals who have different legal bases for claims for redress and remedy of grievances. If the categories are designed to correct the injustices of the past, they do not work.

Basically, Glazer reexamines the system of classification used by the Office of Equal Opportunity. He outlines the current categories of classification and describes unsuspected weaknesses in the fairness of treatment of those in various categories. Later in the essay, Glazer summarizes his argument and the entire process of categorization used by the government in this sentence:

The racial and ethnic categories neither properly group individuals who deserve redress on the basis of past discriminatory treatment, nor properly group individuals who deserve redress on the basis on a present deprived condition.

If you were writing an essay on this subject, you would find that using Glazer's method of development by classification would open many avenues of thought to you that might otherwise have remained closed. You could easily examine any of the categories he has mentioned and see many more subcategories, each with its own problems.

Not everyone who uses classification needs to go quite to the lengths that Glazer resorts to here. The following is an example from a student essay. Christine is interested in making a few points about her early experiences reading magazines, and although she resists classifying them in broad categories, she implies some of those categories because they are implicit in her examples. Here is a case in which illustration by example transforms itself into development by classification because each example implies a classification.

A POPULAR ADDICTION

Magazines are addictive. A walk through the local Walden Books, CVS, or Dairy Mart will reveal dozens of titles and topics. The covers, bold and glossy, beckon potential readers with promises of unique and important revelations: the most effective way to thin thick thighs, newly discovered carcinogens lurking in favorite foods, or the latest waft of fashion panache from "gai Paris." Even the smell of fresh newsprint can be sufficiently seductive to drive a magazine addict to the check-out with one or more of the dream books.

In America we are encouraged, "If you dream it, you can be it." Magazine editors have a knack for packaging up the American dream by convincing laymen that they can cook a "foie gras" like Julia Child, or successfully write off business expenses like a professional financier. Our isolated view of life expands through travel guides, our options increase with career features. Magazines feed our fancy, and we can not resist the flattery.

Magazine addiction is progressive, and may begin early in life with such magazines as *Weekly Reader* and *Humpty Dumpty*. I spent my summers as a child in anticipation of Saturdays, the day my *Weekly Reader* would arrive, rolled neatly into a cardboard tube. A friend of mine recalls designating a large part of her allowance each year for her *Humpty Dumpty* magazine subscription, sacrificing all sweets but M & Ms and chocolate ice cream cones. Both of us eventually moved on to *Seventeen* magazine, from which we learned that boys do not like scholarly girls, and that chocolate reduces young complexions into active battlefields. We converted from word games and wildlife shows to old Joe Namath films, in front of which we sipped tall glasses of Tab. We looked to *Seventeen* for advice and instruction. We had become dependents.

The American public devours magazines by the ton, seeking knowledge, entertainment, and formulas for success. The machinery of high society is well oiled with the monthly boosts it receives from *Town and Country* coverage, and diehard food connoisseurs will not allow a single issue of *Gourmet* to slip by them. Magazines court us with fine words and promises, and we are amenable subjects.

MIXING THE MEANS OF DEVELOPMENT

Later, Christine rewrote the piece with more detailed descriptions of each of the magazines. The final result borrowed something from all three of the means of development we have been talking about in this chapter so far. Her classifications of magazines remained the same, but her descriptions of them, including concrete references to articles and concerns prominent in various issues, made the magazines themselves come much more to life. Further, the items she referred to constituted illustrations by example. They enlivened the piece and helped make her point.

Most professional writers naturally gravitate toward a mixture of the means of development. Your examination of good writing, either that of your peers, or that of the writers you read in magazines and other publications, should turn up numerous examples of the means of development we have discussed. But you will also see that few of them are used purely or singly. Classification naturally benefits from description, just as description thrives on classification. llustration by example would not work very well without the writer possessing some skills at description.

For purposes of illustration, it is relatively easy to show examples of each of the means, but you should always keep in mind that there is no special virtue in keeping the means pure. Mixing them, once you have built up enough conscious awareness of their uses and advantages, is as natural as using them in the first place. Treat the illustrations in this text as examples of a means being dominant but not necessarily being exclusive in its use. (See the box entitled "Tips: Using Classification.")

Tips: Using Classification
- Aim to use classifications that are already familiar to your audience.
- Establish all the subcategories that you feel are relevant to your subject.
- Distinguish your classifications according to quality and kind.
- Be quick to admit any obvious problems in making your categories work in the way you expect.
- Look for opportunities to qualify categories or classifications in unexpected ways so that your audience responds with the sense of learning something new.

Analysis

Analysis applies a close examination of circumstances, events, and complex questions. It usually has a clear goal: the explanation or understanding of a process or phenomenon, or both. It asks the questions Why? and What does this mean?

The analytic approach is based on observation of detail, on the willingness to examine the part without losing sight of its relationship to the whole, and on the belief that the avenue to a total understanding of the whole is reached by a patient meandering through the side streets of the separate examinable elements. If you can understand the parts of something, you can understand how they function relative to each other, and what they each contribute to the whole.

The purpose of analysis is to reveal what is not evident at first sight. Thus, analysis may reveal a subtle relationship among elements; it may reveal the reasons for success or failure of a plan or operation; or it may reveal the implications of a circumstance or situation. A primary function of analysis is usually to reveal the hidden meaning of something, whether it be a physical thing or a series of historical or current events. Analysis is the means of development that is used to see into something. Learning how to use it takes time, and in some ways constitutes an education in itself.

The following example of analysis is related to the question of cause and effect, and it treats the question of racial discrimination. James Baldwin lived in Harlem and became one of America's most distinguished writers. His understanding of racial discrimination was firsthand, and his position as an informed American on this issue was solid. He analyzes here a specific reaction many people have to the question of suffering in impoverished circumstances: pointing to people who have "made it" and assuming that anyone can make it. He uses two frequent examples: Sammy Davis, Jr., and Frank Sinatra. If they made it, why can't other poor people make it? Baldwin takes that, and some other such thoughts, and offers us an analysis that results in a surprise.

Now I am perfectly aware that there are other slums in which white men are fighting for their lives, and mainly losing. I know that blood is also flowing through those streets and that the human damage there is incalculable. People are continually pointing out to me the wretchedness of white people in order to console me for the wretchedness of blacks. But an itemized account of the American failure does not console me and it should not console anyone else. That hundreds of thousands of white people are living, in effect, no better than "niggers" is not a fact to be regarded with complacency. The social and moral bankruptcy suggested by this fact is of the bitterest, most terrifying kind.

The people, however, who believe that this democratic anguish has some consoling value are always pointing out that So-and-So, white, and So-and-So, black, rose from the slums into the big time. The existence—the public existence—of, say, Frank Sinatra and Sammy Davis, Jr. proves to them that America is still the land of opportunity and that inequalities vanish before the determined will. It proves nothing of the sort. The determined will is rare—at the moment, in this country, it is unspeakably rare—and the inequalities suffered by the many are in no way justified by the rise of a few. A few have always risen—in every country, every era, and in the teeth of regimes which can by no stretch of the imagination be thought of as free. Not all of these people, it is worth remembering, left the world better than they found it. The determined will is rare, but it is not invariably benevolent. Furthermore, the American equation of success with the big time reveals an awful disrespect for human life and human achievement. This equation has placed our cities among the most dangerous in the world and has placed our youth among the most empty and most bewildered. The situation of our youth is not mysterious. Children have never been very good at listening to their elders, but they have never failed to imitate them. They must, they have no other models. That is exactly what our children are doing. They are imitating our immorality, our disrespect for the pain of others.

Baldwin's analysis focuses on two smaller aspects of the larger question of racial inequity and the suffering of the black poor: 1. white people are also poor and also suffer, and 2. the determined person can make it out of the ghetto. In essence, Baldwin is quarreling with someone else's analysis. That analysis begins with observation: white people suffer poverty; some people can get out of poverty. It then draws these conclusions: if white people are suffering poverty, then why get so worked up over the fact that black people suffer? And, if Sammy Davis, Jr., and Frank Sinatra can get out of poverty, so can everyone because this is the land of opportunity. Baldwin counters by saying that white poverty does not excuse black poverty, and that although some people can escape poverty, not everyone can. He adds as a footnote the fact that some people who escape poverty do more harm than good.

Breaking the problem down into smaller units is what Alyssa does in the next example of student writing. One summer, when she was in Italy with her mother, she spent some time in Pompeii, a Roman town that was engulfed in an eruption of Mt. Vesuvius. During that visit her mother mentioned to Alyssa that the Roman culture may have perished as a result of widespread lead poisoning. Alyssa decided to write about that possibility. A few paragraphs from her discussion follow—a point by point consideration of whether enough lead entered the body of the average Roman to cause a serious medical problem.

LEAD POISONING IN ROME

Today's city dwelling American is no stranger to lead: he/she absorbs an average of 30 to 50 micrograms of lead a day; lead or lead compounds are pumped into the air by automobile exhaust systems, industrial smelters, or found within paint, waterpipes, and food stuffs stored in lead-soldered cans. How, then, do we explain the Ancient Romans, innocent to the mechanical present and their democracies turned technocracies, who managed to inhale, imbibe, or even eat an average of 250 micrograms of lead per day? What about aborigines of the same period, ignorant of lead's existence or its manufacture, whose natural body levels were fifteen times less than that of their Roman counterparts?

Recent archaelogical finds tell us that lead poisoning may have been a widespread affliction amongst ancient Romans. Previously there was talk, theories, fears of such a possibility, never legitimate tests or the skeletal remains to perform them on: the Romans practiced cremation and left no cemeteries. A discovery of some fifty-five skeletal remains unearthed at Herculaneum (Pompeii's twin city, also covered by lava from Mt. Vesuvius in A. D. 79) provide an excellent "slice" of ancient Roman inhabitants and life. A mean level of 84 micrograms of lead was found within the 55 skeletons, a figure three times that considered safe today. Eight of the Romans may well have been victims of lead poisoning, averaging 100 to 200 micrograms of lead in the body, while two other samples showed the incredible sums of 2,790 and 6,350 micrograms. Such levels are difficult to substantiate, however, for it would seem these individuals ingested lead as part of their daily diet, prompting one to ask, just what were their would-be sources?

History has it that Claudius, Caligula, and Nero were all given to strange bouts of behavior—slurred speech, staggered gait, and mental incompetency, all previously attributed to the effects of alcohol dependency—almost one vinous gallon of it per day. The most damaging factor of which was something on the order of an "ancient additive." Our modern day saccharins and monosodium glutamates are pieces of cake when compared to a particular grape syrup, boiled down in leaded containers, and added to enhance the color and bouquet of wines and prevent their further fermentation. One teaspoon of such a syrup was just enough to cause a chronic case of lead poisoning. Maximilianus used his lead pots, lead pans, lead forks, lead knives, lead water pipes, lead food containers, lead smelted coins, and leaded wine decanter—is it any wonder he might have been an excellent candidate to suffer under the effects of lead poisoning.

Alyssa answers a question: How could the Romans get lead poisoning when they lived in a world that has few of the modern sources of lead poisoning? Her statistics on lead residues in the body establish the fact that there was a possibility. Then Alyssa moved on to the next aspect of the question: How did they get the lead? She looks at the household of Maximilianus—a wealthy citizen of Herculaneum—and sees impressive evidence of the presence of lead in cups and dishware as well as in pipes and utensils. Her analysis is direct and relatively simple. By breaking the entire issue down into manageable parts, and by establishing probable cause, she begins to find answers to her question.

Analysis has an immense number of forms. It can involve the examination of a statement or a question. It can involve breaking down a large question into smaller questions. It can involve examining something like a poem, painting, or piece of architecture for its patterning and its significance or meaning. But no matter what its particular form, it is breaking things down

Tips: Using Analysis
- Restrict yourself to the discussion of a limited number of aspects of your subject.
- Decide exactly what kinds of questions you are interested in answering (or raising): limit your analysis to those questions.
- Analysis usually involves the explanation of the significance of some aspect of your topic.
- Questions of causation and possibility are naturally appropriate for development by the means of analysis.
- Do not lose sight of the whole issue at hand, but be sure to work with aspects of the issue that are small enough to handle comfortably.
- Concentrate on your purposes for analysis, and be sure you accommodate your audience's needs.

into manageable units and always striving to establish the hidden meanings, the unnoticed relationships, the truths that lie beneath the surface. (See the box entitled "Tips: Using Analysis.")

Writer's Workshop: Classification and Analysis

1. What are the appropriate classifications of students at your college? What makes them distinct from one another, and what links them with one another? Concentrate on social and academic distinctions and see if there are any obvious relationships between the two.

2. Choose a piece of athletic equipment, such as running shoes, tennis racquets, golf clubs, basketballs, skis, skates, climbing gear, or anything else and discuss it by using classification as your means of development.

3. Write a commentary on the rooms of your friends, using the means of classification as your principle of development. Try to think up original and witty names for each category.

4. Offer an analysis of the scholarship program of your college. What is the school policy on who gets the scholarships, and on what basis are they offered? You might consider answering the question: Who should get scholarships and why?

5. The argument in favor of nuclear stockpiling usually hinges on the opinion that being well armed is likely to prevent war. Analyze this view by considering the relationship between being armed and being attacked. What are the chief issues to be considered by the nation that feels weapons bring security? Consider, too, the opposite proposition: Would being unarmed increase a nation's security?

6. Using both classification and analysis, consider the following statements that are critical of college sports. Do they constitute an adequate view of the position of sports in colleges?

College athletics is a business, not a sport.
Star athletes are paid to go to college.
Athletics is a social, not an academic pursuit.
College athletics is not really amateur: those who participate are paid in scholarships, extra favors, such as cars and apartments, and some are given special treatment in the classroom.

7. Analyze each of the following statements in an effort to determine its validity:
Legislating the use of seat belts is an infringement on personal freedom.
Flesh magazines like *Playboy* and *Hustler* have damaged the fabric of American life.
Beauty contests like the Miss America Pageant demean all women by making them objects.

Proposed gun control laws would deprive Americans of one of their most basic rights: the privilege of bearing arms.

The more a wealthy person earns, the higher his tax rate should be.

A reverse income tax, whereby those who have no earnings would receive tax payments from the government, would help produce economic equity.

8. Examine the paintings in the color-plate section and establish as many as three or four classifications into which you feel the paintings may fit. What are the classifications and which paintings may best be classified together. Does classification help us interpret the paintings more intelligently?

PART II

Organizational
Principles

Introduction

I N PART, the question of organization has already been considered in the discussions of prewriting, outlines, and some of the means of development. Brainstorming, grouping, clustering, and free writing all produce useful material that needs to be sifted through and organized. Outlines establish what should be part of your writing, and they give you a chance to decide where each part ought to go. The means of development provide guides to segments of a piece of writing. Any long statement on a controversial issue will have sections devoted to analysis, definition, description, cause and effect, and more. The larger question is: Where should each of these be placed in your writing?

Beyond providing the parts, sometimes the means of development can also provide you with an overall structure. For example, you can guide an entire editorial on the subject of the antinuclear movement by the means of comparison. A great many important pieces of writing have comparisons in their titles: *Pride and Prejudice, War and Peace,* and *Rich Man, Poor Man,* to name just a few. Comparison, like the other means of development, offers you a focus and a guide to organization.

Ancient Wisdom

Greek rhetoricians advised their students to follow a direct, clear, and often rigid formula for their works—usually speeches of a relatively fixed length. Their advice is still of great value, although it needs careful interpretation. By no means should we concern ourselves with maintaining rigidity in writing. The ancients insisted that a composition should have three parts:

beginning
middle
end

The problem with this advice is obvious: all writing, good or bad, long or short, has, by definition, a beginning, middle, and end. So on the surface, the advice seems unusable. However, this advice can be made helpful if you establish the needs of your beginning, middle, and end. The following list of suggestions can help you see what the Greeks meant, and at the same time give you an idea for your own structure.

The beginning is the introduction. No matter what you decide to put there, you know that the introduction is the first part of your writing that your audience will see. Therefore its job is to make the best impression it can on your audience. It should keep your audience reading and also inform it about your subject.

The middle of your writing does the work. If you compared the U.S. policy on arms control with the policy of the Soviet Union, the middle would be filled with comparisons of one point after another. Deciding which points to discuss first, second, and third becomes the chief organizational challenge in this part.

No matter what you put in it, your conclusion is usually the last part of your writing the audience will see. In it you will want to reinforce your main points, which you hope will leave the audience knowing what has been accomplished and feeling satisfied, as if the expectations you set up in your introduction have been met.

Following is a small chart showing what the three parts of an essay can accomplish:

Introduction
   Address your audience.
   Establish your subject and your voice as author.
   Clarify your purpose in writing.
   State or imply what your writing expects to accomplish.
Middle
   Approach your subject from the positions implied in your introduction.
   Develop your main points according to your choice of the means of development.
   Order your main points according to your sense of their importance.
Conclusion
   Recapitulate your main ideas.
   Remind your audience what you have achieved.
   Leave your audience feeling satisfied by your approach to the subject.

The chart is appropriately open as a form, because filling in the main points is yet another organizational task. The act of writing is an act of discovery, not only of what you wish to include, but of where you will include it. The outlining process is dynamic; things change as you write. The use of prewriting techniques and the means of development is also dynamic. Some ideas you develop will seem more useful to you than others. How you organize them will depend in large measure on your purposes, which is why the following chapters focus on kinds of writing with different original purposes.

Organizational Demands
of Different Kinds of Writing

The following chapters treat certain kinds of writing that all have their own organizatioal demands. In each chapter specific methods of developing ideas and material will be introduced to supplement the general means of development treated in Part I. The organizational principles appropriate to each kind of writing reveal their special demands and resources.

For example, when approaching the opportunity to write a narrative, you should always keep in mind that narratives are the record of events and activities that have happened in a given time. In narrating a sequence of events you may wish to tell things in the order in which they happen— chronological order—or you may wish to start in the middle of things and later give your reader a flashback to provide the beginning of the narrative. You might also wish to flash back to describe earlier details that supply background.

Informative writing may disregard chronological demands, but insist on an ordering of information according to its importance. In such a case, your job is to sift through the information you wish to communicate and decide which is most and least important. A rule of thumb in journalism is to put the most important information first, and end with the least important. The advantage of that scheme is that the reader will get most of the information right away, and if the reader should stop in the middle, most of the critical information has been transmitted. There is also the question of point of view, or perspective, and the pleasure of writing informative prose is sometimes involved in experimenting with different perspectives. All of these issues are organizational.

Argumentative prose makes its own demands on organization. You cannot write a persuasive piece without developing arguments that persuade. Therefore, your organizational problem will center on where to place specific arguments. Again, ranking your arguments in order of importance can be a useful aid, but very few persuasive pieces use a simple order from most to least important. A certain amount of creative thought has to guide your decisions about what to place where, when you are writing argumentative prose. Even the question of where to place your analysis and refutation of arguments against your position can take on serious organizational overtones.

Writing literary analysis makes its own demands on structure because special kinds of questions are appropriate to this kind of writing just as special terms must be accounted for, such as text, reader, imagery, metaphor, theme, character, action, and so forth. The question of organization might center on deciding which comes first in your discussion, as well as deciding which is most important. This kind of writing depends on the process of gathering evidence and drawing inferences (or conclusions) from that evidence. Which evidence to use, and where to use it will be organizational issues.

All of what has been said here may apply to the research paper. The question of chronology may be crucial for your organization. Or, you may find that in addition to chronology the question of the relative importance of given material is of great significance to your organizational decisions. Most specific to the research paper, however, is the question of where to include a given piece of research in the texture of your own paper. In a research paper you gather a great deal of material evidence. You then must decide how each item weighs in terms of your overall purposes. Then through the process of revision, you can begin to experiment with organizing your material until you find the structure that pleases you.

Each kind of writing discussed in the following chapters makes its own organizational demands, but the demands of one kind of writing can often be applied to another. Chronological order is one organizational principle of narrative that is of great value in other kinds of writing as well. Ranking the separate elements of your writing—arguments, bits of information, pieces of evidence drawn from research—in terms of their importance applies to many kinds of writing. If you organize your writing with the most important element first, and the least important last, you are using a hierarchical principle of organization. If you decide to avoid such a straightforward approach, you will discover that there are others which have been used and which are pleasant to experiment with. But you may find that these principles will be helpful at different times in many kinds of writing.

6

Narrative Writing

Probably no form of discourse is more natural than narrative. To narrate means to tell a story, to describe events, and to record people in action. You do it every day. When you are in the company of friends, one of them sooner or later is going to tell someone about what just happened to him or her. Or, that person may relate the narrative of what happened to someone else. Much of the time you narrate an anecdote, a very brief story with a significance of its own. Joan Didion once began an article with an anecdote about a man who saw a fatal automobile accident in the desert in Nevada. He was in a remote area, and it was growing late at night. The man decided he had to stay through the night with the body because coyotes might come down and damage it. The man felt that would be wrong. And out of that anecdote, Joan Didion began a meditation on the values people hold in that part of the country.

The Anecdote

Narrative is exceptionally powerful. For whatever reason, we have an unusual susceptibility to it. Whenever someone tells us a story—if it's any good at all—we usually stop everything and listen. Once, when reading the *Aeneid* with a group of students, I made some observations on one of the most gory battles in the poem. The narrative depended for its effect on detailed description that bordered on being grisly. Juturnus is described as standing above the man he has just beaten in battle and brutally ramming his spear into his chest, and as I read that painful section of the poem to the class, a woman student rose suddenly in a burst of tears and fled the room. Just a few minutes later I learned that she had recently heard that her fiancé had been killed in Vietnam, and she simply could not tolerate the description that Virgil intended to be read by those who had never known war. Years later, that student wrote me a long letter explaining that she still had not recovered from her experience, but that there was much she needed to say to someone about her fiancé and her feelings. For instance, he had gone into the army to avoid going to prison. He had been a car thief, housebreaker, and general problem in his community. In many ways he was not a nice guy. But she was able to ignore all that and love him anyway, and one of the things she asked me in her letter is how it was possible to love a man who was a criminal, and even worse, how it was possible for her to love a man who was dead. Because that was the situation she was in.

Do you see what I mean? That is an anecdote. It is true, and it is narrative, but only the bare bones of a narrative. Curiously, the bare bones of a narrative are often quite powerful, too.

Writer's Workshop: The Anecdote

Writer's **W**orkshop

1. Write a brief (250 words or less) anecdote relating an event that either you or a friend experienced. Be natural in your telling of the event, and do not strain for effect. Your purpose is simply to relate an experience so that your audience (decide who that is) will have a clear understanding of what happened. As part of your prewriting, refer to Burke's Pentad in Chapter 2 and answer the questions relating to Act, Scene, Agent, Agency, and Purpose. Once you have gathered your ideas and developed some material, write a brief outline of the events of your anecdote. When you are satisfied that you have properly organized them, begin writing your first draft.

2. In your peer editing group, share your anecdotes. Keep careful track of the kinds of questions your peers ask.

Concerning action: What happened? What is the order of events?
Concerning scene: Where exactly did things take place? When did they happen?
Concerning agent: Who are the actors in your anecdote? What are they like? Are they believable?
Concerning agency: Is there a clear sense of how things were done?
Concerning purpose: Do you understand why things were done and what their significance is?

3. Construct an anecdote by referring to the color-plate section. Use the Degas "Self-Portrait," on Berthe Morisot's "Harbor at Lorient" as the basis of an anecdote. Refer to the question above in item 2.

Time: The Power of Chronology

Narratives are organized in terms of time. Events are sequenced and occur one after another. To be a successful narrator, it is essential that you tell a story with both your sense of purpose and audience quite clear. Decide on a time sequence or a plan for that sequence and stay with it until you find the act of writing forces you to alter that plan. But be careful not to drift in your organizational intentions. Revise your plans, do not abandon them.

LINEAR TIME: THE NATURAL SEQUENCE

The simplest way to tell a narrative is to begin with what happened first, then proceed to the next event, and so on until the narrative is complete. Perhaps 90 percent of the time this procedure works perfectly. If you have ever had anyone tell you the narrative of a dream, you will notice that it is always told chronologically, in the order in which the events happened in the dream.

A chronological sequence gives you opportunities to back up in time and make the significance of a current action clear. In other words, you may have to explain what happened in past time that makes the event in present time possible. In drama, this is called exposition. You explain how we got to where we are now so that your audience is not confused or misled.

The following lengthy paragraph from Jane Kramer's *The Last Cowboy* uses time in interesting ways. Overall, her narrative is brisk, almost skeletal —she could provide much more detail—and it follows a straight-on chronological record of what happened when Betsy, the wife of ranch foreman Henry Blanton, started working five years ago. Lots of background is provided to explain the situation, and because the basic means of development of the paragraph is cause and effect, much of it explains what caused some of the events.

Henry had ordered his last saddle from the Stockman's Saddle Shop, in Amarillo, as a kind of compensation when Betsy started working, five years ago. His monthly pay then was only five hundred and fifty dollars, and there was never enough money to buy the groceries, keep the girls in school clothes, settle Henry's debts at the package store, and meet Betsy's Christmas Club payments at the bank. All four Blanton girls were still at home then. They wanted their own horses, and Betsy thought it would be nice if they had music lessons with the new piano teacher over in Perryton —the one who had been doing so well on the concert stage in Oklahoma City until she happened to start a conversation with a handsome cowboy in front of a statue at the National Cowboy Hall of Fame and abandoned her career for a ranch wife's life. As Betsy saw the problem, she had no choice but to take a job, and she took the first one that she was offered. Henry shouted a lot about it, and then he sulked, and finally he left the ranch one morning in the middle of work and drove straight to the sorghum dealer's office. He had been thinking, he said later, about his brother Tom, whose wife, Lisa Lou, had got herself a job in a bakery, and how humiliating it was for Tom to have to stay in the kitchen cooking lunch for everybody when he and the other hands at the Circle Y Ranch were working cattle near his camp. Henry told Betsy's boss that a cowboy's wife had her duty to her husband and to the ranch that paid him. He was eloquent. A foreman's house, he said, was a kind of command post, and a foreman's wife was like a general—well, maybe not a general, but the general's secretary—whose job it was to stay at that post taking messages, relaying messages, keeping track of everybody on the ranch, sending help in an emergency. He talked about the time that winter that he had had a flat tire far from home, in a freezing and remote pasture. He said that he might have died waiting out there in the cold all night if Betsy had not been home to miss him—to call the hands from their supper and tell them where to search. But the sorghum dealer was stubborn. Betsy could type and knew some shorthand, and she looked to him, he said, like a respectable woman—not like one of those town women, with their false eyelashes and skimpy skirts, who thought of a job as the free use of somebody else's telephone. Eventually, he and Henry arrived at a compromise: Betsy would work most days, but whenever Henry was working cattle at headquarters she would stay home and cook the hands a proper branding lunch.

As in drama, the explanation of what had happened before the present begins right after the present event is identified. Everything between the first sentence and the sentence beginning "Henry shouted a lot . . ." is background explaining why Betsy thought it would be a good thing to get a job. They needed some extra money because their daughters wanted horses and Betsy wanted them to take piano lessons. There is yet another narrative implied in the story of the piano teacher, who left a career for the ranch. The bulk of the paragraph thereafter is a straightforward narrative of what Henry did, what he said, and what the results of his efforts were.

If you imagine this paragraph as a sketch for a more detailed narrative, you will see that it has, essentially, the outlines of a plot: wife goes to work to earn extra money; husband gets anxious about her responsibilities as a foreman's wife; husband asks her employer to let her go; employer says she's too valuable; husband and employer find a compromise. These are the seeds for a feminist novel. To be more complete, this paragraph could be filled out with

Act: Full details describing Henry's first reaction to Betsy's going to work; Betsy's search for work; Henry's buying his saddle; Henry making his plea to Betsy's boss.

Scene: A detailed description of the ranch, the saddle shop, and the sorghum dealer's office.

Agent: Clear development of each important character: Henry, Betsy, and her employer, probably through description and samples of dialogue.
Agency: A sample of the eloquence that caused the employer to be willing to compromise.
Purpose: A fuller analysis of the reasons Henry and Betsy had for what they did.

Partly because we are so naturally predisposed toward telling stories, we depend upon narrative in many kinds of writing. For example, the paragraph by Kramer comes from a long book designed to give us insight into what life is like for modern cowboys, and it is generally a work of exposition. The sample that follows is from a research paper by a student who wrote on the career of Buffalo Bill. In order to give us some idea of what his subject was like, David has to narrate a typical event.

BUFFALO BILL

Fame wouldn't allow him to pass unnoticed in the company of his fans. Often it was the habit of Bill and his crew to visit the local saloon of the town they were in after a show for a few drinks, and, as always, they were instantly recognized as celebrities the moment they walked through the door.

The drinks were always on the house and all night long toasts were made to Bill until everyone could talk about how they drank with the famous scout. Bill's social and courteous attitude refused to let him go without participating in toasts to him. By the night's end, he was lucky to escape without being severely intoxicated. Such nights became routine in his life, a daily routine after every daily show, daily. So daily that his wife became concerned for his health. She made him vow not to drink more than four drinks when he went out. Four drinks he vowed and four drinks he would drink and no more. His vow he kept, as it was his morals to do so, but life on the road was rough and after several months his will power began to weaken. He began to look for ways around his vow of four drinks. "What about the size of those drinks," he once confided in his nephew. "Can't I have one the size of two and still call it one?" This he did. Cody also had his nephew keep a bottle secretly hidden in his nephew's trailer so that Bill could secretly sneak a drink when he felt a need to have one.

Cody's drinking came to a climax one winter. The winter had been a bad one at the ranch in Kansas; the snow had been piled high, the mercury had sunk to a new low and the men had nothing to do but drink for two solid months. Bill during this time had become weak, pale, and trembling. He was in such bad shape that one of his farmhands, Reckless, was forced to declare a prohibition on the ranch by hiding all the whiskey in the potato cellar. After about a month, Bill's health began to improve. He regained his strength; his color returned; and he was no longer trembling. But spring had arrived, the snow was melting away, and the Wild West show was on the road once again. Once off the ranch, Bill began drinking again, but this time with a little control.

David

Even though this is a late draft, it could still use some editing. But David has narrated some important events concerning Buffalo Bill's drinking using the means of development by example: his examples are brief narratives. This is a very common and highly effective way to work. Obviously, David's entire essay was not narrative in organizational principle, but this part of it is.

Using the means of organization by example also has its natural organizational opportunities. If you have several examples, you must decide how to organize them. David chose to tell us about each example in chronological order. And it works.

Developing Narratives: The Five Senses

The narratives we have examined have been pretty much skin and bones. Fiction writers, whose primary purposes are narrative, have to supply detail and flesh out the story. This is true for narrative in any context. How does one flesh out a narrative? The first place to start is by using detail supplied by one or more of the five senses. These techniques have been discussed earlier in treating the means of development by description. By including descriptive elements, you can bring an otherwise dull narrative to life.

DETAIL AND DESCRIPTION

David's stories of Bill Cody's drinking problem definitely hold our interest. But when you do not have such interesting stuff you can still hold a reader's interest by keeping two words in mind: detail and description. Detail is names, dates, references to season, colors, and comparisons with specific things that all help to make narrative effective. Description is references to the things that can be perceived by the five senses and help make a narrative complete.

The following example by John McPhee shows one of America's best writers at work. Watch the way he uses specific details to make his narrative lively and concrete. Also note how he appeals to the senses. His description is full, intense, and sensual. It is what makes this brief segment of a narrative work so well.

TRAVELS IN GEORGIA

Although Sam was working for the state, he was driving his own Chevrolet. He was doing seventy. In a reverberation of rubber, he crossed Hunger and Hardship Creek and headed into the sun on the Swainsboro

Road. I took a ration of gorp—soybeans, sunflower seeds, oats, pretzels, Wheat Chex, raisins, and kelp—and poured another ration into Carol's hand. At just about that moment, a snapping turtle was hit on the road a couple of miles ahead of us, who knows by what sort of vehicle, a car, a pickup; run over like a manhole cover, probably with much the same sound, and not crushed, but gravely wounded. It remained still. It appeared to be dead on the road.

Sam, as we approached, was the first to see it. "D. O. R.," he said. "Man, that is a big snapper." Carol and I both sat forward. Sam pressed hard on the brakes. Even so, he was going fifty when he passed the turtle.

Carol said, "He's not dead. He didn't look dead."

Sam reversed. He drove backward rapidly, fast as the car would go. He stopped on the shoulder, and we all got out. There was a pond beyond the turtle. The big, broad head was shining with blood, but there was, as yet, very little blood on the road. The big jaws struck as we came near, opened and closed bloodily—not the kind of strike that, minutes ago, could have cut off a finger, but still a strike with power. The turtle was about fourteen inches long and a shining hornbrown. The bright spots on its marginal scutes were like light bulbs around a mirror. The neck lunged out. Carol urged the turtle, with her foot, toward the side of the road. "I know, big man," she said to it. "I know it's bad. We're not tormenting you. Honest we're not." Sam asked her if she thought it had a chance to live and she said she was sure it had no chance at all. A car, coming west, braked down and stopped. The driver got out, with some effort and a big pouch. He looked at the turtle and said, "Fifty years old if he's a day." That was the whole of what the man had to say. He got into his car and drove on. Carol nudged the snapper, but it was too hurt to move. It could only strike the air. Now, in a screech of brakes, another car came onto the scene. It went by us, then spun around with squealing tires and pulled up on the far shoulder. It was a two-tone, high-speed, dome-lighted Ford, and in it was the sheriff of Laurens County. He got out and walked toward us, all Technicolor in his uniform, legs striped like a pine-barrens tree frog's, plastic plate on his chest, name of Wade.

"Good morning," Sam said to him.

"How y'all?" said Sheriff Wade.

Carol said, "Would you mind shooting this turtle for us, please?"

"Surely, Ma'am," said the sheriff, and he drew his .38. He extended his arm and took aim.

You might be interested to know that from a distance of twelve inches the sheriff fired and missed the turtle twice. The reason I provide that information is that, like the effect of all good narratives, you want to know how it came out. This narrative could be deadly dull if McPhee had not done several things. First, he establishes the characters: a young woman, Carol; a man in his forties, Sam; and McPhee himself. He lets us have a glimpse of Sheriff Wade, but in some ways the most interesting character is the turtle. The turtle is lively because he is described so carefully. Details of coloration and behavior help us see the animal.

After the turtle was mercifully killed, Carol discovered it was female and was just about to deposit its eggs in the sand, which is apparently why it was on the road. She took the eggs and deposited them for the turtle, hoping that they would hatch.

McPhee's technique depends upon detail and description. The five senses are respected: we see colors, read labels, hear the screech of tires. We hear the reverberation of Sam's car and imagine what the sound of the turtle as it was hit might have been. Even the sense of taste is implied in McPhee handing around the gorp. Later in the narrative, Carol prepares soup using the meat of the turtle. The sense of touch is invoked in Carol's picking the turtle up, and the possible terror of the turtle's snapping a finger is included for good measure. McPhee has paid attention to the basics here, and it has paid off.

Writer's Workshop: Sequence of Time, Detail, and Description

Writer's Workshop

1. Search in your journal or memory for an event that could be among the funniest, saddest, scariest, or most embarrassing you have ever had. Brainstorm this event and follow up with free writing. Group or cluster your ideas until you feel you have enough raw material to work with. Then create a brief outline of the most important individual moments in this event. Finally, answer the questions in the Burkean Pentad and revise your outline.

2. Narrate the event you worked on in Item 1. Describe the action in such a way as to include references depending on all five senses. Describe things visually, then describe what would have been heard, then what would have been felt, tasted, and smelled. Once you have satisfied the demand to include all five senses, organize the events in their chronological order.

3. Select an important historical event that you know well enough to write about. Explain what happened by narrating the sequence of actions in chronological order. Be specific enough to use proper names of people and places in which the events occurred. Use the prewriting techniques you find most valuable, but make a special effort to use the Burkean Pentad.

4. Write a single paragraph narrative. Be sure not to have any references that might be interpreted as description from any of the five senses. Do not refer to what might be seen, heard, touched, tasted, or smelled. Then, write the very same narrative again, and include specific references to as many of the five senses as possible. Discuss both versions in your peer editing group. Keep track of the responses you get from your group. What does the second version cause in terms of response that the first version does not? What is the effect of sensual description on your peers?

The Complete Narrative

You cannot have much of a narrative without

characters
a setting
a point of view
a dramatic situation
a shaped action

But when these are present, a narrative can begin to take on life and become satisfying.

CHARACTER

In order to sustain a complete narrative, most writers rely on the creation of character. Because events are ordinarily carried out by people, they need to be described and shown in action. In McPhee's excerpt, the characters are named, shown doing things, and represented by dialogue. Their actions tell us about them, and their dialogue tells us as much about them as the dialogue we hear from genuine people in our own experience.

Character is created in terms of description, action, and dialogue. And the best, most convincing and interesting character is created by writers who observe people. That means if you wish to write adequate narrative, you should begin observing what people do and say. It is important to keep notes in your journal about people you have seen. The journals of professional writers are often filled with scraps of dialogue, description of people, observations and conclusions about folks they have seen and talked with. And writers go back to those journals in order to draw from them for their work. They are like money in the bank. You will find that if you make a few "deposits" in your own journal that the act of writing narrative will be simplified.

SETTING

Narratives always take place in a geographical space. Our reaction to events is often colored by our sense of the locale and awareness of the environment. In many of the previous examples you saw that the setting is carefully described, and its atmosphere sometimes painstakingly evoked. This is achieved as a result of careful observation. In McPhee's narrative, much of the environment is represented by people and objects such as cars.

But in addition to that, McPhee names names. He tells us the bridge went over Hardship Creek and that they were on the Swainsboro Road. Such colorful names evoke a mood and a sense of locale even if you do not know where they are or what they look like. Naming names helps sharpen one's sense of place.

Describing things in appropriate detail—letting the reader know what can be seen, felt, and heard—is another way of making the reader aware of the setting. Because we all live in settings, one of the most important norms we expect of any narrative is an awareness of where things take place and whether or not the environment contributes much to the happenings. Again, one of the great sources of information about places ought to come from your journal. If you take time to brainstorm a locale, or cluster using a physical place as your key word, you will have plenty of details to use in describing the environments in which you spend most of your time. Seeing things is much harder than many people think, and good practice is essential.

When establishing a locale, some writers resort to a simple method. They imagine themselves in the space with their characters (if they are not already there) and ask themselves what they would see if they looked straight ahead. Then they ask what they would see if they looked left, right, up, and down. The point of this exercise is to increase spatial awareness and to demand a kind of inclusiveness of description. It works.

POINT OF VIEW

Someone must tell the narrative. True, some narratives in the third person (using *he said, she said,* but never *I said* or *you said*) seem almost to have no point of view. David's narrative on Buffalo Bill seems that way. David had been told never to use *I* in a paper for an English class, so he cultivated a style that tried to be thoroughly objective in that it refined away any sense of a person telling us about Buffalo Bill. That's all right. It gives a sense of distance to the narrative, and in its way it gives a sense of objectivity and even a bit of official authority. That is the effect David wanted.

Jane Kramer does something of the same kind of thing in her comments on Henry and Betsy Blanton, except that by constantly naming them and staying close to them as she described the action, she makes us feel that the objectivity—the distance—is lessened. We feel much closer to the Blantons than we do to Buffalo Bill, and that is essentially because the point of view restricts us to what the Blantons could have seen, done, and said. There is no author's overview, as there is in David's piece. David uses an omniscient narrator who knows all about his character and even about things his character may not have known at the time. For example, David records what Cody's wife thought and felt about Cody's drinking.

On the other hand, John McPhee uses a first person narrative: "I took a ration of gorp," he tells us early on. McPhee is a character in his own narrative, and therefore he assures us that things happened just as he says they did: after all he was there. We can also evaluate him as a character just as we can Sam and Carol, although you will note that he is less interested in telling us about himself than about the other people. He is a decentered writer in this piece. He is not showing off, telling about his exploits, or pushing his weight around. He is really trying to stay out of the way as much as possible, but he wants you to know that he is not going to tell you anything that he could not have witnessed. He doesn't tell you what Sheriff Wade was thinking, why Carol felt as she did, what the mysterious traveler who stopped and then went on, meant by his comment. He stays only with the observations that are possible for a person in his situation. For that reason, his narrative has a sharp clear focus. It is not muddied with a vague or mixed point of view. It has the simple, direct point of view always associated with first person narrative.

The best advice you can have regarding point of view is to find one that is comfortable and appropriate, and then depend upon it. If you were involved in the narrative events that you wish to write about, then do not be afraid to use *I*. If you were involved, but you do not want to take any responsibility for what happened, then use *he* and *she* and include yourself, if at all, only peripherally. You can report what you saw him or her do and say, but omit your own reactions and responses.

THE DRAMATIC SITUATION

Every narrative has to have some kind of action. In David's narrative, it was Buffalo Bill's drinking, on several different occasions and locales. In Jane Kramer's piece, it was Henry's going in to buy a saddle, then going in to talk to Betsy's employer. However, Jane Kramer's piece reported all of that long after the event and did not try to make it seem immediate, or as if it were happening before your eyes, or even as if it had happened recently. The narrative is of an event that was five years old, so there is not much to be gained by making it seem immediate by describing things as if they were just happening.

On the other hand, John McPhee is interested in the immediacy of the dramatic situation, and by describing events as they occur, and by using dialogue as if it were reported exactly how and when it was spoken, he is able to make us feel as if things were happening right in front of us.

The constant advice given to writers of narrative is

Show us things happening. Don't tell us they happened.

By showing us, McPhee involves us with the action and makes us part of it. This skill does not come immediately to most writers. But it comes eventually if you concentrate on trying for it. Jane Kramer, on the other hand, is not interested in getting you immediately involved with the Blantons. She narrates in order to provide background information. As such, it remains background.

A SHAPED ACTION: THE NARRATIVE PURPOSE

In a complete narrative, the action must be shaped carefully if we are to have a sense of satisfaction in reading it. If you were to write a complete narrative you would have to spend some energy on establishing its purpose and making clear that the narrative you have told satisfies the purpose you had in mind for it. (See box entitled "Tips: Shaping the Narrative.")

Tips: Shaping the Narrative
No one can say in advance exactly how to shape a narrative, but the following are a few principles you can rely on:

Refer back to the beginning. Be sure your narrative has a beginning, middle, and end, and aim to have the end of the narrative cast a new light on the beginning. Consciously refer back to the beginning, so we now see things differently than we had. This is ancient wisdom, but it works.

Make your narrative solve a problem. David solves the problem of Buffalo Bill's drinking by explaining how his winter's experience made him start drinking "with a little control."

Look for a sense of conclusiveness, coming full circle, to a natural resting point. McPhee does that in completing the journey of the turtle, so we feel there is a conclusiveness, a closure. It is the satisfaction of having things tied up and taken care of.

Find a message that can be served in the narrative. If we feel that the narrative has been told to us in order for us to derive a meaning from it, we also get a sense of completion and satisfaction.

You will remember that with John McPhee's narrative, I supplied a few follow-up details: the fact that the sheriff missed when he fired at the turtle, and the fact that after the turtle died Carol buried the turtle's eggs so as to fulfill the turtle's mission in life. I supplied those details in order to help contribute to the shaping of the narrative. The whole business of stopping for a dying turtle takes on completely new meaning when those details are included, because McPhee's narrative now has a shape, a closure. With Carol's depositing of the eggs in the sand, we have a sense of mission accomplished, and we sense an overall significance to the narrative.

The following narrative, by a student, Chester, follows some of these principles fairly well. Chester was anxious to tell a story that would be intelligible to virtually anyone who ever went away from home. He narrates what happened when he went back to see his old buddies after being away at college, and after having realized that he had changed as a result of his college experience. Before you read it, consider the way he works with the principles listed earlier.

> **Refer back to the beginning.** Chester starts his narrative with him on his bed in a dark room; he returns to that imagery and that place in the last paragraph.
>
> **Make your narrative solve a problem.** The problem is how Chester is going to relate to his old friends now that he has gone off to college and they haven't.
>
> **Look for a sense of conclusiveness.** Chester aims for this in his final reference to his friend, and his concern for how he is. We get a sense of conclusiveness by virtue of our finally understanding how the *I* character got into the condition he describes in Paragraph 1.
>
> **Find a message that can be served in the narrative.** Well, you can judge that for yourself. Chester goes through quite a few things in the narrative. Did he learn something from it? Did the events have a moral for him?

TEQUILA NIGHT

My bedroom is dark. You'd think that after lying here for forty-eight straight hours my eyes would be adjusted by now, yet all I can see is darkness; I can feel it. It's pressing in on me and it hurts. I wish it would leave me alone.

My stomach hurts. If I could just breathe a little less, then maybe it wouldn't bother me so much, but I guess I deserve it.

My hands ache a little, too, but I don't care about that; I'm certainly not going to let go of the edges of my mattress. My mattress, good old trusty mattress. I can remember complaining to Mom that I needed a new one; I used to mind flipping it over once a week or so because of the sharp little pieces of broken spring that poke through. I remember arguing that I hadn't had a new mattress since I was ten and the mattress is that old now. Boy, am I glad she never listened. This mattress knows me. It protects me.

The bedsheet is thoroughly soaked near my sweaty palms and I can feel hair clinging to my forehead. If I lick my upper lip, I know it will taste like salty alcohol and I can still feel the tequilla oozing from my pores.

If it hadn't snowed so much the other night, maybe I wouldn't feel so bad now. If things had gone as planned, I'd have taken the hour-long trip to Sue's house, brought her home to meet Mom, gone to the tropical drink party that we were invited to, taken her home for the night, and then driven her back to her house in Stratford in the morning. But I can't think about what was supposed to have happened all night long; it won't change a thing. We had the worst snowstorm Connecticut has seen in my lifetime. Sue didn't come over, and now I'm sick.

It's a shame she never made it here. I went through an awful lot of trouble to make her stay comfortable. Even Mom was anxious to meet the girl who made me want to clean my room for the first time in recent history. I still can't believe I threw out some of that great stuff. There were *Sports Illustrateds* dating back to 1972. There were old letters, empty boxes, broken pens, empty Jack Daniels bottles (which I saved to keep pennies in, but pennies won't quite fit down their necks), baseball, football, and hockey cards, five pairs of almost salvageable sneakers, skate laces, old term papers, and a multitude of other treasures that gave my room personality. Sometimes I wonder if I keep it like that because I enjoy the mess, or because it's such a source of amusement for my friends who come over. Big Ken said it best when he looked around, shook his head, and muttered, "You're unbelievable, Babe."

But those proud days of glowing over my monument to parental insubordination are over. My room was destroyed so that an eighteen-year old girl could spend one night in it, and then it turns out she never even comes.

I know I should have stayed home when the weather reports predicted up to three feet of snow, but I went to the party anyway. The party was just a five minute walk from my house, and even though I wouldn't be able to show off my pretty new girlfriend, I thought I'd have a reasonably good time. Besides, Big Ken would be there. The snowstorm hasn't been born that could stop his truck. His truck was a baby blue, three-quarter ton Chevy, with custom paint, over-sized tires, a gas guzzling V-8, four wheel drive, and a good ol' boy behind the wheel.

In high school, I nicknamed Big Ken "the human keg." He could drink beer with the best of them. Big Ken, me, and the boys used to hang out in the beach parking lot every night during summer vacation, hiding beers under our windbreakers, and playing our country just loud enough to drown out the rock and disco coming from the BMWs and slick Corvettes that always seemed to be there. We were all volunteer firemen and most of us had pickups (or at least wished we did). We were Greenwich, Connecticut, rednecks; simple nine-to-five people miscast in a millionaire's town.

I miss those days of pranking cops, pounding cold brew, and chewing on cigars, but now that I'm in college, I just don't have time to sit around and "cut the bull" every night. And deep down, I guess the old jokes, loud burping, and public urinating just don't seem so funny anymore. Big Ken knows it. I can tell because whenever I drive through the beach, he says something like, "what's the matter, too good to hang around with your old buddies?" The other guys laugh and think he's joking, but I don't know. I can sense that he thinks I feel superior to him now that I'm a college boy. I thought the party would be a good chance to show him that I was still the Babe.

The party: tropical drinks, Hawaiian shirts, leis, and eight inches of snow and counting. Big Ken's truck taxi brought in the crowd. I enjoyed catching up on the latest ethnic jokes, saying some "How've ya beens," and hearing about who's sleeping with whom. The gang hadn't changed a bit.

Rhonda was still on a diet. Milker was still getting picked on, and Stacy pretended that she didn't really care when Big Ken cheated on her. The gang hadn't changed a bit.

Irv was still quiet and weird, Jimmy was drunk, and Big Ken talked way too loudly. The gang hadn't changed, but I had. Although I was enjoying the party, I knew I had become an outsider. My old friends were acting *politely* to me! Linda asked me if she "may" get me a drink. Some of the guys shook my hand, and worst of all, I wasn't privy to the glances and eye talk that mark true friendship. How could they do that to me?

When Big Ken asked me if I wanted to go shot-for-shot with him and a bottle of mescal (Mexican tequilla with a worm in the bottle), I just had to. I had to show him and everyone else that I could still "hang." The fact that I'd already had five or six piña coladas didn't even enter my mind. I just kept licking the salt, pouring in the shots, and sucking on lime wedges. Lick, pour, suck. Before long, the two of us polished off the entire liter bottle. I even ate the worm. I didn't even like the taste of the stuff. It was harsh and acidic. I simply liked the taste of acceptance.

I can't be sure how I got home because I don't remember much after the worm. Mom tells me it took almost an hour to get my drunken carcass over the six-foot mountain the snowplows left in front of the driveway. She says I almost froze to death from falling in the snow so many times. She tells me the ambulance couldn't get to our house because of the storm, but she was in contact with the poison control center all night long. She says I vomited and had dry heaves for over two and a half hours.

All I know for sure is that I'm lying here too scared to sleep, too afraid to let go of the edges of the mattress, too afraid to lose control. The bucket my Mom left near the side of my bed, my aching stomach, and my racing heart are constant reminders of how close I came to dying of hypothermia and alcohol poisoning.

I wonder how Big Ken is.

Chester has chosen not to use dialogue in this narrative, and you can ask yourself whether or not the narrative needs it. Do you get a clear picture of his friends? Do you get a clear picture of what the narrator *I* is like? *I* is in italics because it is not always true that the writer really means for the character to be himself. And, because the *I* is a character like others in a narrative, there is always a sense in which the *I* is fictional, no matter how closely modeled he or she is to the original author. In literary studies, the *I* narrator is considered a persona, an aspect of the author, perhaps, but also definitely a creation of the author.

Paul Delaroche,
The Execution of Lady Jane Grey (1834).

Richard Estes,
Diner (1971).

French Painter, Unknown (often attributed to Constance Marie Charpentier),
Portrait of a Young Woman, called Mademoiselle Charlotte du Val d'Ognes (about 1800).
The Metropolitan Museum of Art, bequest of Isaac D. Fletcher, 1917. Mr. and Mrs. Isaac D. Fletcher Collection.

Jean-Baptiste Dominique Ingres,
Portrait of Monsieur Bertin (1832).
Musee du Louvre.

Edgar Degas, *Self-Portrait* (1857–8).
Sterling and Francine Clark Art Institute,
Williamstown, Massachusetts.

Berthe Morisot, *The Harbor at Lorient* (1869).
The National Gallery of Art, Washington; Ailsa Mellon Bruce Collection.

Chester gives us a report through the narrator's eyes, and therefore everything is tightly controlled by the limited point of view. We know nothing that the narrator does not know, and we see only what he sees. This produces a sharp focus, which in turn intensifies the unity and coherence of the narrative.

The setting is not one of the most important aspects of the narrative, yet in the description of the clean room—and the allusions to the untidy room—we get a good sense of place. The description of the storm, the road conditions, and Big Ken's truck are all detailed enough so that we have a useful impression of place.

The damage the narrator does to himself through drinking so heavily reflects some of the shaping of the narrative to show how Chester bends to peer pressure even when he knows he should not. It also shows the extent to which he has changed. The most touching part of the narrative is the narrator's growing awareness of how different he is from the friends he used to hang out with. This development shapes the narrative. It gives it its point and significance. And although the narrative could be improved, it owes its strength to the fact that it pays attention to each of the principles outlined earlier in this chapter. Even though it is a painful personal story, it would not be successful unless Chester paid attention to the way he unfolded the narrative and the way he satisfied the needs of narrative.

Writer's Workshop: The Complete Narrative

1. Write a complete narrative of a sequence of events that you know gave you insight into your own nature. Rely on any time sequence you choose, but be completely aware of your choice. Decide deliberately to include references to as many of the five senses as possible. Be sure to be specific in referring to places, in alluding to weather and time of day, and in representing the characters who took a role in the events. Use dialogue to represent their thoughts and their observations.

   Before beginning the actual writing, spend time in prewriting. Review your journal for useful material. Use brainstorming, grouping, clustering, free writing, and outlining to gather materials and details. Review the Tips: Shaping the Narrative.

2. If you would rather write about someone other than yourself, go to the library and read something on the subject of an important historical person: Elizabeth Cady Stanton, Abraham Lincoln, Martin Luther King, Jr., John F. Kennedy, or a similar figure. When you feel you have read enough, narrate an important moment in the individual's life. Be sure to avoid depending on the writing you have read. One way to do that is to write your piece from memory, without reference to the texts you have read.

Writer's Workshop

3. Look up the history of Lady Jane Grey in the *Encyclopedia Britannica* or *The Dictionary of National Biography (British)* and refer to Paul Delaroche's painting in the color-plate section. Relate the essential details of the narrative up to and including the moment represented by the painting. Rely on the painting for narrative details.

4. Narrate an event that you witnessed, but which you feel somewhat detached from. Do not make yourself the center of the action. You might choose from among the important events you have witnessed on your campus: a major concert, a campus organization or rally, a sports event, or a lecture. Try as much as possible to re-create the mood of your campus by referring specifically to what you saw and observed with your senses. Be detailed and specific.

5. When you have finished your narrative present it to your peer editing group. Keep track of their responses. In your journal, keep a list of the suggestions they made and what you feel you learned from their analysis.

7

Informative Writing

What Is Informative Writing?

As its name implies, informative writing provides information to a reader who, presumably, needs or wants it. Much of your everyday reading is of informative writing. News stories are generally of this type, and so are many feature stories. Catalogs are informative, often focusing on measurements, colors, dimensions, and a wide range of details that provide enough information for the reader to make a decision about what he or she wants. Business reports provide information about sales, marketing strategies, the competition, the needs of the customer, and the products involved. Annual reports of corporations are also informative.

Researched essays are usually informative, although their central purposes may be to argue for a specific line of action based upon the information in the essay. Discussions of scientific findings are usually informative, even when they narrate how certain discoveries were made, and even if they go on to urge a specific course of action on the part of the reader.

In college, as well as later in life, much of the writing you are asked to do is informational. You do an experiment and then write up a laboratory report. You do some research in your marketing class, and then write up a report explaining what you did and what you think the implications of what you did may be. In a history course you may look into the Treaty of Versailles and write a paper that explains what the signers of the treaty expected to get and, then, what they actually did get. Your paper provides anyone who has not done your research with the information needed to understand what the treaty was and what it meant.

You can easily imagine yourself in the position of being the organizer of an event in your community. You can also imagine how easy it might be for something unpleasant to happen, and then for someone to complain in the local newspaper about such events in general and yours in particular. You would probably want to set the record straight for your community by informing them of your original aims and explaining how things went wrong. Your purpose would be to provide information so that no one would make a rash judgment about such events based on one unpleasant experience.

Gathering Information

Informative prose needs some information. Depending on your purposes and the kind of information you wish to provide, you may have any of a number of possible sources. Consider these as starting points:

> your journal: notes and entries on a subject you knew you would write about
> observations you have made in the field
> newspaper articles, usually available from an index under the headings of your subject
> encyclopedias or reference books on your subject
> books that provide full-length studies of your subject
> interviews with people familiar with your subject
> comments on television or in films on your subject

Naturally there are other sources of information, but relying on these will help you be authoritative.

Informational Goals: Hierarchical Order

Informational writing has the following specific goals:

- to provide complete information
- to provide objective and reliable information
- to organize the information so that it can be interpreted quickly and easily
- to make the information and its value clear to the audience

Because informative writing is as dynamic as any other kind, you must use judgment concerning which of these goals is most important. For example, your sense that you have provided complete information depends on deciding what information is most useful, and what information is dispensable. Only judgment built on experience can tell you that. An assessment of what your audience probably knows, what it needs to know, and what it can do without is essential to such decisions.

The reliability of information is always a problem. Your sources ought to be objective, detached, and unbiased. Your test for such qualities may involve examining a writer's or speaker's background. If you choose a political subject, find out in *Who's Who* or a dictionary of biography whether or not the writer is involved in the politics of your subject. Major university presses and major private presses generally make an effort to ensure that their authors are either objective or that they reveal their biases.

Once you feel that your information is reliable and relevant, then it is necessary to decide how to organize it. The narrative responds well to chronology as an organizing principle, but information may not yield to this kind of organization. Rather, you may find that you have a large number of bits of information that cluster together in subsets. Some, you will see, are less important than others.

One of your first organizational jobs is to establish a hierarchy of importance for your information. One natural procedure in informational writing is to move from the most significant item to the least significant item. This is called hierarchical order. You start with a piece of information that is essential to understanding your primary purpose in writing. The following pieces of information are less important. This implies that in your process of information gathering, you have given each item a value.

A FISH STORY

We can learn a good deal by looking closely at some informational writing. The following item is from a journal that says its goal is "to interpret health information for general readers in a timely and accurate fashion": the *Harvard Medical School Health Letter.* It concerns a discovery about fish in the diet. Recently, researchers have confirmed that those who have a regular intake of fish, especially oily fish, have a significantly lower risk of heart attack. On the surface, this news is curious and needs explanation. The subject is very complex, and the bits of information are numerous and carefully interrelated. Dr. Alexander Leaf must sort out the most important information so that the reader can quickly grasp the significance of the discoveries. The writer imagines a literate audience, but not an audience of professionals.

WHY ARE WE HEARING SO MUCH ABOUT FISH OIL?

Evidence is rapidly mounting that fish oil in the diet can help prevent hardening of the arteries and, therefore, heart attacks. This story began in the early 1970s, with a study of the Eskimos living in Greenland. Danish researchers found that about 40% of the calories in the Eskimo diet come from animal fat. This is a high level—comparable to the amount consumed by urban Danes or Americans. Yet, at any given age the Eskimos have a much lower rate of heart attacks than would be expected from such a high fat intake. A reasonable guess would have been that Eskimos simply are genetically resistant to heart attacks. But those few who move to Denmark and shift to the local diet appear to be as prone to heart disease as native Danes, so that's probably not the explanation.

As the research progressed, another trait provided a clue to the mystery of the Eskimos' resistance to arterial disease: a peculiar tendency to bruise easily. The reason for this proved to be that their platelets (fragments of cells floating in the bloodstream to help with clotting) are less sticky than is typical of Americans or Europeans. This finding suggests the arteries of Greenland Eskimos are being protected by something that alters the way their platelets function.

And this explanation makes sense. We now know that platelets help to initiate so-called hardening of the arteries, or *atherosclerosis*. The process begins with a bit of microscopic damage to the inner lining of the artery, usually caused by rapid, turbulent flow of blood near a bend or fork in the artery. Ideally, the injured spot would just repair itself and the problem would go away. But in many people, the damaged inner surface of the artery attracts platelets, which stick to the injured surface and then release chemical signals. These, in turn, stimulate muscle cells in the artery wall to duplicate themselves and also attract circulating white blood cells to collect at the site of injury. The proliferating muscle cells and white blood cells begin to accumulate abnormal deposits of cholesterol and become even bulkier. In this process, a once healthy area of artery wall is turned into a fatty *plaque*. The artery is narrowed as a result, and blood flow is reduced. With this background in mind, the researchers surmised that the Eskimos were doing something to protect themselves from their own platelets. That "something" appears to be eating a type of oil that comes mainly from marine sources—fish, seal, walrus, and whale.

All the oils we eat are made up of subunits known as *fatty acids*. It has long been recognized that the proportion of saturated to unsaturated fatty acids in the diet makes a difference to the way the body controls levels of blood fat. Eating saturated fatty acids (which predominate in red meat and dairy products) leads to high cholesterol levels in the blood, and a high proportion of that cholesterol is of the LDL (or "bad") type. Eating unsaturated fatty acids (which come from various vegetables or seeds) encourages the body to lower the level of cholesterol in the blood. Fish oils are unsaturated, like vegetable oils, but they have one major structural difference that influences how the body responds to them.

How does fish oil work?
Oils taken in the diet find their way into the membranes of many of the body's cells, including platelets. When the content of fish oil in a platelet's membrane becomes high, there is a change in the way the platelet functions.

A platelet draws on the reservoir of fatty acids carried in its membranes to produce chemicals used to signal both other platelets and cells in the artery lining. These chemicals, known as *prostaglandins*, play a crucial role in the clotting of blood. One in particular, *thromboxane*, makes platelets sticky, and it encourages them to aggregate at sites where the cells lining artery walls are damaged. This action of thromboxane is one of the earliest events in the complex sequence known as atherosclerosis.

Our bodies can't make thromboxane "from scratch." We have to get the raw material, *arachidonic acid* (or AA), in our diets. Grains and seeds are, ultimately, the main sources of this substance. Fish oils provide a very similar, but crucially different material, *eicosapentaenoic acid,* or EPA, which cannot be readily converted into thromboxane. Essentially by getting in the way of AA, the EPA reduces production of thromboxane and thus makes platelets less "sticky."

In itself, this effect would probably be sufficient to limit the ability of platelets to initiate a clot. But the EPA of fish oil has yet another effect. It is also accumulated in the cells lining artery walls. These cells normally pro- duce a chemical signal of their own, but one that *inhibits* platelets from clotting. EPA is readily converted into this material, *prostacyclin.* Thus, fish oils work in two ways, tilting the balance of signals so that stickiness of platelets is diminished. The importance of eating fish oil may be that it acts at such an early stage to inhibit the process of atherosclerosis.

Is that the whole story?

No, it really isn't. So far, studies with fish oil, or EPA, have indicated that it has a variety of beneficial effects, although the influence on platelets may be one of the most critical. Increasing fish oil in the diet leads to a lowering of cholesterol (of the unfavorable LDL type), and it reduces blood pressure as well. In individuals with a hereditary tendency to very high levels of triglyceride in the blood, fish oil leads to a dramatic reduction in the level of this form of blood fat.

In a way, the fish oil story seems almost too good to be true. Not only does this type of oil favor the health of the arteries, but it also appears to act against inflammation, and so it may prove useful in a class of diseases, such as arthritis, in which inflammation gets out of hand.

The basis of this effect may be very similar to the action on platelets. Again, the EPA in fish oil, by competing with the AA in vegetable oil, alters production of chemical messengers. In this case, the compounds that are affected are called *leukotrienes,* which promote inflammation and some immune processes. Animal studies suggest that EPA can improve at least some illnesses that result from excessive inflammatory or immune reactions. The success of animal experiments has led to clinical trials of EPA in arthritis, psoriasis, lupus, nephritis (inflammation of the kidneys), and even some cancers in which leukotrienes are thought to play an important role. Be- cause current treatment for these common diseases is generally inadequate, trials of fish oil are generating a lot of interest.

As usual, one has to say at the outset that much more research and development are needed before firm conclusions can be drawn. The bene- ficial effects of fish oil are probably increased by reducing the amount of other fats in the diet. Nevertheless, on the basis of a study conducted in the Netherlands (and widely publicized last summer), it seems that eating fish, even just a couple of times a week, can lead to a significant reduction in the risk of heart attack.

But I think we should put the subject in perspective. Our understanding of artery disease is still limited, and the major approach to preventing it is through lowering blood cholesterol levels. Now, however, we are discovering that there are several key points in the process by which arteries become narrowed. We will probably find ways to intervene at each of these points and thus lower the total risk of developing heart disease and strokes. Reducing dietary fat, cutting out cigarettes, and getting adequate exercise are still important; these measures lower cholesterol and shift it into the HDL form. Eating fish oil, which seems to work mainly at an early stage of the process, may well make an independent contribution to the health of the heart and blood vessels. It should be remembered, all the same, that the point of reducing saturated fats and total dietary fats is not only to protect from cardiovascular disease but also cancers of the bowel and breast.

Are some fish better than others?
The types of fish that are richest in EPA are those that live in deep, cold waters: salmon, mackerel, bluefish, herring, menhaden. These are also fish that carry fat in their muscles and under the skin. Other fish with a similar habitat, such as cod, tend to have rather dry flesh and store oil in their livers. Thus, cod meat is not a very good source of EPA, but cod liver oil is. However, one must be very careful here. Cod liver oil is also high in vitamins A and D, which can become toxic if taken in large quantities. So it's not a good idea to start taking cod liver oil—at least not in an amount greater than 1–2 tablespoons a day—to obtain EPA; one may get too much vitamin A and D at the same time. It is unlikely that EPA itself will produce serious side effects unless taken in extremely large quantities.

Shellfish also have EPA in them, and the good news is that they are not, as was once believed, high in cholesterol. An error in the measurement method incorrectly led food chemists to identify a different (and harmless) substance as cholesterol. On the whole, I think it prudent for people to consume fish, instead of red meat, at least twice a week. I am not taking supplements of EPA and am inclined to think it's premature to do so until we know how much is needed to achieve benefits and whether the EPA can be simply added to a usual Western diet or whether it is necessary to reduce intake of other fats.

In this country, a great deal of fish oil is produced from menhaden—some 100,000 tons. However, it cannot be sold as a food because it is not on the "generally recognized as safe" (GRAS) list. So the menhaden oil is exported to Europe, where it is partially hydrogenated, making it similar to ordinary vegetable oil. Then it is made into margarine and other substances. A certain amount of fish oil is marketed in the U. S. in capsule form. But it exists in a kind of regulatory limbo—not listed as a drug, in that no therapeutic claims are made for it, and not sold as a food.

If fish oil proves to be as beneficial as now appears to be the case, there would be several ways to maintain an adequate supply. Our current production of menhaden oil could be consumed in its natural form instead of being converted into margarine. There may also be other abundant fish species that aren't much favored for cooking but could supply oil.

Ultimately, though, the source of this oil isn't fish but the microscopic plants of the sea, or *plankton*. The Greenland Eskimos don't get their EPA from fish so much as from whale, seal, and other large sea mammals, which have in turn eaten fish, and the fish have obtained their supply from plants. In the long run, the most practical way to develop a supply of this oil may be to short-circuit this process and extract it directly from plankton, or to synthesize it.

Structural Analysis of the Article on Fish Oil

If you go back to the beginning of the article, you will see that the first paragraph provides a full overview: fish oil in the diet helps prevent heart attacks. Then Dr. Leaf provides some background: the discovery arose from studies of Eskimos. Paragraph 2 brings up the issue of platelets (which aid clotting). Paragraph 3 connects the normal stickiness of platelets to the buildup of material in the arteries. Paragraph 4 shows that the fish oil interrupts hardening of the arteries through buildup of cholesterol. These first paragraphs form a unit: they provide the focus on fish oil, give background, and offer a conclusion.

Paragraphs 5 through 9 concern themselves with the function of oil in the body's cells, with a particular focus on the way fish oil differs from other oils.

Paragraphs 10 through 15 focus on the related benefits of fish oil, reminding us that fish oil not only helps in preventing clogged arteries, but also helps in fighting inflammation and certain types of cancer of the bowel and breast.

Paragraphs 16 through 20 discuss the question of whether some fish are better in helping avoid the buildup in arteries that causes heart attacks. Ultimately, they point out that the source of oil for the fish that provide the beneficial diet is plankton, a microscopic plant. It may be possible to short-circuit the food chain and go directly to plankton to achieve the desired effects that will help us avoid hardening of the arteries.

Schematically, the structure of this article is shown on page 138.

In some ways, the most difficult aspect of the article is the use of unfamiliar names, such as *atherosclerosis, prostaglandins, thromboxane, arachidonic acid, eicosapentaenoic acid, prostacyclin,* and other such medical terminology. However, Dr. Leaf reminds us that it is just terminology, and he gives us a simple explanation each time he uses such a term.

Dr. Leaf is quite aware of his audience and its limitations regarding the technical level of his article. His organization is hierarchical: he begins with the most important observation in the earliest paragraphs: fish oil cuts the risk of heart attack dramatically. Once he has presented the most important

Introduction

> Paragraphs 1 through 4 function as an introduction, stating the findings on fish oil and the background that helps explain the findings.

+

Middle

> Paragraphs 5 through 9 establish the means by which fish oil operates in the body to help control circumstances leading to heart attack.

+

Middle

> Paragraphs 10 through 15 explore the other benefits of fish oil, including anticancer effects.

+

Conclusion

> Paragraphs 16 through 20 act as a conclusion, pointing toward some possible future developments, and making some suggestions for readers.

points, he follows up with other possibilities, including the chance that fish oil may protect individuals from certain cancers.

(See the box entitled "Tips: Informative Writing.")

Tips: Informative Writing
- The writer usually stays in the background, unobtrusively providing the information and maintaining a careful objectivity.
- The writer decides what the primary purpose of the piece is in addition to providing information. The writer usually tries to take into consideration the use the reader has for the information. One purpose might be, for example, to provide enough information to permit a reader to choose between two alternatives.
- Some informative writing will need research, whether in the form of interviews, conversations, bibliographical sources, or careful observation on the part of the writer.
- The writer must decide what the most important information is and in what order it should be presented. This will help determine the structure of the piece.
- Regarding the audience, the writer's questions are "How much does the audience know about the information I am providing? How much background material can I assume the audience already has? How much detail can the audience absorb?"

Writer's Workshop: Informative Prose
The following suggestions should produce a brief essay of about 300 words. Your purpose is to inform your audience as fully as you think it should be. Before each suggestion your audience is identified. Remember to rank your important points in the order of their importance, and aim to have an introductory section, a middle section that contains details and develops ideas, and a concluding section that ties your ideas together.

After you have done your first draft, set up a schematic organization chart of the kind used to analyze the structure of the article on fish oil. Establish clearly which paragraphs are part of the introduction, what material your middle paragraphs treat, and what you include in the conclusion. Revise and reorganize on the basis of your analysis.

1. *Audience:* A friend (preferably at another college). *Suggestions:* Explain what it is like to be a student at your college. Comment on the level of morale in your college, with the purpose of informing a distant friend. Inform your friend what the opposite sex is like in your school. Begin your work on this project by referring to your journal, conducting your

prewriting procedures, and making a brief outline. Organize your bits of information and put them in hierarchical order.

2. *Audience:* Prospective students interested in attending your college. *Suggestion:* Inform such students about what your college is really like. Consider devoting your 300 words to one of the following: the academic climate, your fellow students, opportunities in sports, the extracurricular environment, the general social scene. Be sure to brainstorm, group, and cluster for this project. Develop as much detailed information as possible. Take key words or expressions in your brainstorming and develop clusters from them.

3. *Audience:* A well-informed reader in a given academic discipline. Write an informative piece on a subject derived from your work in another course: psychology, history, sociology, biology, physics, economics, or philosophy. Use the prewriting, outlining, and techniques of structural analysis described in the beginning of this Writer's Workshop.

4. Present your piece of informational writing to your peer editing group. Listen carefully to other pieces that are presented to your group and ask questions about whether or not the writer had ordered the information in a hierarchical fashion. Be specific in your questioning so that you help the writer. Keep track as you listen to the piece (or read it) for each important informational group. Ask, finally, whether or not you felt informed when you finished the piece. What are the questions your peers ask of you? Record them in your journal.

5. Choose either Diego Rivera's cubistic "Zapatistic Landscape" or Richard Estes' superrealistic "Diner" from the color-plate section. Write an informative essay that uses the painting to explain the purposes of Cubism or Super Realism.

Using the Means of Development to Organize Informative Writing

Perhaps you noticed that Dr. Leaf relied on some of the means of development for his organization. Working with the means of development according to definition, comparison, cause and effect, and possibility and circumstance leads not just to expanding your thinking on any issue, but also toward the organization of your writing.

The following brief schema is an aid toward understanding the ways in which Dr. Leaf structured his article:

Definition: Paragraphs 1 through 4 define a series of problems and potential benefits related to heart disease and fish oil.

Comparison: Paragraphs 6 through 9 compare fish oil with other oils, regarding its special benefits.

Cause and Effect: Paragraphs 5 through 15 concentrate on the effects of fish oil on the average person, while also trying to analyze the cause: which is linked to the question of stickiness of the platelets.

Possibility: Finally, the essay ends with four paragraphs on the question of which fish are the best sources of EPA. Leaf raises the possibility that in the future the source of EPA in oil may be plankton or plants instead of fish or other animals.

Dr. Leaf used the means of development in the order we examined them in Chapter 4. The means of development are exceptionally flexible, and, when used together, they tend to provide a full and complete view of any subject. Being thorough, and using the means of development that are especially useful for organizing a piece of informative writing helps Dr. Leaf achieve a satisfying shape for his article.

The use of the means of definition as an aid to organization is as dynamic as any other part of the writing process. The way in which Dr. Leaf has worked, beginning with definition and ending with possibility is practical and effective, although you can choose any order you prefer. You may want to include definitions only after you have aroused the interest of your reader in the issues at hand. Whichever way you do it, your decision should be based on your assessment of your audience's needs and your purposes as a writer.

Remember that the means of development discussed in Chapter 5, description, illustration by example, classification, and analysis are all essentially part of the development we associate with the middle sections of any kind of writing. You may have a good reason at times to begin with description, or even with illustration by example. But your choices should be guided by what it is you wish to say about the information you have at hand. You may wish to use one, none, or a mixture of these means of development. You have a wide range of choice.

DESCRIPTION IN INFORMATIVE WRITING

Description is basic to informative prose, because you often want to impress upon your readers the appropriate details that will make them understand your point. The following paragraph from a student essay on competitive swimming in college, comes from page 3 of a ten-page essay:

Competitive swimming, like other areas in athletics, is based on the athlete's natural abilities. However, when the eight fastest swimmers in the world, all of relatively equal ability, plunge into the pool, ability is no longer the deciding factor. There are several ingredients involved in the preparation preceding top competition. Under physical training, skill mechanics and individual training techniques are crucial to one's performance. These athletes thrust and thrash themselves before a typical meet. A swimmer propels himself 10,000 to 20,000 meters daily before adhering to strict weight training schedules. Hours are spent pumping and lifting weights in a cramped sweaty room giving one a sense of extreme self-sacrifice and deprivation. The swimmer's body is continuously submitted to the unique strains and stresses of the training process; therefore, mobility and stretching exercises are a must. These help increase the range of body movement within key areas, and provide the swimmer with a safety margin against injury, while strengthening and smoothing out his stroke.

Susan

Susan's description does not appeal to visual or aural images. Instead, we have the tactile images of *cramped* spaces; the emotional referent of *deprivation;* and references to the sweatiness of the weight room. Susan is trying to convey what the experience is like, and in order to do this, she must describe at least some of the experience for us.

CLASSIFICATION IN INFORMATIVE WRITING

Classification can structure an entire essay. Suppose, for instance, you want to talk about foods that promote health. You could structure your essay entirely in terms of which classifications of food benefit which parts of our bodies, and which do the most good overall. Establishing the classifications demands that you set up categories, such as foods with high vitamin content, foods that benefit the muscles, foods that contain specific vitamins, foods that have no nourishment value. You could structure an essay in the following manner:

Foods that Promote Health
Foods with high vitamin content:
    Leafy vegetables
    Beans
    Fish
Foods with high protein, benefiting the nervous system and skeletomuscular system:
    Dairy products: milk, cheese, butter
    Poultry: chicken, turkey, game birds
    Red meats: beef, pork
Foods with specific vitamin properties:
    Vitamin A: carrots
    Vitamin C: oranges, potatoes
Foods with little or no nourishment value:
    Celeries

Foods that provide roughage for the digestive tract:
    Grains, cereals, leafy vegetables

You might want to change the order of these classifications by talking about meats first, then move on to specific vegetables because you may feel that vegetables are superior in their capacity to benefit the diet. But however you organize the individual units, you should see that classification can function on an organizational level when you are writing informative prose.

ILLUSTRATION BY EXAMPLE IN INFORMATIVE WRITING

Many writers use illustration by example to organize an essay. Like all the means of development, it is natural to our way of thinking because concrete examples are much more meaningful than generalities, and when you want to make a point, the use of examples is often very convincing.

If you were working with the concept of foods, you might bolster the use of classification with examples showing the effects of specific foods. For example, you might cite that the nutritional value of everyday garden vegetables is much more impressive than that of favorite junk foods. You then could use specific vegetables and specific junk foods as your examples, giving the nutritional value of each.

Avoid the Pitfalls of Illustration by Example

However, there are some pitfalls in using the method of illustration by example as a tool of organization. The most obvious lies in the satisfaction you get as a writer, watching the pages fill with one example after another. Unfortunately, that satisfaction can lull you into a state of stupor. You can forget that each example has to further the overall piece of writing, and that each example is, in some way, different from the last and that the differences and distinctions have to be taken into account along with other qualities.

When you begin stringing one example after another you lose sight of the development of the overall writing. The examples become an end in themselves, rather than expanding the argument or clarifying the situation. The organizational principle begins to resemble a string of beads: there is simply one after another of the same kind of example. However, because examples have great impact in informative prose, it is important to learn how to avoid the pitfalls that often lie in wait for you. (See the box entitled "Tips: Avoiding Problems with Illustration by Example.")

The most important part of this advice is implied in the first tip: be sure to establish differences in quality among your examples. Organizing a piece of writing by example becomes hypnotic because each example gets you closer to the end of the writing task. But it may not get you closer to fulfilling your purpose as a writer.

In the case of classification, you can begin an essay with the intention of talking about five or six different kinds of things relevant to your piece. The distinctions in kind imply a hierarchy, or at least a value judgment. The point of an essay may be just that there are five or six kinds of a given thing. However, when using illustration by example to organize a total article or essay, such distinctions or classifications are often absent.

This problem was very apparent in a recent set of essays from a freshman class that read Homer's *Odyssey.* Some students wrote about hospitality—an important theme in the epic. Some wrote on the importance of women, some on the honor of the main characters, and some on the question of fidelity. One wrote on the power of temptation in the epic. These writers all had one problem in common: they decided to let illustration by example guide the structure of their essays.

The results were not good. The writers shared a common failing: they satisfied themselves with simply establishing the fact that there were examples of hospitality, important women, honorable characters, and faithful people in the *Odyssey.* As I pointed out to them, any reader of the epic would have noticed as much. The fact that the examples they found were genuine examples of hospitality, importance, honor, and fidelity was good. It was true. But it did not serve the purpose of informing a reader as to why these examples were worth examining.

If the writers wanted to inform their readers, they would have had to address an audience who had not read Homer. Because the peer editors had read the work, this was clearly not the case. Further, the purpose of their writing was to have been informative about a given point and its significance. Instead, they settled for informing their readers about the fact of a given point (the presence of hospitality, etc.) rather than going on to offer a thorough understanding of each example. The writers provided the examples. They did not provide a rationale for their pointing to the examples.

In the following, be sure to remember who your audience is, what your purpose in writing is, and how you intend to shape what you write. Include an introduction and a conclusion, however brief they may be. Consider description, comparison, possibility and circumstance, and analysis for individual sections of your work. Experiment with classification and illustration by example in structuring your piece.

1. Write an informative piece of about 300 words on one of the following:

Resisting peer pressure to experience drugs or alcohol
Unofficial dress codes among young people
Getting involved in politics at the grass roots level
Fast food emporiums
Economic opportunities in your hometown
Whether your friends seem unusually materialistic or not
The force of religion in your community or in the country at large

2. Inform your peers of your views on one of the following issues:

The growth of pornography in America
A local community's obligation to its poor inhabitants
Prejudice in your community
Labor unions
Robotics in factories
Buying American-made products
Foreign cars
Japanese competition in the marketplace
Foreign ownership of major U.S. corporations

Be sure to keep your audience firmly in mind, and use the means of development to structure the central portion of your piece.

Process Analysis in Informative Prose

Many organizations rely on process analysis as the basic organizational pattern for informative prose. Like any analytic means of development, process analysis breaks things down into separate stages of development. Let us say, for instance, that you wish to inform an audience about the manner in which it can help pass a necessary law to save lives. Because passage of a law is a complex matter, this can represent a very difficult challenge. You may well have to consult someone who knows more about the legal procedures in your state than you do. But let us assume for the sake of argument that yours is a state in which a legal change can be placed on the ballot in November.

Let us also assume that you wish to introduce a law requiring seat belts be worn in every car in your state. Such laws have been passed in many states, but if yours is not one of them, the following is a possible analysis of the process by which such a law could be placed there and then voted on.

Develop contacts in your college with those who agree with your views: use free spots on the radio, free personals in the paper. Set up a meeting on campus and hang posters where they can be seen.

In your early meetings draft a version of a seat belt law that will draw support from those you have gathered. Draw up a possible version of a petition to be circulated in your state.

When you have contacts on campus, set a committee to develop contacts on other campuses. Have those contacts build an organization like yours, using the same methods you have used. Working through local student government organizations is undoubtedly the most efficient approach.

Establish a committee that will poll legislators and ask for their support for a seat belt law. Their newsletters to constituents can spread their support to people off campus.

Establish committees on all the campuses you have contacted for the purpose of circulating a common petition to place the seat belt law on the ballot in November. If you need 100,000 registered voters to sign, aim for 150,000 in order to account for invalid signatures.

Once the law seems headed for the ballot, establish committees on all the campuses you have contacted for the purpose of showing support for the law. Get information from the Automotive Safety Council, the National Safety Council, and any local safety council to show the statistics concerning how many lives would be saved by seat belts. Publicize the information on local radio, in local newspapers, and on posters through local shops.

Perhaps if you were especially optimistic, you could also begin planning your victory celebration. If you could actually implement a procedure of this sort you might make a strong contribution to automotive safety.

Of course, the point is not just about safety. It is about writing. The details outlined earlier represent a process that is analyzed into steps. You might regard them chronologically and therefore be guided by the principle of time. However, it is more realistic to regard them as being in a procedural order. You have analyzed a complex process to see what must be done to get to the next step in the process. If you were to paint your ceiling, you would probably have to start by getting a ladder, then by getting a paintbrush, then by getting the paint. These three steps in the process are not time controlled. They are controlled by an intricate series of dependencies. In order to reach the ceiling, you must have a ladder. In order to paint it, you must have a brush. In order to use the brush, you must have the paint.

The writer who wants to inform us about how we can get a seat belt law on the ballots and get it passed, must analyze the process into the most reasonable first steps, then proceed to the logical next steps. This is difficult if you are unfamiliar with the process you wish to write about. It is also difficult no matter how much you know about the process if you are not willing to decenter yourself and think clearly about your audience's needs. Often, when you do know a process well, you will forget that your audience may not know it at all. In such a case, there is a breakdown. (See the box entitled "Tips: Using Process Analysis.")

Tips: Using Process Analysis
- Decenter yourself so that you place your audience's needs first.
- Think through the process so that each stage is clear in your mind. Account for all the important steps in the process so that you avoid the omission of any step that could cause misunderstanding on the part of your audience.
- Break down the process into discrete, coherent stages. Establish their connection with the following stage.

Process analysis often treats highly complex issues and is aimed at answering complex questions about those issues. We can imagine process analysis answering such questions as

How does an internal combustion engine work?
How does wax provide traction for a cross-country skier?
Why does water expand as it becomes ice?
What happens if the president and vice president of the United States should both die at once?
How is someone chosen for the Nobel Peace Prize?
How did the Americans break the Japanese code in World War II?

Such questions are endless. If we wish to write answers to them, we must engage in a certain amount of process analysis. Other means of development can be helpful in answering such questions, too. For instance, narrative techniques can easily play a role in answering many of these questions. So the point is that no single means of development is probably going to be used alone in any kind of writing—whether it contributes to the development of an idea or to the organization of a bevy of ideas. We almost always mix our means of development. And if we did not, we would probably be very dull writers.

Process analysis is especially handy as a principle of organization if you are writing about money matters, business, historical situations, and scientific circumstances. For that reason, businesses have begun teaching process analysis to their trainees as if it were, in some cases, the most worthwhile method of organization. Scientists, too, know that procedure is very important in conducting laboratory programs, and developing patterns of research. Therefore process analysis is very useful for writing about science.

An example—a rather famous one—follows. It is by Sir James Jeans, and it answers a very difficult question.

WHY DOES THE SKY LOOK BLUE?

Imagine that we stand on any ordinary seaside pier, and watch the waves rolling in and striking against the iron columns of the pier. Large waves pay very little attention to the columns—they divide right and left and re-unite after passing each column, much as a regiment of soldiers would if a tree stood in their road; it is almost as though the columns had not been there. But the short waves and ripples find the columns of the pier a much more formidable obstacle. When the short waves impinge on the columns, they are reflected back and spread as new ripples in all direction. To use the technical term, they are "scattered." The obstacle provided by the iron columns hardly affects the long waves at all, but scatters the short ripples.

We have been watching a sort of working model of the way in which sunlight struggles through the earth's atmosphere. Between us on earth and outer space the atmosphere interposes innumerable obstacles in the form of molecules of air, tiny droplets of water, and small particles of dust. These are represented by the columns of the pier.

The waves of the sea represent the sunlight. We know that sunlight is a blend of lights of many colours—as we can prove for ourselves by passing it through a prism, or even through a jug of water, or as Nature demonstrates to us when she passes it through the raindrops of a summer shower and produces a rainbow. We also know that light consists of waves, and that the different colours of light are produced by waves of different lengths, red light by long waves and blue light by short waves. The mixture of waves which constitutes sunlight has to struggle through the obstacles it meets in the atmosphere, just as the mixture of waves at the seaside has to struggle past the columns of the pier. And these obstacles treat the light-waves much as the columns of the pier treat the sea-waves. The long waves which constitute red light are hardly affected, but the short waves which constitute blue light are scattered in all directions.

Thus, the different constituents of sunlight are treated in different ways as they struggle through the earth's atmosphere. A wave of blue light may be scattered by a dust particle, and turned out of its course. After a time a second dust particle again turns it out of its course, and so on, until finally it enters our eyes by a path as zigzag as that of a flash of lightning. Consequently the blue waves of the sunlight enter our eyes from all directions. And that is why the sky looks blue.

Thus, Sir James Jeans likens one process with another: the process of ocean waves striking the columns of a pier with the process of waves of light struggling through molecular and other impediments (representing the columns). The concept of scattering, which is what short waves of water and of light suffer, helps explain why the sky, which should not look that way, appears to be blue. Jeans has mixed his means of development here, using comparison at the same time he uses process analysis.

Jeans's technique, using one kind of process to explain another, is useful. He points to a process we have all witnessed, or can at least easily imagine, and likens it to a process that we cannot imagine and of which we could have no direct and useful experience. Jeans's method is, in itself, a kind of process, and one you should use yourself. It is a simple rule of thumb: it is easier to explain a complex process if you can compare it with a similar process that your audience is already familiar with. This is a durable method, and one that can help you explain abstract and complex processes.

Writer's Workshop: Process Analysis

> **W**riter's **W**orkshop

1. Your audience is someone who is unfamiliar with one of the following processes. Choose from the list, or choose another process with which you may be more familiar, and explain it as carefully as possible. Your purpose is to communicate the process to someone who is unfamiliar with it. Naturally, this demands a considerable decentering on your part.

   How one polishes a car
   Registering for classes in your college
   Studying for exams
   Playing a musical instrument
   Preparing for a sports contest
   Impressing the opposite sex
   Lobbying for change on your campus
   Finding a summer job
   Choosing the best newspaper
   Teaching a friend how to play chess
   Deciding what politicians really mean
   How to choose a dentist
   How a digital recording is made
   The proper way to use a computer

2. Analyze the process by which you selected your college, saved for your education, decided to go to college, chose your program of studies, selected a major, or decided to transfer.
3. Briefly describe how water freezes, bees mate, bridges are built, barns are raised, square dances are conducted, TV programs are transmitted, poker hands are evaluated, or the way a dog is trained.

8

Argument

The Nature of Argument

For some people the term *argument* implies a fight or a disagreement, but in rhetoric argumentative prose ordinarily avoids fights and aims to bring readers into agreement with the writer. In no other kind of writing is it more essential to think clearly about how you present yourself as author and about how your audience is likely to react to your position.

Argumentative prose presents and defends a position on a controversial subject. An argument is a point to be developed in defense of your position. Therefore, any argumentative piece may have from one to dozens of separate arguments. Furthermore, you may find yourself writing a piece whose overall structure is informative, or whose purpose is literary analysis or scientific observation—and yet still need to devote a section to argumentative writing. This mixing of purposes is perfectly natural.

Many subjects are controversial because there is no absolute position regarding their truth. For instance, there is considerable controversy over whether or not industrial pollution will produce a so-called greenhouse effect in which the suspended dust in the atmosphere would cause the temperature of the earth to change so much that life would be extinguished. Were you to have a strong view on this question—which could be developed only through wide reading—then you might want to argue that the threat is indeed great unless we end pollution now.

Ordinarily, we do not argue about matters of fact. The fact that gasoline is a fuel that most automobiles run on is not arguable. Arguments center on controversy. For instance, whether or not the lead in gasoline is harmful to the public at large is uncertain. One side of the argument might insist that the quantities of lead left in the air after the gasoline combusts is insignificant to the public health. Another side might insist that even trace quantities can damage a human being because it builds up over the years in the neural tissue of the brain, causing loss of vitality and intelligence.

KNOWING YOUR AUDIENCE

First, you must know your audience well enough to sense whether there is a receptive atmosphere for your argument. If you feel that your audience is open-minded and will listen to your evidence and consider your evaluation of the evidence, then your job is made easier. However, if you feel your audience has already made up its mind and is opposed to your views, then you will have to exert more patience, be willing to claim less, and hope that your audience will listen to enough of what you say so that some change in thinking is possible.

Tips: Working with a Hostile Audience
- Audience: involve the audience as fellow seekers of the truth. Avoid challenging set opinions that counter your own. Let your audience draw its own conclusions, even if you fear they may not be the ones you wish them to draw.
- Writer: present yourself as a seeker after truth examining the evidence in as unbiased a manner as possible. Avoid presenting your own opinions unless substantiated by the evidence.
- Subject material: some subjects—abortion, school prayer, direct involvement in Central America—are going to produce a "knee-jerk" reflex from certain audiences. Try to avoid such a reaction by not using the jargon other writers have used. Avoid stating controversial positions directly: instead, gather evidence and the opinions of experts and present them for evaluation. Let them speak for themselves. Be sure to avoid including such material if it is likely to trigger an automatic negative reaction in your audience.
- Balancing opinion: always be sure to consider evidence for the other side of your argument. By weighting the evidence too far to one side, you appear biased. Even though you feel you have reached an opinion, you should write as if you are still conducting your own inquiry and have not yet fully established your own position. After all, it is possible that by adopting that stance you will discover that your own views are subject to change and growth. If you invite your audience to participate in that change and growth, you may find it will be receptive enough to your argument that it will read on. That is the best you can hope for.

Dealing with a Hostile Audience

Your first strategy is to avoid challenging a hostile audience. You must avoid projecting yourself as superior, enlightened, or pious. The most sensible approach is to treat your audience as an interested party in the search for truth. Then, establish yourself as being one of that party as well.

The most important clue to working with a hostile audience is to position yourself as one of them. You as the author must become one with your audience. Avoid a fight. Offer useful information and make a contribution to the knowledge of your audience. Above all, respect your audience. Your best reward will be in the potential for changing a few minds. Obviously, with a hostile audience you cannot hope to change them all. Changing a few minds must be your goal. (See the box entitled "Tips: Working with a Hostile Audience.")

When Your Audience Is Friendly

A friendly audience is usually an advantage in writing argumentative prose. For example, if you are writing a letter to the campus newspaper in favor of lowering the drinking age in your state to age eighteen so that freshmen can have beer at their social engagements, you can be sure that the

> *Tips: Working with a Friendly Audience*
> - Audience: encourage your audience to think clearly and without self-interest about your argument. Treat your audience as people who earnestly seek the truth and who are serious about looking closely at the evidence. Do not play to their emotions, even if the temptation to do so is intense.
> - Writer: avoid becoming chummy with your audience and encouraging sloppiness in their thinking. Do not insult those who may think differently from you. Do not insult the opposition: it weakens your authority.
> - Subject material: if you feel that your audience will too readily accept your position on the subject, remind them that there are two or more reasonable points of view. Avoid settling for the easy position on a serious subject.
> - Balancing opinion: consider opposing views with as much vigor as you bring to views that you instinctively support. This means that you should present counterarguments for your audience to consider. You know your audience will read your work, and it is a contribution to their knowledge and background to include views they might not readily listen to if presented by a person perceived as a hostile speaker. This is essential to intellectual rigor and sincerity.

majority of your audience—undergraduates who read the campus paper—will favor your position. You needn't fear hostility unless your campus is committed by its very nature to temperance, as is the case with many campuses that have a religious orientation.

However, it is also true that one of the worst temptations of addressing a friendly audience is that instead of demonstrating the truth of a position, you simply reinforce the audience's prejudices. Therefore, it is all too possible that you might ignore important evidence and simply pander to established opinion. A friendly audience can make you sloppy and unthorough in your approach. When that is true, your argument will do nothing but convince those who are already convinced. (See the box entitled "Tips: Working with a Friendly Audience.")

One useful approach to constructing an argument is to put yourself in the place of the reader. If you can imagine why someone would disagree with you, your chances of writing a good argument are increased. Your sympathetic approach to your opposite-minded readers will pay off because only that approach will assure you that you will have readers.

Some issues are so loaded with emotion that no one is likely to listen only to reason. People have emotional investments in issues such as abortion, legalizing marijuana and other drugs, putting a stop to pornography, gay rights, and dozens more such issues. When working with such controversial subject matter, you need to be extremely careful about offending the sensibilities of your reader. If you adopt the view of a mutual seeker after truth, and if you avoid assuming a position of superiority, then you may have a chance of having your thoughts considered carefully rather than dismissed abruptly.

Writer's Workshop: Constructing Arguments

Writer's **W**orkshop

1. Choose one of the following positions. Identify your audience as friendly. Write three sentences, each a reason or argument in favor of the position. Then write three arguments in opposition to the position. Finally, rewrite these arguments to address a hostile audience. Discuss all of your arguments with your peer editors and keep a record of their questions and reactions.

Contraceptive advice and devices should be advertised on television and radio.

Military service should be mandatory for everyone over 18 years of age.

Unilateral nuclear disarmament on the part of the United States is desirable in the next decade.

International terrorism is not an effective political weapon.

Social inequities result from unequal social advantages.

conscience

CLARIFYING YOUR PURPOSE

Whenever you write argumentative prose, your most likely purpose is to persuade your audience to agree with you. A second purpose might be to explain or clarify something. For example, to explain why a pencil in a glass of water appears broken, you might have to argue for a theory of refraction. Another purpose in constructing an argument is to find the truth about something: you examine the circumstances and the reasons underlying both sides of a position to see what seems true. Finally, there is the argument whose purpose is to help you draw the best conclusions about something.

When Your Purpose Is to Persuade

You are used to the persuasive powers of argument in commercial advertising. For instance, when you are told that the "Hum-Buggy" automobile has the best paint job in the industry, the best safety-test record, the best handling, smoothest performance, the longest warranty, the greatest owner loyalty, you are reminded that you should buy a Hum-Buggy. The logic behind the argument is that if this is the best car, then you would naturally want to buy it. If you accept the logic, then you are persuaded that the Hum-Buggy is the car for you.

When Your Purpose Is to Explain

When something odd happens, you sometimes need careful reasoning and close argument to figure out why. For instance, when a predator enters a territory occupied by a species of bird, one bird will begin making noise to warn the rest of the birds. In the process, that bird signals its position to the predator, making it vulnerable to attack. Ordinarily, it would seem that evolution would be at fault in such a circumstance: the individual is at risk. However, by constructing an argument that assumes the evolutionary process is at work, one realizes that by risking the genes of one bird, the genes of the group as a whole stand a better chance of survival. Consider it this way:

Evolution favors either the individual or the group.
The individual by signaling the group risks death.
The group, once signaled, avoids the predator and lives.
Therefore, evolution operates to protect the group, not the individual.

This argument establishes that evolution does not necessarily work on an individual basis—as, for example, the popular image of ruthless survival of the fittest has long suggested. Rather, this argument suggests that evolution works on the level of the gene pool of the group. Evolution aims to protect the entire gene pool and will sacrifice an individual when necessary.

When Your Purpose Is to Establish or Uncover the Truth

In Shakespeare's play, Hamlet set out to discover if his uncle really murdered his father. He wrote some lines to be inserted into a play he called

"The Mousetrap" which was to be performed by strolling actors before his uncle, the king. The lines reenacted in close detail the manner in which Hamlet was told (by his father's ghost) that his father had been murdered: by having poison poured in the porches of his ear. Hamlet was testing his uncle's reaction, assuming that if the king reacted badly to the play, he would be admitting guilt. Consider the following argument:

> If the king reacts badly to the play, he is guilty.
> The king does react badly—running out of the hall.
> Therefore, the king must be guilty.

There may be many reasons for the king to run out of the hall, and it is not possible to know from this argument which reason is the right one. However, Hamlet was convinced there could be no other reason, and he acted on it. For him this argument uncovered the truth.

When Your Purpose Is to Help Draw Appropriate Inferences

Another scene following immediately after "The Mousetrap" illustrates the means of drawing inferences. When he enters his mother's bedroom, Hamlet is looking for her husband, the king. He sees that there is a man hiding behind the curtain that insulates the stone wall. Because the man is in his mother's bedroom he draws the instant inference: it must be the king. He then stabs through the curtain and kills Polonius, the wrong man. This indicates how dangerous some forms of argument and logic can be. Consider the argument Hamlet constructed:

> If there is a man in his mother's bedroom, it must be his mother's husband, the king.
> There is a man in his mother's bedroom.
> Therefore, it must be the king.

Obviously, the first part of his argument is wrong, however reasonable it seemed at the time. Hamlet ruled out the possibility that his mother's advisor, Polonius, may have convinced her to permit him to overhear her conversation with Hamlet.

The Structure of an Argument

Like all pieces of writing, argumentative prose has a beginning, middle, and end. Like other kinds of writing, the argument is dynamic and changes in response to your purposes. Your flexibility of mind is important for deciding what is going to be included in any given section of your piece of writing.

Still, when you are in your early stages of drafting, it is sensible to keep some simple and effective principles in mind. (See the box entitled "Tips: Constructing an Argument.")

> *Tips: Constructing an Argument*
> Beginning of an argument:
>
> - Identify your subject and its importance.
> - Establish that there is a controversy.
> - Clarify your position on the subject (carefully if your audience is unfriendly).
> - Suggest how you will argue your position.
>
> Middle of an argument:
>
> - Review any necessary background.
> - Establish a limited number of points to argue.
> - Argue each point in turn.
> - Rebut any important counterarguments to your position.
>
> End of an argument:
>
> - Review your basic position.
> - Summarize your arguments and what they imply.
> - Encourage your reader to share your position, or show what needs to be done to arrive at a fully conclusive position.

THE BEGINNING

What you decide to say in the beginning of your argument is going to depend on your analysis of your audience and your relation to it. You have a choice of being direct or indirect. You can try to win the confidence of your audience or not. If you are confident that your audience is with you, you can begin developing your views immediately; if not, then you may have to be more cautious. In no other kind of writing is an analysis of your audience going to be more important to you.

THE MIDDLE

The middle of an argumentative piece includes the points that you wish to argue. The most important question you might ask is how you decide what those are, and where these arguments might come from. First, you usually begin with a commitment to a viewpoint. For example, you might react to an essay defending capital punishment by saying to yourself, "Capital punishment is wrong. It doesn't work." From that you can begin to develop an argument. What you begin with ordinarily is a personal commitment. From that you can build a careful and reasonable argument.

USING THE MEANS OF DEVELOPMENT

Some of your best resources for developing arguments are the means of development. Each of them can develop a single argument. Together, they can produce a series of arguments that constitute your position.

Following is a group of simple arguments for opposing capital punishment. They were constructed by applying the means of development described in Chapters 4 and 5. From each, we could build an argument that can stand as a single point or be developed in a full paragraph or perhaps several paragraphs.

Development by definition:
Capital punishment is institutionalized murder.

This example defines capital punishment in terms of a word that most law-abiding citizens recognize as negative. Any argument using this approach is going to involve the emotions of the audience. One of the problems of this argument is to establish that murder is the appropriate word: can a government ever murder someone? That must be argued, too.

Development by comparison:
Capital punishment is a throwback to primitive societies.

This example invites a discussion of the practices of primitive societies and presupposes some background knowledge. The comparison does not cast modern society in a good light. The society that summarily kills its thieves or adulterers is sometime pagan, or barbarous. If this argument can be developed fully, it can be effective. It can also be useful to compare the crime rate in a society that practices capital punishment with one that does not.

Development by cause and effect:
Capital punishment has not caused a reduction in crime.

This is potentially a powerful argument. People recommend capital punishment because it is supposed to deter crime. Yet, it can be argued that in times when capital punishment was most popular, as in eighteenth-century Britain, crime was rampant. Capital punishment did nothing to stop it.

Development by possibility:
Innocent people have sometimes been executed.

The possibility of the innocent dying at the hands of the state is real. This can best be developed by using yet another means of development: that of example.

Development by example:
Joseph Frank, a Jewish employer in the American South, was condemned and imprisoned, then lynched by an angry mob. Yet, he was innocent, and was recently pardoned. His pardon does not help bring him back to life. A number of innocent people have been condemned and executed in highly emotional situations, and we know it can happen again.

Development by description:
One way of bringing home the meaning of capital punishment is to describe a typical death in graphic detail. It may help your audience see capital punishment as a human and touching event rather than as something abstract and remote. This would naturally involve reaching the emotions of your reader, and you should be cautious of that strategy.

Development by classification:
Certain kinds of criminals, such as police killers, are often recommended for capital punishment. You might argue that instead of capital punishment, the society should classify its most dangerous criminals and guarantee their permanent imprisonment.

Development by analysis:
Capital punishment may be a sign of the failure of a society to detect and control its most dangerous criminals. It also may be a symbol of vengeance, a need on the part of society to gain retribution and revenge. If so, then it can be pointed out that such a desire is counter to the Judeo-Christian philosophy of our culture. Rather, it is typical of pagan cultures. An analysis of the hidden motives for supporting capital punishment may be very useful.

PUTTING YOUR ARGUMENTS IN ORDER

All arguments are not equal. For example, in the preceding section, each means of development helped produce an argument. If you were to write an essay on capital punishment, you might wish to use some or all of them, but you would also see that some are more powerful in their implication than others. A comparison with primitive cultures might not influence someone bent on executing a mass murderer. However, showing that someone much like those in your audience could be falsely accused and executed might be a very strong argument. The argument defining capital punishment as murder can also be very strong, because it involves a moral issue. If a society is opposed on moral grounds to murder by individuals, how can it not oppose murder by the society?

Nestorian Order

Ancient orators concluded that one of the strongest structures for an argumentative piece of work was to place the arguments in this order:

First: the second-strongest argument

Second: the weakest arguments in order

Finally: the very strongest argument

This technique has the advantage of beginning with a powerful argument that might arrest the attention of the audience. Once its attention has been gained, it will be willing to listen to your less powerful arguments. And before you lose their attention, you conclude with the most powerful argument of all, thus leaving the audience with its strongest impression of your views.

Hierarchic Order

Another alternative is to rank your arguments according to their likely appeal and strength. Then use them in the order of their strength: the first is the most powerful, whereas the last is the least powerful:

First: your strongest argument

Second: your next argument

Third: your next argument

Fourth: your next strongest argument

Fifth: your weakest argument

Naturally, you can have any number of arguments in this system, but you must place them in descending order of strength.

You have yet another choice: reverse hierarchic order, in which you begin with the weakest argument and proceed to the strongest. This is not a bad way to structure an argumentative piece, but your decision should depend upon your analysis of your audience. Will it read long enough to get your strongest point?

Ranking your arguments is instructive because it gives you a chance to think clearly about their impact. You may find, for instance, that in the process of organizing your piece you will discard some arguments as being ineffective, and at the same time develop new ones to fill in gaps that you discover while analyzing your position.

THE END

The most satisfying ending for an argument involves permitting your audience to draw its own conclusions, especially if you know that your middle development of the argument is so conclusive that there is little or no chance that your audience will ignore your position. The ending usually draws the main lines of the argument together and examines their implications.

Likewise, if the argument is not totally resolved by your discussion, as is often the case, you may wish to encourage your audience to continue the examination. Certain lines of development may be possible, in which case you might want to give your audience some direction. Then again, you may wish to end your essay with an especially important or powerful argument. In such a case be sure that the argument has a clear conclusion and that your audience is likely to share it.

Writer's Workshop: Constructing Arguments

1. Rank the arguments against capital punishment which were developed in the preceding section. Which is most important? Which is least important? Which would you begin with if you were to write an editorial opposing capital punishment?

2. Your job is to write an editorial defending capital punishment. Construct new arguments in favor of capital punishment by using the resource of the means of development as follows:

definition
comparison or contrast
cause and effect
possibility and circumstance
description
example
classification
analysis

3. Choose a controversial subject for an editorial for your college paper and work up arguments to help establish your position. Use the means of development to help you, and then rank each argument in terms of its strength: 1 is the strongest, 2 next, etc.

rank:
   definition
rank:
   comparison or contrast
rank:
   cause and effect
rank:
   possibility and circumstance
rank:
   description
rank:
   example
rank:
   classification
rank:
   analysis

4. Choose a subject on which to argue, or select one of those listed here:

No college varsity sport should be permitted to engage in intercollegiate competition unless at least 80 percent of its athletes graduate with a diploma.

Secondary and primary schoolteachers should be tested periodically in their knowledge of their subjects.

Rock and roll music has a divisive effect upon families.

The federal government should support nonprofit theaters in inner cities.

Workfare programs are beneficial to all members of society.

You may argue against any of these statements if you wish. First, work up arguments using the means of development, then rank them in order of importance. Finally, write a short editorial fully developing and ordering the arguments as you think they are most effective.

Some Examples of Argument

We begin by looking at a sample of argument that takes the form of two very brief opposing statements. They are essentially like miniature editorials of the sort we find in our daily newspapers, each holding to a specific point of view and each arguing rationally and carefully. The subject they argue is whether or not secondary schoolteachers should get merit pay if they can be shown to be above average in their performance. It is a knotty question, but many people think they can answer it without much reflection. This is not the case, as you will see. The opponents in this argument are Lamar Alexander, governor of Tennessee, in favor of merit pay and Willard McGuire, president of the National Education Association, opposed.

First read Alexander's position in favor of the argument:

If you want the best results, you hire the best people. In this day and time, you can't hire the best people with a pay scale that rewards mediocrity. Our present system features low wages, lifetime contracts, little real evaluation—and not one penny of extra pay for outstanding performance. Unless we change, we won't be able to keep and attract the teachers we will need to lead our crusade for excellence in education.

Lamar Alexander develops a single argument using cause and effect as his means of development. He tells us first that the best people produce the best results. Second, the effect of a "pay scale that rewards mediocrity" is that the best people cannot be hired. He tells us in his last sentence that the present situation, if maintained, will cause us to fail in producing "excellence in education."

The Power of Premises

A premise is an assumption that an argument depends on for its success. Usually, a carefully argued position examines the most important premises openly. Sometimes, on the other hand, a writer will hide his premises, hoping that the reader will not observe them or call them into question. In that case, the reader is expected simply to assume them, too. Lamar Alexander relies on the following premises:

The best people produce the best results.
The best people will be attracted or maintained by a merit pay system.
Three things (lumped together in one sentence) are bad:
    low wages
    lifetime contracts
    little real evaluation

These three things are totally different from one another, and lumping them together is tricky because we will agree low wages are bad, but must we then agree that lifetime contracts are bad, or that there is, indeed, little real evaluation? We can summarize his points by restating them in terms of cause and effect: the current situation causes mediocrity. If he is right, then he is also right in wanting to change the current situation.

However, there is also another side to the argument, which Willard McGuire defends:

Merit pay has been used time and time again in the past to pay a few people more so that many more could be paid less. We object to that, especially at a time such as we face in 1983 when all teachers must receive substantial increases or else the teaching profession will continue to be shorn of many of the good people in it and will have greater problems attracting bright, capable young teachers.

It seems that if you find any fault with the idea of merit pay, then people assume you favor mediocrity or something other than merit. That certainly isn't true of the National Education Association. We're opposed to merit pay as it has been described in the past and continues to be described. But that doesn't mean we oppose the idea under any and all circumstances.

McGuire also depends upon cause and effect for his argument. He says that the real effect of merit pay is that most teachers get paid less than they ordinarily would. He implies that one of the reasons for instituting merit pay is to pay teachers less. One basis of agreement between him and Lamar Alexander is in the assumption that low pay discourages good people from entering the profession of teaching.

In his second paragraph, McGuire has provided a counterargument. He realizes that there seems to be a hidden premise in his response: that if he opposes merit pay he may also oppose meritorious teaching. He counters this by resorting to definition: "We're opposed to merit pay as it has been de-scribed," which is to say, as it has been defined by people such as Lamar Alexander.

McGuire implies that one of the hidden premises of those who recommend merit pay is that the procedure is useful for punishing teachers as well as rewarding them. McGuire realizes he must take into account his audience's concerns because, if he represents teachers and does not defend merit, then he seems contradictory—or worse: it looks as if he thinks that teachers are not meritorious enough to qualify for extra pay. That is why he immediately attempts to clarify his overall position on merit pay by saying that his association is not opposed to it "under any and all circumstances." There are some circumstances under which it might be agreeable.

This argument will be a lively issue for some years to come. One problem is that there is no means by which a meritorious teacher can easily be identified. Another problem is that teachers selected for merit pay may end up being the favorites of a given school system rather than the best teachers, as happens in some systems today. Identifying a good teacher seems, on the surface, relatively easy; in practice, it has turned out to be exceptionally difficult. The cause and effect relationships that these experts accept need more careful analysis if this argument is to move in a direction which promises some resolution.

The next article discusses the influence of television on American politics, particularly on the presidency. Its author is interested in the subject because he is in a business related to television. Moreover, he has cause to relate it to a recently published book on the question.

TV IS WEAKENING THE PRESIDENCY
by Merrill Pannitt

BEGINNING

The author begins by focusing on an important book and what it argues concerning the presidency.

Direct quotations give us a chance to see how Ranney's argument is expressed.

A new book by a leading political scientist concludes that television news may be interfering with our political process by increasing distrust of government, weakening Presidents and possibly discouraging voting. Austin Ranney, former president of the American Political Science Association and presently a resident scholar at the American Enterprise Institute, argues in his recently published Channels of Power that television's relentless concentration on the White House causes Presidents to realize "that it is at least as important to look good as to do good," and tempts them to "inflate their rhetoric out of all proportion." This leads to rising expectations as to what Presidents can accomplish and ultimately a loss of public confidence when they can't deliver on their promises. Ranney writes that while all the ways in which American politics has changed since World War II cannot be blamed solely—or perhaps even mainly—on the advent of television, "It seems clear that the glare of televisions's attention has helped significantly to weaken the ability of Presidents and Congressmen to govern."

MIDDLE

Pannitt relies on cause and effect as his means of development. There is a consensus of the effect of television on the presidency.

This paragraph considers the effect of TV on the "inadvertent audience," those who watch or hear the news while waiting for dinner.

An effect: TV has replaced other experts or social groups that helped form political opinion.

This begins a new concern: still related to cause and effect. We must consider three points:

As network news departments prepare for the Presidential primary season, it may be appropriate to review what Ranney and other political scientists have learned about television's effect on politics and government.

It should go without saying that they do not agree on all aspects of that effect, but there is a consensus on some important points, one of which is that television is giving us more political information than people feel they need—or want.

Television has an "inadvertent audience" for political news, writes Michael Robinson, who has reported on his studies in several scholarly works. He has found that viewers generally tune to the local news for the weather and sports and then leave the sets on while they are eating dinner or waiting for it to be cooked. Although they are passive about political material, viewers tend to trust television reports more than those in other media partly because they have come to know the men and women who appear on their screens. These newscasters have replaced, to a large extent, pre-television sources of political information—either parents, teachers, churches and social groups; or "opinion leaders" who, having an interest in politics, collected information and passed it along to less interested and less informed citizens.

Is television news biased? There are observers who believe it slants toward the left, embracing at very least "liberal" causes, and those who believe it slants toward the right, working to perpetuate the political and economic status quo in the interest of those who own the television industry. Ranney and several other prominent scholars believe that the bias in television news is not so much political as structural, a result of the constraints that shape newscasts. These constraints include: 1) the economic need for high ratings that compels the networks to seek out the new, the unusual and the aberrant and stories with "good visuals," such as American troops setting fire to peasants' huts in Vietnam; 2) the time limitations that force compression of news into snippets that are really daily updates on continuing themes—the economy, the Arab-Israeli impasse, America vs. the Soviet Union—and that are most effective if all the snippets can be related to an overall theme; and 3) such legal restraints as the equal-time rule and the Fairness Doctrine. Says Ranney: "Network newspeople take the anti-establishment stance that most journalists take, in part because they feel it is their professional obligation and in part because it makes for more interesting stories, more Emmys, larger audiences, and all the good things that larger audiences bring."

1) Success is a clear effect of high ratings; therefore sensational news is more likely to be produced.

2) Time limits cause important news to be treated in snippets.

3) Fairness rules have the effect of limiting certain coverage.

Says Michael Robinson: "Although it has been only recently and partially documented, network journalism tends to be more 'anti-establishment' than print journalism, especially compared to the non-prestige newspapers. . . . One important outcome of this usurpation of the parties by the media has been that network news has emerged as 'the loyal opposition,' more so even than the party out of office. It is now the networks that act as the shadow cabinet."

This paragraph treats the first point in the preceding paragraph: being anti-establishment is more striking and newsworthy than going along with the standard position.

A result of this network journalism—and of the way politicians are portrayed in entertainment shows—was found by Robinson in data compiled by the Center for Political Studies of the University of Michigan. Respondents who used television as their main or sole source of political information were divided from those who used other media as well. Those who used television as a main source were found to be more confused and more cynical than those who used other media. Those who used television only were the most confused and cynical of all. Yet politicians see television appearances as second in effectiveness only to eye-to-eye contact and a warm handshake as a way to become known by the electorate.

This paragraph considers the effect ("result") of this kind of coverage.

Television produces confusion, cynicism.

The analysis of Robinson's data develops this point.

This is especially evident in primary elections, where voters are offered a list of names and are more likely to vote for someone they have heard of than an unknown. Television's influence in primaries, then, is even greater than in general elections, by which time the candidates have become known quantities. In 1980, nearly three-quarters of the delegates to the national conventions were chosen in primaries, and most were pledged to vote for a particular candidate. The consequence, according to Ranney, is that the national conventions no longer make decisions on their own, but merely register decisions made in primary elections held weeks and months before the conventions. By deciding which primaries—and which primary candidates—are most worth covering, television plays a vital role.

This section establishes television's effect on primaries—using the research of Michael Robinson to clarify the argument.

Michael Robinson, in his study of the 1976 primaries, found that New Hampshire, which gave Jimmy Carter his first primary victory, cast 82,381 Democratic votes. On the day after the primary, the three networks carried 2100 seconds of total news time on the New Hampshire results. New York cast 3,746,414 Democratic votes in a primary won by Sen. Henry Jackson.

Pannitt presents and analyzes statistics to show the effect of media coverage.

The following day the three networks combined devoted only 560 seconds of total news time to the results. Thus, Robinson concludes, the New Hampshire results received 170 times as much network news time per Democratic vote as did the outcome in New York.

This introduces the means of development by considering what's possible. McGovern's going beyond what was thought possible becomes, then, an important point. Television's decision about what is possible affects the way the news is reported.

The networks—and the print press—also set political ground rules by deciding how well primary candidates are expected to do. In the 1972 New Hampshire Democratic primary, Edmund Muskie received 46 percent of the vote, George McGovern 37 percent. The media had predicted that Muskie would win more than 50 percent of the vote and McGovern 25 percent. Not Muskie's victory, but McGovern's "strong showing" became the news story. As a result, Muskie went down in the polls as McGovern rose and the second-place winner in New Hampshire eventually won the nomination.

During the presidential race itself, television focuses on personalities rather than on issues.

After the conventions, the Presidential election campaign is a matter of issues to the candidates, of a horse race between personalities to television and therefore to the public. A year after he was elected, Jimmy Carter told a reporter: "it's a strange thing that you can go through your campaign for President, and you have a basic theme that you express in a 15- or 20-minute standard speech that you give over and over and over, and the traveling press—sometimes exceeding 100 people—will never report that speech to the public. The peripheral aspects become the headlines, but the basic essence of what you stand for and what you hope to accomplish is never reported."

The needs of the network cause candidates to say things that are newsworthy, which may also be distortions.

Since the networks and the press have their own needs and their own ideas of how best to serve them, Ranney writes, candidates who depend upon free television exposure have no alternative but to accommodate their schedules and try to find material the networks will find worth broadcasting—no matter how much they deplore trivialization of the campaign.

Pannitt presents Robinson's views in support of his own.

The political scientists express concern over the glare of television's attention, which some feel has weakened the ability of Presidents and Congress to govern once they are elected. Writes Robinson: ". . . the increasingly greater reliance on the media for nomination, election, status in the Congress and reelection is one sign of a new congressional character—one more dynamic, egocentric, immoderate, and perhaps, intemperate. . . . In a final irony, . . . although more policy information is directly available to members than ever before, members themselves spend no more time with that information than they ever did. Public relations, after all, has become more and more demanding on the members' time. Policy can be more efficiently handled by staff or subcommittee."

Television coverage of the president produces a fantasy of "an all-powerful Chief Executive."

The President faces the same problem, Ranney writes: "The fantasy of an all-powerful Chief Executive enthroned at the top of an ordered hierarchy of departments, bureaus, and agencies, issuing orders that are rapidly received and faithfully executed, has long since evaporated under the hard light of dozens of reports by Presidents and thousands of analyses by scholars. Even so, many observers say that the power of Presidents in recent years, especially since the mid-1970s, has declined significantly, and some believe as I do, that television has an important though not an exclusive or perhaps even primary, role in that process.

"My reasoning is simple: political nature abhors a vacuum in the executive branch. Hence to the extent that a President has to spend more of his limited time and energy dealing with his vast public-relations problems, exacerbated as they are by the adversarial way in which television and the press contrast the feebleness of his performance with the greatness of the office, the less time he has to spend on everything else."

Television coverage causes the president to spend too much time on grooming a public image.

The Ranney book is a serious, objective examination of how modern media—especially television—are in many ways reshaping our political process. In a calm, reasoned, clear and readable way, he sums up the conclusions of respected scholars, offers his own, and leaves us pondering problems much more serious, perhaps, than who will win which primary election.

END

Summary: Television has affected the political process.

The essay is almost all middle. The beginning barely introduces its subject: television and the presidency. Because he is writing in *TV Guide*, Pannitt assumes that his audience will think the relationship between the two is essential, so he does not try to intrigue readers or vie for their attention.

The essay develops one argument after another, while also analyzing the arguments of others. The middle of the essay is devoted to examples and specifics that relate to how television has affected presidential campaigns and presidential matters. Its three parts each undertake a specific task.

Finally, the end of the essay is exceptionally brief. Because the author, Merrill Pannitt, seems to accept Austin Ranney's views, he adds that it may have even wider implications than Ranney realizes. The ending leaves the reader to decide where the truth lies and to evaluate the implications of Ranney's arguments.

Principles of Argument, Logic, and Reasoning

Argumentative prose usually relies on logic and reasoning. Most acts of reasoning involve two or more people who agree on certain principles, but disagree on others. The areas of agreement are usually established early, then the exploration of the disagreement follows. When you argue, your goal is to produce as clear a position on your subject as possible. You want to feel that what you write is logical.

EVIDENCE

Evidence can be facts, statistics, or details gathered on a given subject. It can be statements made by important authorities who have studied the subject, or it can be drawn from your own experience. In a competent argument, you need to gather evidence and sift through it to select what is most reliable.

In the largest sense, evidence is data, and it is best gathered in a manner that will guarantee its authenticity, accuracy, and relevance to the issues. Arguments that produce no data for their support are often ignored by readers, and for good reason. They are likely to be expressions of a personal rather than a reasoned view.

INFERENCE

Evidence must be examined and then interpreted. Statisticians are sometimes accused of being able to distort statistics to prove any case. This is not necessarily true. What is true is that anyone who argues can usually find some statistics somewhere that will support an argument. This involves interpretation: downplaying one statistic or overemphasizing another. All evidence needs to be discussed and interpreted in order to establish its usefulness to the argument.

Interpreting evidence is called inference—drawing a conclusion from the evidence. In Merrill Pannitt's essay, a reference is made to a poll conducted by Michael Robinson for the University of Michigan. First, the connection with a distinguished university helps establish the significance, validity, and objectivity of the evidence. The poll compared those who relied on television for all their news with those who used it for only some of their news. The results demonstrated that "those who used television only were the most confused and cynical of all."

The poll represents evidence, but Pannitt does not go on to draw the inferences: instead, he relies on the reader to do so. One possible inference is that the presentation of television news causes those who rely on it entirely to become cynical and confused. However, there is no way to verify that causal relationship from the evidence at hand. It may well be that people who do not read newspapers and news magazines, but rely entirely on television news, are already cynical and confused before they watch the news. We have no way of knowing. To make that piece of datum effective, Pannitt or Robinson, or both, would have to establish a causal relationship. They cannot. But that does not mean that the reader cannot do so on their behalf.

Inductive Reasoning ──────────────────

In the following excerpt, Paul Fussell's approach to the question of social class uses a specific form of reasoning: induction. It depends upon observation— usually of a great many examples or instances of a phenomenon. Then, on the basis of specific observations, some general principles are drawn that seem true. One strength of this form of reasoning is that it is closely linked to observation and facts—most of which can be verified or examined by a reader. One weakness of this form of reasoning lies in the limitations any individual has in making enough observations upon which to base a conclusion. If the sampling of observations is not complete, then the conclusions will be limited and possibly untrue.

INDUCTION AND EVIDENCE

Induction draws its strength from evidence and observation. If an inductive argument is to be convincing, the reader must accept the evidence and the premises that are naturally implied by the evidence. The more reliable the evidence and the more there is of it, the stronger the inductive argument will be. Evidence consists of examples, details, and other information gathered by the writer or reliable sources.

It is not clear how much hard evidence appears in the following excerpt, although there are many recognizable details that may or may not ring true for the reader. Fussell includes not only his own observations—in the shopping malls, for instance—but also a quotation from a diet book.

NOTES ON CLASS

The time when the evening meal is consumed defines class better than, say, the presence or absence on the table of ketchup bottles and ashtrays shaped like little toilets enjoining the diners to "Put Your Butts Here." Destitutes and Bottom Out-of-Sights eat dinner at 5:30, for the Prole staff on which they depend must clean up and be out roller skating or bowling early in the evening. Thus Proles eat at 6:00 or 6:30. The Middles eat at 7:00, the Upper Middles at 7:30, or if very ambitious, at 8:00. The Uppers and Top Out-of-Sights dine at 8:30 or 9:00 or even later, after nightly protracted "cocktail" sessions lasting usually around two hours. Sometimes they forget to eat at all.

Similarly, the physical appearance of the various classes defines them fairly accurately. Among the top four classes thin is good, and the bottom two classes appear to ape this usage, although down there thin is seldom a matter of choice. It is the three Prole classes that tend to fat, partly as a result of their use of convenience foods and plenty of beer. These are the classes too where anxiety about slipping down a rung causes nervous overeating, resulting in fat that can be rationalized as advertising the security of steady wages and the ability to "eat out" often. Even "Going Out for Breakfast" is not unthinkable for Proles, if we are to believe that they respond to the McDonald's TV ads as they're supposed to. A recent magazine ad for a diet book aimed at Proles stigmatizes a number of erroneous assumptions about body weight, proclaiming with some inelegance that "They're all a crock." Among such vulgar errors is the proposition that "All Social Classes Are Equally Overweight." This the ad rejects by noting quite accurately:

Your weight is an advertisement of your social standing. A century ago, corpulence was a sign of success. But no more. Today it is the badge of the lower-middle-class, where obesity is *four times* more prevalent than it is among the upper-middle and middle classes.

It is not just four times more prevalent. It is at least four times more visible, as any observer can testify who has witnessed Prole women perambulating shopping malls in their bright, very tight jersey trousers. Not just obesity but the flaunting of obesity is the Prole sign, as if the object were to give maximum aesthetic offense to the higher classes and thus achieve a form of revenge.

Apart from a brief quotation, Fussell's evidence is his own observation. We may not agree with him but we may verify his conclusions by matching our observations with his. If we have had similar observations, we will probably agree. If we have not, then we may not be convinced by his analysis of the evidence.

PREMISES AND INDUCTIVE REASONING

A premise is the building block of an argument. It is a statement based on observation, report, and other evidence. In an inductive argument, a premise is established after the evidence forces you to agree on what seems true. Usually, you establish several premises in the hope that your reader will agree with them. If your reader does agree, then the conclusions you draw will bring your reader into agreement with your argument. Most premises are not stated directly. They are implied. Some arguments are difficult to rebut because the premises are not evident. For that reason, you need to analyze the argument and examine the premises individually.

Paul Fussell is quietly basing his argument on premises that seem to be drawn from observation and experience. Any careful argument will demand that the writer and reader come to agreement on what seems to be true. This means that they will agree on the premises of the argument and then go further to agree that the premises imply a conclusion. When they agree on the conclusion, the argument is over.

Paul Fussell, like many writers, does not state his premises directly. He implies them. That means we need to use some analysis to discover his premises. Here are two of his premises:

Patterns of behavior determine social class.
Dinnertime represents a pattern of behavior.

The first question we ask as readers is whether we agree with these premises. As a counterargument you might say, "No, patterns of behavior are unrelated to social class." Or, even more radically, you might say, "No, there is no such thing as social class in America." In either case, you have dismissed the

premise and are not likely to agree with Paul Fussell. The second premise would then be meaningless. But let us assume you agree with the first premise. Then, would you also agree with the second? If you do, then you will probably agree with Fussell's conclusion: Social class can be determined by a person's dinner hour.

Induction's greatest strength lies in the weight of evidence. If Fussell were to be truly inductive in this argument, he would mass the observations of many people, not just his own. As it is, he is asking us to join him in observation. If our observation agrees with his, then we will find his argument persuasive. If not, then his is a weak inductive argument.

PREMISES AND THE QUESTION OF TRUTH

Whether or not Fussell's argument is true will depend on the truth of the premises. First, look at the premises. Are there such things as patterns of behavior? You would agree there are. Are there such things as social classes in America? Some people will agree. Can you, through your own observation or that of others, satisfy yourself that social class can be determined by patterns of behavior? If so, you then agree with the first premise. The second premise is not so difficult. After all, most people tend to have dinner at roughly the same time every day.

The question you would raise about the second premise is whether sitting down to dinner at the same time indicates anything about social class. Even if you agree with the first premise, this second premise seems to be stretching things.

For example, if you agree that behavior determines class, is it enough to look at only one kind of behavior, the dinner hour, to determine class? Of course, Fussell is aware of that limitation, too, and he offers other forms of behavior to consider. He focuses on slenderness and obesity, and he develops further premises:

Thin people belong to the upper and lower classes.
Obese people belong to the Prole classes.
Proles spend their free time bowling and roller skating.
Out-of-Sights engage in lengthy "cocktail" sessions.

Are all these premises verifiable by observation? Fussell says yes. How do you respond? These premises depend on earlier premises: that social classes exist and that they are determined by behavior. Fussell believes that obesity and slenderness are results of behavior and that they are therefore determiners of class. Bowling and roller skating are forms of behavior. Do you accept his view that the Proles, not the upper or lower classes engage in them? If you do, then you accept Fussell's premise, and probably will agree with his argument.

Examining your own premises carefully will make you much more con-

fident in the strength of your position. Your arguments will be strengthened first by listing your premises. Then your premises should be tested carefully to be sure that each aspect of the subject and what you say about the subject can be agreed upon by you and your reader. Is what you say verifiable by observation? Will your observation support all that you say about it, or are you going too far?

Deduction: Data, Claim, and Warrant

Deduction moves from the general to the specific. Deduction usually begins with a general established premise, then makes a range of specific claims that can be validated by probability or further observation. Paul Fussell, for example, acts inductively to create his premises. Then, once his premises are accepted by his reader, they become the basis of further claims that are deductive.

This is, in fact, one of the problems with Fussell's argument. Even if you accept his evidence and all that he has to say as reasonable and true, the argument has problems on a deductive level. For instance, if you see a thin person, can you then deduce that you are looking at a member of the upper or lower (but not Prole) classes? If Fussell's premises are accurate, then the answer should be yes. But can you truly believe that every obese person you see belongs to the same class, much less the class that Fussell calls the Proles? You can see that Fussell's argument has problems on the deductive level.

Stephen Toulmin, in an important discussion of argumentation (*The Uses of Argument* [Cambridge: Cambridge University Press, 1958]), offers some examination of premises and the basis of argument. He asserts that there are three steps involved in establishing an argument:

> *Data:* A fact, series of facts, observations, or conditions.
> *Claim:* A conclusion drawn on the basis of the data.
> *Warrant:* The reason one is entitled to make the claim.

Toulmin uses the following structure to help us:

Data ——————————————————————————— So, Claim

Since,
Warrant

Consider how this relates to Paul Fussell's argument:

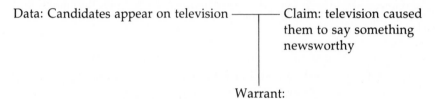

Data: People eat at 6:00 or 6:30 ———— Claim: so, they must be Proles

Warrant
Since,
Proles have to be out roller skating or bowling by early evening

Another pattern that Toulmin has put forward is one that includes back-ing—evidence drawn from observation, facts, or information that gives strength to the warrant. The following example is drawn from Merrill Pan-nitt's essay on television:

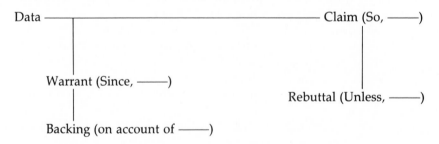

Data: Candidates appear on television ———— Claim: television caused them to say something newsworthy

Warrant:
Since television news only reports what is newsworthy
Backing:
on account of the fact that television has very little time for reporting, it forces those who wish to appear on it to be newsworthy.

Toulmin recognizes that there could be exceptions to the claims that are made on the basis of data and warrant. So there is yet another pattern:

Data ————————————————— Claim (So, ——)

Warrant (Since, ——)

Rebuttal (Unless, ——)

Backing (on account of ——)

We can illustrate this pattern from Paul Fussell's argument:

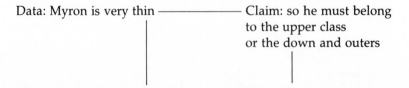

Data: Myron is very thin ———————— Claim: so he must belong to the upper class or the down and outers

Warrant:
Since thin people are in
upper class or the down
and outers

Backing:
on account of the fact
that Proles are overweight
from eating too much
convenience food

Rebuttal:
Unless he is seriously
ill

or,
Unless Fussell's concept
of social class is
simply fallacious

These patterns may appear at first a bit unusual. But they are the kinds of sentences you use in everyday arguments. For example, the material in the preceding diagram can be written:

Unless Fussell's concept of social class is wrong, or unless Myron is dangerously ill, he can't be a Prole because only the upper class or the down and outer class ever gets that thin.

Such statements are common in argument. You have often used them without consciously being logical. Toulmin's diagrams are useful in studying your own arguments and assuring yourself that you are being forceful, effective, and convincing.

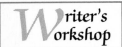

Writer's Workshop: Data, Claim, and Warrant

1. What are some possible premises underlying each of the following arguments? The first one is done for you as a model, but be aware that there are several ways of establishing the premises of any of these arguments. Each may, in its way, be equally effective.

   a. Manufacturing more nuclear weapons makes the world safe from war.
      Premise: The more nuclear weapons we have the less likely it is that a nuclear war can be won.
      Premise: No one would fight a war that cannot be won.
      Premise: As long as we have more nuclear weapons we will have no war.

   b. Manufacturing more nuclear weapons makes the world more dangerous.

   c. Posing in the nude makes a young woman unworthy to be Miss America.

  d. Posing in the nude does not make a young woman unworthy to be Miss America.
  e. Good lawyers defend clients even when they know they are guilty.
  f. Good lawyers do not defend clients they know are guilty.
  g. When I want a good doctor, I find one who drives a Mercedes.
  h. When I want a good doctor, I find one who drives a Volkswagen.
2. Analyze the following statements in terms of data, claim, and warrant. Use Toulmin's diagram to help you see what the data, claim, warrant, possible backing, and possible rebuttals might be. Remember that in an analysis of this kind, different people will come up with different ways of breaking down these arguments. The first one is done as a model to show you some of the possibilities.
  a. Manufacturing more nuclear weapons makes the world safe from war.

Data: America is manufacturing more ———— Claim: So America is
    nuclear weapons   helping to prevent
                                            war

Warrant: Since no nuclear war can be
won, none will be fought   Rebuttal: Unless, a
                                        mad leader does not
                                        care as much about
                                        winning as about
                                        destroying

Backing: On account of the total
destruction which nuclear war will
produce, the human race will perish   or,
in a war. There is no such thing as a   Unless some country
limited nuclear war. Nuclear war is   mistakenly thinks it
equivalent to suicide.   can win a nuclear
                                         war

  b. The more nuclear weapons we have the more likely we are to have a war.
  c. Miss America stands for positive moral values.
  d. The struggle between skilled adversaries serves our legal system well.
  e. Because medicine is a well-paid profession it attracts the brightest students.
  f. Segregation in schools produces inferior education for all races.

The Analysis and Rebuttal of Arguments _____

The ultimate goal of analyzing arguments is to help you be more precise and convincing in your own writing. Examine the following argument and its analysis.

INCAPACITATING CRIMINALS
James Q. Wilson

When criminals are deprived of their liberty, as by imprisonment (or banishment, or very tight control in the community), their ability to commit offenses against citizens is ended. We say these persons have been "incapacitated," and we try to estimate the amount by which crime is reduced by this incapacitation.

Wilson contends that incapacitation works but reminds us that justice must also be served.

Incapacitation cannot be the sole purpose of the criminal justice system; if it were, we would put everybody who has committed one or two offenses in prison until they were too old to commit another. And if we thought prison too costly, we would simply cut off their hands or their heads. Justice, humanity, and proportionality, among other goals, must also be served by the courts.

Incapacitation does not involve changing behavior, as does rehabilitation.

But there is one great advantage to incapacitation as a crime control strategy—namely, it does not require us to make any assumptions about human nature. By contrast, deterrence works only if people take into account the costs and benefits of alternative courses of action and choose that which confers the largest net benefit (or the smallest net cost). Though people almost surely do take such matters into account, it is difficult to be certain by how much such considerations affect their behavior and what change, if any, in crime rates will result from a given, feasible change in either the costs of crime or the benefits of not committing a crime. Rehabilitation works only if the values, preferences, or time-horizon of criminals can be altered by plan. There is not much evidence that we can make these alterations for large numbers of persons, though there is some evidence that it can be done for a few under certain circumstances.

Three conditions have to be met for incapacitation to work.

Incapacitation, on the other hand, works by definition: its effects result from the physical restraint placed upon the offender and not from his subjective state. More accurately, it works provided at least three conditions are met: some offenders must be repeaters, offenders taken off the streets must not be immediately and completely replaced by new recruits, and prison must not increase the post-release criminal activity of those who have been incarcerated sufficiently to offset the crimes prevented by their stay in prison.

First condition: most prisoners are repeat offenders.

The first condition is surely true. Every study of prison inmates shows that a large fraction (recently, about two-thirds) of them had prior criminal records before their current incarceration; every study of ex-convicts shows that a significant fraction (estimates vary from a quarter to a half) are rearrested for new offenses within a relatively brief period. In short, the great

majority of persons in prison are repeat offenders, and thus prison, whatever else it may do, protects society from the offenses these persons would commit if they were free.

The second condition—that incarcerating one robber does not lead automatically to the recruitment of a new robber to replace him—seems plausible. Although some persons, such as Ernest van den Haag, have argued that new offenders will step forward to take the place vacated by the imprisoned offenders, they have presented no evidence that this is the case, except, perhaps, for certain crimes (such as narcotics trafficking or prostitution), which are organized along business lines. For the kinds of predatory street crimes with which we are concerned—robbery, burglary, auto theft, larceny—there are no barriers to entry and no scarcity of criminal opportunities. No one need wait for a "vacancy" to appear before he can find an opportunity to become a criminal. The supply of robbers is not affected by the number of robbers practicing, because existing robbers have no way of excluding new robbers and because the opportunity for robbing (if you wish, the "demand" for robbery) is much larger than the existing number of robberies. In general, the earnings of street criminals are not affected by how many "competitors" they have.

Second condition: new criminals do not automatically fill the "openings" left by criminals incapacitated by prison.

The third condition that must be met if incapacitation is to work is that prisons must not be such successful "schools for crime" that the crimes prevented by incarceration are outnumbered by the increased crimes committed after release attributable to what was learned in prison. It is doubtless the case that for some offenders prison is a school; it is also doubtless that for other offenders prison is a deterrent. The former group will commit more, or more skillful, crimes after release; the latter will commit fewer crimes after release. The question, therefore, is whether the net effect of these two offsetting tendencies is positive or negative. All studies of the extent to which prisons reform offenders are also, in effect, studies of whether they *deform* them. In other words, when we compare the post-release crime rates of persons who have gone to prison with the crime rates of similar persons who have not, we can ask whether prison has made them better off (that is, rehabilitated them) or made them worse off (that is, served as a "school for crime"). In general, there is no evidence that the prison experience makes offenders as a whole more criminal, and there is some evidence that certain kinds of offenders (especially certain younger ones) may be deterred by a prison experience. Moreover, interviews with prisoners reveal no relationship between the number of crimes committed and whether the offenders had served a prior prison term. Though there are many qualifications that should be made to this bald summary, there is no evidence that the net effect of prison is to increase the crime rates of ex-convicts sufficiently to cancel out the gains to society resulting from incapacitation.

Third condition: prison cannot become a "school for criminals;" it must be a deterrent.

Wilson says no evidence points to prison as making convicts more criminal.

In short, the three conditions that must be met for incapacitation to reduce crime are in fact met. What remains is to find out how much crime is reduced by sending offenders to prison and then to ask whether those gains in crime reduction are worth the cost in prison space and (possibly) in justice.

Conclusion: the conditions are met.

The core of this argument breaks down in this way:

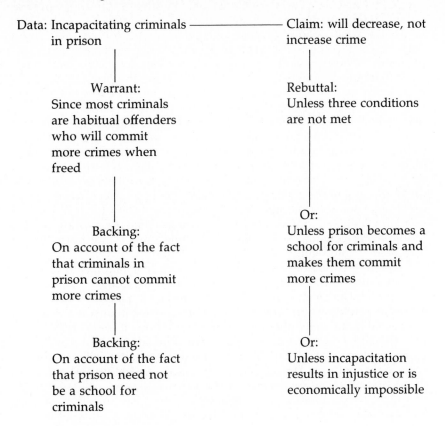

Data: Incapacitating criminals —————— Claim: will decrease, not
in prison   increase crime

Warrant: Rebuttal:
Since most criminals   Unless three conditions
are habitual offenders   are not met
who will commit
more crimes when
freed

Backing: Or:
On account of the fact   Unless prison becomes a
that criminals in   school for criminals and
prison cannot commit   makes them commit
more crimes   more crimes

Backing: Or:
On account of the fact   Unless incapacitation
that prison need not   results in injustice or is
be a school for   economically impossible
criminals

Let us consider this analysis step by step:

The Truth of the Data, Claim, and Warrant
On the surface of things, it appears reasonable to assume that incapacitation will produce a drop in the crime rate and that the three conditions can be met.

The Presence of Evidence and the Fairness of Inference
The evidence, as established in scholarly studies and reports, is plausible,
and the author is careful not to claim too much.

On the basis of the evidence, the inference, and the consistency of data,
claim, and warrant, therefore, the argument seems substantial. If you disagree with it, you would have to question it on grounds other than its logic or
consistency. This usually means you will have to examine its premises, both
stated and unstated.

Wilson's Premises

Rehabilitation works only for a small number of inmates.

Inmates are mostly repeat offenders who would commit crimes if let go.

The three conditions that must be met for incapacitation to work effectively are, in fact, true.

Prison does not make inmates more criminal than they already were.

You may feel there are other important premises to consider, but these will serve to help you begin a rebuttal if you wish to do so. See the box entitled "Tips: Testing Premises" for questions you can raise of any premises, and the answers that will help you establish a counterargument.

Tips: Testing Premises
- Is the premise verifiable by evidence or observation?
- If not verifiable, does the premise seem reasonable or plausible?
- Does the premise offer a desirable consequence?
- Is a counterpremise equally true and desirable?

There are four premises to consider:

Premise 1

Rehabilitation works only for a small number of inmates.

Evidence suggests some people can be rehabilitated, but we cannot tell how many. It is a plausible premise, but not easily verifiable.

Premise 2

Inmates are mostly repeat offenders who would commit crimes if let go.

If two-thirds of the inmates currently in prison are repeat offenders, then the evidence would suggest that any one of them, if let go, would go back and commit more crimes of the sort they have already committed. This premise is reasonable.

Premise 3

The three conditions that must be met for incapacitation to work effectively are, in fact, true.

The first two conditions seem apparently met: Most inmates are repeat offenders. Putting a robber in jail does not seem likely to provide an "opening" for a new robber. But the third, that prison does not make people more criminal (it is a school for crime) is not self-evident.

Premise 4

Prison does not make inmates more criminal than they already were.

This premise is the third condition that Wilson feels may be met. But it is not readily verifiable by evidence or observation. Wilson defends the premise by saying "there is no evidence that the prison experience makes offenders as a whole more criminal." In a way, Wilson defends the premise by lack of—rather than presence of—evidence. Although, he suggests that some, especially young, offenders are deterred by a prison sentence from committing more crimes.

Does the premise seem reasonable or plausible? That depends. It would appear likely that criminals, when put together, will discuss the "tricks of the trade." And it would also seem that criminals in prison would force others to be like them if only for the purpose of survival. The popular image of prison is something like that of the jungle in which only the strongest, or most savage, can survive.

Wilson's argument is careful and prudent. He concerns himself with the question of whether justice will be done by incapacitation and whether the costs of extra prison space will be worth the results. These are, themselves, potentially powerful counterarguments which anyone arguing with Wilson would take into considertion. An effective counterargument could build itself on the following premises:

> Prison makes criminals; longer terms will make more criminals.
> Longer terms are not a substitute for rehabilitating criminals.
> Abandoning efforts at rehabilitation is a form of injustice.
> Incapacitation will mean more prisons—perhaps more than our resources will allow.

Writer's Workshop: Testing Premises

1. Refer back to Merrill Pannitt's essay on television and politics. List three principal premises of his argument. One of the most important is: The way in which the news must be reported on TV helps determine what is reported.

2. Examine each premise in light of the testing premises tips listed earlier:

   - Is the premise verifiable by evidence or observation?
   - If not verifiable, does the premise seem reasonable or plausible?
   - Does the premise offer a desirable consequence?
   - Is a counterpremise equally true and desirable?

3. Examine each premise for its data, claim, and warrant. Set up a Toulmin diagram like the one on page 175. Every premise will be analyzable in relation to Toulmin's pattern.

4. Find an argumentative essay—or a section of one—in a magazine, newspaper, or collection of essays. Identify its premises and analyze them for their validity, using the questions in Item 2.

5. Write a brief argumentative piece on a subject of your choice. Clarify your premises by listing them at the end. Offer an analysis of two of your premises using the Toulmin diagram.

Fallacies of Argument

Unfortunately, certain kinds of statements that seem very reasonable are, underneath it all, quite unreasonable. Fallacies in argument have been talked about for thousands of years, and it is useful to review some of the most important. Each demands some analysis, and each should be avoided if you want your argument to be powerful and effective.

GENERALIZING FROM LIMITED EXPERIENCE

Inductive arguments are powerful because there is a great deal of experience and evidence to force you to a conclusion. However, some people try to argue from limited experience and therefore risk deriving false conclusions. Everyone is likely to be guilty of this fallacy at one time or another, but it is important to resist jumping to any conclusions on the basis of limited information.

For example, in a recent case in Florida, a family was bombed out of its home because it was known that some of the children had AIDS. Many people jumped to the conclusion that the family had used drugs intravenously—one likely cause of AIDS—when, in fact, the disease was the result of blood transfusions necessitated by chronic illnesses of the children. Almost 20 percent of AIDS cases are not accounted for by the usual high risk factors, such as sexual activity, homosexual activity, intravenous drug use, and blood transfusions. No one knows what causes that 20 percent disease rate, although some observers suspect mosquitoes, fleas, or ticks. That conclusion in itself is an example of generalizing from limited experience, because no scientific studies have clarified causality by insect bite.

FALLACIOUS CAUSAL ANALYSIS

Because it is often impossible to establish the exact cause of something, people sometimes feel free to suggest that because one thing happened first, what follows was caused by it. In professional sports, it is a custom not to talk about a pitcher who is in the last innings of pitching a no-hitter baseball game. It is thought to be bad luck. When, in a recent game, the announcer ignored baseball lore and mentioned in the last inning that the pitcher on the mound was throwing a no-hitter, people became enraged. And when the pitcher threw a pitch that was hit out of the stadium for a home run, people mobbed the station complaining that the announcer caused the pitcher to lose his no-hitter. Obviously, there is no causal connection between these events.

In your own writing, be sure that your causal analysis has something stronger to go on. If it does not, you will seem to be holding on to a fallacy to keep your argument afloat.

BEGGING THE QUESTION

Whenever you present a questionable argumentative premise as if it were an absolute fact, you are begging the question. Currently, Asian students are exceptionally high achievers on national science tests, such as the Westinghouse Awards. In 1988, eleven of fourteen winners in New York City were Asian. Such a fact has encouraged some people to argue by begging the question. For example, "Since Kim is Asian, she will be a science whiz in school." Such a statement is unreasonable. It does not take into account the differences among individuals and it assumes that what is true of some people in a group will be true of all of them.

In other cases, people argue that a given quality in an individual demands a given response. Sometimes they set the premise up in a way that most people can see through. Consider the following examples:

Crack addicts deserve prison because they are addicted.
Unless you have published a novel, you should not criticize one.
Only a statesman can judge a statesman.
If you are tall, you should think about being a basketball player.
She is a woman, so she is sensitive and understanding.

AVOIDING THE QUESTION

When the issue centers on one important thing, and the person arguing avoids approaching it directly, a fallacious line of argument can develop. In the 1950s the Russians in the UN were sometimes challenged on the mass arrests, imprisonments in the Gulags, and the mysterious disappearances of its citizens. When challenged on these points, Representative Molotov often responded by asking about "The lynchings in your own South."

Such a ploy is only a ploy. Most people see through it. Instead of answering the question, Molotov shifted the grounds of the argument and avoided it entirely. In 1988, when a newsman challenged a candidate for the presidency to explain his stand on an important issue, that candidate responded by challenging the newsman about an incident in the newsman's past when he walked off a show. That is not argument, it is avoiding argument.

ARGUING TO THE PERSON

One especially difficult form of fallacy is argument *ad hominen*—arguing to the person rather than the issue. Instead of continuing an argument on the points that are important, a fallacious approach diverts attention to the background or beliefs of the person arguing.

Some examples are the following statements:

> You cannot expect to understand what it means to be oppressed; you are a doctor.
> Mr. Diazo would naturally have sympathy for the Marielitos who rioted in two federal prisons—he is Puerto Rican.
> The testimony given by the Pallazo Company predictably implies that the public water supply is bad. They own a spring-water company.
> This man is a known criminal. He has had three parking tickets in the last decade, and his views on how we can improve the police force are going to be questionable.
> What can you expect from Diana Jones? She flunked math. She cannot be thought of as a potentially successful businessperson.

THE FALSE DICHOTOMY

One fallacy that should be transparent to most readers is, unfortunately, all too often effective. It is the fallacy of establishing two alternatives and pretending they are the only choices available. When someone says, "If you are not with me, you are against me," that person is setting up a false dichotomy. There may be many other positions on an issue. One may agree, but have reservations about part of another person's position. Does that mean one is against the other person? No. But in a situation in which only two choices are given, then the fallacious claim may be made.

Usually, a person who depends upon a false dichotomy is desperate. The sense of desperation usually shows through the argument, and therefore it is often quite transparent. However, emotions enter into such arguments, and therefore it is sometimes possible that an audience will accept this fallacious view. People who believe in school prayer sometimes accuse their adversaries of being godless or atheistic. Such a charge is unfounded, because there may indeed be churchgoers who believe in the separation of church and state. By not allowing that possibility, a fallacy is introduced into the argument.

Some examples of this fallacy are the following statements:

> Either you vote for the president, or you are opposed to freedom.
> Either we support the resistance, or we forsake democracy.
> People who watch television don't read.
> The newspaper is filled with either murders or terrorism.
> You have a choice. Either accept my solution on garbage disposal, or end up wallowing in your own garbage forever.

Constructing Argumentative Essays

Avoiding the fallacies discussed in this chapter is possible if you can learn to spot them. Sometimes they are tempting, but your audience will usually be quick to recognize them. They are a lazy person's way of arguing.

The purpose of examining fallacies and the questions of evidence, argument, and logic is to point you toward constructing arguments of your own. Naturally, all of us argue. It is one of the most basic ways we use language. Probably the most usual purpose in our writing is persuasion. Therefore, it is important that you learn to write effective arguments. (See the box entitled "Tips: Constructing an Argumentative Essay.")

> *Tips: Constructing an Argumentative Essay*
> - Clearly establish the subject of your essay.
> - List your arguments. Remember that the means of development are useful for developing arguments.
> - Analyze your arguments in terms of data, claim, and warrant.
> - Gather evidence supporting your arguments.
> - Take the most important counterarguments into consideration, showing how they can be rebutted.
> - Decide on the order in which you should present your arguments: Nestorian, hierarchic, or other.

Each of the tips is built on what you have already examined in this chapter and can be developed further and studied in some depth.

Sample Argument

The following sample argument is built on the tips for constructing an argumentative essay. The title is:

Automobiles Should Not Go More Than Thirty Miles an Hour

Clearly Establish the Subject of Your Essay

Many writers feel that the subject of an argumentative essay is best established in its title. Here are a few titles of possible argumentative pieces:

Gun Control Can Save Lives
Why We Must Discontinue Metal Money
Television Has Warped the Minds of a Generation
Rock and Roll Can Save the World
College Students Should Invest in Common Stocks
Automobiles Should Not Go More than Thirty Miles an Hour

An Argumentative Thesis

These titles imply an overall thesis that will guide the entire argument. For instance, the first of these could have a thesis such as "Arguments in favor of gun control are based on the principles of individual liberties, but the cost of such liberties is too high. Guns cost over 10,000 lives a year in America alone, and it is clear that gun control is the key to saving lives in this country." The advantage of the sample titles is that they can be rooted in a clear thesis that can guide your entire essay. That makes your job as a writer much easier.

In the last example, the thesis is clear: automobiles should be limited in their speed. It will be difficult to defend this thesis because you know it is not a popular position.

List Your Arguments

The means of development can help produce arguments if none occurs to you spontaneously.

Definition: Several points need attention here because some definition of automobile is necessary. (For instance, does the argument really include ambulances, fire trucks, and police cars?) You would have to define what *limited* means: by law or by design. If by design, then automobiles would be manufactured to go no faster than thirty miles an hour.

Development by Comparison: Other ages and other places have done without the high speeds we seem to rely upon. Were they worse off?

Development by Cause and Effect: several arguments can be constructed:
    Reducing highway speed will reduce highway deaths.
    Reducing highway speed will help cars last longer.
    Lower speeds will reduce auto-related crime.

Development by Possibility: Arguing from the question of possibility, we can develop this argument:
    It is possible to reduce auto liability and collision insurance costs by reducing highway speed.

Analyze Your Arguments in Terms of Data, Claim, and Warrant

It is not necessary for you to analyze all the possible arguments at this time, but look at two so they will act as models for later analysis.

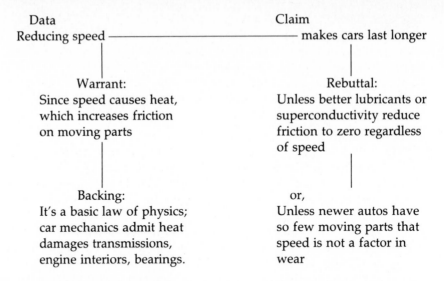

Data   Claim
Reducing speed ——————————————— makes cars last longer

Warrant: Rebuttal:
Since speed causes heat,   Unless better lubricants or
which increases friction   superconductivity reduce
on moving parts   friction to zero regardless
                                                        of speed

Backing: or,
It's a basic law of physics;   Unless newer autos have
car mechanics admit heat   so few moving parts that
damages transmissions,   speed is not a factor in
engine interiors, bearings.   wear

This procedure gives you full control over your argument. You can fairly evaluate your premises, and therefore your argument, before you commit yourself to writing. This technique puts you in control of your own argument, while also giving you a chance to reflect on the possibilities of counter-argument.

You can do the same with this argument:

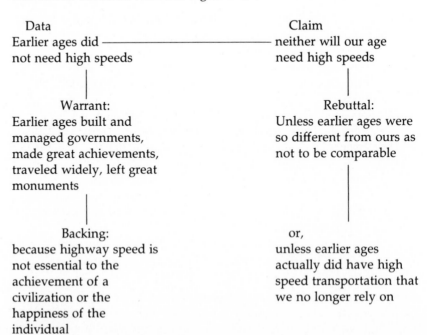

Data   Claim
Earlier ages did ——————————————— neither will our age
not need high speeds   need high speeds

Warrant: Rebuttal:
Earlier ages built and   Unless earlier ages were
managed governments,   so different from ours as
made great achievements,   not to be comparable
traveled widely, left great
monuments

Backing: or,
because highway speed is   unless earlier ages
not essential to the   actually did have high
achievement of a   speed transportation that
civilization or the   we no longer rely on
happiness of the
individual

This procedure is ideal for clarifying a variety of potentialities in your arguments. By considering the questions raised in the warrant, backing, and rebuttals, you will not only have considerable strength in your essay, but you will also have enough material for a complete, convincing essay.

Gather Evidence Supporting Your Arguments

Once you have examined your arguments in terms of data, claim, and warrant—and in the process, of course, revised and refined them—you will know what kind of evidence you will need in order for your argument to be effective. In this sample argument, you would need evidence that will support the view that

1. high speed is a factor in highway accidents.
2. high speed is a factor in premature wear of automobiles.
3. high speed is a factor in promoting automobile-related crimes.
4. high speed is a factor in automobile damage, thus raising insurance costs.
5. earlier ages did not need high speeds to achieve happiness.

Where will such evidence come from? Because automobile insurance companies spend incalculable sums on accident claims every day, they represent one of the best places to begin. A visit to an insurance agent will produce a number of free handouts with details concerning the important factors in automotive safety. Examine them to see if speed is an issue. Further, you might speak to an insurance agent and ask directly whether he or she feels that speed is as important a factor as your argument assumes it is. Keep notes on your conversation and ask, at the same time, whether or not the agent feels limiting automotive speed to thirty miles an hour would reduce highway fatalities. Ask also what the likely reactions to such a proposal might be. In this way, you may discover some other points to rebut in your essay.

Highway safety is a major issue in both newspapers and magazines, and an examination of the *Ulrich's International Periodicals, Reader's Guide to Periodical Literature,* or the *New York Times Index* will be sure to turn up more than enough material on the subject of safety and speed. The problem will be that there is too much material rather than too little, and therefore you will have to be carefully selective. Remember that you will be looking for evidence establishing causal relationships between speed and both highway deaths and highway damage. You would expect considerable resistance to your basic position because people seem to enjoy speeding very much.

Take the Most Important Counterarguments into Consideration, Showing How They Can Be Rebutted

Because there will be resistance to your position, you should be able to plan for arguments opposed to your view. We have already spotted one:

Speed is essential for doing the world's work. You could argue that we have become used to high speed, but that it is a convenience, not a necessity. By pointing to the achievements of past eras, you can demonstrate that speeds higher than thirty miles an hour (as well as automobiles themselves) are not necessary for important achievement.

The basic argument against this position is that most people simply enjoy speed. By weighing their enjoyment against loss of life and property damage, you should be able to argue that mere enjoyment is not significant enough to outweigh the lives that would be saved by reducing speed.

Another counterargument will be that speed saves great amounts of time. Things get done more quickly, people get places faster. But, again, you can weigh that view by reminding your reader that perhaps 30,000 of the 55,000 people killed on the highways each year in America alone would be alive if the speed of automobiles were reduced. Weighing the convenience of several hours saved against the years that people who are killed lose permanently is an obvious way of disposing of that counterargument.

The Strategy of Counterargument

The strategy of your response to counterarguments is to admit that something is lost—convenience, fun, thrills—but that something much more important is gained—life. This strategy is effective because it admits other points of view while showing them to be limited or shortsighted.

All good argumentative pieces anticipate important counterarguments. By doing so, you make your work powerful and thoughtful. You give it substance and depth.

Decide the Order in which You Should Present Your Arguments: Nestorian, Hierarchic, or Other

Once you have your arguments chosen, you can put them in their most convincing order. Choosing the order of your arguments provides you with the structure of your essay. In this sample argument, you could use Nestorian order:

1. It is possible to reduce auto liability and collision insurance costs by reducing highway speed.
2. Reducing highway speed will help cars last longer.
3. Lower speeds will reduce auto-related crime.
4. Counterargument: Earlier ages did not miss the speed and neither shall we.
5. Reducing highway speed will reduce highway deaths.

You can imagine the structure of a five-page discussion on this topic taking the approximate structure shown on pages 189–191.

Introduction: begin, if possible, with a narrative explaining why your subject is important. Explain why it is desirable to take the position you favor.

Argument 1: Explain why it is possible to reduce liability and collision rates by reducing highway speed. Give some indication of the amount of money spent on these insurances and then indicate how much in dollars would be saved by the recommendation that you are making.

Argument 2: Explain why reducing highway speeds will help cars last longer. Establish that there is a cause and effect relationship between speed and wear. If possible, get some quotations from mechanics or other experts to verify your claim. Estimate what the life span of an automobile would be if speeds were dramatically reduced.

Argument 3: Begin establishing that speed is a factor in automobile-related crime and that by reducing speeds criminals will be less likely to escape from the scene of the crime and therefore less likely to commit crimes. Point out, too, that the incidence of car thefts alone will be dramatically reduced by forcing cars to go more slowly.

This is a place in which you can insert some statistics or estimates of the number of car-related crimes. Ask a local police force for information.

Argument 4: Naturally there will be intense resistance to your argument, so here is the place to give it voice. One counterargument will be that it is fun to drive fast. Another will be that speed is necessary for the world's work. Because other ages did without it, you can point out that we can too.

You can also point out that the fun people have is costing lives.

Argument 5: Your fifth argument is your strongest. Be sure to begin by pointing

> out that the average death toll in America is around 55,000 people a year, about the death toll of American military in the Vietnam War. Establish the connection between speed and death on the highway—and stress that the value of a single human life is incalculable. Remind your reader that high speeds cause a huge loss of life.
>
> Finally, end with a reflection on the importance of saving lives, saving time. Remind your reader that speed kills.

Every argumentative essay will demand its own structure depending upon the strength of its arguments and on the opposition you can expect from your audience. But no matter what structure you choose, the procedure of examining the premises of your arguments and testing them according to the principles of data, claim, and warrant will help you develop each argument fully.

Audience and Planning

The act of writing any piece, no matter how careful the planning, will alter the structure you may have conceived for it. If you find that an argument begins to look weak after you've developed it, then by all means be sure to reduce its importance in your essay. Do the same if an argument proves to be much stronger than you expected. The act of writing only completes the act of planning, and because it implies discovering things that you didn't know before you started, you can expect to make changes as you go along.

It is always helpful to bring things to a human level by narrating a personal experience, telling the story of someone who may have suffered because of excessive speed, or by some means getting us involved with the human element implied in your argument. Just setting out one argument after another will not do. Always spend part of your planning time looking for a humanizing anecdote or for a specific instance that will bring the importance of your points home. Then, after an appropriate introduction, you can begin to structure your detailed arguments. (See box entitled "Tips: Designing the Overall Structure of an Argument.")

Tips: Designing the Overall Structure of an Argument
- Introduction: details, anecdotes, events, narratives, or other humanizing elements that will help establish the human importance of your subject.
- Your first arguments.
- A disposition of possible counterarguments.
- Your final argument (your strongest, if in Nestorian Order).
- Conclusion, which also helps reestablish the human element by considering your arguments in human terms. This might come in the form of considering a quotation from a person you have interviewed, or a quotation from a source you have researched.

Writer's Workshop: Constructing an Argumentative Essay
1. Using the arguments and suggestions in this chapter, write a piece entitled "Automobiles Should Go No Faster than Thirty Miles an Hour." Decide on the order of your principal arguments and add any new arguments of your own. Try to anticipate the counterarguments that you need to account for.
2. Instead of defending the argument in Item 1, write a piece that argues for allowing automobiles to go as fast as current manufacturers permit. You will have to invent your own arguments and treat the arguments developed as counterarguments. Be sure to take advantage of the processes of invention by spending time in brainstorming, free writing, grouping, and clustering. Develop as much material as possible before beginning your outlining. Use the means of development to work up arguments to use in the piece. Once you have done your prewriting, follow this procedure:

- Clearly establish the subject of your essay.
- List your arguments. Refer to Chapters 4 and 5 to give you useful means of development that can help you find arguments.
- Analyze your arguments in terms of data, claim, and warrant.
- Gather evidence supporting your arguments.
- Take the most important counterarguments into consideration, showing how they can be rebutted.

- Decide on the order in which you should present your arguments: Nestorian, Hierarchic, or other.

3. Write your own argumentative essay on a subject that is important to you. Follow the procedures outlined in this chapter as carefully as possible. Be sure to use the means of development to work up arguments. If you have trouble finding a subject of your own, choose from among the following topics:

Pornography should not be protected by the constitutional guarantee of free speech.

Gun control can reduce the amount of violence in American life.

Metal money is an unnecessary waste of natural resources.

Television has warped the minds of a generation.

Rock and Roll is moral music.

College students should invest in common stocks while they are in college.

Environmental issues will be the major challenge of our time.

Nuclear weapons are a necessary evil.

You may certainly take the opposite side of any of these arguments. Writing on both sides of any of these issues is excellent training.

9

Literary Analysis

Creative Insight: Literary Critic As Reader

Your audience for a piece of literary analysis may be peers or scholars interested in a specific literary work and its complexities, or readers of a campus or local paper interested in your review of a book or poem. As a writer, your general intention is to present yourself as objective, observant, and inquiring. Your subject is either already known to your audience or not, and if it is not, you will have to provide a helpful summary. Your purposes as a writer are usually to present a case or argument in favor of an interpretation that has resulted from your own careful response to and analysis of the work. Sometimes, your purpose may be simply that of presenting information or interpreting the facts of the work. But ordinarily, the literary critic's purpose is persuasive.

It is also true that when you write about literature you are revealing your habits and skills as a reader. Being aware of yourself as a reader of a literary work—as a member, that is, of the work's audience. You can make many useful observations about the expectations the work seems to have of its readers. Does the work, and therefore the author, assume a reader with a wide background in the classics and the Bible, as John Milton does? Or does the writer assume a reader with no such background, as Sylvia Plath does? Does the author create an audience by using some of the strategies discussed in Chapter 1?

The good literary critic demonstrates a high level of reading skill. When you are writing literary criticism, you actually deepen your reading abilities, because in many ways a great piece of literature alters the habits of its readers. Some people go so far as to say that good literature creates good readers. Attentive reading educates your capacity to read.

ANNOTATION: LOOKING FOR PATTERNS

Your preparation for writing literary analysis involves keeping track of important lines, expressions, or phrases that may be useful to you. As a literary critic, you make several passes through a piece of literature: first, a careful reading looking for details such as unusual descriptions, characterizations, and observations. Then, another reading may yield insight into the primary themes or statements of the author or major characters. A later reading may aim at establishing patterns and relationships between major elements in the work. For example, certain kinds of descriptions of darkness, shadow, and light may begin to be meaningful when you notice what the author leaves in darkness and what in light. Analysis, as a means of development, usually implies a search for meaning, so literary analysis usually tries to establish the meaning of such patterns. If it seems to fit in with what you perceive as the meaning of the entire work, then you can feel assured that you are developing useful insights.

Enjoyment: The First Level of Reading

All literature is meant to be enjoyed. Close reading of literature is designed to deepen our awareness of what literature does and says, and properly done, it should deepen our pleasure. As in anything in life, studying literature gives you more information and produces more awareness of the resources available to you.

You read some literature without worrying about what you might have to say regarding it. Often you remember that kind of reading as most pleasurable. When you begin writing about literature, you necessarily increase your attentiveness and your insight. The result of performing careful literary analysis is a heightening of awareness, observation, and responsiveness to all your subsequent reading. Part of this is a result of your growing capacity to discover pattern, development, thought, and values as they are expressed in literary works.

The Power of Annotation: The Art of Questioning

The literary analyst's usual question is *Why?* Why does a character step into the shade at a given moment? Why does another character pretend he has not heard a threatening comment? Why does the author pause in the middle of an action to describe a scene and a setting that figured long ago and which seems not to have a direct relationship to the current action? Why is the story told to us by a person who seems not to have had a hand in it originally? Every piece of literature will provoke its own questions. Therefore, the first stage of prewriting in literary analysis is learning to develop good questions. Questions based on Kenneth Burke's Pentad (Chapter 2) relating to Act, Scene, Agent, Agency, and Purpose are a powerful aid to developing a subject to write about in relation to a work of literature.

You may refer back to Chapter 2 to examine the detailed questions built around Burke's Pentad, but consider the usefulness of these questions as a starting point in observing any piece of literature, regardless of its genre:

Act
What has happened in this work? What are the different aspects of the action? Is the action a unified plot, or is it a collection of episodes? What is the importance of the action for the characters or for the reader?

Scene
How carefully is the setting described? In what terms is it described—the terms of the characters, or the author/narrator? How important is the setting in relation to plot or character?

Agent
Are the characters fully developed psychologically, or are they relatively one dimensional? Who are the most important characters? What importance have the lesser characters to the action?

Agency
By what means did the main characters achieve what they did? How do they expect to accomplish their goals? Is their means of action supported by a principle, or is it supported by force or persuasion? Is the means by which the characters achieve their ends worthy and desirable? Is there any means they should have used that they did not?

Purpose
What are the primary motivating purposes of the characters in the work? Are their purposes clear and intelligible? Do you approve of them? Should you? Do the characters expect you to approve of them? What do you feel is the ultimate purpose of the piece in relationship to you the reader?

During your rereadings, ask questions by underlining and writing in the margins of your text (or in your journal if the text is from the library). You can begin with the general questions listed in this section, and then move to more specific questions, such as: "Why does the image of a stone fence appear here?" "Is the reference to the *Odyssey* supposed to mean that this hero is like Odysseus?" "Am I supposed to like this character? If so, why do I feel so ambiguous about her?" "Are the birds supposed to be symbols?" "How does this reference to a rowboat tie into the narrator's worries about his conscience and his sense of mission in life?" Such questions function as pointers. They give you possible direction in your further readings. You are looking for answers to difficult questions that you yourself have formulated.

Being Original

One of the most important aims you have as a literary analyst is being original in your thinking. You may feel that most pieces of good literature have been gone over again and again by experts and that you are not likely to find anything they have not discovered. But that is not quite the point. You are a unique individual, and you have a unique sensibility to art and literature. What you observe is not likely to be identical with what anyone else observes. Therefore, your biggest difficulty would actually be in trying *not* to be original.

Insights are observations you develop about a work of literature as you read it. Sometimes they begin as guesses or hunches. But they almost always result from the asking of questions. Of course there are those moments when it suddenly occurs to you that a given pattern of imagery implies a meaning that you didn't suspect at first. But even then, the sudden insight is preceded by a questioning attitude, a wondering about something. In the earliest stages of reading, you should cultivate the best questions you can in your annotations. They are to be treated as a resource. Without them, you are likely to flounder, and to have little or nothing to say about a piece of literature.

Developing Your Own Way In: An Approach Through Argument

Because its purpose is persuasive, literary analysis is usually related to argument. You establish a body of evidence for examination—the data, making a claim regarding that data, then discussing the warrants that will support your claim. The literature supplies the data, which you can work up by using the Pentad or the means of development. Your observations about the data should be stated clearly so that your audience can react to them and consider them against what its own views might be.

Whatever you claim, you will need to examine the evidence before you. You will have to develop warrants that are reasonable, and you will want to guide your reader toward accepting your views. Your claims depend on your careful reading of the work.

DEVELOPING INSIGHTS

Every good piece of literary analysis is built around an insight into the work of literature. The act of writing a first draft will refine your insight by limiting, focusing, and qualifying it. The first draft, as in other kinds of writing, will naturally follow your process of developing ideas through brainstorming, grouping into patterns, and clustering. Responding to the Burkean Pentad is also a natural step in this process. Once you have performed some of these early stages of writing, you may find yourself in a position to express a thesis that will draw together your observations uncovered in the process of annotation. A thesis, or overview, permits your audience to know what it is that you are about to examine and what kinds of conclusions you feel you have been able to draw. It gives shape and order to what you write while helping your reader not only follow you, but absorb your conclusions and assess the value of your insights for his or her own reading of the work.

SUMMARY AND ANALYSIS

Some writers profit from summarizing a work for themselves in the early process of writing. It is a stimulus to observation, and sometimes will reveal valuable insights. A careful summary will sometimes be a strong persuasive device for your reader.

Summary serves two useful purposes for the literary critic. One is to help clarify an ambiguous narrative point in a text that has raised unsettled questions. If it is not absolutely clear what happens in a given section of a text, then a summary may be useful just to establish a common ground between you and your reader. The other is in a situation in which you know that your reader has not read the literature to which you refer. If you are in doubt in a classroom situation, you can usually assume that your audience has read the literature, and therefore a summary is not necessary. However, if you are writing for a newspaper, say, or for a general audience in a literary magazine, then it may be useful to offer a brief summary. But you must remember that a summary is never a substitute for analysis: it can only be prelude to it.

Annotating a Sonnet: Shakespeare

Annotating a sonnet is not altogether different from annotating other literature, and because a sonnet is relatively short, it can serve as a useful example. The following sonnet is one of the best known in English, and you may have seen it before. First, the underlined passages struck the reader as having special importance, and they are underlined in order to act as a reference. They are something to return to later, to examine in depth in relation to other parts of the poem. Then, the questions that the poem excited follow afterward.

You can see that the underlinings and the questions are somewhat like a brainstorming session. In effect, after reading a poem like this, it is always useful to jot down every question that comes to mind, even questions that may seem silly. You never know when you are at this stage of analysis what kinds of ideas you'll have, and you never know what will be valuable. Later on, you can sort through the questions and throw out the unusable ones, but at first you need to gather as many as possible.

Free association, clustering, random questions—all these are part of the process of prewriting when you are searching for an original way to analyze a piece of literature. The following is Shakespeare's Sonnet 73:

> That time of year thou mayst in me behold
> When yellow leaves, or none, or few, do hang
> Upon those boughs which shake against the cold,
> Bare ruined choirs, where late the sweet birds sang.
> In me thou see'st the twilight of such day
> As after sunset fadeth in the west;
> Which by and by black night doth take away,
> Death's second self that seals up all in rest.
> In me thou see'st the glowing of such fire,
> That on the ashes of his youth doth lie,
> As the deathbed whereon it must expire,
> Consum'd with that which it was nourished by.
> This thou perceiv'st, which makes thy love more strong,
> To love that well which thou must leave ere long.

In a poem like this, everyone's underlinings and questions will differ. Even though this is a very brief poem, it is packed with significance, and its density is such that a first, or even a second reading is not likely to reveal everything that we want to know. The following questions are annotations developed specifically in reaction to a line-by-line reading of the poem. You may be able to add to them.

Questions
Why is there talk about seasons? The first line implies that the poet is in his *autumn*.

Do the yellow leaves only mean it's fall, or are they symbolic?

The "cold, Bare ruin'd choirs" suggest a church—why? And what are the birds doing? Why singing? Are they associated with the church?

Why the twilight and sunset imagery? Is there a connection with the fall? Maybe the end of the season? Could it be a connection with the poet's life ending?

The images of black night and death must relate to the poet. Why?

This must be why the image of the fire—it was cold in line 3—and its ashes get mixed up with the "ashes of his youth." Why is the poet talking about his youth getting burned up?

What does that line "Consum'd with that which it was nourished by" mean? It seems important. Could it mean life is consumed by life?

And why does looking at the poet's autumn of life make "thy love more strong"? Is it just because of the realization that the poet is aging?

I wonder who the poet is talking to. I also wonder what the poet wants and whether the person he's addressing is going to do something after reading the poem. The church image is curious. How does it fit into the whole poem?

Some of these questions are very big. And not all of them can be answered. Yet, some of them begin to show some patterns. For instance, there is the pattern of the seasons ending, the barrenness of the boughs, the ending of the day, the dying of the fire—all these point to a comparison with the aging of the poet. Even the birds could refer to the songs the poet sings—these birds are gone, according to the word "late," which implies they were here, but are not here now. We use that word to refer to someone who has recently died, "The late Mr. Clifford." This pattern of imagery could form the basis of an interpretation of the poem. Another focus for a brief analysis of the poem could be the church: why a holy place in a poem that talks about love? Another focus could be the question of what the reader is meant to learn from the poem.

There are two other larger questions that could form the basis of an interesting analysis. First, if the birds are gone, and the implication is that the poet's skill is waning, why does the poet say so in a great poem? And second, because this is Sonnet 73 in a group of more than 150 sonnets (and also we know that the great plays are not yet written), what is Shakespeare getting at? Is he the poet who speaks these lines? Or has he invented a character who speaks them?

Writer's Workshop: Annotation and Asking Questions

1. Provide your own underlining and annotations for one of the following poems. Make a list of your questions.

THE ROAD NOT TAKEN

Two roads diverged in a yellow wood
And sorry I could not travel both
And be one traveler, long I stood
And looked down one as far as I could
To where it bent in the undergrowth;

Then took the other, as just as fair,
And having perhaps the better claim,
Because it was grassy and wanted wear;
Though as for that the passing there
Had worn them really about the same,

And both that morning equally lay
In leaves no step had trodden black.

Oh, I kept the first for another day!
Yet knowing how way leads on to way,
I doubted if I should ever come back.

I shall be telling this with a sigh
Somewhere ages and ages hence:
Two roads diverged in a wood, and I—
I took the one less traveled by,
And that has made all the difference.

Robert Frost

HOLY SONNET 10

Death, be not proud, though some have called thee
Mighty and dreadful, for thou art not so;
For those whom thou think'st thou doest overthrow
Die not, poor Death, nor yet canst thou kill me.
From rest and sleep, which but thy pictures be,
Much pleasure; then from thee much more must flow,
And soonest our best men with thee do go.
Rest of their bones, and soul's delivery.
Thou art slave to fate, chance, kings, and desperate men,
And dost with poison, war, and sickness dwell,
And poppy* or charms can make us sleep as well
And better than thy stroke; why swell'st thou then?
One short sleep past, we wake eternally
And death shall be no more; Death, thou shalt die.

John Donne (1633)
*opium

632

The Brain—is wider than the Sky—
For—put them side by side—
The one the other will contain
With ease—and You—beside—

The Brain is deeper than the sea—
For—hold them—Blue to Blue—
The one the other will absorb—
As sponges—Buckets—do—

The Brain is just the weight of God—
For—Heft them—Pound for Pound—
And they will differ—if they do—
As Syllable from Sound—

Emily Dickinson

Using the Means of Development _____

The means of development discussed in Chapters 4 and 5 are useful for critical analysis. They can produce good insights as well as help guide the structure of your writing. And although the means of development by analysis is the most normal to use for literary criticism, most of the other means of development can be put to good use as well.

COMPARISON

Comparative studies of pieces of literature take several forms. Some of the possibilities are comparisons of

- works of the same kind (two poems, two short stories, two novels, two plays)
- works by a single author
- works on a single or similar theme
- works of the same period
- works from the same or different periods and cultures
- works of the same form (sonnets, rhymed couplets, odes, dramatic monologues)
- segments of different works (descriptive passages, use of similes, metaphors, imagery, and other technical devices)
- characters, plots, settings, mood, atmosphere, themes

Comparative essays have an interesting advantage in that they encourage you to be specific. Using the means of development by comparison will suggest ideas and insights that show up in relationship to other similar pieces of literature. Sometimes it is difficult to find something to say about a single literary element, but it is usually much easier to comment about one thing as it relates to another.

For example, Shakespeare's and Donne's sonnets allude to death. Donne is very direct, addressing death as if it were a character. And Donne chides death by reminding it to be more humble, because it will cease to exist at the Last Judgment Day. By contrast, Shakespeare does not address death directly, but he does refer to sleep as "Death's second self that seals up all in rest," which tells us that he is concerned with death. He also mentions "the glowing of such fire,/That on the ashes of his youth doth lie," and then tells us that it is a "deathbed" "Consum'd with that which it was nourished by." (The virgule [/] indicates the end of one line and the beginning of the next when quoting poetry.)

This is a very different approach. Donne speaks directly to death and is optimistic in his tone. Shakespeare speaks directly to an unknown person, possibly one he loves, and he is relatively pessimistic in tone. In Donne's poem, death is not to be feared. In Shakespeare's poem, death is consuming the poet's life, and it must be reckoned with. Because death is consuming the poet, the person whom he addresses is told "To love that well which thou must leave ere long."

Such a comparison focuses on two things: the person addressed by the poems and the differing representations of death and the poets' attitudes toward it. With those qualities in mind, you could begin to develop a full essay that would open some of the more interesting aspects of the poems to our examination.

DESCRIPTION

It may not be immediately apparent, but a good deal of literary analysis is description. Much of the earlier discussion of comparison involves describing what is in the poems. For instance, the commentary on Donne's use of direct address needed a description of Donne's procedure. Some of the description includes quotations that serve to validate the observations: as a reader you can verify whether or not the writer's description is accurate. Sometimes, alas, a writer will assume something is true which you, as reader, can see is false.

If the writer's description of the work is faulty, then a misreading is naturally going to occur. Therefore, it is important to be able to make your description accurate and as precise as is necessary for your purposes.

Literary description establishes what is perceptible in the work and clarifies its nature.

Its function is to point to the literary evidence upon which you will base your observations about the work or works.

Emily Dickinson's poem can be described as follows:

It is structured in three parts, with each part establishing a comparison of the brain with something else: the width of the sky, the depth of the sea, and the weightiness of God. Each part of the poem is a stanza of four lines, with the second and fourth lines rhyming. The poem uses simple, everyday language, with mostly one-syllable words. Many of the words are capitalized, but it is not clear why. It has no punctuation, except for the dashes, which do not have a clear apparent function. The poem does not seem to be spoken by a character other than the poet, and it has no specific audience —it is not written to a friend or a special reader.

Description such as this is often useful before you begin writing. On the basis of this description, you might want to write about Dickinson's use of dashes. No one really knows why she added them, or what they are supposed to do. So your observations may make a genuine contribution to what has been said and thought about the poem.

The only problem with development by description is that the result cannot stand alone. It is only part of your argument. It is a prelude to analysis, an aid to analysis. On the basis of careful description—which qualifies as data—a claim can be made. If you do not go on to draw conclusions from your description, then your description will not help you in your criticism.

CAUSE AND EFFECT

Cause and effect is one of the most central means of development in literary analysis. In the nineteenth century, literary analysts were very much concerned with knowing what caused certain works of literature to be written. Usually, critics at that time linked the works with events in the lives of the writers. In a way, the critics' function was to explain the works by showing how they related to the life of the author. For instance, if a poem was sad, and it could be shown that the author was experiencing unhappiness at the time of composition, then it became "clear" that the unhappiness was caused by personal tragedy.

But this approach eventually became bankrupt. Aesthetic critics pointed out that there is no easy way to relate sad poems to sad circumstances in writers' lives. Indeed, there were many cases in which writers on the verge of death wrote joyous and uplifting works. In modern times, we have concluded that the emotions expressed in a literary work rarely have much to do with the personal emotions of the artist. It is more common to see the artist transcending the limitations of a personal emotional circumstance.

However, you can see that this approach has some intriguing angles. For instance, we would be very interested in knowing why Shakespeare wrote Sonnet 73 and to whom it is addressed. Many suggestions have been given, but we do not have enough information to be sure of the validity of any of them. One of the most intriguing questions concerns whether the poem is addressed to a man or a woman.

Sometimes we learn from letters that a given work was excited by a specific event—in a sense it was *caused* by that event. Henry James talks about the "germ" of a novel, the incident, observation, or idea that actually begets a novel. He comments that one of his most famous books, *The Ambassadors*, was begotten by his witnessing a man and a woman in a small boat, rowing on a river in France. He was taken by the woman's parasol and her colors. The scene was so striking to him that he began to work on his novel at once, planning to use it as a climactic moment. And, indeed, it appears as the climactic moment in Strether's realization that the young American, Chad Newsome, is having an affair with Madame de Vionnet.

In the case of Robert Frost's poem, "The Road Not Taken," there are several incidents that were said to have "caused" the poem. One was his walking in the woods and seeing another person coming from a sharp angle toward an intersection with his path. The other person, Frost thought, looked so much like Frost himself that he was startled and stopped still until that person had passed. He reported that he began the poem shortly after, reflecting on the fact that he could only have taken one road at a time. In another comment, however, Frost said that he had been out walking in the country with a friend who when confronted by a choice of roads always complained that they should have taken the other road. Because of this complaining, Frost contemplated the choices that one has, using the two roads to symbolize different paths of life.

Research into such questions constitutes, in a sense, analysis of cause and effect, although it regards the literary work as an effect of a specific cause. This is sometimes plausible, as in the example of Frost's poem, for which we have some testimony from Frost. But in the case of Shakespeare, it is very speculative and does not contribute much to our understanding of the work.

Much more useful is discussion of the elements within a work that cause it to have the effect it has on its readers. This is not to say we can ever really summarize the effect that a complex work has on us. Indeed, it may have different effects on different readers, depending on their preparation and experience. Careful analysis of the details of a work of literature, examining them for what they contribute to the whole, actually helps produce an effect in the reader because it makes the reader more aware of what elements are functioning in the work.

ILLUSTRATION BY EXAMPLE

Unfortunately, illustration by example has a serious pitfall built into it, and therefore ought to be used carefully in literary analysis. The pitfall is a temptation to list one example after another to prove a thesis. For example, if your thesis is that Hamlet does not trust the people about him because he feels they are corrupted by the court of his uncle, Claudius, it would be easy enough to choose several examples that show how this is true. The problem is that your thesis may well have been proved after two examples; five or six represent overkill.

Examples of all kind are necessary in literary discussions, but development by example needs to be guided by one basic concept. Examples are designed to prove a point and do not constitute a point in and of themselves.

ANALYTIC TECHNIQUES

The means of development by analysis concentrates on finding evidence within a work of literature that, upon examination, implies a relationship or meaning that a more casual reader might not observe. Your commentary on the evidence is analytic in nature. The earlier commentary on the sample poems is analytic in part because it treats a limited aspect of the poems: their imagery, use of language, and mode of address. It is also analytic because by commenting on a specific element of the poems, it aims to reveal some of its larger meaning. By examining an isolated element, the analysis reveals the generally organic nature of the entire poem. It shows us how carefully and artistically integrated its elements are.

One aim of analysis is to produce a heightened sense of awareness. A piece of literature involves its readers and makes them forget they are reading. Sometimes a reader has a sense that something wonderful has been achieved, but that it is not clear just what it is. The literary critic aims to examine the work to see how its effects have been achieved. Along the way, the critic may also point to meanings and effects that the average reader did not notice. This enriches the experience of the reader and enlarges the scope of the work.

---

*W*riter's *W*orkshop

Writer's Workshop: Using the Means of Development

1. Offer a discussion of either or both of the following poems by Walt Whitman. They resulted from Whitman's involvement as a war nurse during the American Civil War, and they are both dated 1865. Develop your discussion by means of definition, comparison, cause and effect, possibility, description, classification, use of example, or analysis. Rely on only one of these.

CAVALRY CROSSING A FORD

A line in long array where they wind betwixt green islands,
They take a serpentine course, their arms flash in the sun
 —hark to the musical clank,
Behold the silvery river, in it the splashing horses loitering
 stop to drink.
Behold the brown-faced men, each group, each person a
 picture, the negligent rest on the saddles,
Some emerge on the opposite bank, others are just
 entering the ford—while
Scarlet and blue and snowy white,
The guidon flags flutter gayly in the wind.

BY THE BIVOUAC'S FITFUL FLAME

By the bivouac's fitful flame,
A procession winding around me, solemn and sweet and slow
 —but first I note,

The tents of the sleeping army, the fields' and woods' dim
    outline,
The darkness lit by spots of kindled fire, the silence,
Like a phantom far or near an occasional figure moving,
The shrubs and trees, (as I lift my eyes they seem to be
    stealthily watching me,)
While wind in procession thoughts, O tender and wondrous
    thoughts,
Of life and death, of home and the past and loved, and of those
    that are far away;
A solemn and slow procession there as I sit on the ground,
By the bivouac's fitful flame.

2. Instead of commenting on these poems using only one of the means of development, use a combination. Once you have written your commentary, explain your choice of means of development, and comment on your sense of satisfaction with what you produced.

Reader Response Criticism

Reader response criticism begins with a careful discussion of the effects of aspects of a work of literature on its reader. The writer often anticipates a specific audience and attempts to control that audience's response, or at the very least produce a response to the work. By examining the kinds of response you give as a reader to a work, you can develop some important critical insights into the work.

As a reader you have certain expectations. You expect, usually, that literature will represent life, either in a realistic, fantastic, or mixed fashion. And sometimes an author will play with your expectation, as in science fiction, which may begin in a most realistic fashion, but reveal itself to be concerned with an as yet impossible world. Some readers expect to be entertained in an escapist way by a book, whereas others expect to be challenged and made to think. Some expect to have a book excite their emotions in such a way as to make them feel deeply about important things.

Your expectations will color much of your response, at least during the first reading. Once you have read a work and know its outlines, your successive readings will have different expectations. Surprise, amusement, and shock will probably not be among them. At the stage of successive readings your expectations must center on deepening your awareness and sharpening your emotional responses.

As a reader you will have different expectations of a novel than of a poem, play, or essay. Your expectations of a historical novel will differ from those of a science fiction or romance novel. If the work was written in the Middle Ages you will have one expectation, whereas if it is modern you will have another. If it is centered in Renaissance Rome, your expectation will be different than if it is centered in contemporary Chicago.

Kathleen McCormick has worked up a series of questions that help center a reader's response to a literary text (*College English* 47, no. 8 [December 1985], 840–41). An adaptation of them is presented in the box entitled "Tips: Reader Response Criticism."

Tips: Reader Response Criticism

1. **What is the predominant effect of the text on you?**
   Confusion, suspense, identification with characters, interest, boredom, amusement, terror, sorrow for the characters, fear, etc. An answer to this question should explore the complexities of multiple effects. It also benefits from keeping track of your reactions in a journal.

2. **Why do you think the text had that effect?**
   a. In order to answer this, you should consider the differences in social customs, language, social organization, moral and ethical assumptions between the work and your own norms. You should consider the familiarity or unfamiliarity of situations, circumstances, references and allusions, or special background assumed by the text.
   b. You also must consider your own preparation for the text. Are you familiar with the literary conventions of the work in question? Do you have special preparation for reading literature of certain periods or of certain kinds? Are you prepared to respond to the historical or social contexts of the literature? Does a possession of a special background help or hinder your response to the work? Does your gender or expectation of gender behavior affect your response to the work?

3. **What does your response tell you about yourself?**
   What do you learn about your preparation for reading, your approach to the act of reading, your assumptions about literature? What do you learn about our social standards, the limits of an author's social awareness, your own social awareness? Is your sense of normality or conventionality tested by the literature you have read? What kinds of limits do you sense in yourself as a reader? What strengths do you have?

_____ Reader Response: Shakespeare and Dickinson

In the case of Shakespeare's Sonnet 73, you may respond to the imagery of fall, ashes, and aging very sympathetically. You may actually respond by feeling a degree of personal sympathy for the poet. The question one might ask is to what extent Shakespeare had anticipated your response.

In one sense, the fact that Shakespeare seems to have addressed this poem to a specific person tells us that he anticipated a careful response. He knew his audience intimately and that the images of the church choir would mean something important to it, and that the ashes on the fire would be palpable enough so that they needed no elaboration. Shakespeare even tells his reader what an appropriate response to the imagery and details of the poem should be: to value life because it is perishable.

Emily Dickinson's poem is quite different because it seems not to have been addressed to a specific person and may have been intended only for the poet's eyes. Many of her poems were discovered after she had died, some written on scraps of paper, and very few of her poems were published. In this case, the expected response of the reader is complicated.

The form is suggestive of a children's poem: short lines, simple rhyme. The pattern of each stanza is virtually the same, beginning with "The Brain is." If we think about what expectations we have in children's rhymes, then we expect pleasant sounds that amuse us and perhaps stick in our memory, but we do not expect profundity. Yet Emily Dickinson is giving us just that, especially in her final stanza, which implies a very unusual correlation between the human brain and God—which might explain why she capitalizes Brain throughout the poem. That correlation might offend or shock some readers; others may find the correlation enlightening. Still others might not even notice it.

One response is to marvel at the simplicity of the poetry, while admiring the complexity of the thought. The disjunction between the two is apparent because the form of the poem builds clear expectations of the reader and evokes certain responses in advance. This poem is unlike some modern poetry that anticipates a response of bafflement on the part of the reader. Some poetry is quite obscure, and because the reader is not going to understand everything at first, the poet can count on producing certain responses to the text. If the poet can make good use of those responses, then the poem may ultimately be satisfying to the reader.

READER PREPARATION

There is, along with the anticipation of response, the fact of preparation. All readers of literature need to be responsible to the text. This involves several things. For one thing, it involves reading with an open mind and with an informed ear. You cannot know everything about poetry before you read a poem, but you should be knowledgeable about certain formal demands. For example, Shakespeare expects his reader to know that the sonnet has fourteen lines, that each line has ten syllables, that the rhyme scheme is ababcdcdefefgg. He also expects his reader to know the meaning of the words he uses, so when he says, "bared ruin'd choirs," he expects his readers to know he is talking about a specific place in a church.

Writing literary criticism involves preparation for reading. One way of preparing yourself is to learn some of the conventions associated with specific genres. Such preparation provides you with a set of reasonable expectations to use in your reading.

Naturally, you cannot expect to be thoroughly prepared for each novel, short story, play, or poem you read. There will be specifics that you need to learn in order to read the work intelligently. There will even be specific literary conventions that you may not be aware of at first, and in order to read better you will need to learn about them. This is all part of reader preparation.

Because every piece of literature prepares you anew for reading literature, one of the jobs of the literary critic is to keep an open mind about the work at hand. Be willing to learn something new, and be willing to work on what may at the moment appear to be obscure. Learning to read literature involves clearing away obscurities by acquiring the background necessary to place specific literary elements in their proper perspective.

Genre and the Reader's Expectations

Literature is usually approached differently depending upon its genre: fiction, poetry, or drama. Within each of these are many subgenres, but virtually all those subgenres will respond to any critical approach designed to open up avenues of insight into the general category. In some cases, a critical principle will cross over generic boundaries and apply to several kinds of literature. For example, the setting in a play may be of immense importance, as, for example, the Danish court, filled with darkness and intrigue in *Hamlet*. But considerations of setting (e.g., Burke's Scene) are not exclusive to drama. Many poems, such as Frost's discussed earlier, are interesting for their setting, and most short story authors are careful to inform us thoroughly about their setting. We can study the setting in any kind of literature—but only when it is an element of that literature. What can we say, for instance, about the setting of Emily Dickinson's poem? Virtually nothing because her poem does not rely on setting. The same is true of considerations of plot and character. They are often of great value and importance in a literary work, but sometimes—again as in Dickinson's poem—they are of no interest except for being absent.

From a rhetorical perspective, you can regard the considerations appropriate to each genre as topics about which to write criticism. Setting in drama is a topic to be analyzed and discussed, just as is character and action. Once you have considered the theme of a piece of literature, then it will be productive, critically, to ask whether or not there is an organic relationship between theme, character, plot, action, and whatever other aspect of the literature you feel is pertinent to your analysis. Much of this has already been discussed in Chapter 2 in considering the Burke Pentad as a means of development.

Because the most important first stage of criticism is observation—literally perception of what is there—you can best begin by establishing exactly what you perceive in a literary work. Remember as you progress through this section that much of what is true for one genre will be true for another.

FICTION

Fiction ordinarily means prose narrative: short stories and novels. Sometimes fiction is told in a linear way: first one thing happens, then another. Sometimes the author plays with time and permits us to see the action in terms of flashback, filling us in on previous action. Sometimes the narrative is furthered by using letters: *Pamela,* the first English novel, for instance, is entirely told by letters. What we expect in good prose fiction is a significant theme, an interesting and involving plot, strong character, and a social setting in which to consider the plot and character.

Theme

Short stories and novels, both varieties of prose fiction, have a good many qualities in common. In each we look for a theme. The theme is what the work is about, a statement that sums up the subject of the work. It can sometimes be the author's statement about life, about the world. In some fiction, theme is elusive. We can see, for instance, that the story's subject matter may be hunting for a whale, as in Herman Melville's *Moby Dick,* or striking out on an adventure, as in *Huckleberry Finn.* But in each of those novels, the theme is something else, something much deeper. In both novels the theme has to do with the nature of good and evil in the world. One way of stating the theme of *Moby Dick* is to observe that a person's obsession with evil is usually destructive—even self-destructive. But this is an overriding theme of the book. There are many other themes that you may feel are almost as important.

Poems usually have themes, too. Emily Dickinson's poem, "The Brain," has very little in terms of character or action, but its theme is very important: the Brain is like God: it includes the world in its thought. The differences between Brain and God are like the differences between syllable and sound: not as much as one might think. In one sense, this is a daring poem, especially for its time, because it seems to liken human qualities with those of God.

The theme of a work of fiction is intelligible only after some reflection and analysis. It involves looking deeply into the work and stripping aside many of the superficial distractions of plot. Moreover, your sense of what the theme of a novel is may differ from someone else's. To a large extent you will have varying opinions because you may perceive something of importance that will not be noticed by someone else. This is not a problem, because the question of theme will depend on exactly what you do see in the work: it is not carved in granite.

You may think of the theme as being a statement of the significance or the meaning of the work, particularly as it relates to the overall human condition.

Plot

Fiction involves people in action, and the action is usually called the plot. But consider the term: a plot is something planned, something worked up, something thought out and participated in by characters. Therefore, not all action is plot. The plot is the organized action that produces revelation or insight. Some short stories are heavily plotted, whereas others are lightly plotted. To understand what that means, consider O. Henry's heavily plotted short story, "The Gift of the Magi." It is about two young people who are married, but who have so little money they cannot afford to buy Christmas presents for one another. They decide to sell their most precious possessions —he sells his pocketwatch, and she sells her beautiful long hair to a wig-maker. Meanwhile, he buys her a beautiful comb for her hair, while she buys him a chain for his watch. The result is ironic: things work out exactly opposite from the way the characters want them to be.

By contrast, there are stories in which very little happens. In James Joyce's lightly plotted "Araby," a young boy decides he must go to a bazaar called Araby. He depends on his uncle for the money, but his uncle comes home late, eats his dinner, and only then remembers to give the boy his money. The boy then takes a train (like an overground subway) to the bazaar and arrives almost at closing time. Essentially, the story is almost plotless. The conflict in the story occurs within the boy's own consciousness, his sense of himself, and he ends the story deriding himself for his vanity and weakness, because his going to Araby was a kind of mission—like that of a crusading knight—to return with something to impress a young girl in the neighborhood.

So, one critical approach to discussing plot concerns the level of complexity that the action achieves. Is there a great deal of complication in the interrelation of characters? Does the action take a number of ironic turns and depend upon the unexpected for its effect? Or does the action follow a pattern of normal expectation? Then it is possible to ask what constitutes the conflict in the story. Is the conflict in terms of action—as in an adventure story? Both *Moby Dick* and *Huckleberry Finn* include intense conflict in their action, and thus both pay close attention to plot. In some narratives, as in Joyce's, the conflict lies within the characters, thus reducing the significance of the plot.

Some narratives, such as suspense stories, are carefully plotted. You read along wondering how things will come out. On the other hand, there are some stories in which the action seems to have been extracted from a moment in the characters' lives and there seems to be no twisting of the action to achieve a desirable outcome. Heavily plotted fiction can seem artificial. Life, as you already know, rarely ever seems to traffic in irony and twists of fate. Ordinarily, it is the smooth following of one activity after another, with no sense of plottedness. Slice-of-life fiction follows the activities of people over a period of time, as if there were a silent reporter on the scene jotting everything down. The significance of such stories is usually implied in the relationship of the characters, and in the things they do that do not seem important to them but are important to you because the author has provided a perspective from which to regard their actions.

Point of View

Point of view is the name we sometimes give for the perspective that the author provides. All fiction has to be told from some point of view. Among the choices are

The omniscient narrator: A narrator who knows everything, including what the characters think, what they feel, what will happen, what has happened. The narrative is usually told in the third person: "Benker paused. He looked thoughtfully at Hilda and wondered whether he should tell her about the will." Usually such a narrator has no name in the action, and often such a narrator is associated with the author.

The restricted narrator: A narrator who, like you, knows what is visible and apparent, but nothing more. This can be told in the third person: "Benker watched Hilda turn her face from him. He stood by the garden seat. They appeared to be angry with each other." Or, it could be told in the first person: "I never thought I would see Benker again. And yet, there he was, as odious as ever, standing childlike by the garden seat."

Another kind of restricted narrator is one who has a name and a place within the action. Occasionally this kind of narrator is unreliable. That is to say, you need to be cautious accepting information supplied by such a narrator because the narrator may wish to hide something. In a famous example in the vein of mystery stories, Agatha Christie created a narrator who told a mystery that seemed extremely difficult for the reader to solve as the narrative went on. The reason was that the narrator was the murderer, and thus lied to the reader, as murderers are sometimes wont to do.

Finally, when you discuss plot in fiction, one crucial question is How does the plot reveal the significance of the action? Remember that the action is what the characters do, or what is done to them, whereas the plot is the organization of that action. Therefore, the plot unfolds the action in a specific way, aiming for specific effects. There may be a climax, a moment of intense revelation in the story. If so, does that moment *open* the story up for you? Does the plot contribute to producing insight into the entire story?

Characterization

Ordinarily people act in fiction. The quality of the characterization in a story or novel is something you can examine. You can ask whether the characters are full psychological beings or merely types. In George Orwell's *Animal Farm*, the characters are not people, but animals. Their psychology is less interesting than the types they represent. The beast fable, which tells stories with animals as the main characters, has been popular since the Middle Ages, and its value is that it can tell a political tale (which is one of its primary functions) without having to name names. It uses types, such as the overbearing tyrant, the sniveling lieutenant, the warlike military person, the coward, the do-gooder, and many more.

Types are very useful in fiction, and have been in service in drama for millennia. The *miles gloriosus*, the braggart warrior, appears in Plautus, Shakespeare, George Bernard Shaw, and many more besides. He shows up in contemporary novels and in short stories. However, our modern predilection is toward fully individualized characters. We can think of Emma Bovary as a type in Gustave Flaubert's *Madame Bovary*. She is a foolish woman who commits adultery out of boredom, and whose lovers are even more foolish than she. We can think of the bored housewife as a type if we wish. But in Flaubert's novel, Emma Bovary becomes complex, intensely human, and mercilessly revealed to us. What happens to Emma Bovary seems less interesting to us than our sense of who she is. The brilliance of Flaubert's revelation of her to his readers is what attracts us finally to the novel. The book is one of the most masterful achievements in characterization in all of literature.

The same is true of many plays as well, such as *Oedipus Rex, Antigone, Dr. Faustus, Hamlet, King Lear*, and many more. Each of these is named for its hero, and in each a full development of character is essential for the narrative to achieve its end.

Characterization may be flat or round—that is to say, underdeveloped or fully developed. Minor characters are sometimes appropriately flat, because they play a small role in the action. When you find minor characters with full development—when you know a good deal about their internal sense of themselves, their moral and emotional life—there is usually a reason, and your job as critic is to establish what that reason may be. Likewise, if a major character is underdeveloped, you need to search out the reason for that. It may be a commentary on the character that is meant to be picked up by the reader and treated as a value judgment.

Sometimes an author will not give the leading character a name. In Ralph Ellison's award-winning novel, *Invisible Man*, the main character is unidentified. The effect of this is very unsettling for the reader. You are used to knowing the name of the character who demands your attention, especially when the character's point of view dominates the narrative, as it does in this novel, which is told from the first person. But Ellison has a reason for handling the characterization in this way: his character is black, growing up in America in the 1930s, living in Harlem, trying to participate in the American Way. He discovers that as far as his culture is concerned, he is invisible. America does not see him, does not recognize him, and essentially disowns him. This is part of the theme of the novel, and the lack of identity for this character is part of the means by which Ellison helps clarify his theme.

Setting

Most fiction is set in a recognizable historical/physical locale. Ellison's novel is, in many ways, a study of the setting in which his characters move. He begins with a dramatic moment sometimes published separately as a story, called "Battle Royal," in which a group of young blacks are pitted against one another in a bloody fistfight for the amusement of a white men's club in the South. After the fight, the boys are offered money, but it is lying on a rug that is electrified, and when they grasp at the coins and bills, they get shocked terribly. When that ordeal is over, the narrator is invited to give a speech to the people assembled. They are the social leaders of the community, including the superintendent of schools. The narrator, even as he swallows his own blood, delivers the speech he had prepared, emphasizing the concept of social responsibility, as he had planned. This is an ironic comment on the action at hand, in which the leaders of the community were being socially irresponsible.

In many works of fiction, the setting takes on great importance. As a critic, you may wish to establish the relative importance of the setting. Does it reflect a time and place accurately? Does it evoke the qualities of that time and place in your imagination? Is it drawn in such a way as to help illuminate the characters or clarify the theme? What qualities should the careful reader observe in the setting? Is the environment responsible for the behavior of the characters? How different is your own time and place from that of the text? Does this difference produce special problems for the reader?

Some novels, such as William Kennedy's Albany trilogy *Legs, Billy Phelan's Greatest Game,* and *Ironweed,* have been praised as putting a community on the literary map. Before Kennedy wrote those novels, Albany was not apparent in any literary gazetteer.

F. Scott Fitzgerald captured the mood and sense of place of 1920s' Long Island in *The Great Gatsby,* whereas William Faulkner concentrated on revealing old Mississippi in novels such as *As I Lay Dying, The Sound and the Fury,* and *Absalom, Absalom!* Mark Twain captured life on the Mississippi River in Missouri after the Civil War, just as Saul Bellow revealed the social mores of Chicagoans after the Second World War. John Updike's characters are usually from Pennsylvania or New England, and they populate a roughly contemporary world. Philip Roth's characters are usually from New Jersey, where he was born. Edna O'Brien's settings are generally Dublin or London, and her characters are usually Irish. James Joyce wrote a book of short stories and three novels; all are set in the heart of Dublin. Most writers of narrative fiction are known for relying on a limited number of settings that they know well. And they often provide the reader with a special insight into that setting.

As a critic, your attention should be drawn to the setting. Is it detailed? What effect does it have on character? How satisfying is it for you to read about the setting?

POETRY

In addition to questions of theme, character, and setting, poetry invites other observations on qualities of imagery, rhythm, diction, metaphor, symbol, rhyme, and structure. Some poems are narrative and involve many of the same ingredients that we encounter in fiction. However, when we think of poetry, we think of certain qualities that are more specific to poetry than some other genres. One of these is imagery.

Imagery

An image is a descriptive passage that asks you to imagine what is described. The appeal is usually through a specific sense, such as the sense of sight or sound. Occasionally, an image will appeal to more than one sense at a time, resulting in a special device called synaesthesia. When you say someone's tie is *loud,* you are using synaesthesia, because the term applies to sound, but your expression refers to color. Imagery is common to most poetry. Modern poets often rely on it heavily, sometimes avoiding connecting statements that could clarify the theme or the situation, therefore making the poems difficult to understand.

In her poem, "Poppies in October," Sylvia Plath opens with "Even the sun-clouds this morning cannot manage such skirts." The image is that of the poppies as bright red skirts, which gives you a sense of their shape and invites you to imagine them looking up at the sky. Wilfred Owen, the World War I poet, begins "Dulce et Decorum Est" (Sweet and fitting it is to die for one's country), one of his most powerful poems about a mustard gas attack, with "Bent double, like old beggars under sacks,/Knock-kneed, coughing like hags, we cursed through sludge."

Metaphor

If you have already studied poetry carefully, you may have noticed that the two images quoted in the preceding paragraph are also metaphors. A metaphor is an implicit comparison of two unlike things. It is designed to impart a sense of freshness to the primary thing under discussion, while pointing up perhaps unnoticed similarities. The first, Plath's reference to poppies as skirts, is a normal metaphor: it makes its comparison without notifying us that it is doing so. And because few of us would think of the poppy as a skirt (we'd have to turn it upside down in our mind to do so), this is a very refreshing metaphor.

The second use of metaphor is a special form called simile. It is denoted by the use of the terms *like, as, as if,* or *such as,* which tell us that a poetic comparison is coming. To decribe the marching soldiers "Bent double, like old beggars under sacks" is to invoke both a strong visual image and to make a comparison that is a simile. In another poem, "The Show," Owen describes the battlefield before him as "Gray, cratered like the moon with hollow woe,/And pitted with great pocks and scabs of plagues." The imagery of the moon is appropriate enough: the bombshells are like moon craters, and the barrenness of the moon is imparted to the once fruitful earth before him. But the metaphor of the plague is a surprise: the pocks become like the scars of bubonic plague, and metaphorically the earth is fallen victim. The plague suggests the situation Thebes is in when Oedipus solves the riddle of the sphinx and takes the throne: the irony there is that Oedipus is the cause of the plague. In Owen's poem, people have caused the plague, and the plague is war.

Such a metaphor helps us to feel the emotional qualities Owen himself felt. Metaphor is a device that we respond to unconsciously: the concept of the plague would affect us even if we did not analyze its elements consciously. We do so in order to help deepen the response we give the metaphor. Being aware of the ways in which poets work does not harm your capacity to enjoy and respond to a poem. It intensifies it.

Symbol

Closely related to metaphor, a symbol is an object, place, animal, person, or situation that is used to evoke a wide range of meanings related to the primary subject at hand. For example, in *Moby Dick,* the great white whale becomes a symbol of evil to Captain Ahab, who vows to hunt it down and kill it. The whale stands for all that is untameable in nature, for the immense power in nature that sometimes erupts and kills mankind. For Ahab, the whale was evil. For the reader, however, the whale is less evil than it is natural. To the reader, Ahab seems to be loading the whale with a meaning it does not possess. A symbol can shift its meaning at times, as it does with the great white whale. It can sometimes resonate with several meanings, enriching your experience. The reason poets and writers use symbols is that they penetrate our unconscious. As Freud observed, symbols are the language of our dreams, and literary symbols affect us on an unconscious level, forcing us to respond much more deeply to a piece of literature than we might otherwise do.

Unraveling a symbol—analyzing its conscious meanings—can sometimes be difficult. Because the author wants us first to feel the significance, rather than know it, there is usually no effort to tell us that we are confronting a symbol. We must sense it, as in the following poem by A. E. Housman:

Into my heart an air that kills,
   From yon far country blows:
What are those blue remembered hills,
   What spires, what farms are those?

That is the land of lost content,
   I see it shining plain,
The happy highways where I went
   And cannot come again.

                                      1896

Housman uses the country air to symbolize the freshness, the odors of his youth when he went upon "happy highways" of innocence. As a child he was innocent and not worldly wise, as he was when he wrote these lines. He was content in those days, but experience has caused him to lose his sense of contentment and thus has made it impossible for him to travel again in the land he once knew as his.

He has symbolized his lost youth as a landscape he cannot return to, but can only contemplate from a distance. Even a whiff of that air can kill him because it causes him to remember the innocent past and see how far he has fallen from that innocence. The convention of symbolizing the innocent past as a landscape is ancient: the Garden of Eden is such a landscape, and as John Milton tells us in *Paradise Lost*, the human race can contemplate its innocence, but never return to it.

Just as the metaphor compares two things, the symbol implies a comparison: an outer real landscape, with the inner moral landscape of the poet. We understand in concrete terms the meaning of the impossibility of returning to a youthful state of contentment.

Diction

Poetry naturally economizes because it is shorter (in general) than fiction. Therefore, each word must be specially weighted. Diction is the word choice of the poet. Some poets insist, along with William Wordsworth and Samuel Taylor Coleridge, that poetry use the ordinary language of everyday speech. On the other hand, many poets feel that poetry can employ special kinds of words to achieve special kinds of effects.

In some poetry you can detect a rather formal diction, relatively distant from the language of everyday speech. David Jones begins a section of "In Parenthesis" with an allusion to Malory's *Morte D'Arthur*, itself known for its special diction: "So thus he sorrowed till it was day and heard the foules sing, then somewhat he was comforted." To say that a character "sorrowed" instead of "was sad," and to use the term "foules" for the more common "birds," is to create a diction that is consciously distant and formal. By contrast, T. S. Eliot includes a snatch of conversation in a London pub in his poem, "The Waste Land":

When Lil's husband got demobbed. I said—
I didn't mince my words, I said to her myself,
HURRY UP PLEASE ITS TIME
Now Albert's coming back, make yourself a bit smart.

The slang "demobbed" means demobilized, being let out of the army after World War I. The interjection, "HURRY UP PLEASE ITS TIME," represents the pub keeper shouting that it is time to close the pub. This is surprisingly close to the kind of conversation and language one could expect to hear even today in a London pub.

Jones's very formal diction, and his allusion to much older literature gives you a fresh and unexpected relationship with his poem. It causes you to establish a specific set of expectations and you thus approach the poem more formally yourself. In the middle of "The Waste Land," Eliot's conversational interlude is a total novelty. The relatively formal tone of the poem is broken unexpectedly, and you find yourself suddenly shifting gears in an effort to understand what is happening in the poem. Ironically, the shift into ordinary conversation causes confusion and makes the poem more difficult to understand.

When approaching a poem to examine its diction, ask yourself whether or not there are words or terms that surprise you. What expectations are established by the poem? Are they shifted at any time? To what use does the poet put your expectations? What pleasures do you derive from shifts or changes in expectation?

Rhythm and Rhyme

The rhythm of a poem refers to its apparent movement of sound, the way the natural accents of speech affect syllables and pace a reader through the work. If you think of poetry as spoken, and of the sounds as comparable to musical tones, you can get a sense of the possibilities of rhythm in a poem. Some poets plan a poem out in terms of rhythm. Percy Bysshe Shelley, for instance, planned a poem out in terms of lines that, in the first draft, read something like: di da di da, di da di da. And even today, poets often begin their work only after having sensed an authentic rhythm for their thoughts.

The principal way of commenting on rhythm is to examine lines for their meter. Meter means measure, and meter is the measure of the rhythm of verse lines. Meter is expressed in terms of feet. A foot consists of syllables in a given pattern of stressed and unstressed sound. A line of poetry may have anywhere from one to a dozen or more metrical feet.

> With rue my heart is laden
>   For golden friends I had,
> For many a rose-lipt maiden
>   And many a lightfoot lad.

>By brooks too broad for leaping
>The lightfoot lads are laid;
>The rose-lipt girls are sleeping
>In fields where roses fade.

This poem has a distinct rhythm, which is accented by the fact that each line is end-stopped (you feel the need to stop and pause at the end of each line), and the rhymes are full and complete. Two kinds of rhyme are in evidence here: one is masculine rhyme, in which one syllable rhymes with one syllable: "had" and "lad." But there is also feminine rhyme, in which two syllables rhyme with each other: "laden" and "maiden." Nicely, Housman has used his reference to a male in his masculine rhyme and to a female in his feminine rhyme, but actually the names have nothing to do with the gender of people. They refer to the gender of words in Latin and romance languages. Housman was a teacher of the classics.

The rhythmic movement of the poem depends on a kind of balance, almost like the pause in a swing of a pendulum, at the end of the second line of each stanza. Then there is a full pause at the end of the fourth line. Each stanza is nearly identical in rhythm, and rhyme patterns. And that is an irony as well, because the first stanza speaks of living, and the second of dead youngsters.

The poem's easiness produces the expectation of lightness and an upbeat theme. But although light and upbeat in rhythm, the poem is really dark in its ultimate meaning. The disjunction between its rhythmic form and its meaning is an example of Housman playing on our sense of irony—the difference between what we expect and what we get in the poem. He is reminding us that no matter how lightfooted or "rose-lipt" we are when young, we must eventually die.

Many readers feel that the opening line has a weightedness to it, and that it rhythmically acts out its content. You are almost forced to pace yourself through that line, pausing very slightly at "rue," "heart," and "laden." The rhythm is that of a funeral cortege. One detail contributes to keeping the rhythm moving: the pronunciation of "many a." Housman makes it come out as: "manya." The effect is to produce a swinging rhythm in the third and fourth line of the first stanza.

The rhyme contributes very much to the rhythm because every time you hit a rhyme word, you must pause. You build up an expectation after the first two lines, and Housman realizes that you demand satisfaction by hoping for a return of the familiar rhyme sound. This is a very powerful psychological fact. Poetry that does not rhyme—free verse—usually depends heavily on rhythmical patterns of pause, rush, and rest.

DRAMA

Drama emphasizes plot and action, characterization, and setting. At times, it can also possess the qualities of poetry: imagery, rhythm and rhyme, metaphor and symbol, and much more. Shakespeare's plays are poetry, and some of them use a good deal of rhyme.

The primary difference between drama and other forms of literature is that you expect to witness it, not only read it. Today you can see live drama in a theater, on city streets, in parks, on outdoor stages. You can see drama in movie theaters on film, or on television, and on tape. The chances are that you have been exposed to more drama than any other kind of literature.

Time and the Unities

Dramatic literature puts special pressure on time. The Greek dramatists insisted that the most effective way of staging a play was to make sure the dramatic action took exactly as much time to unfold and complete itself as the play itself took to act. That was the first unity: the unity of time.

The unity of character implies that a character is to be the same in the beginning of the play as at the end, and sometimes it implies that one of the characters in the play must be the primary character, with only a small number of supporting characters. Along with this, the unity of place insists that the action of the drama take place in a single locale, usually in a public space in front of a building that characters can enter and exit from.

The best serious plays, the Greeks felt, had only one plot. To introduce a subplot was to weaken the main action. Today, most television miniseries are woven together using a number of subplots—each with its own cast of characters—which ultimately come together in a climactic moment sometimes anticipated by the audience. Sometimes they come together in a surprising or shocking way, and your surprise is part of the delight of the literature. The unity of action—having only one plot—is more often adhered to in the most serious dramas, and least adhered to in comedies and farces.

Obviously, the unities are not well maintained in contemporary drama. It is normal for a play that runs less than two hours to cover years of dramatic time. Films regularly engage in flashbacks—dramatic action of a past time reenacted as an interruption of the main plot. They regularly cut from one day to another, from one moment to another, and in some cases even flash forward to what is going to happen.

Comedies often use multiple plots, with sometimes intentionally confusing intersections and overlaps. On television, you expect a multiple plot in almost any drama that is longer than half an hour. Critics may be correct in pointing to this practice as evidence of a fundamental weakness in the dramatic material itself. That is a critical judgment you can consider in working with any dramatic material you examine. Plays like *Hamlet* have a single plot, with very few distractions from the main action, even though the main action—Hamlet's avenging his father's death—is delayed almost painfully through the play. A comedy like Shakespeare's *Much Ado About Nothing* has multiple plots and uses them to good effect. Your critical observation of the nature of the plot or plots will help you decide the success or failure of the play on that count.

When working with plot, several important questions should be raised. The first concerns the clarity of the action. Is the plot direct, clear, intelligible? Is it probable, given the nature of the play as realistic or a fantasy? Does the important action happen onstage, or is it offstage? The relationship of onstage to offstage action is always interesting: why does something happen offstage? If the play is in one act, is the action satisfactorily completed? If it is in several acts, how is tension maintained at the end of an act? Are the expectations we have at the end of one act satisfied or frustrated in the next? Why?

Dramatic Reversal

Much drama is built upon a premise of reversal. Oedipus begins *Oedipus Rex* as the king, secure in possession of the throne, with wealth, a wife and children, and the respect of his kingdom. By the end of the play, he learns that he murdered his father and married his mother, who then committed suicide. He then blinds himself, turns the throne over to his brother-in-law, and accepts banishment for life. Such a reversal is especially interesting to most audiences in part because we know that reversals of fortune can happen to anyone. Indeed, that was one source of the wide appeal of Greek tragedy. The ordeal of the tragic hero evoked pity and sympathy from the audience, but the audience also knew enough to realize that such a reversal—if it can happen to the king—can happen to anyone.

Reversals of less dramatic weight occur in all kinds of drama. On a television situation comedy an apprehensive parent waits to meet the daughter's new boyfriend. Instead of greeting an undirected, laidback partygoer, the parent learns that the new boyfriend has just been admitted to medical school. This is an ironic reversal, and may produce comic results, especially if the parent has just thrown a fit about the daughter's usual boyfriends.

One result of the use of dramatic reversal is the recognition of the truth by the main character or characters. It might be said that the general structure of serious drama is based on three moments: the search for a truth, the discovery and recognition of that truth, and the suffering which facing that truth reveals.

The Genres of Drama

Just as fiction has several genres: short story, novella, and novel, drama has several genres: tragedy, comedy, and tragicomedy. Tragedy is a drama of high seriousness, in which a character of great personal worth is brought from a high place to a low place. Often the heroes and heroines of tragedy live on after the end of the play, but more often they die. Tragedies seem to have their origin in a religious ritual whose basis may derive from ancient sacrifices. Tragedy has come to demand intense responses from an audience as well as great significance from the action and the characters. You expect a tragedy to treat matters of life and death. These are the highest issues of human concern. When you approach a tragedy, therefore, you expect full psychological development from characters and a clear, logical plot that rises from the characters and not from the situations. In tragedy, the characters provide the rationale for what happens.

Comedy, besides being funny, is irreverent and often a weapon of social reform. Usually a comedy ends in marriage, and many comedies focus on the efforts of amorous young people to come together over the protestations of spoilsport old people. The comedies of Molière are filled with such predicaments. In comedy, the young lovers always win out. Marriage implies a renewal, a rebirth, new hope. In a sense, comedy is the renovation of tragedy.

Subplots, minor characters in great number, and unbelievable complications and situations are the staple ingredients of comedy. The comic material is frequently generated from the improbability of the characters' circumstances. In Shakespeare's *Comedy of Errors,* long-lost twin brothers show up with equally lost twin servants at the same time in the same town. But each brother and servant pair is unaware of the presence of the other. The result is hilarity when they each meet up with citizens who mistake them for one another. The humor does not result from any deep psychological intelligence on the part of the brothers or servants; instead it derives from the improbability of the circumstances.

Tragedy is said to be virtually impossible to write in the modern world. There is no hero whose stature is so great that we can make him tragic. Arthur Miller's *Death of a Salesman* is perhaps the closest we have to a modern tragedy, and in that play Miller elevated a failed salesman to the heights of a tragic hero. But most serious plays written in this century have been part tragedy, part comedy, and for that reason have been described with a hybrid term: tragicomedy. Plays like Henrik Ibsen's *Ghosts* and *Hedda Gabler* are very serious in their intentions, and in their mood. Yet neither Mrs. Alving nor Hedda fulfills the requirements of a tragic hero, whose moral and social elevation is far above that of the audience. If anything, they are on an exact par with the audience. They are powerful characters, but they have more than a single tragic flaw, and they do not dominate their world in the way they would like.

The essence of drama is contrast. Plays develop in less time than many longer narrative forms. If an audience is to be kept alert and concerned, the dramatist needs to set the actions and the characters of the play in sharp contrast. This means that an intensity of feeling—the expression of the characters and the responses of the audience—must be evident for drama to succeed.

_____ A Student Sample: Sylvia Plath's Blood Imagery

When you write literary criticism and pause to quote a line or a passage that illustrates your point, the convention is to indent lengthy quotes (forty words or more) in your text without using quotation marks, so they are set apart and are easily visible. When quoting only a line or two, use quotation marks and run the lines into your text.

When you quote from a secondary source—a letter written by the author you are studying, or a commentary by another literary critic—you should be sure to provide a footnote (see Chapter 10 for appropriate form) that includes the author, title, place of publication, and page. The following sample from a freshman essay on Sylvia Plath's book *Ariel* contains references to Plath's poetry. Each poem is identified, but because the class used *Ariel*, Gregg did not need to refer to page numbers. His essay is carefully focused on one of the most important aspects of Plath's poetry: her imagery. Further, Gregg was drawn to one kind of imagery, because he had gathered numerous examples of it in his passes through the text. By pulling them together and offering a commentary on them, he gives us insight into an aspect of the poetry that might have escaped us. You may feel that for an essay of this brevity, Gregg quoted too much, and you may be correct. But one advantage of his quoting so much—at least for using his work here—is that you get a good sampling of Plath and can follow what he says. Ordinarily, you would wish to restrict your quotation to the most important examples in order not to pad your essay.

Gregg began his study with some insights in his journal over a period of time:

> There's so much blood in these poems. And red. I noticed that red is there, too. Blood and red. She even cuts herself and makes a big deal out of it. So it must be important. Like excitement, maybe? After all, it's red. That's exciting. Lady Lazarus is a poem that's got some of that stuff in it. I'm going to check this out later, see if other poems do it too. I should go back and check on some earlier poems. This might be good for part of the paper.

> Poppies. I saw it again. Poppies are red, like the poppies they sell in the Mall on Memorial day. Red, like the blood. Prof. Jacobus said something about the fields where the French and Germans died in WWI being covered in poppies and people thought there was something connected there with the blood of all those soldiers. And there's a lot of German stuff in these poems. Was her father a Nazi? Or a soldier? Weird.

> I'm beginning to get the idea, I think. The blood is a life force. But it's perishable. It can die. Like us.

> Plath associates life blood and birth. She associated it with death, too. Which is it? Maybe that's a focus for me.

Later, after writing a few sample paragraphs and developing an outline, Gregg tried to work on a thesis:

> In <u>Ariel</u>, there are two kinds of blood imagery. One is connected to life, and one to death. And Sylvia Plath seems to see that they are related to each other, but that life is stronger.

Eventually, Gregg became convinced that the two kinds of imagery were not opposed to each other, but that they revealed two aspects of nature: life and death.

He had heard in class that Sylvia Plath had a very intense life with an unhappy ending. His insight developed from his annotating the poetry and noticing a constant reference to blood and the images associated with it. As he gathered examples, he saw that two contradictory patterns emerged: one associated with death, and one associated with life. In the opening paragraph of his essay, Gregg shapes a thesis statement that he felt balanced these patterns. His job in the essay is to decide how the images are used. In the process, he brings into play the several examples that he had kept track of in his note-taking.

SYLVIA PLATH'S BLOOD IMAGERY

> In <u>Ariel</u>, Sylvia Plath develops a complex image of blood. At times blood is good and is related to life. But at other times, blood is evil and is related to a draining of life. These blood images are found throughout the book and stand for a constant contradiction that is basic to all life and part of the problem of facing up to life.

> In the first few references to blood, Plath develops a relationship between it and powerful positive feelings. Blood excites her in "Cut." "What a thrill," she exclaims after she has cut herself. Plath writes later in the same poem,

> > A celebration of this is.
> > Out of a gap
> > A million soldiers run,
> > Red coats everyone.

> In the poem, "Lady Lazarus," Plath says,

> > There is a charge, a very large charge
> > For a word or a touch
> > Or a bit of blood.

In these examples, blood is equated with a life force which Plath finds very exciting. In these poems, blood is proof of life. A few lines from "Poppies in October" provide even more evidence of the relation between blood and the life force. Plath writes,

> Nor the woman in the ambulance
> Whose red heart blooms through her coat so astound-
>   ingly.

In these lines, the blood blooms. This choice of words creates a definite image of growth and life. These same words are used in "Nick and the Candle-stick," where Plath writes,

> O embryo
> Remembering even in sleep,
> You crossed position,
> The blood blooms clean.

The same feeling of growth and life is associated with blood here, except here the presence of an embryo, a new life, makes the imagery and the connection between blood and a life force even stronger.

Blood is not, however, always associated with life in Ariel. It is also associated with exhaustion and death, the antithesis of vitality and growth. Plath's poem, "Poppies in July," has four lines which support this point. She writes,

> And it exhausts me to watch you
> Flickering like that, wrinkly and clear red, like
>   the skin of a mouth
> A mouth just bloodied.
> Little bloody skirts!

The relationship between exhaustion and blood not only appears in this poem, but also in "Lesbos," where Plath writes,

> You are so exhausted . . .
> Flapping and sucking, blood-loving bat.

Yet the most conclusive piece of evidence which sup-ports the hypothesis that blood and a life-draining force are related is found in "Medusa." Plath writes,

> Flat and red, a placenta
> Paralyzing the kicking lovers.

```
Cobra light
Squeezing the breath from the blood bells
Of the fuchsia. I could draw no breath,
Dead and moneyless.   .   .   .
```

It is quite clear that this poem draws a close association between the bloody placenta and its paralyzing
and even murderous effects on life. The placenta also
offers a striking contrast to the embryo in "Nick and
the Candlestick." After birth, the embryo, now a baby,
grows and lives, while the placenta dies and shrivels up.

What these dual images of blood are supposed to symbolize is difficult to guess, but quotations from some
of the poems seem to provide us with some possibilities, perhaps all of which are true. The blood in
Plath's poems may be a symbol of the world created by
humankind. In "Totem," Plath writes "The world is
blood-hot." An application of the relationships of
blood to the world would indicate that at times the
world gives life, and at other times it steals away. We
know this is true, for in the world there are hospitals
dedicated to the preservation of life, and wards which
serve no purpose but to destroy life.

Another thing which blood could be a symbol for is
poetry. In "Kindness," Plath says, "The blood-jet is
poetry." Writing poetry is certainly an exhausting
task. Scrawling out one's feelings on paper takes tremendous energy and effort. Yet, poetry is also uplifting. In Plath's poem, "Years," she writes,

```
What I love is - -
The piston in motion
My soul dies before it.
And the hooves of the horses,
With their merciless church.
```

Here, the piston in motion and the hooves with their
endless church are symbols for the rhythm of a poem.

It is also interesting to note how the relation between blood and both good life-giving forces and life-
draining forces can be related to a woman. To a woman,
blood can be either life-giving or life-draining.
Blood can be either a healthy sign of vitality or fer-
tility, or it can be a sign of death, wounds, and ste-
rility. Plath was certainly aware of this correlation.
In "The Munich Mannequins," she writes,

```
Perfection is terrible, it cannot have children.
Cold as snow breath, it tamps the womb,
```

> Unloosing their moans, month after month, to no
>   purpose.
> The bloodflood is the flood of life.

In conclusion, I reiterate the point that this imagery is very complex. I have probably only scratched the surface of the endless interpretations of these blood images, but it fascinated me, and I was delighted to at least attempt to shed some light on this aspect of Plath's poetry.

Writer's Workshop

Writer's Workshop: Writing Literary Analysis

Note: Before working on an individual piece of literature, review the special for each genre discussed earlier. Use this review as a refresher to help you approach the literature with the freshness and completeness that it deserves. Ask yourself the reader response questions that we examined earlier:

1. What is the predominant effect of the text on you?
2. Why do you think the text had that effect?
3. What does your response tell you about yourself?

After you have finished your annotations, be sure to use some of the prewriting techniques mentioned in Chapter 1. Brainstorming, clustering, and free writing are especially useful when working with a specific piece of literature. The Burke Pentad in Chapter 2 is an especially effective aid to working up good ideas for discussing literature.

1. Choose a group of three poems by one author. If possible, choose with a related theme or with qualities in common. Begin by listing your responses to your first and later readings of the works. Then examine annotations for insights and queries that center on one of the following:

   imagery
   word choice
   rhythm and meter
   metaphor

   Examine these qualities for patterns of development within the poems. As you examine the poems, look for a hypothesis that you feel explain the choices the poet has made and which would give your audience insight into the skills of the poet. Write a brief analysis of one aspect of the poems you read, assuming you are writing for a literate audience that may read the poems before. Put the information provided under the genre of poetry to establish in your mind (and the reader's if necessary) exactly what your expectations should be of the works. Decide to what extent the author has led you to expect certain responses.

2. Examine a short story from an author whose work you admire. Establish its point of view and characterization. Then identify its theme and go on to offer an analysis of the relationship of characterization and plot to that theme. To what extent is the relationship more subtle than the average reader might suspect? What efforts has the author made to integrate theme characterization, and plot? Are the efforts successful? If possible, read several other stories by the same author in order to get a sense of what the expectations of theme, characterization, and plot might be in that author's work.

3. Select a play whose genre you recognize: tragedy, comedy, or tragicomedy. Examine it for its characterization and for its approach to the unities. What devices does the playwright use to help develop theme and action? Is imagery metaphor, or special use of language apparent in the play? How and why are your expectations of the genre rewarded or frustrated by the play?

4. Choose a play by Shakespeare and check with your library to see if you can see it on videotape. All the plays of Shakespeare are on videotape and most of them should be available in your library. Read the play, keeping an eye out for details and speeches that seem especially important because of their relationship to the theme of the play, to the characterization, to the setting, and to the plot. Establish the plot (or plots) and comment on their resolution. After you have read the play carefully, view the play on tape. Be sure to have your text with you, and annotate it as you view it. What different observations do you make about plot, characterization, theme, and dramatic conflict as a result of your seeing the play as opposed to reading it?

5. Television situation comedies are among our most popular forms of drama. Study a situation comedy carefully. If possible, record a specific show, then run it back several times so you feel you have a good understanding of its principal elements: plot, characterization, use of language, dramatic conflict, and theme. Consider the kind of setting it uses and how important it is to the action of the show. If possible, write to the network that produced the show and request a copy of the script (this is not something you can depend upon—you can only do it with a great deal of lead time). If you do not have the script, be sure to jot down important lines as you watch the program. Use them as quotations if necessary in your own essay. Once you have seen and re-seen it, write a critical essay on the show.

6. Creative writing: Use one of the paintings in the color-plate section as the basis of a short story or a poem. Rely on the painting for sources of description, imagery, character, and narrative. Be as detailed as the painting will allow you.

10
The Research Paper

The Starting Point: Prewriting

In one sense, you come to college in order to learn how to do imaginative research on subjects of your choice. When you sign up for a course in history, psychology, sociology, economics, or virtually any other discipline, you expect that a research paper is likely to be asked for at the end of the term. You could say that getting an education is almost synonymous with learning how to do research. That ability helps you grow intellectually throughout your life.

When Your Subject Is Chosen for You

When you approach the job of a research paper you will either have a topic chosen for you or choose one of your own. If the choice is yours, you should begin to keep notes in your journal as soon as you know the project is due. Write down the names of people who interest you, books that you feel would be useful to read, and events you know might have relevance to the area of your research.

In your journal keep track of all the leads for books, magazine articles, newspaper clippings, or references that you come across as you begin the process of thinking about your project. Gathering a wide variety of material is the key to making your research both involving and complete. As much as possible, try to work on a subject that already interests you, something you have always wanted to know about.

Once you have a subject, you will find that the techniques of brainstorming, free writing, and clustering are useful at several points in the process of working. For instance, they are helpful in finding a subject. If you find your mind blank, you can usually get some ideas by referring to the texts in the course, or you can ask your instructor for suggestions. If you are in a situation in which there is no course or instructor, then your best source of information is the library or your general reading. Take a subject that seems rewarding and brainstorm it to see how much you can get out of yourself. It is worth repeating this procedure for several subjects.

Later, when you have done some research on your subject, you will find that brainstorming and free writing can help you find your own way into shaping the essay. Be sure to take a moment to account for the basic ingredients of the writer's situation: audience, writer, subject, and purpose.

DEVELOP A PERSONAL ANGLE OR THESIS FOR YOUR ESSAY

A research paper involves gathering material. Your goal is to be sure your reader will have access to the most up-to-date views in your area of research. But beyond that you have the obligation to take a stand on your material. That means you should be able to understand your material well enough to add a personal note. Your investigations should help your readers form their own judgment on the matter at hand.

Your research paper is like an argument. Your materials of research are the evidence on which data, claim, and warrant are based. Your reader should understand the value of the arguments you uncover in your research and also be given complete access to counterarguments that you need to resolve as you write. As in any argument, the terms must be clear, and the material itself must be controversial enough to warrant discussion.

The best way to make your research paper interesting to your reader is to develop a thesis that you feel is defensible and provocative. Most instructors will not give you a thesis to defend in a research paper. Instead, they may provide a general subject from which you are expected to develop a thesis. The following list is a sample from a history course. Students are asked to choose from the suggested topics and come up with their own thesis as a result of their research.

John Brown and the raid on Harper's Ferry, 1859
Elizabeth Cady Stanton: the Seneca Falls Convention, 1848
Robert E. Lee, his refusal to accept command of the Union Armies, 1861
Sam Houston and the founding of the independent nation of Texas, 1836
Mary Lyon: the founding of Mt. Holyoke, the first American women's
  college, 1837

In each of these cases, the instructor has provided a limited subject, but the details to produce a thesis are omitted so that you can work them up from your own research.

Using the Means of Development to Guide Your Research Goals _____

JOHN BROWN: THE RAID ON HARPER'S FERRY

After choosing a subject, one of your first prewriting jobs is to explore the means of development to see if they can help you narrow your subject and give your research good direction. Once you have found an appropriate direction, you will have read enough to develop a preliminary thesis. You can see how this technique works for the subject of John Brown.

Definition

If you write on John Brown, your first research job is to establish what the raid at Harper's Ferry was. Biographical, historical, and other sources quickly reveal that it was an attack on a U.S. arsenal for the purpose of getting arms to help free a number of slaves using violent means. As you read, you will discover that John Brown was an abolitionist, part of a widely organized movement in America to free the slaves in the South. The question of how violence figured in their goals is of first importance to your research. You would also wish to define John Brown's personal position on violence in the name of freeing the slaves.

Comparison

As you conduct research, you will find other comparable incidents. For example, there were numerous skirmishes in Kansas, where there was a dispute concerning slavery. Kansas was not a slave state, but some people wanted it to be one. John Brown was involved in a raid at Pottawatomie Creek in which his men killed a number of proslavery settlers. A goal of your research might be to see if there is a legitimate comparison between Potta- watomie Creek and the incident at Harper's Ferry.

Because Brown had a long, flowing white beard and looked like an Old Testament prophet, you can make a fascinating comparison. To what extent did Brown act like an Old Testament figure? He was deeply religious—did he pattern his behavior on that of a biblical figure? Is there anything biblical about what he did? Some people think so.

Cause and Effect

The cause of the raid and its effect on the American public, particularly on its attitude toward slavery, could provide you with a thesis for your essay. The question of whether or not the raid could have been effective intrigues historians even today. Because it appeared that such a raid was totally futile, the suggestion has been made that John Brown set out to make a martyr of himself. When the Union Armies took the field only two years later, they sometimes sang a song inspired by the raid: "John Brown's body lies amouldering in the grave, but his soul goes marching on." One goal of your research might be to establish whether or not the cause of freedom had been positively affected by the raid.

Possibility

Brown's sense of what would be possible as a result of his raid is interesting. One of his ideas was to establish a heavily armed black army that would operate from a mountain stronghold in Virginia and conduct skirmishes against slaveholders. The question of whether such a scheme was even remotely possible should figure high on your list of inquiries. Whether any of Brown's schemes would have ended slavery any more quickly is central to an understanding of the importance of the raid. Any inquiry into the raid at Harper's Ferry would have to account for the circumstances that surrounded the event, and some of your research should be directed toward clarifying them.

Analysis

The various elements of the raid: what Harper's Ferry was, what it represented, why it was raided; who John Brown was and why he took it upon himself to act as he did; what the government did, and why it took so long for the U.S. Marines under Robert E. Lee to finally surround him; why the government decided to execute Brown as quickly as it did—all of these are elements needing careful examination and analysis. Your research will uncover numerous such elements. You cannot analyze all of them. But if you keep track of the most important ones, you can decide at the appropriate time just which of the elements most need development and analysis.

Further Means of Development

You will also have plenty of opportunity to use description, classification, and illustration by example in your research paper. However, these means of development pertain more to the actual writing of the essay than they do to guiding the early stages of your research.

Writer's Workshop: Developing Ideas for a Research Paper

Writer's Workshop

1. Choose one of the research topics listed earlier, or choose from the following list:

President Harry S. Truman and the dropping of the first atomic bomb
The current situation in arms control
Drugs and their effect on the rise of crime
The U.S. Supreme Court and the nature of its recent decisions
The Execution of Lady Jane Grey

Corruption in local government
The role of varsity sports in the life of your university or college

2. After either doing some research or some thinking on your topic, develop some ideas that might help guide your potential research paper, using the following means of development:

definition
comparison
cause and effect
possibility
analysis
further means of development

When You Choose Your Subject

Some of the prewriting is already done for you when you have specific assignments. But when the topic is entirely open, your job is quite different. In any assignment you begin with a certain number of givens. First, you have a subject area such as economics, design, or biology. Were you to be given an open-ended assignment in economics, for example, you would begin by making lists. Because you would be taking a course in economics, and already know a good deal about the area, the best way to proceed is to list important subjects, events, or people whose significance you would like to know more about, such as the following:

capitalism
theories of production
Adam Smith, *The Wealth of Nations*
production and wealth

From such a brief list—developed from class notes and from annotations in the textbook—could come innumerable research papers. But doing more research (such as reading Smith's book and looking up commentary on his theories) will produce a sharper focus, and eventually a thesis for your own research paper.

The list, although brief, constitutes a step in prewriting. The reason it is so short is that when you make it, you already have a great deal of information and a number of things that interest you. That is normal in any course in which you will write a research paper. The course acts as an aid to prewriting.

CHOOSE SOMETHING YOU'VE ALWAYS WANTED
TO KNOW ABOUT

If you are offered an open-ended assignment, you should choose something you have always wanted to know about. This is especially true if you are writing a research essay for a subject area that is important to you. Working on something personally involving will help you make the piece better than it would be otherwise. Besides, you will also feel much better as you work, and your sense of satisfaction when the job is done will naturally be greater.

Treat the opportunity as the chance to get acquainted with (or more acquainted with) something that has intrigued you, but that has had to be put on the back burner because of the pressures of school. Make your goal twofold: please yourself, and inform your audience. The best research work done on any level, professional or apprentice, usually comes from someone who is so wrapped up in a subject that it almost becomes a personal extension of that person's life.

Writer's Workshop: Choosing Your Subject for Research

1. You have your choice of any subject to do research about. If you have something you have wanted to know more about, sketch it out in your writer's journal.
2. If you have no specific ideas in mind for a research essay, use the following procedure:
   a. List the academic disciplines that interest you most.
   b. Name an important event in one of those areas.
   c. Name an important person associated with that event.
   d. Spend one minute brainstorming this person and this event. Write down everything you can think of that is associated with them. Use the Burke Pentad to help you gather information.

      Act
      Scene
      Agent
      Agency
      Purpose
   e. Group your random observations into related subtopics.
   f. Choose one of those groupings as the basis of a research paper. What is it, and what kind of essay might develop from it?
   g. What are the chief problems your research must solve?
   h. What is the most important question you can ask about your topic?

W riter's W orkshop

Materials of Research: Where to Look _____

The first place to start your research is in your college or university library. In most cases you will be restricted to using the material that you find there. And one of your first moves should be to request help from your librarian in locating reference material in the field you are researching.

Your questions should be as specific as possible at this early stage of the process. You may know, for instance, that you are going to write a research paper on a specific topic, such as John Brown's raid at Harper's Ferry or the Shroud of Turin. Or you may still be at the stage of knowing you want to work in the area of economics and that you want to look up some material on Adam Smith. In either case, your librarian will direct you.

Your library has a number of important resources:

Online computer searches: computer databases are being compiled for many special subject areas. Most will cost a small fee, but they can save time. More and more advanced students use these services—it is a good idea to become acquainted with them as early in your career as possible.

Catalog: usually a card catalog, but increasingly today, an online computer catalog.

Reference room: contains biographies, guides to periodicals, encyclopedias, specialized commentary on the literature of innumerable subjects, and those most important of all reference works: dictionaries.

Microfilm and/or microfiche collection: contains important historical materials, much of which will be newspapers.

Periodical room: contains current journals, magazines, and other publications.

Interlibrary loan office: where you can arrange to borrow books from other collections.

Special collections: houses manuscripts and unusual materials, such as literary magazines of a given era, or the gifts of collectors of specialized books, pamphlets, and documents. This could be a great source of material for an original research project, and one of your first options should be to check to see what the holdings are and whether or not they can be used.

Support services: provide searches for books that are out on loan, and the indispensable copy machines that permit you to "take notes" using photocopies.

ONLINE COMPUTER SEARCHES

More and more libraries are connecting with centralized services that maintain an online search capacity. One of the most common in American universities is OCLC, Online Computer Library Center, the world's largest database of bibliographic information. So far, over 6,000 libraries have access to it and it contains more than thirteen million entries. You usually conduct searches by subject with the aid of a librarian.

If you were to search for information about John Brown and Harper's Ferry, you could search each topic either separately or together. By searching them together, you would be sure to get both the proper John Brown and information about the raid at Harper's Ferry and its aftermath. Were you to search the Shroud of Turin, you would find that your first searches under that title would yield nothing. But after searching again under Turin you would find that bibliographic entries concerning the shroud are under Holy Shroud of Turin.

The following example is a printout from an online search in Boston College's Thomas P. O'Neill Library, showing fourteen citations that are in the library. Were you to get a result as promising as this in your own library, you would then request information on each of the books cited, thus getting their call number and a more detailed description of their contents. This kind of searching saves an incredible amount of your time and assures you of finding information on your subject.

```
071 THOMAS P. O'NEILL LIBRARY -
GEAC LIBRARY SYSTEM KEYWORD SEARCH


Your title keyword: TURIN          Matches 12 titles
                    No. of citations in entire catalog
1 The Economics of public service: Proceedings of a
confere>
1
2 Fiat invites you to an encounter with Jean Dubuffet:
Turin>1
3 Holy Shroud of Turin /
1
4 Inquest on the Shroud of Turin /
1
5 life of the Venerable Joseph Benedict Cottolengo :
founder
of>    1
6 Portrait of Jesus? : the illustrated story of the
Shroud
of>      1
```

```
7 Publication du Centre d'études franco-italien des
Universitat>1

8 Report on the Shroud of Turi /

1

9 In search of the Shroud of Turin: new light on its
history>

1

10  Shroud of Turin.

1

11  The Turin fragments of Tyconius' commentary on Rev-
elation

1

Type a number to see more information -OR-
FOR- move forward in this list    CAT- begin a new search
```

Some of these items are useful and some not. Items 3, 4, 6, 8, 9, and 10 are clearly on the subject of the Shroud of Turin. To get more information about these books, you would punch their respective numbers and learn about their contents. If they look promising, an inquiry will determine if the book is in, and then you can check it out.

This search only finds books in the library. To find articles and books that are not in the local library, you can conduct a full online search.

Special Online Resources

An online search costs money according to how many entries you find. Most fees are modest and some libraries absorb the cost. Online searches are conducted in two stages. First you search for your subject, then you look to see if your library has the material you have uncovered. You can expect your library to have only a few of the items the search uncovers. But what it does not have, it can locate in other libraries, and then request through interlibrary loan. This method can take time, and is one of the best reasons to start your research early.

The sample on pages 239–240 is a result of online searching through the DIALOG service and the *American history and life* database for John Brown and Harper's Ferry. Almost 120 items were retrieved in a matter of seven or eight minutes. The search was conducted by a librarian in consultation with the person who had the inquiry. The keywords were John Brown and Harper's Ferry. The first two pages of the report are included. All the items are published after 1972, which is a common limit of these resources. Obviously only some of them will be useful, and all of them will supply you with more bibliography. The especially valuable aspect of this search is that it uncovered current periodical materials, which ought to be available in most large college libraries.

DIALOG   **File 38: AMERICA: HISTORY & LIFE—63–87/ISS24A3   (Copr. ABC Clio Inc.)**

882528   24A-06317
"THE GREATEST SERVICE I RENDERED THE STATE": J. E. B. STUART'S ACCOUNT OF THE CAPTURE OF JOHN BROWN.
Thomas, Emory M
Virginia Magazine of History and Biography 1986 94(3): 345–357.
Note: Based on Stuart's letter to Elizabeth Letcher Stuart and primary and secondary sources: 32 notes, 3 photos, illus.
Document Type: ARTICLE

James Ewell Brown Stuart helped in the capture of John Brown after his abortive raid on Harpers Ferry, Virginia, in 1859. Stuart was serving as a lieutenant in the army in Kansas, and was visiting Washington, D.C. when news of Brown's revolt reached the War Department. He accompanied Robert E. Lee to Harpers Ferry as an aide. Brown and other abolitionists had hoped to make Harpers Ferry the first in a series of mountain strongholds for southern slaves. Includes an 1860 letter written by Stuart to his mother describing Brown's capture. (C. Marsden)

879683   24A-03571
THE MISSISSIPPI PRESS'S RESPONSE TO JOHN BROWN'S RAID.
Phillips, Adrienne Cole
Journal of Mississippi History 1986 48(2): 119–134.
Note: Based on newspaper accounts, manuscript collections, government documents, and published secondary sources; 79 notes.
Document Type: ARTICLE

Traces the psychological impact of John Brown's raid on Mississippi as reported in the state's newspapers. Press response depended largely on whether the paper was unionist or secessionist. Topics analyzed in both types of papers include the loyalty of the slaves; the mental state of Brown; who, besides Brown, were responsible; and antislavery and unionist sentiment in the North. Although the unionist papers protested against the fire-eating journalism of the secessionist papers, the fears aroused by the Harpers Ferry raid helped push Mississippi toward secession in 1861. (M. S. Legan)

878214   24A-02157
A CENTENNIAL VIEW OF THE JOHN BROWN HOUSE.
Emlen, Robert P.
Rhode Island History 1986 45(1): 15–21.
Note: Secondary sources: 5 illus., 12 notes.
Document Type: ARTICLE

The American Architect and Building News first publicized the John Brown house of Providence in January 1887 by reproducing sketches done by E. Eldon Deane, probably from photographs made in 1886. In 1936 John Nicholas Brown purchased the house and soon opened it to the public. (P. J. Coleman)

866653   24B-00654
Where Industry Failed: Water-Powered Mills at Harpers Ferry, West Virginia.
Gilbert, Dave; Hyde, Charles K
Charleston, W. Va., Pictorial Hist., 1984. 86 pp.
Document Type: BOOK
Book Review:
Hyde, Charles K. Technology and Culture   27 (Jan 86) 148–150.

866240   24B-00241
Young Howells and John Brown: Episodes in a Radical Education.
Cady, Edwin H; Arms, George; Habegger, Alfred
Columbus: Ohio State U., 1985. 116 pp.
Document Type: BOOK
Book Review:
Arms, George, Habegger, Alfred, Am. Literature 58 (May 86) 279–281.   New England Q.   14 (June 86) 294–298.

767587   22B-03485
Ambivalent Conspirators: John Brown, the Secret Six, and a Theory of Slave Violence.
Rossbach, Jeffery; Parrish, William E.; Howard, Victor B.; Turner, Thomas Reed
Philadelphia U. of Pennsylvania Pr., 1982. 298 pp.
Document Type: BOOK
Book Review:
Parrish, William E., Howard, Victor B., Turner, Thomas Reed.

DIALOG   **File 38: AMERICA: HISTORY & LIFE—63–87/ISS24A3**   (Copr. ABC Clio Inc.)

Historian 47 (Nov 84) 121–122. Ohio Hist. 93 (Sum–
    Aut 84), 189–190. Virginia Mag. of Hist. and
    Biog. 93 (Jan 85), 111–112.
See also 22B:1460. 21B:3470.
Pease, Jane H, Hess, Earl J, Crofts, Daniel W. Am.
    Hist. Rev. 89 (Apr 84) 520–521. New York Hist.
    64 (Oct 83) 442–443. North Carolina Hist. Rev.
    61 (July 84) 411–412.
See also 21B:3470.

688590   21C-09027
**"John Brown Gordon: Soldier, Southerner,
American." (Vol. 1–2)**
    Eckert, Ralph Lowell
    DAI 1984 44(9): 2860-A, DA8400113
    Louisiana State U. 1983. 447 pp.
    Document Type: DISSERTATION

687517   21C-03076
"Responses in Mississippi to John Brown's Raid."
    Phillips, Adrienne Cole
    DAI 1983 44(3): 845-A. DA8316187
    U. of Mississippi 1983. 303 pp.
    Document Type: DISSERTATION

686663   21B-03470
**Ambivalent Conspirators: John Brown, the Secret
Six, and a Theory of Slave Violence.**
    Rossbach, Jeffery; Field, Phyllis F; Bruce, Dickson
    D, Jr; Kraut, Alan M; Friedman, Lawrence J; Dillon,
    Merton L; McKivigan, John R; Casdorph, Paul D
    Philadelphia: U. of Pennsylvania Pr., 1982. 298 pp.
    Document Type: BOOK
    Book Review:
    Field, Phyllis F, Bruce, Dickson D, Jr, Kraut, Alan
M, Friedman, Lawrence J, Dillon, Merton L,
McKivigan, John R, Casdorph, Paul D. Civil War Hist.
    29 (Sept 83) 281–282. Georgia Hist. Q. 67 (Fall
    83) 392–394. Hist.: Rev. of New Books 11 (Sept
    83) 235. J. of Am. Hist. 70 (Sept 83) 417–418. J.
    of Southern Hist. 50 (Feb 84) 127–128. Rev. in
    Am. Hist. 11 (Dec 83) 521–525. West Virginia
    Hist. 44 (Spr 83) 249–251.
Rev. art.

683433   21A-06242
**THE SANTA FE TRAIL, JOHN BROWN, AND
THE COMING OF THE CIVIL WAR.**

Easley, Larry J
Film & Hist. 1983 13(2): 25–33.
Document Type: ARTICLE

The treatment of Civil War history in the 1940 film,
    Santa Fe Trail, is similar to that of many films of
    its era; the conflict is portrayed as having been
    triggered by fanatical Northern abolitionists.

667229   20B-03275
**The Journey: A Biography of the American-Jewish
Freedom Fighter Who Rode with John Brown in
Kansas.**
    Litvin, Martin; Stern, Norton B.
    Galesburg, Ill.; Galesburg Hist. Soc., 1981. 473 pp.
    Document Type: BOOK
    Book Review:
    Stern, Norton B. Western States Jewish Hist. Q. 15
    (Oct 82) 95.

666771   20B-02817
John Brown: A Cry for Freedom
    Graham, Lorenz; Greene, James S, III
    New York: Crowell, 1980. 180 pp.
    Document Type: BOOK
    Book Review:
    Greene, James S, III. Hist. Teacher 15 (Aug 82) 585.

578191   20A-04076
**JOHN BROWN'S RAID AT HARPERS FERRY
AND GOVERNOR HENRY ALEXANDER WISE'S
LETTER TO PRESIDENT JAMES BUCHANAN
CONCERNING THE INVASION.**
    Woodward, Isaiah A.
    West Virginia Hist. 1981 42(3–4) 307–313.
    Note: Based on the correspondence and journal
articles.
    Document Type: ARTICLE

Discusses the letter from Governor Henry Alexander
    Wise to President James Buchanan with regard to
    John Brown's Harpers Ferry raid in 1859. (J. D.
    Neville)

571631   19C-10858
**"The Political Career of John Brown Gordon, 1868
to 1897."**

Widely Available Electronic Databases

AGRICOLA   Information provided by the U.S. Dept. of Agriculture.

AMERICAN HISTORY & LIFE   General service for American history.

AMERICAN MEN AND WOMEN OF SCIENCE   Details on scientific people.

ART LITERATURE INTERNATIONAL   The J. Paul Getty Trust has gathered literature on art.

BOOK REVIEW INDEX   You can check numerous reviews of a book that may be central to your research.

BOOKS IN PRINT   A valuable resource for finding current books on your subject.

CA SEARCH   Chemical abstracts for science projects.

COMMERCE BUSINESS DAILY   Information from the Dept. of Commerce.

CONGRESSIONAL RECORD ABSTRACTS   Information on legislation direct from the Congressional Record.

ECONOMIC LITERATURE INDEX   Information in the area of economics.

ERIC   National Institute of Education, Educational Resources Information Center. This long-established database includes a wide range of information on subjects related to education, sociology, history.

MLA BIBLIOGRAPHY   Useful for any literary research.

NATIONAL NEWSPAPER INDEX   You can search a news item and see how it has been handled by different newspapers.

NURSING AND ALLIED HEALTH   For any project involving health services.

PAIS INTERNATIONAL   A useful database for anything touching on public affairs. It has a wide coverage and can produce excellent leads.

RELIGION INDEX   For searching any subject related to religion.

SCISEARCH   Scientific information from 1974 to the present.

SOCIALSCISEARCH   For the social sciences.

ULRICH'S INTERNATIONAL PERIODICALS DIRECTORY   This is a major resource for information on periodical literature and articles in numerous academic fields.

UPI NEWS   Up-to-the-minute reportage of events.

U.S. POLITICAL SCIENCE DOCUMENTS   For information about political science in America.

WASHINGTON PRESS TEXT FULL TEXT   Articles from newspapers from the nation's capital.

WORLD AFFAIRS REPORT   Political information on a global basis.

ZOOLOGICAL RECORD   Information on wildlife, animals, and their environments.

All of these, and hundreds more, can be of use to you. But two prerequisites are obvious: first, give yourself time to make use of the resources. And second, ask your librarian to give you full information on the resources before you begin using them.

THE CATALOG

The catalog, electronic or conventional, consists of entries for each of the books and holdings in your library. Each item in the catalog will have a call number, the number you use to find it on the shelf. Usually, you will discover that other books on the same or a closely related subject will be on the shelf with the book you look up, and therefore, it is wise to look closely around you when you have found the book you want. That means, too, that even if a book you want is not in the library you should go to the shelves and look for other books on the same subject.

Cataloging Systems

Books are catalogued in the United States in one of two ways, using the Library of Congress classification scheme, or the Dewey Decimal scheme. Many older libraries use both, with the older part of its holdings in the Dewey system, and the later material in the Library of Congress system. The two systems look like this:

Dewey Decimal	Library of Congress
821.1	PR3567
M296	M26
1954	1984

A sample of a catalog card as supplied to a library using the Library of Congress System appears on the top of page 243.

The Library of Congress number is in the upper left corner. The designation *H25* includes the first initials of the author's last name (it could be just *H*) and a number that is a code assigned to the author. If the book were catalogued under a Dewey Decimal number, it would, as the bottom of the card indicates, look like this:

510.78
H12
1962

```
HF5548      Halacy, D    S
H25         Computers, the machines we think with.
1st ed.
New York, Harper & Row 1962
279p. Illus. 22 cm.




            1. Electronic Computers   2. Automa-
               tion
            I. Title


HF5548.H25      510.78      62-14564
```

Including the year of publication (here, 1962) is optional.

The bottom of the author card has suggestions for cross-referencing the book. The number *1* refers to the general subject. The number *2* refers to yet another subject heading, and a card is provided in the catalog for that. Finally, there is a roman numeral *I* for the title card. Checking the bottom of the card is helpful in the early stages of your research because it will provide you with the appropriate subject headings that you can refer to for finding more material.

Remember that when you are looking up material on a research project, you have a number of important resources. There is the author card for each book, and then a number of subject cards. The library is doing all it can to help you find the resources you need. The catalog is where you should begin your research, because in the shortest amount of time you can come up with the greatest amount of material. You know the material is, or can become, available to you quickly because the catalog lists the actual holdings of the library.

Writer's Workshop: Your Library
1. What is the catalog system of your library: Library of Congress or Dewey Decimal System?
2. What is the physical location of books on literature? On art? On science?

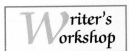
Writer's Workshop

What is the physical location of bound periodicals?

Where can you conduct an OCLC search? A PAIS search?

3. Conduct an online search for your subject either with OCLC or with your own library's online catalog. Copy out the catalog entry on at least three related books in your library. Comment on the kind of information you can get from the catalog entries.

4. If you have access to a PAIS or UPI NEWS search or any of the specialized services that may be relevant to you, get a printout of your search and discuss it with your peers. Share as much information as possible about the experience of using specialized databases.

THE REFERENCE ROOM

The resources of the reference room in your library are vastly more expansive than you might think. To begin to make use of them, be sure you speak with your reference librarian as you begin to narrow down your subject. Although there are many more, some of the most important resources of the Reference Room are

Dictionaries

The Oxford English Dictionary. 13 vols. plus four supplements (New York: Oxford University Press, 1933, 1972, 1977, 1986). This reference is usually referred to as the *OED* and is generally regarded as the most thorough dictionary of the language. It is good for its historical information regarding the usage of words.

Webster's Third New International Dictionary of the English Language (Springfield, Mass.: G. C. Merriam, 1961). This is an unabridged dictionary that is especially useful for American English.

Among the many other dictionaries available are rhyming dictionaries and dictionaries of synonyms, usage, pronunciation, slang, quotations, and more.

Encyclopedias

The New Encyclopedia Britannica, 15th ed., 30 vols (Chicago: Encyclopedia Britannica, 1979). The structure of this new version of a great encyclopedia is novel: the one-volume *Propaedia* gives you a large overview of any subject or figure you wish to know about, with suggestions for where to look for more information. The ten-volume *Micropaedia* gives you brief articles on subjects, whereas the nineteen-volume *Macropedia* provides the in-depth entries on subjects.

Encyclopedia Britannica, 11th ed. (New York: Encyclopedia Britannica, 1910). This is still the most valuable edition for historical or classical information.

Encyclopedia Americana, 30 vols. (New York: Americana Corporation, 1977). This is useful for any projects involving American history or American subjects.

You have many specialized encyclopedias to consult. However, you should be aware that encyclopedias are by their nature outdated, sometimes opinionated, and always much too brief. Do not rely on them for anything more than a convenient overview of your subject and a brief introduction to its bibliography.

Biography

Dictionary of American Biography, 11 vols. (New York: Scribner's, 1974, 1977). This is a good source of biographical information on Americans who are not living today.

Dictionary of National Biography, 21 vols. (London: Oxford University Press, 1938, 1960). This is the source of biographical information for British figures of importance who are not alive today.

Biographical references are important starting points when working on any kind of research project. For example, you can get an excellent overview by looking up John Brown in the *Dictionary of American Biography.* The same is true if you were to look up Robert E. Lee. You would also learn the names of other important figures who affected Brown's behavior and possibly get some clues for further research that would help you make your essay more valuable.

Special Material: General Resources

INDEXES

If you are researching current material, you will want to use the *New York Times Index.* It is usually two months behind the current date, and has a page in the back explaining special symbols and how to put it to use. The sample page from the issue for April 16–30, 1987, concerns the subject of Europe. The numbers after each entry refer to the date, section, page, and column of the item. If you are researching current events, this index will be very useful. (See page 246.)

A sample from *The New York Times Index*, April 16–30, 1987.

other headings — **Europe. See also**
Air Pollution, Ap 24
Apparel, Ap 25

main heading — **With several deft moves, Mikhail S Gorbachev has maneuvered US into awkward political corner by exploiting West's ambivalence about arms control;** *summary* — by offering to rid Europe not only of Soviet and US medium-range missiles, but of shorter-range missiles as well, Soviet leader has left US with three uncomfortable choices: it can persuade allies to swallow agreement that many Western Europeans fear would strip away too much of their nuclear protection and leave them at military disadvantage, it can sign in spite of Western European concerns, or it can risk being portrayed as culprit in collapse of arms control

(M) is medium length article —
negotiations (M), Ap 16,I,1:4

(L) is long article —
Sec of State George P Shultz says that treaty eliminating medium-range nuclear missiles in Europe is within reach, despite

(S) is short article —
continued differences over how to verify accord and what limits to set on short-range missiles; Shultz's cautiously optimistic assessment at news conference in Moscow seems to be shared by Soviet Foreign Min Eduard A Shevardnadze, who says there is 'rather good prospect' of summit meeting in Washington this year to sign accord, but members of US negotiating team say that serious obstacles remain;

date
section
page
column
photo of Shultz and Shevardnadze (M) Ap 16,I,1:6

Pres Reagan says talks in Moscow between Sec Shultz and top Soviet officials 'hold promise' for accord on medium-range missiles 'at some point in the not-too-distant' future' (S), Ap 16,I,14:4

Excerpts from Sec of State Shultz's news conference in Moscow on negotiations to eliminate medium-range nuclear missiles in Europe, Ap 16,I,15:1

Editorial urges US and its NATO allies to accept in principal Mikhail S Gorbachev's proposal to ban short-range as well as medium-range missiles from Europe and 'get on with negotiating the hard details of arms control', Ap 16,I,22:1

Secretary of State George P Shultz briefs NATO allies in Brussels on his talks in Moscow, and several express concern about Soviet proposal to eliminate both short-range and medium-range nuclear missiles in Europe; Shultz himself appears more welcoming to Soviet proposal, raising possibility that issue could become source of contention between US and its allies; under medium-range agreement, US would destroy 316 warheads on its Pershing 2 ballistic missiles and ground-launched cruise missiles in Western Europe while Soviet Union would destroy 1,434 warheads on its single-warhead SS-4 and triple-warhead SS-20 missiles within its European territory; illustration (M), Ap 17,I,1:6

David K Shipler analysis contends that Soviet proposal to remove all short-range nuclear missiles from Europe has caused discomfort among Pentagon hard-liners and some West Europeans, who worry that it might be step toward 'denuclearization' of Europe and resulting West European vulnerability to superior Soviet conventional forces; Sec of State George P Shultz illustration (M), Ap 17,I,8:1

Pres Reagan says that he will consult with allied leaders at economic summit meeting in Venice in June on Soviet proposal to eliminate not only medium-range missiles, but also shorter-range missiles from Europe (S), Ap 17,I,8:2

Soviet Foreign Ministry spokesman Gennadi I Gerasimov says that Sec of State George P Shultz had come to Moscow unprepared to bargain on arms control, and 'left hiding behind the backs of their allies' (M), Ap 17,I,8:5

Flora Lewis Op-Ed column contends that confusion in Western Europe over Moscow's proposal to rid Europe of nuclear missiles spotlights failure of US and its allies to develop contingency planning for arms control alongside military planning; maintains that arms-control agreement would be triumph for Pres Reagan after serious setbacks (M), Ap 17,I,31:2

New York Times Index, April 16–30, 1987.

A sample from *The Reader's Advisor*.

Conservation

Adams, Alexander B. Eleventh Hour: A Hard Look at Conservation and the Future. *Putnam* 1970 $7.95

Allen, Thomas B. Vanishing Wildlife of North America. *National Geographic Soc.* 1974 $4.25
"An encyclopedic approach to a sad subject—the potential for extinction of many reptiles, fish, birds, and mammals in North America"—(*LJ*).

Amory, Cleveland. Man Kind? Our Incredible War on Wildlife. *Harper* 1974 $8.95
"Outraged at the decimation of animals by hunters, Amory laces his documented polemic with ironic humor"—(*Booklist*).

Atkinson, J. Brooks. This Bright Land. *Doubleday* Natural History Press 1974 $5.95
"As much a naturalist as a Pulitzer Prize winner and drama critic, Brooks Atkinson demonstrates a real concern for the plight of America's natural beauty and wildlife heritage . . . This is not a long book but one that should be required reading for every person in America"—(*LJ*).

Clepper, Henry E., Ed. Leaders of American Conservation. *Ronald* 1971 $10.95
Origins of American Conservation. *Ronald* 1968 $5.95
"A valuable historical handbook"—(*LJ*).

Curry-Lindahl, Kai. Let Them Live: A Worldwide Survey of Animals Threatened with Extinction. *Morrow* 1972 $9.95 pap. $3.95
The author "deals with all known vertebrate species and subspecies that have become extinct or are declining so rapidly that they soon may be. Continent by continent, region by region, these animals and their problems are surveyed and discussed"—(*LJ*).

Ehrenfeld, David W. Conserving Life on Earth. *Oxford* 1972 $10.00
"My role in writing this book," the author says, "has been that of an advocate for the natural world." As such, Ehrenfeld has examined in depth the problems of overpopulation, technology, the extinction of animal and plant species, pollution, urban blight, the gradual decay and destruction of our environment"—(*LJ*).

Evans, Howard Ensign. Life on a Little-Known Planet. *Dutton* 1968 $8.50; *Dell* Delta Bks. pap. $2.45
"The 'little-known planet' of the title is the earth; and Evans is pleading for a greater understanding of earth life—even unto the smallest bug. Seldom, if ever, has the case for the natural sciences—and for conservation—been presented with such reasoned, convincing eloquence"—(*N.Y. Times*).

Fitter, Richard. Vanishing Wild Animals of the World. Introd. by Peter Scott of the World Wildlife Fund; fwd. by the Duke of Edinburgh; 43 color plates *Franklin Watts* 1969 $7.95

Graham, Frank, Jr. Man's Dominion: The Story of Conservation in America. *M. Evans* 1971 $8.95
"The author of *Since Silent Spring* tells the troubled story of the conservation movement. . . . It is obvious from the book that the battles of the past, once considered over and won, will continually reoccur"—(*LJ*).

Where the Place Called Morning Lies: A Personal View of the American Environment. *Viking* 1973 $6.95
"The book is a plea for controlling the inroads that industry is making on the rural areas of Maine, and the problems that modern technology has brought"—(*LJ*).

A more general aid to research is *The Reader's Advisor: A Layman's Guide to Literature*, 12th ed., 3 vols., ed. Jack A. Clarke (New York: R. R. Bowker, 1977). This useful volume covers fields from history to science. See the page of entries in science, under conservation (on page 247). In the opinion of its editor, the entries represent the most important books to refer to for this subject.

INTERLIBRARY LOAN

The interlibrary loan facility in your library helps you locate a book you may need at another library, and then arranges to loan you the book from that library. This is an excellent service, but its use is limited, and the book you wish to order may not be as important to you as you think.

If you are uncertain of the value of a given title, one resource to double check is the *Book Review Digest,* a monthly publication from the H. W. Wilson Co. It does not review government publications or textbooks, but it reviews most other kinds of publications. The sample provided below is from the May 1986 copy. The entry under Francisco Scarano was developed from the subject index at the back of the digest, under Puerto Rico. If you were researching the sugar industry in Puerto Rico or in the West Indies, you would locate this title. If it is not in your library, you would want to check its reviews as sampled here to see if the book would be useful to you. If it is, you can order it through interlibrary loan.

A sample from the *Book Review Digest*.

SCARANO, FRANCISCO A. (FRANCISCO ANTONIO).
Sugar and slavery in Puerto Rico; the plantation economy of Ponce, 1800–1850.
242p il maps $21.50 1984 University of Wis. Press
306 1. Sugar industry and trade 2. Slavery—Puerto Rico 3. Plantation life 4. Puerto Rico—Economic conditions
ISBN   0-299-09580-0   LC 83-40271

The author seeks to "reconstruct the growth of [Puerto Rico's] sugar economy out of a subsistence and livestock economy. He examines the . . . assumption that slavery was comparatively unimportant to Puerto Rican sugar production and . . . documents its errors. He [attempts to] reconstruct the internal organization of sugar haciendas, their sources of initial capital (immigrant funds), the slave trade that supplied labor, and their sugar technology." (Choice) Bibliography. Index.

"On the foundations of solid archival research, Scarano convincingly shows that sugar development in early nineteenth-century Puerto Rico was based on slave labor, as was the case on every other Caribbean sugar isle. . . . A detailed portrait of the functional aspects of social and economic life has resulted from this microapproach. This is largely owing to the rich documentary sources available at the local level: land and slave registers, notarial protocols, population censuses, and data on individual units of production. These kinds of sources are not available on an island-wide basis

and heretofore have been untapped by historians. . . . This volume is not only a pioneering addition to Puerto Rican historiography but also a valuable contribution to the literature on Latin American socioeconomic development.''
  Am Hist Rev 90:522 Ap '85. Laird W. Bergad (460w)

"Although the study is confined to the Ponce valley, it is generally applicable to Puerto Rico. The work contributes a meticulous and valuable body of local material to the growing scholarship that may soon be synthesized for an expanded understanding of plantation society in colonial America. For upper-division undergraduate and graduate collections in Caribbean and Latin American studies.''
  Choice 22:479 N '84. R. Berleant-Schiller (200w)

Writer's Workshop: Using the Reference Room

1. Write a brief biography of one of the following individuals using the resources of the reference room:

Frédéric Bartholdi	Ferdinand Foch	Christopher Wren
Junípero Serra	Friedrich Nietzsche	Cynthia Ozick
Eve Curie	Janis Joplin	Frederick Douglass
George Stilwell	Frédéric Chopin	Walter Hagen
Artemisia Gentileschi	Sitting Bull	Virginia Woolf
Witter Bynner	Isadora Duncan	Scott Joplin

2. List the most important reference books in your library in the field of American history.
3. Which are the most important computer services available for research in your library?

The Collection and the Periodical Room

When you have a subject, whether general or specific, your next move is to go to the holdings in your library, find the books, and browse among them. Look to the left and right of the books, the call numbers of which you have found in the catalog. Among them will be related titles, and some of them may be useful to you.

Tips: Scanning a Book
- Examine the table of contents for references to your subject.
- Examine the index for references to your subject.
- Search especially for a bibliography and see if there are entries on your special area of interest.
- Look into a section or chapter that seems to relate to your subject and assess its value to your project.

If you discover that a book on the shelves near the items you have already discovered relates to your subject, be sure to take it off the shelf and scan it. If the book seems valuable, check it out. (See the box on page 249 entitled "Tips: Scanning a Book.")

BEGIN WITH BIBLIOGRAPHY

One reason for your choosing the most current books and examining them first is that good researchers will provide you with up-to-date bibliographies. These will not only save you time, but they will help you narrow your subject and focus your research. You should always depend on your own library's resources, but a review of the bibliographies of books important to your project will give your research an edge. All professional researchers build a bibliography in this manner.

PERIODICAL LITERATURE:
READER'S GUIDE, *ULRICH'S*, AND *NEWSBANK*

The *Reader's Guide to Periodical Literature* is an index to articles that appear in general magazines and many important journals. It is published in annual volumes with a monthly supplement and is therefore among the most up-to-date resources you can use. In the sample entry on page 251, you can see that subject and author entries appear together. The title of the item is followed by an abbreviation of the name of the periodical—a list of abbreviations appears at the beginning of the *Guide*.

NewsBank is a resource on microfiche. It offers a wide range of material in an easy-to-use form. See the entry under parenting (on page 253), with interesting subtopics such as arrests and statistics.

The *Reader's Guide* tends to be very generalized, so you ought to supplement it with more academic guides such as *Art Index*, *History Index*, and *Business Periodicals Index*. Check with your periodicals librarian to see if there are special guides in the subject areas that interest you.

Ulrich's International Periodicals is a very important guide for the college student. (See pages 254–255 for sample entries.) The *Reader's Guide* is for the general reader and does not include references to the most scholarly publications. For that reason, although it is easy to use and widely available, it is not the best source for you. *Ulrich's* is the source you should go to first if you have access to it. Many libraries now have this reference either as a compact disk database, or as an online database that you can search.

A sample from the *Reader's Guide to Periodical Literature*.

Drugs and artists
Acid test [LSD and creativity; study by Oscar Janigar] R. B. Tucker. *Omni* 10:16 N '87

Drugs and children *See* Drugs and youth

Drugs and employment
Doctors square off on employee drug testing. C. Holden. il *Science* 238:744–5 N 6 '87

Drugs and judges
Betrayal. H. S. Scott. *New Repub* 197:12–13 D 14 '87

Exit the smoking judge [D. Ginsburg] I. Austen. il por *Macleans* 100:32 N 16 '87

The Ginsburg test: bad logic. C. Krauthammer. il *Time* 130:102 N 23 '87

Pot & politics [D. H. Ginsburg's Supreme Court nomination; cover story] A. Press. il pors *Newsweek* 110:46–52 N 16 '87

Sins of the past [drug use by D. Ginsburg derails Supreme Court nomination] M. Hornblower. por *Time* 130:18–20 N 16 '87

Up in smoke: the undoing of a High Court nominee [D. Ginsburg] B. Duffy and D. Baer. il por *U S News World Rep* 103:24–6 N 16 '87

Drugs and politicians
After the Ginsburg debacle, a chronicler of the sixties ponders the new politics of pot [interview with T. Gitlin] M. Wilhelm. il por *People Wkly* 28:124+ N 23 '87

Test cases for a new political generation. J. Alter. il *Newsweek* 110:48–9 N 16 '87

Drugs and sports
Another NCAA fumble [judge rules against testing policy] B. Newman. il por *Sports Illus* 67:100 D 7 '87

Athletes and steroids: playing a deadly game. R. W. Miller. il *FDA Consum* 21:16–21 N '87

The case for the defence [lawyer's account of baseball player F. Jenkins' narcotics case; excerpt from Greenspan] E. L. Greenspan and G. Jonas. il pors *Macleans*——— *name of periodical* 100:48–50+ O 19 '87

Expos' Youmans enters drug treatment clinic. *Jet* 73:50 N 2 '87 ——— *volume*

Offshore racing's image problems. D. Wallace and C. Davis. il *Mot Boat Sail* 160:42–5+ D '87 ——— *pages of article*

Steroids: the stuff of synthetic supermen? [anabolic steroids] M. S. Kreiter. il *Curr Health* 2 14:14–16 D '87

Time to rise and shine [drug charges against Phoenix Suns players] C. Neff. il *Sports Illus* 67:30–2+ N 23 '87 ——— *title of article*

Drugs and the aged
Monitoring drugs for the aged. W. I. Bennett. il *N Y Times Mag* p73–4 D 13 '87

Drugs and women
"Boy, could I use a . . ." (a) drink, (b) pill, (c) joint. If you filled in the blank you could be a preaddict. ——— *author of article* W. Gallagher. *Mademoiselle* 93:210–11+ O '87 ——— *date of periodical*

Drugs and youth
See also
Drug education ——— *further topic headings to see*
National Teen Challenge (Organization)

Drinking, drugs and kids: what to say. L. Salk. il *McCalls* 115:65 O '87

Drug abuse: who says it can't happen to your kid? M. O'Connell-Cahill. il *U S Cathol* 52:20–5 O '87

Drug use: down, but not in the ghetto. M. Miller. il *Newsweek* 110:33 N 23 '87

Kids can be drink and drug free. il——— *illustrated* *Parents* 62:22 O '87

"My mom saved my life" [daughter of comedienne C. Burnett] A. W. Petrucelli. pors *Redbook* 170:108–9+ N '87

The new kid [undercover narcotics cop G. Raffield murdered at Midlothian High School in Texas] por *Time* 130:61 N 9 '87

Teen to teen: drugs aren't cool. il *Curr Health* 2 14:19–21 N '87

NewsBank: **Usage Instructions.**

——— How to Use NewsBank® ———

STEP 1.

Turn to your research topic in the **NewsBank Index**, which is arranged alphabetically by subject. An explanation of the index appears at the bottom of each left-hand index page. A key to the abbreviations for NewsBank's subject categories appears at the bottom of each right-hand page.

You may find a "See" reference which will tell you that NewsBank has indexed this information under a different term.

> *EXAMPLE:*   Welfare
> > *See* Public Aid (Welfare)

You may also find a "See also" reference, which will suggest other terms where you can find related information.

> *EXAMPLE:*   Public Aid (Welfare)
> > *See also* Energy Assistance Programs: Food Assistance Programs, Medicaid, Social Services

SAMPLE INDEX ENTRY

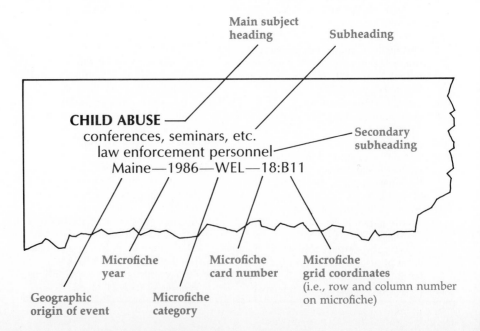

NewsBank: **Sample Entries.**

PARAMILITARY AND SURVIVALIST GROUPS

activities
  Aryan Nations Church
    Utah: West Jordan—1987 SOC
    115:B9, 115:B10–11, 115:B12,
    115:B13
  skinheads
    Michigan: Detroit—1987 SOC
    115:C10–12
  White American Resistance
    Colorado: Denver—1987 SOC
    115:B14
  white supremacist groups—1987
    SOC 115:D2–3
  white supremacists
    Georgia: Atlanta—1987 SOC
    115:C1
leaders
  Beam, Louis, Jr.—1987 SOC 114:G8
    arrests and indictments—1987
    SOC 114:F11–12, 114:F13–14,
    114:G1–2
    arrests and indictments (chart)—
    1987 SOC 115:C2–3
neo-Nazi groups
  violence
    Illinois: Chicago—1987 SOC
    115:C4
opposition and opposition groups
  . . .
    Utah—1987 SOC 115:C5–6
  Salt Lake Area Chamber of
    Commerce
    Utah: Salt Lake City—1987 SOC
    115:C7
trials
  The Order
    Colorado: Denver—1987 SOC
    115:C8, 115:C9
  White Patriot Party
    North Carolina: Raleigh—1987
    SOC 115:C13

violence
  skinheads—1987 SOC 115:C14–D1
white supremacist groups
  protests, demonstrations, etc.
    California: Glendale—1987 SOC
    115:D4–5

PARAPSYCHOLOGY
    See **Psychic Phenomena and
    the Occult**

PARENT ABUSE
    See **Elderly Persons**—abuse

PARENTING
    See also **Mentally Retarded
    Persons**—marriage and family
    relations; **Pregnancy**
attitudes and opinions
  discipline for teens (chart)—1987
    SOC 115:D6–8
mothers, full-time
  studies and reports
    California: Los Angeles—1987
    SOC 115:D9–10
parents, working
  babies in workplace
    South Carolina—1987 SOC
    115:D11–12
  studies and reports
    Michigan: Ann Arbor—1987
    SOC 115:D13–E3
teenagers
    See also **Pregnancy**—teenagers
trends
  studies and reports
    Utah—1987 SOC 115:E4

PARENTS' RIGHTS
    See **Abortion**—minors; **Birth
    Control**—minors

How to use the NewsBank index (Sample Entry)	**AIR POLLUTION** ◄[1] 1986 ◄[7] automobiles ◄——[2] [4][5][6] smoking vehicles ◄—— [3] ►Colorado: Denver—ENV 79:B3	1—Major Subject Heading 5—Microfiche Card Number 2—Sub-Headings 6—Microfiche Grid Coordinates 3—Geographic Location 7—Microfiche Year 4—Microfiche Category (at top of index page)

Copyright NewsBank, inc. 1988

Ulrich's International Periodicals: Sample Entries.

SAMPLE ENTRY

DEWEY DECIMAL CLASSIFICATION —— 535.544.6

COUNTRY CODE —— CN ISSN 0045-5105

MAIN ENTRY TITLE —— CANADIAN JOURNAL OF SPECTROSCOPY. (Text

YEAR FIRST PUBLISHED —— in English and French) 1963. bi-m. Can. $80

FREQUENCY OF PUBLICATION

PRICE

LANGUAGE NOTATION —— (Spectroscopy Society of Canada) Polyscience

CORPORATE AUTHOR

PUBLISHER NAME AND ADDRESS —— Publications Inc., 555 Legendre E., Suite 24, Montreal, Que. H2M 1G2, Canada. TEL 514-381-0442. Eds.

EDITOR —— I.S. Butler & T. Theophanides. adv. bk. rev. charts.

SPECIAL FEATURES —— illus. index. circ. 1,200. Indexed: Biol.Abstr.

INDEXED IN:

CIRCULATION —— Chem.Abstr. Curr.Cont. Met.Abstr. Sci.Abstr. Sci.Cit.Ind. Abstr.Bull.Inst.Pap.Chem. Anal.Abstr. GeoRef. Mass Spectr.Bull. World Alum.Abstr.

FORMER TITLE —— Supersedes: Canadian Spectroscopy (ISSN 0008-5057)

ANNOTATION —— *Spectroscopy*

Ulrich's Sample Entries (cont.).

820 US ISSN 0013-8304
E L H. (English Literary History) 1931. q. $19 to individuals; institutions $52.50. Johns Hopkins University Press, Journals Publishing Division, 701 W. 40th St., Ste. 275, Baltimore, MD 21211. TEL 301-338-6987. Ed. Ronald Paulson. adv. circ. 2,000. (also avail. in microform from UMI; reprint service avail. from UMI) Indexed: Curr.Cont. Hum.Ind. M.L.A. Arts & Hum.Cit.Ind. Abstr.Engl.Stud.
History
810 US ISSN 0093-8297
E S Q; journal of the American Renaissance. 1955. q. $15 to individuals; institutions $20. Washington State University Press, Pullman, WA 99164-5910. TEL 509-355-4795. Ed. Robert C. McLean. bk. rev. bibl. charts. illus. circ. 625. Indexed: Curr.Cont. M.L.A. Amer.Hum.Ind. Arts & Hum.Cit.Ind. Abstr.Engl.Stud. Ind.Bk.Rev.Hum.
800   US
EADS BRIDGE; a literary review. 1972. s-a. $4. St. Louis University, English Department, St. Louis, MO 63108.

TEL 314-658-3010. Ed. Avis Meyer. circ. 500.
810 US ISSN 0012-8163
EARLY AMERICAN LITERATURE. 1966. 3/yr. $9 to individuals; institutions $10. (Modern Language Association of America) University of North Carolina Press, Box 2288, Chapel Hill, NC 27515. TEL 919-966-3561. Ed. Everett Emerson. adv. bk. rev. bibl. cum.index. circ. 650. Indexed: Curr.Cont. Hist.Abstr. Hum.Ind. M.L.A. Amer.Hum.Ind. Arts & Hum.Cit.Ind. Amer.Hist. & Life. Abstr.Engl.Stud. Rel.Ind.One.

EARTH'S DAUGHTERS; a feminist arts periodical. see *WOMEN'S INTERESTS*

700 CK ISSN 0012-9410
ECO; revista de la cultura de occidente. 1961. m. $22. Libreria Buchholz, Av. Jimenez de Quesada 8-40, Bogota, Colombia. Ed. J.G. Cobo Borda. bk. rev. circ. 4, 500. Indexed: M.L.A. Hisp.Amer.Per.Ind.
839.5 NO ISSN 0013-0818
EDDA; Nordisk tidsskrift for litteraturforskning. (Text in English and Norwegian) 1914. 4/

yr. $50. Norwegian University Press, Kolstadgt. 1, Box 2959-Toeyen, 0608 Oslo 6, Norway (U.S. address: Publications Expediting Inc., 200 Meacham Ave., Elmont, NY 11003) Ed. Asbjoern Aarseth. adv. bk. rev. index. circ. 950. Indexed: Can.Rev.Comp.Lit. Ind.Bk.Rev.Hum.
890 US ISSN 0364-6505
EDEBIYAT; a journal of Middle Eastern literatures. 1976. s-a. $12. University of Pennsylvania, Middle East Center, 838 Williams Hall/CU, Philadelphia, PA 19104. TEL 215-898-6335. Ed. William L. Hanaway. adv. bk. rev. index. circ. 300. (back issues avail.; reprint service avail. from ISI) Indexed: Curr.Cont. M.L.A. Ind.Islam. Arts & Hum.Cit.Ind.
801.955 US ISSN 0276-7589
EFFECTIVE SPEECH WRITER'S NEWSLETTER. 1975. bi-m. $15. Effective Speech Writing Institute, Box 444, University of Richmond, VA 23173. TEL 804-282-0388. Ed. Jerry Tarver. bk. rev. bibl. circ. 500.

Building a Bibliography

Be sure to keep track of all the bibliographic items you come across. The simplest way to do this is to maintain a 3×5 card file, each with a bibliographic entry. Cards can be alphabetized and will aid in compiling your bibliography of works cited at the end of the research paper. Some researchers use 5×8 cards to take advantage of additional space. Others use regular typing paper with the bibliographic entry at the top, and then write their notes on the book or article below.

SAMPLE BIBLIOGRAPHY CARDS

Some sample entries are:

call number
author's last name, first name. Collaborators if any.
title of book (underlined), or "Title of article," in quotation marks

If it is a book, follow with city of publication:

publisher, date
If an article, the journal (underlined), volume number, issue number, (date), and page reference.

BF 431

S2

Sagan, Carl. <u>The Dragons of Eden: Speculations on the Evolution of Human Intelligence.</u>
New York: Random House, 1977.

SAMPLE BIBLIOGRAPHIC ENTRIES

The bibliography is typed double spaced, with entries in alphabetical order. The first line of an entry begins at the left margin, but any subsequent lines are indented another five spaces. Here are a few sample bibliographic entries showing you how to handle some of the items you are likely to find:

When there is one author for a book:

Denny, Frederick Mathewson. <u>An Introduction to Islam.</u> New York: Macmillan, 1985.

When there are two or more authors for a book:

Michaels, Leonard, and Christopher Ricks. <u>The State of the Language.</u> Berkeley: U of California P, 1980.

When a book has an editor:

Angus, Douglas, and Sylvia Angus, eds. <u>Contemporary American Short Stories.</u> New York: Fawcett, 1960.

When you have two books by the same author, list them alphabetically and use three hyphens as a substitute for the author's name in the second listing:

Jones, Stephen. <u>Drifting.</u> New York: Viking, 1975.
- - -. <u>Turpin.</u> New York: Macmillan, 1968.

A reference to a signed article in an encyclopedia:

Nevins, Alan. "Ulysses S. Grant." <u>Encyclopedia Britannica.</u> 1976 ed.

A reference to an unsigned article in an encyclopedia:

"Brown, John." <u>Family Encyclopedia of American History.</u> Pleasantville: Reader's Digest, 1975.

An article in a journal or magazine:

Vandenbroucke, Russell. "Athol Fugard: The Director Collaborates with His Actors," <u>Theater</u> 14, No. 1 (Winter 1982): 32-40.

An article in a journal with continuous pagination:

Freedman, Carl. "Writing, Ideology, and Politics: Or-
     well's 'Politics and the English Language' and En-
     glish Composition." College English 4 (1981):
     327-340.

An article from a newspaper:

Flange, Bernard. "Nuclear Reactor Failure in Virginia."
     The Washington Post 17 September 1986, sec. 3: 16.

or

"Geologic Faults Pose Problems for L.A." San Francisco
     Chronicle 13 August 1986, sec. 1: 1.

A book by one author, edited by someone else:

Shakespeare, William. Complete Plays. Ed. Peter Alex-
     ander. London: Oxford U P, 1939.

An interview:

Heller, John. Personal [or Telephone] interview. 15 Mar.
     1987.

A lecture:

Heller, John. "Saving the Shroud." Religious Studies Lec-
     ture Series, Severance Hall. Boston, 12 Feb. 1986.

A film:

Allen, Woody, dir. Hannah and Her Sisters. United Artists,
     1986. (If you do not know the director, begin with the
     title of the film.)

A play performance:

<u>Master Harold . . . and the boys.</u> By Athol Fugard. Dir.
   Lloyd Richards. Yale Repertory Theater, New Haven,
   CT. 12 Mar. 1982.

   In every case, your purpose is to be clear and to provide all the information you or your readers could need in order to find the reference.

Compiling the Bibliography

The bibliography that accompanies your research paper should appear at the
end on a separate page or pages, headed by *Works Cited,* depending on the
style of citation you are instructed to use. The appropriate styles are described
later in this chapter under the headings MLA Style and APA Style. The items
listed in your bibliography should include the books, articles, and other
materials you have gathered and used in the paper. The works are to be
gathered in alphabetical order, using the last name of the authors as the
first entry.

   Your goals are always clarity, completeness, and accuracy. It pays to keep
a complete bibliographic record of everything you uncover right from the
beginning of your research. It is not necessary to separate different kinds of
entries, such as books, articles, references to encyclopedias, and so on. Simply
list all your sources in alphabetical order so that your reader can have a handy

---

Tips: Compiling the Bibliography
- The bibliography is always on a separate page at the end of your
  essay.
- The title *Works Cited* should be centered one inch down from the
  top of the page. The first entry begins two spaces below that.
- All the entries are alphabetical by author (last name first) or title
  (ignore *A, An,* or *The*).
- All entries are double spaced, with two spaces between them.
- The first line begins at the left margin, but subsequent lines are
  indented five spaces.
- When there are two or more authors, begin with last name, first
  name, but the second and subsequent authors are listed with first
  name first.

guide to research in one place. Your bibliography, like the bibliographies of the authors you read, will serve as a guide to further inquiries for your reader. (See the box entitled "Tips: Compiling the Bibliography.")

Writer's Workshop: Bibliography

1. Compile a bibliography of available articles and books on one of your own research subjects or one of the following subjects. Aim for at least five and no more than ten items. Use the appropriate form.

   St. Peter's, Rome
   Carmen Cavallaro
   The Sextant
   St. Thomas
   Sir Lawrence Olivier
   Cleveland, Ohio
   Bacon
   Fast food
   Miguel de Cervantes
   Miles Davis
   Lou Gehrig
   Basketball
   Poverty in America
   Rudolf Valentino
   The Verazzano Narrows Bridge
   The Sears Building, Chicago
   McKim, Mead, and White

2. Compile a bibliography of items available in your library on one of the following subjects:

   John Brown
   The Shroud of Turin (The Holy Shroud)

Keeping Your Notes

Your notes are a valuable research tool and should be kept in good order. (See box entitled "Tips: Note-Taking.")

Tips: Note-Taking

- Keep complete bibliographic information at the top of your note card.
- Survey the source, book, or article, and begin with a comment on the general nature and value of the item.
- If possible, cite the author's general purpose.
- List the major points the author makes, or the major subjects the author covers.
- On subsequent note cards, each identified with the author and source, keep
  a. quotations, using quotation marks, which you feel may be useful in your paper.
  b. your opinions about the usefulness, value, or importance of what the author has said.
- Be sure to keep careful track of the page reference for any quotation. Before you include a quotation, check it for accuracy.

SAMPLE NOTE CARD: GEORGIA O'KEEFFE

The following is a sample note card for a research paper on the subject of sexual symbolism in the work of the American painter, Georgia O'Keeffe (1887–1985). The student was interested in the difficulties O'Keeffe faced because she was a woman artist, and in the degree to which she used sexual symbolism to make a statement. The student found an entry in a book that specifically concerned itself with women artists.

N43
F56
Fine, Elsa Honig. <u>Women and Art: A History of Women Painters and Sculptors from the Renaissance to the 20th Century</u>. Montclair: Allanheld & Schram, 1978. The entry on Georgia O'Keeffe is on pages 191 to 194. Fine says that women artists have special problems because the art establishment tends to ignore them. 191. O'Keeffe showed her work in 1923 at Alfred Steiglitz's gallery, "291." Steiglitz was a famous photographer. He married O'Keeffe in 1924.

Fine says: "After the meeting with Steiglitz, the struggle for recognition as an artist was over for O'Keeffe; her reviews were consistently favorable and she always had a place to show."

192. Fine quotes O'Keeffe: "Although the artist em-phatically denies it, claiming that 'the critics are just talking about themselves, not what I am think-ing,' there is obvious sexual symbolism in both her abstractions and representational paintings."

Fine says there is sexual symbolism; O'Keeffe says no. One thing I want to check is whether or not O'Keeffe ever says there is such symbolism. I'll have to see what others say. I see some symbolism my-self in Open Clam Shell. It seems pretty obvious.

Fine calls it "Vaginal Iconography": p. 193. p. 194: Good quote: "For her independent lifestyle during the early years of the 20th century, Georgia O'Keeffe was labeled a 'new woman.' That spirit still remains. Suspicious of all the words that have been written about her, the artist wrote and super-vised the publication of her own monograph at the age of eighty-nine."

p. 229, Bibliographic lead: "Georgia O'Keeffe," Whitney Museum of American Art, New York, October 8-November 29, 1970. Catalogue essays by Lloyd Good-rich and Doris Bry.

I'll probably have to get this on interlibrary loan.

These are notes taken in the early stages of reading for her essay, and this student was not ultimately able to find the catalog for the Whitney Museum show. However, her university museum had an original O'Keeffe that she was able to look at, and one thing this student did was to set up an interview with the curator of the collection. Fortunately, the curator had once met Georgia O'Keeffe and was able to provide the student with some interesting material.

Always indicate quotations by using quotation marks, as in this example. This is much more important than it may seem because it is essential for you to know exactly what your own comments are and not to make the mistake of thinking that something you quoted is your own work. Using quotation marks accurately right from the beginning is the best way to avoid such an error.

PLAGIARISM

Plagiarism is the use of someone else's statements or ideas as if they were original with you. When you are working on a research project, you need to depend very heavily on your sources. Your contribution to your reader is to gather the most important material together for examination, and then to find an original point of view—a personal angle—from which you can write your own observations about your subject. If you are sloppy about keeping track of your quotations and your own comments, then you may unwittingly find yourself guilty of plagiarism by using someone else's ideas when you thought they were your own.

If you do not quote your source directly, but summarize a source, then be sure to indicate so clearly in your notes. The best thing is to use this method:

```
Elsa Honig Fine:  She says that O'Keeffe was already
famous when her husband died, but only after that did
O'Keeffe go to the southwest, where all her great paint-
ings were made.
```

When you are making your own comments on your note cards, use a similar kind of indicator:

```
Me:  O'Keeffe may have been given a special boost because
she got married to a famous artist. I wonder what would
have happened to her if she had not gotten married at all.
If she had never been involved with a man, would she have
been so successful?
```

The penalty for plagiarism in some programs is extremely severe—usually the failure of a course. Therefore, it is all the more important to keep very careful track of your own comments and those of your sources. Save all your notes until you have your paper back.

PLAGIARISM AND PARAPHRASE

Paraphrasing is restating something you have read into different words, ordinarily trimming the original material to a quarter or a third of its length. On your note cards, such paraphrase is often of great help in keeping track of what you have read. If you use a paraphrase in your paper, give a citation indicating its source.

SOURCE

"In the early 1880s each of the great Impressionists became obsessed with problems of style and went through a crisis of doubt. In each case the causes were different, but the basic problem may have been the very success of the techniques these artists had invented—techniques which opened so many new possibilities of further exploration. The Impressionists may have become afraid (as Picasso was so often to be afraid) of growing merely slick, since they were all artists of considerable virtuosity" (Phoebe Poole, *Impressionism* [New York: Oxford U P, 1967], 216).

Sample from a student essay (this is plagiarism):

```
In the 1880s the important Impressionists were concerned
with style and went through a period of doubt. The causes
were different in each case, but the problem, basically,
was in the success of the techniques the artists invented.
The Impressionists were probably afraid of becoming
merely slick, especially since they were all virtuoso
artists.
```

In this case, the writer has consciously shifted words and phrases around, has pretended that the ideas and expressions were his own, and has not mentioned Phoebe Poole at all. Even if there were a footnote to this passage, it would be plagiarism because it literally steals the original author's expression. The only way such a passage could be used in the way the student uses it is to quote it accurately in its original form with quotation marks.

There is, however, an acceptable way of using material of this sort, and that is to use a paraphrase with a citation. The following is not plagiarism:

Phoebe Poole concludes that the great Impressionists went through a period of crisis and self-doubt in the early 1880s because they feared that they would become "merely slick."

The footnote would then provide a complete reference to the source of the paraphrase.

Writer's Workshop: Keeping Note Cards

1. Develop two note cards on books or articles relevant to your research project. Be sure to follow the procedures outlined earlier, and include complete bibliographic information.
2. Demonstrate your ability to paraphrase by offering a paraphrase of the following paragraph by Frank Beaver:

> In modern cinema few artists can challenge Ingmar Bergman in prominence. The consistency of his vision and the intensity of his personal and philosophical ruminations greatly enhance the best traditions of Swedish culture. His abilities as a film practitioner suggest genius, one capable of drawing great performances from a favored stock company of players, of exposing the face as a mask for human suffering while willing at the same time to reveal the medium in which he works as an illusory device incapable of fully grasping the mysteries of human existence.

Writer's Workshop

Conventions of Citation

Citation is the accurate documentation of source material gathered for your research paper. You will need to know about three kinds of citations: the bibliography that appears at the end of your essay under the heading *Works Cited*, the specific notes that are signaled with a number in the text and are gathered at the end of the essay under the heading *Endnotes*, and the citations within your text.

THE PURPOSES OF CITATIONS

Citations indicate your thoroughness in research. They also show whether your sources are well balanced and of high quality. For some audiences, your citations will offer a starting place for further reading on a subject. It is possible, for instance, to have your essay act as a stimulus to further research on the part of the reader.

Your citations also help establish the validity of your argument. A good researcher is fair to the sources of information. That means the good researcher ought not to quote information in a context that distorts its meaning, nor permit a source to be twisted around to say anything other than what the original author intended. By using your citations accurately, you can make it possible for a reader to look up material that might seem doubtful, but which supports your views.

What You Should Mark with a Citation

You should mark every use you make of secondary sources:

direct quotations
paraphrases of your sources
references to interviews or lectures
reference to theories or views held by your sources
use of graphs, charts, or visual materials from your sources

The point is to be sure to give the proper credit for all materials you have developed in your research and you want to use in your paper.

In every case, your citations will authenticate your work, and act as a guide to your reader. Therefore, they must be clear, accurate, and consistent. To that end, several styles of citation have been developed in order to establish a uniform style for publication in various fields. They now guide research of virtually all kinds, including books written for a popular audience. By learning these systems, you make yourself part of the tradition of research throughout the world.

THE LENGTH OF YOUR CITATION

Ordinarily, your source will be noted in parentheses after the passage in quotation marks in "this fashion, marked by quotation marks, and then given a citation" (Goldblatt 75). The author and the page number will refer to the works cited bibliography at the end of your text. The end punctuation of your sentence comes after the parenthesis. However, when something you wish to quote is longer than four lines of text, then you would indent ten spaces and double space the quotation.

(handwritten margin notes: "10 spaces", "NO QUOTATION MARKS", "IF LONGER THAN 4 LINES", "NOT 1 PERIOD")

> Judging from the evidence that has been gathered regarding the Shroud of Turin, there is some cause for concern regarding forgery. . . . The predilection of medieval forgers for reproducing items associated with Jesus was such that Europe was virtually flooded with pieces of the cross, the crown of thorns, the cloak, the sandals and innumerable objects . . . all proven worthless. (Goldblatt 75)

The ellipsis (three dots: . . .) indicates that you have left something out of the quotation. You have the right to edit any quotation, as long as you remain faithful to its original intention and meaning. The first ellipsis in the example has four dots with a space between them, and the first dot indicates the period for that sentence. This means the material omitted covers two or more sentences. The second ellipsis, simply the three dots, means that you have omitted a clause or phrase within a sentence.

When you indent a long quotation, as you would also do for four or more lines of poetry, you do not need quotation marks. The indentation—preceded by double spacing, and followed by double spacing—tells your reader that the material is a quotation.

What Not to Cite

When you are unsure or worried about plagiarism, you can easily go overboard on citations. The rule is a commonsense one: cite what you consciously use from another source. You do not need to cite common knowledge. For example, if you were researching the Shroud of Turin and learned that Turin was in Italy, you would not need to cite that information. Even though you may not have known it when you started, Turin is definitely in Italy, and that is common knowledge.

Try to avoid overdoing your citations. Try a sample on your instructor if you are in doubt. Finding the appropriate balance is important in the early stages of your writing.

The MLA Style Parenthetical Citation

The Modern Languages Association has established a style for citations that has become a worldwide standard. It is used in a great many journals in several fields, such as literature, history, art, and others. Before preparing a research essay in a course, you should check to see what the preferred style citation form is for that discipline. The current edition of the *MLA Handbook* is 1984.

The MLA style tries to include all the documentation in parentheses following the citation. This has several advantages: you can put the parentheses right after the citation, even if it appears in the middle of the sentence; you can include several citations for different sources in one sentence; and you can clean up your text by avoiding superscript numbers.

THE CITATION IN YOUR TEXT

In order for the MLA style to function, you must have a detailed bibliography (Works Cited) at the end of the paper, because the new style includes the barest information necessary to understand the citation. Following are some samples from what would be the text of your essay.

When you do not mention the author's name in your text:

```
One investigator says that scientists are approaching
the investigation of the shroud with some skepticism
(Heller 77).
```

Note: The author's name is used in this fashion if there is only one work cited in the bibliography. No comma comes between the author and the page; the final punctuation goes outside the parenthesis.

When you mention the author in the text and the author has more than one work in the Works Cited:

```
Why does Heller say that the scientists are approaching
the investigation of the shroud with "almost fanatical
suspicion?" (Report 77).
```
or (Heller, Report 77)

Note: This sample assumes there is more than one item in the bibliography by Heller, and *Report* is the shortened form of the title of the item to which this documentation refers. When you end with a quotation, the parenthesis follows the last quotation mark, but the sentence ends with a period, the final punctuation mark. When a question mark or an exclamation mark is in the original quote: "almost fanatical suspicion?" a period still follows the parenthesis. If a period ended the quotation, omit it and follow the original form as shown here. You always supply the end punctuation after the documentation.

When you mention the author's name in the text and there is only one item in the Works Cited to refer to:

```
Heller makes a point of saying that the scientists who
study the shroud approach the task with suspicion (77).
```

Note: This sample assumes there is only one item by Heller in Works Cited, so you need only the page number in the parenthetical documentation. Your reader can easily turn to the back of your paper and see the title of Heller's work.

When you cite a work in several volumes:

> Zask, in his multivolume work on church icons, has only one extensive reference to the shroud (4:542).

Note: This sample assumes a work of four volumes. The reference is to page 542 of the fourth volume. You do not need *vol.* as part of your documentation.

When you have a long quotation that is set off from your text, you provide the parenthetical documentation at the far right after the end of the quotation:

> The scientists who worked on the shroud had as many different reactions as any group might (Heller 84).

SAMPLE ENDNOTE

Most of your endnotes will be explanations or comments on bibliography rather than documentation of sources. Because the parenthetical documentation is usually complete and easy to manage, your notes will look something like the following:

> Each of these investigators found that his theories about the Holy Shroud changed during the investigations. But some of them changed their thinking in almost predictable ways.[3]

When your endnote 3 appears, it will be something like this:

> [3]Heller's argument is especially important because he is a scientist himself, whereas Zask and Minnery are reporters. One of them is a reporter for a religious monthly publication, and he may have a hard time being objective.

WORKS CITED

In the MLA format, the Works Cited should be prepared very carefully, because every citation in the body of the paper will be keyed to this list. In general, the list of Works Cited constitutes your bibliography. (See box entitled "Tips: Citing Works Using MLA Format.")

| TIP | *Tips: Citing Works Using MLA Format* |

- *p.* and *pp.* to refer to pages are usually omitted unless some confusion might result.
- *vol., ch., sec.* are usually omitted and included as arabic numerals followed by a colon (:) in this fashion: (4: 542–44), which means volume 4, pages 542 to 544.
- after the name of a journal, there is no comma before the volume number, which is arabic; and after the date there is a colon (:), not a comma:

  Author. Title. *Journal* 22 (1986): 121–30.

Here is a sample of Works Cited in the MLA style:

WORKS CITED

Anonymous. "The Five Brave Negroes with John Brown at Harper's Ferry." Negro History Bulletin 27 (1964): 164-69.

Askew, Margaret. Virginia Cavalcade 29 (1979): 14-21.

Cady, Edwin H., George Arms, and Alfred Habegger. Young Howells and John Brown: Episodes in a Radical Education. Columbus: Ohio State UP, 1985.

Rossbach, Jeffery, Jane H. Pease, Earl J. Hess, and Daniel W. Crofts, Ambivalent Conspirators: John Brown, the Secret Six, and a Theory of Slave Violence. Philadelphia: U of Pennsylvania P, 1982.

Simpson, Craig. "John Brown and Governor Wise: a New Perspective on Harper's Ferry." Biography 1 (1978): 15-39.

Whitman, Karen. "Re-evaluating John Brown's Raid of Harper's Ferry." West Virginia History 34 (1972): 46-84.

The APA Style Citation

The style of the American Psychological Association is widely used in the social and behavioral sciences. It is detailed in its *Publication Manual of the*

American Psychological Association, 3rd ed. (Washington: American Psychological Association, 1983).

Its ideal is to have no footnotes, no endnotes, no numerical citation. All the relevant information for a reference is given in parentheses in the text, and keyed to the *References* at the end of the paper. References is equivalent to Works Cited in the MLA style.

THE CITATION IN YOUR TEXT

Because all the sources you used will appear in a numbered list at the end of the paper, what you need to do is refer to (author, date, and page) in your text to document a specific source.

Here are four samples:

Only one of the authors I consulted (Smith, 1978, pp. 5-7) went on record as a person who believed the shroud's authenticity.

Smith (1978, p. 48) consulted with several specialists before discussing the shroud with the scientists.

"Carbon dating would tell us nothing more than we already know," one author (Smith, 1978, p. 235) said.

In his brief article Heller (1981) says the Shroud is more problematic than he had thought.

If Smith had written two pieces in 1978, you would list them in proper alphabetical order, and if your reference were to the later of the two publications, you would use this form: (Smith, 1978b, p. 235).

The convention is to cite page numbers in a general reference, such as the first example, if you are referring to a book. If your reference is to a short article, as in the last example, then no page reference is needed.

REFERENCES

The APA style conforms more with international practice than the MLA style. For a book:

Last Name, Initials. (date in parentheses). <u>Title underlined.</u> Place of publication: Publisher.

Wilcox, R. K. (1977). <u>Shroud.</u> New York: Macmillan.

Piven, F. P. & Cloward, R. A. (1971). <u>Regulating the poor.</u> New York: Random House.

Only the first letter of a title is capitalized.

For a journal article with two authors:

Last Name, Initials, & Last Name, Initials, (Date), Title, but not in quotation marks. <u>Journal underlined, vol. number underlined</u>, first page–last page.

Stevenson, K. E., & Habermas, G. R. (1982, April) Verdict on the shroud. <u>Saturday Evening Post, 4</u>, 64-67, 120.

Note: the second and subsequent lines of bibliographic entries are indented three spaces in from the margin. The *Saturday Evening Post* has a volume number, 4. 64–67, 120 is the page reference. The numbers 64–67 mean that the article appears on all pages from 64 to 67, while the later number, 120, means it also appears on that page—but the comma rather than the dash tells us that it does not appear on pages between 67 and 120.

The following is a Reference List in the APA style:

REFERENCE LIST

Arlow, J. (1956). <u>The legacy of Sigmund Freud.</u> New York: International Universities Press.

Balogh, P. (1972). <u>Freud: A biographical introduction.</u> New York: Scribner.

Clark, R. W. (1980). <u>Freud: The man and the cause.</u> London: Cape.

Fine, R. (1962). <u>Freud: A critical reevaluation of his theories.</u> New York: McKay.

Freeman, L. (1980). <u>Freud rediscovered.</u> New York: Arbor House.

Freud, S. (1965). <u>New introductory lectures in psycho-analysis</u> (James Strachey, Ed.). New York: Norton.

Fromm, E. (1970). <u>The crisis of psychoanalysis.</u> New York: Holt, Rinehart and Winston.

Klein, N. (1983). Freud's insights into compulsion. In
    Frank Walker (Ed.), <u>Modern essays on Sigmund Freud.</u>
    (pp. 27-54). New York: Dagda Books.

Masson, J. M. (1984). <u>The assault on truth: Freud's sup-
    pression of the seduction theory.</u> New York: Farrar,
    Straus and Giroux.

Rosenfeld, I. (1970). <u>Freud: Character and consciousness.</u>
    New York: University Books.

Writer's Workshop: Conventions of Citation

1. Use the following bibliographic information to complete the assign-
    ments:

An Introduction to English Architecture written by Frank Hoar and pub-
    lished by Evans Brothers Limited, London, 1963.

Mary R. Lefkowitz. "Women in Greek Myth," published in *The American
    Scholar* in Spring 1985, pages 207 to 220. This is a periodical that
    paginates continuously from the first to the last volume of a calendar
    year.

"How It Strikes a Contemporary," an essay by Virginia Woolf appearing
    in her book *The Common Reader*, published in 1953 by Harcourt Brace
    Jovanovich. The essay occupies pages 236 to 246.

a. Make a reference to each of these in the MLA style and the APA
    style.

b. Cite each of these in your text in the MLA style and the APA style.

Writing the Paper

The information and suggestions in Chapter 3 "Writing and Rewriting: From
Thesis to Draft" are valid for research essays. In some ways, research papers
are less problematic than other essays at the prewriting stages because the
materials of research—your notes, your references to other authorities, and
all the material you have gathered—tend to focus your attention and give you
a more concrete attitude toward the job of writing. After all, if you have a
series of subtopics you know must be treated in order to convince your
audience of a specific view, then a good part of your job is done for you: you
know what must be taken into consideration in a given section of your essay.

In writing the research paper, your notes will sometimes do the work of the journal. But it is still a good idea to carry a journal with you so that you can jot down good ideas when they strike you. Ideas are vastly too precious to throw away, and even if you have a good memory, you will find that the jotted-down notes will be fuller and more detailed.

SELECTING THE THESIS: BE FLEXIBLE

Developing a good thesis grows out of practice. The thesis for your first draft should be thought of as dynamic, something whose shape and nature can change in the act of writing. In a research paper, there is good reason to establish a series of theses: one to govern the entire essay, and one for each subsection of the essay.

THE THESIS IN RELATION TO THE EVIDENCE

Before constructing a thesis, you will have quotations, paraphrases of important arguments, opinions of your own derived from your reading, and many other items, including visual or statistical information. All of this material constitutes evidence that must be interpreted. The act of writing is often the act of choosing evidence and deriving inferences from that evidence.

Before beginning to write, survey the evidence and see how it can break down into subsections. Label them, then gather your research into folders— or into stacks of cards—corresponding to these sections. Ask yourself: What does the evidence force me to believe? If you can come up with an answer to this question, you will have the raw material from which to construct your thesis.

Remember that the thesis states your subject and your propositions regarding it. However, avoid the clichéd approach of "My purpose in writing this essay is to demonstrate that John Brown remained inside the arsenal at Harper's Ferry much longer than he needed to in order to be certain that he and his men were captured and martyred." Anyone reading your sentence knows you are writing an essay, so you do not have to say so. This approach is too obvious.

Instead, your thesis might be "The raid on Harper's Ferry may have been a futile act, but it was a gesture that placed the cause of abolishing slavery at the center of the struggle brewing between the North and the South. In one sense, John Brown gave the North a clear cause for fighting and hastened the end of slavery in America."

Such a thesis is broad enough to sustain an essay of several large subsections. And one of those subsections could deal with the question of why John Brown remained in the arsenal long after his goals were achieved. The same

thesis statement quoted in the previous paragraph could then be modified as follows: "John Brown probably remained inside the arsenal at Harper's Ferry much longer than he needed to in order to be certain that he and his men were captured and martyred."

Subordinate Theses: Smaller Tasks

As you outline a long essay, you can break it down into small, manageable parts, each governed by a subordinate thesis. Just as you might want to argue a position regarding why John Brown hesitated leaving the arsenal, you might want to do the same when considering why it took Robert E. Lee so long to get to the arsenal to quell the raid. Each of these issues represents a subsection of the overall essay. If you develop a thesis to govern such subsections, what you will discover is that you have broken down a very large task into smaller, much more manageable tasks.

When a professional writer approaches the task of writing an entire book, he or she may be intimidated. After all, the job of writing a huge book of 600 or 700 pages looks both exhausting and impossible. But every writer knows —professional or apprentice—that at any one moment at the pad, typewriter, or computer, all that can be written is a few words. Anyone can write a few words at a time. And in a single sitting, all that can be written is a small section of a large project. Obviously, writing three or four pages is much less daunting than writing hundreds.

Each part of the research essay can benefit from having a clear subordinate thesis. If you want to define what the raid at Harper's Ferry is, consider how much space you will need, and then construct a thesis that will help you achieve your goal. You might say, "The raid at Harper's Ferry was not just a futile act by frustrated men. It was one man's test of the will of an entire government. It was the first blow of the Civil War." This gives the writer a focus and a sense of what must be achieved in the section dedicated to definition.

Your thesis should be a statement you can defend with the argument you construct from your evidence. There may be cases in which you feel a narrow thesis may be inappropriate. For example, you may be writing on a very controversial subject, and your research may not have convinced you of either side of the argument. If so, then it is reasonable to establish a broader thesis, one in which you admit that certainty is not yet possible, but that the argument is ongoing. The point of your research essay will then be to inform rather than convince. You will provide the materials of the dispute and invite your audience to review them to see if it is willing to take a stand on the issues.

The Thesis Is Only a Guide

In the first draft stages of writing, a thesis has to be thought of as something tentative. It is a statement that you test through your writing. That is why, when your analysis of the evidence begins to contradict your thesis, your strategy should be to abandon it and form a new thesis that better respects the evidence.

Just remember that the thesis you come up with in the early stages of writing is only a guide, and like all guides, it can change and shift as you work. Locking yourself in with a thesis at any stage in the process of writing an essay—except when making your fair copy of the final version—can be damaging. Many authorities on writing insist that sticking with a thesis for the sake of having a thesis can be dull and destructive to good writing and good thinking.

GATHERING YOUR MATERIALS

As you do your research, you should look for any natural order that seems to develop with the material. If none develops at first, look for means by which you can key your material.

Keying Your Notes

Essentially, your notes are likely to cover a wide area, but at the same time, you will see references to specific issues appear in different sources. In writing about John Brown the following issues will appear:

> Brown's motives for the raid
> Brown's hesitation at leaving the arsenal
> The comparison of Brown with Old Testament prophets
> Abolitionists and their reactions
> Public reaction to the raid in the North
> Public reaction to the raid in the South
> The execution of John Brown and his sons
> The ultimate results of the raid

You can key each of these issues with a capital letter, a number, or a one-word title. Some researchers use different color markers. But whatever you use, remember that your purposes are basically retrieval. You want to be able to gather your material under different headings so that you can have quick access to it when you need it in your writing.

Keep your notes separated out according to source—because you will have access to the bibliographic information that way. If you give letter *A* to the question of motives, and *B* to the question of hesitation, then you can go through your sources and label quotations and comments with a specific letter.

Computers work exceptionally well at a task of this type. If you have access to a computer, you can set up computer files keyed to your subject. You will want to use one of the database systems, such as PC-File, File Express, or

D-BaseIII, which sets up a number of categories under which you can search a file. You can arbitrarily establish a dozen or so fields in which you can search your notes. Some of the fields will be blank at first, but as your research continues, you can fill them in. Therefore, a list of the kind of areas to search in writing about John Brown could be reduced to a number of key terms:

motives
hesitation
Old Testament
abolitionists
Northern reaction
Southern reaction
execution
results

Searching files involves the computer finding all the quotations, comments, and source material that you originally thought was related to a given field. A search would go through all your notes to see which ones, for instance, related to the reaction in the North, which to the reaction in the South. The search would gather all that material and you then could save it in a special file. To do this properly, you must have complete bibliographic information connected with each item. That would be done automatically when you set up the program.

Note cards can be keyed by hand on the same principles as the computer, and the job can often be done more quickly for an essay of ten pages. One advantage of note cards is their ease in being assembled together once you have keyed them. Another is their ease in being assembled into gatherings that you did not realize you'd need until late in the stage of composition.

Keying and Structure

One value of keying your notes is that it will produce clues for the structure of the essay. In an essay that begins with the following thesis

> The raid on Harper's Ferry may have been a futile act, but it was a gesture that placed the cause of abolishing slavery at the center of the struggle brewing between the North and the South. In one sense, John Brown gave the North a clear cause for fighting and hastened the end of slavery in America.

you can assume that a number of the keyed items in your research will be developed by a separate subordinate thesis. These possible subordinate theses were developed from the keyed items listed earlier:

> John Brown's motives were not just to succeed in stealing weapons, but to place the cause of freedom, the freedom of the slaves, at the center of the national debate in 1859.

Brown's hesitation at leaving the arsenal was probably a result of his realizing that if he failed, he might affect the conscience of America better as a martyr than as a successful raider.

Many newspapers and lecturers compared Brown with the Old Testament prophets because he looked like one, and he acted with the same kind of violence and wrath they associated with the angry god of the Old Testament.

The abolitionists in the North reacted with excitement and hope even though the raid failed. They realized that the raid focused attention on their efforts to abolish slavery in America.

In the South, the reaction was of horror. They saw the Northern abolitionists as violent and dangerous.

The final result of the raid was probably to make the freeing of the slaves one of the most emotional and popular causes in the federal government's struggle against secession.

These subordinate theses can provide you with a clear purpose in the subsection in which they appear. The best theses will tell you what you have to accomplish in each section. In the research essay, one key to structure lies in combining the use of the means of development you have already learned with the material that your research uncovers.

Selecting Quotations and References

Once you have established key sections with research material for support, select the best quotations, references, statements, and materials for your essay. Judging their relative value may be difficult outside of the essay itself, but every item you have found is useful. Selecting them according to their relative worth will make your job easier.

From your keyed material you need to find the most important items for actual use in your essay. If you have done your job of research well, you will have more material than you can use. So the result is that you will have to select what is most important and what you feel will best establish your argument. If you have keyed all your research material in the order in which you plan to use it, then when you move from subsection to subsection you will have your material right at hand.

As in any responsible piece of work, you will find arguments opposing the position you wish to support. Giving fair weight to counterarguments will always be a measure of your seriousness and your fairness in handling the material. If you uncover arguments that go directly against your own, quote them or paraphrase them accurately and explain why you find the arguments unacceptable.

THE OUTLINE

Like your thesis, your outline is a dynamic concept. It will shift and grow as you redraft your essay. Before beginning the outline of your research essay, refer back to Chapter 3 and the suggestions for outlining. They work as well for the research paper as for any other kind of writing.

Keeping your outline flexible is important. Things change as you write, and you need to restructure your outline as you go along. Make an outline at the beginning, then revise your outline as you revise your essays. Once you have a reasonable first draft, retype your outline and examine it for changes. Before your second draft, edit your outline looking for structural changes—moving sections from place to place as necessary. Once that is done, use the new outline to guide the final draft.

A Sample Research Paper: "The Shroud of Turin: Real or Forgery?"

The following is an outline and research paper on the Shroud of Turin. The outline reflects the structure of the paper as well as acting as a guide to the reader. The essay, although not perfect, is engaging. Joanne was extremely interested in the Shroud of Turin, especially because just before she began work on the project, the shroud was subject to a number of interesting scientific investigations. Therefore, in this case, the subject chose Joanne— she would have wanted to know more about this phenomenon whether or not she were assigned a research paper.

She realized when she wrote her first draft that she could not take a clear stand on whether or not the shroud was authentic. There was disagreement even among those who were in the Shroud of Turin research project, so she felt it was her job to present the evidence and let the reader make the decision. Therefore, the thesis of the essay is in the title: it is a question that Joanne admits cannot easily be answered.

The history of the shroud of Turin is a lesson in up-to-date research methods. What Joanne could not know is that in 1988 the Archbishop of Turin permitted scientists in three countries to take one square centimeter samples from the shroud for carbon-14 dating. The official report from these tests was not released as this book was going to press. But unofficial leaks from several sources report that the shroud material is medieval. Assuming it is a medieval forgery, one wonders how it could have been so skillful as to baffle the scientists whose work Joanne reports on. While one aspect of the mystery may be solved, there are many more that remain.

The Shroud of Turin: Real or Forgery?

Joanne Wosahla

English Composition

Prof. Jacobus

March 26, 1985

A separate title page is not essential, but it is a useful addition to a research paper.

The Shroud of Turin: Real or Forgery?

This outline is especially detailed and guides the reader into the paper.

Outline

I. Introduction
    A. Secondo Pia: photographer
    B. The first photograph of the shroud
        1. A positive of the negative shroud
        2. Did Pia see the face of Christ?

II. Historical background: the record
    A. The history of the shroud
        1. Joseph of Arimathea
        2. Uncertainty of origins
            a. No carbon dating
            b. Geoffrey de Charney
            c. Arculph: 640
    B. Connection with art history
        1. Byzantine art and details of the shroud
        2. Ian Wilson, first century in Edessa

III. Verifying the shroud
    A. Scientific tests
        1. Pollen dating
        2. Textile evidence
            a. Herringbone twill
            b. Linen and cotton handspun
    B. Scriptural authenticity
        1. Dr. Pierre Barbet's anatomy research
            a. The anatomy of crucifixion
            b. Importance of his research
            c. Archaeology: Jehohanan

2. Details on shroud correspond with Bible description
    a. Facial injuries
    b. Shoulder, knee injuries
    c. Chest cavity expanded
    d. Spear wound
    e. Unbroken legs
    f. Misspelled Roman coins
    g. Body is unwashed

IV. Shroud of Turin Research Project
  A. The questions
    1. What were the body images and bloodstains made of?
    2. How were both formed?
  B. John Heller and the committee
    1. Committee members
    2. Credentials
    3. Relation to religious groups
  C. Job: prove the shroud is real or not
    1. Gayet collection of funerary linens
    2. Chemical studies
    3. Is it a painting?
  D. Jet Propulsion Lab
    1. Lack of linear directionality
    2. VP-8 Image Analyzer
  E. Blood tests
    1. McCrone resigns: the shroud is painted
    2. Backup studies: Bruce Cameron
  F. Did a statue act as a stand-in?
  G. The scorch hypothesis
    1. Jackson: efforts to produce a scorch on linen

                2. The 1902 vaporgraph theory

          H. Flash fotolysis

                1. A resurrection event?

                2. Examining the evidence

V.   The opposition

          A. Jack Jennings

                1. Skepticism for the shroud

                2. Faith and doubts

          B. Negative reactions from believers

VI.   Conclusion

The Shroud of Turin: Real or Forgery?

Title 1 inch from top of paper

Secondo Pia stared in astonishment and chilling awe as he held the dripping negative plate up to the red light. What appeared before him on that night of May 28, 1898? The negative slowly developed and revealed--what?--a positive image? Before his eyes he saw developing a scourged yet tranquil face with closed eyes, a mustache and beard, a long and prominent nose, and strands of matted hair. Pia later stated that "I was so filled with fear that I almost fainted. For there grew plainly visible on the plate the face and body of a man whose head was covered with blood, whose wrists carried stigmata, whose expression was that of untold majesty" (Smith 50). Was Pia the first man in history to gaze upon the actual appearance of Christ as he lay in his tomb?

That question remains unanswered to this day. Pia had photographed the Holy Shroud of Turin, an ancient linen measuring 14 feet, 3 inches long, and 3 feet, 7 inches wide, a cloth kept in Saint John's Cathedral in Turin, Italy. It has long been venerated as the burial cloth of Jesus Christ. Pia's photograph, the first ever taken of the Shroud, stirred questions and controversy as people desired to know if, in fact, it could be proof of Christ's resurrection. But the desire to know more about it has led to numerous questions: Is it historically legitimate? How old is it? Where did it come from? Do the scientific findings correspond with Scripture? Is the cloth truly the authentic cloth Jesus was placed in by Joseph of Arimathaea in Golgotha some 2,000 years ago, or is it the burial linen of an unidentified crucified man, or for that matter, is it the work of a clever forger? How was the image formed and of

Four spaces between title and text

Introduction includes a humanizing event

Background details on shroud

Chief questions

½ inch from top of page to number

what is it composed? And, on another level, what do the scientific findings mean to Christians and non-Christians of today? Scientists and theologians say that claiming it is definitively Christ's shroud will forever remain outside the bounds of proof, but a close look at the studies lead to some interesting and leading conclusions to say the least.

Uncertainty is part of the thesis

The uncertainty regarding where we got the cloth has created debate over the Shroud's authenticity. Up to this date, a Carbon-14 test has not been performed, so we do not know the exact date of the cloth.[1] What evidence we have to authenticate the linen goes back only as far as 1353 with documentary evidence, for we know that Geoffrey de Charney of France founded a church at Lirey where "the true Burial Sheet of Christ" was exposed (Sullivan 785). We do not know how he obtained it, though, but he does speak of "spoil of battle." In 1203, a shroud bearing "the figure of our Lord" was seen by Robert de Clari, a chronicler of the Fourth Crusade, but he wrote that the following year it disappeared when the Byzantine capital was looted. It could be the same as the Lirey linen, but the only one who would have known was de Charney, and he never recorded if they were one and the same (Weaver 734). The House of Savoy obtained it from Margaret de Charney in exchange for two castles in 1453 (Sullivan 785) and while there in Chambery, it was damaged by a fire in 1532. In 1578 it was moved to Turin, and remained there. The real uncertainty comes from the time before 1353.

Medieval history of shroud

Ancient history of shroud

What we do know is that around 640 there is a documented reference to the burial linen of the Passion by Arculph, claiming that he kissed the "Lord's winding sheet" in Jerusalem, and in 631, Saint Braulio wrote that the Shroud was a known relic then (Sullivan 785). In the 5th or 6th

century, Saint Nino referred to a shroud of Christ (Saint
Nino was a Jerusalem Native and Apostle of Georgia).

In Byzantine art Christ was frequently represented
with details visible on the Holy Shroud of Turin (Otterbein 13: 187). An article in <u>National Review</u> points out
that Christ's physiognomy in portraits changed about the
year 300, and we can see that these features correspond   *Details of Christ's*
with details on the Shroud; these details include the rec-   *portrayal*
tangular design above the nose, random spots of blood, a
forked beard, one raised eyebrow, abnormally swollen or
shaded cheeks, and a line across the throat, which is actually a wrinkle on the Shroud. The article suggests that the
Shroud may have been taken from the original tomb to Rome
so as to be closely protected by the Christians during the
period of persecution (Sullivan 787). Ian Wilson, a British scholar, found that a portrait of Christ existed in the
first century in Edessa, but notes that the artistic representation of Christ "changed dramatically during the
sixth century, and believes the nature of the changes indicated the renewed accessibility of the Shroud during
that century" ("News" 656).

The historical evidence remains inconclusive, but some
studies of the actual linen as a textile have revealed important findings. Max Frei, a Swiss criminologist, formerly of the Zurich Police Scientific Laboratory, collected 48 pollen samples, and found that several were
identical to pollens found in 2000-year-old sediment in   *Scientific tests*
Lake Generazeth. It could have moved through Palestine,
Asia Minor, and Savoy. The problem with pollen dating is
that it is unreliable, since pollen can travel far in the
wind (Murphy 57).

Though the pollen tests are not definite, Gilbert Raes,
director of the Laboratorium de Meulmeester Voor Techno-

Murphy and Weaver are cited at end of paragraphs as sources of information

logie der Textilstaffen at the Rijksuniversiteit-Gent, Belgium, found that the herringbone twill weave was occasionally manufactured in the Middle East during Christ's time. The linen has traces of a cotton of a Middle East variety, and two aspects reveal ancient practices: one, the thread appears to be hand spun--after about 1200 A. D. European thread was spun by a wheel; and two, the threads seem to have been bleached before weaving, which is an ancient practice (Weaver 747).

Questions of scriptural authenticity are raised here

So what good is this cloth that lacks documentation and radiocarbon dating that would prove it is from the first century A. D.? This brings us to the scriptural authenticity and these findings help give credence to the assertion that it was Christ's, since historical evidence leaves us wondering. Especially instrumental was the work of Dr. Pierre Barbet, a French surgeon who, in the 1930s, verified the anatomical accuracy of the marks. He found that the nail marks were on the wrists, not the palms, as has been depicted in art, and he worked with cadavers in order to prove these were where they should actually be. A nail driven through the palm would not support the hanging body, but it would if driven through the wrist. Ian Wilson points out that "although this experiment was carried out forty years ago, it has been recognized by medical men even today as a brilliant piece of research, and one of the many which carry absolute conviction for the Shroud's authenticity" (27).

Wilson's name is in text, so quotation needs only a page reference in parenthesis

Barbet's study was confirmed by archaeology, for in 1968 the bones of crucified slave Jehohanan were found in an ossuary. On the inside of the radius, a well-defined scratch mark and worn place remained from where the nail had driven through (Weaver 747). Barbet's work is especially significant in disclaiming the Shroud as a forgery, for medieval artists routinely painted Christ with nailed palms, and the forger would have to have medical knowledge to know to put the marks in the wrist. There is no record of an artist studying anatomy until Donatello, born thirty years after the Shroud surfaced in France (Murphy 56).

Anatomy is a modern science

The presence of facial injuries corresponds with Christ's being struck on the face by the High Priest's men and Pilate's soldiers. The scourge marks are patterned like those inflicted by a Roman whip called a "flagrum," a multithonged whip with lead or bone on the tip.

The anatomy of the Shroud shows a right shoulder chafed raw, chafed over the scourge marks, which, according to Dr. Willis of England, is consistent with the carrying of a heavy beam (Wilson 21). The knee showed heavy damage, and Ian Wilson comments that "it hardly needs mentioning that Jesus' difficulty carrying the cross, specifically recorded in the Gospels, strongly implies repeated falls (25).

In the 1960s, Msgr. Ricci, an archivist at the Vatican, worked with Dr. Miani, a professor of anatomy at Rome's Sacred Heart Medical School, and found that the bar must have weighed between 66 and 88 pounds, and was tied with rope to the arms, shoulders, and left ankle. He would not have been able to ease his fall, instead falling squarely on his forehead or nose. A cut forehead and broken nose are shown in the image ("Secret" 81).

The anatomy further shows an expanded chest cavity, held in a state of rigor mortis, which would correspond with an attempt to draw air into the lungs (Goldblatt 415). The air gets trapped in the lungs during crucifixion and the victim dies from asphyxiation. Also evident is this victim's attempt to raise himself by the nail in the foot: "The 10-degree variance of the two blood flows on the

Goldblatt not mentioned in text, so he is cited in parenthesis

forearms of the Shroud image reflects precisely this up-
and-down prelude to death" (Goldblatt 417).

The Shroud shows that a spear was thrust on his side,
for there is evidence of an elliptical wound in the right
side. Jesus did not have his legs broken, as did most crucifixion victims (prevents them from lifting themselves
and breathing), and this man's legs were not broken. The
wounds on the head indicate that a cap of thorns was worn.
Wilson calls this "virtually signatory" (37).

Some experts believe that Roman coins were on the man's
eyes, and speculate that because of a spelling error on the
coin the body could have been wrapped at the time of crucifixion. The coin says UCAI, but the "c" may be a spelling
error; it could be an error for a "k" for Tiberious Kai-
saros. In 29 A.D. and 32 A.D., Pontius Pilate issued misspelled coins, and this corresponds with the time of
Jesus' death (Maggiori 9).

The body of this shroud was obviously not washed, contrary to Jewish customs, but Gary Habermas, an associate
professor of apologetics and philosophy at William Tyn-
dale College, noted that those executed by the government
were left with blood on the body, a token of the person's
payment for illegal actions (Minnery, "Not a Forgery"
44). Also, the best exegetes do not contest the idea that
there was no time for Jesus' body to be washed before the
Sabbath (Jesus died on the eve of the Passover Sabbath)
(Wilson 40). Also detectable is evidence of bound hands,
head, and feet, consistent with Jewish custom. Ethnolo-
gist Carleton S. Coon has also determined that the image is
of a man of the physical type found among the Sephardic
Jews and noble Arabs of modern times (Wilson 22).

Background and aims of STURP

John Heller, a member of the Shroud of Turin Research
Project (STURP), remarked that "nothing in the findings

contained a single datum that contravened the Gospel accounts. . . . Nor was there anything else on the Shroud
that would negate the actual presence of a scourged, crucified man lying in that linen" (217). Heller's opinion is
not to be taken lightly, for it comes only after several
years of intensive studies on the Shroud by STURP.

STURP began work on the Shroud in 1978. It was formed
with the desire to answer two key questions: What were the
body images and bloodstains made of? and How were both
formed? (Heller 206). Its members included specialists
within the fields of physics, biology, and chemistry. Although the forty members were either agnostics, Mormons,
Jews, Catholics, or Protestants, and could seemingly be
ecumenical and unbiased, several points must be realized.
For one, none of the STURP members had a professional stake
in this investigation. Each was well established in his
field. Secondly, they wanted to make sure it would be a
purely scientific investigation. Team member Jackson
stated that "the major purpose of STURP is to ensure the
integrity of this project. No church, no religious group,
no group of any kind, will or can influence STURP" (Heller
77). Thirdly, all findings were reviewed by what Heller
calls an "uncompromisingly and painfully tough and thorough" group of STURP scientists. Fourthly, STURP filed a
suit against Servant Publications when it published Verdict on the Shroud in 1981, for the team did not want the
public to think it represented its findings and conclusions. Although the injunction was overturned, it is important to note that STURP wanted to present their research in a nonbiased, scientific manner.

STURP may not conclusively state the decision toward   *Author's opinion*
which their research points, but the results of the find-
ings provide enlightening information.

Foremost in STURP's task was to prove or disprove the Shroud as real or fabricated. This particular shroud was unique because of the image. Heller pointed out in his book <u>Report on the Shroud of Turin</u> that there are "thousands and thousands" of pieces of funerary linen that go back to millennia before Christ, and there are the linens of the Coptic Christian burials. No image of any kind is on any of these linens (220). These Coptic Christian burial cloths are kept in the Gayet collection in the Louvre, and according to the archaeologist Gayet (excavated in Egypt near Antinoe around the turn of the century), these cloths had been used in burying Jesus' followers in Egypt, people known as Coptic Christians. On these cloths it is hard to distinguish blood stains. The comparison of this Shroud to others left open the big question of what the image was made of and how (Wilcox 60).

Technical information provided by Stevenson, cited in parentheses

Extensive chemical studies revealed that the image was the result of dehydrative acid oxidation with the formation of a yellow conjugated carbonyl chromophore of the cellulose. Chemically the image was determined. Use of the microscope and electromagnetic examination revealed that no chemical was present on the cloth in any appreciable quantity (Stevenson 66). So, the Shroud could not have been altered by chemicals. But how did the image get there?

The widely postulated notion of the image being the result of a painting proved definitively to be false. The light yellow coloring lies only on the topmost surface of the threads. If it was painted or rubbed on, the coloring would diffuse or soak into the threads, run down the sides of the threads, and leave deposits between them. STURP found none of these aspects on the cloth. The Shroud survived a fire in 1532, and the heat should have altered the color of organic pigments if they were used. The color

change would be closest to the burned area, yet the unifor-
mity of the yellow image remains right up to the edge of the
burns, unaltered. Also, the water thrown on to put out the
fire would have caused ink to run, but that did not happen
(Weaver 751). Each stained fibril is an identical shade,
and the darker areas only reflect a greater number of
stained fibrils. Acid painting was also ruled out, because
it produces densities which differ from those of the yellow stains on the Shroud.

According to Dr. Donald Lynn and Jean Lorre of the Jet
Propulsion Lab, and members of STURP, the lack of linear
directionality indicates that the cloth was not painted.
Their computer work analyzing the facial region revealed
that the feature-generating mechanism was probably direc-
tionless, for the image "is composed of a wide range of
spatial frequencies which are oriented in a random fashion" (Culliton 237). Heller (202) gives us a clear idea of
how difficult it would be to forge it due to the limitations of the nervous system:

*Heller and page num-
ber cited in text*

*Lengthy quotation in-
dented ten spaces, dou-
ble spaced*

> One would need a twentieth-century micromanipu-
> lator, which would have to work hydraulically at
> a distance of one or two meters. It would have to
> be rigged to a device called a waldo, which is an
> invention of the atomic era. Also, the artist
> would have to know how many fibrils to paint
> qualitative, and do the whole thing in reverse,
> like a negative.

The VP-8 Image Analyzer at the Air Force Weapons Lab revealed further insight. The VP-8 is a sophisticated instrument that converts image intensity to vertical relief. The Shroud rendered a perfect 3-dimensional image of

a crucified and scourged man, but when Jackson, a physi-
cist at the Air Force Academy, asked several artists to try
and reproduce the image of the man's head, the image analyzer failed to produce a proper 3-dimensional relief from
their work. Each rendering only gave a distorted, gro-
tesque result (Heller 151). Ordinary paintings and photographs simply do not have such accurate 3-dimensional information.

Many rigorous tests for blood were conducted, since the
image only penetrates the top 1/5000th of the cloth, but
the red marks penetrate through (Maggiori 9). Before doing
blood tests, it was ruled out that the "blood" stains
could be a long-lasting, heat-resistant colorant. It
could not be the hypothesized Tyrian purple dye made from
seashells as Professor Max Saltzman of UCLA, "the ultimate authority on ancient linen colors" found (Heller
123). These studies were confirmed by Dr. George Ruggiere,
the director of the New York Aquarium and marine biologist.

Walter McCrone, a team member who later resigned because he was insulted by the rigorous review of his papers
on the Shroud, claimed that the images and bloodstains
alike were all paint. McCrone was convinced that the
Shroud was a fraud, for as Heller remarks, "he merely
quoted his own microscopic observations and reiterated
that the whole shroud was paint" (Heller 184). He dismissed the results of the physical findings or of the presence of blood, yet these findings have been rigorously
conducted. Among these are microspectrophotometric scans
of crystals and fibrils, reflectance scans of the Shroud,
positive hemocromogen tests, positive cyanomethemoglobin
tests, positive tests for bile pigments, and tests for
characteristic hemeporphrin fluorescence. The hemoglobin
found was in the acid methemoglobin form and it was dena-
tured and very old. Heller and Adler confirmed their find-

ings by contacting Bruce Cameron, a scientist with a double doctorate dedicated to hemoglobin in its many forms,
who verified it as blood (Heller 147). Heller states that
"any one of these is proof of the presence of blood, and
each is acceptable in a court of law. Taken together, they
are irrefutable" (186). Furthermore, the blood markings
correspond to studies done on the angles of the blood
flows, which show that they are consistent with a crucifixion position. And, in the side wound, clear serous
fluid has been found along with the blood. (Incidentally,
this corresponds with John's Gospel account which states
that water and blood flowed from the side wound) (417).

Other details provide insight. Eric Jumper and Sam Pel-
licori found dirt on the heal image, on the tip of the nose,
and on one knee when examining it under a microscope.
Heller questions, "what could be more logical than to find
dirt on the foot of a man who has walked without shoes?"
(112).

So, if the image was not painted and shows real blood,
we are still left with the question of how the image got on
the cloth in the first place. A popular hypothesis of German writer Blinzler asserted that it could have been
formed with the aid of a statue. According to this notion,
the statue was coated with a substance able to produce an
image, and blood was added in approximate areas (Wilson
18). However, this theory proves inconclusive after examination.

For one, had the image been created using a hot statue,
deeper scorches would appear on high spots like the nose.
Secondly, no one has been able to reproduce a comparable
image on cloth, neither mechanically nor naturally.
Thirdly, and most significantly, the statue would have to
have been done before much was known about the anatomy of
circulation, according to Robert Bucklin, forensic pa-

Questions remain, topic shifts to how the image got on the cloth.

thologist and assistant coroner for Los Angeles County
("Shroud of Scientific Questions" 260). Certain details
of the image, like clotted blood and distention of the rib
cage, reflect a degree of anatomical knowledge not available in the 14th century. According to deputy coroner and
forensic pathologist Joseph Gambescia, the chairman of
medicine at Philadelphia's St. Agnes Medical Center,
pathological and physiological evidence is unquestion-
able, and represent medical knowledge that was not even
known 150 years ago (Heller 2).

Another image-creating theory proved false is the
scorch hypothesis. In the scorch theory, if heat and timing are carefully controlled, an experimental scorch can
yellow cellulose fibers as those on the Shroud were. The
image resembles the scorches from the 1532 fire also (Stevenson 67). However, none of the fibers were burnt or damaged as would be expected in the transfer process. The
scorch lies only on the surface fibers, and every time
STURP member Jackson tried to reproduce a light scorch on
linen, the burn affected more of the fiber than did the
image on the Shroud. When he tried scorching it with a
three-dimensional object, the precise effect failed to
reproduce (Minnery, "Hung Jury" 69).

*Minnery has two items
in Works Cited. An ab-
breviated title gives us
a clear reference*

In 1902, internationally noted zoologist Yves Delage
and his biologist assistant Paul Vignon thought they knew
how the image was formed. In their vaporgraph theory, they
believed that the image may have vaporized onto the cloth
by the chemical interaction of ammonia produced by the
urea in the morbid sweat and the aloes and olive oil used to
prepare the body for burial. This theory proposed that the
ammonia diffused from the corpse to the cloth and produced
a stain when it reacted with the aloes and oils.

STURP found problems with the vaporgraph theory. If
vapors caused the image, the detail would not be there.

Vapors diffuse in the air; they do not travel straight upward or in parallel lines. Chemists concluded that more
sweat would have been necessary to produce enough ammonia
for such a reaction. Even if enough ammonia had been produced, the chemical reaction would have permeated the
threads of the cloth. A damp cloth would be necessary in
the vaporgraph theory, but had it been damp, the cloth
would have tightly clung to the body in many places
which would cause the image to be distorted grossly (Stevenson 67).

   How was the image formed then? Scientists are left with
this one looming question. Eric Jumper has hypothesized
that a very brief molecular burst could have caused radiation and formed the image, a process called flash photoly-
sis. This sounds a lot like a resurrection event, but STURP
refuses to officially state such a conclusion since there
is no way to scientifically prove such a conjecture.

Author reviews possi-
ble conclusions

   A good look at the evidence does cause one to lean toward such a conclusion, though: proof of the time period of
twenty-four to thirty-six hours of being in the cloth (no
more, no less) corresponds almost exactly to Scripture;
this conclusion was reached because there are no signs of
decomposition and decomposition would have destroyed the
image (Goldblatt 418); the bloodstains are intact and precise anatomically, so the body could not have been removed
normally--smearing would have occurred ("Secularism"
1397); Christ could not have still been alive and then have
walked away because there are signs of rigor mortis and evidence of post-mortem exudations (serous fluid from the
pores, and oozings of liquid blood with serum) (Goldblatt
418); also, in the ancient world, the dead were usually
left undisturbed because decomposing bodies were considered unclean (Sullivan 787).

   According to Heller, the team has been forced to conclude that the Shroud "is an extracanonical witness to what happened to Jesus Christ, whether the man in the Shroud was Jesus or not" ("Shroud Scientist" 63). STURP's wording must be careful in light of the unique position Jesus holds in history, and Heller points out that "it is certainly true that if a similar number of data had been found in the funerary linen attributed to Alexander the Great, Genghis Khan, or Socrates, there would be no doubt in anyone's mind that it was, indeed, the shroud of that historical person" (219).

Anonymous article is cited by a short version of complete title: "A Shroud of Turin Scientist Speaks Out: Evidence that Nearly Demands a Verdict"

So what about all this scientific proof? Are we being given the same opportunity to assuage our doubts about Christ 2,000 years later than Thomas? Thomas, in John 20:25, refused to believe until he saw the nail holes, put his fingers into them, and put his hand in Christ's side. Some see the studies as enlightening and for the best, yet a vehement opposition has been expressed.

Author recapitulates and asks questions

STURP member Rogers of the Los Alamos Scientific Lab expressed a personal, not group, view in 1978, saying "What better way, if you were a deity, of regenerating faith in a skeptical age, than to leave evidence 2,000 years ago that could be defined only by the technology available in that technical age?" (Culliton 239). Deacon Frank Driscoll of the Church of the Good Shepherd in Seymour, Connecticut, believes that "whether we believe that the image on the Shroud is Jesus or not, by studying it we are brought closer to Him through contemplation and thought. It is a great tool for increasing our faith" (Maggiori 10). Heller believes the Shroud's important message for today is to reaffirm the gruesomeness of the "passion that has been sanitized through time" ("Shroud Scientist" 64).

Others are not as ready to believe so optimistically. Jack Jennings, a United Presbyterian Minister from Montana, wrote that "faith needs neither proofs nor props. Clinging to relics such as the True Cross or the Holy Shroud can only encourage infantilism instead of maturity." He encourages "healthy skepticism," for a shroud is not needed to confirm or establish faith (554). An article in the Saturday Evening Post reflected the mild attitude that if "by science and reason we could prove Christ's resurrection, for his death alone is meaningless, then what would we have? Something dry and stale, for there will always be doubts, and the purpose of religion is to assuage doubt by faith, not fact" (Smith 51). A Newsweek article pointed out that the resurrection "is one mystery that will always require the illumination of faith," reflecting a middle of the road perspective (Woodward and Matthews 95). Anthony Burgess reflects the unthreatened attitude by looking to other issues: "The real wonder of Christianity lies in its doctrine of charity and tolerance. We need to weave this living tissue, not examine an old shroud. The real miracle is still to come if we let it." He does not believe "orthodoxy is really assailed by the theories of modern medicine" (12).

Though some view the Shroud mildly, there are those who feel studies are offensive. When one reader of Christian Century heard about the Air Force Academy planning on making a 3-dimensional replica of the image, she became enraged: "a plastic Jesus, six feet tall, courtesy of the U. S. Air Force? Trouble is, I can't think of many words of Jesus that the Air Force would care to quote. How about 'Father, forgive them, for they know not what they do?' " (Lindskoog 934). A commentary in Science News reveals the fear of some that the Shroud may become a marching banner for fundamentalists, literalists, and rigorists: "If past instances are any guide, they are likely to be used by controversialists who have little or no appreciation of what the pretensions and limitations of science really are" (Thomsen 211). Martin Marty wrote in <u>Christian Century</u>, "leave the dead to bury their own dead, and have the Shroud crowd wrapped up with the deathly cloths. But go ye and produce a Barnabas, or be a Barnabas, being the gospel, disclosing the power of the resurrection" (391).

CONCLUSION

Conclusion

Whether or not one accepts the Shroud as actual proof of the resurrection will ultimately be up to the individual himself, for such proof will remain outside the realm of science. But one must consider all the evidence found by scrutinizing scientists, and consider the odds. Kenneth Stevenson, a Dallas computer engineer, has calculated the odds as 83 million to one that the Shroud belonged to Jesus ("Secularism" 1397).

Real or fake--you decide.

Works Cited

Abbott, Walter M. "The Shroud of Turin." <u>America.</u> 13
    April 1957: 49-50.

Burgess, Anthony. "Notes from the Blue Coast: The Truth of
    the Shroud." <u>Saturday Review.</u> 25 Nov. 1978: 12.

Culliton, Barbara J. "The Mystery of the Shroud of Turin
    Challenges 20th-Century Science." <u>Science.</u> 21 July
    1978: 235-39.

Filas, Francis L. "The Shroud." <u>America.</u> 11 Jan. 1964:
    52-53.

Goldblatt, Jerome S. "The Shroud." <u>National Review.</u> 16
    April 1982: 415-19.

Hart, Jeffrey. "Truth & Culture." <u>National Review.</u> 2
    Sept. 1977: 992-95.

Heim, S. Mark. "The Shroud Study's Unanswered Ques-
    tions." <u>The Christian Century.</u> 4 Nov. 1981: 118-19.

Heller, John H. <u>Report on the Shroud of Turin.</u> Boston:
    Houghton Mifflin, 1983.

"Image Problems for Shroud of Turin." <u>Science News.</u> 17
    Oct. 1981: 245.

"Is This What Christ Really Looked Like?" <u>Life.</u> Feb.
    1984: 37.

Jennings, Jack A. "Putting the Shroud to Rest." <u>The
    Christian Century.</u> 1 June 1983: 552-54.

"Letters." <u>National Review.</u> 26 Oct. 1973: 1146.

"Letters." <u>Science.</u> 1 Sept. 1978: 774.

"Letters." <u>Science News.</u> 13 Jan. 1979: 19.

"Letters." <u>Science News.</u> 20 Jan. 1979: 35.

Lindskoog, Kathryn. "That Man in Question." <u>The Chris-
    tian Century.</u> 19 Oct. 1977: 934.

Maggiori, Dee. "The Shroud of Turin: Imprint of Jesus or
    Forgery?" <u>Fairfield County Catholic.</u> 2 March 1985:
    9-10.

Martin, Frank W. "Is That an Image of Christ? Two Young
    Americans Probe the Shroud of Turin Mystery." Peo-
    ple. 27 Nov. 1978: 27-28.

Marty, Martin E. "M.E.M.O.: Proof-Shroud." The Christian
    Century. 2 April 1980: 391.

Minnery, Tom. "The Shroud of Turin: A Hung Jury." Chris-
    tianity Today. 6 Nov. 1981: 68-69, 88.

- - -. "The Shroud of Turin: Scientists Conclude It's Not a
    Forgery." Christianity Today. 20 Feb. 1981: 44-45.

Murphy, Cullen. "Shreds of Evidence." Harper's. Nov.
    1981: 42-65.

"News on the Shroud." National Review. 10 June 1977: 656.

Nickell, Joe. "The Shroud of Turin--Unmasked." The Hu-
    manist. Jan./Feb. 1978: 20-22.

Otterbein, A. J. "Shroud, Holy." New Catholic Encyclope-
    dia. 1967.

Rinaldi, Peter M. "Requiem for the Shroud." The Christian
    Century. 20-27 July 1983: 20-22.

"Secret of the Shroud." Newsweek. 29 April 1968: 81.

"Secularism: Closing Time." National Review. 27 Nov.
    1981: 1397.

"Shroud of Scientific Question." Science News. 25 April
    1981: 259-60.

"The Shroud of Turin." Newsweek. 10 Dec. 1973: 83.

"A Shroud of Turin Scientist Speaks Out: Evidence that
    Nearly Demands a Verdict." Christianity Today. 7
    Oct. 1983: 62-64.

Smith, Sebastian. "The Shroud." Saturday Evening Post.
    April 1978: 50-51.

Stevenson, Kenneth E. & Gary R. Habermas. "Verdict on the
    Shroud." The Saturday Evening Post. April 1982:
    64-67, 120.

Sullivan, Barbara M. "How in Fact Was Jesus Laid in His
    Tomb?" National Review. 20 July 1973: 785-89.

Teitelman, Robert. "Time Machines." <u>Forbes.</u> 12 Sept.
    1983: 194.

"That Damned Shroud." <u>National Review.</u> 25 Dec. 1981:
    1526-27.

Thomsen, Dietrick E. "Turin Shroud: Nature and Superna-
    ture." <u>Science News.</u> 30 Oct. 1981: 211.

Weaver, Kenneth F. "The Mystery of the Shroud." <u>National
    Geographic.</u> June 1980: 730-52.

Wilcox, Robert K. <u>Shroud.</u> New York: Macmillan, 1977.

Wilson, Ian. <u>The Shroud of Turin.</u> Garden City: Doubleday,
    1978.

Woodward, Kenneth L. and Christopher Matthews. "Christ's
    Shroud." <u>Newsweek.</u> 18 Sept. 1978: 94-95.

Zeik, Michael. "Getting the Picture." <u>Commonweal.</u> 1
    (1984): 341-42.

11
Writing for Business

Business Writing

Even if you do not plan a career in business, some day you will probably want to apply for a summer job, a temporary job, a grant or a fellowship. The principles remain the same whatever your motives. Only the details will change. The most important principle to remember is that your writing, and only your writing, will represent you when you apply for a job or when you write on behalf of a company.

Before you become part of a business, you are responsible for certain kinds of correspondence. The first is the résumé, in which you establish your background and your credentials, while at the same time clarifying your job goals. You should prepare the résumé in advance of needing it. If possible, you should keep it on a computer so it can be updated periodically. There are many services at copy centers and secretarial centers that will keep a copy of your résumé on a disk to be updated as you need it. They will also run off copies on a good quality printer.

The second type of correspondence is the letter of application—applying for a job. Some people make the mistake of thinking this is first, and the résumé second. If you think that way, you will find yourself trying to turn out a résumé under pressure while at the same time turning out a letter of inquiry while under pressure. The results are rarely good.

Recently a publisher in Boston advertised an entry-level job that would have been ideal for innumerable recent college graduates. The publisher received 260 letters in response to the advertisement. The first stage of screening was simple: 200 of the letters were set aside because of spelling mistakes or inaccurate usage and writing. Publishers are not the only employers who use this method. What it means is simple: when you write a letter

304

to a professional audience you have the obligation to make it accurate. That is the first requirement.

After that, of course, you need to make your writing significant and pertinent to the purposes at hand. You might think that one requirement is to be unusually interesting. Perhaps. But I recall being shown a very cute letter from a man who wanted a job with the company that I worked with. He sent a résumé with a picture. He had a family with six or seven children. On the picture it said, "Our Dad produces." My boss, who was responsible for hiring at the level this man was aiming for, thought the letter was cute enough to show around. But he thought it was too cute for the kind of person he would have hired. You may not agree with it, but the world of business is relatively conservative and expects a more solid and dignified approach. That, in a word, means businesslike.

Some companies will want to see samples of your writing. Therefore, it is important to put together a small portfolio of your writing. The purpose will be to show that you can write accurately, that you have some experience in writing, and that your writing reflects intelligence and thoughtfulness. These qualities are prized in business because they mean that you can learn new systems quickly. Slow learners cost businesses too much money.

In your portfolio include a good letter, preferably to a business. A good letter to an editor, or to a legislator will also be valuable. If you have published something in a high school or college publication, include a copy. If you have written a paper or a creative piece that you are especially proud of, then by all means include it. Do not include more than four or five pieces. Make them short, but representative. If you have written something that is especially pertinent to the type of business you are applying to, be sure to include it.

Before you are employed, then, you should learn how to prepare

a résumé
a letter of application
a portfolio of your writing

Once you are in a company you will find yourself with a good many kinds of writing to do. The more responsibility you have in a firm, the more likely you are to be asked to write several kinds of pieces. Most of them will be letters, some will be reports. If you are involved in technical writing as part of your job, you will get special training to satisfy the needs of the task. But in a general situation you may be asked to write

letters of inquiry
letters of response
letters of complaint
monthly, quarterly, and annual reports
memoranda
news releases

KNOWING YOUR AUDIENCE

As in all kinds of writing, if you know your audience, you have a good chance of writing successfully. But more than that, even if you do not know your audience, remembering that you have an audience, that the audience is observing you, and that it cares about what you are writing, is essential to writing successfully in business. And there are times when writing successfully in business is equivalent to *being* successful in business.

Your audience is composed of busy people. They have specific needs and are looking at your writing to assess whether or not you are answering their needs. They do not want elaborate detail, inessential meandering, or colorful writing. They want to read someone who gets to the point and does not waste time. The saying in business is that time is money.

When you write a letter asking about a job, you may spend a good deal of time worrying over details. You may examine every phrase, and you may rewrite many times. But you will not think of yourself as spending ten or twenty dollars an hour for the time it takes you to write. When you get a letter, you must realize that it represents a considerable expense on the part of the business. Usually a person has written the letter, given it to a secretary who has typed it, who in turn passes it on to the mail room, which sorts it. The expense of an average letter, even one that is very brief and uncomplicated, averages $7.50.

Not only is there an expense entailed in writing a letter, but there is an expense entailed in reading a letter in business. Therefore, your most important starting point must be showing respect for your audience's time and talent.

Preparing the Résumé

The résumé is a brief document that has to do a great deal of work. It must be strong, clear, direct, and efficient. It must project the image of yourself that you feel is most desirable, the image you will feel most comfortable with. And, if you want the job badly enough, you will want to take into consideration the image that the company seems most likely to want.

There is a potential problem here for some people. Most of us know that the standard company wants you to dress conservatively. Women know that most businesses want them to wear dresses or suits of a conservative type. You may feel you are compromising yourself by adopting standards that are alien to you. If you are uncomfortable about this, my advice is that you talk with a placement counselor and then to someone who works in a company of the sort you would like to join. Some companies, such as the recent young computer firms that have sprouted up around the country, are very informal in dress and in attitude. They look for people who are good at what they do, and they do not always care how they dress or how conformable they are.

For your own sake, and for your own happiness, you must honestly assess your personal qualities. They may well be included indirectly in your résumé, and this may help you find the job that you will enjoy.

Sometimes a company will listen to your suggestions and make changes that will accommodate you. One young woman took a summer job at the new local mall after her freshman year in college. The job was to serve as the hostess for the mall, greeting children, answering questions from adults. The problem was, she discovered, that the people who hired her expected her to wear a skimpy red outfit with black net stockings. She explained to them that in her opinion this was demeaning to women—no man would be expected to do anything similar. She told them that she was unwilling to wear such a getup, but she also said that she was willing to wear a clown costume—which she happened to have—and to be an entertaining hostess rather than just an enticing hostess. This was a feminist issue with this young woman, and the people who hired her had enough respect for her feelings to agree to her suggestions.

Not only did this person stick to her principles, but she also offered a positive alternative suggestion for her employer. In essence, she perceived a problem and offered a solution. The consideration of how you wish to project yourself to a potential employer is prior to any consideration of how to prepare a résumé and what it should look like.

PREWRITING: MAKING LISTS

What do you need to include on the résumé? First, make some lists, including your educational background. Begin with dates and places, starting with the most recent:

1982-1986 Western Connecticut State University

English major

Dean's list 1985-86

Worked as a stringer for the campus newspaper

Secretary of Mountaineering Club

Published poetry in Conatus, the literary magazine

1980-1982 Joel Barlow High School

The Camping Club

Member of Student Council

Played Tom in Glass Menagerie, our senior play

What experience have you had that shows your interest in working? It is important to scour your memory for any jobs that you performed for others, such as baby-sitting, and part-time work of any kind. Here are some suggestions:

Summer 1985   Intern at the <u>Danbury News-Times</u>; wrote captions for photos; worked in classified dept

Summer 1984   Worked as a cook at Wendy's, Rte. 7, New Milford

Summer 1983   Clerk at Caldor's in the Appliance Department, Rte. 7, Danbury

Summers 1981 and 1982   Mowed lawns with my brother

If you have any special interests or special skills, you should be sure to mention them.

Special interests:

I enjoy writing. I enjoy working with people, especially as part of a team or a group. I enjoy working with customers.

Who can write a good letter of recommendation for you? You will need three references. If possible, one of them should be a former employer. If your college has a placement service, you will be asked to get three references for the dossier that will be assembled for you. It usually includes a transcript of your work in college, with evidence of your graduation, as well as a number of academic references that will stay on file.

Three references:
Prof. Richard Moryl
Dept. of Music
Western Connecticut State University
181 White Street
Danbury, Connecticut 06810

Mr. Darryl Hawkins, Manager
Appliance Department
Caldor's
Route 7
Danbury, Connecticut 06810

RÉSUMÉ

Stanley M. Myers
45 Revolutionary Road
Redding, Connecticut 06875
(203) 555-1212

<u>Career Goal:</u> Entry-level job in publishing.

<u>Education:</u> 1982 to present: Western Connecticut State
University. Graduation: May 1986.
Major: English and American Literature
Dean's List 1985-1986.

1980-1982 Joel Barlow High School

<u>Extracurricular Activities:</u> Reporter on the <u>Campus Weekly</u>,
the college newspaper, 1983-1986. Secretary of Mountaineering Club, 1985-1986. Poetry published in <u>Conatus</u>, literary
magazine, Vol. 18, Spring 1985; Vol. 20, Winter 1986. High
school: Camping Club; Student Council; Tom in Tennessee Wil-
liams's <u>Glass Menagerie</u>, the senior play.

<u>Employment:</u> Summer 1985   Intern in the editorial section of
   <u>The Danbury News-Times.</u>
Summer 1984   Clerk at Caldor's in the Appliance Department,
   Rte. 7, Danbury.
Summer 1983   Worked as a cook at Wendy's, Rte. 7, New Milford.
Summers 1981 and 1982   Mowed lawns.

<u>Special Interests:</u> Writing. Experience with literary maga-
zine, college newspaper, and city newspaper. Portfolio of
pieces may be seen on request. I enjoy working with people,
especially when part of a team.

<u>References:</u> Dossier is on file at the Placement Office, West-
ern Connecticut State University.

<u>Personal References:</u>
Prof. Richard Moryl
Dept. of Music
Western Connecticut State University
181 White Street
Danbury, CT 06810

Mr. Darryl Hawkins, Manager   Mrs. Margaret Gardner
Appliance Department   Department of English
Caldor's   Joel Barlow High School
Route 7   Redding, Connecticut 06875
Danbury, Connecticut 06810

Mrs. Margaret Gardner
Department of English
Joel Barlow High School
Redding, Connecticut 06875

One more thing to consider as you list some of the important items that will go into a résumé is what kind of job you want. Usually, a résumé is prepared with the idea that it will be useful for applying to more than one company. That means you would be wise to list your career goals. If you are applying for a summer job, then you need to be specific—usually you will be canvassing an area and looking for any kind of opportunity the company might have. Be explicit, and say you are looking for a summer job. A review of your past experience might give an employer an idea of your range of abilities.

However, if you are graduating from college and looking for a job leading to a career, then you should have a clear section marked career goals. Most businesses like to know that you have clear goals in part because setting and meeting goals is one of the basic ingredients of doing business wisely.

SAMPLE RÉSUMÉ

See the sample résumé on page 309. Notice that it is on one page. Most employers do not want to read a résumé that is more than one page in length. This résumé, written by Stanley Myers, is designed to use in applying for a career job at graduation time.

Writer's Workshop: The Résumé

1. Prepare a list of the past jobs you have had.
2. Name three people who can be called upon to be references for potential employers.
3. Identify your long-term career interests and your immediate job needs.
4. What are your chief extracurricular activities?
5. Use the information in Items 1–4 to prepare a résumé you could use for applying for a job now or for the summer. Be sure to follow the format described in the text.

The Letter of Application

Every résumé, unless it is handed personally to a potential employer, should be accompanied by a simple, brief letter of application. The purpose of the letter is to introduce you to the employer and to represent you as favorably as possible.

For obvious reasons, this letter, as well as your résumé, must have no errors. Carelessness in proofreading is taken to mean carelessness in general. Even if you do not feel this is fair, you must be certain to read your letter and your résumé with great care. For insurance, have someone you know who writes well read them for you. Sometimes another pair of eyes is needed to spot problem errors.

The tone of the letter of application is crucial. You should always avoid the "know-it-all" tone, which usually offends potential employers. Your letter does not have to prove anything: if you are applying for a job in writing, you need not show off your imagery. Rather, you should try to assess your skills as best you can, and indicate how you feel you can be a benefit to the company to which you are applying. If you know the job for which you are applying, you will want to suggest what qualifications make you suitable for the position. (See the box entitled "Tips: Writing the Letter of Application.")

Tips: Writing the Letter of Application
- It should be accurately typed on good paper.
- It should have your name and address.
- It should indicate which job you are applying for and how you heard about it.
- It should be about three or four paragraphs, and no longer than one page.
- It should sound as if it were personally written to this employer and should not sound as if it is a form letter.
- It should be courteous, but relaxed, and it should not repeat information in your résumé.

SAMPLE LETTER OF APPLICATION

The letter on page 312 was written in response to a specific job advertised in a newspaper. However, if Stanley wanted to write a letter "on the blind" to a publisher, he would have included everything except the reference to the advertisement. Instead, he would have simply inquired as to whether or not there was an entry-level job available at the publisher for which his skills and interests would be appropriate.

It is useful to prepare a letter of application in advance, so you do not have to start from scratch with each of your inquiries. Most of the sample letter, except for the references to audio tapes and to the specifics of Jeffrey Norton Publishers, could be used to write to any publisher. But notice that Stanley found out the publisher's specialties and demonstrated his willingness to do a little homework.

March 19, 1986

Ms. Jan Yates, Vice President
Jeffrey Norton Publishers
Guilford, Connecticut 06437

Dear Ms. Yates:

    Your advertisement in the Sunday <u>Danbury News-Times</u> for a copy-writer for your new series of audio tapes for schools sounds inter-esting, and I would like to apply for the job. I used one of your tapes when I was in high school to help me learn my lines for our senior play. I have asked some of my teachers about your company and they tell me that you publish many different kinds of tapes for schools, colleges, and self-education. One of my professors showed me a bro-chure you sent her for a series of lessons in Italian. It seemed to be a well thought-out program.

    Although I have not had any direct experience with audio tapes, I have worked for my college newspaper writing short feature stories. One of my best stories was based on my riding the baseball bus when we went to Florida to start practicing between semesters. I also worked as an intern for the <u>Danbury News-Times</u> where I learned to write cap-tions for photographs in news articles. I also worked in the classi-fied department and helped customers write good classified ads.

    My writing experience should be helpful to me in filling the job you advertise. I want to begin a career in publishing, and I would like to talk to you about the job. My résumé is enclosed and I will be happy to answer any questions you may have about my background and my writing abilities.

Sincerely,

Stanley M. Myers

Stanley M. Myers
45 Revolutionary Road
Redding, Connecticut 06875

(203) 555-1212

Enclosure

His letter sounds personal, as if it were written especially for Ms. Yates, not as if it were rehashed from a form letter. This makes a great deal of difference to a potential employer.

Writer's Workshop: The Letter of Application

1. Make a list of three jobs advertised in your local college or community newspaper for which you might apply.
2. Write a letter of application for a job you want. If you need a job, then send it, along with your résumé, and see how you do. If you are asked for an interview, then you did this assignment well. If you plan to go to the interview, be sure to read the next section very carefully.

The Interview

Although the interview is not a form of writing, it is worth a few words in passing. Ideally, the letter and the résumé that Stanley wrote ought to result in an interview. The letter and résumé are door openers, and once the door is opened, it is up to Stanley to be able to reveal in himself the qualities that would make him useful to the company.

Here are some obvious recommendations that can prove very useful in an interview:

1. *Share the airwaves:* don't monopolize the conversation, but especially avoid giving one-syllable answers to the interviewer's questions. The interviewer wants to get to know you, so it is essential to use some of the principles discussed in early chapters: develop your ideas when you are given a chance to talk.
2. *Present yourself neatly:* remember that you will have to fit into the company, so be sure to look the way you feel you should for the kind of job you want.
3. *Shake hands and maintain eye contact:* this may sound odd, but interviewers base their reactions on first impressions. That is all they have. A firm, but not bone-crushing handshake is essential. Maintaining eye contact is very important, because many people think they can detect sincerity or insincerity by looking others in the eye. Avoiding eye contact makes you seem insecure, uncertain, and perhaps too timid.
4. *Avoid smoking, chewing tobacco, or chewing gum.*
5. *Be prepared for some tough opening questions:* many interviewers have a set pattern of opening questions. Some might be: What can you do for this company? What makes you think you can do this job? Are you

interested in a career, or are you just trying things out? How far do you want to go in this company? What do you think you will be doing ten years from now? What are your chief weaknesses? Giving these questions a bit of thought ahead of time will give you an edge. Notice that most of them can be answered with an approach based on the means of development that you have already learned in Chapters 4 and 5. That is also true of any question thrown at you.

6. *Do not play hard to get:* you may have other jobs you are interested in, and you may think your prospects are good. But you should interview for a job as if your livelihood depended upon it. You should impress your interviewer with your desire and your willingness to work hard to succeed.

7. *Keep your energy level up:* interviewers are astonished at the lackadaisical fashion of some people looking for a job. They are especially interested in weeding out the slow-moving, slow-thinking, half-asleep prospect. Be sure that you get plenty of rest for the interview. Psych yourself up for every interview.

8. *Be well informed about the company you are applying to:* this means you should know who the president and major officers are, what the company does, and something of its history. It is amazing to consider that most people research the colleges they go to in any one of a number of college guides. But very few graduates will do the same for the companies they plan to work for—and they might be with a company for much longer than four years. Check your library for information in the Dun & Bradstreet Reference Book, Standard and Poor's Corporation Records, Thomas's Register of American Manufacturers, or any other source your reference librarian recommends. Request an annual report of the company and read it. The more you know about the company in advance of your interview, the more impressed your interviewer will be. Your seriousness will be evident. Use the skills you learned in writing the research paper for this part of the process.

Business Letters

In business, much of the minute-by-minute correspondence is done using the telephone. Someone has a thought and calls up to communicate it to someone else who can carry through on it. A product engineer notices that a critical report is missing, so he or she calls up and asks for a replacement. Most phone calls satisfy immediate needs.

However, most phone calls are not recorded and cannot be referred to at a later time. The information that is transmitted by phone is of temporary value, and it cannot be consulted in detail later. The virtue of the business letter is that it can be consulted years later, if necessary, to verify a crucial decision, to clarify a cloudy point, or to modify a previous position. The letter is concrete and historical; the telephone conversation is evanescent and transient. Letters are by no means less expensive than telephone calls. They may cost more, but they also last longer.

You will find that most of the writing you will do in business will fall into several categories:

business letters
reports
memoranda
news releases

You may also be expected to write technical reports of various kinds, depending on your area of expertise and on your training and background. But most of the day-to-day writing done on the job involves communication designed to respond to someone else's need for information. That information may be needed immediately, in which case you would write a letter or a report that would be sent right away. Or it might be needed at some future time, and thus a memorandum may be needed that can be responded to later.

In any event, your first obligation is to provide clear information, and therefore the skills and techniques you learned in Chapter 7, especially process analysis, will be immediately useful in writing for business. Because your obligation is to provide information, you must do all you can to guarantee that your information is accurate, up to date, and clearly presented.

In some cases, your obligation will include the granting or denying of requests from someone else. If you were in a personnel department, you might get inquiries from people looking for a specific kind of employment. Depending on the inquiry you receive, you may grant or deny the request. In this second instance, you must keep in mind that your obligation in that case is not to anything as abstract as information, or even to a given job, but to the person to whom you are writing.

Your aim when writing letters that grant or deny a request must be to respect the feelings and integrity of the person to whom you write. Business is not just a matter of shuffling papers, selling products, manufacturing, and service. It is also a matter of serving human needs. Modern Japan has built a remarkable industrial power whose basis is, in many ways, still closely tied to traditional values of honor, cordiality, and personal respect. These are essential values for doing business well.

Therefore, your knowledge of your audience should be supplemented by a respect for that audience. You should respect both your reader's feelings and immediate needs. Being courteous, thoughtful, and concerned will always achieve one very important goal: it will leave your reader respecting your company. And because your happiness with a firm will often depend on the kind of respect it commands, you not only do your reader a service by being thoughtful, you do yourself a service.

BUSINESSLIKE FORMAT

Each company for which you work may ask a slightly different format for its letters. You will be given models you can follow, but all of them will be variants of a basic form that has served business and industry for many years. The elements of that form are standard:

the return address
the date
the complete name and address of the recipient
the subject of the letter
the body of the letter
the closing salutation

The format of these elements will vary only slightly from company to company.

The Return Address

In most cases, your correspondence will be on company stationery, and the return address will be printed at the top of the first page of the letter. Any subsequent pages will be blank at the top, because it is unnecessary to duplicate the address inside the letter. When you are using unprinted stationery, and when you are privately corresponding yourself with a business or a client, set off your address at the upper right of your letter an inch and a half down from the top:

```
Taken for Granite Antiques
Thimble Islands Road
Stony Creek, Connecticut 06405
August 20, 1988
```

The left margin of the return address is justified (the first letter in each line is in the same column, as illustrated). The left justification is standard in business correspondence because it produces a clean, efficient look, and it is easy to read.

The Complete Name and Address of the Recipient

Because a business letter is a record that will be kept on file perhaps indefinitely, the practice of including the full name and address of the recipient is essential. For one thing, it saves considerable time in follow-up letters because you will not have to pause to look up an address. This is especially important when you are writing to someone for the first time, or to someone whom you will address only infrequently. In some ways, this is the most critical detail in writing business letters. Here is a sample address. Note that it is left justified, set a space down from the return address, and a space above the opening salutation, which ends with a colon. If you were well known to the addressee, you would end the salutation with a comma. The colon is formal, the comma, informal in style.

```
Ms. Arden Cavallaro
2687 Rochambeau Avenue
Bronx, New York 10211

Dear Ms. Cavallaro:
```

The address is left-justified in the first column of the letter, which is the left margin. The left margin should be an inch and a half from the left edge of the paper. The subject of the letter is included beneath the salutation. It is not always necessary, but if you suspect that your reader receives many letters a day, you may want to clarify the nature of your correspondence immediately by establishing what you are writing about. The proper form is

```
Subject: Marble-topped dark oak vanity table
```

Sample Format

The body of the letter is your message. Each paragraph should begin in the left margin. Indentation is not necessary if you set each paragraph apart by a single space. The sample letter on page 318 is very brief to illustrate the usual format of business letters.

The sample letter is composed of a number of short paragraphs, each of which addresses a different topic. The writer reminds the reader of the agreements they had verbally, an important detail should there be a later misunderstanding. The format is suitable whether the letter concerns antiques, the shipment of a million tires, or the commissioning of a new power plant.

BUSINESSLIKE STYLE

Unfortunately, some business writing has gotten a bad reputation. It is marked by a prefabricated, cliché-ridden style filled with openings such as, "Enclosed please find," "As per your request of the 28th instant," "Re yours of the 19th," and closures such as "I remain," "Thanking you in advance, I am," and many more such wooden expressions. When you get such a letter

```
                                        TAKEN FOR GRANITE ANTIQUES
                                        Thimble Islands Road
                                        Stony Creek, Connecticut 06405
                                        August 20, 1988


        Miss Arden Cavallaro
        2687 Rochambeau Avenue
        Bronx, New York 10211


        Dear Miss Cavallaro:


        Subject: Marble-topped dark oak vanity table


        When you were here last you left a $50 deposit on the marble-topped
        vanity table I had on display. We agreed that I would find out the
        color and origin of the marble and send you the dimensions of the table.

        We also agreed that if the marble were domestic in origin, or if the
        dimensions were too large for your space, I would refund your deposit
        by September 1. Well, I had the marble examined by Sol Harmon of Guil-
        ford, an expert furniture restorer, and he assures me that the marble
        is from Cararra, Italy, and that the official color is pearl. He also
        gave me a bottle of marble cleaner which, if you like, you can use to
        help restore the top.

        The dimensions of the table are 29 inches high by 23 inches wide by 42
        inches long. I believe you said you could not use anything more than
        45 inches long, so I think this will fit your space.

        As we agreed, I will hold the table for you until September 1. If you
        will stop in before then and pay the balance of the bill of $250, I
        will immediately arrange shipment of the table. If you have a prob-
        lem, please call me at 481-5157, and we will work out the details.

        Sincerely,

        Stacia Porter
        Stacia Porter
```

you feel that the writer is uncaring. The sad thing is that often people will assume this artificial, stilted style thinking that they are being businesslike. They think the jargon somehow qualifies them as being objective and efficient. (See the box entitled "Tips: Achieving Businesslike Style.")

> *Tips: Achieving Businesslike Style*
> - Establish your audience and your purpose for writing.
> - Use simple and direct language.
> - Keep your sentences short.
> - Focus each paragraph with a topic sentence.
> - Write slowly and carefully.
> - Keep your letters to one page when possible.
> - Avoid any phrases that sound clichéd or stereotypical.
> - Keep your audience's needs uppermost.
> - Be relaxed; imagine speaking the words you write.
> - Be specific in your references: name names, avoid vague pronouns.
> - When appropriate, use a list of important points set off from your text as this list is.
> - Close with explicit suggestions rather than vague promises.

Using a simple and direct style will help give you a sense of confidence and communicate an assurance. You want to communicate with your audience, not impress it. People who impress their audience are putting themselves first; when you put your audience first, then you speak simply, directly, clearly.

Short sentences help you clarify sometimes complex thoughts. The same is true of short paragraphs. A bulky paragraph filled with long sentences can be very uninviting. By thinking about the format of your letter, and keeping it short and direct, you will be helping your audience read your letter efficiently. Most letters can be limited to a single page—but it may take planning.

Once you have planned your letter—you know who is going to read it and why you are writing it—then the process of writing should be slow and deliberate. You may not have enough time in business to redraft a letter, so aim to write it well the first time. You will have the chance to edit lightly, but a major draft may be impossible.

Being relaxed in letter writing often comes with experience. By the time you are expected to write in a business setting, you will have amassed considerable writing experience. Be sure you draw on that experience as you write. Remember that the principles of audience, writer, subject, and purpose, as discussed in Chapter 1, will be useful in all business correspondence. The principles you learned in relation to the means of development are equally pertinent to business writing. Definition, comparison, cause and effect, description, classification, and analysis are all essential to making a letter or a report full, intelligible, and useful.

The Cover Letter

Because the cover letter is not in itself of first importance, it can be short and simple. Usually, the cover letter accompanies a report, such as an annual report, or a catalog, such as a parts or sales catalog, and its purpose is to introduce the item it accompanies or "covers" to the reader.

The cover letter can be summarized as follows:

Audience: someone who has requested the item the cover letter introduces, or someone who is presumably interested, on the basis of research or past experience, in the item.

Writer: the writer is usually unknown to the reader, and although the writer may be of interest to the reader, the writer is objective and distant, although not cold or brusque.

Subject: the subject is usually introduced in the first sentence. It should be clear and specific.

Purpose: the cover letter introduces something. Therefore, its purpose is to give the reader a reason for receiving the item enclosed, a sense of the usefulness of the item, and a clear indication of what might be expected as a response to receiving the item. In terms of the means of development, one can say that the cover letter is responsible for defining the item, describing it briefly, then suggesting the effect that the item might be expected to produce.

A Standard Form

The most common cover letter is usually a form letter. Form letters are addressed to a general public, not a specific reader, and, like certain loose-fitting T-shirts, one size fits all. A sample of a genuine form letter, on the inside front page of a catalog, will serve to identify the genre:

Executive Photo invites you to enjoy the convenience of shopping at home or in your office at the lowest possible prices.

Dear Customer:

The management and staff of Executive Photo & Supply Corporation are happy to extend this invitation to you.

We maintain one of the largest inventories of photographic equipment and supplies. We also carry extensive audio, video, computer, and office equipment at most affordable prices. Because of the limitation of space we cannot list as much of our stock as we would wish. If there is anything you want or need, not shown in this catalog, please call our toll free number (except N.Y. State) and we will be happy to give you the information you desire.

> Sincerely,
>
> Executive Photo & Supply Corporation*

This letter is abbreviated, but not brusque. The reader holds the catalog while reading the cover letter, so a simple introduction is all that is necessary. The cover letter clearly establishes the products that are in the catalog, and it further indicates that the reader can inquire about other items which the company may sell, but which are not listed. The emphasis of the letter is on the extent of the inventory and the low prices, because these, along with the convenience of mail order, are the key factors in ordering from a catalog.

The Personal Touch

A form letter of the kind illustrated by the sample on pages 320–321 is usually written by a specialist and then approved by committee, which is one reason why it seems objective and impersonal. However, the cover letter that an individual might have to produce in a normal business situation would have more of a personal touch, because it would usually result from a direct request. See the sample letter on page 322.

The Letter of Inquiry

Asking questions is the job of the letter of inquiry. When you respond to an advertisement for a position in a firm, you are writing a letter of inquiry. When you ask if a company carries a particular line of products, you are writing a letter of inquiry. When you write such a letter, you usually have needs that are clarified in the process of writing. The more specifically you state those needs, the more effective the letter of inquiry will be.

The main elements of the letter of inquiry can be summarized as follows:

Audience: a business firm that usually will not know who you are or who you represent. That firm may be positively or negatively disposed to provide you with the information you request. You will have to modify your letter in the same way you modified your argumentative prose: to anticipate a negative response before you get it. If you know your reader will be positively disposed toward you, then you can take a more direct course.

Writer: the writer is usually unknown to the reader, and although the writer may be of interest to the reader, unless the request is very unusual or sensitive, you need not reveal more about yourself than

---

* 120 West 31st Street, New York, N.Y. 10001-3485

DAWSON ROLLER BEARINGS
Salem, Massachusetts 01970

July 1, 1986

Mr. Mark Zaitchik
17 Granary Road
Marblehead, Massachusetts 01974

Dear Mr. Zaitchik:

Thank you for your interest in our marine type roller bearings. The project you have set up for yourself in rebuilding the diesel engine in your sloop sounds very challenging. We wish you good luck with it.

I have included our latest catalog of bearings designed to do marine service. Our products have been consistently praised by customers in the field and, as you may know, we have been supplying marine grade bearings to the United States Navy since 1934. You may find the replacement bearings you need, or you may find a suitable substitute.

You may order the bearings you need by contacting your local dealer, Marblehead Marinas, or you may call me directly. We have an engineer who is interested in rebuilding marine diesels, and I am sure he would be glad to advise you if you have questions.

Sincerely,

Frederick Perkins

Frederick Perkins
Sales and Service Department

who you are and what you plan to do with the information you request.

Subject: in a letter of inquiry, your subject may be complex or difficult to explain. It is important to be as clear as possible and as specific as possible in order to help your reader understand what you need.

Purpose: the letter of inquiry requests information from someone. Therefore, one purpose is to establish efficiently and clearly what you need.

Another is to assure the reader that your intentions are positive and good, and that you will not misuse the information.

The letter of inquiry is almost always written to order. The only time you would encounter a form letter of inquiry is in a mass mailing that might ask for statistical information, consumer product information, or customer satisfaction. Again, like most form letters, such a letter would be written by a company specialist, then gone over by a committee of those responsible for working with the information the letter might gather.

Any letter of inquiry you might write would likely arise out of an immediate question or need. Usually you will be inquiring about the availability of a product or a service from a business firm. The letter inquiring about a job is a specialized form of the letter of inquiry.

When you are on the job, the letter of inquiry can be relatively direct and uncomplicated. Usually, you have been presented with a specific problem, and you need a specific solution. Therefore, your letter will be simple, focused, and direct. However, when you are not on the job, your tendency with the letter of inquiry may be to become self-conscious. That usually results in an awkwardness marked by your not knowing quite how to present yourself. Remember that you need say no more about yourself than who you represent and what you plan to do with the information you receive. The sample letter on page 324 shows one approach to the inquiry.

The sample letter describes a complex situation in which the writer is performing a service for a customer as an act of goodwill. You will note that he clearly establishes the model numbers of the items in question, the problem itself, and the question he is asking the reader. He also establishes that the firm he is addressing no longer makes the parts available, and therefore there is no conflict of interest on the part of Dawson Roller Bearings.

The writer of the letter is as specific as his information will permit. Because the enclosure gives all the dimensions of the bearings, as well as the technical data, it is not necessary for the letter to include dimensions and tolerances. However, the letter does include the information regarding model number and application of the bearings.

Another item the writer is specific about is the date when the information is needed. This can sometimes be a delicate issue, because you do not want to sound pushy regarding a response. The fact that the plant closes for two weeks at a given period is important information and will be helpful in guiding the recipient of the letter.

Letter of Response

When you are responding to an inquiry, your obligation is to satisfy your customer or your business correspondent. If you were responding to the inquiry concerning the sleeve bearings a customer wishes to use in a given application, you would need to do several things in advance of responding:

DAWSON ROLLER BEARINGS
Salem, Massachusetts 01970

August 13, 1986

Product Manager
Doppler Diesels
Los Gatos, California 93074

Subject: Replacement drive bearings

Dear Sir:

We have received a request from a customer in Marblehead, Massachusetts, for two of our number 45-8760-331 bearings to be used in rebuilding a vintage Doppler Diesel, Model M-36/SN/8845. As I understand it, these are sleeve bearings which will be used to replace the upper and lower bearings on the main drive shaft.

Our customer does not have drawings or blueprints for his engine, nor am I familiar with that particular model. He has taken some measurements which agree with the dimensions of our bearings, but I want to ask you to examine the descriptive material I have enclosed to see if the tolerances would allow you to recommend using our bearings in this application.

The specification sheets I have enclosed give exact dimensions and tolerances of the bearings, as well as heat ranges and breakdown ranges. If you need more information to make a judgment, I will be glad to provide it.

Our customer has been told by your office that you no longer make the parts that would be used to rebuild his engine. As you probably know, we have been making marine grade bearings for more than fifty years. I would appreciate hearing from you by September 13, since we have a two-week plant closing beginning at the end of September.

Thank you for your attention.

Sincerely,

Frederick Perkins

Frederick Perkins
Customer Service

1. Check the specifications for the original parts used in your engine.
   a. Establish dimensions
   b. Establish tolerances for load bearing and for heat ranges.
2. Check the specifications provided by Dawson Roller Bearings.
   a. Compare the dimensions and tolerances with the original bearings.
3. Establish that there is or is not reason to use the Dawson bearings as a replacement.
   a. If there is reason to use them, respond by saying there is a probable hope of success in replacing the bearings.
   b. If the bearings are not usable in this application, explain why, and make a suggestion for choosing an alternative bearing.

The main elements of the letter of response can be summarized as follows:

Audience: a customer or a member of a business firm—yours or another's. You probably will not know the person to whom you are responding. Your approach to your reader should be courteous and efficient in providing an adequate response.

Writer: you will probably not be known to the reader, and your job will be to establish the fact that you have the credentials to respond with authority on the subject that interests the reader. Your job title may be sufficient to clarify this point. If it is not, you might want to give the source of your information, or else qualify it by pointing out that your expertise is limited.

Subject: at the opening, a letter of response should clarify its subject and indicate what the letter is responding to.

Purpose: the letter of response aims to satisfy the needs of another person as expressed in a letter or telephone conversation. To be sure that you are achieving this goal, you will want to write with the letter or the inquiry directly in front of you. It helps to itemize the requests in a given letter so that you know whether or not you are covering all the needs of your correspondent.

Usually the letter of response is very specific. Someone might ask for information regarding the application of a given product, for information concerning the adequacy of supply of a specific product, or for information concerning the availability of service of a specific sort. The range of possibilities is immense, but in every case the letter of response is designed to serve a need that is clarified in the letter to which you are responding. That is one reason why it is useful to annotate that letter so you can be sure you are providing the appropriate responses.

The sample letter of response on pages 326–327 is addressed to a customer who has asked about the availability of a product that is not listed in the company's catalog. The writer has specified the date of the letter to which she is responding, and in addition has offered a brief summary of its major points. This establishes the fact that the writer understands the questions in the original letter.

MARVEL CABINETS
Industrial Park
Waughtown, North Carolina 27107

August 20, 1988

Mr. Arthur Lopes
145-67 Avery Avenue
Danville, Indiana 46122

Subject: Contemporary light fixture model M-24567-85-9206A

Dear Mr. Lopes:

In your letter of July 30, 1986, you indicate that you are trying to match the dark finish of your antique bathroom cabinet with one of our light fixtures. I will take each of your questions in turn.

1. Your cabinet style, Dark Oak, does have a fixture designed to match it in color and style, but it is the one you have seen, with a skirt-style lampshade for each of the four bulbs. We do not make another style lampshade for this fixture, nor do we make the Contemporary model with a Dark Oak finish.

2. You may substitute our Contemporary model, cited above, but the color of the wood will be light oak.

3. We cannot make Dark Oak wood panels available for the Contemporary model because the design of the panels is very different.

4. You will not be able to darken the oak on the Contemporary model because we treat all our bathroom cabinetry with a special chemical formula to prevent staining, therefore making it impossible to darken the finish without losing the wood grain.

I appreciate your interest in our Contemporary light fixture, and I am sorry that I cannot supply this in Dark Oak. There are two suggestions that I can make, based on my conversation with the woodworkers in our assembly plant in Winston-Salem. The first is to paint the wood with a dark brown oil-base paint. This will result in the loss of the wood grain, but you may find in your application that the tones will be close enough for that not to be a noticeable problem.

The second suggestion requires some woodworking knowledge on your part, or on the part of a carpenter. Since there are only two strips of oak on the fixture, you or a carpenter should be able to replace them with new wood, obtained locally, which can be stained to match your original cabinet.

I am sorry to have to make a suggestion that involves your having to modify our fixture. But at least that way you will have fixtures that match. Our policy, unfortunately, is not to grant a rebate if you choose this latter course of action. However, I have personally talked with people in the design shop and conveyed your request that the Contemporary lighting fixture be made in Dark Oak as well as Light Oak.

Sincerely,

Madeleine Jackson
Vice President

The tone of the letter is very important. Mr. Lopes was very angry to hear that the cabinet he installed in his bathroom did not have a matching light fixture in the color he needed. The company had decided that the contemporary fixtures were to be in light colors, whereas the antique fixtures were to be in dark. Mr. Lopes did not realize his choice of a dark cabinet locked him into using an antique style of lighting fixture that he did not like.

Madeleine Jackson researched the problem with various departments in her company before responding to Mr. Lopes. At least Mr. Lopes knows he has been listened to by someone who is both in authority and in sympathy with his position. But as Ms. Jackson knows, the letter must be disappointing because it still leaves the problem to be solved by Mr. Lopes.

BOILERPLATING

Computers have made boilerplating a standard procedure in business letters. Boilerplating is the preparation of paragraphs that can be inserted into a letter to deal with a problem that recurs frequently. The term comes from the practice of stamping out steel into standard sizes for manufacture into steam boilers. Sheets of similar size could be used in any one of a number of applications in manufacturing the boilers.

Suppose, for example, you were in the automotive business and you discovered that there was a leak in the air conditioner of a given model. Suppose, too, that the manufacturer had discovered this leak and had made allowances for it by providing a free part that solved the problem. If you received correspondence in the form of complaints about this problem, you might have to write a simple explanatory statement over and over again. It would be better to write it once and reuse it. This is boilerplating.

Here is an example of a paragraph that could be inserted into a letter to a customer complaining of such a problem:

```
Saab has discovered that in some of its four-door
models for the years 1984-86, the air conditioner will
leak onto the passenger-side floor. You may make ar-
rangements with your local dealer to solve this problem
with the installation of a plenum that will catch the
moisture from the air conditioner and drain it outside
the car. This installation should take no more than an
hour, and it is a free service.
```

A paragraph of this kind could appear in a letter that treats other subjects and may respond to other needs on the part of the person addressed. Boiler-plating is not appropriate for a mass mailing, because inevitably a form letter is used for such a purpose. However, some institutions, such as universities, hospitals, and charitable organizations, will also create form letters that use boilerplating.

For example, if an institution is keying a drive for raising funds, there may be specific appeals that can be made to individuals within certain groups. There may be an appeal that can be specially made to those of a given age group (which for some institutions can be determined by a computer code of graduating years, or even a record of the recipient's age). There may be an especially important appeal made in terms of the region of the country in which the addressee lives. This can be determined by the zip code. Any number of variables may be relevant in a given letter, and depending on the variant, a boilerplate paragraph may be very valuable.

If you use boilerplating techniques, be sure not to lose the personal approach or the personal touch. You may wish to write some personal letters to friends, for instance, in which you repeat the same paragraphs—perhaps news about yourself. If your friends compare notes and discover you have done so, you will find them properly insulted. They will feel you think they are not worthy of individual letters.

Boilerplating is a useful tool. But it must be controlled. It should not become a substitute for thoughtful correspondence.

Writer's Workshop: Business Letters

Writer's **W**orkshop

1. Write a letter of inquiry to a local large business. If you do not have a personal reason for writing to the company, follow these suggestions:

Ask for an annual report or a description of the principal activities of the firm.

Ask the firm what it feels is the best educational background for its executive employees. You may wish to specify a department: sales, service, manufacturing, personnel.

Ask the firm what kind of personnel it is currently looking for and hiring.

Ask the firm what kind of community support it engages in.

Ask the firm if a representative would speak at a specific student organization to which you belong (clear it with your organization first).

2. Write a letter of inquiry to a government agency.

Ask your town representatives for the town annual report. Ask for information concerning the state's contribution to the annual budget of your town.

Ask your state representatives for the state annual report. Ask for all special reports on the operation of the state universities and colleges.

Ask your state representatives to give you information about the state's arts associations and the programs they have for state artists.

Write to the United States Government Printing Agency in Washington, DC 20002, and ask for a list of the free government pamphlets available to you. Specify a special interest in areas that have particular appeal to you.

3. Monitor your own mail for the next three days (or the last three days). If there is a letter from a business asking for your response, write a letter of response using the models and information described earlier. Your parents or a friend may have such a letter if you do not.

4. If you have recently purchased a product that has some kind of deficiency, write to the company asking for advice on how to have the problem solved.

5. You may adapt any of the earlier suggestions and apply them to an organization or agency at your own school. Write a letter of inquiry or response to a school organization, using the same format and tips provided earlier in the chapter.

The Memorandum

Memorandums serve the purpose of record keeping and communication within a company. Ordinarily, they are not seen by outsiders. They are more than just letters within a company, however, because sometimes a memo is written by someone who will be the only person to read it. It acts as an aid to memory (hence, memo) that may be invoked at a much later date. In that case, it may be a record of a sequence of events, a process that is repeated only three or four times a year, or a record of a telephone conversation or personal chat.

The format of the memo is standardized in each company, which usually prints up forms that satisfy its needs. In general, the heading of any memo will contain four instructions that will look like this:

TO: **DATE:**
FROM:
SUBJECT:

The rhetorical situation regarding memos can be summarized as follows:

Audience: yourself, or an associate in the company. Whether you know the person or not, you should be certain to give his or her title in the first line of your memo because the memo may really be addressed to the person holding that position rather than the person named. If in ten months or so that person moves to another position, your memo will serve to help the next person in that position.

Writer: the writer is usually known to the reader, but because the memo serves as an historical record, the job title of the writer may be as important as who the writer is. Ordinarily, the memo is a strongly decentered document. Personal details are not important.

Subject: the subject is clearly isolated and should be stated in a few words. Memos may or may not be read by administrators, depending entirely on their subject.

Purpose: the memo is designed to keep a record of something or to supply some information needed by someone else in the company.

The style of a memo may be more brisk than that of a letter. Because the point is to keep a record of something, an abbreviated style is adequate. Most people reading memos are pressed for time and expect the memo to distill a great deal of material into the space of a few lines.

Some memos—perhaps most—are very short. Many companies have memo forms that are a half page in length. However, there are also many companies that make provision for complete memos of two or three full-length pages. These are sometimes called memorandum reports. As in most writing that you will do, the length will depend on the needs you are trying to satisfy. But, whatever the length, the memo should be

as short as possible
accurate
clear
focused

The memo, although brief, is not to be treated lightly. Memo writing benefits from the following principles stressed in this book:

- Prewriting: The memo should be generated after a careful review of the principal points it should cover.
- Clustering: This very well may involve the use of clustering and brainstorming or list making.
- Drafting: Because the memo is going to be a permanent record, you should write a rough draft on ordinary paper, then revise and redraft on the appropriate form.
- Development: The memo is especially responsive to the means of development discussed in Chapters 4 and 5. Definition, comparison, cause and effect, description, illustration by example, classification, and analysis all have important roles in the writing of memos. Because the memo is abbreviated, full development is not possible; instead, a brief development with basic information provided is usually adequate.

SAMPLE MEMOS

Service Memo

The memo on page 332 serves as a record of a service call, detailing the fact that a service call was made, what the problem was, and what was done. This will be useful later in the event a second service call is necessary.

SERVICE MEMO   **PARKER TELEVISION CABLE CO.**   **DATE:** 6/26/88

CALL BY: Stanley Hriko
Marty Powell

CUSTOMER: F. Bograc

ADDRESS: 45 Millicent Ave, Apt. 4

COMPLAINT: Distorted picture

DIAGNOSIS: Superband power fall-off; moisture trap

ACTION TAKEN: Cable booster box on pole replaced. Old box was wet so there must be a leak. We found corrosion but only the superband was affected. Low and middle bands were functional, with 10% power drop-off. Could not bring superband up to 100% power. Recommend a follow-up to check for moisture. This may be one of the starling situations we had down the street, where the bird uses the box to crack acorns.

A memo of this kind can be of great use for another service person if there is a later call and the customer is still not satisfied. The second service person can see what has been done, and what should be done later. For example, another service person would look closely for moisture if a further visit is necessary. The service memo is an important historical record; therefore it must be accurate and complete.

Interoffice Memo

When correspondence between various people or departments requires a written record, the appropriate format is the interoffice memo. In most companies, a specific form is provided for you. Again, you must communicate clearly and simply and keep the historical record in mind.

INTEROFFICE MEMORANDUM   DEFORREST COMPUTERS

TO: Sylvia Hampstead   **FROM:**   Walter DeForrest

Title: Head   **Title:**   President

Dept: Customer Service   **Dept:**

SUBJECT: The Rollins Account   **DATE:**   June 10, 1988

Two things: first, Mrs. Rollins dropped me a line complimenting you on the way you handled the mixup on the installation of the Networking IBM-PS/2s. Eventually she wants to connect to Ethernet, and without the appropriate add-on boards, she would have had a hard time.

She did not realize the boards were missing, so you earned some credits with her for getting to her before she was aware of it. Apparently, she really admired your letter and your instructions as well as your speed and honesty. It's nice to hear good news for a change.

The second thing is that I'd like you to talk with Hirsch Yachts in St. Thomas. See if you can find out what software they are using on their PS/2s. Rollins Charters is in a similar business, and we installed the Hirsch system in September, so I know they have got it up and working. By now there must be a market leader in the software these folks use in keeping track of charter orders, availability of boats, captains and crew, and other such details. Boatsoft was the first program available, but I will bet there is a better one out there now. Mrs. Rollins is depending on us to find something for her, and Boatsoft is sending me a sample disk. But see what you can find out from Hirsch.

See if you can get something to me by Friday the 13th.

In a memo of this sort, in which the news is generally good, it is pleasant to see a company person in a higher position praising the work of someone who has taken initiative. The tone of this memo is not as cold as in, say, a service memo, because it is not just an historical record, it is a communication of praise for an employee.

At the same time, there is a job to be done. The president is interested in finding some information that would be of help to a client. Therefore, the second part of the memorandum asks for some specific information. A course of action has been suggested: call the Hirsch company, a yacht chartering company in St. Thomas, to find out what kind of software they use to keep track of their business. The president also wants to be sure that he gets the information he wants in three days. If Ms. Hampstead can get through on the telephone, this should be reasonable.

Telephone Memo

The telephone is indispensable for doing business today. However, it is not a useful business tool if a record of an event is needed. Therefore, the telephone memo is used in many firms to keep track of verbal instructions, commitments, and agreements. There are times when a letter will naturally follow a telephone conversation, in which case the letter will act as a memo. It will mention the date of the conversation and the topics covered as well as any conclusions reached.

Because the telephone memo is kept in a file, it is not addressed to a second party. Instead, it is kept on hand to make sure that a proper understanding was reached. It is usually a relatively brief document. (See the telephone memo on page 335.)

The purpose of this memo is to record the conversation and any action taken on it. If Mr. Weisbroke should make the same mistake again, this memo could be produced to show that a similar event had happened in the past.

The Memo Report

Many reports in business are cyclical. For example, every quarter there must be a sales report as well as a revision of the projected earnings for the year. Businesses operate on four three-month quarters, so it is natural to repeat certain kinds of reports almost as if they were being updated. Stockholders are given formal quarterly reports, but they all begin as memo reports from various departments. The director of investor relations then takes those reports and assimilates them for the investors.

Memo reports are simplified, short reports designed to supply basic information much the way a progress report does. Usually, the memo report is one to three pages in length. As in most other business correspondence, the shorter the better. (See pages 336–339 for an example of a memo report.)

Some of the features of the memo report are

- an abstract: a summary of the report
- statement of purpose: what the report covers
- background
- the use of subheadings to guide the reader

SAUGUS PHOTO-FINISHERS
TELEPHONE MEMO

FROM: Leonie Barton
CONVERSATION WITH: Paul Weisbroke

SUBJECT: Complaint on order
DATE: May 14, 1986

ACTION: Paul Weisbroke called about the Moyles wedding pictures we processed on May 11. He complained that he had ordered the 5 × 7 special but got our 4 × 6 standard prints. These were in addition to the 11 × 14 portraits, which were done to his satisfaction.

Weisbroke has made this complaint before. I checked the original order and saw that he did not specify 5 × 7. I explained that when no size is specified, the default is 4 × 6. He did not have a copy of his original order, and I don't think he believed me. I am sending a photocopy of our copy for his files.

This time I okayed a reprint of the whole order at 5 × 7 with no charge. But I also told him that he must specify the size in writing. I said this to him twice, so if this happens again we will not be responsible.

- recommendations (where necessary)
- follow-up suggestions

The memo report can be very flexible. The tone of this report is relatively relaxed. However, a report of a more formal nature might have a more objective tone. The function of the report is to gather information, record it, and point to the results of the report. This report is the record of a series of events and aims to keep the sequence of things straight. In this sense, it combines some of the qualities of the narrative with those of process analysis. The sequence of events, chronologically, is very significant.

MEMORANDUM REPORT   DEFORREST COMPUTERS

TO: Walter DeForrest, Layne Simpson,   FROM: Sylvia Hampstead
Peggy Marrant, Bob Slote, Francine
Barenboim, Carlos Bamas   DATE: July 8, 1988

ABSTRACT

A telephone conversation with Hirsch Charters resulted in an invitation to survey their computer installation. Their setup was installed by Layne Simpson in September, sold by Carlos Bamas, our local rep. I discussed software applications, their present uses of the system, and their plans for expansion. My recommendations were to add four Model 50s, a Bernouli Box to connect them, and two 2400-band (switchable to 1200) modems to connect the Charlotte Amalie office with St. John and with New York. All this to be done by September.

BACKGROUND

Hirsch installed its system and had it working within a week, relying on Boatsoft (Boston) for its software. Boatsoft Version 3.1 is currently $2400. They supply up to ten free copies to Hirsch for that price. The program is copy-protected and has a lock on it. My original contact with Hirsch was to get information about the software.

MEETING AT HIRSCH

I flew to Charlotte Amalie on July 5 and was met at the airport by Peggy Fernandez, a vice president of the company. She had made arrangements to put me up at Yacht Haven, the hotel adjacent to the marina in which the company operates.

(continued)

I examined the computer setup on July 6, after a good rest. Hirsch
uses the computer system to

> keep their customer accounts up-to-date
> do billing
> pay accounts
> follow up on leads
> keep inventory of boats
> track potential captains and crews
> maintain location of boats
> plan charter dates
> test availability of craft
> plan maintenance
> track age of boats
> compile reports for investors
> customer correspondence
> interoffice communication

The fleet consists of 34 52-foot Morgan yachts, 28 46-foot Morgans,
and a total of 41 other boats of differing dimensions. Plans are to
replace 30 of the Morgans in the next 3 years with a new boat currently
being built in Taiwan. About 75% of Hirsch's business is bare-boats—
chartering to people who know how to sail. The remainder involves
providing a captain and crew for people who wish to charter, but not
sail the boats.

SATISFACTION WITH SYSTEM

Peggy Fernandez was quick to tell me that the system is a lifesaver. I
think she was being witty. Their business has increased by 18% over
the same period last year, but they have not needed any more office
staff, and some of the staff is freed for important work onboard.

(continued)

The first question Peggy had for me is what I recommended for expanding the system. See my recommendations below.

BOATSOFT SOFTWARE

Boatsoft is owned by Zdravko Habl, a former sailor, who was the first programmer to work out a system for charter boats. Hirsch is satisfied with the system and helped Habl refine it so that now with Version 3.1, Hirsch feels the system is functional and efficient. I worked with it only for a short time, and it seemed to be efficient, if a little slow, in most functions. The spreadsheet program was both small and slow, but Hirsch felt it was adequate. The word-processing features are primitive, but again Hirsch's needs are limited in this area. The program shines in data keeping and the billing procedures, the two most important functions Hirsch needs.

We can recommend this software to other clients in the charter business. As far as Hirsch knew, there is one other program, Yachtbol, available, but it is more expensive and seems to do nothing more, except that it is programmed for color. At this moment, I pointed out, the color feature is of no distinct advantage to Hirsch.

NETWORKING

Hirsch is interested in networking its computers. I told them Layne could set the system up for them in two weeks, but they were not aware they could share databases from computer to computer and had been relying on the phone.

Writer's Workshop: The Memorandum

1. Write a memo report to yourself covering the last meeting of one of the extracurricular activities you enjoy.
2. Write a memo recording the principal details of the most recent important telephone conversation you have had. You may wish to record the next conversation and then take notes as you talk.
3. If you have a part-time job, write a memo to your boss, suggesting one way in which your job could be streamlined in order to save money for your company.

(continued)

What this means is that they will need two more computers at their St.
John office, a Bernouli Box in Charlotte Amalie, two more computers
and two modems, one in St. John, another in New York. Carlos is meeting on Friday to begin processing the order. Apparently Carlos had
mentioned networking to them, but Peggy was the key figure and had not
been contacted. My conversation with her began very casually, but
quickly I realized she saw a real need. It was a lucky meeting.

RECOMMENDATIONS

I have recommended they install four Model 50s, a Bernouli Box, and
two 2400-band modems. These are the kind that are switchable to 1200
band. Carlos should go over this with them, since he may have a
slightly different suggestion. Peggy was sure the price range I mentioned would be okay.

One thing I did not think of until I left was that they might make one
of those machines a COMPAQ portable or a Zenith Z181 laptop, so they
can take it on board a boat if need be. Carlos should check that out
with Peggy.

More important, I discovered that a follow-up visit like this one
produced new business and helped cement relations. Could I recommend
that we experiment by visiting a few more recent installations and
seeing what we can learn? This one turned out to be a valuable meeting.

4. Go to your local librarian and ask for information on how you can use
   computer databases to search out information on the activities of businesses you are interested in. After your interview, write yourself a
   memo which includes the important information, so that when you
   are looking for a job, you can refer to it for help.
5. If you belong to a student organization, write a memo to one of its
   officers explaining how you feel membership in the organization can
   benefit the individual and the college community. You need not send
   this (or any other) memo if you do not wish to.

The News Release

The news release is a specialized form of writing that is designed to give public information about an event or activity related to the business. Ordinarily, most businesses have a special department that handles news releases. Indeed, that department regularly handles all the material that is released by the company to the press or media. For that reason, your likelihood of writing a news release is not as great as writing a letter. But often individuals in a business will provide the news department with a release that may be edited or slightly changed to fit the requirements of the local papers.

For most releases, the same rules that might apply to any news article will apply. The journalist's questions, who, what, when, where, why, and how, will guide the writer of releases. But beyond the need to include all the information that is relevant is the need to present the news in an interesting way. Generally, a news release is sent from a company to a newspaper in the hopes that it will be used. If it is used it will not only announce the news and give useful information about the company, but it will also act as a positive form of advertising. People are much more likely to read a news article about a company than they would a paid advertisement. (See the box entitled "Tips: Writing News Releases.")

Tips: Writing News Releases
- Make the release newsworthy. Be sure the information is worth printing and not just a puff for the company.
- Include all relevant information.
- Indicate that the release is current, and that it may be used immediately.
- Provide enough background on the company so that the average reader will know what its products are and what it does.
- Follow a journalist's pattern, putting the most important information first.
- Be sure the release can be printed as is, with no necessary editing.
- Use a standard form that any of the media can use.

SAMPLE NEWS RELEASES

Most companies have a form they use for news releases. If the company does not have such a form, you would prepare the release on company stationery with **For Immediate Release** centered on the top of the page. The release should be typed double spaced and should end with ### or -30-, the traditional journalist's symbols for ending. The release should also have a

ECHLIN   **Corporate Headquarters**
Echlin Inc. 100 Double Beach Road,
Branford, Connecticut 06405   203-481-5751

NEWS RELEASE

For Further Information Contact:

Paul R. Ryder
Director,
Investor Relations

Branford, Connecticut, October 4, 1985—Mr. John E. Echlin, a
founder of Echlin Inc., was inducted on September 26 into the Automotive Hall of Fame in Midland, Michigan. The Automotive Hall of Fame
annually recognizes outstanding business leaders for their significant contributions made to the automotive industry. Mr. Echlin joins
a distinguished group of seventy-seven such leaders, including pio-
neers such as Henry Ford, Alfred P. Sloan, and Walter P. Chrysler. Inducted with Mr. Echlin this year were Edward G. Budd, founder of Budd
Co. and Heinz Nordhoff, who was instrumental in building Volkswagen.

Mr. Echlin and his brother, Earl, started their business in 1924
in San Francisco where they manufactured automotive ignition compo-
nents. Under Mr. Echlin's direction, the company grew to become a
major ignition parts manufacturer known for its innovative marketing
programs.

Today, Echlin Inc. is a worldwide manufacturer of electrical,
fuel, brake, and power transmission replacement parts for a wide variety of motor vehicles, with annual sales of $900 million. Mr. Ech-
lin's emphasis on quality products and customer service, upon which
the company was founded, continues to produce successful results.

Mr. Echlin holds an honorary Doctor of Business Administration
Degree from the University of New Haven, where he served on its Board
of Governors from 1964 to 1973. The John E. Echlin Hall at the university was recently named in his honor.

Mr. Echlin and his wife, Beryl, reside in Boca Raton, Florida.

###

name for the person to contact in the event that the paper or radio or television station wishes to have more information.

The first release (above) concerns the induction of the founder of a
company into the Automotive Hall of Fame. That is a newsworthy event, and
the release explains its meaning while also providing a short background of
the founder and a profile of the activity of the business.

ECHLIN   **Corporate Headquarters**
Echlin Inc. 100 Double Beach Road,
Branford, Connecticut 06405   203-481-5751

NEWS
RELEASE

For Further Information Contact:

Paul R. Ryder
Director
Investor Relations

Branford, Connecticut, October 11, 1985—Echlin Inc. earnings per share for its fiscal year ended August 31, 1986, rose to $1.10. This represents a 4 percent increase from the $1.06 earned in fiscal 1984, and includes 7 cents per share loss due to Echlin's 26 percent equity investment in Raymark Corporation. The per share results take into account the 2 for 1 stock split which was effective August 7, 1985.

Sales in fiscal 1985 totaled $771.4 million, up 12 percent from last year's $689.0 million. Excluding acquisitions made in fiscal 1985, sales of Echlin's comparable operations decreased about 2 percent, and included price increases of about 1 percent. The softness in sales was across most product lines and in most markets, as the motor vehicle replacement parts industry has experienced only a small increase in sales over the last twelve months.

In Echlin's fourth quarter, sales increased 17 percent to $205.0 million, up from $174.7 million last year. The increase was due entirely to acquisitions made in fiscal 1985. Earnings per share increased 11 percent to $0.30; the effect from Echlin's equity investment in Raymark Corporation was negligible.

''We expect the total aftermarket industry's unit sales to show slowly accelerating growth through 1986, rising to about the 4 percent level,'' Mr. Mancheski said. ''Unit sales increases, coupled with the turnaround of acquisitions made in fiscal 1985, should help us achieve our minimal annual growth objective of 15 percent in earnings per share in fiscal 1986.''

This release, from the same company, is a report on earnings for the fiscal year of 1985. Such reports are usually made directly to stockholders, but it is also common to provide business publications and local media with this information. The release is quite frank about the sales figures, indicating that they could be better, and explaining that they reflect an industry-wide pace.

(continued)

Comparative audited results for the fiscal years ended August 31 were:

	1985	1984
Sales	$771,390,000	$688,971,000
Income before taxes	76,646,000	76,017,000
Taxes	31,043,000	32,197,000
Net income	45,603,000	43,820,000
Earnings per share	$1.10	$1.06

Unaudited results for the fourth quarters ended August 31 were:

	1985	1984
Sales	$205,003,000	$174,689,000
Income before taxes	20,654,000	19,197,000
Taxes	8,366,000	8,048,000
Net income	12,288,000	11,149,000
Earnings per share	$0.30	$0.27

All earnings per share data reflect the 2 for 1 stock split effective August 7, 1985.

###

Because news releases are a relatively specialized kind of writing, you need not practice them. However, it is apparent that the means of development, such as definition, analysis, comparison, and possibility are all in evidence in such exercises. In the normal course of things, the raw information that goes into the releases is provided for you, even if you need to conduct interviews or do some research. Outlining is very useful for news releases, especially after a first draft has been written.

The emphasis, however, is always on what is new. By making sure that you focus on what is new and by making it as interesting as possible, you can be more confident that your release will end up in print instead of in a wastebasket.

PART III

Style

Introduction

THE THIRD PART of rhetoric is style, which governs many of the choices you make in writing. The focus of this part will be on word choice, sentence patterning and structure, and paragraphing. In addition, your attention will be directed to the style of certain writers in an effort to recover something of an old tradition, the imitation of fine writers. The great stylists of other ages learned to perfect their writing through the close analysis of the choices of recognized writing "stars." Some of our own great modernists did the same.

The focus on word choices begins with the question of tone and the concern for ways in which you can establish a voice that will suit your purposes. Each of us speaks in a recognizable voice, and learning how to project a voice in prose writing depends on word choice, rhythms of speech, and imagery. Imagery is one of the stylist's most interesting resources, and is often connected with metaphor and other intensifying devices. Most writers know about those devices, and many use them at times, although often unconsciously. The same is true of the distinction between connotation and denotation. We use both these approaches to language, but learning how to control style means learning how to control such devices.

The primary function of the chapter on words is to identify some of the choices that are always available to you as a writer. Then, you will examine the choices individually to see what kinds of results they produce. After you have had some experience using the various devices of imagery and metaphor, you should begin to get a sense of which ones are useful for you and in which situations. You may find that some of them are eye-openers that unleash a hitherto unknown power in your prose but you may also find that some are better saved for a specialized kind of writing.

The chapter on sentence structure explores some of the advanced ways of analyzing sentences. Sentences are classified according to their grammatical structures: the simple, compound, complex, and compound/complex sentences represent variations on a single basic theme. Yet the writer must know these variations in order to exercise the range of choices that should be available in any prose work. An accomplished writer does not use sentence patterns by accident. Instead, most of the choices are examined and reexamined at all stages of composition, from the earliest drafting through all the stages of revision. Knowing what the choices are, seeing how they can affect you as a reader, and then trying them out for yourself can help you see how to improve your later drafts.

The grammatical structure of sentences is only one consideration. The sentence has certain rhetorical forms based on the concepts of parallelism, accumulation, and periodicity. Parallelism involves balancing similar structures one with the other. Accumulation involves establishing a basic structure, then adding elements one after another until the sense of the sentence is complete. A periodic structure involves holding the main point of the sentence off until the end. There are good reasons for using all these rhetorical strategies, and careful study will show you that none is mysterious and all are available to you.

Because paragraphing is so little understood, you will find that examining some current thinking about its structure and principles will help you gain confidence. Naturally, the concept of the topic sentence comes up in our discussion, but you will see that it is a dynamic concept, like many others you have already studied. The style of the paragraph has altered considerably in the last century, which tells us it is a structure that is responsive, like all others, to the demands of the age as well as to the individual writer.

One important stylistic issue concerns the function of the paragraph. You will see that the opening and closing paragraphs of any written piece have specific functions, and they need to respond to these functions in their form. The developmental paragraphs, by contrast, can be more flexible and respond in various ways to the demands of unity and cohesion.

All these concerns—choosing the appropriate words, fashioning responsive sentences, and effective paragraphs—are discussed in Chapter 15, "Imitating Accomplished Writers." In our age the concept of imitation is not widely promoted. There are good reasons for a reluctance to imitate others. But language is interesting for the fact that it is learned by imitation, and writers constantly remind us in their diaries and journals of how much they learned by imitating other writers whom they admired. Famous painters usually have dozens of canvases showing how they imitated the old masters in order to better learn their craft.

Writers—especially apprentice writers—can learn a great deal by studying the choices of skilled professionals. But such study involves a close analysis and careful examination. Chapter 15 helps you learn to make such close studies and then to put your discoveries to good use. Two kinds of examination are demonstrated. The first examines a piece of writing for its subsurface features: for its structure. You then write your own work imitating the structure. The second examines the surface features, such as uses of repetition, choices of metaphors, manner of address, tone, and emphasis. In response to your analysis, you are asked to write your own piece using these tricks of the trade.

Style is an advanced concern for writers. Once you have begun to master the elements of prewriting, invention, and organization, the issues of style reveal themselves to be subtle and intriguing. Invention is a process that you employ at all stages of writing, just as you make organizational choices at all stages. The same is true of all stylistic choices. But we study them at this point because our desire is to respect the richness of opportunity implied in every stylistic choice. In many ways you will be going over familiar ground, but with new eyes and with a new sense of purpose. The hope is that you will make new discoveries that will help your writing be lively and involving.

347

12

Style: Words and Figures of Speech

Tone and Voice

When we talk about tone in written prose, we use an analogy from spoken language. Tone is shorthand for *tone of voice.* Yet because you can use different words to approximate the same meaning, writers make their word choice to convey some of the emotion that lies behind the tone of voice. By altering your tone of voice in conversation, you can project sensitivity, alarm, indifference, haughtiness, pretentiousness, contempt, anger, and apprehension. In writing, the best way to project such a voice is to choose your words carefully and to use expressions that suggest the tone you desire.

Beginning writers usually have so much to worry about as they write, that the thought of modifying their word choice to accommodate subtle shifts in tone rarely comes up. But as you grow more accomplished, you will realize that every word choice tends to project a tone. Your job is to control and choose the appropriate tone for your rhetorical situation.

Your choices will depend on your analysis of your audience, yourself as a writer, your subject, and your purpose in writing. Tone is a subtle item. Sometimes it is difficult to know just what tone a writer establishes. Sometimes you can detect a certain tone—almost like a taste or an odor—but not be exactly sure what it is.

The differences you perceive in tone invariably result from the posture you take as a writer in relation to your audience. If you respect and admire your audience, you will choose from one range of tones. If you have a low regard for your audience, you will choose from another.

IT'S NOT WHAT YOU SAY, BUT THE WAY YOU SAY IT

What are some of the tones your writing can adopt? A few are demonstrated in the following sections. The fact that they can be named shows you how useful they are. They are frequently used by writers to achieve specific

348

effects. However, you must realize that tone is infinite, and this is only a tiny range among the choices you have.

YOUR TONE WHEN YOU ARE ON THE SAME LEVEL WITH YOUR AUDIENCE

Informative: the tone we find in informative prose. There have been some complaints about apathy on campus, and I wanted to help respond to them. Because apathy is a complaint that seems to have been leveled at college students throughout most of this century from time to time, it needs to be put into perspective. Apathy seems to be a behavior that is unacceptable to the person complaining. It also seems to be defined in terms of what is not done: protests are not conducted, charities are not supported, concerns are not aired, interest in certain areas does not seem to exist. Perhaps the time has come to define apathy in terms of what it is, rather than what it is not.

Resolute: an unwavering firmness found usually in argument. You have seen the signs of apathy. Your fellow student turns away from you when you are raising funds for African food relief. You see your roommate ignoring the mail that comes almost daily urging him to vote. You find yourself wondering if giving blood does any good. Things are happening in South Africa, Northern Ireland, and the Middle East. You turn the page. Our generation has dropped out of life. We are the walking "apathetes." If we expect to live in a healthy world we must change our ways.

Conciliatory: a willingness to come to terms, also found in argument. Perhaps some people on modern college campuses are apathetic. I suppose it is true that some people care more about Michael Jackson than they do about apartheid. And maybe some people should take a better interest in politics. Congressional and presidential elections should take a bigger place in our awareness. But my sense is that there really is not much more apathy on college campuses today than there was ten years ago, or even thirty years ago.

YOUR TONE WHEN YOU HAVE A LOW REGARD FOR SOME OF YOUR AUDIENCE

Ironic: saying one thing, but meaning another—hoping that your true audience will understand and that those you criticize will be a bit puzzled by your tone.

I walked around campus yesterday with a bullhorn, shouting out a simple slogan: "Why is this campus bathed in apathy?" You must realize that I did not whisper this slogan, and I put in a full day reciting it. From eight in the morning to twelve noon, I concentrated on lower campus and the dorms. A serious-looking fellow in Harbinger Dorm stared out his window at me for a while, then waved nicely and disappeared. One of my professors looked at me for a moment, then, in between my slogan raising, said, "I missed seeing you in class yesterday."

My only break was for lunch, when I rewarded my sore throat with some lemonade. In the afternoon, I spotted two sunbathing freshmen and gave them my message. They had on headphones with a thundering concert insulating them from me. My own dormmates saw me coming and turned the other way. So far as I can tell, by the end of the day, no one noticed me. No one complained, no one disagreed, no one said anything about my observation. Could this be a sign of apathy?

Supercilious: the word literally means *raised eyebrows,* which results in placing the reader in an inferior social or intellectual position. This does not involve showing contempt, but rather broadening the distance between reader and writer.

Obviously, you haven't observed it. Or if you had, you certainly haven't taken much interest in it. You may even be part of the problem. And the problem is apathy. No one on this campus wants to get involved in worthy causes. Charities that once were staffed to the brim with eager students are forced to place ads in the paper and on the radio. Big Brother associations have reported a 64 percent drop in student applications for a little brother. The Women's Crisis Center is staffed by five weary volunteers, when there are seats for twenty. If you were a Boy or Girl Scout, send your merit badges back to headquarters. Your campus is the epicenter of yawn. Apathy has moved in like a fog.

YOUR TONE WHEN YOU FEEL YOUR AUDIENCE IS ABOVE YOU IN STATION

Respectful: when you show respect and aim not to offend your reader. This is essentially a tone that you might take in writing to your priest or rabbi, your dentist or surgeon, or your lawyer or professor.

Apathy is a problem of this campus, and from what I can tell, it is a problem on other college campuses, as well. *Time* magazine ran an article last fall comparing the campuses of the mid-1980s with those of the mid-1950s and came to the conclusion that there is really very little difference between them.

My own feeling is that college students on all campuses and in every generation spend so much time in their courses and, for some of us, at jobs that keep us in school, that most of us do not have time to become involved in all the activities that we would like to engage in. The result, often, is the appearance of apathy. Personally, I care about apartheid, about the famine in Africa, about the problems of exploiting illegal aliens from Mexico, and quite a few problems beyond those. Yet, I realize that there will always be some apathy on campus.

At this point in your writing, you should have two concerns regarding tone. The first is to be sure it is appropriate to your needs by establishing a clear sense of your audience and your relationship to it. The second is to be sure to know what tone your writing projects—in other words, do not project a tone that is not intended.

This second point is very important. Many people—perhaps all of us—have been guilty at one time or another of hurting someone's feelings by saying the wrong thing. Actually, it may not have been the wrong thing so much as saying it the wrong way. In writing, you can occasionally project a tone you do not really intend. The only way to avoid that is to let what you write sit for a time and then reexamine it.

How can you recognize tone? It comes from reading with an eye for it, comparing your observations of tone with those of others, and keeping track of the tone of pieces you read. It comes down to practice. Students of reading realize that the recognition of tone in a piece of writing can be a difficult skill to learn.

Writer's Workshop: Tone

1. Write a paragraph that adopts the tone of one of the previous examples. Choose your own subject, or choose from the following:

public transportation
living with your parents
college sports
the homeless in America
Japanese products
the equality of men and women

2. Write a paragraph that achieves one of the following tones—as best you can imagine it:

brusque
pious
cordial
authoritative
tentative
folksy

Writer's **W**orkshop

amused
uncertain
distant
friendly

3. Comment on the tone of the following excerpts. Examine the passages for the contrast between formal standard English and colloquial English, for the percentage of sentences that could have issued from simple conversation as contrasted with sentences that seem revised, polished, and refined. Examine unusual words and try to clarify the effect they have on the reader. What name would you give to the tone you perceive? (You may choose from those listed earlier or a name of your own.)

A. He did not go to the college called Harvard, good old Alma Mater as she is. He was not fed on the pap that is there furnished. As he phrased it, "I know no more of grammar than one of your calves." But he went to the great university of the West, where he sedulously pursued the study of Liberty, for which he had early betrayed a fondness, and having taken many degrees, he finally commenced the public practice of Humanity in Kansas, as you all know. Such were *his humanities,* and not any study of grammar. He would have left a Greek accent slanting the wrong way, and righted up a falling man. (Henry David Thoreau)

B. I remember being startled when I first saw my grandmother rocking away on her porch. All my life I had heard that she was a great beauty and no one had ever remarked that they meant a half century before. The woman that I met was as wrinkled as a prune and could hardly hear and barely see and always seemed to be thinking of other times. But she could still rock and talk and even make wonderful cupcakes which were like cornbread, only sweet. She was captivated by automobiles and, even though it was well into the Thirties, I don't think she had ever been in one before we came down and took her driving. She was a little afraid of them and could not seem to negotiate the windows, but she loved driving. She died the next summer and that is all that I remember about her, except that she was born in slavery and had memories of it and they didn't sound anything like *Gone with the Wind.* (Lorraine Hansberry)

C. Squirrels are quite a different thing. The squirrel hunter, at his best, is an American traditionalist. Unlike the quail man, whose hunting manners come, like his shotgun design, from Europe, the squirrel hunter is a rifleman. His exemplars are Boone and Crockett; he moves well and quietly through the woods, or waits with great patience for the chance to place a difficult, well-calculated shot. Ideally, though the practice could hardly be called widespread, the squirrel hunter will use a muzzle-loading rifle—there is considerable trade in them among enthusiasts. And with it he will shoot as the frontiersman did, not to hit the squirrel directly but to bark him—that is, to strike the limb just under the squirrel's head, so that the animal is killed instantly, by concussion, from the impact of the heavy lead ball against the wood, with no visible wound. There is another sort of dedicated rifleman around, it should be added, whose weapon is the most technologically advanced—scoped and custom-fitted, embodying esoteric ballistic principles in the way its ammunition is loaded. But these riflemen are not generally after squirrels; their engineering natures require open shots at long ranges for fulfillment, and it is the groundhog by a distant burrow, the crow on a far limb, which most engages them. (Vance Bourjailly)

D. In our society (it's the only one I've experienced, so I cannot speak for any other) the razor of necessity cuts close. You must make a buck to survive the day. You must work to make a buck. The job is often a chore, rarely a delight. No matter how demeaning the task, no matter how it dulls the senses or breaks the spirit, one *must* work or else. Lately there has been a questioning of this "work ethic," especially by the young. Strangely enough, it has touched off profound grievances in others, hitherto silent and anonymous. (Studs Terkel)

E. A student is often told to think positively. He learns that having a bad attitude about himself will make his performance become lower. In today's environment, if a student is negative about everything, then other people will see that he has no self-confidence. When other people's attitudes are positive, and this student's attitude is negative, then the ones who are positive thinkers will not want to associate with those who are negative thinkers; the positive thinkers do not want to be accustomed to negative thinking (a student sample).

4. Spend some time listening to the conversation of your friends. Then write a paragraph that imitates that conversation as exactly as possible. You may change things—words, expressions, emphases—as you like, but try to make the written prose approximate the spoken prose as much as possible. If you can do this with someone else, exchange samples and comment on the things you have done that work well to achieve the effect of reproducing conversation.

Choices of Words: Levels of Diction

You can often get a powerful effect simply through deciding which words best convey your emotional, as well as logical, meaning. You can choose a formal language, which will produce a formal tone by impressing or by reassuring your reader. That will always depend on who your reader is. Or, you can choose a very informal language—such as slang or colloquial expressions—which will produce a tone that can relax, shock, or amuse your reader. Again, that will depend on who your reader is.

Tone that reveals itself in an unusual or special word choice often depends on imitation. It is something you pick up from someone else. Look at the following sentences and ask yourself where they originate—what kind of person said them, and how do other people begin to pick up their peculiar twist or quality:

1. According to usually reliable sources, the exchange between the secretary of state and Mr. Gorbachev was unusually frank.
2. We need a significant input on the supply side if we expect to impact the situation positively in the near future.
3. Darlings, you really must come by and see me some time.
4. Man, that is one cool dude you got there.
5. Brothers and sisters, do you realize the threats to our peace and our sanity that drugs like crack and cocaine present?
6. You say you have never seen a homeless man? You say you have never seen a woman pushing all her belongings in a shopping cart down a dark street at night? You say you have never seen the poor huddling around a garbage-can bonfire? You say you have avoided the lines of the soup kitchens as they stretch around city blocks?
7. Marsha—they tell me I have only a year to live. But it's not me I'm worried about. It's little Joshua. Where will he go? Who will take him in when I'm gone?
8. Yeah, so I played him tight on third, right up the line, like, and I figured if he's goin' for extra bases it'll be up the line like I said, and whaddya know? I see the ball comin' back at me before I picked up the sound of the bat 'n I scooped it up and pegged to first and got 'im by a hair.
9. Go ahead, make my day.
10. Despite the fact that Mr. Divine is currently incarcerated in a maximum security facility, our position is that he has maintained his innocence because he was unjustly accused, mistakenly convicted, and slanderously maligned by the press. This is a case of media exploitation which has worked to the detriment of one of our city's most noble, self-sacrificing servants. We expect this verdict to be rescinded at the appellate level and we are currently optimistic about tomorrow's decision.

Each of these is distinctive in its own way. Some are echoes of the popular media, especially television and films. Many words and expressions become suddenly popular because a celebrity has said them on a TV series or a talk show. Most of the samples are representations of spoken expressions, such as "Go ahead, make my day." Even the soap opera ("Marsha—they tell me . . .") contributes to our language and we absorb its expressions into our writing and speaking. The newspaper or news magazines, with their equivocations: "usually reliable sources," "normal relations have been resumed," and more, contribute an odd indirectness to some writers' expression. The influence of certain fields—like computers in the second sample—sometimes shows up in your writing.

CULTIVATING A GOOD PLAIN STYLE

Between the extremes of a highly learned, specialized style, and the low-down, gut-bucket style of the streets is a durable, direct, democratic, and supple style that has been developing steadily in English since the early seventeenth century. It is characterized by a word choice that prefers simplicity to complexity, directness to obliqueness, and clarity to obfuscation. It says things simply and directly. It makes clarity a primary goal, so it prefers simple, often short words (as it prefers short sentences), and it avoids pretension.

Some critics of contemporary styles have complained that the plain style is barren and devoid of expression. They feel that a style that uses more Latinate vocabulary should be promoted with the same vigor that we promote the plain style. Their fear is that the plain style homogenizes thought and feeling, and thus recommending it will rob writers of the chance to be expressive and imaginative.

There is some truth to these complaints. Nonetheless, I recommend cultivating the plain style for several reasons. First, it is a very democratic style. It communicates with a wide variety of readers and does not appeal only to the well read or the intellectual. Second, it is flexible and can be used for almost any purposes you have in mind, from informative to narrative to argumentative prose. And third, once mastered, it can be molded and shaped so that it can absorb elements of the high or the low style and remain unusually effective. It is a style that sets off short bursts of a learned or low style with great effectiveness. It is also the style that I have been recommending all through this book.

One reason for advocating the plain style is that it is a tough style with a peculiar resilience. Careful revision can produce a reasonable polish, and—maybe most important—nobody is going to laugh at it because of its snootiness or its refusal to say simple things the way they should be said: simply. Just consider the comic qualities of the following brief essay, "If God Were Process-Oriented." This anonymous piece was meant to be funny, but you can see yourself that the reason it is funny is that it is so close to what some people really write.

IF GOD WERE PROCESS-ORIENTED

If God were process-oriented, the Book of Genesis would read something like this: "In the beginning God created the heavens and the earth." The earth was without form and void, so God created a small committee. God fully balanced the committee by race, sex, ethnic origins and economic status in order to interface pluralism with the holistic concept of self-determination according to the adjudicatory guidelines. Even God was impressed. So ended the first day.

And God said: "Let this committee draw up a mission statement." And behold the committee decided to prioritize and strategize and God called this "process empowerment," and God thought it sounded pretty good. Evening and morning with the second day.

And God said, "Let the committee determine goals and objectives, and engage in long-range planning." Unfortunately, a debate as to the semantic differences between goals and objectives preempted almost all of the third day. Although the question was never satisfactorily resolved, God thought the process was constructive. Evening and morning were the third day.

And God said: "Let there be a retreat in which the committee can envision functional organization and engage in planning, being objective." The committee considered adjustment of priorities and consequential alternatives to program directions. And God thought it was worth all the coffee and doughnuts. So ended the fourth day.

God said: "Let this committee be implemented consistent with the long-range planning and strategy and commitments. And consider the guidelines and linkages and structural sensitivities and alternatives and implemental models." And God saw that this was very democratic. So would have ended the fifth day except for the unintentional renewal of the debate about the differences between goals and objectives.

On the sixth day the committee agreed on criteria for adjudicatory assessment and evaluation. This wasn't on the agenda that God had planned. God wasn't able to attend the meeting, having to take the day off to create day and night, heaven and earth, seas, plants, trees, seasons, years, sun, moon, earth, fish, animals, and human beings.

On the seventh day God rested and the committee submitted its recommendations. As it turned out, the committee recommended forms for things identical to the way God had already created them. So the committee passed a resolution commending God for God's implementation according to the guidelines. It was expressed (very quietly of course) in some opinions that mankind should be have been created in the committee's image.

And God caused a deep sleep to fall upon the committee.

Anonymous

A deep sleep would fall on anyone who had to read this kind of prose day in and day out. One of the problems with such prose—apart from its being silly and high-falutin'—is that it is evasive. It hides what it means. That is a sign of a vicious style. It is often used by evil politicians and people who don't want you to know what is really going on. What, for instance, is "adjudicatory assessment and evaluation"? And would you be happy knowing you had to undergo it?

Unfortunately, it not only sounds reasonable to some readers, it actually sounds attractive. Much of what you take to be a matter of style is basically absorbed by imitation, either conscious or unconscious. Even though we have been recommending a plain style to the students of America for more than a generation, we still see such inflated and pretentious styles.

Style: Some Student Samples

The following sample from an essay on poverty was intended to express strong personal feelings. Do you feel it does?

Poverty is a social problem to the extent that widespread, sustained, collective actions are directed at circumstances widely perceived to cause suffering, damage, or disruption. There is an important distinction to be made between poverty and other social problems. Indigence seems to augment the consequences of social problems while wealth diminishes those consequences. A rich black man is respected much more than a poor one, just as a corporate executive who abuses alcohol is not a Skid Row bum like the alcoholic who can barely afford to buy his liquor. Poverty intensifies all other social problems.

Jim

The most problematic sentence here is "Indigence seems to augment the consequences of social problems while wealth diminishes those consequences." A translation is "Poverty makes social problems worse; wealth lessens them." Indigence is not a bad word, but you can see that it is used here only because Jim doesn't want to say poverty again. Indigence establishes a different tone, but Jim cannot control it.

The two examples, a rich black man and an alcoholic executive, do not come alive in the discussion. Being black and being alcoholic may or may not be social problems—but they are certainly two issues of a totally different order and should not be lumped together here.

Here is what Jim would have wound up with if he had said things in a good, honest plain style:

Poverty is a social problem that requires widespread community action to reduce its suffering, damage, and disruption. Poverty is different from other social problems, such as racism or alcoholism, although such problems are much worse for the poor than for the rich.

Not only is this revision clear, but look at how short it is. It is only 42 words, as compared with Jim's original 96 words. So, you can see just why

Jim was happy going along with his old style: it meant he could get through a 1,000 word essay with only 500 words' worth of ideas. Getting Jim to give up that inflated style was not easy. He knew deep down what its advantages were—provided nobody read what he was writing.

Something else is revealed in the revision: Jim's ideas are not well developed. He thought his method of development was definition, but he sidestepped definition with his long words and evasive approach. If poverty is a social problem, what makes it so? Why is it not a personal problem? I am poor because I do not have any money. Why is that a social problem? Is alcoholism a social problem? Jim just assumes it is. He does not establish why. To do so would demand an analysis of cause and effect: the effects of poverty are evident on the whole society, which has to supply food, clothing, housing, and many other services to the poverty stricken. And there is much more beyond that, but Jim did not write about those further details. His failure to control word choice and tone prevented him from doing the job he set out to do.

Jim aimed for an elevated tone. Consider the authoritative quality of expressions such as, "circumstances widely perceived," "an important distinction to be made," and "Indigence seems to augment the consequences." Silently, in your mind's ear, say these expressions to yourself. Under what circumstances can you imagine using that kind of language? And for what purposes? Because you do not talk that way—and neither does Jim—you would have to be adopting that language and the tone that goes with it. And if so, it is for a purpose.

Imagery: The Language of Specificity and Detail

Jim's word choices have some other interesting consequences. The most important is that they sacrifice specificity and avoid detail. What, for example, is poverty in Jim's sample? What details do you have about it that make it real for you? Is there anything in the paragraph that forces you to the conclusion that poverty is a social problem?

Jim has not used imagery. Imagery is created by language that appeals to the senses. An image is the mental picture we get from language that is detailed, draws a picture, suggests a texture, touches upon odor or taste, or produces the memory of sound in our mind's ear. To make a clear point about poverty, Jim might have resorted to a careful and detailed description to make us understand at the deepest level what he is aiming at.

Just bring to mind the examples of poverty you have seen, whether they are isolated instances of men wrapped in bedraggled old coats sleeping in hallways or subways, or instances of unemployed young men drinking out of brown paper bags, wavering and taunting one another on the street corner in a slum area. If you wanted to make the point that poverty is a social problem, you could hardly do better than to develop such a paragraph through the means of description.

Here is a student sample that makes a very clear point and depends on specific, concrete language to do it. The writer is thinking about images. The language is detailed and descriptive, suggesting a scene that you could actually be part of.

MY NATIVE NEW ENGLAND

California on December 21st: winding lines at suburban post offices; tacos and avocado dip at a Christmas party; colored lights outlining rectangular housefront after affluent rectangular housefront; Christmas cards with holly and snowscapes beside the sandy-beached, palm-treed surfing magazine covers. In California I was not able to convince myself that Christmas was a mere four days away. Huge red and white signs proclaiming "Merry Christmas" on garage doors failed to convince me. The traditional fantasy gingerbread house apparent on the cover of *Good Housekeeping* magazine failed to convince me. And the thin Santas in lightweight North Pole costumes lifting suntanned children onto their laps failed to convince me. I am a New Englander.

In New England we do not stand for hours at the post office waiting to mail Christmas packages. Most of my relatives live within a three-hour radius; most of our gifts are delivered personally. Traditional party fare in New England is just that—traditional. We continue to light the plum puddings of our English forebears. Spicy thick eggnog with a bit of spirit and hot buttered rum complement the abundance of holiday cookies which are rarely store bought and often baked with the cooperation of kids, parents, and grandparents. Colored holiday lights, mere beacons in the dark in the balmy West, gently reflect off of snow-drifted bushes, creating a dual radiance. Christmas card displays blend with the covers of *Yankee* and *Connecticut* magazines, uninterrupted by Sun & Fun journals.

My partiality toward New England has taken a full lifetime to develop. I vacationed as a child in the raw beauty of obscure Maine beaches, jumping in the numbing salt spray and racing my siblings on jagged rocks. Camping deep in the woods of New Hampshire, we watched the orange sun set over an inky purple lake, then retreated to the campfire to tan our marshmallows over flames alive with the same brilliant color. We went ferrying to Martha's Vineyard and dawdled through the streets of specialty shops and pastel houses, leaving sufficient time, of course, to get a quintessential quick burn on the beach. We learned what Boston, Providence, Hartford, and New York had to offer—museums, stage companies, orchestras, shopping—all one to four hours away.

Christine

RELYING ON THE SENSES

Christine's primary appeal is to the visual sense. We *see* the skinny santas, the signs on the garage doors, the colored lights on the tree, and much more. We also are invited to recall the taste of spicy thick eggnog and even to contemplate the feeling of the winter air when we look at the snow on the covers of New England magazines. Then she invites us to feel the numbing Maine waters, and the quick burn on the beaches. She treats us to the heat of the campfire, the roasting of the marshmallows. She is appealing to almost all the senses, with the sense of sound implied in stage companies and orchestras.

The techniques for doing this are treated in full in the section on Developing Narratives: The Fives Senses in Chapter 6, "Narrative Writing." Even when you are not explicitly narrating a story—what is Christine's story?—you can make language come alive by making a direct appeal to the senses.

This is what it means to use imagery in your work. Your word choices need a directive, and the directive is simply to bring your writing alive by avoiding the dull and the abstract, and choosing the vital and the concrete. In order to do this, it takes commitment and the willingness to remember that it should be done, and that when it is done, it makes all writing better. (See the box entitled "Tips: Using Imagery.")

Tips: Using Imagery
- Imagery depends on details and detailed observation.
- Imagery depends on language that appeals to the five senses.
- Imagery makes your writing concrete and specific.
- Imagery is effective because it involves the reader on the level of a shared experience.
- In order to use imagery, you need to remember to use it.

However, there are so many things to keep in mind when writing that it is not a surprise that such a demand might be forgotten. There is a great deal to remember. Demanding a lively imagery from your prose should become one of your chief priorities.

The following student example was the fourth piece out of eight that were written that semester, and it was inspired by reading an essay of E. B. White's called "The Ring of Time." Deborah was a basketball player, and White had motivated her to think about the rituals she went through playing basketball at college and in the neighborhood. She balances general, relatively abstract language in the first paragraph with a somewhat more detailed, descriptive second paragraph. The third paragraph is from page 3 and describes the game in more detail.

BASKETBALL

A performance is a practiced routine. It is a scheduled array of events. There is often little freedom in a performance done for a crowd of paid spectators. The body is free to move as the mind tells it, yet the mind has been conditioned, trained to instruct the body to perform a select pattern of motions. Complete freedom, on the other hand, can be obtained in a practice session. The relaxed atmosphere and the intent of perfecting previously learned skills initiates a response in every performer. No matter what the sport, no matter what the skills, dedicated athletes rely on practice to prepare themselves for the time they will be required to prove themselves.

An example of freedom "in practice" is the pickup basketball game, which can be seen in many neighborhood parks. The players are young and old and come from many different ethnic backgrounds. The teams are picked at random, with those not picked forming a team to challenge the winners. There is no jump ball to signal the start of the game. There are no referees to call the fouls. There is a lot of swearing, a lot of humor, a lot of exhibition. The slam dunks and the rowdy jeers from the players waiting for their chance to show off are all part of the game. A slap on the hand, back, or rear is the only recognition a player receives for a well-executed play. The players push themselves to their limit because they don't want to lose. They are driven by desire and need. They give the game all they've got. After a while they earn respect and find themselves picked for many starting teams.

. . .

The ball is shot, it comes off the rim at an odd angle. More than six hands reach to grab it. The players push and bully each other to get at the ball. One possesses the ball. He gives a quick head fake and dribbles to the opposite corner. He pulls up for a quick jumper. His defender anticipated that move and he reached for the sky as he left his feet to block the shot. His fingertips made contact and the ball, deflected to the right, is caught by his teammate. The sprint down court was expected. The players set up for their offensive moves. John saw Yancy slide behind a defensive player unnoticed. The pass was quick and hard. The ball went down one, two, the dribble stops as he pivots. He lifts his body into the air with startling momentum and effortlessly finger rolls the ball. The rebound of the backboard is perfect. The score is now 7 up.

Deborah

Deborah made an effort to use imagery in this sample. As she moves toward the action that most interests her, she becomes more and more specific. However, if you did not know how basketball is played, and if you did not know specialized terms like *dribble* and *backboard,* much of this could be confusing. The kinds of motions basketball players make could be described more visually, and the noise that always accompanies the pickup game could be evoked. And what about the body contact, the feel of the ball, the heat of the asphalt under your feet? These are an intimate part of the game and could intensify the imagery.

The use of imagery begins with a reliance on the senses. Jim's sample has little imagery because he has ignored his senses when he writes. It is not that Jim could not be more immediate, nor that he could not use images. It is simply that he does not. It has not occurred to him. His peer editor reminded him with a little sign:

Rely on the five senses.

The following passages are from a very accomplished writer, the novelist and essayist, Virginia Woolf. Her work is noted for its skillful style, and for the immediacy of her language. The subject of her essay is the past, her own earliest memories. Obviously, Virginia Woolf was intensely responsive to visual and aural stimuli from earliest childhood. Such sensitivity is natural to all of us, but it is especially noticeable in successful writers.

THE FIRST MEMORY

This was of red and purple flowers on a black ground—my mother's dress; and she was sitting either in a train or in an omnibus, and I was on her lap. I therefore saw the flowers she was wearing very close; and can still see purple and red and blue, I think, against the black; they must have been anemones, I suppose. Perhaps we were going to St. Ives; more probably, for from the light it must have been evening, we were coming back to London. But it is more convenient artistically to suppose that we were going to St. Ives, for that will lead to my other memory, which also seems to be my first memory, and in fact it is the most important of all my memories. If life has a base that it stands upon, if it is a bowl that one fills and fills and fills—then my bowl without a doubt stands upon this memory. It is of lying half asleep, half awake, in bed in the nursery at St. Ives. It is of hearing the waves breaking, one, two, one, two, behind a yellow blind. It is of hearing the blind draw its little acorn across the floor as the wind blew the blind out. It is of lying and hearing this splash and seeing this light, and feeling, it is almost impossible that I should be here; of feeling the purest ecstasy I can conceive.

Virginia Woolf goes on later to talk about the curious melding of the visual imagery and the sound imagery: the colors and the sound of the waves and of the blind. She admits that she really cannot distinguish between the visual and the aural, although they are both intensely powerful in her imagination. For us, distinguishing between them is unimportant. The intensity of the colors she recalls, those of the flowers on her mother's black dress, and the color yellow of the blind, is quite distinct. We definitely perceive these imaginatively. Much the same is true of the splashing of the waves, and of the dragging of the acorn—the weighted end of the drawstring for the blinds—across the floor. These are virtually palpable to us.

Virginia Woolf's conversational tone is also intriguing in this passage. She is not imagining her audience as a group of formal critics, or of student writers, or of anyone distant and objective. Instead, she writes as if she is writing a letter to a friend. She uses pleasant, conversational expressions, such as "I suppose," after she thinks the flowers may have been anemones, and "which also seems to be my first memory," when she admits that the memory of the waves and the blind also seems to be her first memory. Her tone is relaxed and friendly.

Finally, she communicates yet another aspect of the memory, the feeling of pure ecstasy she recalls from lying there in a state wavering somewhere between sleep and wakefulness. This is a feeling state that cannot really be described in sensual detail. We have little or no imagery to convey these feelings. But, you know yourself what it is like to be half between sleep and waking. And if you can imagine that state, then you can add to it the feeling of wonderfulness that Virginia Woolf associates with her memory.

Writer's Workshop: Imagery

1. Write a paragraph that tells us about your earliest memories. Be sure to build your description around an appeal to our sense of sight, sound, touch, taste, and odor. Although it is not essential that you get all five senses involved, be sure that some of them are developed. If you wish to refer back to the tips on description in Chapter 6, be sure to do so.

2. Write a brief passage centered on an activity that you have recently taken part in. It may be a political campaign, a sport of some kind, a social gathering, a party, an academic event, a concert, a family picnic —or anything that you feel you wish to describe to others. Make your language responsive to the five senses.

3. In a brief paragraph, describe the imagery in "The Harbor at Lorient" by Berthe Morisot in the color-plate section. Rely on the information in the box entitled "Tips: Using Imagery," and be as detailed as possible.

4. Write a brief passage that communicates to others your feelings about the region of the country in which you live. Make your language appeal to the senses and create vivid images. Imagine yourself writing for an audience that has not visited your region.

5. Use one of the following subjects (they are obviously abstract in their present form) as the basis of a very brief essay:

poverty	fear
wealth	prejudice
vanity	sexism
peace	delight

Be sure to develop examples, and then use a language that is especially concrete and specific. Make your language create images.

Metaphor: A Mode of Thought _____

Metaphor is a special kind of comparison used to intensify emotional impact. Its effect depends on finding an unexpected relationship between the two things that are part of a comparison. For example, a few years ago, popularizers of science were fond of talking about spaceship earth. This metaphor works very quietly: it compares the earth with a spaceship, although the expression does not come out and say the earth is *like* a spaceship, but just goes right ahead and assumes the comparison. It is a bit surprising, too. It takes an act of imagination to realize that because the earth is hurtling through space the way a spaceship might it can be thought of as a spaceship, too. And if that is so, we are its inhabitants, and we are shooting through space as well.

An assumed comparison, a sense of surprise, and an act of imagination are the key elements of metaphor. The fact that the comparison is not expressed with "like" or "as" makes the metaphor sometimes rather subtle. When you say, "The crowd roared in approval," you may not realize that you are metaphorically comparing people with animals. Lions roar. People shout. The same is true when you say, "His hopes were dashed." Hopes are not physical and cannot be dashed and broken—except metaphorically. When you come home from a date and say, "I struck out," your audience does not assume you were playing softball.

An immense amount of everyday language is metaphorical. Some language theorists have insisted that metaphor rules language. Words themselves are often compressed metaphors, like *daisy*, which is a compression of "day's eye." Everyday expressions such as "He was in pain" are basically metaphorical—this one compares pain to a container that someone can be in. You can see already that none of us can say very much to one another without being metaphorical in some way.

The effective metaphor usually includes a surprise, and the surprise is usually pleasant because it rewards the reader with an unsuspected conceptual relationship. E. B. White wrote about a book by Will Strunk, one of his college professors. He revised it for publication and commented on the job:

The Strunk book, which is a "right and wrong" book, arrived on the scene at a time when a wave of reaction was setting in against the permissive school of rhetoric, the Anything Goes school where right and wrong do not exist and there is no foundation all down the line. The little book climbed on this handy wave and rode it in.

This brief paragraph is like a deviled egg: it's stuffed with metaphor. The word *scene* is a drama metaphor, just as the word *arrived* is metaphoric—

etymologicially meaning "to come to the water's edge." The wave of reaction is a water metaphor, and the word *school* is a metaphor, because there is no genuine school—it is imaginary. "Foundation" is an architectural metaphor, and "all down the line" is a naval metaphor. Finally, to suggest that the little book could climb, compares it with something animate. And the "handy wave" and "rode it in" are two more metaphors. We are left with the image of the little book as a boat. Or perhaps today you get the image of the little book as a daring surfer riding the wave of reaction.

The surprise and pleasure of contemplating this metaphor come from the unexpected relationship of the book to a boat. It is sent out into the world and will sink or float on its own. Like a boat, it is filled with cargo: information on how to use the language. Like a boat, it depends on the tide and on the waves. Like a boat, it depends on the good fortune of the weather. And the weather in the case of the boat is the atmosphere—the general mood of the people who will use the book.

To be effective, metaphor must be controlled. Its effects are sometimes quite strong, even when the reader is unaware that it has any effects at all. This is one of the most impressive qualities of metaphor. It invokes an emotional response without the reader's conscious awareness. It also acts as a means of increasing the specificity and concreteness of language, because the metaphor often compares something abstract with something concrete. The result is that it imparts the same kind of vitality to language that imagery does.

Here are a few metaphoric expressions of varying levels of subtlety. Some will be familiar to you, and a few may be new.

William Shakespeare was in the twilight of his life when he wrote Sonnet 79.

This year the manager of the Oakland Raiders has taken on a great deal more than he can chew.

She was brilliant as a young woman, but in later years her genius went into eclipse.

Parker was simply not a self-starter. He'd clutch at the last minute, and if someone tried to give him a job, he'd put on the brakes and come to a screeching halt. He's going to live life in the breakdown lane unless he radically shifts gears.

Did you see how slowly he thought that out? You could literally see the wheels turning up there.

Are you in the class?

What's up?

Say, that's cool.

His theories are built on sand. They will topple in the first tremor of argument.

The first of these compares Shakespeare's life with the duration of a single day: his last years equal the hours of twilight. The second compares the job of the Oakland manager with that of a diner, who must choose a menu according to his ability to deal with it. The third is a much used solar metaphor—her career resembles the brilliance of the sun until it disappears suddenly, when it resembles the eclipsed sun. Parker is drenched in an automotive metaphor. Again, this is one used very frequently in conversation or writing. Seeing the wheels turning has long been a metaphor for observing someone thinking things out slowly. It derives from the fashion of grandfather clocks, when the clockwork movement was on a level with a person's head. The *in* in the next example is rarely recognized as a metaphor, but it implies that the class is a container capable of holding a person. The direction *up* is metaphoric in the next example: there is no literal up or down in the expression; there is only a metaphoric direction. Notice that contemporary slang inverts the direction: What's going down? The equivalence of anything with cool is metaphoric: there is no specific degree of temperature implied in the expression. Building on sand—or quicksand—is a common metaphor for anyone who does not properly prepare something.

Imagination is essential in employing metaphoric language skillfully. Sometimes, it is a matter of extending a metaphor, as in the example of Parker, and drawing out every last association. In that case, you must have a good reason to use such a metaphor. If Parker were a garage mechanic, or if he had a special relationship with cars, then it might be useful. But if that is not true, then your readers will think you are simply being fancy when you could have been plain.

METAPHOR IS NOT DECORATION

When metaphor becomes decoration it loses its power. It becomes self-conscious. Ordinarily, metaphoric language should be used only when it arises from some logical connection with the primary subject. Then, and only then, is metaphor deep in the fabric of the writing. And when it is deep in the fabric of the writing, it will emerge from a pattern of thought. It will be part of a continuing development of ideas.

Metaphor is much too often the result of an unconscious process that has not been filtered through an artistic consciousness. Many writers use metaphor without knowing they have done so. Usually that results in inappropriate or embarrassing moments. For example, one essay commented on Alabama Governor George C. Wallace's position on racial segregation by saying, "He didn't have a leg to stand on." This student was embarrassed when it was pointed out that the governor is confined to a wheelchair.

Other such unsuspecting uses of metaphor often embarrass apprentice writers because they have not developed a metaphoric way of thinking. Once they do so, however, they find that it is a natural way of thinking, and it is not especially difficult to control metaphors in their writing. Controlling metaphors—not producing them—is the most important part of the process.

Using metaphor wisely and well can help you make your writing more effective. It can stimulate an audience, and it can even help you develop insights into your material. But it is perfectly possible to write well without developing special skills in using metaphors. Most of the student prose you have seen in this text does without metaphors. Much of the professional writing you read does without them.

But—and this is a very large *but*—writers of real power use metaphor as a basic device in their work. They also depend on imagery and they control their language and tone to get the exact effects they wish. But beyond that they use metaphor to probe into the emotional core of their audience. They use it to subtly convince an audience and win it over. In an important sense, they use the audience's beliefs to help them make their own point.

Martin Luther King, Jr.: The Use of Metaphor

There are few better examples of the effective use of metaphor than the writings of Martin Luther King, Jr. He was skilled in almost every stylistic device a writer could employ. And he wrote on behalf of a cause that few Americans could say was wrong: equality. His speech "I Have a Dream" is conspicuous for its use of metaphor. Its very title is metaphoric: the word *have* is used for possession, and one questions how anyone could possess a dream. But we use such an expression in "I had a dream last night," when possession really is not the point. The concept of the dream is used to mean a vision of how things can be in the future. Metaphorically, it is like a dream in that it is only imagined. It is not real. Look at the intensity of metaphor in the first four paragraphs of his speech:

I HAVE A DREAM

Five score years ago, a great American, in whose symbolic shadow we stand, signed the Emancipation Proclamation. This momentous decree came as a great beacon light of hope to millions of Negro slaves who had been seared in the flames of withering injustice. It came as a joyous daybreak to end the long night of captivity. But one hundred years later, we must face the tragic fact that the Negro is still not free. One hundred years later, the life of the Negro is still sadly crippled by the manacles of segregation and the chains of discrimination. One hundred years later, the Negro lives on a lonely island of poverty in the midst of a vast ocean of material prosperity. One hundred years later, the Negro is still languishing in the corners of American society and finds himself an exile in his own land. So we have come here today to dramatize an appalling condition.

In a sense we have come to our nation's capital to cash a check. When the architects of our republic wrote the magnificent words of the Constitu-

The shadow is a metaphor. The beacon light and the flames of injustice are metaphors.

Metaphorically segregation and discrimination have manacles and chains. Poverty is an island; wealth is an ocean; society has corners and the poor are exiles—all metaphorically.

The banking metaphor begins. Justice is "owed" to everyone. Blacks are not having their checks honored.

America is like a bank, but it is defaulting. It issues a bad check. Justice is a bank; it has vaults. Gradualism is a drug, segregation is a dark valley, racial justice is a sunlit path. Racial injustice is a quicksand; brotherhood is a solid rock.

tion and the Declaration of Independence, they were signing a promissory note to which every American was to fall heir. This note was a promise that all men—yes, black men as well as white men—would be guaranteed the unalienable rights of life, liberty, and the pursuit of happiness.

It is obvious today that America has defaulted on this promissory note insofar as her citizens of color are concerned. Instead of honoring this sacred obligation, America has given the Negro people a bad check, a check which has come back marked "insufficient funds." But we refuse to believe that the bank of justice is bankrupt. We refuse to believe that there are insufficient funds in the great vaults of opportunity of this nation. So we have come to cash this check—a check that will give us upon demand the riches of freedom and the security of justice. We have also come to this hallowed spot to remind America of the fierce urgency of *now*. This is no time to engage in the luxury of cooling off or to take the tranquilizing drugs of gradualism. *Now* is the time to rise from the dark and desolate valley of segregation to the sunlit path of racial justice. *Now* is the time to open the doors of opportunity to all of God's Children. *Now* is the time to lift our nation from the quicksands of racial injustice to the solid rock of brotherhood.

Dr. King's mode in this opening can be said to be almost totally dependent on metaphor. There are so many that one is almost dazzled. I have pointed to the most important in the outside margin, but you may certainly see others. One of the most important powers of metaphor is that it makes you believe certain things even independent of what is being said. For example, at the end, when King says segregation is a dark valley and racial justice a sunlit path, he depends on our belief that a sunlit path is brighter, happier, more positive, and more desirable than a dark valley. And as a minister, he holds in the back of his—and your—mind the allusion to the valley of the shadow of death in the Twenty-third Psalm. Metaphor reinforces the positive meaning of his statement.

The same is true of his metaphor of America as a bank dispensing justice. We are well disposed to the thought that justice should be dispensed to all. We, too, realize that if justice had vaults that they would never be empty. If the American nation bounced a citizen's check (a common metaphor) on that bank, then we would definitely know it was not because there was no justice, but because someone did not want to provide it. In itself, that would be an unjust act.

In a sense, the entire nation is like a bank: there is a national wealth and a national store of well-being that should be available to every citizen as a birthright. The fact that the wealth is not shared, that the wealth of opportunity is limited to a few, is also central to the metaphor.

Dr. King has chosen metaphors that are within the experience of virtually every reader: the valleys, the paths, the quicksands and the rocks, as well as the banking metaphor. He begins with a metaphor of light: first in the beacon light of the mariner, designed to guide seafarers in the darkness. But then, he moves to the light of the fire of injustice, which sears its victim. In the case of the metaphor of the beacon light, we have a concrete reference. But in the case of the flames of injustice, we are working with an imaginary flame, a total metaphor. Yet, we instinctively know that if injustice produced light, it would be a fire that would devour the innocent.

METAPHORS AND OCCUPATIONS

Dr. King has depended on a basic approach to using metaphor in writing. He has drawn his primary metaphor from a well-known occupation: banking. One way to help yourself develop a metaphoric way of thinking is to adopt the special language of a given occupation and see how well it works in your writing. In the case of banking, we have useful metaphors: checks, funds, deposits, withdrawals, interest, penalties, loans, notes coming due, vaults, collateral, security, and many more such terms. But note that each term implies a concept and an activity, which the writer can use to good effect. Dr. King uses only a few of these concepts and terms. He needed only a few.

Here are a few well-known occupations and some of the terms appropriate to them. If you wanted to use them as the basis of an extended metaphor such as Dr. King's, they represent ideas, concepts, and comparisons that could be very interesting and suggestive in your writing.

Occupational Metaphors

The Military	Law	Sales
headquarters	court	store
draft	defense	goods
promote	prosecution	deal
march	judge	bargain
attack	jury	inventory
retreat	case	back order
withdraw	plead	catalog
keep watch	complaint	counter
pincer operation	witness	display
platoon	testify	advertise
shore leave	plaintiff	complaint
bivouac	counsel	supply
maneuvers	appeal	demand
ship out	writ	costs
shape up	habeas corpus	profits
bomb	convict	overcharge

Any one of these special terms could be applied metaphorically to something in your writing. Some simple examples:

Military: Because she was engaged, Betsy was not amused at his flirtatious maneuvers.
Law: Ortega knew she thought he was guilty of flirting with her: she convicted him with her eyes.
Sales: He figured that it was not profitable to advertise his feelings around her anymore.

A great many of the most powerful metaphoric passages derive from using the terminology of a given calling or profession in a totally unexpected and unusual context. The very act of doing so implies a kind of surprise and gives the writer a chance at freshness of expression. Dr. King's banking metaphor is an example, as is E. B. White's boating metaphor.

Student Samples: The Use of Metaphor

Using a given profession as the basis of an extended metaphor can be useful for focusing our attention. The following example from a student composition represents the opening paragraphs of an essay on fast food.

"Thirty-nine cent hamburgers." "Forty-nine cent cheeseburgers." "Flame broiling beats frying." "Aren't you hungry?" "America's meat and potatoes." The burger war is raging and the giants of the fast food industry are barraging us with well-placed salvoes which explode with catch phrases and taste-tempting visual images. Until recently, the burger battle has been between Burger King and McDonald's, but now a third major power has joined the fracas. Wendy's! One visit to the newest superpower of the burger world and a person can see that Wendy's possesses several weapons, tactical warheads in other words, that will enable it to become the victor in the war for number one.

The first of these weapons is innovation. Wendy's was the first one to have a salad bar, Burger King eventually followed suit, and McDonald's still has not realized that man does not live on burgers alone. Wendy's most recent innovation is Hot Stuffs, baked potatoes stuffed with such palate-pleasing items as cheese, bacon, and chili. While the jury is still out on Hot Stuffs, at least we know that Wendy's is striving to find new ways to please us.

Jeff

Jeff is less interested in the surprise value of his metaphor than in the simple fact that it works so well. Competition is, as the language we often use to describe it tells us, very much like a war. Therefore, our imaginations help us easily conceive the kind of engagement Jeff describes. In the second paragraph there are only two instances of metaphor: *weapon* and *jury.* The first continues the metaphors of the first paragraph, but the second introduces a new metaphor, drawn from the legal profession. You might ask yourself how effective that is.

The following example is not an extended metaphor, but rather an example of finding metaphoric opportunities. Dolores was simply looking out for appropriate chances to use metaphor.

A walk in the woods is an experience which can yield surprising insights into the life of planet Earth, which carries on day after day despite our general neglect. As we career from home to school or work and back again on the lifeless stretches of pressed pavement we know simply as roads, Mother Nature conducts a symphony of revivification in those woods that you see off to your left. She, however, is not content to merely patch over the furrows in her work as are the state crews in their lumbering, bright orange trucks; nature must rejuvenate itself from the beginning, from the spawning of a fragile seed. How much the cycle of our woodlands is akin to the cycle of our own lives (not to mention essential to it), and how often we simply overlook it—take it for granted except for the occasional weekend hike to climb a mountain on the Appalachian Trail. A walk in the woods is a way to reforge our link with life, a way to return to our roots.

Dolores

Dolores admitted that she was trying a bit too hard, and that her effort was in many ways overwritten. *Career* implies a billiard metaphor that she was unaware of—and it is not really appropriate to the subject of nature reviving itself. *Mother Nature* is already a metaphor, and because it is so common, it is a cliché. Dolores thought she had used it well because she had Mother Nature metaphorically conducting "a symphony of revivification." She soon realized that the metaphor was vague, and that it needed a clearer visual or aural imagery for it to work.

The metaphoric comparison of nature reviving itself and the patching over done by the road crews in the summer is imaginative, but her peer editors felt it was both strained and inappropriate. They did not get anything new or vital about the way nature revives itself, because they already knew that natural things spawn from seeds, and that rejuvenation begins with the smallest thing. Reforging a link with life is a metaphor from the world of chains, and chains have nothing to do with returning to the roots of things— even though the two items are in the same sentence.

Dolores was using metaphor as decoration, not as a way of seeing more deeply into her subject matter. In her own defense, she pointed out that in using so many metaphors she was imitating the variety we find in nature. Moreover, she defended her road-patching metaphor because its inadequacy mimicks the inadequacy of humankind in approaching the job of patching nature.

Though this was not a fully successful piece, she felt she had developed insight into her subject as she wrote. She thought she had written with more vitality than in her earlier efforts.

MIXING METAPHORS

Dolores, in using so many metaphors drawn from different occupations or activities, ended up mixing metaphors. That very expression is a metaphor (mixing is usually applied to physical things). Generally, it is not good form to mix metaphors. Writers have always been warned away from doing so because mixing metaphors tends to dilute their effect. Here is an example drawn from the sentences that illustrated the three earlier occupational metaphors:

> Because she was engaged, Betsy was not amused at his flirtatious maneuvers. Ortega knew she thought he was guilty of flirting with her: she convicted him with her eyes. He figured that it was not profitable to advertise his feelings around her anymore.

This example has the basic problem associated with mixed metaphors: the reader cannot help but wonder why the metaphors are there. What is the point? Could this not be said just as well without recourse to any metaphors at all? The military metaphor by itself might have some point here, but only because of the old concept of the war between the sexes. But the other metaphors are obviously strained. These metaphors are decorative and extraneous. Rather than being a deep, significant element of thought, and a fundamental concept of the writing, metaphor is a fancy detail. It does not imply a richness of meaning.

On the other hand, you can see that Martin Luther King mixes his metaphors rather liberally. Some critics might feel that he could have used fewer

> *Tips: Using Metaphor*
> - Metaphor is not decoration, it derives from a mode of thought.
> - Using terminology associated with an appropriate occupation or activity can be effective in constructing a metaphor.
> - Metaphor can be conceived as extended—controlling an entire paragraph or group of paragraphs—or specific, limited to a single expression.
> - Mixing metaphors is rarely successful—it blurs the metaphoric effect.
> - The effective use of metaphor almost invariably depends on a conscious awareness of its function. Using it badly almost always results from using metaphor without knowing it.
> - Even though the use of metaphor must be conscious, often its effect is unconscious: metaphor affects the emotions of the reader. You must know why you are doing so in order to maintain control of your language.

metaphors and mixed them less vigorously. But Dr. King controls his use of metaphor. None is accidental. Each is effective within its own right. The real problem with mixing metaphors concerns control. If you are mixing metaphors without knowing it, then you are almost certainly likely to lose their potential effectiveness. (See the box entitled "Tips: Using Metaphor.")

Writer's Workshop: Metaphor

1. We hear commonly used metaphors such as, "He really threw a curve ball at me with that exam," "That guy was a monster when it came to calculus," and "I was sunk on that last question." In your journal, jot down a list of the common metaphors you hear in conversation or see in print in the next twelve hours.

2. List expressions associated with the following occupations:

professional sports   medicine and nursing   politics and government

3. Which other occupations or professions have a special language of their own that can be useful for constructing metaphors?

4. Write a brief essay of two or three paragraphs in which the controlling metaphor is drawn from one of the occupations listed in Item 2. Before you begin writing, review the language that is natural to the occupation you choose, and concentrate to develop a mind-set that accepts the language as natural, and that will help you apply it. Write about anything that interests you, or choose from among the following:

going out on a blind date
a visit to the local shopping mall
registering for classes
your last debate about politics
what your choices on TV were the last time you looked
your most recent talk with your parents
what cars will be like when we run out of oil
how the Russians might describe an American college
life in a small town
life in a city

5. In your journal, keep a record of the most interesting uses of metaphor you see in the next day. Show the material to your peer editors and discuss the way you think it works. Find an example of an instance that you feel works well, and one that you feel does not.

Word Choice: Connotation and Denotation _____

Careful writers begin by being careful about their choice of words. They choose them for their

- denotative meaning within the context of the sentence
- contribution to creating an appropriate tone
- contribution to producing imagery
- possible effect on the emotions of the reader
- connotative meaning

The connotative meaning of a word or a group of words is defined in terms of their secondary meanings and the associative values that they excite. Denotation is the dictionary definition of a word. Connotation is like body English. It provides a little extra punch even though it may not change the literal level of meaning.

Connotation is what words imply, not what they necessarily state. The control you have over the implication of words is surprisingly great, although connotation is like the use of imagery and metaphor. In order to use it in your work, you need to remember to do so.

Here is a sample of three ways of saying the same thing: each is a comment on someone who talks more than enough. But for obvious reasons, each expression casts a different light on the same activity. Connotation can change the emotional meaning of a neutral statement:

I am an interesting conversationalist.
Sometimes you talk too much.
He's a blabbermouth.

These are mildly amusing, but they are also commonly heard. You know plenty of people who use the double standard: when you do something it's almost a crime, but when they do it then it's okay.

CONNOTATIVE PROSE IS JUDGMENTAL

Connotative prose can positively or negatively color what you wish to say because it has the capacity for distortion. When you write, ordinarily your purpose is to be objective and straightforward. However, there are times when you know your audience is so much opposed to your thinking that you need to color what you say in order to give yourself a fair chance.

Frankly, that is putting the best face on the matter. The problem with a connotative style is that it is sometimes used to cover up the truth. And that is one goal which, as a writer, you must never have. On the other hand, as a writer and thinker, you need to know when someone else is using connotative language to your detriment.

A Sample: Gloria Steinem

Gloria Steinem sees that language sometimes controls the way we judge some basic issues. For instance, she admits that there have been times when she was embarrassed at the thought of a natural (and in terms of social values, neutral) physical event that women experience: menstruation. She began to think that because "it is a man's world" the concept of menstruation was engineered by a male society to be embarrassing, that everything associated with it is negative. But she then thought that if things were different—if men could menstruate—why then the connotative values of all the language associated with menstruation would be reversed.

IF MEN COULD MENSTRUATE

So what would happen if suddenly, magically, men could menstruate and women could not?

Clearly, menstruation would become an enviable, boast-worthy, masculine event:

Men would brag about how long and how much.

Young boys would talk about it as the envied beginning of manhood. Gifts, religious ceremonies, family dinners, and stag parties would mark the day.

To prevent monthly work loss among the powerful, Congress would fund a National Institute of Dysmenorrhea. Doctors would research little about heart attacks, from which men were hormonally protected, but everything about cramps.

Sanitary supplies would be federally funded and free. Of course, some men would still pay for the prestige of such commercial brands as Paul Newman Tampons, Muhammad Ali's Rope-a-Dope Pads, John Wayne Maxi Pads, and Joe Namath Jock Shields—"For Those Light Bachelor Days."

Statistical surveys would show that men did better in sports and won more Olympic medals during their periods.

Generals, right-wing politicians, and religious fundamentalists would cite menstruation ("*men*-struation") as proof that only men could serve God and country in combat ("You have to give blood to take blood"), occupy high political office ("Can women be properly fierce without a monthly cycle governed by the planet Mars?"), be priests, ministers, God Himself ("He gave this blood for our sins"), or rabbis ("Without a monthly purge of impurities, women are unclean").

Male liberals or radicals, however, would insist that women are equal, just different; and that any woman could join their ranks if only she were willing to recognize the primacy of menstrual rights ("Everything else is a single issue") or self-inflict a major wound every month ("You *must* give blood for the revolution").

Street guys would invent slang ("He's a three-pad man") and "give fives" on the corner with some exchange like, "Man, you lookin' *good!*

"Yeah, man, I'm on the rag!"

This is both amusing and serious. It will come as no surprise to you to know that Gloria Steinem has been a leading feminist for years. She makes a series of value judgments with her language. It is tolerable to us, because although it is naturally distorted for effect, we sense that there is more than a grain of truth to what she says. You can verify that from a few instances: men tend to drink and get rowdy much more than women do, just as they tend to get into brawls more than women do. Yet, the language that describes these activities is much more likely to be filled with praise for male masculinity and aggressiveness than it is to be filled with the kind of condemnation such behavior really merits.

Steinem's prose is judgmental, which is true of any highly connotative prose. She says that if men controlled society and if men menstruated, then they would have invented a language and a set of social mores that would approve, rather than disapprove that activity. Steinem implies that men determine much of the value judgment of the society, and as a result our language reflects male-dominated points of view. She takes the male-dominated language and turns it around.

The effect of her prose is dependent on her choice of words. She plays with advertising jargon: John Wayne Maxi Pads, and so on. Think of the parodic nature of her imitation of the language of Congress, creating a National Institute of Dysmenorrhea. Each of her quoted expressions parodies a kind of standard language that we see in the newspapers and magazines or hear on radio or television. Each is completely turned around in the typical way that parody works. Yet Steinem's purposes as a writer are not limited to comedy: she wants to make her audience think about the seriousness of her underlying point.

Even though connotative prose is judgmental it is not always parodic, as in Steinem's example, nor is it always as pointed and obviously one-sided. Some writers try to moderate, either because they realize they are talking negatively about something that everyone is doing, or because they want to appear to be objective, or at least reasonable.

A Sample: Richard Rhodes

Richard Rhodes, a former Hallmark Cards employee, opens his essay on the greeting card business with a relatively veiled judgment. His title gives him away, of course, because his choice of words includes a judgment: "Packaged Sentiment" implies something negative. Sentiment—emotions and feelings—are natural, unbridled, expressive. To package them connotes a negative, prefabricated approach to a person's emotional life. In fact, that is his point, but notice how carefully he dances around it.

PACKAGED SENTIMENT

Christmas is come, the holiday season, and with it our annual deluge of cards, whose successful dispersal across the land the Postal Service heralds to justify failing us for the rest of the year. "By God, we moved the Christmas cards!" Well, half of all the personal mail moved annually in the United States is greeting cards. Cards for Christmas but also cards for New Year's, Valentine's Day, Easter, Mother's Day, Father's Day, Independence Day and Thanksgiving and Halloween, the official holidays of the American year. And for the occasions greeting-card people call "Everyday," although they are not, births and birthdays, graduations, weddings, anniversaries, showers, vacations, friendship, promotion, hello, love, thanks, goodbye, illness and bereavement, and even to have Thought O'You and for a Secret Pal. We are a nation not of letter writers but of card signers. If the personal letter is long dead, maimed by the penny post and murdered by the telephone, the mass-produced card thrives, picturing what we haven't skill to picture, saying what we haven't words to say. Cards knot the ties that bind in a land where a fourth of us change residence with every change of calendar and where grown children no longer live at home. They show us at our best, if in borrowed finery. You may buy a card made of pansies and doggerel or you may buy a card made of da Vinci and the Sermon on the Mount. Whoever receives it will understand what you meant, and that you meant well.

Rhodes starts off in a neutral way, telling us that the Christmas season is marked by the sending of quite a few greeting cards, but then he surprises us by going on to say that half the personal mail we send or get is greeting cards. That's when he begins to become connotative and judgmental.

When he says, "We are a nation not of letter writers but of card signers," he casts a connotative slur. We implicitly get the point that being a letter writer is superior to being a mere card signer. A card signer is packaging his or her emotions, a letter writer would at least be giving them shape, form, and life. When he says that greeting cards "show us at our best, if in borrowed finery," he is being judgmental. Borrowed finery is not ours; it is not good. We should wear our own finery because this metaphoric finery—words, pictures, expressions of feeling—ought to reveal us to our friends. Instead, we borrow the finery of others and misrepresent ourselves.

Finally, he builds to a connotative crescendo when he tells us slyly that we can "buy a card of pansies and doggerel." Pansies are not your most elegant flower, and doggerel is verse that limps along like a dog. The thought that anyone would settle for crummy verse and inelegant flowers is unpleasant. Yet, he tells us that is what the entire nation is doing. Even those well-meaning folks who aim for a higher tone and choose illustrations by Leonardo da Vinci, and the expressions of Jesus in the Sermon on the Mount are seen somehow to be desecrating those masterpieces. After all, what does Leonardo or Jesus have to do with the banality of greeting cards?

In one paragraph Rhodes has told us what he thinks of the practice of sending greeting cards instead of writing an honest letter. Yet, Rhodes has been much more cautious than Steinem. He has been careful to ease into his connotative excursion so that he would not lose his audience. And he takes a remarkable risk: because half the mail in the country is greeting card mail, many of his readers are greeting card senders.

His purpose as a writer is neither to be caustic nor outrageous in the manner of Gloria Steinem. Yet, his purpose is not just to be informative. After all, who cares if half the personal mail in America is greeting card mail unless there is some judgment to be drawn? The remainder of the essay is largely informative, developed by circumstance: telling us the history of the greeting card; comparison: citing European contrasts and similarities; and then illustration by example, with plenty of discussion and analysis of the samples. The connotative style changes after the first paragraph, but the message returns later in the essay. We get the picture: our national reliance on greeting cards for what we say to one another is not desirable.

A Student Sample

Most connotative prose style is used in argumentation. It is natural to argue a position that you know may not be popular with your audience. And in the process it is natural to try to put your subject in the best possible light. However, it is also important for you to avoid distorting things in order to avoid the truth. (See the box entitled "Tips: Using Connotative Prose.")

> *Tips: Using Connotative Prose*
> - Connotation depends on words that color the meaning of an otherwise neutral expression.
> - Connotation draws on the secondary meanings of words and on associations whose values are positive or negative.
> - Connotative prose is usually obvious to the reader, so be sure to establish a good relationship with your reader if you plan to use this technique.
> - Connotation slants your meaning: it must be used in defense of worthy causes.

The following student sample begins an argument in favor of euthanasia, the killing of a terminally ill patient. The argument is conventional, based to some extent on the concept of freedom of choice. But you will also see that Tom goes to some length to represent the circumstances of the ill as hopeless, including going so far as to beg the question by telling us that anyone who was rational would agree with him.

EUTHANASIA

Due to the many medical advancements of this age, euthanasia is now a very controversial topic. Should a person be kept alive physically, even though he or she is dead, mentally? The most reasonable answer to this question is definitely not. What transpires in the brain is the true essence of life—a body without an active brain is worthless. Such a person is not only worthless to himself, but he is also a heavy burden to others. The emotional and economical strain put on the person's relatives is immeasurable. In addition, these mentally nonexistent people take up valuable hospital and nursing home space that could be used for mentally alive, but physically ill people. Freedom of choice is important in our democratic society, and the choice of life or death should be left up to each individual to decide for his or herself. It is terrible to think that one might spend one's final months, or even years, as a burden to those one loves, simply existing, attached to a machine, unable to think or truly live. Faced with a decision of this type—a merely physical existence, relying on drugs or a machine, or a merciful death—anyone with a rational mind would pick euthanasia.

Tom

Tom colors things here with connotative expressions. Consider how "a merely physical existence" contrasts with "the gift of life," which he could have used in this example. And "a merciful death" contrasts with "the abrupt end of life," both of which mean much the same thing in this context. He did not use the latter words because their connotation is the opposite of what Tom wanted. Think of how he emphasizes words such as *burden* and *strain* in this discussion. The ideas they represent could be expressed in connotative terms that imply the opposite of what he is driving at.

Tom is arguing a position here. But you will see that the expressions cited are not reasons—they are connotative expressions whose slant or coloration is designed to convince. Consider a term describing someone who is brain dead (which is the kind of patient Tom describes) as "worthless to himself." That is not provable, and therefore not a reason for or against Tom's position. Instead, it is a connotative choice designed to slant the argument.

Tom does have several reasons for defending his view: people should have a free choice, even to die; terminally ill patients are a burden on their family; they take up valuable room in the hospitals; it is awful to think you can end up that way yourself. But Tom does not trust his reasons alone. He loads his language in such a way as to use connotation to sway your thinking.

Writer's Workshop: Connotation

1. In the following instances, provide the missing expressions. You job is to say essentially the same thing, but either in a neutral, negative, or positive fashion. In the first example, all three expressions are provided as a model.

Neutral: Margot shops somewhere every day.
Negative: Margot is always out in the stores buying a lot of junk.
Positive: Margot is shrewd and always finds the best bargains.

Neutral: Priscilla and Hector read many books.
Negative:
Positive:

Neutral:
Negative: Lupe wears the weirdest clothes I've ever seen.
Positive:

Neutral: No one volunteered to give blood this month.
Negative:
Positive:

Neutral:
Negative:
Positive: My father says the president is standing tall on Russia.

Neutral:
Negative: Percy was very sly in not volunteering.
Positive:

Neutral: The professor asked Lucy a question.
Negative:
Positive:

2. Write a single paragraph on one of the following subjects. Determine in advance whether your paragraph will be positive or negative in its connotation.

vegetarianism
sexism
college sports as farm teams for the pros
buying on credit
materialism
adopting children of another race
soap operas
banning pornography

3. Rewrite Richard Rhodes's essay on greeting cards to make your connotation positive rather than negative toward the question of having half the personal mail in America come in the form of greeting cards.
4. Rewrite Tom's paragraph on euthanasia so as to make the terminology as neutral as possible. Try not to produce a negative or positive connotation.

13

Style: A Rhetoric of the Sentence

The kinds of sentences you write determine a great deal about the impact of your prose. Your choice of words will establish your tone, clarify your emotional appeal through metaphor and imagery, and perhaps qualify your position through connotation. Your sentences will naturally complement your word choices, and to some extent they contribute to tone, particularly insofar as they may resemble conversational patterns or establish a level of formality. But they also have an important effect in guaranteeing clarity of expression —because the various elements of the sentence, the subject of the main clause or clauses, and the qualifying ingredients of various subordinate clauses and phrases must be in clear and intelligible relation to one another.

Beyond their capacity to clarify meaning, sentences also have the quality of penetrating the unconscious of your reader through their rhythms. Some writers cannot begin to write without sensing an inner rhythm to their opening sentences, then looking for that rhythm to develop throughout the piece. Inexperienced writers find this sometimes astonishing. Yet, time and again, you can see in the work of the best writers a sense of rhythm and timing. Long, undulating sentences will be balanced against sharp, clipped sentences in an effort to establish a pleasing variety of rhythms for the reader. The pacing of sentences implies a concern for prose rhythms.

Sentences, Grammar, and Rhetoric

There are two main ways of classifying sentences. One is according to their structure in traditional grammar; the other is their rhetorical structure. Both of

381

these systems of classification have limits, particularly for an inexperienced writer. One reason this chapter comes late in the study of style is so that some of the main considerations about sentences will already be familiar to you, and so you can see what is useful for helping you fashion more interesting sentences. Being more mature in your thoughts about writing will help you find this chapter more valuable.

It is important to get some basic points clear from the outset. First, the discussion of grammar here is meant to be informative and not prescriptive. In other words, it is to help you learn the descriptive language that refers to specific parts of the sentence so you can discuss it clearly with others. Second, the rhetorical patterns of sentences are often impractical for apprentice writers to concern themselves with. Spending time writing sentences in the three rhetorical patterns that follow is useful mainly for showing you what the resources of the patterns are. It is sometimes said that any writers who start out aiming to write a periodic sentence, for instance, would probably choke on the complications that naturally arise from the patterns. Maybe so. But it is also true that good writers use the rhetorical approaches that follow, and although you may be reluctant to use them often (and probably rightly so), you deserve to know what they are and what they offer.

The material in this chapter does not pretend to tell you what to do. Rather, it offers you some opportunities to study what writers do. You will have chances to experiment with the various approaches to the sentence. Take what you find helpful and leave the rest for later consideration.

SENTENCE CLARITY

Most writers aim for clarity. A good, well-structured sentence is basic to achieving clarity. Things go wrong for the apprentice writer at the level of the sentence, whereas most positive stylistic achievements in prose begin there. The sentence can be discussed in terms of its grammar or its rhetorical function. Both of these merge into one at many levels, but each can be examined to learn how to strengthen the effect of a sentence.

Moreover, there is no predicting exactly what effect what kind of sentence will have on a reader. Each sentence always must be examined in light of what it says, where it is found in a larger composition, and what structural choices are made. All these elements work together to impress upon the reader the exact effect the writer desires.

The grammatical issues regarding the sentence concern themselves with accuracy and completeness. Each sentence needs a clear main clause, and any peripheral clauses or phrases added to that must be attached sensibly and function in logical relationship to the main clause. Therefore the writer needs to have at least a basic understanding of some of the grammatical issues underlying sentence structure. Toward that end, the following section reviews the primary grammatical classifications of sentences and examines their various elements.

The rhetorical effects of a sentence are not divorced from grammatical concerns. If anything, the two are interdependent. Most beginning writers compose sentences of the same general length and structure, which means they are unaware of the demands sentences make upon style. Any person who speaks in a dull monotone will put his audience into slumberland. If you use the same basic sentence structure again and again you will dull your readers into inattention. Readers get tired. They have needs; they have feelings. Good sentences will satisfy those needs and stimulate those feelings, but not unless you are aware of their rhetorical power and their effect on your audience.

THE ELEMENTS OF THE SENTENCE: GRAMMATICAL VALUES

Some Definitions

The sentence is constructed from three basic building blocks. The first, and most indispensable, is the independent clause, which includes a subject and a predicate and stands alone as a complete thought. The second building block is the dependent clause, which also has a subject and a predicate, but which needs the independent clause to complete its thought. Finally, there is the phrase, which is a group of words that usually has either a subject or a predicate, but not both. Sometimes it has neither.

The Independent Clause

Because it does not depend upon something else for completing its meaning, the independent clause can stand alone as a sentence. Each of the following examples from student work is a clause that can be added to either before, after, or within to make it more detailed. But more important, it can happily stand alone.

> Freud developed a strong mind.
> Friends support each other.
> The ERA amendment almost passed.
> Life on a college campus brings out two sides of every student.
> Aristotle once said that myths are more true than history.

The first three examples contain nothing but the basic elements of the independent clause: subject + verb + object. But in the last two examples additional material is included, primarily prepositional phrases in the first sentence, and a noun clause in the second (these are discussed later).

The Dependent Clause

Dependent clauses are incomplete statements having both a subject and a predicate. Most are introduced by adverbs such as *when, after, because, before, until, except for, instead of,* and *although.* Noun clauses, which serve as subjects, objects, or complements, usually begin with *that, whoever, what, whose,* or *which.* They are also dependent and cannot stand alone. Adjective clauses usually begin with *who, which,* or *that.* Most of the time, you will recognize dependent clauses simply because they sound incomplete. You expect another structure to complete their meaning.

Adverb Clauses (underlined)
<u>after Einstein proposed the theory of relativity</u>
<u>until we began to think seriously</u>
my friends went <u>to camp</u>
anyone <u>with the proper credentials</u> could arrive

Noun Clauses (underlined)
<u>Who steals my purse</u> steals trash. (used as subject)
Lincoln saw <u>what his generals could do.</u> (used as object of a verb)
The ancient Romans were <u>a people one could easily admire.</u> (used as complement of a verb)
Michael's gift was appropriate for <u>anyone he wanted to amuse.</u> (used as object of a preposition)

Adjective Clauses (underlined)
President Jefferson, <u>who was respected by his colleagues</u>, was both politician and scientist. (modifying *Jefferson*)
His was an action <u>that brought dissension among us all.</u> (modifying *action*)
Before he knew it, the Black Prince was into something <u>that even he could not control.</u> (modifying *something*)

THE SIMPLE SENTENCE

A sentence requires at least one independent clause. After that, there can be any number of further independent clauses, dependent clauses, and phrases. In describing the various grammatical types of sentences here, the identifying elements are the clauses; the presence or absence of phrases will not affect the naming of the structure of the sentence.

Tips: Using the Simple Sentence
- The simple sentence is reliable and effective; however, like every other kind of sentence, it must not be overused.
- Make it active: use strong, active verbs where possible.
- Use it in contrast with longer sentences that rely on different structures.
- Use it to make a strong point. It has real value as a punch line.

The simple sentence is a single independent clause, often including modifiers and phrases. An independent clause is a structure that includes a subject and a predicate that can stand alone as a complete thought. (See the box entitled "Tips: Using the Simple Sentence.") The very first sentence of Joyce Maynard's essay "Clothes Anxiety" begins with the simplest of simple sentences:

I love clothes.

The subject is *I* and what is predicated about the subject is that it loves clothes. The classic pattern of English is present in this structure:

$$\boxed{\text{Subject} + \text{verb} + \text{object.}}$$

A very durable structure, it does excellent service in the hands of writers as different as William Shakespeare and Annie Dillard. Most writers admire it.

Good writers use the simple sentence to good advantage. The first paragraph of Joyce Maynard's essay has the job of holding the attention of a reader. It has to reveal the subject of the essay and hint at the kinds of things the writer will say about it. As you read it, look for the variety she achieves in her sentences.

CLOTHES ANXIETY

I love clothes. But sometimes I wish I had the kind of occupation that requires a uniform. As it is, I can spend 45 minutes getting dressed, change outfits a dozen times, and see myself reflected in a store window half an hour later, looking a mess. I have tried so hard to master this casual, thrown-together look I see in magazines. But my mascara smudges. My curls never last. Fashion eludes me.

Joyce Maynard

These sentences are carefully structured. The first is the simplest of sentences. The second, beginning with *But* may surprise you. Some people say it is wrong to start sentences with *and* or *but;* however, professional writers often do so, and Joyce Maynard does it twice in one short paragraph. In a structural sense, this is a form of "cheating." By ending her first sentence where she does, she achieves her rhetorical purpose of starting with a sentence that is something like a left jab.

After the first short sentence come three longer sentences. They provide a good deal of background information and begin her development through cause and effect: she tried to achieve the effect of being in fashion, but failed. The longer sentences establish the causes—what she does in order to achieve the desired effects. Then, she reveals in a spurt of short punchy sentences what the effects really are:

But my mascara smudges. My curls never last. Fashion eludes me.

These sentences could be easily joined into one. Just add two commas and an *and.* But the effect of rapid fire would be lost. The sense of punctuating an ending of a series of thoughts would be lost.

Joyce Maynard has thought carefully about what kind of sentence goes where in the paragraph. The most important sentences are usually in the beginning or the end of the paragraph. In the beginning, they establish the atmosphere of the passage; in the end, they stay with the reader and carry over into what follows. In this example, the most important sentences are the shortest. They appear both in the beginning and the end, as if the author were taking no chances on losing her audience. Because she was writing for a general readership in the *New York Times,* she was confident that her technique would be effective.

Writers take the time to revise their work so that they can get the effects they want. John R. Trimble, talking about how writers work with sentences, has this to say:

Each of these authors instinctively understands one of the chief secrets of artful writing: you must keep the reader in a state of near-perpetual surprise. Not suspense, but *surprise.* It's like baseball. A skilled pitcher mixes up his pitches. He'll throw a fast ball, then a curve, maybe a change-of-pace, then a knuckle ball. Skilled writers are constantly feeding the reader's appetite for novelty, be it with a fresh idea, a fresh phrase, or a fresh image .

For Trimble, most writers are like a baseball pitcher: they consciously decide what kind of sentence must go where. Unlike baseball pitchers, writers have a chance to "throw a pitch" again, and the act of revision is the writer's chance to achieve the second time what could not be achieved the first. Instinct and conscious decision naturally work together in all writers, and what a writer lacks in instinct can be made up in thoughtful training.

Types of Phrases

The simple sentences illustrated earlier are short independent clauses, but it is not true that all simple sentences are short. Some are of moderate length, and some are quite lengthy. The term *simple* implies only a single grammatical fact: that the sentence is one independent clause. It can have any number of phrases attached to it. A writer has a great many choices among phrases.

The Prepositional Phrase

A prepositional phrase consists of a preposition and its object, including any modifiers of the object. The use of the prepositional phrase is to clarify relationships and to provide information about the words they modify. In the following examples, the preposition is the first word in the phrase; its object is underlined. Prepositional phases often function as adverbs.

against <u>interpretation</u>
of no real <u>importance</u>
on the right <u>track</u>
between theatrical <u>engagements</u>

Some common prepositions are *in, on, of, at, with, from, to, up, out of, over, above, below,* and *like.* If you look at the text of the preceding pages, you will notice how frequently *in, of,* and *to* are used to make connections between elements of a sentence. They are the mainstays of writing.

The Participial Phrase

The participial phrase consists of a participle (the *-ing* or *-ed* or *-en* form of the verb) followed by its object and modifiers. The participle, object, and modifiers are all connected after a comma with their subject. Their subject is also the subject of the following clause, whether independent or dependent. That way, the subject benefits from a double value: it is preceded by verbal information of some importance, and then it is followed by the all-important predicate.

Some common present participles are *beginning, slowing, having, being, seeing, doing, understanding, looking.* Some common past participles are *anticipated, understood, begun, slowed, seen.*

One usefulness of the participial phrase is that it introduces a verbal action to a sentence without having to become a full verb/predicate structure. In other words, the participial phrase does some of the work of a clause without having to be a clause. Most of us are familiar with the participial phrase as coming at the beginning of a sentence. It establishes a condition or situation, then leaves the rest of the sentence free to make a predication about its subject. The introductory participial phrase always modifies the subject of the next clause. Therefore that subject must follow the participial phrase after the comma that separates them. The most common pattern is

Participial phrase, subject + predicate.

Some examples, with the participial phrase underlined are

<u>Beginning his final descent</u>, the astronaut shut down the engines.
<u>Having made his point clear</u>, Patrick Henry sat down in his chair.
<u>Avoiding the appearance of overconfidence</u>, Dolores sought some way to downplay her successes.

Chester Nimitz, <u>giving the final signal to begin the seige</u>, looked for a way to shorten the battle. (Here the subject comes first, the participial phrase comes second.)

<u>Amused by all the talk about his accomplishments</u>, Felix just smiled knowingly and walked on. (Here, the past participle *amused* is filled out by two prepositional phrases, beginning with *by* and *about*.)

The participial phrase is often, as in the last three examples, composed of a participle and prepositional phrases; they work together. Regardless of its length, the grammatical function of the participial phrase is always the same: it acts as an adjective, modifying a noun or pronoun subject. Therefore the rule about having the subject follow right after the participial phrase (or right before it) is imperative for the sake of clarity. The participial phrase often functions as a smooth transitional element in a sentence.

The Infinitive Phrase

The infinitive is a form of the verb: to + verb. Some infinitives are *to be, to have, to do, to invent, to signify, to insinuate, to suggest, to understand*. Every verb has an infinitive form, and when the infinitive is followed by an object and its modifiers, it becomes an infinitive phrase. Like other phrases, it can have any number of modifiers without losing its identity.

And like the participial phrase, the infinitive phrase draws some of its power from the fact that it depends on a verb form for its identity and therefore adds verbal power to a grammatical structure that is not a verb. Just as the participial phrase is always an adjective, the infinitive phrase is always a noun. It is used as the subject of a verb or as the object or complement of a verb.

Some examples of the infinitive phrase, with the infinitives underlined, are:

<u>to seem</u> deeply concerned
<u>to have</u> an overwhelming interest
<u>to expect</u> another chance
<u>to differentiate</u> among a wide variety
<u>to submit</u> to an entirely stupid ritual

The infinitive phrase can be the subject of the verb. The following infinitive phrases are underlined:

<u>To have three chances</u> was like a dream come true for Tommy.
<u>To be self-assured, poised, and unspoiled</u> seemed the ambition of each of our interesting guests.

The infinitive phrase can also be the object or complement of the verb. Here the entire infinitive phrase is underlined:

Frederick wanted <u>to assure us</u> all of a fair deal.
Penelope demanded <u>to be heard</u> on this issue.
The ambition of our mayor was <u>to clean up the entire city.</u>

The infinitive phrase can be the object of a preposition, and therefore part of a prepositional phrase:

He would not move except <u>to show contempt.</u>

Finally, the infinitive phrase can be used as an adverb, modifying a verb or another adverb:

Mordecai was smart enough <u>to know how to get the most</u> from his abilities. (There are two infinitive phrases in a row here: one modifying *enough* and one modifying *how*.)

The Gerund Phrase

The gerund is another verbal whose form is the *-ing* ending of the participle. But instead of being used as an adjective, it is used as a noun. The gerund *doing, having, sensing, appointing, admiring, buying, selling,* and so on, is completed in the phrase with an object and its modifiers. The gerund can be the subject of a verb, the object or complement of a verb, or the object of a preposition.

In the following examples, the gerund phrase is underlined. When the gerund has a subject, it is in the possessive case: *her* doing; *his* having; *our* deciding; *Martin's* thinking; *Judy's* anticipating; *my* concluding. When the gerund is used as an object of a preposition, it often has no subject. The gerund uses the *-ing* form of the verb to name the action that the verb stands for. Thus, because it is a name, it is a noun; and that makes the *-ing* form a gerund. Here are some examples, with the gerund phrase underlined.

Gerunds as the subject of a verb:

<u>Fred's holding on to the rail</u> could have caused the accident.
<u>Our looking forward to a time when people would value trees</u> is what conservation of the forest means.

Gerund phrases as the object of a verb:

Alastair wanted <u>his loving his brother as himself</u> to be the norm, not the exception.
After my training, I immediately noticed <u>Lucas's breathing</u> from across the room.

Gerund phrases as the object of a preposition:

Martina had a real affection for <u>handling thoroughbred ponies.</u>

No one who was involved in <u>tasting coffee</u> as a profession could have objected to Carlos's decisions about <u>selling the overstock</u> or <u>changing the date</u> for <u>returning</u> the unused portions of the last shipment.

Extending the Simple Sentence with Phrases

The last example of gerund phrases demonstrates that some simple sentences can be longer than one might expect. The expedient of adding phrases to a basic structure of the independent clause can help flesh out the meaning of that clause by providing important information that might otherwise have to come in a succession of choppy, short sentences.

The following simple sentences are all extended by phrases. In each case the type of phrase is identified.

Having served   under the commander   of the third Pacific fleet
  (part.)   (prep.)   (prep.)
for more than three years   before setting sail,
  (prep.)   (prep. with gerund)
Rear-Admiral Smith had immense confidence   in Nimitz's
                    (ind. clause)   (prep.)
knowing   when to give chase   and when to lay   in wait.
(gerund)   (infin.)   (infin.)   (prep.)

I once went   to Kansas City   for the express purpose
(ind. clause)   (prep.)   (prep.)
of making a grand tour   of its great restaurants.
(prep. with gerund)   (prep.)

Calvin Trillin

You will quickly come   to detect the difference
  (ind. clause)   (infin.)
between a true surgeon and a mere product   of the system.
  (prep.)   (prep.)

Richard Selzer

THE COMPOUND SENTENCE

Joining together two or more independent clauses produces a compound sentence. The compound sentence does not include any dependent clauses, although it may contain any number of phrases. Usually, the signal for such sentences comes in the form of a coordinating conjunction: *and, or, but, nor, for.* Or, it might come in the form of punctuation, the semicolon (;) or the colon (:).

Because each independent clause could stand alone as a sentence if it were detached, joining them together must always have a purpose. One purpose is to make a meaningful connection that the reader might otherwise be unaware of. The significance of the connection need not be explained; it is implied. (See the box entitled "Tips: Using the Compound Sentence.")

Tips: Using the Compound Sentence
- Connect independent clauses of generally equal importance or value.
- Make the reasons for the connection apparent: understand them yourself first.
- Remember that without the relief of other kinds of sentences, the compound sentence can become flabby and dull.

V. S. Naipaul, in the following opening paragraph, has a very good reason for relying on compound sentences: he is making a personal connection with another culture. His writing connects us both to him, through his reactions, and to Teheran, through his impressions and reportage. The compound sentence, then, serves a rhetorical purpose: to underscore the point of his essay.

We made a technical stop at Kuwait, to refuel; no one left the plane. It was dark, but dawn was not far off. The light began to come; the night vanished. And we saw that the airport—such a pattern of electric lights from above—had been built on sand. The air that came through the ventilators was warm. It was 40 degrees Centigrade outside, 104 Fahrenheit, and the true day had not begun.

We can schematize the first three sentences; each independent clause is placed on a separate line here for clarity:

> We made a technical stop at Kuwait
> no one left the plane
> It was dark
> dawn was not far off
> The light began to come
> the night vanished

Naipaul uses conjunctions and punctuation to relate stopping and staying, dark and light, the airport from above and from ground level. The warmth of 104 degrees Fahrenheit and the heat that would follow when the true day arrived is also implied in the last sentence. This opening passage establishes critical connections at the heart of the essay. Instead of relying on the short, jabbing sentences that make one declaration after another, as in Joyce Maynard's work, Naipaul relies upon connectives, both stated and implied. There is in his paragraph less a sense of urgency, more a sense of slow, unraveling discovery. Maynard implies she knows exactly what the nature of her clothes anxiety is, but Naipaul implies that the nature of his experience in Iran is still unfolding.

THE COMPLEX SENTENCE

The complex sentence has one independent clause and at least one dependent clause. Sometimes, complex sentences have numerous dependent clauses, and they can become involved and sinewy. You may have to read them twice, or at least to ponder them carefully. Their effect is usually the opposite of the simple sentence. They cause you to reflect and consider, perhaps even to probe and examine.

They are useful for raising important issues whose nature or outcome may be uncertain. The rhetorical effect is to put you in a receptive and reflective mood. You sense that you are not necessarily going to be told things, but that you will be asked to think about things. The connections, when they are made, will be made in an environment of wide-ranging choices, some of which you may not yet wholly appreciate or understand.

Complex sentences have numerous signs to indicate their structure. Among them are adverbial conjunctions such as *if, whether, when, unless, so that, since, as, before, after, while, as soon as, although, otherwise, because, despite*, and many more. Some are relative conjunctions like *which*, or *that*. The usual punctuation mark used to signal the complex sentence is the comma. An introductory dependent clause is always followed by a comma. The independent clause can come anywhere in the sentence: beginning, middle, or end. Placing it at the beginning can help in proposing a problem whose solution might be implied in the following dependent structures; burying it in the middle will emphasize the qualifying nature of the dependent clauses; putting it at the end may help imply a resolution to the uncertainties posed by the dependent structures. Wherever it is placed, it will achieve an effect upon the reader. The careful writer will want to control that effect.

Walter Lippmann was a powerful columnist who addressed significant political issues in American life. He often confronted the most complex problems, particularly regarding the role of government in everyday life. The first paragraphs of ''The Indispensable Opposition'' introduce ideas whose complexity is reflected in the structure of the sentences, and you are carefully led to consider his points. In a sense, Lippmann's choice of sentence structure, predominantly complex, tips us off to the seriousness of his message.

Were they pressed hard enough, most men would probably confess that political freedom—that is to say, the right to speak freely and to act in opposition—is a noble ideal rather than a practical necessity. As the case for freedom is generally put to-day, the argument lends itself to this feeling. It is made to appear that whereas each man claims his freedom as a matter of right, the freedom he accords to other men is a matter of toleration. Thus, the defense of freedom of opinion tends to rest not on its substantial, beneficial, and indispensable consequences, but on a somewhat eccentric, a rather vaguely benevolent, attachment to an abstraction.

It is all very well to say with Voltaire, "I wholly disapprove of what you say, but will defend to the death your right to say it," but as a matter of fact most men will not defend to the death the rights of other men: if they disapprove sufficiently what other men say, they will somehow suppress those men if they can.

Walter Lippmann

We can schematize the first sentences of the first paragraph to reveal their independent and dependent clauses:

Independent clause	**Dependent clauses**
1.	Were they pressed hard enough
most men would probably confess	
	that political freedom is a noble ideal rather than a practical necessity
2.	As the case for freedom is generally put to-day
the argument lends itself to this feeling	

The first sentence begins with a dependent clause of condition, with _If_ implied ("If men were pressed hard enough"). The dependent clause in the second sentence, "As the case for freedom is generally put to-day," is also a clause of condition, explaining how things are put now. The entire passage, and most of the rest of the essay, develops in terms of such sentences because Lippmann's ideas are subtle.

THE COMPOUND/COMPLEX SENTENCE

If one were to add an independent clause to a structure consisting of a subordinate and an independent clause, the result would be a compound/complex sentence because there would be at least two independent clauses and at least one dependent clause. An example:

People who have the insecurities attributed to Nietzsche can be brilliant while feeling depressed, and it may also be true that people who are eminently secure, like Wagner, are aware of brilliance only as it contrasts with depression.

The structure, quite abbreviated, can be schematized:

Independent clauses	Dependent clauses
People can be brilliant	who have the insecurities
It may be true	that people are aware of brilliance
	who are eminently secure
	as it contrasts

In this case, there are two independent clauses and four dependent clauses. The first dependent clause is embedded in the first independent clause and gives information about *people*. The second dependent clause modifies *true*, the key word of the second independent clause. Some of the important information in this sentence is provided in phrases—which do not enter into the distinction made between compound and compound/complex sentences.

The rhetorical effect of the compound/complex sentence varies from example to example, but because it is a large, usually sprawling sentence, it demands thoughtfulness of the reader. Because it presents a considerable amount of information, and may at times seem to develop in a number of different directions, it is a sentence that is used sparingly by modern writers. (See the box entitled "Tips: Using Complex and Compound/Complex Sentences.")

Tips: Using Complex and Compound/Complex Sentences
- Double-check each sentence for clarity.
- Be careful to establish a clear relationship between the parts of sentence, particularly of the two or more independent clauses.
- Use one of these structures when you have to balance alternatives or consider complexities of thought that derive from the relationship of the ideas in the various clauses.

A few more examples follow, with the independent clauses underlined for convenience.

> <u>The focus of her disapproval fluctuated</u>; first, <u>she eyed me rather strongly</u> because as the sunlight fanned brighter, <u>waves of heat blew through the broken windows</u> and <u>I had removed my jacket</u>—which she considered, perhaps rightly, discourteous.

> ***Truman Capote***

This sentence has two independent and four dependent clauses. It has an ambulatory quality and seems to pass from one observation to the next, linking each as it goes. It tends to be an amalgam of a sentence, gathering details, sensing developments, and picking up interesting bits as it grows.

Another sentence with two independent and two dependent clauses follows, but notice how different the effect of it is. It describes the result of a nuclear weapons explosion:

> The intense but comparatively short-lived radiation from the weapon would kill people in the first few weeks and months, but the long-lived radiation that was produced both by the weapon and by the power plant could prevent anyone from living on a vast area of land for decades after it fell.
>
> *Jonathan Schell*

The two clauses which are not underlined, "that was produced both by the weapon and by the power plant," and "after it fell," are dependent clauses. The first is a noun clause defining which radiation is under consideration; the second is an adverb clause of time. In each case the dependent clause establishes a point of information important to the independent clause to which it relates.

Writer's Workshop: Types of Sentences

1. Choose three of the following subjects (you may substitute one of your own) and write one paragraph on each, following the directions below:

hesitation	rewarding work	drunk driving
being aggressive	snobbishness	make-believe
jealousy	political guile	being on time
boredom	naïveté	talent

After you have chosen your subjects, but before you begin writing, go through your journal for an event or specific reference that could be an illustration or focal point for writing. You may wish to reflect on the subject, recalling events that can act as a seed or beginning point for writing. If, for instance, you can recall a moment in which hesitation has produced a specific effect in your life, use it as a beginning. Use the prewriting techniques of clustering and free writing before you do a first draft.

a. In your first paragraph use simple sentences for your key statements.

b. Make your second paragraph depend upon compound sentences.

c. Construct your third paragraph mainly from complex and compound/complex sentences.

What effect do the instructions here have on your choice of a subject for each of the paragraphs you write?

Writer's Workshop

2. Rewrite what you have written for Item 1 and concentrate on achieving sentence variety. How does it affect the quality of your prose? How difficult is it for you to achieve variety?

3. Write a brief essay in which you balance various sentence structures within your paragraphs. Identify the kinds of sentences that predominate in various paragraphs. Does the logic of your thought support the kinds of sentences that you have written? Fill out the following chart indicating the relative proportion of sentence types:

simple sentences
compound sentences
complex sentences
compound/complex sentences

4. Consult the color-plate section and choose a painting that you can describe best in a single paragraph. Indicate which sentence types predominate in your paragraph. Is there a clear relationship between them and the simplicity or complexity of the painting?

Rhetorical Sentence Structures

There are other ways of conceiving the structure of a sentence. The following sentences may be thought of as simple, compound, or complex, but such a description is limited. I want to add three important principles: parallelism, accumulation, and periodicity.

PARALLELISM

In its simplest form, parallelism is repetition of a structural pattern: a phrase, a clause, or even a sentence. Sometimes this means repeating the same phrase or clause with minor variation, either in a group of sentences, or within a single sentence. Generally, certain kinds of conjunctions, called coordinating conjunctions, are used to link parallel elements within a given sentence. The most frequently used are *and, or, nor, for, not only, but also, either, or, neither, nor.*

Traditionally, parallelism has been forceful in political speeches. Part of its power comes from its implicitly comparing similar things. When you say about a friend: "Julia was witty, sensitive, and thoughtful," you are paralleling three qualities. You can schematize this kind of parallelism in this fashion:

$$\text{Julia was} \begin{cases} \text{witty} \\ \text{sensitive} \\ \text{thoughtful} \end{cases}$$

Each of these qualities is linked together, and our natural impulse is to think of how they differ from one another and how they relate to one another. Is it common, for instance, to find these qualities in the same person?

Parallelism works in many ways and takes many forms. A sentence with a similar structure, but using different elements to parallel is "My experience shows me that people who like to wear bright clothes are fun loving, those who like to wear dark clothes are introspective and cautious, and those who wear exotic clothes are totally unpredictable." This can be schematized as follows:

My experience shows me that
$\begin{bmatrix} \text{people who like to wear bright} \\ \text{clothes are fun loving} \\ \text{those who like to wear dark} \\ \text{clothes are introspective} \\ \text{those who wear exotic clothes} \\ \text{are totally unpredictable} \end{bmatrix}$

In each of these cases there are three elements paralleled. The reason for this is that we have gotten used to thinking of such elements in groups of threes. Writers frequently rely on the pattern, so much so that we think of it as natural and almost automatic. It is also easy to parallel two elements, which we sometimes think of as balance: "When I thought of them years later, I realized that Maisy would always stare wistfully out to sea, while June would sit there and knit furiously with her back to the ocean."

I realized that
$\begin{bmatrix} \text{Maisy would always stare wistfully out to sea} \\ \text{June would sit there and knit furiously with} \\ \text{her back to the ocean} \end{bmatrix}$

The two items paralleled are entire clauses. The repetition of the helping verb *would* emphasizes the parallelism. Such a detail—which is not absolutely necessary for clarity or intelligibility—is a mark of style, and it helps your reader appreciate your parallelism. (See the box entitled "Tips: Using Parallelism.")

Parallel Sentence Patterns

Abraham Lincoln is famous for his use of parallelism. The following passage relies on an absolute repetition of the same phrase: "You cannot." Like the Ten Commandments, it develops a tone of remarkable authority by use of negatives (the Ten Commandments uses "Thou shalt not") and aims to encourage a positive kind of behavior.

You cannot bring about prosperity by discouraging thrift. You cannot strengthen the weak by weakening the strong. You cannot help the wage earner by pulling down the wage payer. You cannot further the brotherhood of man by encouraging class hatred. You cannot keep out of trouble by spending more than you earn. You cannot build character and courage by taking away man's initiative and independence. You cannot help men permanently by doing for them what they could and should do for themselves.

Lincoln's tone is resolute. He speaks as if there were no question about what he says. The restatement of the slightly biblical beginnings has a distinct flavor that invites us to accept what is said; it is only after we have read and accepted it that we begin to realize that the language of religion has been adapted to the purposes of economics.

Parallel Clauses

Parallel structure applies to parts as well as to individual sentences. The following example provides signposts to tell us there will be parallelism. The expressions "Just as there is" and "so there is" tell us that we are being held in suspension for a moment while the sentence unwinds itself. This is an enormous sentence, set off as a single paragraph, and its structure parallels two independent clauses with two dependent clauses.

Just as there is only one species of human being on earth, and all divisions into races, cultures, and nations are but man-made ways of obscuring that fundamental truth, so there is only one scientific endeavor on earth—the pursuit of knowledge and understanding—and all divisions into disciplines and levels of purity are but man-made ways of obscuring *that* fundamental truth. (Isaac Asimov)

Parallelism is not only structural, but it also controls thought. This example parallels the sameness of all humanity with the sameness of all science. By making the structure of the comparison equal, he helps underscore the equality that is at the center of his statement.

Parallel Phrases

When you want to emphasize similarity, your choice is to parallel several phrases. The following paragraph includes, at its very center, a lengthy sentence designed to parade before us the images of one lovely beauty after another. Helen Lawrenson reports on the running of the bulls in Pamplona, an event that figured strongly in Ernest Hemingway's novel, *The Sun Also Rises*. It is a romantic ritual of proving male courage by racing down the early morning streets amid the bulls that are to fight in the arena that day. And just as it drew many romantic young men out to prove themselves, it drew young women to cheer them on. Helen Lawrenson is interested in their beauty.

However, the pretty girls, who are perversely attracted by heroic bloodshed, listen with attention as rapt as it is stimulating, and try to nod knowingly at the right intervals. Pamplona during fiesta is one of the world's greatest pick-up centers. Crowds of men come unattached, on the theory that taking your own girl to Pamplona is like taking your own beer to Munich. I doubt if I've ever seen so many pretty girls in one place, all of them looking well-bred and chic and expensively reared. The plainest among them were girls who would have been outstanding in any other group: it was only that they were eclipsed at Pamplona by the number of really sensational beauties there: cream-skinned Spaniards with aquamarine eyes; ravishing Roman girls with pale, full lips, violet eye shadow, and an unmatched Italianate elegance of dress; English girls with chablis-colored hair in high, wrapped beehives; dozens of vivid Americans, alluringly tawny, with lovely legs; and sultry French teen-age sorceresses, Nouvelle Vague style. There was one paralyzing Belgian beauty whose long, straight hair was the color of the under side of a mushroom, and on it she wore a witch's peaked hat of black straw, from under which peered her amazing face, pale and cool and delicate, with enormous navy blue eyes. She moved about like a young queen bee, always in the center of a swarm of buzzing males.

Lawrenson offers us seven sentences in this paragraph. Her imagery is strong, her description exact, and her closing metaphor suggestive. She uses two simple sentences (2, 7), two compound/complex sentences (1, 6), and three complex sentences (3, 4, 5), the last of which contains the series of phrases describing the beautiful girls. This balance of sentences tells us something important. Professional writers of the stature of Helen Lawrenson, who was once editor of *Vanity Fair*, like to vary their sentence structure to take advantage of opportunities for more gracefully expressing themselves.

Lawrenson's fifth sentence contains five parallelled phrases, each of which is descriptive. Not all of these phrases are exactly alike structurally; Lawrenson has varied them so that some are short and pithy, while others are more expansive. Because she is describing girls, she has been careful to avoid repeating the term *girl* too often. She has been as attentive to the needs of variety among these phrases as she has been to the need for sentence variety in the paragraph.

THE CUMULATIVE SENTENCE

The cumulative sentence is a less studied technique, and it produces a more relaxed and easygoing tone. Most of us think in accumulative or associative patterns. Parallelism is effective because it imposes a clearer order on things that might otherwise be linked associatively, whereas the cumulative sentence usually begins with an independent clause and then goes on to add one thought after another, almost in imitation of the way a series of ideas will occur to you.

A famous example of such a sentence comes from the letter of Bartolomeo Vanzetti to Dante Sacco, the son of the man with whom Vanzetti had been accused of murder during a payroll holdup. Sacco and Vanzetti were almost certainly convicted and executed for their political beliefs, not for the crime, and their names have become celebrated memorials to the kind of political hysteria and injustice that was experienced in many nations in the first half of this century.

Remember, Dante, remember always these things; we are not criminals; they convicted us on a frame-up; they denied us a new trial; and if we will be executed after seven years, four months and seventeen days of unspeakable tortures and wrong, it is for what I have already told you; because we were for the poor and against the exploitation and oppression of the man by the man.

Vanzetti's punctuation is very individual, and the semicolons tend to give the sentence a choppiness (but also an intensity) that might have been avoided with different choices. However, the seriousness of Vanzetti's thought, the importance of his message—all this comes through with immense clarity.

George Orwell, in the following example, shows the process of accumulation throughout an entire paragraph, although it is most evident in the first and last sentences. If it were not for the second sentence, a short simple declaration, one would be almost unaware that it is a political statement about the results of colonialism.

When you walk through a town like this—two hundred thousand inhabitants, of whom at least twenty thousand own literally nothing except the rags they stand up in—when you see how the people live, and still more how easily they die, it is always difficult to believe that you are walking among human beings. All colonial empires are in reality founded upon that fact. The people have brown faces—besides, there are so many of them! Are they really the same flesh as yourself? Do they even have names? Or are they merely a kind of undifferentiated brown stuff, about as individual as bees or coral insects? They rise out of the earth, they sweat and starve for a few years, and then they sink back into the nameless mounds of the graveyard and nobody notices that they are gone. And even the graves themselves soon fade back into the soil. Sometimes, out for a walk, as you break your way through the prickly pear, you notice that it is rather bumpy underfoot, and only a certain regularity in the bumps tells you that you are walking over skeletons.

In one sense, Orwell's subject is taking a walk. He begins and ends "out for a walk." The ambulatory quality of the paragraph leads to the accumulation of detail. First, it has to do with the observation of things, then with thoughts about things. Colonialism produces some of the phenomena Orwell observes—and he uses cause and effect as his means of development. However, his focus is not so intensely on cause and effect; rather, it is on the details themselves, accumulating them slowly as to give us a fuller experience.

Accumulating information, details, or observations in a sentence or a paragraph should have a rationale or purpose. Its effect is to build awareness and emotional involvement, although the nature of the involvement may be mild and engaging rather than intense and exciting. (See the box entitled "Tips: Using the Cumulative Sentence.")

Tips: Using the Cumulative Sentence • The cumulative sentence is a reliable all-purpose sentence. It is probably the sentence you will use most in your writing. • Accumulation may follow a simple add-on process, or it may rely on embedding information between a subject and its predicate. • The cumulative sentence is probably best used when providing information or description. • The rhetorical effect is easygoing and relaxed: usually the first part of the sentence bears the weight of meaning, because the main clause is usually first.	TIP

PERIODIC SENTENCES

The periodic sentence has a Latin flavor because it was favored by Cicero and other Roman stylists. The structure of the sentence is dominated by decisions regarding subordination. Its special qualities have to do with the fact that the most important part of the sentence, the most significant independent clause, comes at the end. What come first are usually a number of qualifiers to establish the situation clarified by the final clause. First, look at some examples with the final clause underlined:

When the last pages of the history of our struggle are written, and if the historian is a woman who has suffered the injustice of prejudice and unequal treatment at the hands of men who had little regard for her or for other ambitious members of her sex, may it be said that although we struggled for change, change was precious slow to come.

Since the Germans had built up a southern defensive, fearing an invasion from Marseilles, and hoping that an impending storm would forestall any effort of a channel crossing, Hitler entrusted Normandy to the Vichy French and exhausted German defenders.

The next example is a paragraph whose sentences possess periodicity, although the last sentence is technically its periodic sentence. We wait until the last moment to fulfill the promise of the first sentence. This paragraph illustrates the most interesting rhetorical effect of the principle of periodicity: suspense.

Thirty years have passed, and Voltaire, now at the height of his fame, holds a pair of scissors in one hand and a slug in the other. Let me repeat: in the one hand he holds a large brown slug, and in the other a pair of scissors. The slug is of Swiss extraction, and comes off one of his estates, where it has been eating the lettuces. *Ecrasez l'infame?* But no: he reserves it for another purpose. Looking into its face, he surveys the gloomy unresponsive snout which is all a slug offers, he compares it with the face of a snail, so much more piquant, and both with the face of a man. All three are different, but all are faces, and he does not know whether he trembles at the edge of a great discovery or of a joke. Beneath him are the blue waters of the Lake Leman, beyond them the walls of Mont Blanc, he stands with one foot in Genevan territory to escape the French, and the other in France, to be safe from the Swiss. He stands triumphant, all his possessions are around him, thousands of his trees grow, his contented peasantry work, his invalid cousin dozes, the bells of the church he built chime—and he cuts off the slug's head. (E. M. Forster)

This is an amusing beginning for a serious discussion of the French philosopher Voltaire's scientific methods and scientific inquiries. A study of the sentences in the paragraph will show that E. M. Forster has aimed at a thoroughly periodic effect and achieved it; however, he has varied his sentences in length and in structure. He uses balance and parallelism in sentences 1, 2, and 3. Sentence 5 is cumulative, and the final sentence is periodic. None of the sentences is unusually difficult, nor unusually simple. Forster has found a middle ground in which his sentences have a generally comfortable shape and size.

Sometimes, periodicity can take on the quality of an interruption. It can be used to hold off an effect until the necessary details for its appreciation are clarified. Edmund Wilson reflects on the area in which he was born and to which he has come back to live out his days. He is not particularly happy with the arrangement, but he nonetheless describes what he sees with some sharpness.

I look out across the Hudson and see Newburgh: with the neat-windowed cubes of its dwellings and docks, distinct as if cut by a burin, built so densely up the slope of the bank and pierced by an occasional steeple, undwarfed by tall modern buildings and with only the little old-fashioned ferry to connect it with the opposite bank, it might still be an eighteenth-century city.

Wilson's conclusion, that Newburgh, with its crisp engraving-like landscape, resembles an eighteenth-century city, is withheld until we have absorbed the specific details of description, whose purposes are unrevealed until the end of the sentence (which begins a paragraph). The gist of the paragraph is that everything associated with the house to which he returns, including many of the values and aspirations of his own family, is antiquated, left behind, and dated. The periodicity of this sentence helps build a suitable emotional aura to accompany the entire flow of his thought.

Periodicity conveys a sense of orderliness, of thoughtfulness, and of timing. It also gives the writer a particular kind of control over the material, because it provides a chance to build up details, thoughts, items essential to giving the final statement more power than it would have if it were offered without adequate preparation. (See the box entitled "Tips: Using Periodic Sentences.")

Tips: Using Periodic Sentences

- The rhetorical weight of the periodic sentence is at the end, because the main clause always comes at the end of the sentence.
- The periodic sentence depends for its effect on withholding basic information until the reader is thoroughly prepared to understand it.
- Periodicity has the potential for both suspense and surprise.
- Overuse can produce a highly mannered and artificial quality in writing.
- Occasional, careful use can reflect both control and thoughtfulness on the part of the writer.

TIP

Writer's Workshop: Rhetorical Sentence Structures

1. Choose three sentences from your recent writing. Decide whether they are grammatically simple, compound, complex, or compound/complex. Find examples from your own sentences of parallelism, accumulation, or periodicity.
2. Rewrite some of your own sentences from earlier compositions to make them reflect rhetorical sentence structures: at least one sentence using parallelism, one using accumulative principles, and one using periodicity.

3. Examine some of the sample essays and paragraphs in earlier chapters for the types of sentences good writers use. Keep a record of the sentence types by maintaining the following checklist:

Title of essay:
Number of simple sentences:
Number of compound sentences:
Number of complex and compound/complex sentences:
Uses of parallel structure:
Uses of accumulation:
Uses of periodicity:

What does your research tell you about the choices made by good writers?
4. Perform the same experiment using your most recent essay. What similarities and what differences do you discover in your approach to writing sentences as compared with that of professional writers?
5. Rewrite a recent essay with the goal of achieving sentence variety and of using the best structural options available. How different is the quality of your prose? Is your thinking clarified, or do your ideas develop as you do this exercise?

Revising Sentences for Accuracy

Problems with individual sentences fall into certain patterns. Some of them are relatively basic and involve choices that introduce confusion. For instance, the two most common problems I see in the early stages of anyone's writing are the sentence fragment and the run-on sentence. The sentence fragment is a group of words that lacks a subject or a predicate and is not, therefore, a complete sentence. A run-on sentence is the joining of two sentences into one, without the appropriate conjunction that would make them relate intelligibly to one another.

EDITING SENTENCES

The following examples are from student work. Most of them are from work done in the first two or three weeks of a college course in writing. They represent various kinds of problems in writing the sentence, from the basic problems of fragments and run-ons, to the more sophisticated questions of making the most of opportunities to revise sentences according to the major principles already discussed.

The Sentence Fragment

Good writers sometimes use sentence fragments. They can be effective in a journalistic style. They can add punch and a casual tone to writing, and good writers make use of those qualities. Apprentice writers, however, usually do not know that they are writing fragments. That fact usually compromises their effectiveness. It is either sloppiness, or perhaps a typographical oversight, or possibly the failure to know that the fragment is incomplete that causes people to use fragments. The result is a lack of clarity, or a sense of bewilderment.

The first examples are all from a single student's work. You may find the examples relatively familiar, because these are problems common to many people's writing.

> Children are new at life and hence experience things for the first time. With the first experience being the most significant to them.

This is typical. The second group of words looked like a sentence to David because *being* seemed to him a verb. However, *being* is a verbal here, a participle. A way of rewriting this sentence to improve it is to join the two elements into a single, coherent sentence:

> Children are new at life and their first experience of things is the most significant to them.

Here is another from David's work:

> I remember the first car I drove. A gray 1979 Olds Delta 88.

This example is better in that there is no confusion introduced by the fragment. The problem is simply that David put things down more or less the way he spoke. Sometimes this is a good strategy. It can be effective in prose that aims for an easy, conversational tone, or that imitates the atmosphere of a student union or conversation pit. But this piece of writing was attempting a formal tone, and David's choice here was an accident. He could have easily improved it:

> I remember the first car I drove, a gray 1979 Olds Delta 88.

Finally, another example:

> I was always very careful driving it because this was 1980. Which qualified the car as still new.

The *Which* clause seemed to be a sentence to David because it has a subject (*Which*) and a verb (*qualified*). Unfortunately, David thought *car* was the subject, which did not help things much—either way he has an adjective clause that cannot function properly in the environment he has set up for it. A clear, improved version is

> I was always very careful driving it because in 1980 the car still qualified as new.

You can see that these simple changes make the sentence accurate and clear.

Run-on Sentences

David had as much of a gift for the run-on sentence as he did for the sentence fragment. The problems you see in these next examples are the result of paying little or no attention to basic principles of sentence structure. Once David saw these problems and heard our suggestions for improving his difficult sentences, he began to take the job of structuring his sentences seriously. It eventually made a stupendous difference in his writing.

> I remember my first experiences in driving, experiences because when one drives a car there are many different situations, parking a car is a lot different than driving down a highway, which is where most of my experience came from.

The problems with this sentence are several: David is trying to say too many things at once. He needs to make up his mind and simplify. The first clause "I remember my experiences in driving" has four elements: *I, memory, experience,* and *driving.* Which is the key element? You are led to believe it is the last word *driving,* but after the comma comes an explanation about another word, *experiences,* which leads David to distinguishing between parking and highway driving. He ultimately ignores the other three elements of his opening clause. This stands as an entire paragraph in his piece, and it is marred by a lack of focus and a lack of development. What is his means of development?

It is not easy to revise a sentence of this kind because David needs to rethink the entire point he is making. As he has written it, there are no clear distinctions, and no clear message. One improved version is

> My first experiences in driving centered much more on highway travel than on parking.

The question of memory is omitted: if David can talk about his first experiences, he can remember them and does not need to tell us so. He had two kinds of experiences to mention, and they are both clearly here. If David had written this last sentence, he would have seen clearly that he did not have a paragraph and that he needed to develop his thoughts.

A more simple form of the run-on sentence is called the comma splice, in which two sentences are joined together by a comma instead of a conjunction. We will look at another student's work for this example:

> Machiavelli's thoughts on this matter are distorted, often contradictory, and absolutely wrong, as the end result, they may contribute more to the decline of the power of state rather than the preservation of the former.

It is by no means easy to know what Ken meant by this sentence. He seems to be contrasting the decline of the state with the preservation of the state. The comma that is at fault here comes before "as the end result." In revision he needed first to divide the two sentences that are run together, then he needed to clarify the second sentence.

> Machiavelli's thoughts on this matter are distorted, often contradictory, and absolutely wrong. As a result, they may contribute more to the decline of the state than to its preservation.

It should be no surprise to find that sentences marked by fragments or run-ons often include confusions and uncertainties. They result from a lack of attention to the basic ingredients of the sentence. The writers do not know which of their clauses are independent, which dependent. They do not realize they are writing phrases. Here is a final example of these relatively banal (but pervasive) problems:

> Responsibility was an adult term to me then, adults were responsible and being responsible made like an adult.

As in many of these cases, you get the general idea. However you have to do a great deal of work to make sense out of the assemblage of words you are given. This is clearly two sentences. Here is the simplest kind of improvement:

> At that time, responsibility was an adult term to me. Adults were responsible and being responsible made me feel like an adult.

Revising Sentences for Style

The problems of fragments and run-ons represent serious inaccuracies that can be avoided, but which developed from misunderstandings or errors. For a few pages, I would like to direct your attention to the kinds of things you can do for your own writing to take advantage of the principles of grammatical and rhetorical sentence structure discussed earlier. The remaining examples here are student work, but instead of their being examples of errors in prose, they are examples of missed opportunities. The samples are fine as far as they go. The question is, how would they look if they had benefited from a good redrafting and revision?

EDITING FOR VARIETY

First, let us look at a good example. This is a brief paragraph that uses many of the basic principles we have been discussing.

They have arrived. In this male America they may be judges, lawyers, doctors, construction workers, business executives, cab drivers—or wives and mothers, but they'll never be the same submissive creatures they once were. Across America, from government to business, from courtrooms to church pulpits, women's lives are changing, and with them the traditional roles of the sexes. America has not entirely given up the stereotype of the typical dominating male, but U.S. women today are fast changing that.

Sylvia

This comes from Sylvia's last piece of writing in a semester-long course in composition. It uses the snap of an opening simple sentence balanced by longer sentences; therefore, it scores well on the question of aiming for meaningful variety. The parallelism of the occupations in the second sentence is well handled, but so is the periodicity of that sentence: the point comes at the end. The remaining sentences use balance, parallelism, and periodicity. The paragraph is simple and direct. It sets the stage for fuller discussion and development.

The next example is an earlier piece from the same class. We had not yet discussed the questions of style that are the focus of this chapter, although Tony felt his sentences were accurate, which is true enough. But he also felt he made some effort to vary them, which is not as true as he thought. Except for his last two sentences, the rhythms of his prose are dull and repetitive. He uses the same sentence pattern again and again.

Huge universities give students a poor and inadequate education. A university is characterized, as opposed to other schools, by its large size. Its large population requires a large campus. Gigantic dormitories and lecture halls are also needed to house the many students. As a result of this situation, anonymity is present. One's absence or presence in a class is rarely if ever known. Because of large student populations, personal contact with the faculty is rare. Classes of three hundred people permit few question and answer periods; most students remain quiet. Physical mobility is curtailed, in many instances, by long waiting lines, student number disagreements, or university procedures.

Tony

Tony's peer editors agreed with his opinion regarding large schools. I pointed out the fact that Harvard and Berkeley are huge universities and that they have a reputation for being places in which you can get a good education, but I don't think it convinced Tony. In any event, Tony's choppy sentences dull a reader so much that by the end of the paragraph it is difficult to worry about whether he is right or wrong.

There is vastly too much sameness here, and Tony admitted that this is basically a first draft that he left as is. He thought it would do, and did not revise it. My suggestion was to revise with an eye toward incorporating the stylistic principles considered earlier. I suggested aiming at a variety of sentence structures of both the grammatical and rhetorical types. Here is a revision—which, whether the argument is right or wrong, avoids some of the repetition of the original.

Huge universities give students a poor and inadequate education. Their large population, huge campus, gigantic dormitories and lecture halls all produce anonymity. Because there are so many students in a class, the presence or absence of an individual goes unnoticed, and the chances of personal contact with a faculty member are few. Classes of three hundred rarely give students a chance to ask questions. Even physical mobility is stifled by waiting lines, office errors, and elaborate university procedures.

Read each of these one after the other and ask yourself which version is more convincing. The second has a variety of sentences, although there is no straining for variety—it is simply a matter of looking for opportunities to improve dull sentences.

In the revision, the first simple sentence was retained. It is effective, clear, and to the point. Then the second sentence uses the parallelism of population, campus, dormitories and lecture halls to produce an effect: anonymity. Cause and effect also directs the next compound/complex sentence, which begins with a subordinate clause ("Because . . . in a class"), follows with an independent clause ("the presence . . . unnoticed), and links the second independent clause ("the chances . . . are few") accurately with the conjunction *and*. The next is a simple sentence, and the last again depends on parallelism (*lines, errors, procedures*) for its organization.

The principle of the revision is simple: look for chances to achieve variety while also improving clarity. Avoid repeating the same sentence pattern unless you can take advantage of the chance for parallelism. One way to improve the clarity in all these examples of revision is to keep in mind the means of development of the main ideas. Cause and effect is the obvious means of development here, but in other examples you will find other means used to clarify the thought.

EDITING FOR OPPORTUNITY

Each of the examples in the last section is revised with an eye for finding the opportunity to use an alternative structure that works better than the original. This distinction will apply to your efforts at revision of otherwise acceptable sentences. The chance to use a variety of grammatical sentence structures is an opportunity, but it exists only for those who know it exists. If you had no awareness of their existence, you might never use certain of the grammatical structures available to you. Many writers seem to fall into a dull pattern of using the same kind of sentence again and again.

The best opportunities for revision are probably at the later stages of revision. Then you can see what you have that is good, and go on to seize the chances of improving the rest. You can see if you need sentence variety. You can see if you have taken advantage of periodicity where appropriate, or parallelism when you have similar or contrasting elements to discuss. You can see if you have written too many, or too few cumulative sentences. You can begin to tell whether the rhythms of your sentences are dull and repetitive. You have the opportunity to do something about it.

Linda's example, which follows, is a paragraph that was on the second page of a four-page discussion of a passage from the autobiography of Frederick Douglass, an American slave who escaped to New England and freedom shortly before the Civil War. Linda is talking about emigration and the quest for freedom as it affects many people.

For the few that leave, getting used to the new country is very hard. Many of them flock to the big cities. They are drawn by the excitement and the promise of some kind of job. Many of them are from small towns and are not used to the kinds of people found in the city. Most take any kind of work they can get and usually end up working way below minimum. The so-called sweat shops of the big cities are full of immigrants. Some turn to a life of crime to survive. A few are as lucky as Douglass and find someone to help them. It is up to the individual to decide if freedom is worth the cost. He must decide whether it is better to be in a foreign land where there is freedom or to remain with his family in a country where personal freedom is not important. If the need for freedom is strong enough, the answer is clear. Freedom must be obtained at any cost.

If you count the words you will see that most of the sentences are of approximately the same length as the first and most of the sentences are either compound or simple. There is little or no use of parallelism or accumulation and no periodicity of any kind. You might wonder why you would wish to revise this paragraph. The answer lies in the middle, where one

choppy sentence after another appears flat-footed and dull. These sentences cry out for revision. There is great opportunity here for improvement.

Many immigrants flock to the big city, where they have excitement and the promise of a job, but getting used to their new country is not easy. Many, from small towns, are unused to city ways and have to take low paying jobs in sweat shops, while some even turn to a life of crime. Only a few, like Douglass, find friends who can help. The question of whether freedom is worth the heavy price some immigrants pay depends on whether their need for freedom is strong enough. If it is, then it must be obtained at any cost.

These sentences, although varied, are essentially cumulative in kind. The original paragraph does not offer many opportunities for parallelism: there are no explicit contrasts, no lists of things. The need for suspense or withholding information is absent, therefore the most clearly useful rhetorical kind of sentence is the cumulative. Moreover, the most useful grammatical form is the compound/complex sentence, which is often the form the cumulative sentence takes.

In short, even when a group of sentences seems to be more or less acceptable, you can usually revise for variety and for opportunities to match your rhetorical choices to your purposes. Like so many other editing situations, you cannot make use of your opportunities until you realize they are available.

Writer's Workshop: Revising Sentences

1. Revise the following sentences for accuracy:

Though Machiavelli wrote his essay for princes of his time, his advice should be heeded by all, critics are incorrect in saying he is a cynic.

It seems that wearing the colors of our country on the Fourth of July is becoming outmoded, people have somehow gotten it into their heads that only children dress up for such occasions.

This made me nervous. Because I didn't want to drive that day. The fear of collision was instilled in me like an omen.

Death is not a comfortable topic for anyone to discuss. But it is a tragic mistake to attempt to shield a child from anything. Regardless of how upsetting or unpleasant the subject matter.

2. The most important use you can make of the suggestions for revision in this chapter is to take a paragraph from your last piece of writing and revise each sentence. Follow these suggestions:

Revise each sentence for accuracy.
Revise each sentence for variety.
Revise each sentence for opportunity.

Writer's Workshop

Be especially careful to avoid a host of same-structure grammatical forms. Then, go on to look for chances to make use of what you know about parallelism, accumulation, and periodicity.

3. Sometimes you can gain distance and objectivity by looking first at someone else's work. The following paragraph is by a student in the early stage of a writing course. Revise each sentence in the paragraph with an eye for accuracy, variety, and opportunity to use the rhetorical principles of parallelism, accumulation, and periodicity.

Gun control. Gun control is not necessary in the United States today. Yet gun control bills have been vetoed time and time again by state and federal legislators. The reason cited for the veto of gun control bills is that the United States Constitution states that the citizen has the right to bear arms. Although other clauses of the United States Constitution have been amended and changed, the gun control clause has remained untouched. It appears in the Constitution because at the time of its writing, the life style of many people, plus the frontier, required gun usage. But our life style today bears few resemblances to that of our forefathers. Many laws have changed with the times, with the Civil Rights Acts as just one example. The gun control law has not.

4. Revise the following brief paragraph, using the principles discussed in this chapter.

Fifty years ago, few people would have thought it possible for men and women to live in a co-ed dormitory. I, for one, have lived in both; an all-female dormitory and a dormitory co-ed by rooms. After living a year in both, I've come to the conclusion that co-ed living has more benefits. My perspectives on life and the male sex have both broadened and changed.

14

Style: A Rhetoric of the Paragraph

The Paragraph: Background

The paragraph is a creation of style, history, and rhetorical purpose. No adequate definition exists for the paragraph, and no description of it will satisfy the ways in which it is used by competent writers. You are often taught in school that the paragraph is a group of meaningfully related sentences governed by a topic sentence that usually comes first. However, examination of paragraphs written by experienced writers has time and again demonstrated that such a definition does not always describe the way in which paragraphs are really written. Some writing specialists have gone so far as to say that proposing such a structure for the paragraph will actually impede the creativity of a writer, which certainly is a possibility if the paragraph is not well understood.

Historically, the paragraph is a new thing. Classical writers did not use it at all, and it was not until the latter part of the Renaissance, in the 1580s, that it began to be seen in printed books. Unlike the sentence, it is not a product of spoken language. It is a product of the printed page. For that reason it is somewhat less natural to use, and rhetorical experience based on speech does not always relate directly to writing. To a certain extent, the paragraph is a visual structure as much as a semantic structure. It is designed to help the reader by breaking blocks of sentences into related groups.

Rules for the design of the paragraph—such as its needing a topic sentence and the desirability of its following a specific means of development—were devised in the 1860s and found their way into the schools not long after. The paragraph has changed dramatically since then. In the nineteenth century paragraphs were long, often a page or more, densely packed, and developed sometimes according to a tangled pattern of reasoning. In the early twentieth century, paragraphs were typically bulky and dense. But in the

413

latter part of the twentieth century, paragraphs have become much shorter as a means of pacing a reader more briskly through the prose.

We even see paragraphs of a single sentence in contemporary writing.

Different kinds of writing will treat the question of paragraphing much differently. Newspapers and magazines observe the width of the column in their decisions about paragraph length and will even re-edit copy to make better visual use of paragraphing. Obviously, the narrower the column, the fewer sentences there will be in a paragraph. If a magazine is written for a general audience, the paragraphs will be shorter and often reflect an opening topic sentence, whereas if the publication is for a specially educated readership, the paragraphs will become longer and denser. And this is the point: every publication knows its audience. Matching the style of paragraphing with the needs of the audience is part of the rhetorical function of the writer.

The Paragraph: Two Theories

You may have noticed that your essays rarely come back with much comment on paragraphing. If your paragraphs are very long, you may be asked to split them in two or three sections. Except for certain relatively common and consistent mistakes, most writers have little trouble with writing paragraphs. However, for the very reason that most of us think relatively little about paragraphs, you can learn a great deal about them by examining them in detail.

There are two popular theories about the rhetorical nature of the paragraph, and both of them may be wrong. Yet, they are very widespread. The first, and the most common, treats the paragraph as an essay in miniature. The theory observes that, like an essay, the paragraph has a thesis; and like an essay, it develops that thesis until it has made a statement which seems finished or largely complete. The paragraph, then, is joined to what follows it much as vertebrae are joined together to form a spinal column: each is a related and conjoined entity which, to some extent, resembles the whole.

The second, more recent, theory is that the paragraph is based on the structure of a sentence. Just as a sentence has a main clause from which everything else depends either in a subordinate or coordinate relationship, the paragraph has a topic sentence—which comes at the beginning—and which acts as an umbrella under which all the other sentences are joined. Moreover, this theory sees the paragraph as developing much as cumulative sentences develop: by the principle of addition. One important thought is added to a previous thought until the purpose of the paragraph has been achieved.

It is also possible to see the paragraph as related to a sentence based on parallelism. Some paragraphs repeat patterns from sentence to sentence within the paragraph (see the example of Lincoln's writing in the section on parallelism in Chapter 13) and emphasize their balance and rhythms. Likewise, some paragraphs seem to save their punch for the end, imitating the pattern of the periodic sentence. Such paragraphs may have their topic sentence, for example, coming at the end instead of at the beginning. This theory has a great many adherents, and it bears thinking about, especially because if you have mastered some of the principles of sentence structure in Chapter 13, you can use them here in constructing paragraphs.

Neither of these theories needs to be thought of as excluding the other (as often happens in the work of theoreticians). You may feel that both are useful when you set about constructing a paragraph. In some cases, when you are not sure of what you want to say, thinking of the paragraph in terms of the sentence will help add important refinements of thought one piece at a time. You look back through a paragraph and decide what might come next, what you can coordinate with the main idea, what you can subordinate to the main idea or those that follow. On the other hand, you may see in the process of revision that some of your paragraphs treat a self-contained aspect of the total subject of the essay. In that case, you may wish to go back over the paragraph in an effort to be sure that it does, indeed, represent the entire issue in a manner that a short essay might.

No definition will be adequate to describe all paragraphs. However, you will find this limited definition useful as a starting point:

The paragraph develops a concept, idea, subject matter, or thesis in a group of related sentences. When a new subject matter is introduced, a new paragraph begins.

Commonsense Suggestions for Paragraphing

THE TOPIC SENTENCE

The topic sentence is most useful when your primary purpose is absolute clarity. By establishing the topic and the way it is to be developed, you help your reader understand what you are trying to do. If you find it difficult to do this, consider this strategy: use the topic sentence in the first draft of a paragraph if possible; otherwise, write until you feel you have a full paragraph, then in the process of revision search your material in order to formulate a clear and effective topic sentence. Then revise your paragraph.

The following topic sentence is from the work of Louise, a composition student. Her topic sentence is strong and direct, although it also includes a great deal of information. The overall topic is death, but her specific focus is on the question of whether or not it is appropriate to talk with children about death. Her conclusion is that it is not only appropriate, but essential. That conclusion is revealed in her topic sentence.

> Death is not a comfortable topic for anyone to discuss, but it is a tragic mistake to attempt to shield a child from anything, regardless of how upsetting or unpleasant the subject matter.

COHESION

Because the paragraph unifies a group of sentences under one general concept, each sentence must relate to the sentences before it and after it. Cohesion is achieved if you can establish the connection between each of the sentences in the paragraph; at that point you can say that the paragraph holds together.

Louise continues her paragraph by thinking about the questions that arise in regard to talking with children about death. She is particularly concerned with the effect that not telling the truth has on children, and her paragraph achieves cohesion in part by focusing on cause and effect as a means of development.

> Death is not a comfortable topic for anyone to discuss, but it is a tragic mistake to attempt to shield a child from anything, regardless of how upsetting or unpleasant the subject matter. The time to address this problem is before a death actually occurs. Not many people can do this. Even adults find it impossible to discuss their mortality among each other. For children this reluctance can have devastating consequences. Sometimes they blame themselves for the demise of a loved one, or develop a morbid fascination that can lead to nightmares or other such manifestations. Children who know nothing about death are forced to delve into their imagination in search of answers. This unfortunate process can lead to distorted conclusions.
>
> *Louise*

UNITY

Unity, as the word implies, is the achievement of oneness. Trying to stay with one aspect of your subject matter in a paragraph is important for giving the reader the assurance that you have the subject matter in appropriate focus. If you do this, you give the reader confidence in your control and in your ability to handle your subject matter.

Louise achieves unity by avoiding the temptation to go off in other directions, even if they may be important. Louise's paragraph could be more detailed and more specific—the question of nightmares seems to come out of nowhere and it is as if she had a specific instance in mind, but did not mention it. Mentioning it, or being specific, would not have hurt the paragraph's unity. It would have made the paragraph more satisfying. One thing we do not know, for instance, is what the age range of the children she refers to might be.

LENGTH

No one can say how long a paragraph should be. Consequently, establish your own guidelines. In the last decades of the twentieth century, paragraphs ranged from five to fifteen sentences. But remember that there may be times when you will wish to be shorter or longer in your paragraphs. Your decisions about length must rest on your decisions about your audience and the best way to handle what you are writing about. A breezy, personal essay may benefit most from very short paragraphs. A serious expository essay on a difficult subject may demand longer paragraphs. Your decision on this point depends on your attitude toward your material and your audience.

MEANS OF DEVELOPMENT

A paragraph develops your thinking on a given subject. Therefore, the effectiveness of your paragraphs will be directly affected by the extent to which you rely on some recognizable means of development. Your first choice should be to rely on the techniques you mastered in Chapters 4 and 5. They are especially useful for fully developing a paragraph. Deciding on a good means of development in the first stages of writing helps you achieve clarity and unity. Revising in the later stages of writing—even if you decide to change your method of development—will help you achieve polish and a sense of inevitability.

You have seen examples of well-developed paragraphs in Chapters 4 and 5, relying on an entire range of different means of development. The following example, by a student, John, writing his fifth of eight essays in a freshman composition course, relies on cause and effect for its means of development. However, the paragraph is mixed in development, because it begins with definition, the definition of the Laffer Curve, a technical economic term. Then it concerns itself with a single cause, a government reform to take advantage of the insights of the Laffer Curve and its two effects: the intended effect and the actual effect, and so in a sense, it is also using comparison as part of its means of development.

In 1974, at the University of Southern California, macroeconomist Arthur Laffer developed a curve which illustrates that as the rate of taxation increases above the 50% mark, lower revenues are collected from people in higher income brackets. This is primarily a result of delinquency in paying taxes by people who fear they are being overtaxed. The Economic Recovery Tax Reform Act, instigated in 1981, sought to rectify this situation and promote national economic growth by increasing the individual's disposable income. The act sought to accomplish this goal by cutting taxes, allowing the use of individual retirement accounts, higher investment tax credits, and most of all by implementing the accelerated tax cost recovery system. The rationale behind this plan was that if the people in the highest income brackets had higher disposable incomes, the net effect would be higher aggregate demand and supply, raising the Gross National Product, which would spur economic expansion and inevitably increase tax revenues. Unfortunately, the tax reform was a means to an end which was nowhere in sight because it aided those in the highest income brackets and neglected those in the lower and middle ones. Hence this reform created a present tax system which is overwhelming and confusing to people because of its complexities, which provides new loopholes for individuals who really don't need them, and which generally moves intolerably toward being regressive.

John

By keeping his eye on the principles of development that are central to his purposes, John is able to keep a very complex paragraph under control, despite the great temptation to veer off in any one of numerous directions.

This tip, that you should rely on a strategy of development of a single specific idea in a paragraph is of immense importance. Paying attention to it could help you improve your writing quickly.

VARIETY

Varying the length of your paragraphs, your approach to the topic sentence, and your means of development will always improve your writing. Monotony can bewilder and depress a reader.

Writer's Workshop: Paragraphing

1. Begin by examining a recent essay of your own. From the body of your essay, copy out a paragraph that you feel has a clear and strong topic sentence. Describe the paragraph by establishing the relationship of each of the following sentences to the topic sentence. Do you find agreement with peer editors concerning the clarity, strength—or even the existence—of the topic sentence you identified? Is there agreement concerning the relationship of other sentences to the topic sentence?
2. Choose a paragraph of your own that has no obvious topic sentence. Copy it out and repeat the experiment in Item 1 of describing how

each sentence relates to the unstated topic of the paragraph. Is the paragraph, now that you have examined it, effective? Is the subject matter clear? Are the sentences unified and is there cohesion in the paragraph?

3. Revise a previously written paragraph in order to give it a stronger topic sentence. As you do so, be sure to revise all the sentences in the paragraph to make their relationship with that topic sentence more exact and clear. Follow the suggestions for paragraphing in this chapter. Does establishing a topic sentence, choosing a clear method of development, and achieving unity produce the improvement which you expect careful revision to produce? Do your peer editors agree with you?

4. Begin with new subject matter and write a paragraph with a clear topic sentence, unified and coherent follow-up sentences, and a reliable approach to development. Below that paragraph, describe your process: did you feel it was more or less difficult to follow the suggestions for paragraphing than to use your conventional approach to paragraphing? Did you feel more or less satisfied with the final results than you usually do with your paragraphs? Did you feel that constructing a careful topic sentence impeded your creativity? What changes in your usual strategy were you aware of? Do your peer editors notice a difference in your approach?

5. Revise the student paragraphs that follow. Aim to create a single paragraph using the materials in these scattered observations. Develop a strong topic sentence and decide on a strategy of development. You may naturally alter the content of this material as you see fit, but do your best to keep your version a recognizable variant of the original.

Myths are used for many different purposes and are used in many different societies. Myths play a big part in each society and have a common thing: they are used to explain the unknown. The Greek myths responded to the social needs of their society, dealing with basic questions such as death, birth, and hardship. By telling these myths, they were also used as a source of entertainment.

There is no neat definition for myths other than the purpose of explaining the obscure. Myths constantly change as conditions change. They change with such things as the immigrations of people and also with the change in morals and religion. The Orient brought over a great many myths to Greece, explaining many mysteries of life.

Aristotle once said that myths are more true than history because they show the truth of people. This is very important even though the writers of these myths are often considered uneducated. To be truthful about what goes on in a society does not take an educated person, just an honest one.

The most important function of myths is to give security to a society. They give people an understanding of what is going on in their society and why; this puts many people at ease. Being ignorant of something can be one of the scariest things. It's important to remember that even though myths explain a lot, their explanations are not always true.

Theodore

The Paragraph Zone

One proposal resulting from analysis of the contemporary paragraph is that we think of paragraphs as a spatial unit controlled by an overriding idea. That means that one basic thesis or topic can govern two, three, or even four groups of sentences that can be formatted as paragraphs. However, each of those groups contributes to the whole, and therefore the unit forms a paragraph zone rather than a single unbroken paragraph. To some extent, that concept directs Theodore's sample on Greek myth.

The primary value of this theory is that it helps explain what journalists, in particular, do in their writing. Moreover, it helps you remain flexible in your thinking about the paragraph, recognizing its potential and recognizing your extended range of choice.

Looking at Paragraphs

These are the beginning three paragraphs from an essay by one of the most distinguished of modern writers, C. S. Lewis. In the left column are some comments on his paragraphing.

THE TROUBLE WITH "X" . . .

The topic of the entire essay appears in the first sentence. But it also appears in the title. The topic sentence may be said to extend through both of the opening sentences.

I suppose I may assume that seven out of ten of those who read these lines are in some kind of difficulty about some other human being. Either at work or at home, either the people who employ you or those whom you employ, either your in-laws or parents or children, your wife or your husband, are making life harder for you than it need be even in these days. It is to be hoped that we do not often mention these difficulties (especially the domestic ones) to outsiders. But sometimes we do. An outside friend asks us why we are looking so glum; and the truth comes out.

On such occasions the outside friend usually says, "But why don't you tell them? Why don't you go to your wife (or husband, or father, or daughter, or boss, or landlady, or lodger) and have it all out? People are usually reasonable. All you've got to do is to make them see things in the right light. Explain it to them in a reasonable, quiet, friendly way." And we, whatever we say outwardly, think sadly to ourselves, "He doesn't know 'X.' " We do. We know how utterly hopeless it is to make "X" see reason. Either we've tried it over and over again—tried it till we are sick of trying it—or else we've never tried it because we saw from the beginning how useless it would be. We know that if we attempt to "have it all out with 'X' " there will either be a "scene," or else "X" will stare at us in blank amazement and say "I don't know what on earth you're talking about"; or else (which is perhaps worst of all) "X" will quite agree with us and promise to turn over a new leaf and put everything on a new footing—and then, twenty-four hours later, will be exactly the same as "X" has always been.

The entire essay is developed, as each of these paragraphs is, by relying on circumstance.

This paragraph concerns itself with possibility.

One principle of development is the hypothetical example.

You know, in fact, that any attempt to talk things over with "X" will shipwreck on the old, fatal flaw in "X's" character. And you see, looking back, how all the plans you have ever made always have shipwrecked on that fatal flaw—on "X's" incurable jealousy, or laziness, or touchiness, or muddle-headedness, or bossiness, or ill temper, or changeableness. Up to a certain age you have perhaps had the illusion that some external stroke of good fortune—an improvement in health, a rise of salary, the end of the war—would solve your difficulty, But you know better now. The war is over, and you realize that even if the other things happened, "X" would still be "X," and you would still be up against the same old problem. Even if you became a millionaire, your husband would still drink, or you'd still have to have your mother-in-law to live with you.

A continuation of the concern for possibility: all efforts to confront "X" will fail.

C. S. LEWIS'S TOPIC SENTENCES

This is, in many ways, a traditional style. Yet, it would be very difficult to represent the first sentence of each of these paragraphs as adequate topic sentences. Instead, they point to an aspect of the topic, a part of the problem, and lead the writer into adding further sentences that expand, explore, and develop it. The first paragraph begins with possibility: the possibility that seven out of ten readers will have problems with someone. The rest of the paragraph suggests possible people with whom the reader may have a problem.

Development: Hypothetical Examples

The second paragraph is developed by referring to hypothetical examples—made up out of possible advice, in the form of possible dialogue "spoken" by friends. What might they possibly say? One could ask whether the first sentence of the second paragraph is adequate as a topic sentence; it is not certain that—in the abstract—it is. However, because the second paragraph is a group of examples of what people might advise us, we hardly need a strong topic sentence. The topic of the paragraph is clear without it. And Lewis does not veer off into minor considerations; he stays with a limited number of possible pieces of advice and presents them clearly.

Cohesion and Unity

The first sentence of the third paragraph *includes* the topic of the entire paragraph: the fact that all advice will fail because of the character flaws already observed in "X," but, again, this is not the model of a topic sentence. It is a model for a sentence that continues the discussion of the previous paragraph. Instead of announcing a new topic it continues the topic already under discussion. Therefore, the effect is one of unity, cohesion, and consideration of all aspects of the problem at hand. Rhetorically, the effect is one of patient, thoughtful, caring attention. Even if the writer has given "X" a "bum rap" and is wrong himself, he does not seem so.

The third paragraph patiently establishes that the possibility of change was thought to be reasonable, but that was in the past. The future might hold change, but the likelihood is slight. All in all, the possibility of anything being done to better the relationship between the writer and "X" is not good.

These three paragraphs may be said to constitute a paragraph zone. They really develop a single topic: the fact that most of us have a difficult friend about whom we are given typical advice that is basically doomed because our friend cannot or will not change.

The fact that the paragraphs lack a definitive series of topic sentences does not make them weak. Rather, it makes them appear more coherent because they seem to need one another all the more for being incomplete alone. This effect is always achieved much more fully if the writer avoids the practice of announcing boldly the new topic of the new paragraph. If the paragraph focuses clearly on that topic, it is not really necessary to state it explicitly.

In the beginning of his essay on King Kong, X. J. Kennedy takes a somewhat different approach, building each paragraph carefully around an isolatable topic sentence. Each is then developed by example.

WHO KILLED KING KONG?

The topic sentence appears first: it proposes the possibility that King Kong has been seen by huge audiences.

Comparison is used to flesh out the paragraph.

The ordeal and spectacular death of King Kong, the giant ape, undoubtedly have been witnessed by more Americans than have ever seen a performance of *Hamlet, Iphigenia at Aulis,* or even *Tobacco Road.* Since RKO-Radio Pictures first released *King Kong,* a quarter-century has gone by; yet year after year, from prints that grow more rain-beaten, from sound tracks that grow more tinny, ticket-buyers by the thousands still pursue Kong's luckless fight against the forces of technology, tabloid journalism, and the DAR. They see him chloroformed to sleep, see him whisked from his jungle isle to New York and placed on show, see him burst his chains to roam the city (lugging a frightened blonde), at last to plunge from the spire of the Empire State Building, machine-gunned by model airplanes.

Though Kong may die, one begins to think his legend unkillable. No clearer proof of his hold upon the popular imagination may be seen than what emerged one catastrophic week in March 1955, when New York WOR-TV programmed Kong for seven evenings in a row (a total of sixteen showings). Many a rival network vice-president must have scowled when surveys showed that Kong—the 1933 B-picture—had lured away fat segments of the viewing populace from such powerful competitors as Ed Sullivan, Groucho Marx and Bishop Sheen.

The first sentence establishes that Kong has staying power.

The proof is in the example of its TV popularity.

But even television has failed to run King Kong into oblivion. Coffee-in-the-lobby cinemas still show the old hunk of hokum, with the apology that in its use of composite shots and animated models the film remains technically interesting. And no other monster in movie history has won so devoted a popular audience. None of the plodding mummies, the stultified draculas, the white-coated Lugosis with the shiny pinball-machine laboratories, none of the invisible stranglers, berserk robots, or menaces from Mars has ever enjoyed so many resurrections.

Again, a clear topic sentence tells us that despite TV Kong is popular in many cinemas. He is then compared with other monsters.

X. J. KENNEDY'S TOPIC SENTENCES

Although Kennedy uses clear topic sentences for each paragraph, none of them actually gets to the stated subject matter of the entire essay: the question of who killed King Kong. That is reserved for later, after it has been established that *King Kong* is among the most popular of Hollywood's monster epics. The first three paragraphs, using the means of development by comparison, make the point very clearly. After that point is established Kennedy can go on to discuss some of the implications of the film for American life.

Here are the topic sentences:

> The ordeal and spectacular death of King Kong, the giant ape, undoubtedly have been witnessed by more Americans than have ever seen a performance of <u>Hamlet, Iphigenia at Aulis</u>, or even <u>Tobacco Road</u>.
> Though Kong may die, one begins to think his legend unkillable.
> But even television has failed to run <u>King Kong</u> into oblivion.

These sentences relate to one another through their subject matter, King Kong. Otherwise, each treats a different aspect of the overall subject, and the second two seem to have grown out of something which was said in the previous paragraph. This helps achieve cohesion and establishes transition from one paragraph to the next.

Cohesion and Unity

Paragraph 1 ended by telling us Kong was machine-gunned. Paragraph 2 begins by taking up that point and qualifying it. Paragraph 2 has brought up the subject of TV, so paragraph 3 opens with a qualification of the effect of TV on Kong. Beginning the second two paragraphs with conjunctions makes the transitions and glues the paragraphs together. Kennedy produces a tight structure that is thoroughly cohesive. The decision to begin such paragraphs (much less sentences within a paragraph) with a conjunction is based on rhetorical effect, not on rules of grammar: Kennedy knows he is using an effective strategy for achieving cohesion.

In exactly the same fashion as C. S. Lewis, Kennedy has kept each paragraph on one aspect of his subject. By sticking with a single aspect, Kennedy is naturally going to achieve unity. The first paragraph discusses why one can assume so many people have seen the film. The second gives evidence—a single example—of why Kong's legend can be expected to live. The third qualifies his popularity in relationship to other monsters. Nothing extraneous is added; there are no distractions.

The Topic Sentence As a Form of Outline

If topic sentences are chosen carefully, either in the first stages of the first draft, or in the process of revising a later draft, they can become the basis for an outline of the essay. In certain kinds of writing such an outline can help you establish a cohesive structure for an entire piece. (See the box entitled "Tips: Writing the Topic Sentence Outline.")

> *Tips: Writing the Topic Sentence Outline*
> - If your essay is a researched piece of work, you can gather the materials of your research under headings, work out the more detailed subheadings, and before writing establish your probable topic sentences. Your final revision will naturally reflect your discoveries during writing but your topic sentences can still resemble an outline.
> - If your essay is an argument that you have thought out in advance, you will profit from stating your position as a topic sentence, then stating your reasons, or the chief arguments you wish to defend, as the topic sentences of individual paragraphs. The same is true of the arguments against your position.
> - If your intention is to be precise in presenting information about a process or a circumstance, the technique of outlining with topic sentences will be effective.

ROBERT GOTTFRIED: "THE STIRRINGS OF MODERN MEDICINE"

In Robert S. Gottfried's book, *The Black Death,* Chapter 6 is entitled "The Stirrings of Modern Medicine." The author is an historian trained in research methods, writing for a sophisticated audience, but not exclusively for professional historians. His book was chosen for a major book club designed to reach the general reader, probably because of the clarity with which he presented a great mass of researched material.

The following sentences are both the first sentence and the topic sentence of each paragraph. They are in the exact order in which they appear in the chapter, and they constitute the first section of the chapter.

1. One of the most important legacies of the Black Death was the destruction of the existing medical system and the beginning of its modern successor.
2. In order to understand the first stages in this evolution it is necessary to look at the old system.
3. Most of the medical corpus was of classical origin or inspiration, but the format in which it was studied was medieval, modeled after the scholastic method popularized around 1100 by Peter Abelard, a teacher at the cathedral schools in Paris.
4. The basis of preplague medicine was the theory of humors.
5. When one's bodily humors were in equilibrium, one was in good health; this was called Eukrasia.
6. By the fourteenth century, Europe had six principal medical schools, located in Salerno, Montpellier, Bologna, Paris, Padua, Oxford.
7. The medical schools at Bologna and Paris came into prominence in the thirteenth century.
8. By the time of the Black Death, the medical school at the University of Paris was generally considered to be the most prestigious in Europe.
9. If university-trained physicians were at the top of the medical profession, surgeons stood second.
10. Barber-surgeons were distinct from surgeons proper and made no pretense of being an elite.
11. Apothecaries were more difficult to classify.
12. Finally, there was a group of unlicensed or nonprofessional medical practitioners, people with no formal training, organization, or regulation.
13. This, then, was Europe's medical community in the fourteenth century.

The first topic sentence establishes that Gottfried's development is by means of cause and effect. He begins with the medical profession, which was strained by the effects of the epidemic. His thesis, revealed in that sentence and the following topic sentences, is that the Black Death caused an overhaul in medical practice resulting in the founding of medical schools and the establishment of a medical hierarchy.

Cohesion and Unity

Each of Gottfried's paragraphs stays with its single subject and uses a variety of means of development. The most common is the presentation of examples drawn from the research. However, the rhetorical effect is not one of smooth transition from paragraph to paragraph, as in the work of C. S. Lewis and X. J. Kennedy. Rather, we have the feeling that we approach individual blocks of information in each paragraph; the cohesion is achieved in terms of meaning: the basic subject of the chapter does not change from paragraph to paragraph. Rather, each paragraph introduces a subtopic related to the general subject: the effect of the Black Death on medicine.

The concept of the paragraph zone, observed in the work of Lewis and Kennedy, is not at work in Gottfried's chapter. Rather, each paragraph establishes itself a task, then quickly accomplishes it.

In a book such as Gottfried's, this is workable. You read it to gather information, to understand an historical change, and to evaluate the thesis. It is not a contemplative essay; it is an informative essay. Most writers of such essays would readily admit that it would be ideal to be able to establish the structural principles of a chapter (or segment of it) with as much ease as Gottfried.

Writer's Workshop: Achieving Cohesion and Unity

1. Write a paragraph or paragraph zone using development by example. Choose your own topic sentence or use one of the following:
   a. King Kong is quite different from the monsters in modern films.
   b. More people than you might expect seem to believe in some form of extrasensory perception (ESP).
   c. The more money my friends have, the more they seem to waste.
   d. One of the most dangerous things you can do is drink too much at a party, then get in the car and drive home.
   e. People think that flying in an airplane is dangerous, but the statistics suggest that in comparison with other forms of travel it may be almost as safe as staying at home.
2. Choose a recent essay from your own writing and write out each of the topic sentences, one after the other in a list similar to the one prepared from Gottfried's chapter. Do they constitute an outline of your essay? Should some sentences be placed elsewhere? Should some be rewritten to help achieve better cohesion or unity in the overall essay?
3. In your next essay assignment, write out each of the topic sentences (or main sentences) in a list after you have completed the first draft, but

before you begin the second or the final draft. Before you write the final draft, produce as clear a sentence outline as possible. Use it to develop the final version of your essay. In a postscript to your essay, describe the process: did you find it difficult? Impossible? Helpful? An unnecessary problem? Do your peer editors agree with your judgment of the process and the end result?

Methods of Paragraph Development

By examining each of Gottfried's topic sentences, you can begin to determine the most likely means of development of the paragraph. This is partly because Gottfried has built in his method of development already, thus making the job of writing easier. Such a procedure is difficult on the first draft, but by the second or third draft, it should be easier. Let's examine some of Gottfried's paragraphs.

Beginning: Development by Cause and Effect

The first three paragraphs, as their topic sentences reveal, establish the medical system in use at the time (the late Middle Ages) and relate it to the past ("old system") from which it developed. Topic sentence 2 is quite bold in stating that the job of its paragraph is "to look at the old system."

Development by Definition

Because specialized material is to be presented, definition is important. Paragraph 4 cannot assume we know the theory of humors, so it must be defined:

The basis of preplague medicine was the theory of humors. The human body had four humors—blood, phlegm, yellow bile, and black bile—which, in turn, were associated with particular organs. Blood came from the heart, phlegm from the brain, yellow bile from the liver, and black bile from the spleen. Galen and Avicenna attributed certain elemental qualities to each humor. Blood was hot and moist, like air; phlegm was cold and moist, like water; yellow bile was hot and dry, like fire; and black bile was cold and dry, like earth. In effect, the human body was a microcosm of the larger world (p. 106).

Development by Comparison

Paragraph 9 implies a comparison in its topic sentence, which attempts a distinction between the theoretician of the medical Middle Ages, the physician, and the "mechanic" of medicine, the surgeon. The paragraph is developed in a straightforward way, showing the individual background of each, the nature of their work, and their social standing in the community.

If university-trained physicians were at the top of the medical profession, surgeons stood second. They had a professional standing of sorts, were incorporated into the university program in southern European medical schools, and were granted some recognition in the schools of the North. Before the Black Death, surgeons were clearly second-class medical citizens, regarded primarily as skilled craftsmen best-suited to bleeding and closing wounds. Many of them were literate and had some textbook training, but most of their knowledge was based on experience. Unlike physicians, who often never touched their patients, surgeons performed operations, including trephining (a kind of medieval brain surgery), phlebotomy, and cautery, and did much of the bone setting that is basic to medicine. While university-trained physicians were accounted the social equal of wealthy merchants (though not the equal of great bankers and long-distance traders) and lawyers, surgeons were rated at a lower level, with notaries and goldsmiths (p. 108).

Development by Illustration and Example

Development by example is implied in sentence 6, which names six medical schools; you expect to learn something about each, and do. Sentence 7 names two medical schools, and you learn why each is important: you are provided with facts about each school. Sentence 8 explains that one school, Paris, was most prestigious: the reasons for its prestige are enumerated. The next four paragraphs take the same approach: 9 gives information about physicians and surgeons; 10 about barber-surgeons; 11 about apothecaries; 12 about related nonprofessionals. Paragraph 12 becomes a kind of summary or conclusion.

Most paragraphs are developed using a mixture of means. If definition is the basis of the development of paragraph 4, there is also a touch of comparison used in defining each humor, just as there is a reliance on example to make the definition clear. However, in the case of Gottfried's examples, the mixture, whatever it might be, usually has a dominant and recognizable mode of development. This is in keeping with the clarity of his work and his intention to inform his readers.

The following is a group of individual paragraphs whose methods of development offer useful instruction. Because each of these paragraphs does an individual job, it can be examined alone; however, you must not forget that each exists in a context within an essay. Each of these is in the middle of an essay, not the beginning or end.

SAMPLE PARAGRAPHS

Chronological Presentation of Facts

The following is from a discussion of barbed wire:

Whether or not Glidden was the original inventor, he certainly was the more successful businessman. He made his first wire in 1873, forming the barbs with a converted coffee grinder and twisting the twin wires in his barn with a hand-cranked grindstone. He sold his first wire, and took out his patent, in 1874. That same year he formed a partnership with a neighbor, I. L. Ellwood, and built a factory in De Kalb. Before the end of the next year, their factory was turning out five tons of wire a day, using improved steam-operated machines. In 1876 Glidden sold a half interest in his invention to the Washburn and Moen Manufacturing company of Worcester, Massachusetts, which had been supplying him with plain wire; in payment he got $60,000, plus a royalty of 25 cents for every hundredweight of barbed wire sold. (John Fischer)

This is a transitional paragraph, moving from one subject, a discussion of who, among two neighbors in De Kalb, Illinois, was the true inventor of the modern method of making barbed wire, to the next subject: Glidden's success in business. Hence, the first sentence is not the topic sentence. Because this paragraph is a recitation of the known facts of how Glidden set himself up in business its topic is implied: it needs no stated topic sentence. John Fischer follows the simple chronology of events, a system that is practical and clear.

Development by Description

Describing people, places, and things is one of the writer's basic jobs. The following shows how one writer works out an entire paragraph devoted to the behavior of children. Two subtopics are developed in the paragraph. The first is the way children walk; the second is the way they dawdle.

But then, children don't walk like people, either—sensibly, staidly, in a definite direction. I am not sure they ever acquire our grown-up gaits. They canter, they bounce, they slither, slide, crawl, leap into the air, saunter, stand on their heads, swing from branch to branch, limp like cripples, or trot like ostriches. But I seldom recall seeing a child just plain walk. They can, however, dawdle. The longest period of recorded time is the interval between telling children to undress for bed and the ultimate moment when they have brushed their teeth, said their prayers, eaten a piece of bread and catsup, brushed their teeth all over again, asked four times for another glass of milk, checked the safety of their water pistols or their tropical fish, remembered there was something vital they had to confide to you, which they have forgotten by the time you reach their side, switched from a panda to a giraffe and back to the panda for the night's sleeping companion, begged to have the light left on in the hall, and finally, being satisfied that your screaming voice is in working order, fallen angelically into slumber. (Phyllis McGinley)

This is also a transition paragraph, as the first sentence demonstrates, linking itself to the thought that preceded it. Phyllis McGinley makes this paragraph work because of her fertile imagination. She virtually exhausts the subject in producing a virtuoso list of dawdles. Such a list could have evolved from a series of journal entries that kept track of typical things children do when faced with the proposition of going to sleep. The exactness, the familiarity of these details—along with their obvious concreteness—makes the paragraph irresistable.

Development by Question/Answer

As you know from perusing any one of dozens of contemporary magazines, many articles are almost exclusively developed in terms of questions and answers. You can do the same with a paragraph. The following example is a question that spreads over a paragraph zone:

Well, is it true that the black community is edging into the middle class? Let's look at income, the handiest guide and certainly the most generally agreed-upon measurement. What income level amounts to middle-class status? Median family income is often used, since that places a family at the exact midpoint in our society. In 1972 the median family income of whites amounted to $11,549, but black median family income was a mere $6,864.

That won't work. Let's take another guide. The Bureau of Labor Statistics says it takes an urban family of four $12,600 to maintain an "intermediate" living standard. Using that measure, the average black family not only is not middle class but it earns far less than the "lower, non-poverty" level of $8,200. Four out of five black families earn less than the "intermediate" standard.

What about collar color? Occupational status is often considered a guide to middle-class status, and this is an area in which blacks have made tremendous gains, breaking into occupations unheard of for non-whites only a decade ago. When you look at the official occupation charts, there is a double space to separate higher-status from lower-status jobs such as laborer, operative and service worker. That gap is more than a typographical device. It is an indicator of racial separation as well, for the majority of working whites hold jobs above that line, while the majority of blacks are still confined to the low-pay, low-status jobs below it. At the top of the job pinnacle, in the elite categories of the professions and business, the disparity is most glaring, with one out of four whites in such middle-class jobs in contrast to every tenth black worker. (Vernon Jordan)

This paragraph zone is typical of publications such as news magazines, which have narrow columns and need to paragraph frequently in order not to discourage the reader. The opening question controls the shape of the following paragraphs and states their general topic. However, it is not clear exactly in what sense it is a topic sentence. It states the topic of the following paragraphs, but it does not give us an idea of how the topic is to be worked out or developed. The methods of development are definition and comparison. How can we tell what we mean by middle class without a definition? Our recourse is comparison with other groups. Both these methods of development are plausible in the strategy of question/answer.

Writer's Workshop: Methods of Paragraph Development

1. Write a paragraph on a subject of your choice. After you have a good first draft, examine it to see which means of development is best to

guide your revision. Remember that you can mix them. Choose from among definition, comparison, possibility, cause and effect, description, illustration by example, classification, or question/answer.

2. Write five paragraphs on one of the paintings in the color-print section. Make each paragraph rely on a different means of development for its primary way of exploring the painting. You will need to shape your topic sentences differently for each of these paragraphs.

3. Find a paragraph you have already written and revise it so as to have it develop according to any of the means of development listed in Item 1. If possible, find a paragraph that you wrote without the conscious purpose of using one of the means of development. To what extent is the paragraph improved? How would you describe the differences between the two versions?

4. Develop the following topic sentences into appropriate paragraphs. Title each paragraph with the method of development you have used.
   a. One of the newest tourist attractions on both coasts is whale watching.
   b. Proximity is probably the most crucial factor in an undergraduate romance, probably even more important than age.
   c. Undergraduates in the 1980s have different interests than their counterparts in the past.
   d. The rewards for choosing the right course of study and doing well in college ought to be fairly clear to most of us.
   e. According to the media, the long-range weather forecast points to some interesting possibilities. [Check your local newspaper, TV weather report, or weather phone, if available.]

5. Use each of the following methods of development for a paragraph on subject of your choice (write three paragraphs in all):
   a. use of descriptive detail
   b. use of chronological presentation of facts
   c. question/answer

6. Write an essay on one of the following subjects, using as many as possible of the methods of paragraph development described in this chapter.
   a. The revival of patriotism in your state
   b. The most important use of tax dollars in your community
   c. Taxes: their fairness and unfairness
   d. How architecture in your community (or one nearby) affects the way people live
   e. Why should art and artists be supported by the society as a whole?
   f. Should towns purchase privately owned land for use as bird sanctuaries, open spaces, or protected forests?

When your essay is complete, append a list of the methods of development you used in the order in which you used them. Comment on your own experience in using such conscious processes as those required by the assignment. Does being conscious of choosing a method of development change the way you write? Do your readers feel it is an improvement? Do you?

Opening Paragraphs

The paragraphs so far discussed have all been within an essay. They are developmental, working up aspects of the general subject of the essay, or an important related subject that will cast light upon the whole. However, the first and last paragraphs of an essay do special jobs. Opening paragraphs are designed to catch and maintain the attention of the audience. Their rhetorical function is to establish a good relationship with the audience, to qualify your purposes, and to present yourself as a writer. (See the box entitled "Tips: Writing the Opening Paragraph.")

> *Tips: Writing the Opening Paragraph*
> - The opening paragraph, or paragraph zone, will usually state or imply the thesis of your work.
> - It will also establish your voice: qualifying the tone of your entire piece.
> - It will act as an invitation to read on; it will catch the reader's interest either through its general importance, its fascinating subject matter, or its special relevance to the individual reader.

ESTABLISHING THE IMPORTANCE OF THE SUBJECT MATTER

Sometimes it is essential to defend a decision to write about something important, and it is necessary to qualify the significance of the subject matter of an essay. The following paragraph, by historian Barbara Tuchman, is from the beginning of a book on the fourteenth century. It was published in a time of turmoil: after the Vietnam War and during the Watergate crisis.

At a time when everyone's mind is on the explosions of the moment, it might seem obtuse of me to discuss the fourteenth century. But I think a backward look at that disordered, violent, bewildered, disintegrating, and calamity-prone age can be consoling and possibly instructive in a time of similar disarray. Reflected in a six-hundred-year-old mirror, a more revealing image of ourselves and our species might be seen than is visible in the clutter of circumstances under our noses. The value of historical comparison was made keenly apparent to the French medievalist, Edouard Perroy, when he was writing his book on the Hundred Years' War while dodging the Gestapo in World War II. "Certain ways of behaving," he wrote, "certain reactions against fate, throw mutual light upon each other."

This is a very direct approach. The author confronts an issue that may have represented a source of anxiety and motivated her to write her book: the study of the past gives us insight into the present. Looking at past centuries helps us understand ourselves in this one.

The opening paragraph reveals the author's subject matter, the fourteenth century, and gives us a hint of her approach. She is likely to employ some comparison with that century and with our own. Her ultimate purpose will be to reveal to us "ourselves and our species." One means by which she encourages us to read on is that she promises to discuss violence, disorder, and disintegration, all qualities that to one degree or another fascinate us—particularly in reading (rather than in real-life experience).

INTRIGUING YOUR AUDIENCE

Catching the attention of the audience is sometimes a good strategy for beginning an essay, and one way to do it is to spread the introduction through several paragraphs, in a paragraph zone, ladling out the information and the thesis as one goes along. The following beginning could have been constructed as one paragraph, although each of the units of this paragraph zone treats slightly different aspects of the overall topic, which is stated in the title of Marilyn Machlowitz's "Never Get Sick in July." Notice that its strategy, in relation to the audience, is to be very direct and to imply that the audience is personally involved and should pay close attention—or else.

One Harvard medical school professor warns his students to stay home —as he does—on the Fourth of July. He fears he will become one of the holiday's highway casualties and wind up in an emergency room with an inexperienced intern "practicing" medicine on him.

Just the mention of July makes medical students, nurses, interns, residents, and "real doctors" roll their eyes. While hospital administrators maintain that nothing is amiss that month, members of the medical profession know what happens when the house staff turns over and the interns take over each July 1.

This July 1, more than 13,000 new doctors will invade over 600 hospitals across the country. Within minutes they will be overwhelmed: last July 1, less than a month after finishing medical school, Dr. John Baumann, then twenty-five, walked into Washington, D.C.'s, Walter Reed Army Medical Center, where he was immediately faced with caring for "eighteen of the sickest people I had ever seen."

The subject matter of the essay is implied in its title, and the audience is almost involuntarily forced to ask a question of the author: "Why shouldn't I get sick in July?" The author begins by quoting some research. She then goes on to suggest what kind of testimony one would get from two groups: "real doctors" and the administrators of hospitals. The quotations around the first of these groups implies that the interns, whose statistical presence constitutes the matter of the third of these paragraphs, are somehow not "real." By undermining our faith in the doctors flooding the hospitals in July, she encourages us to read on. After all, most of us will be out there watching fireworks on the fourth—so unless we plan to be hermits, we have a stake in what she is talking about.

ESTABLISHING YOUR TONE

Machlowitz's tone is fairly formal, particularly in her third paragraph. She assumed an audience who is more interested in her information than in who she is. However, there are times when you need to introduce yourself as an expert—either in a subject or in your own experience. In that case, you have the choice of writing in the first or third person, but each choice implies a distance from the audience. A rather intimate tone is achieved by using the first person; a more formal tone is achieved by using the third person. In the case of the following example, Dick Gregory, because he is known to the audience, is able to adopt a relaxed, first person mode of address, but his language is generally formal—no colloquialisms (except one: "got me a little old handkerchief")—but it is relaxed.

I never learned hate at home, or shame. I had to go to school for that. I was about seven years old when I got my first big lesson. I was in love with a little girl named Helene Tucker, a light-complexioned little girl with pigtails and nice manners. She was always clean and she was smart in school. I think I went to school then mostly to look at her. I brushed my hair and even got me a little old handkerchief. It was a lady's handkerchief, but I didn't want Helene to see me wipe my nose on my hand. The pipes were frozen again, there was no water in the house, but I washed my socks and shirt every night. I'd get a pot, and go over to Mister Ben's grocery store, and stick my pot down into his soda machine. Scoop out some chopped ice. By evening the ice melted to water for washing. I got sick a lot that winter because the fire would go out at night before the clothes were dry. In the morning I'd put them on, wet or dry, because they were the only clothes I had.

Several qualities make this paragraph an appealing beginning. It begins in what seems a chronological fashion, with a story about his "first big lesson." It also tells a story about what happened to him when he was a little boy in school, falling in love with a pretty girl. Because all of us were once little, and most of us were in school, we can relate immediately to the situation he describes. We share his feelings and can imagine what it would have been like for us if we were to have shared his experiences.

Concluding Paragraphs

Just as opening paragraphs have special jobs to do, concluding paragraphs have their own responsibilities. They come at a time when the thesis has been revealed, the approach the author has taken is either clear or not, and the subject matter has been developed as far as possible. The final paragraph may spend some time establishing what has been accomplished, what the upshot of the essay is, and possibly what the implications for the reader might be. (See the box entitled "Tips: Writing the Concluding Paragraph.")

Tips: Writing the Concluding Paragraph
- One strategy for the concluding paragraph is to review what is implied in the material gathered together in the essay, essentially answering the question: What must we conclude from what has been said?
- Another strategy is to suggest what the future holds now that the current situation has been reviewed and appraised.
- A third strategy is to reflect philosophically on the implications of the essay.
- A fourth strategy is a return to the beginning to clarify the implications of the original thesis.

Some essays do not need a concluding paragraph because they set themselves a job to do which, when done, is simply done. There is no need to review it, restate it, or summarize it. The job is done, and you know it. So you can relax. Narratives that are chronological in structure have a final moment which, when told, acts as the concluding paragraph.

On the other hand, most essays need a conclusion, and there are a great many ways to bring an essay to a satisfactory ending. Most of them respect the tips for writing the concluding paragraph. Most pieces of writing benefit from a wrapping up, a reflection on what has been said, and a backward glance on what has been done.

CONCLUDING WITH A PHILOSOPHICAL REFLECTION

Annie Dillard, famous for her personal essays reflecting on her own way of life and its implications, tells the story of preparing for a total eclipse of the sun. The body of "Total Eclipse" describes her preparations for traveling to the exact place at which the eclipse could best be seen, her anticipation of the event, and the behavior of those around her who shared her excitement at seeing something which, in Yakima, Washington, where she was, would not occur again for more than a hundred years.

Apparently people share a sense of these hazards, for when the total eclipse ended, an odd thing happened.

When the sun appeared as a blinding bead on the ring's side, the eclipse was over. The black lens cover appeared again, backlighted, and slid away. At once the yellow light made the sky blue again; the black lid dissolved and vanished. The real world began there. I remember now: we all hurried away. We were born and bored at a stroke. We rushed down the hill. We found our car; we saw the other people streaming down the hillsides; we joined the highway traffic and drove away.

We never looked back. It was a general vamoose, and an odd one, for when we left the hill, the sun was still partially eclipsed—a sight rare enough, and one which, in itself, we would probably have driven five hours to see. But enough is enough. One turns at last even from glory itself with a sigh of relief. From the depths of mystery, and even from the heights of splendor, we bounce back and hurry for the latitudes of home.

This is a paragraph zone, including a single-sentence paragraph that links what is to come with a previous discussion of the hazards of everyday living not just for those who, like some people in her immediate environment, are unimpressed by such miracles as eclipses, but for those who are suitably impressed. Those who are aware and involved in life can be surprised by fate, and it is as if, as she tells us, in the presence of such a strange and mighty event as a once in a lifetime total eclipse people are aware of the dark forces in their lives, the forces beyond their control. It is why they vamoose while the event is still in progress.

Chronologically, this is the last moment in the journey to see the eclipse, but that is not why the essay concludes here. It is because Annie Dillard drew from the events surrounding her departure a conclusion about people: they "were born and bored at a stroke." It is one of the things her experience taught her.

CONCLUDING WITH A SUMMARY REFLECTION

Michael Arlen, a television critic for *The New Yorker*, wrote a thoughtful essay on the subject of death on television during a specific week's worth of viewing. Arlen concluded that television was extremely offhand in its treatment of death, using it largely as a plot necessity in crime shows, and being indirect and evasive on news shows. The essay is filled with statistics and references to specific shows, and the final paragraphs clearly need to provide something of a conclusive summary that helps tie things together.

But it's not only children in our society who are isolated from death by our communications organizations. Virtually all the rest of us have been left to shift for ourselves in dealing with this great, commonplace matter—have been made enemies of death, terrified and stricken by its seeming uniqueness, frozen at gravesides into our separate overcoats. One has heard it said that everyone must deal with death on his own, and perhaps that's true in terms of the physical act of one human being's dying. But for much of history both the dying and the survivors (soon to be the dying) have devised systems—tribal custom or religion—whereby it was possible to place death where it belonged, as part of the continuous, collective cycle of human life. In our era, television has pushed its way into the void left by the fading presence of religion and tribal authority. Television is, if not a formal system, at any rate a huge, cool authority, and also a kind of family, and juggling act, and troupe of players—and priesthood. Indeed, once, with the Kennedy deaths and the death of Martin Luther King, it showed what it could do in incorporating into the community not just a particular or famous death but *death*. Since then, however, it has been mainly silent on the subject. We do not die, apparently, except in numbers, or in Rangoon, or with blank faces in a gunfight. The institution of television often claims to be a mirror reflecting our society, and often many of us are agreeable to thinking that this is so. Perhaps it's more and more worth realizing that it is a mirror that reflects only a part of us. Our deaths, at least—that mass collective act—are not yet part of this reflection.

CONCLUDING WITH A RETURN TO THE BEGINNING

To construct a conclusion that reflects back on the opening statements of an essay requires planning of the sort that usually comes in revision, after you realize where the essay is heading and what has been established. In one of the most well-known essays on aberrant psychology, Bruno Bettelheim describes "Joey: A 'Mechanical Boy' " who, he says in the end of his opening paragraph, "was a child who had been robbed of his humanity." Joey was convinced he was a mechanical boy, and everything he did was done exactly as a machine would have done it. It took him a great deal of time and effort to return to normal. The final paragraph zone treats that process in abbreviation, with the very last paragraph acting as a postscript that addresses the issue raised by the last sentence of the opening paragraph of the essay.

Joey at last broke through his prison. In this brief account it has not been possible to trace the painfully slow process of his first true relations with other human beings. Suffice it to say that he ceased to be a mechanical boy and became a human child. This newborn child was, however, nearly 12 years old. To recover the lost time is a tremendous task. That work has occupied Joey and us ever since. Sometimes he sets to it with a will; at other times the difficulty of real life makes him regret that he ever came out of his shell. But he has never wanted to return to his mechanical life.

One last detail and this fragment of Joey's story has been told. When Joey was 12, he made a float for our Memorial Day parade. It carried the slogan: "Feelings are more important than anything under the sun." Feelings, Joey had learned, are what make for humanity; their absence, for a mechanical existence. With this knowledge Joey entered the human condition.

Bettelheim's concluding paragraphs are spent in summing up. The body of the essay described in great detail the nature of Joey's fantasies about himself; it was left for the last paragraph to assure us that Joey broke through the fantasies and recovered. The means by which that was accomplished may have been interesting, but they were not part of the essay. Therefore, the ending of the essay is brisk and reassuring; the connection between being human and having feelings, which brings us back to the beginning of the essay, is central to the strategy of producing a sense of conclusiveness.

Writer's Workshop: Opening and Concluding Paragraphs

1. From your most recent essay, abstract the opening and the concluding paragraphs. Revise them using the most useful suggestions from this chapter. Has the shape of your paragraphs changed markedly? If not, why not? If they have, are you satisfied with the revision?

2. Write an opening paragraph on a theme that can be illustrated from your own life experience. Establish a conversational tone, assuming an audience of people of your own age, but people who do not know you very well. Attempt, through your tone, and through the examples you allude to, to present yourself in a favorable light. Comment, after you have written the paragraph, on what strategies you worked up for yourself, and what effects you feel most satisfied with in the paragraph.

3. Rewrite the paragraph you have written for Item 2 above and address it to a judgmental adult, one who you fear may not be sympathetic to you. Keep in mind that this is an opening paragraph and that in the body of your essay you would have a chance to soften your audience's resistance to you.

4. Write a single paragraph that describes the primary differences between the paragraphs you have written to satisfy Items 2 and 3 above. In other words, analyze your own performance, making reference to the processes which you used to create the paragraphs and the relative success—in your estimation—of each paragraph.

5. From the same essay you consulted for Item 1, take the final paragraph and evaluate it as a concluding paragraph using the suggestions and tips for writing the concluding paragraph. What are its strengths; what are its weaknesses? What qualities does it possess that are not discussed in your response to Item 1?

6. If you feel your concluding paragraph is not satisfactory, revise it using as many of the tips and suggestions in this chapter as are relevant to your purposes.

15

Style: Imitating Accomplished Writers

You learned language through a process of imitation, a natural intellectual function of mimicking what you heard, and in many cases what you saw. Aristotle once declared that he would rather be born blind than deaf, because if he were deaf he could not learn language through imitation of sounds, and if he could not learn language, he could not be civilized.

The patient reproduction of what you hear produces language and understanding. Through experimentation and attention to detail, you begin at an early age to master the most amazing and complex of human inventions. As you grow older, you learn to mimic not only the basis of language, but special turns and twists of phrases that contribute toward a special style associated with your friends, your neighborhood, your region. Different social groups develop an approach to language that depends entirely on association and imitation. Black teenagers in Newark, New Jersey, have a different approach to language from white teenagers in Waterville, Maine, or Hispanic teenagers in Miami, Florida. All of these groups differentiate themselves through imitation, usually within the group.

The vitality of spoken language is especially noticeable in dramatic programs on television, or in films. Rural programs, such as the now defunct "Waltons" or "Mayberry RFD," and networks such as Nashville have one approach to language. It is infectious, and when programs are popular, you will hear twists of phrases in current use, and probably pick them up yourself. The same is true of inner city shows, such as "Hill Street Blues," "Miami Vice," and "St. Elsewhere." The writers of these shows listen carefully to the rhythms and style of language and imitate them in their characters. We in turn pick up expressions and add them to our repertoire, especially when we want to seem in vogue.

439

Imitation is the careful attention to nuance, detail, and style—then the effort to reproduce those qualities in your own language.

Imitation: Sentence Architecture

A good writer doesn't just read. A good writer reads in order to learn how to develop the skills of a writer. In this sense anyone who wishes to learn to write well has an astonishing advantage. Good writing is available to be examined and absorbed by anyone; there is no fee. But it is a challenging experience to look at the achievement of a good writer and compare it with your own work. As apprentice writers, you are usually overwhelmed by the excellence of the work, and cannot hope to emulate it. Or, you may read a writer whose style is so idiosyncratic that it is not only impossible, but useless to try to imitate it.

It is not enough to examine the end product of a good writer's work. You must think about the processes by which the work was achieved. This requires detailed examination, paying attention to the writer's word choices, the tone, the approach to imagery, metaphor, connotation. It requires a careful study of sentence patterning and the ways simple sentences balance complex sentences, and how accumulation contrasts with parallelism and periodicity.

Further, studying writing requires a consideration of the overall patterning of paragraphs, the use of topic sentences and where they appear in the paragraph, and what means of development are used to explore ideas.

You have been doing this throughout this book. The examples that appear in the chapters devoted to the means of development, as well as the chapters devoted to style all have examples which are there for study. In a sense, they are there for you to learn from by imitation.

Looking at Structure

Looking at structure is an architectural approach to imitation. You are going to be asked to examine the plans for a piece of writing. Sentences and paragraphs are like any other structures: they have parts and those parts are positioned according to plan. They can be moved, altered, reshaped, and the results will be a new structure.

The most interesting result is that no matter how hard you try, you can never duplicate the original, and so you will quickly see that this approach to imitation is totally unlike plagiarism. Plagiarism is the taking of someone else's work and representing it as your own. If you change anything, you change it only slightly. But imitation requires a total change of the surfaces of the piece you are imitating, while it also requires that you adhere to the structure that lies beneath.

WORKING ON SENTENCES

In Chapter 13, "Style: A Rhetoric of the Sentence," you spent some time examining the grammatical structure of a sentence. Some of that will come in handy now, and you may wish to review those pages as you consider the following.

The instructions for imitating sentences will make it sound as if you must do everything exactly correctly. However, there is a considerable latitude implied in what I am about to say. As I tell my students, the point of this is not to do it perfectly, but to try to do it at all. In other words, the discipline of the attempt is what produces results. Perfection is not possible. (See the box entitled "Tips: Imitating Sentences.")

Tips: Imitating Sentences

- Spend some time examining the underlying structure of the sentence you wish to imitate. Analyze it in terms of its major parts: independent clauses, dependent clauses, and subordinate phrases.
- Choose a totally unrelated subject matter so as to avoid interference with the original.
- Avoid as much as possible using the same connective words (except for *and*).
- Aim in your imitation to reproduce the same kind of parallelism, periodicity, or cumulative techniques that the original uses.
- If you cannot imitate a sentence in exact detail, get as close as you can and make your sentence as strong and effective as possible.
- Remember your ultimate purpose in imitation: to learn from the inside how other writers make their sentences work. Concentrate on absorbing their techniques.

TIP

It is useful for you to know the main elements of the sentence, because the analyses depend on our mutual understanding of the parts of a sentence. The following symbols are based on Chapter 13, and I list them here for convenience:

IC   This is the independent clause: an independent subject and verb that could stand as a sentence.

DC   This is the dependent clause: it has a subject and verb, but is dependent: a noun clause; adverb clause; adjective clause.

SP   This refers to all types of subordinate phrases: they have a subject or a verb, but not both; sometimes neither (e.g., ''very well''). They can be participial, infinitive, gerund, adverbial, adjectival, prepositional.

( )   Means that one structure interrupts another structure.

+   Means that one structure is linked to another.

Few working writers actually analyze their sentences in the fashion you are about to do. Just as good golfers do not analyze their swing when they are on the back nine in a PGA tournament, and just as performers of a high-wire balancing act do not stop to take measurements of angles of thrust, writers work out of a discipline of learning that has become virtually instinctive to them. The point of imitation, however, is to begin a conscious analysis so you can begin to develop some of the instincts of the writer. Learning how to get inside a sentence will give you some insights that it might take years to discover otherwise.

The point of imitation is not for you to use it later in your work, but to learn basic principles. Fundamentally, what you are learning is that sentences grow and develop, and that if you have an understanding of their parts and how they are positioned, you can create a polished and well-made sentence of your own. Then, once you can do that, you can go on to do the same with paragraphs.

DETAILED IMITATION: OPENING SENTENCES

The opening sentence is of special importance, because it must somehow maintain the interest of the reader while also providing some insight into the way the piece of writing will develop. All writers work hard on their opening sentences, and they are especially well polished.

The simplest method of analysis is used for each of the following sentences. You are to concern yourself only with the independent clause, the dependent clause, and any subordinate phrases. This means, in the simplest sense, that when prepositional and other phrases are part of the clauses, independent or dependent, they do not need to be identified separately. This is in the interest of your examination of the major parts of the sentences. In your own imitations, you may add such phrases as you like without altering the fact that they are independent or dependent clauses.

Imitation: Sample Sentences

The following samples are imitations of the opening sentences of essays by fine writers. Below them you will find the sentence that was the basis of the imitation. Then you will see an analysis of the sample, with the imitation analyzed in the same way. The analyses will show you how the imitations were developed.

1. No one can tell me, despite my inexperience, that photography is not art.

2. People love to flock to country fairs: they enjoy the livestock and produce during the day and they like the excitement of the rides at night.

3. Some uninformed people insist that the First World War, when it began in Europe, was caused by territorial ambitions, failed technologies, and tyranny: but it was just as much a product of overpopulation, colonial ambition, and insane patriotism—Europe had not seen a major conflagration since Napoleon and the war of 1812, which was still the basis of modern military strategy.

The originals, their analyses, and the analyses of the imitations are as follows:

1. *Original:* I have often done my best to consider, in various aspects, what is really the matter with Sightseeing. G. K. Chesterton ("On Sightseeing")

   Analysis: I have often done my best to consider,: independent clause
   in various aspects,: prepositional phrase
   what is really the matter with Sightseeing: dependent noun clause

   Imitation: No one can tell me,: independent clause
   despite my inexperience,: prepositional phrase
   that photography is not art: dependent noun clause.

2. *Original:* Soothsayers and fiction-writers have a case: one day the Earth will collide with a bright comet or its dark corpse and the result will be world-wide mayhem. Nigel Calder ("The Comet Is Coming")

   Analysis: Soothsayers and fiction-writers have a case: independent clause
   one day the Earth will collide with a bright comet or its dark corpse: independent clause
   and the result will be world-wide mayhem: independent clause

   Imitation: People love to flock to country fairs: independent clause
   they enjoy the livestock and produce during the day: independent clause
   and they like the excitement of the rides at night: independent clause

3. *Original:* We all remember that Queen Victoria, when she died in 1901, had never got to see a helicopter, a television set, penicillin, an

electric refrigerator; yet she had seen railroads, electric lights, textile machinery, the telegraph—she came about midway in the industrial and technological revolution that has transformed our world. Randall Jarrell ("The Taste of the Age")

> *Analysis:*   We all remember: independent clause
> that Queen Victoria, (. . .), had never got to see a helicopter, a television set, penicillin, an electric refrigerator: dependent clause
> (when she died in 1901): dependent clause
> yet she had seen railroads, electric lights, textile machinery, the telegraph—: independent clause
> she came about midway in the industrial and technological revolution: independent clause
> that has transformed our world: dependent clause
>
> *Imitation:*   Some uninformed people insist: independent clause
> that the First World War (. . .) was caused by territorial ambitions, failed technologies, and tyranny: dependent clause
> (when it began in Europe): dependent clause
> but it was just as much a product of overpopulation, colonial ambition, and insane patriotism—: independent clause
> Europe had not seen a major conflagration since Napoleon and the war of 1812: independent clause
> which was still the basis of modern military strategy: dependent clause

This method may seem an unusually detailed way of going about imitation. But consider some of the alternatives. If, as an aspiring writer, you admire the work of someone whom you would like to emulate, what might you do to begin? You might read incessantly until the rhythms of the person's prose began to ring in your ears. And although that is not a bad thing, even then you may find when you begin to write yourself that you pick up only some of the surface elements instead of the deeper structure of the style.

Ask yourself exactly what you would do to imitate the following two opening sentences without submitting them first to the preceding kind of analysis:

THE FUTURE IS NOW

Not so long ago I was reading in a magazine with an enormous circulation some instructions as to how to behave if and when we see that flash brighter than the sun which means that the atom bomb has arrived. I read of course with the intense interest of one who has everything to learn on this subject; but at the end, the advice dwindled to this: the only real safety seems to lie in simply being somewhere else at the time, the further away the better; the next best, failing access to deep shelters, bombproof cellars and all, is to get under a stout table—that is, just what you might do if someone were throwing bricks through your window and you were too nervous to throw them back. (Katherine Ann Porter)

The task of imitating these sentences becomes very difficult, because without detailed analysis everyone's sense of them is merely impressionistic. You can only regard them in a vague way, and your imitation would be only an approximation of the original. Detailed analysis is essential to making the principles of imitation work. Without a detailed analysis into their basic parts, the imitations of these sentences have only one quality in common: there is one relatively short sentence followed by a relatively long one.

Detailed imitation requires the careful analysis of the sentence into its major parts. And you as a writer benefit because you discover that it is easier to imitate an independent clause or subordinate phrase than an entire sentence.

Analyzing sentences into their major parts makes the job of imitation much easier. It also simplifies the process of learning how good writers construct their sentences, and how they achieve variety of structure.

Writer's Workshop: Imitating Sentences

1. Imitate the following sentence. Be sure to follow the analysis carefully. Construct an independent clause joined by *that* to a dependent clause that explains the meaning of a key word in the independent clause.

   More significant than those major encounters are the never ending little skirmishes that wear us down (Hans C. von Baeyer, ''The Wonder of Gravity'').

   Analysis: More significant than these major encounters are the never ending little skirmishes: independent clause
   that wear us down: dependent clause

   Your imitation:

   _____ independent clause
   _____
   _____ dependent clause
   _____

2. Imitate the following sentence, using a subordinate phrase of time (*After, Now, Soon,* etc.) or of place (*Where, Near, Beyond,* etc.) as your opener.

   When I used to ask my mother which we were, rich or poor, she refused to tell me (Eudora Welty, ''A Sweet Devouring'').

Writer's **W**orkshop

> *Analysis:*   When I used to ask my mother: dependent clause
> which we were, rich or poor: dependent clause
> she refused to tell me: independent clause
>
> *Your imitation:*
>
> _____ dependent clause
> _____ dependent clause
> _____ independent clause

3. Imitate the following sentence. Use a short independent clause and two infinitive phrases. Notice how Azimov fleshes out his infinitive phrases.

   It is easy to divide a human being into mind and body and to attach far greater importance and reverence to the mind (Isaac Azimov, ''Pure and Impure: The Interplay of Science and Technology'').

   > *Analysis:*   It is easy: independent clause
   > to divide a human being into mind and body: infinitive phrase
   > and to attach far greater importance and reverence to the mind: infinitive phrase
   >
   > *Your imitation:*
   >
   > _____ independent clause
   > _____
   > _____ infinitive phrase
   > _____
   > _____ infinitive phrase

4. Imitate the following sentence. Aim for a good parallelism of the final three subordinate phrases.

   In former years, American University students have at times distinguished themselves by such newsworthy antics as the swallowing of live goldfish, panty raids on the dormitories of girl undergraduates, and the pelting of police (Helen Lawrenson, ''The Bulls of Pamplona'').

   > *Analysis:*   In former years: subordinate phrase
   > American university students have at times distinguished themselves by such newsworthy antics as: independent clause
   > the swallowing of live goldfish: subordinate phrase
   > panty raids on the dormitories of girl undergraduates: subordinate phrase
   > and the pelting of police: subordinate phrase
   >
   > *Your imitation:*
   >
   > _____ subordinate phrase
   > _____

————————————— independent clause
————————————— subordinate phrase
————————————— subordinate phrase
————————————— subordinate phrase

5. The next sentence is the beginning of a famous meditation on nature, life, and death. Notice that some parts of the sentence, such as the modifier of the first subject of the first independent clause, can also be clauses. The first dependent clause, an adjective clause, is embedded in the entire independent clause. In your imitation, use an embedded clause to modify your first subject.

Moths that fly by day are not properly to be called moths; they do not excite that pleasant sense of dark autumn nights and ivy-blossom which the commonest yellow-underwing asleep in the shadow of the curtain never fails to rouse in us (Virginia Woolf, "Death of a Moth").

Analysis: that fly by day: embedded dependent clause (adjective clause)
Moths (that fly by day) are not properly to be called moths: independent clause
they do not excite that pleasant sense of dark autumn nights and ivy-blossom: independent clause
which the commonest yellow-underwing asleep in the shadow of the curtain never fails to rouse in us: dependent clause

Your imitation:

————————————— dependent clause (adjective clause)

————————————— independent clause

————————————— independent clause

————————————— dependent clause

Looking at Paragraphs

A CLASSROOM EXERCISE: IMITATING JAMES BALDWIN

One of the exercises that most benefits my writing students is the analysis and imitation of a seven-sentence sample from the work of the masterful essayist, James Baldwin. This may be difficult for those who have not closely analyzed sentences in the earlier examples, but if you have done some of the analyses you will find yourself able to do the following exercise.

Student writers who have done this exercise say that the results are so striking that they sound, for the first time, like the writers whose work they read. There is a reason for this: they are doing consciously what professional writers (for the most part) have learned to do unconsciously, through experiment, trial, error, and imitation of their own.

A STUDENT SAMPLE

Before going further, let us look at a student sample. This was the best work of a student up to this point in a writing course, and it wowed his colleagues when they heard him read it. As you read it, ask yourself whether, apart from the fact that you have been told it was produced by a process of imitation, you would ever suspect that it was anything but a well-made paragraph.

The first cut of the gilded cards revealed the devil. As the next nine cards were also turned, the images of my past, present, and future materialized before me. The specters that the gypsy conjured to complete the reading were both enticing and disturbing. I saw then that the gypsy's face, which had remained implacable as she revealed my destiny, had become turbulent. Her hands shook, spilling the rest of the deck which landed haphazardly upon the floor; of course, logic told me, I was sure that I was going to be shocked by Madame Lucia's exorbitant fee before I went home. I was inclined to be skeptical of the old gypsy on the beach in Atlantic City by the big orange sign on the popcorn stand at the end of the boardwalk. When I finally paid her and left, I started to reflect upon her musings, and at the same time chuckled at myself, wondering whether, for my twenty-five dollars, I had learned my true destiny.

Ethan

The virtue of Ethan's paragraph lies in its vividness of detail and the rhythms of sentences, particularly in the way in which they change and alter their patterns. The detail and the color come from Ethan, however much they may have been inspired by James Baldwin. But the structure of the sentences is all James Baldwin's. Ethan said that this was a very difficult exercise to do. It was the first of its kind that he had ever done, and partly because of that it took him much longer than he thought it would. His feeling at the end, however, was that of satisfaction. He learned something about style that he would not have using any other method. His subsequent work in the course demonstrated that what he learned stayed with him.

Here is the sample paragraph that Ethan relied upon with the sentences numbered for later analysis. After you have read it, go back and reread Ethan's paragraph.

A SAMPLE FOR PARAGRAPH ANALYSIS

(1) The day of my father's funeral had also been my nineteenth birthday. (2) As we drove him to the graveyard, the spoils of injustice, anarchy, discontent, and hatred were all around us. (3) It seemed to me that God himself had devised, to mark my father's end, the most sustained and brutally dissonant of codas. (4) And it seemed to me, too, that the violence which rose all about us as my father left the world had been devised as a corrective for the pride of his eldest son. (5) I had declined to believe in that apocalypse which had been central to my father's vision; very well, life seemed to be saying, here is something that will certainly pass for an apocalypse until the real thing comes along. (6) I had inclined to be contemptuous of my father for the conditions of his life, for the conditions of our lives. (7) When his life had ended I began to wonder about that life and also, in a new way, to be apprehensive about my own.

The analysis of the paragraph follows:

1. **IC**

   IC: The day of my father's funeral had also been my nineteenth birthday

   This is one independent clause with a prepositional phrase ("of . . . funeral") embedded between the subject ("day") and the verb ("had . . . been"). It is an example of a strong simple sentence stating the theme of the paragraph.

2. **DC + IC**

   DC: As we drove him to the graveyard

   IC: the spoils of injustice, anarchy, discontent, and hatred were all around us. A dependent clause followed by a main clause: a basic complex sentence.

3. **IC + D(SP)C**

   IC: It seemed to me

   DC: that God himself had devised . . . the most sustained and brutally dissonant of codas.

   SP: to mark my father's end

   An independent clause with a noun clause as the object of *seemed*, with a subordinate phrase (infinitive) embedded in it. This is another complex sentence.

4. **IC + D(DC + DC)C**

   IC: And it seemed to me, too

   DC: that the violence . . . had been devised as a corrective for the pride of his youngest son.

   DC: which rose all about us

   DC: as my father left the world

   Similar to sentence 3, except that the noun clause has two dependent clauses, an adjective clause (*which*) and an adverb clause ("as my father left"), embedded in it. It too is a complex sentence.

5. **IC + DC + I(DC)C + DC + DC**
   IC: I had declined to believe in that apocalypse
   DC: which had been central to my father's vision
   IC: very well . . . here is something
   DC: life seemed to be saying
   DC: that will certainly pass for an apocalypse
   DC: until the real thing comes along.
   The first independent clause is followed by an adjective clause (*which*); a prepositional phrase, and then, after the semicolon, the second independent clause begins a new understanding. This is a compound/complex sentence, and an example of accumulation.

6. **IC + SP + SP + SP + SP + SP + SP**
   IC: I had inclined to be contemptuous of my father
   SP: for the conditions
   SP: of his life
   SP: for the conditions
   SP: of our lives.
   This is a main clause subject and verb ("I had inclined") with an infinitive phrase ("to be") as the object of the verb *inclined*, followed by a series of prepositional phrases: (*for, of, for, of*). This is a true cumulative sentence, quite like many durable, ordinary sentences.

7. **DC + IC + SP + I(SP)C + SP**
   DC: When his life had ended
   IC: I began to wonder
   SP: about that life
   IC: and . . . to be apprehensive
   SP: in a new way
   SP: about my own.

This is complicated: the second independent clause has its subject and verb ("I began") implied, rather than restated. Baldwin is saying: "I began to wonder and (I began) to be apprehensive." The rest of the sentence is direct enough.

The following example is that of another student using the same model. His name is Uk, and he is Korean born, with only a year in the United States. English is not an easy language for him, but this exercise helped him rewrite an essay he had been working on about Latin America. He still shows signs of some difficulty with the language, but they are few, and easy enough to correct. This is exactly as he wrote it:

Mining at Nicaraguan harbors by CIA may surprise many Americans. When we remember the past United States foreign policy towards Central America, few people would be surprised. It was in the early 1910s that the United States government intervene in Columbia to weaken its influence on Panama Canal. It was in 1954 that the Guatemalan government which was established through election was overthrown by the United States due to independency policy from the United States corporations. The United States government were always proud of its intervention under the name that the United States try to defend justice at the world level: more specifically saying, they are defender of democracy and they prevent the evil of communism from growing. Many people from Central America are likely to accept the advancement of American democracy for the development of Central America and for the development of Central American people. However, when American democracy is forced to be accepted, it may also look like evil, especially for the concerned people.

Uk

Uk had been in the United States for only a year when he wrote this piece. He works hard and he listens well. His comment on this exercise was that he felt that he was somehow getting inside this paragraph when he wrote it. He also felt keen satisfaction from the result. Later, Uk went on to write an extensive research essay on the policies of our government toward Central America, using the sample here as one of his paragraphs.

Writer's Workshop: Imitating Paragraphs

1. Here is your chance to try the same experiment in imitation. Refer to the James Baldwin's paragraph, then note the analysis here. Choose a subject that is unrelated to Baldwin's.

Writer's **W**orkshop

1. **IC** _____

2. **DC + IC** _____

3. **IC + D(SP)C** _____

4. **IC + D(DC + DC)C** _____

5. **IC + DC + SP + I(DC)C + DC + DC** _____

6. **IC + SP + SP + SP + SP** _____

_____

_____

_____

7. **DC + IC + SP + I(SP)C + SP** _____

_____

_____

_____

2. Using the paragraph below as your model, construct your own imitation on a subject of your choosing.

> It's still natural today to speak of "audio-visual aids" to teaching, for we still think of the book as norm, of other media as incidental. We also think of the new media (press, radio, TV) as _mass media_ and think of the book as an individualistic form—individualistic because it isolated the reader in silence and helped create the Western "I." Yet it was the first product of mass production. (Marshall McLuhan)

In this example, try to imitate the relative length of the sentences, and the punctuation, including the parenthesis and the dash.

1. **IC** _____
   SP _____
   SP _____
   SP _____ ,
   IC _____
   SP _____
   SP _____ .
2. **IC** _____ (_____)
   SP _____
   SP _____
   DC _____
   DC _____ .
3. **IC** _____ .

3. Choose a paragraph you admire. Analyze it as best you can, in terms of IC (independent clause), DC (dependent clause), and SP (subordinate phrase). It is not necessary for you to be exactly accurate with the description, as long as you can determine the general shape of sentences in the paragraph.

Once you have made your analysis, create your own paragraph in imitation of your original.

Observing Style

Any critic of the technique of imitation as I have described it will point out the obvious: that imitation is artificial. Such a critic might also point out that writers rarely use the technique. The critics are right on all counts. However, you should keep in mind the goals established at the outset for the use of imitation. It is a technique designed to help you gain access to the inside of a piece of writing. You are not expected to use this method directly in your writing.

The complaint that imitation is artificial is also correct. Artificial means "made by art," and that is precisely the point. The sentences and paragraphs we have looked at are constructed by an art that is very mysterious if all you do is look at the finished product. The mystery starts to clear when you begin to look beneath the surfaces of the art and see that the whole has parts and that you can examine those parts and create them on your own. Obviously, any complex structure is artificially analyzed into its parts. And clearly any complex structure is easier to understand when its parts are separated out for us. Art is artificial, and the art of writing is no exception.

Looking at the structure of sentences and paragraphs is one way of observing details of a writer's style. There are others. The principles of imitation can be applied to the problems of word choice. If you look at a writer who takes a special approach to word choices, you have a chance to analyze what those choices are and to learn from them. That is true for the use of special technical words, for the use of words that praise or insult, and for the use of affectations like the use of slang, colloquialisms, or Latin quotations. The key to this kind of imitation is nothing other than observation. If you look for the unusual use of words, you will find it. If you find it and observe it, you will be able to imitate it, however approximately.

The following example is somewhat different. It is the opening paragraph of a complete essay. Joan Didion is one of the most successful and acclaimed of contemporary essayists. Her work covers many different kinds of subjects related to the way in which we live in contemporary America. Her style is complex, and it is closely related to her attitude toward her subject matter and her audience. This is exactly as it should be.

OBSERVING JOAN DIDION: "ON THE MALL"

ON THE MALL

They float on the landscape like pyramids to the boom years, all those Plazas and Malls and Esplanades. All those Squares, and Fairs. All those Towns and Dales, all those Villages, all those Forests and Parks and Lands.

Stonestown, Hillsdale. Valley Fair, Mayfair, Northgate, Southgate, Eastgate, Westgate, Gulfsgate. They are toy garden cities in which no one lives but everyone consumes, profound equalizers, the perfect fusion of the profit motive and the egalitarian ideal, and to hear their names is to recall words and phrases no longer quite current. Baby Boom. Consumer Explosion. Leisure Revolution. Do-It-Yourself Revolution. Backyard Revolution. Suburbia. "The Shopping Center," the Urban Land Institute could pronounce in 1957, "is today's extraordinary retail business evolvement. . . . The automobile accounts for suburbia, and suburbia accounts for the shopping center."

This is a skillful piece of prose aimed at an upbeat audience that knows Didion's subject matter and that she expects will respond positively to her implied criticism. The following schematic breakdown highlights the most important techniques Didion uses here.

1. The opening sentence uses a striking comparison: the shopping malls "float like pyramids." The comparison reminds us that for our time, the shopping mall is just about as important and culturally symbolic as the pyramids were for the Egyptians. If the Egyptians were most centrally concerned with religion and the afterlife, our culture is most centrally concerned with shopping. The metaphor *float* has numerous associations, but in the context of pyramids it makes us think of the floating of a mirage on the desert landscape.
2. The next few so-called sentences are fragments—"All those squares and fairs." Didion is using the technique of the list: listing one popular name after another. Each of us has a shopping mall with such a name nearby.
3. The metaphor that defines the malls as "toy garden cities" in which no one lives is also striking. Didion stresses the egalitarian nature of the mall: everyone is a consumer.
4. Then follows another list in the form of sentence fragments: "Baby Boom. Consumer Explosion." And more.
5. Finally she ends with a quotation from the Urban Land Institute. It gives special authority to her statement.

The key to the passage is in Joan Didion's treatment of the shopping mall, using a couple of striking metaphors, and the very curious technique of the list in the form of the sentence fragment. Ordinarily it is never recommended that an apprentice writer practice the sentence fragment—after all, such writers use them too often unconsciously. But one of the obvious realities of writing is that good writers use them for good effect. It is clear that the effect here is to relieve the tedium of the list. It works.

The metaphors help develop emotional interest. The lists relate the experience to each of us, and the quotation lends authority to Didion's views. As a result, this opening paragraph holds our interest and makes it possible for us to compare our own experiences with hers.

Here is a sample imitation of this paragraph. It does not attempt to break down each sentence and follow its grammatical structure. Instead, it aims at using the basic devices: striking metaphors, lists, and a final quotation.

A STUDENT SAMPLE: "ON THE ROAD"

ON THE ROAD

They leap and pounce, corner and glide all around us, the denizens of the modern asphalt jungle, all those gleaming new automobiles. All those Jaguars and Panthers. Cougars and Colts. Mustangs, Impalas, Falcons, Rabbits, Lynxes. Their animal names transform us into hunters once again, calling us back to our primitive urges and, even if only temporarily, joining us with primal nature, giving us, for a price, domination over the most robust beasts. How unlikely it would be for the moguls of automotive magnificence to name our automobiles after vegetables. Can you imagine pulling up to your favorite restaurant in a Toyota Turnip? Isn't it clear why we will never see a Ford Tomato on the road? Or Plymouth Potato, Renault Radish, Chevrolet Carrot, Datsun Cauliflower, or a Volkswagen Acorn Squash? Consumer's Union said it clearly, "Consumers want to borrow some of the glamour of their automobiles, which is why manufacturers continue to use names that imply freedom, power, and animal grace."

Josh

The effect of this kind of imitation is quite different from what is achieved by relying only on the grammatical structure of a paragraph. Here, you observe the explicit devices that the writer uses, then get inside them by using them yourself.

You would never use a piece of imitation produced in this fashion in your own work. Your purposes for studying such a paragraph and imitating it are primarily to give yourself a chance to follow in the footsteps of a successful writer and learn firsthand some of the tricks of the trade. Once having mastered such approaches, you can then have a free hand at structuring your own prose and developing your own techniques.

Here is another paragraph that seems quite natural at first reading. It is snappy, effective, and interesting. It is also written by one of our most endeared writers, Margaret Mead.

MARGARET MEAD: "NEW SUPERSTITIONS FOR OLD"

NEW SUPERSTITIONS FOR OLD

Once in a while there is a day when everything seems to run smoothly and even the riskiest venture comes out exactly right. You exclaim, "This is my lucky day!" Then as an afterthought you say, "Knock on Wood!" Of course, you do not really believe that knocking on wood will ward off danger. Still, boasting about your own good luck gives you a slightly uneasy feeling—and you carry out the little protective ritual. If someone challenged you at that moment, you would probably say, "Oh, that's nothing. Just an old superstition."

But when you come to think about it, what is a superstition?

Some of the important techniques used in this paragraph are

1. The relaxed opening, "Once in a while," is almost in the same category as "Once upon a time."
2. The use of a quotation from you—not one you actually said, but one you might say. Then, another quote after a moment of reflection.
3. Then a moment of reflection on the main point just made.
4. With a final quotation, identifying the meaning of your first quotation.
5. And a single-sentence paragraph posing a question.

The following imitation tries to use most of the techniques in a very different kind of approach.

A STUDENT SAMPLE: "A BLIND DATE"

A BLIND DATE

Every so often somebody comes up to me in the Union or in the dorm lounge and starts asking what I'm doing for the weekend. "Uh-oh," I say to myself. "He's got a girlfriend who's got a girlfriend, and. . . ." I can see it coming: the blind date syndrome. "How come he singles me out again," I can't help but ask. Is it because my girlfriend goes to a college a thousand miles away? Or is it that he thinks I'm just anxious to help out when I can? Why can't I just say no? Why do I have to hem and haw until I find myself saying, sure, I'll help you out? I've never really had any fun on a blind date, so I should just say, "Forget it."

Of course, I sometimes think I might meet someone interesting: after all, in those cases I'm a blind date myself, right?

Loring

The subject matter is very different, and the natural development of ideas takes a new direction. Loring wisely followed the shape of Margaret Mead's paragraph as far as seemed practicable. When he had to innovate—as in asking the rhetorical questions near the end of the first paragraph—he did so. The result is a natural-sounding paragraph and the beginning of an interesting meditation on blind dates.

Loring took the opportunity to learn something about how writers make choices about style. As he did so, he added stylistic details of his own and became aware of the process of choice that involves every writer in every piece of writing. Style is choice. Studying the style of other good writers is helpful in several ways: it helps you see the kinds of choices such writers make, but it helps even more in that you begin to realize that choices are available that you may not have known about.

In the simplest sense, the question of style is essentially related to the awareness of options. When you know the options are there, you can take advantage of them. When you are unaware, you simply let opportunities slip by.

Imitating the Right Teacher

The work that goes into imitation will be well spent only if you study good writing. When I referred earlier to great writers developing their style through the process of reading other writers and then absorbing details of style, I meant that the writers they read were the best available. I also meant that such writers usually imitated others who were trying to write the same kind of work: novelists reading novelists, poets reading poets, essayists reading essayists.

When you begin to think about looking for writers to study in detail, you should look at essayists. If you have a special field of interest, such as history or science, then look at essayists who also specialize in that field. Be sure to read essayists who are fairly contemporary and who write in English—as opposed to reading a translation.

Further, you should examine those writers whose work does not "wow" you. In other words, see whether or not you feel that with a little work you actually could write something of a similar quality. Some writers are simply so dazzling that most of us have little or no hope of coming close to what they do. Imitating such a writer is frustrating and unproductive. Study the style with this thought in mind: Can I possibly construct a sentence as this writer does? Can I ever hope to emulate the choice of words, the essential strategies?

Examine the style of such writers to make sure that it is not, like that of Tom Wolfe, Erma Bombeck, William Buckley, or Hunter Thompson, mannered and especially quirky. Obviously, many fine and successful writers are quirky. That is part of their charm, but for you such quirkiness is useless. Your concerns at this point in your writing are not to pick up the mannerisms of trendy writers, but to develop insight into the more durable questions of style.

Some of the modern writers who I recommend are

Machael J. Arlen	Toni Morrison
Isaac Asimov	Norman Mailer
Russell Baker	John McPhee
James Baldwin	Samuel Eliot Morison
Gwendolyn Brooks	George Orwell
Annie Dillard	Katharine Anne Porter
Ralph Ellison	Lewis Thomas
Nora Ephron	Eudora Welty
Ellen Goodman	Edmund Wilson
Stephen Jay Gould	Virginia Woolf
Edward Hoagland	E. B. White
Martin Luther King, Jr.	Richard Wright

If you examine good writers, you give yourself the chance of improving your own writing in a direction that will benefit you throughout life. After considering some of what I have said about imitation, it may be clearer now why writers are always advised to study other writers. It is for the same reason architects go to school to study the work of other architects.

Writer's Workshop: Imitation

1. Examine the following paragraph and its brief analysis. In the space provided, write your own paragraph using imitation to produce similar effects. In this exercise you do not have to imitate the exact grammatical structure of each sentence.

A HANGING

It was in Burma, a sodden morning of the rains. A sickly light, like yellow tinfoil, was slanting over the high walls in to the jail yard. We were waiting outside the condemned cells, a row of sheds fronted with double bars, like small animal cases. Each cell measured about ten feet by ten and was quite bare within except for a plank bed and a pot for drinking water. In some of them brown, silent men were squatting at the inner bars, with their blankets draped round them. These were the condemned men, due to be hanged within the next week or two.

George Orwell

This paragraph is notable for several qualities:
1. The first sentence establishes the place and the season.
2. The second sentence includes a simile, "like yellow tinfoil," to make the sensory experience more vivid.

3. The third sentence establishes the point of view, telling us where the narrator and his colleagues were.

4. The next sentences concentrate on exact measurement, precise details of the contents of a space, and specific information.

5. The final sentence brings the experience home by qualifying the people who are in this place.

2. Imitate the paragraph in Item 1 by revising your version to conform to the grammatical structure of each sentence in the paragraph. Analyze the sentences the way Baldwin's sentences were analyzed. You need not be absolutely accurate; just do the best job you can.

3. Which of these experiments in Items 1 and 2 produces the more interesting final product? Which of these paragraphs are you more proud of, and which pleases your peer editors more? In a very brief statement of, say, 200 words, establish which of these methods of imitation is more productive and successful for you. If possible, examine the process you used to write your paragraphs and comment on the relative difficulty or relative satisfaction you get from each.

PART IV

Memory

Introduction _____

THE ART of memory was highly refined among speakers and writers during the thousands of years in which there were no, or few books. Many of our greatest pieces of literature were originally memorized rather than written down. Homer's *Iliad* and *Odyssey,* parts of the Bible, and all the Koran were originally committed to memory and remained that way for many centuries. Muslims memorized the Koran from the lips of Mohammad and transmitted it to the true believers. At one time in the history of Islam, entire armies were distinguished by the fact that each soldier knew the Koran by heart. Interestingly, it was widely thought during the early days of manuscript books, that a piece of literature would last forever if it were kept in the memory, but that when it was kept in a book it risked loss.

This view of things is strange to us because we have so many books. Libraries such as the New York Public have giant collections numbering upwards of ten million volumes. Books are relatively cheap in our culture, so the time and the discipline that used to be spent in memorizing texts can now be used in other ways.

Speakers still need to use some of the older techniques of memorization, using symbols or catch words to remind them to include or develop a given point. But writers have long abandoned memorization, preferring journals to keep track of random thoughts, and note cards to help organize them.

Chapter 16 will show you how to create a piece of writing that will stick in the memory of the reader. Many special techniques have been developed to aid memory in writing. One of their values is to help you grow confident that what you say will not be dismissed. Because the key to memorization is repetition, an entire range of techniques exists that use repetition in clever, unnoticeable ways. They are not simply redundant or repetitious in the way an unconscious writer can be—repeating for no reason except forgetfulness or haste. Rather, they are designed to reinforce ideas and issues. Among the most effective are the poetic devices, rhyme and alliteration, and the more traditional prose device of enumeration, the numbering of segments of a piece of writing and then treating each in turn.

Techniques of concatenation are especially interesting. Concatenation means the joining together of separate parts. In a piece of prose, the separate parts are words, phrases, ideas. The first element that concatenates them is grammar, which shows their relationship. The next is the simple placing of words on the same page, in the same paragraph, in the same sentence. However, then the subtlety begins. Finding ways to interlink ideas from sentence to sentence, from paragraph to paragraph will help your writing remain with your reader. The examples in Chapter 16 show that concatenation is not based on mere repetition, but skillful and careful use of this device to imply links from one idea to another.

Another key to memorization is boiling something down to an easily portable expression, such as an aphorism. "A stitch in time saves nine," is such an expression, and it uses a form of rhyme just to make it easier to memorize. In other ages, one of the prime ends of writing was to arrive at an aphorism that the reader could take away from the piece and use as an epitome, or summary, of what was said.

This is still an effective technique, but like all techniques of repetition or abbreviation, it must be used sparingly. Techniques designed to make your writing more memorable will not work if they are used without thought or reason. They will not work if they are used so often as to deaden your reader's response.

Therefore, as in all applications of writing techniques, the keys to success are caution and judgment. You develop judgment by using the techniques as carefully as you can, then examining the responses that your peer editors and others will give you. The process of writing, being read, and evaluating your reader's responses is essential to learning any of the skills of writing.

16

Memory: Being Memorable

Rhetoric and Memory: The Tradition

In traditional rhetoric, memory is on an equal basis with invention, organization, and style. Originally, memory was invoked as a discipline to help someone keep in mind the key elements that were to go into a talk or speech. Ideally, those who were to speak wanted to appear spontaneous, and so it was important to develop methods that would permit them to memorize key ideas, arguments, and issues.

Although you may not need to memorize what you write, the very ambition of creating something memorable is helpful to writers. Most writers would like to think that after a piece has been written and read, some of it will stay in the reader's imagination. Often, the only pieces likely to be remembered will be very good ones. Therefore, writers' desire to be memorable is connected to their desire to create a fine piece of prose.

The modern writer only rarely expects to say something that will be remembered. Even Abraham Lincoln, at the dedication of the graveyard at Gettysburg, began his speech by saying that "the world will little note, nor long remember what we say here." He was quite wrong, especially because the Gettysburg address is regularly memorized by thousands of schoolchildren. But Lincoln, like many great writers, was obviously conscious of the fact that memory is an issue in speaking and writing. You cannot help but feel that Lincoln, by saying what he did, was actually making a bid to be remembered.

Traditionally, memory in rhetoric is dedicated to the act of memorizing. Today, however, it is devoted to the entire issue of how one crafts a prose that could be memorable. In other words, it concerns itself with those elements of style that aim specifically to make it easy for readers to retain what you have written.

Memory: Beginning with Titles

Sometimes it is enough to create a memorable title, which can make your writing seem more appealing from the first. You may not be able to make the rest of the piece memorable, but if you can make the title noteworthy, at least you know that will stick in the imagination and probably carry with it much of the point of what you write.

CONNECTING WITH THE FAMILIAR

As any expert in memory will tell you, one of the best ways to keep something in memory is to connect it to something else that is already memorized. It is good advice. Titles are especially susceptible to this strategy. Amanda Cross once wrote a successful mystery novel called *The James Joyce Murders.* Amanda Cross is actually Caroline Heilbrun, professor of English at Columbia University, so she aimed her book at an audience of literary people. For that audience, the title was unforgettable and she undoubtedly sold many copies just on the basis of her title. In addition, she did something very witty. She knew that anyone who would respond to her title would know James Joyce's book of short stories, *Dubliners.* So she titled her chapters after the stories in that book, beginning with "The Sisters," and ending with "The Dead." In one simple but remarkable stroke, she fused her book to the memory of the readers who might buy it.

One problem with connecting with familiar sayings or existing titles of books, movies, or plays, is the danger of becoming cute. Titles such as "A Rolling Scone Gathers No Sauce," "A Glitch in Time Saves Nine," "All's Well that Ends Period," "The Merry Wives of Dubuque," "Feeders' Digest," and "Some Day My Prints Will Come" all suffer from strain. They are much too obvious in their effort to connect. As a result, they do not work. All they do is make the reader wince.

On the other hand, a title such as Marilyn French's *Women's Room* works very well. It addresses a specific audience of women, while also connecting its title with something familiar in everyone's memory. The recent novel by Alison Lurie called *Foreign Affairs* is about a college professor who goes to Europe to do research in the summer and ends up having an affair that changes her life. Her title's immediate reference is to the scholarly journal of political science of the same name, but the additional double entendre is obviously effective in this context. Writers often search for such titles, hoping to find something that will wittily or meaningfully connect.

1. Create some titles for a piece that could appear in your local college newspaper as a feature story. Some possible subjects are listed. You supply a title that connects with something that your student audience would know. Your sources should be book titles, plays, films, TV shows, musicals, music groups, popular or classical pieces of music, magazine titles, or local campus groups. If possible, write at least one title that has an appropriately amusing double meaning.

   the college marching band
   your student union
   one athletic team
   your theater group
   dormitory life
   eating places on campus
   social societies on campus
   campus landscaping

THE DOUBLE MEANING

Television programs are often titled in such a way that they can mean any one of several things. The reason for this is simple: our amusement at the double meanings helps fuse the title in our mind. Because television executives cannot survive unless people remember to watch their shows, they use great ingenuity in their titles. Consider just a few from recent (and some defunct) shows. "Hill Street Blues" might sound like it should feature guitars and slow drag rhythms, but of course it is about policemen, who in America wear blue uniforms. "M*A*S*H" sounds like a crushing experience, and in a way it is, although the title is an acronym for Mobile Army Surgical Hospital, and the show is about a group of nurses and doctors in the Korean War. "St. Elsewhere" is a baffling title for another show about doctors and nurses, but its connection with all the "St." hospitals in our country guarantees it familiarity.

Shows like "Magnum, P.I." and "Remington Steele" obviously play on the double meaning involved with our association of their names with guns. The "Untouchables" connects with outcasts. Shows like "Moonlighting," "Bosom Buddies," "From Rags to Riches," and "Family Ties" all depend on your knowing their title as an ordinary, everyday expression. "The Dukes of Hazard" were not English dukes, but a pair of brothers named Duke. Such opportunities for expanding the apparent meaning of a title are rarely passed up by producers. "Miami Vice" is not self-evident in meaning until one knows the show is about the vice squad in Miami.

One of the most interesting television titles is "Kojak," a show that ran for many years and made its star internationally known. The name is related to George Eastman's famous photographic product, Kodak. Eastman spent a good deal of time trying to invent a title for his camera and his film. He wanted it to be very simple, one or two syllables in length, pronounceable in any language, and to seem to have meaning although actually having none. Kodak was his eventual choice, and in light of what he wanted to achieve, a totally memorable trade name, it was a brilliant success. Another word that has a similar kind of quality is *okay*. These words are so universal that someone once pointed out that if you say *Kodak* or *Okay* in virtually any country in the world, you are speaking the native language.

Memory and Structures of Repetition

The ultimate key to memory is repetition. If you wish to memorize something, the only dependable technique available is repetition with attention to detail.

As a result of this fact, many of the most interesting devices at the rhetorician's disposal are called schemes of repetition. In a sense, they represent microelements of repetition because they, in miniature, repeat an important structure or detail, thus helping a concept or idea to dig itself into the memory of the reader.

RHYME

One such device is rhyme. We are familiar with it in poetry, and the rhythmic structure of the line of poetry is usually repeated in such a way that the rhymes come around at a specific point each time, building up a sense of expectation. Thus in a poem such as:

> Jack and Jill
> Went up the hill
> To fetch a pail of water
>
> Jack fell down
> And hurt his crown
> And Jill came tumbling after

not only do the word sounds rhyme at the end of the lines, but the number of strong accents repeat in each line, so that each line has the same, or almost the same, underlying structure. As a result, these words are in the memory of almost every English-speaking person. It must be the repetition of rhyme and meter that makes these lines so memorable: after all, could you defend them on the grounds of how important their ideas are?

In prose, you are not urged to use rhyme. It would sound precious, and probably distract your reader. However, you should also realize that many phrases are turned in prose that depend on their effectiveness wholly because they seem to make more sense by virtue of their rhyming. Here is a simple list that you can easily add to. All have appeared in print in the popular media.

> The best in the West
> The least in the East
> The mouth of the South
> Take a pot shot
> The fleet feet . . .
> A zoot suit
> The late great . . .
> Even Steven
> Loose as a goose
> A low blow
> Supersaver
> Live at five
> The best of times, the worst of times
> Lean Cuisine
> Tough stuff
> Cool Yule

ALLITERATION

Alliteration depends on repeating the same letters from word to word. Here's an extreme example from the poet Algernon Swinburne: "Life is the lust for the light of the lamp that is dark till the dawn of the day when we die." Fortunately, he was playing around with the *l*'s and the *d*'s here—basically trying to be funny. However, this is a line actors often memorize—easily. The repetition of the letters *l* and *d* at the beginnings of words makes it memorable. After all, you certainly cannot translate the line into anything significant, so it has to be the patterning of letters that makes it memorable.

Alliteration works in three ways: initial (repetition at the beginning of a word); medial (repetition in the middle of a word); and terminal (repetition at the end of a word). The letter sound *s* is alliterated in all three ways:

Initial: Super Sunday
Medial: My persuasive assistant
Terminal: Sauce for cooks

Using the resources of alliteration in all three ways at once or in sequence can be very effective. Here is an example:

Initial: Double duty.
Initial, medial, and *terminal:*   Double duty indeed!
Terminal, initial, medial: Take care of the microphone.

Here are some examples of alliteration, shifting from one letter to another. The intention in each case is to write a statement that will stick in the memory.

Some disappointed freedom fighters found solace in the promise of medical supplies from the Red Cross.

Parking problems have produced inappropriate solutions to the lack of lots for all our colleagues: one professor proceeded to asphalt his front yard and charge a fee for fellow sufferers.

Making more money is not the only solution to helping us be happy.

This technique is one of the more persistent devices of advertisers, especially those advertising cigarettes and beer. Advertisers know alliteration gets into your unconscious and sticks there. Even against your will. Alliteration sells an untold number of products everyday.

ENUMERATION

Enumeration is the device of breaking up your discussion into a small number of parts. When you say, "There are three things I want you to remember," you use enumeration. Ordinarily, three or four items or ideas will be the most effective number for enumerating. It is a simple and effective technique. It has the advantage not only of establishing a pattern of repetition, but of establishing a structure. Here, in miniature, is the way it works:

Apart from conditions of mass starvation, sudden and calamitous crop failure, or other temporary problems that sometimes arise to prevent a people from feeding itself, it is to the disadvantage of a developing nation to accept gifts of food from the United States. In point of fact, there are three good arguments against America's sending free food to an underdeveloped nation that is not suffering famine. First, that nation builds an immediate dependency upon the food and will neglect its own crop production. Second, the local farmers will inevitably fail to sell their crops if we provide free food, and therefore their failure will perpetuate the local problems. And third, one of the problems we have seen in the past is that some local governments use free American food as a political weapon and give it only to those communities that support their goals. People unpopular with the government die.

James Tucker

In this example the discussion has been partitioned into three arguments: 1. nations become dependent; 2. local farmers can't sell their crops if U.S. food is free; 3. U.S. food can become a political weapon. These separate arguments have simple tags: first, second, and third.

Enumeration has one absolute advantage: it aids in the clarity of any discussion. You know you have several strands of information to discuss. You inform your audience in advance how many there are, and you thus build up a sense of expectancy in the reader that is rewarded by following through on your promise. The aid to memory in enumeration comes in part by connecting to what all of us know, a sequence of numbers. We all know the terms *first*, *second*, and *third*.

Enumeration has another interesting effect. It makes you sound authoritative—like an author—which is exactly the way you wish to sound. When you begin a segment of a discussion by saying, "There are three important factors to keep in mind when regarding the possibility of there being an economic crash in the 1990s," you sound like a person who has thought about the problem. You sound, in short, prepared.

If you can use enumeration at all, you probably are prepared. The confidence that you impart to your readers is usually warranted. Therefore, well-prepared writers often use enumeration to underscore the work they have done to organize their thoughts and to guide the thinking of their readers. To a large extent, when a writer states that there are three major points to consider on a given issue, the reader is usually satisfied that this is indeed the case.

The advantage of enumeration in this situation is that the first paragraph can state the three major themes—the three lines of argument, as in the case of the example about food and famine. Then those themes can be repeated later in the essay. One could follow this as a structure:

Paragraph 1 identifies three
arguments, using the device of
enumeration.

+

Paragraph 2 and additional
paragraphs develop
enumeration number 1.

+

Enumeration number 2 is developed
in the next group of paragraphs.

+

Enumeration number 3 is developed
in the next group of paragraphs.

Here are some samples of chiasmus, using these terms, which, for the sake of convenience, are opposites. Because they are opposites, they have an especially clear relation to one another, a relation that will not become blurred when they are reversed in order.

1. Wealth has been said to be the cure for poverty, but poverty is often less of a disease than wealth.
2. When I was young, I found myself yearning for the complex and settling for the simple, but now that I'm older, I pray for things to become simple, knowing they will be as complex as ever.
3. Freedom is not slavery, but slavery sometimes masquerades as freedom.

ANAPHORA

Anaphora is the repetition of the same word or phrase at the beginning of a phrase, clause, or sentence.

The repeated item or idea usually has a special significance, a seriousness that demands and supports the repetition. Like every device used for repetition, anaphora must be used sparingly. Overdoing it simply robs it of its power. Here are a few samples:

Andrew Carnegie did not trust the Jefferson Company. He did not trust its president. He did not trust its board of directors.

Reluctantly, the pilgrims began the journey up Mt. Siloa. Reluctantly, they arrived on its summit and bathed their feet in its sacred stream. Just as reluctantly, they returned to the bustle of the city streets below.

While America slept, they struck. While we slept, they announced an overwhelming victory.

Never will I permit our friends to be so insulted. Never have I have seen such rudeness.

Mild variation works just as well with anaphora as exact repetition. Repeating an item once, twice, or even more often is sometimes very effective. A great many important moments in political writing have been marked by anaphora because of its power to intensify the meaning of any statement. Here are some samples from important historical figures:

We must recollect . . . what we have at stake, what it is we have to contend for. It is for our property, it is for our liberty, it is for our independence, nay, for our existence as a nation; it is for our character, it is for our very name as Englishmen, it is for everything dear and valuable to man on this side of the grave. *William Pitt*

Individuality does not consist in the use of the very personal pronoun I; it consists in tone, in method, in attitude, in point of view, it consists in experiences of inflation may actually amount to less than the victory on Getting Ahead Day, but the sense of loss far outweighs the memory of gain.

Second, there is the problem of property. Another testimony to the actual economic strength of the middle class is that the number of property owners with estates ranging from $60,000 to $200,000 rose from 2.3 million in 1958 to over 10 million in 1972. This is an enormous gain in the number of modestly propertied families. It is also an enormous increase in the number of households who watch with impotent alarm as their savings accounts melt, their life insurance policies lose value, their bonds deteriorate in purchasing power, and their stocks go nowhere (from 1965 until the present boom, stocks have essentially moved sideways, with no net gain at all).

Last, there is the fact that the two years of inflation and recession since 1974 *have* ground down on the economic middle class along with everyone else. The process of staying ahead of inflation has depended on economic growth. For almost two years, until very recently, our economic growth has been negligible or even negative. Probably the burden of recession has hurt families in the working-class income brackets more severely than those in middle and upper brackets, but better-off families have also felt its impact, either in reduced incomes or in frozen ones, or even in unemployment.

Thus it is understandable that we believe in the myth of a killing inflationary experience for the middle class. Inflation is psychologically painful, hell on property, fierce when it is accompanied by recession. Nonetheless, inflation over the last twenty-five years has been more than matched by growth, in both income and property. Over this period, the middle class has not been killed—in fact, it has done extremely well.

From the first, Heilbroner is interested in the contrast between myth and reality. And when he reaches the question of why the middle class feels so squeezed, he begins the next paragraph with: "Three answers suggest themselves. One is that the psychological costs of inflation are greater than its economic gains." The next paragraph begins: "Second, there is the problem of property." The following paragraph begins: "Last, there is the fact that the two years of inflation and recession since 1974 *have* ground down on the economic middle class along with everyone else." These sentences are like elements of an outline. They signal the material that is to come, and they guide us through this segment of the essay.

So, for the reader, enumeration prepares us to watch each item unfold, one after the other. We know how many items there are, how they relate to the overall subject, and how they will develop. Enumeration makes the job of reading easier, just as it makes the job of writing easier.

CLIMAX

In the earlier examples, there are almost always three elements in the enumerations. The use of three segments in enumeration is a form of rhetorical climax. For some reason, three items in a sequence has always seemed to us the right number: not too few, not too many. If you listen to people talk, you will notice that they often veer toward lists of three: "He was tall, dark, and handsome." "She moved in first, stayed an hour, then left." "We can defend this case on three points: the motivation, the opportunity, and the question of possibility." "The attack took place simultaneously on land, sea, and air."

Some elaborate theorizing has gone on about this fact. For example, some people have said that when you start listing four items in such a series, you indicate that you are not really as sure of yourself as you are when you list three. It is as if you are padding things to make them look good.

However, when you use enumeration, you do not have to worry about having four or more elements. The right number is the number that you feel is relevant. If there are five things to point to, then point to them without worrying about it. But, keep in mind that traditionally, and for good psychological reasons, three things usually work best.

CHIASMUS

Good writers use special repetition devices sparingly. Like metaphor, they should not be thought of as ornamental, or something that you add on later. Rather, they should become part of thinking as you are writing. Learning to use a device such as chiasmus needs practice.

Chiasmus is the repetition of two items in this fashion:

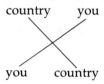

Or, as in John Kennedy's famous statement:

> "Ask not what your country can do for you, ask what you can do for your country."

The sayings of famous people, especially politicians, are sometimes set up in this fashion. Again, it is psychologically satisfying to see this pattern emerging in a sentence because the use of balance gives the words an extra force of reason. The statement seems true because the words fit together so well.

Chiasmus is a Greek word alluding to X and associated with *scissors*, and you can see that shape in the X used to link the repeated words. It is usually, like President Kennedy's statement, short and pithy. A well-known example, by a British politician, Sir John Seeley, illustrates the power that a short chiasmic statement can have. Note how effective it is as an aid for memorization:

> "History is past politics, and politics present history."

Chiasmus is flexible, and not limited to an exact repetition of single words or phrases. It can include the similar repetition of entire clauses, or clauses that are approximately structured in similar ways. Abraham Lincoln liked this device and used it frequently. He said,

> "I claim not to have controlled events, but confess plainly that events have controlled me."

He also showed the flexibility of the device in a famous expression that uses chiasmus, then moves right on from it:

> "You can fool all the people some of the time and some of the people all of the time, but you can not fool all of the people all of the time."

Once, when he was asked to comment on a book, he said,

> "People who like this sort of thing will find this the sort of thing they like."

This structure obviously cries out for memorization. You find it easy to remember any use of chiasmus because it seems to be inevitable, and it seems to be right. Moreover, because it juggles a small number of items, just two, in a balanced way, it becomes memorable even against a reader's will. For that reason, it is usually used for a sentence that seems to imply or demand a conclusion. It sews things up.

For the average writer, chiasmus may look like a gift of the gods, or a device reserved only for the inspired. But that is not really true. What it takes to use chiasmus is the willingness to look for the chance to put it into action. You need two items, and only two items. And if you keep in mind that the second time you refer to the two items you reverse their order, then you can begin to experiment with it.

For instance, if you take these pairings, you can try to use chiasmus in any of a number of ways:

wealth	poverty
poverty	wealth
simple	complex
complex	simple
freedom	slavery
slavery	freedom

The structure of this section of the essay echoes the structure of the lead-off paragraph. You can repeat your main points without being repetitious, and therefore you drive your main points home in the imagination of the reader. And, perhaps just as important, by using enumeration you solve the problem of organization for this segment of your work. You know that it will be cohesive, positively enhance your discussion, and be satisfying to your reader.

Robert Heilbroner: Middle-Class Myths, Middle-Class Realities

The following brief excerpt from an essay by economist Robert Heilbroner is part of a larger piece that works almost entirely by the device of enumeration. Heilbroner is careful to avoid repeating the tags *first*, *second*, and *third*, but he does enumerate his subject and his discussion. The title implies two parts: myths and realities, and this sample constantly reminds us of the myth and then informs us of the reality of inflation versus income growth. Even when Heilbroner says, as in the beginning of this sample, "One thing emerges . . . ," he appears to be using enumeration.

One thing emerges very clearly from this look at the economic realities. The economic middle class is a lot less rich (as well as a lot less large) than most people think. This delusion lends support to a second general myth about the middle class. It is that the middle class has been caught in a ferocious squeeze between rising prices and rising taxes.

Let us begin with inflation. Consumer prices have doubled since 1950, and have risen by two thirds since 1965. Hasn't this inevitably taken its toll of middle-class well-being? The answer is that it hasn't, because middle-class incomes have risen even faster than prices. In 1974, it required an income of $15,000 to enter the top 40 percent of families, where the middle class is found. Back in 1950, however, to get into the top 40 percent required an income of only $3822. An extraordinary fact, but true. In those days the poor included all families with incomes of less than $1661, and the upper class—the top 5 percent—began at a family income of only $8666. If we doubled those 1950 amounts, we would keep everyone approximately abreast of inflation. But actual incomes have far more than doubled. That marginal upper-class family of 1950 has not doubled its $8666 income, but has quadrupled it.

Thus, in "real" terms—that is, with full allowance for inflation—the middle class has fared very well. Then why does the middle class *feel* squeezed by rising prices?

Three answers suggest themselves. One is that the psychological costs of inflation are greater than its economic gains. Once every year or so, we get ahead of the inflationary spiral, when salaries are raised, promotions are won, year-end profits are shared. On that day there is a real sense of moving ahead, an acute moment of economic triumph. But the triumph is followed by 364 days of irritation as shopping bills rise. The small defeats of 364 saying things in such a way that you will yourself be recognized as a force in saying them. *Woodrow Wilson*

Old age brings along with its ugliness the comfort that you will soon be out of it,—which ought to be a substantial relief to such discontented pendulums as we are. To be out of the war, out of debt, out of the drouth, out of the blues, out of the dentist's hands, out of the second thoughts, mortifications, and remorses that inflict such twinges and shooting pains,—out of the next winter, and the high prices, and company below your ambition,—surely these are soothing hints. *Ralph Waldo Emerson*

In your own writing, the technique of anaphora can emphasize a crucial point or establish a position. It is simple to use and very effective.

ANALOGY

One of the constant tips in books on memory is that if you want to remember something new, attach it in your mind to something you already know. My license plate is 872-DYB. I remember the numbers because 8 is the month of my birth, 7 is one less than 8, and 2 is the number of numbers that come before it. I remember DYB by associating it with "Do You Believe?" This may seem weird to you, but it works for me. The advice of the memory books is to associate what you want to remember with what you already know. If you meet someone whose name is Dean James, associate that name with James Dean; if a person is named Green, think distinctly of the color when you are introduced.

Analogy is a form of association. It links a well-known process, experience, or object to the subject at hand. It resembles metaphor—and in many cases is an extended metaphor—because it borrows from one known sphere of activity to lend to another.

The device can be profoundly effective and memorable. One of the most famous instances in English comes from the *Essays* of Francis Bacon, and it was written in its original form in 1597. In his essay "Of Studies," he discussed the act of reading by comparing it with the act of eating:

Some books are to be tasted, others to be swallowed, and some few to be chewed and digested; that is, some books are to be read only in parts; others to be read but not curiously; and some few to be read wholly, and with diligence and attention.

Like so many of the examples you have seen in this chapter, this analogy operates in three parts, using totally familiar terms to describe a process that does not have the same kind of terminology built into it. As a result, you have a much clearer sense of his recommendations concerning reading and what his attitude is toward books. And you have a memorable passage.

Analogy works in a very direct way. You could use the experiences of an airport: takeoff and landing; of an army: advancing and retreating; of a college education: matriculating and graduating. Virtually any experience that is well known could be used analogously to help make your writing fresh and memorable.

Here are a few instances using the three suggestions in the previous paragraph:

> His mind was like a terminus, with ideas taking off every few seconds and insights landing with the regularity of a commuter shuttle.
> Darwin signaled the advance of a new era in science. He garrisoned the forces of evolution in the abandoned theaters of old theories. And ironically, it was only after having gained victory over the rear-guard forces of science that his discoveries settled in for a century-long siege on the minds of the public.
> Unfortunately, all too many users of "recreational" drugs graduate into the ranks of the addict. Dependency is a matter of degree.

The way to use this device is to associate your subject with a process you understand: driving a car, starting a band, cooking a meal, going out for a date. Whatever it is, it will help enliven your subject. And like most of the techniques in this chapter, it should appear in your early drafts. It should be part of your thought, not a detail of ornamentation. The example from Bacon comes from the 1597 edition of the *Essays* (although it is modernized). In the 1612 and 1625 editions "Of Studies" was expanded and changed, but this passage was still retained from the first edition. The concept came to him early on, and he found it effective.

Writer's Workshop: Structures of Repetition

1. Write at least two paragraphs of an essay on a topic of your own choice. Use enumeration as the basic structure of your paragraphs. However, either in your early planning or in your revision stages, use at least two of the following techniques:

rhyme
climax
chiasmus
anaphora
analogy

Concatenation

Good writers have a complex way of tying their thoughts together. Their paragraphs seem to be welded and virtually seamless, like a piece of sculpture. The separable elements of their paragraphs are interrelated and depend upon echoes, especially of the key ideas or terms.

The linking of ideas and relationships is called concatenation. Latin *catena* means chain, and concatenation is a technique of interrelating elements in writing in such a way as to make them seem chained to one another. The technique is really a collection of techniques. It is not a device. It is not like metaphor or anaphora. Rather, it is a means of repeating key phrases, ideas, terms, and other words so as to give the reader the sense that the paragraph is tight, unified, and weighty.

Concatenation produces a sense of inevitability. Certain pieces of writing seem to exist in only one imaginable form—"To be, or not to be," is an example. We cannot imagine this said in any other way, and other versions of the same statement seem almost ridiculous. Well, this sense of the inevitable can be produced in ordinary writing, too, although one can hardly hope for the absolute perfection that Shakespeare was able to develop.

The capacity of concatenation to affect the memorability of prose is not exactly clear. A carefully concatenated paragraph or group of paragraphs insinuates itself into the imagination or memory, but not in as exact a way as analogy or anaphora may do. Rather, it is less exact, embedding the concepts, or impressions of the subject matter into the reader's mind. We pass from one carefully concatenated paragraph to another, gathering impressions, taking away with us a sense of what has been said rather than an exact replica.

In the following example, in order to show the relationship of the elements that have been chained together by repetition, I have circled words, boxed them, underlined them, and then connected them with lines to one another. The care with which all the separable elements in the paragraphs have been united through repetition is instructive. The repetition is not dull, not even repetitive. It is reinforcing. Laurie Lee uses quite a number of the devices mentioned in this chapter, including analogies of many sorts.

CHARM

Charm is the ultimate weapon, the supreme seduction, against which there are few defences. If you've got it, you need almost nothing else, neither money, looks, nor pedigree. It's a gift, only given to give away, and the more used the more there is. It is also a climate of behavior set for perpetual summer and thermostatically controlled by taste and tact.

True charm is an aura, an invisible musk in the air; if you see it working, the spell is broken. At its worst, it is the charm of the charity duchess, like being struck in the face with a bunch of tulips; at its best, it is a smooth and painless injection which raises the blood to a genial fever. Most powerful of all, it is obsessive, direct, person-to-person, forsaking all others. Never attempt to ask for whom the charm bells ring; if they toll for anyone, they must toll for you.

As to the ingredients of charm, there is no fixed formula; they vary intuitively between man and woman. A whole range of mysteries goes into the cauldron, but the magic remains the same. In some cases, perhaps, the hand of the charmer is lighter, more discreet, less overwhelming, but the experience it offers must be absolute—one cannot be "almost" or "partly" charmed.

Charm in a woman is probably more exacting than in a man, requiring a wider array of subtleties. It is a light in the face, a receptive stance, an air of exclusive welcome, and almost impossibly sustained note of satisfaction in one's company, and regret without fuss at parting. A woman with charm finds no man dull, doesn't have to pretend to ignore his dullness; indeed, in her presence he becomes not just a different person but the person he most wants to be. Such a woman gives life to his deep-held fantasies and suddenly makes them possible, not so much by flattering him as adding the necessary conviction to his long suspicion that he is kind.

In addition to demonstrating concatenation, this passage also illustrates the movement through two of the means of development mentioned in Chapter 4: definition and comparison. In the rest of the passage, Lee continues his comparison of charm in women by discussing it in men. Most of his discussion may be considered a form of definition, but he also offers development by example, cause and effect, and analysis.

The paragraphs above are interesting for the repetition of key words or ideas. Laurie Lee seems intent on exhausting what we know about charm, and rather than let us lose sight of his subject, he carefully zeroes in on it again and again. By the time we finish, we feel that we have had a workout and that we do finally understand something about that elusive subject, charm.

Frankly, I find the technique of interconnecting elements within a paragraph and from paragraph to paragraph a mark of highly subtle, very polished, and professional writing. Most apprentice writers are unable to do this, although one reason is merely because they never think to try. This is not a technique likely to appear in an early draft of a piece of writing. Rather, I think it is more reasonable to assume that it will be an aim of later revision. If so, then you can see that it is not an impossible goal.

A STUDENT SAMPLE

The following is a sample from the beginning of a freshman class essay. We had been reading Friedrich Nietzsche's essay, "Apollonianism and Dionysianism," from *The Birth of Tragedy from the Spirit of Music.* The terms represent two aspects of everyone's personality. Apollonianism is the cool, rational mind, whereas Dionysianism is the irrational, the sometimes frenetic and inspired mind.

We will first look at a third draft sample that makes a good attempt at developing some of the technique of concatenation. Then, we will examine it once more with a further revision aimed explicitly at improving the concatenation.

ORIGINAL

Friedrich Nietzsche was correct in stating that life was a continual struggle between Apollonianism and Dionysianism. The fact that life is a struggle also means that all areas of life are a struggle between these two opposing forces. Even in our modern-day pastimes, the conflict is present. The sport of football is more than a game: it is a representation of life. Life is a battle fought between the forces of Apollonianism and Dionysianism. As a representation, football points out the necessity of the mutual existence of both expressions of life.

In Nietzsche's essay, "Apollonianism and Dionysianism," he defines these two contradictory, but necessarily coexistent, terms. Apollonianism is an aspect of human society or mankind in general. It is characterized by rational thinking on the part of the individual. Emotions are downplayed to such an extent that they are almost nonexistent. Order, on the other hand, is especially important. Everything has its own niche. Through Apollonianism, the individual gains confidence by thinking thoroughly about a problem and discovering a solution logically.

Dionysianism is a direct opposite of Apollonianism. It is, basically, controlled insanity or controlled chaos. Rational thinking is a stranger to Dionysianism, which is unplanned and uncontrolled. Groups that are suddenly transformed into frenzied mobs exhibit Dionysian behavior. Emotion rather than calm thinking, accompanies Dionysian actions.

Glenn

Glenn went on to talk about a specific game in which he saw some fathers of schoolboy players eventually become so irrational that they tried to fight with the coach. His own experience as a player showed him the validity of Nietzsche's insights into the forms of behavior that reveal basic sides of human psychology. In this version and the revision following, key elements are repeated. In the revision, the most important elements are repeated in such a way as to help link the line of thought from the beginning to the end of a specific paragraph, then from paragraph to paragraph. The key elements are those which are circled and linked together:

Apollonianism

Dionysianism

life

opposing forces

football

chaos

control

rational thinking

emotion

continual struggle

psychology

These terms, when listed as they are above, give a clear sense of the content of the passage. By reiterating them carefully, and linking them from paragraph to paragraph, Glenn gives them special emphasis and importance. And while it is not possible simply to memorize the passage on one reading, you would discover that it would be relatively easy to memorize if you gave it real effort and went over it a number of times. For the one-time reader, this technique helps the passage penetrate into the imagination.

REVISION

Friedrich Nietzsche was correct in stating that life was a continual struggle between the psychological expressions of Apollonianism and Dionysianism. These two necessary but opposing forces are apparent in the built-in conflict we find in many of our pastimes, especially sports. For example, the sport of football is more than a game: it is a representation of life — life as a battle fought between the forces of Apollonianism and Dionysianism. As a representation of life, *football* points out the necessity of the mutual existence of both of these psychological forces.

Nietzsche defines "Apollonianism and Dionysianism" as contradictory, but necessarily coexistent, terms describing extremes of human psychology. Apollonianism is characterized by rational thinking on the part of the individual. Emotions are controlled to such an extent that they do not interfere with the rational function. Order is especially important: everything has its place, everything is controlled. The Apollonian individual gains confidence by thinking problems through and discovering a solution logically.

Dionysianism, the opposite of Apollonianism is controlled insanity or controlled chaos. Rational thinking is absent from the unplanned and uncontrolled Dionysian behavior that is present usually in groups. Groups that are suddenly transformed into frenzied mobs exhibit Dionysian behavior. Emotion rather than calm thinking, accompanies Dionysian actions.

Football, with the careful planning of the coach and quarterback calling plays that are rational, carefully thought out and Apollonian, also has its Dionysian side. The chaos and frenzy of the pileups that accompany a fumble, the roaring of the crowd when they tear down the goalposts, the jubilation of the victorious team at the end of the game — all these are Dionysian qualities. Football is a game like life. It has those two necessary, but opposite forces in continual struggle for all to see.

 **Writer's Workshop**

Writer's Workshop: Concatenation

1. The most profitable exercise you can do for this workshop is to find a paragraph from one of your own recent essays, then rewrite it to improve its concatenation. This is an act of revision.

2. In the following paragraph, circle the repetitions that help improve its

concatenation. Do not forget anaphora, alliteration, analogy, reference to familiar titles or double meanings.

LEARNING HOW TO DANCE
by Andre James

Every so often, I hear some of the same old waltz music that used to echo off the walls of my grade school gym during our late-afternoon "voluntary" dance classes. Teachers and parents alike seemed to think it was a good idea for all gangly pre-adolescents to learn to dance. What they didn't know is that we were scared to death to get that close to each other. The teachers tried to match us by size. Even though I was the tallest sixth-grade boy, I usually danced with a girl who towered over me by three or four inches.

And we were awkward. The music would drone out of the same squawking public address system they used for basketball games and I would start by stepping on Gertrude Giddlehofer's foot. "Accidentally," she would clip me with an elbow. The music would bounce and we would bounce. My legs were too long and wouldn't do what I told them to. Gertrude would get huffy, and the song would end with a jolt. We would rush off to the walls of the gym and segregate ourselves into knots of giggling girls and sullen boys.

Those afternoons seemed endless. I would try to hide from Mrs. Knapp's eagle eyes when she was deciding who was holding back too much. But she always saw me. I would limp out to the floor, bow to my partner—who in any normal school event wouldn't even talk to me—and take her clammy hand in mine, and waltz. "ONE-2-3, ONE-2-3," I would keep saying to myself, but it never did any good. I still don't dance. When I hear those old tunes, I involuntarily flinch, as if Mrs. Knapp were still after me.

3. Rewrite the following student paragraph with the aim of improving its concatenation. Circle the elements that you feel are effectively repeated, and which therefore help create the concatenation.

Despite America's literary achievements, our music, and the performing arts, football dominates our cultural lives. Chances are many more people know of Joe Namath than know of Kurt Vonnegut. More Americans have probably seen football games than ballets. And not even a rock concert promoter would schedule a performance on Super Bowl Sunday. It is unlikely he could sell enough tickets to cover expenses when televisions in an estimated 17 million homes are tuned in to the Bowl game. Americans are lazy and they adore aggressive and competitive activity. It is these traits that have allowed people to appreciate football more than literature, music, and the arts.

Isobel

The Memorable Phrase: Aphorism _____

For thousands of years, writers have realized that one of the best things they can give their audience is a pithy, memorable statement as a means of emphasis. Such statements are called aphorisms, statements which "oft were thought, but ne'er so well expressed."

The aphorism is a compression of meaning. It contains much in a small space, and it seems almost to be a piece of folklore, as if it had always been in the language. The sense of timelessness that characterizes aphorisms is one of their strongest and most impressive qualities. That is why the aphorism is so popular, and why many writers work hard to produce it in their prose. Statements like "A penny saved is a penny earned" seem immortal, but someone thought it up first. Indeed, it is possible to invent aphorisms, but before you can do so you need to know what they are. The best way to understand aphorisms is to examine a few:

> A pessimist is a man who has been compelled to live with an optimist. (Elbert Hubbard)
> What does not destroy me, makes me stronger. (Friedrich Nietzsche)
> All women become like their mothers. That is their tragedy. No man does. That is his. (Oscar Wilde)
> To choose time is to save time. (Francis Bacon)

Each of these is essentially true—at least up to a point. You may want to argue with Wilde's statement, and possibly all of them. But in effect, each is reasonable and in its way convincing.

In fact, one of the problems with the aphorism is that it always sounds convincing. That is why writers use them. But like many things, the source of the strength of the aphorism is also a source of its weakness. As a writer you have a moral obligation to use the power of the aphorism in the name of truth. In other words, do not abuse it. Respect its power and be sure that you have put it to a worthy use.

Some writers use aphorisms written by Benjamin Franklin, Niccolò Machiavelli, Samuel Johnson, William Shakespeare, Oscar Wilde, and any number of other writers who are especially known for using them. But it should also be remembered that these writers created aphorisms of their own (and adapted those of others, too!).

It is probable that some writers have a special ability to produce aphorisms because so many good aphorisms have come from a small number of writers. One reason why so many good aphorisms come from a small number of writers is that they are the writers who make a point of trying to use them. Some writers, like Machiavelli and Francis Bacon, made it their business to look for any opportunity to turn an otherwise forgettable sentence into a memorable aphorism. I suspect this is a process that takes place during revision, although there may be some writers for whom the process begins early, in a first draft, perhaps. I am sure it works differently for different people. But looking for chances to make use of an aphoristic structure will certainly boost anyone's chance of being able to use aphorisms.

APHORISTIC STRUCTURES

To get a sense of how you can increase your use of aphorism, look at some examples with a commentary on each one. The first is based on the structural relationship of X is the X of X, which will usually produce an aphoristic feeling, especially when the relationship is: NOUN is the NOUN of NOUN:

Necessity is the mother of invention. (Anon.)
Fear is the parent of cruelty. (J. A. Froude)

The power of these aphorisms comes from their brevity, six words, and their capacity to reveal a cause and effect relationship through means of the metaphor of parent and offspring. Here are a few examples based on that structure:

War is the amusement of fools.
Industry is the playground of millionaires.
Style is the cousin of insecurity.
Politics is the exercise of deception.

You can take virtually any two closely related terms (war/fools; industry/millionaires; style/insecurity; politics/deception) and link them with a third term to produce an aphorism. If the middle term is metaphoric, the power of the aphorism is increased immensely.

A second structure is based on balancing opposite things. A great many aphorisms are delightful because they bring opposites together, or press them further apart. This is the principle behind Oscar Wilde's aphorism asserting that women become like their mothers and men do not, and that each in its way is their tragedy. Wilde resolves two contraries wittily into a third term that includes them both. Samuel Johnson in the following aphorism contrasts four things: marriage/celibacy and pains/pleasures.

Marriage has many pains, but celibacy has no pleasures.

To put this structure to work, you need only the appropriate contrasts. Here are some examples:

education/ignorance	good health/illness	impossible/possible
democracy/tyranny	profits/losses	youth/age

Here are some aphoristic statements constructed on this model:

> Education may not always produce profits, but ignorance inevitably points the way to losses.
>
> In our age democracy is theoretically impossible, but by contrast, tyranny appears everywhere dangerously possible.
>
> Good health is something we take for granted in youth, while illness is something we fear in age.

A third structure is based on a pattern of similarities. You can imagine it fulfilling this pattern: The more we X something, the less we X something. Here is an example by Anton Chekhov:

> The more we love our friends, the less we flatter them.

The similarity between love and flatter may not be obvious right away, but it is based on the likelihood that the people you love deserve to be flattered. This is reasonable. To make this structure work, you need a topic— friends—and two verbs—love and flatter—with a sense of similarity built into them. Here are some sample topics and verbs, followed by aphorisms built on the model of Chekhov.

topic: professional athletes   verbs: pay/value
The more we pay professional athletes, the less we value them.

topic: books   verbs: read/understand
The more we read our books, the less we understand them.

topic: automobiles   verbs: complain about/abuse
The more we complain about our automobiles, the less we abuse them.

APHORISMS IN ACTION

The first rule about using the aphorism is to use it rarely. It has great weight and power, but it is, like a battleship, noticeable. Therefore, by using it sparingly you will not outwear it.

You must also realize that this is not an age in which the aphorism is fashionable. And yet, it is still respected and admired when it is used well. For example, John Kennedy's famous statement, ''Ask not what your country can do for you, ask what you can do for your country,'' has taken on the status of an aphorism. It is pithy, implies obvious truth, and when the chiasmus is used in a brief statement, it often sounds like an aphorism. It is worthwhile to return to my earlier comments on chiasmus and note that they often indicate a connection with the aphorism.

In a sense, the aphorism is best used either as a focal point for discussion —something in the manner of a topic sentence in a paragraph, or as a final summary statement. Either way, your focus on the aphoristic statement will help give it added weight. The following sample gives us a good idea of how an aphorism can function in a paragraph:

The rebuilding of American cities has been an ongoing project for more than forty years, and it is about time to demand a progress report. In the old days, a city was a place where people lived. When they needed an office building, they figured out how to support it. When they needed a store, someone built it and fit it in among their homes. When a neighborhood became a slum, some people moved to better places. So far as anyone can tell, the old-fashioned slums have been replaced by projects which have been re-named ghettos. The downtown districts of yesterday are now glassed-in malls where every third shop seems to be selling shoes and where bloodless music pours quietly out of hidden loudspeakers to entertain listless shoppers. The old ornate brick office buildings and banks have been replaced by square, glass-sided monsters. Ethnic areas have disappeared to make way for expressways, and theaters seem to have been replaced by parking garages. Today's city is the child of commerce.

In this case, the aphorism is the last sentence, which implies a judgment that will have to be explored in the following paragraphs. Indeed, the entire paragraph is filled with judgment: there is a distinct sense that the modern city is a kind of failure. The aphorism implies the cause of that failure.

The next example shows the aphorism developing within the paragraph, where it has been prepared for by specific details, and where it can be followed by material to develop its implications. It is the fourth sentence.

Tabitha was yellow and white, with suspicious eyes and a nervous, switchy tail. When I first met her, I was convinced that she was a deprived, lonesome beast, and that all she needed was a touch of old-fashioned loving attention. Well, a half-dozen cold stares, a scratch or two later, I devised that I was dead wrong. The more affection you give a cat, the less it gives you. Maybe I am being extreme, or just reacting badly. But in a way it stands to reason. Tabitha had a good thing going. She got fed regularly in the kitchen, had the run of the yard and governed the barn. What did she need from me? It was I for whom affection had a special meaning. For her, it was simply an interruption of an otherwise smoothly running afternoon.

Revision and the Art of Memory

By now it should be apparent that writing memorable prose involves the willingness to master certain skills. They are the subject of this chapter, and I have named them in this order:

connecting with the familiar
using a double meaning
rhyme
enumeration
climax
chiasmus
anaphora
analogy
concatenation
the memorable phrase, or aphorism

Each of these is in its way a form of repetition. When you connect with a double meaning, you are echoing something that already exists—it is a way of referring to something that is already in the memory of your reader. This is the basis of most memory training, and each of these approaches reinforces that training. Even the aphorism is to an extent a repetition, because it echoes other pithy expressions that we associate in our memory with a form of wisdom. Skillful repetition is the key to writing memorable prose.

In addition to mastering each of these skills, you need to add the skill of judgment, something that is a result of two factors. The first is the opportunity to write and to gain experience. I have often referred in these pages to experienced and inexperienced writers. Experience improves your judgment. When you ask yourself whether a specific kind of repetition is too much, or whether it is not enough, you will be able to answer the question better if you have had a good deal of experience.

On the other hand, until you have had experience, you can best develop your judgment by relying on the observation of others: a good friend who has more writing experience than you have, your colleagues in a writing class, or the instructor with whom you are working. The point is that someone else can give you perspective and can respond specifically enough so that you can tell whether what you are trying to do is effective or not.

And the final advice I have on the matter of writing memorable prose is to think of your revisions as opportunities to make bland and colorless sentences and paragraphs memorable and strong. One specific goal you can aim for is

Revise for memorable prose.

Without this intention you will be like an archer without a target. You will not know what to aim for. But with it, you can hope to improve the impact of everything you write. Being memorable depends on your willingness to revise.

Writer's Workshop: Being Memorable

1. Write an aphorism for each of the patterns described in this chapter:
   a. NOUN is the NOUN of NOUN:
      Necessity is the mother of invention.
      _____ is the _____ of _____ .
      _____ is the _____ of _____ .
   b. Balancing things opposite:
      Marriage has many pains, but celibacy has no pleasures.
      modern/old fashioned   efficient/inefficient
      loud/quiet   good/bad
      Choose your own patterns of opposites.
   c. Using similarities: The more we X something, the less we X something.
      The more we _____ _____ , the less we
      _____ _____ .

2. Take one of your early essays, preferably a one-page effort, and rewrite it using the techniques discussed in this chapter. Aim to create not only a clear and well-structured piece of writing, but also to make it as memorable as possible. How much alteration of meaning is involved in this process? Is any essential meaning changed because of your efforts to make your writing memorable?

3. Take a recent paragraph or group of paragraphs (no more than three) and revise them to take into account as many of the structures of repetition as possible: rhyme, alliteration, enumeration, climax, chiasmus, anaphora, and analogy. If possible, share your efforts with other people doing the same assignment. How do you react to their efforts, and how do they react to yours? Do you feel your own effort is more memorable than it was?

4. Memorize the result of your work in Item 3. Commit your paragraph or paragraphs to memory. Keep a record of how long it takes you to do so. How difficult a job is that to do? Rate it on a scale of 1 to 5 with 5 being most difficult and 1 being least difficult. Compare your ratings with those of others.

PART V

Presentation

Introduction

THE WAY in which you present your work to your reader will have a great effect on how it is received. In a college setting, you may find that minor grammar and spelling errors will not count heavily against you. It has been traditional in recent years to suggest that a knowledge of grammar is not absolutely essential to writing well and that spelling is a demon that affects people who are very bright as much as anyone else. Outside a college setting, however, such errors will count very heavily against you. In some cases poor spelling will count much more against you than you know it should. It can lose you the respect of colleagues.

Part of the reaction outside colleges is dependent on the assumption that grammar and spelling are simple subjects that most people should learn in grade school. In professional life, knowledge of grammar and spelling are marks of distinction and affect judgments about promotion, hiring, and the general regard a person might be given in a chosen walk of life. For that reason, it is important for you to take matters of presentation very seriously.

The Modern Writer's Stylebook, which follows, includes extensive discussion of the kinds of grammatical issues important for the writer. It focuses on basic issues that help produce clear and accurate writing. Certain kinds of grammatical problems tend to affect many writers, and these are targeted carefully to give you the help you need when you need it. The stylebook addresses problems with verbs, sentences, agreement, modifiers, and punctuation. These are the chief areas where most writers need to pay special attention.

Punctuation is something that many writers do by feel. When they think a pause is necessary, then they put in a comma; when they feel things have come to a stop, they put in a period. Sometimes this will do well enough, but there are basic rules that are not difficult to review and learn, and if you follow them you will know you are accurate rather than just approximate in your approach to punctuation. Each of the major forms of punctuation is addressed separately, with enough review and discussion to help you learn its principles.

Spelling is a problem. It does not respect intelligence. For that reason, it is sometimes handy to have a list of the words that are being most misspelled these days. Such a list is in the stylebook. If you know you have a spelling problem, go through this list and circle the words that you know have given you problems in the past. Reviewing them will help. And there are rules for spelling that work most of the time (alas, not all). Reviewing them before writing will help you. If you compose on a computer, you can take advantage of the spell-checkers that will go over each word, find those misspelled, and suggest the proper spelling to you.

Sexist language is also a problem for some writers. Today, the writer no longer assumes that all unnamed references are *he* or masculine. Rather, we assume no specific gender. The simplest way out of the trap of sexist language is to convert singular pronouns such as *he* to *they,* which is not gender linked. Keeping this point in mind will help you avoid offending your audience.

Finally, the physical form in which you present your work will always affect the person reading it. Anything that is slapdash, with cross-outs and messy additions, will affect your readers negatively, even if it affects them unconsciously. It is natural, human, and predictable to expect that a neat, carefully prepared piece of writing will get much more favorable attention than its opposite.

Some commonsense suggestions for preparing work by hand, typewriter, and computer end the stylebook. These should be of use to you from the first moment you begin writing, because they cover most of the issues relative to the physical form of your writing. Contemporary research into writing reminds us that the presentation of a piece of writing has a direct effect on how it is valued by the people receiving it. If you hold it in high value by taking pains to be accurate, your audience is likely to do the same.

17

A Modern Writer's Stylebook

Basic Grammar for the Writer

Although it is generally agreed that there is no connection between a mastery of grammar and a mastery of writing, you need to know a minimum of grammar in order to revise your work and profit from the editing of peers and professionals. You were asked to consider grammatical principles in the earlier chapters on sentences and on imitation. Difficult problems of communication arise when you are not sure of the most basic grammatical principles. The information in this section concentrates only on reviewing what you need to know as a writer.

Before beginning this section, turn to Chapter 13, "A Rhetoric of the Sentence," and review the distinctions between subject and predicate, and between phrase and clause. We begin with the parts of speech.

NOUNS: WORDS, PHRASES, AND CLAUSES

Nouns are the class of words, phrases, or clauses that name something and act in a sentence as a subject, object, or complement. Sometimes their function in the sentence defines them as nouns, and sometimes they are, like proper nouns, identified by the fact that they clearly name something.

gr

Words

Common nouns name *general* people, things, places, and concepts. They are only capitalized when they begin a sentence. Proper nouns name *specific* people, things, places, and concepts, and they are always capitalized.

494

Common nouns:

people, boys, laborer, boxes, boats, dog, table, book, cities, neighbor-hood, street, parlor, kitchen, magic, faith, war, theory, caution, alarm, forgetfulness, height, weight, credibility.

Proper nouns:

Elizabeth Cady Stanton, Niccolò Machiavelli, May Sarton, Fernando Va-lenzuela, Wayne Gretsky, Tom Cruise, Glenda Jackson, Andreas Vol-lenweider, Van Halen, Bix Beiderbecke, Stevie Wonder, the Hope Dia-mond, the Cray Computer, Chevrolet Camaro, Argentina, the Virgin Islands, New Jersey, Ohio, Miami, New York City.

Noun Phrases

Sometimes a group of words will name something and function as a noun. A sentence will always include a word that is a noun, and add other words that modify it and complete its meaning. A noun phrase is distinct from a noun clause in that it does not have a complete subject and a complete predicate. In the following examples the noun phrases are underlined:

The man in the gray uniform explained it to me.
Marco told me about a crazy scheme.
Luis is a man with a sense of mission.

Noun Clauses

A clause can also act as a noun. It names something and usually serves the sentence in the ways a simple noun would do. The noun clause is estab-lished as a noun clause by its function in the sentence: it can act as a subject of a verb, as the object of a verb, or as the complement of a verb. It can also modify another noun. In the following examples the noun clauses are un-derlined:

What he saw was another instance of general neglect. (Subject of the verb *was*)
Linda asked that she be given another room assignment. (Object of the verb *asked*)
A reliable person is anyone we can trust the way we trust Hector Cha-voya. (Complement of the verb *is*)
The police waited for someone who could come forward and identify the victim. (Modifies *someone*, the object of a preposition)
The citizens who protested vigorously against closing the school were rewarded with an apology from the mayor. (Modifies *citizens*, the sub-ject of the sentence)
Noun clauses often begin with the following words: *who, whoever, that, whatever.*

PRONOUNS

You often need to refer to a given person, place, or thing more than once in a paragraph. To avoid useless repetition, you normally employ pronouns —words that stand in the place of nouns.

The most frequently used are the following personal pronouns:

Subjective Singular	Plural	Possessive Singular	Plural	Objective Singular	Plural
I	We	My/Mine	Our/Ours	Me	Us
You	You	Your	Your/Yours	You	You
He/She/It	They	His/Hers/Its	Their/Theirs	Him/Her/It	Them

TIP

Pronoun Tips: Misusing **This**

- One recurrent problem in apprentice writing is the failure to make *this* refer back to something explicit. The failure stems from an inadequate consideration of your audience. It is the situation where you know what you are referring to, and you assume everybody else does, too. You must remember that *this* has to refer back to a specific noun or noun phrase.

Here is a case in which *this* is misused:

John Brown wandered across the state of Kansas trying to halt the spread of slavery and to make sure that when Kansas joined the Union it was not one of the slave states. This made him famous.

What noun or noun phrase does *this* refer to: is it "to halt the spread of slavery"? It cannot be "John Brown wandered" because it is not a noun phrase. The referent must be a noun or noun phrase for which *This* specifically substitutes. In the sentence above, *this* seems to stand for an idea that underlies the entire sentence, not a grammatical group of words.

Here is an acceptable use of *this:*

John Brown's crime was breaking into a federal armory. This brought federal troops into action against him.

This refers back to "crime" (or, you may interpret it as referring back to the explanation of the crime: "breaking into a federal armory"). In either event, *This* refers to an explicit group of words, each of which is either a noun or a noun phrase.

Relative Pronouns

Relative pronouns refer back to something that has already been mentioned. The most common are: *who, which, whoever, that, whom.*

Demonstrative Pronouns

Pronouns that refer to explicit or specific people, places, or things are demonstrative: *this, these, those, that.*

Reflexive Pronouns

Reflexive pronouns (e.g., myself, ourselves, themselves) should not be used alone as subjects in a sentence. For instance, it would be unacceptable to write: "Myself is going to the store." You may may use the pronoun reflexively, however: "I myself am going to the store." This use tends to lend emphasis, even though it is basically redundant.

Indefinite Pronouns

Pronouns that do not refer to specific people, places, or things and that are often used as adjectives are: one, another, other, both, some, many, much. Ordinarily we use them to refer to one person, another friend, other times, both feet, some coffee, many chances, much luck.

The names of the classes of the pronouns may not be of first importance to you as a writer. However, using the pronouns effectively is. Examine the following passage as a sample of pronoun use. Each pronoun is underlined.

> You who struggled toward a concept of freedom that will stand some of us in good stead in years to come have yourselves established our sense of what is right and have identified for many of us what we could not have identified on our own.

ADJECTIVES

adj

A word that adds to or clarifies the meaning of a noun or pronoun is an adjective. Most descriptive words fall into this category. They are not names, but references to qualities. They make it possible to specify information concerning nouns, and thus they can make your writing more vivid. The material in Chapter 5 concerning description is to some extent dependent on the careful understanding of adjectives and their use.

Adjectives can provide information relating to the five senses: colors for sight, odors for smell, flavors for taste, sounds for hearing, size and texture for feeling. Here are some adjectives, underlined, which provide information relating to the senses.

red shoes   loud noises
stinky sneakers heavy barbells
sour milk

Adjectives can sometimes be doubled up, ordinarily using a comma to separate them, as in these examples:

<u>large, round</u> apples
<u>tall, dark-haired</u> beauties
<u>moderate, intelligent</u> politicians

Adjectives can also complete the meaning of a sentence when the verb *to be* is used for the purpose of describing its subject. In the following samples the underlined group is an adjective phrase. You could as easily substitute a single adjective.

Some people are <u>talkative, noisy, and boisterous</u>.
My friend Franny Gonzalez is <u>lanky and easygoing</u>.
His plans for the future were <u>indecipherable, vague, and probably wrong</u>.

Adjectives have degree. They can be positive, comparative, and superlative. So if you think something is *good*, then it is positive; if comparative, it is *better*; if superlative, then it is *best*. Each of these adjectives implies that something is good, but the use of degree tells us how good. Here are some examples:

Positive	*Comparative*	*Superlative*
small	smaller	smallest
frightened	more frightened	most frightened
some	less	least
much	more	most
mighty	mightier	mightiest

Problems arise with adjectives of degree when you use two comparatives or two superlatives together. They work against each other when you do so. For instance, it is improper to say: "the most mightiest wrestler." *Mightiest* is sufficient. The same is true of an expression like "The more taller of the two." *Taller* does the job alone.

VERBS

verb

Verbs put the punch in sentences. They express, define, and delimit action instead of naming something. When you *kick* the wall in disgust, you *verb* the wall in disgust. When you *play* the guitar, you *verb* the guitar.

Verbs can be singular or plural. That means they can express action committed by one person or a number of persons. Here are a few singular verbs and their plural counterparts. They can also be in the present tense, the past tense, the future tense, or the present or past perfect tense. Each verb is linked with a pronoun or noun subject and object.

Present Tense

Subject	Singular Verb	Object
Alex	catches	bluefish.
I	can see	tourist sights.
Every sport	defies	description.
Chick Correa	plays	subtle piano.

Present Tense

Subject	Plural Verb	Object
Nina and Josh	catch	trout.
People	tell	many stories.
We	force	ourselves too much.
Some Nigerians	play	interesting percussion.

Past Tense

Subject	Singular Verb	Object
Benny	aced	the test.
Louisa Miller	assumed	nothing.
Argentina	fought	Great Britain.
Someone	saw	flying objects.
No one	minded	what I said.

Past Tense

Subject	Plural Verb	Object
Ginny and Sal	had	problems.
People I know	saw	red when you said that.
The Ugandans	made	bread in the morning.
Chinky and Phil	mocked	everybody else.

Future Tense

Subject	Singular or Plural Verb	Object
Jamie	will take	classes later.
You	will need	economic independence.
My aunts	will prepare	a new production.
I	will study	the ground plans.

Perfect Tenses

Subject	Singular Verb	Object
Present Perfect		
Eduard	has been	on the dean's list.
I	have had	a few problems here.
You	have seen	several baseball games.

Past Perfect

Margot Ibanez	had fought	any negative critics.
I	had lost	my nerve.
They	had forgotten	their violins.

Future Perfect

Mr. Stanley	will have had	breakfast by now.
John Denver	will have reached	stardom at age 22.
The dance	will have been over	by ten-thirty.

---

vbl

VERBALS: INFINITIVES, PARTICIPLES, AND GERUNDS

In addition to the verbs, there is a class of words which are verblike, but that fall short of being verbs. These are the verbals, which name an action rather than transmit it. They come in three forms:

Infinitives: to have; to sense; to improve; to challenge; to have; to see; to think; to show; to complain. The sign of the infinitive is *to* plus the first person singular form of the verb.

Examples in a sentence: *To know* you is *to love* you. He wanted *to have* you come over for dinner. What are you permitted *to eat?*

Participles: they act as adjectives, clarifying the meaning of a noun or pronoun. They have two forms, present and past. The sign of the present participle is the *-ing* ending: moving; insisting; approaching; allowing; falling. The sign of the past participle is *-ed, -en,* or one of the irregular forms, such as done; begun; come; sung; lost; torn; sprung; held; caught; kept; worn; swum.

Examples in a sentence: *Approaching* the on-ramp, I began my turn. With the performance *improved* by my design, I made it easily.

Gerunds: singing; playing; thinking; doing; having; throwing; fooling; praying; studying; expounding. The sign of the gerund is the *-ing* form of the verb when it is used as the name of the action of the verb. The gerund functions as a noun in a sentence.

Examples in a sentence: *Parking* was not allowed, but *standing* was permitted for a short time. *Singing* in church was fine during the hymns, but not otherwise. Fritz was amused by my *stopping* at the intersection.

ADVERBS

Adverbs do for verbs and adjectives what adjectives do for nouns and pronouns. They clarify verbs by providing more details and information about how they operate. If you see someone lifting a typewriter, and she is lifting it *easily,* then you have used an adverb to clarify how she is lifting it. Adverbs can be used to qualify adjectives. If something is big, for instance, and you want to know how big, you use an adverb:

The scab was <u>very</u> big
Tony's <u>unusually</u> fast delivery
My friend's <u>purposely</u> exaggerated expression

Adverbs can also clarify the meaning of other adverbs. So if there is something you wish to make clear about how an adverb works, the word that you can use to help out is going to be an adverb. Here are some examples of paired adverbs:

very emotionally
quite desperately
more slowly
less advantageously
just after

Many adverbs end in *-ly,* although sometimes you can use an adverb without its *-ly* ending. Here are some examples of adverbs that have two useful forms: slow, slowly; full, fully; quick, quickly.

When adverbs clarify the meaning of verbs, they usually give information about how something is done, when it is done, or where it is done. The following examples, with the adverbs underlined, offer a range of the way in which adverbs function when they give information about verbs.

Everyone treated Alicia <u>cautiously</u>.
Pimm spoke with the dying man <u>after</u> the incident.
The police interrogated Alicia's cousin <u>near</u> the scene.

PREPOSITIONS

You have already encountered prepositions in Chapter 13, ''A Rhetoric of the Sentence.'' All prepositional phrases begin with a preposition. The job of the preposition is to connect nouns, noun phrases, or noun clauses with other parts of the sentence. Fortunately, they function very smoothly in the work of most beginning writers, so most of us encounter very few problems with them. Some of the most common prepositions are as follows:

at	concerning	into	over
as	despite	in spite of	regarding
about	down	instead of	since
above	during	like	to
by	except	near	unlike
because	for	of	until
beneath	from	on	with
beside	in	onto	without

The prepositions in the following sentences are underlined:

Ferdy got <u>into</u> trouble last night.
I was asked to come <u>in because of</u> the mess he caused.
<u>Upon</u> hearing <u>of</u> the strangeness <u>of</u> the situation, we decided to see him <u>instead of</u> calling him.

CONJUNCTIONS

conj

Conjunctions join parts of a sentence together. Unlike prepositions, which are also joining words, the conjunctions usually do not give additional information, such as why, how, or where the joining takes place. You can see why when you look at a list of the principal conjunctions:

and, or, nor, but, for, so, yet

Paired conjunctions—which usually work together—set up a recognizable pattern:

either, or	neither, nor
not only, but also	whether, or
both, and	as, as

The conjunctions are underlined in the following examples:

<u>Either</u> Hector leaves this room, <u>or</u> I do.
Fred <u>and</u> Phyllis opened an ice cream shop together <u>but</u> found out that Alaskans are not crazy about ice cream in January.

The relationship between adverbs and conjunctions is often very close. In some cases, we actually call certain connecting words conjunctive adverbs, because the distinction is so slight. As a writer, you need not worry about the exact difference. What you need to know is that the relationship between all connecting words is close, and that making them function smoothly is achieved primarily by recognizing their general function rather than their explicit and exact name. Some conjunctive adverbs appear underlined in the following examples:

No one would trust him <u>thereafter</u> because of the robbery.
Percy was undoubtedly related to the fellow you saw near the school, <u>thus</u> your recognition exposed you to danger.
You heard Mr. Camacho, <u>nonetheless</u> you chose to ignore him.

ARTICLES

The nice thing about articles is that they always precede a noun, and there are only a few of them in two classes: indefinite articles: *a, an,* and the definite article: *the.*

Those whose native language is not English will have trouble with articles because other languages handle the concept very differently. Therefore, a few rules can be established for the use of the articles. (See the box entitled "Tips: Using Articles Correctly.")

Tips: Using Articles Correctly
- *The* is used when the following noun is definite and already familiar to the reader. If you are talking about a specific book, then you say *the* book, as in this sentence: I was reading *the* book Hemingway gave to Laura's father. However, if you do not specify a definite book, then you would use the article *a,* as in this sentence in which the writer implies that Hemingway gave several books to Laura's father, and the reader is only looking at one, making the indefinite article necessary: I was reading *a* book Hemingway gave to Laura's father.
- When the following noun is singular, use *a* or *an.* When it is plural, use *the.* Examples: an ocean, a camper, a nation; the oceans; the campers; the nations.
- *The* is not used with certain plural nouns, such as collectives, in which the entire class of that noun is intended by the sense of the sentence. If, for example, you wished to use *writers* to apply to all writers as a class, your use in a sentence would be: The Nobel Prize honors all writers. It would be improper to say: "all the writers" in this instance. If you were specifying a subclass of writers, however, you would use *the:* The Nobel Prize honors all *the* writers who have been its winners. In the second case *the* implies a limitation to a specific group: only Nobel Prize winners.

Articles are one of the greatest problems for non-native speakers. Conventionally, in our language we refer to these collective or mass nouns when they represent all of their class *without* using *the:* diplomacy, communism, slavery, politics, democracy, women, men, justice, ideals, persecution, and many more. Here is a sample of this kind of usage:

> In contemporary American politics communism is often represented as fostering a kind of slavery, whereas democracy is said to be based on the ideals of justice for all.

When referring only to a specific kind, part, or group of these collectives, it is proper to use *the.* Notice how the sense of the sentence limits the collective noun to a specific class or selection among that collective in the following example:

> The politics of Great Britain is still far removed from the politics of the United States, just as the communism of Russia is far removed from the communism practiced in Mao's China.

Parts of the Sentence

sent

The grammatical identity of any word or phrase depends on how it used in the sentence. Therefore, a review of the parts of the sentence and what their function is can help you establish the grammatical situation.

Much of this will be found in detail—and with slightly different emphasis—in Chapter 13, "A Rhetoric of the Sentence."

Every sentence must have a subject and a verb, and to be grammatically accurate, every sentence must have at least one independent clause. The independent clause must have a subject and a verb. And although it is not required, the independent clause usually has an object or a complement in addition to the subject and verb.

The four principal elements of the sentence are as follows:

> The subject is the core of the sentence. It is the name of the person, place, thing, or idea that dominates the action of the sentence. It is the topic of the sentence.
> The verb is the action center of the sentence. It states what the subject is or does. It describes a specific action or state of being.
> The object is the noun or pronoun that receives the action of the verb.
> The complement completes the action of the relatively actionless verbs, such as the verb *to be.* It does not receive action; it describes or renames the subject.

THE INDEPENDENT CLAUSE

A clause is a group of words that contains a subject and a verb. There are two kinds of clauses: the independent clause that can stand alone as a sentence, and the dependent clause that is incomplete and cannot stand alone as a sentence. Examples of the independent clause, with the subject, verb, and object or complement labeled are as follows:

Subject	Verb	Object
The wolfman	annoyed	his psychiatrist.
My electrician	inspected	the wiring.
Idealism in industry	aroused	suspicion in Congress.
John Kenneth Galbraith	has studied	poverty in America.

Subject	Verb	Complement
Margaret Mead	became	a great anthropologist.
Plato's Theory of Forms	is	serious about realism.
I	will be	ready soon.
You	are	an astute young woman.

THE DEPENDENT CLAUSE

The dependent clause contains a subject and a verb, but it needs an independent clause to complete its sense. Often, the dependent clause will begin with a subordinating conjunction to signal the fact that it needs to be joined to something else. Here are some samples:

Subord. Conjunc. Adv.	Subject	Verb	Object/Complement
whether	Jamie	observed	the New York scene
unless	my Aunt Jennifer	explained	the situation to me
while	someone	was moving	my furniture
because	Ragusa	is	tall and skinny

subord

Each of these has a subject and each has a verb, but none can stand alone without something else to complete its sense.

PHRASES

phr

A phrase is a group of words that has a subject or a verb, but not both. Occasionally, it can have neither. Here you will find only a brief series of definitions of the most important grammatical forms of the phrase. For more information, examples, and details, refer to Chapter 13, "A Rhetoric of the Sentence," under the subject of phrases.

Noun and Verb Phrases

Groups of words that function as a subject, object, or noun complement in a sentence are naturally noun phrases. Here are some examples:

a group of candidates
my friend Agnes Da Silva
Archie Hamilton's two dogs
the Woody Allen films about New York
ideas Edison used in his work

Groups of words that constitute the verb often include helpers that indicate the present or past participle and are therefore all part of the verb. Here are some examples:

would have been convinced
should have seen
had been
might have signified
can have thrown
could have anticipated

The Prepositional Phrase

A prepositional phrase begins with a preposition and includes the object of the preposition and any words that modify the object. Most apprentice writers have no trouble with prepositional phrases. Here are some examples:

in the dead of the night
at the top
by the near wall
in front of the castle
beside the large oak tree
after this car

The Participial Phrase

The participial phrase begins with a participle and includes its object and any words modifying the object. It always modifies a noun. The participial phrase modifies a noun or pronoun largely because it has no subject of its own; therefore it must relate to another word, a noun. It functions as an adjective in the sentence—because any word that modifies a noun is an adjective. The following participial phrases are underlined:

<u>Assuming the very worst</u>, Luiz hesitated at the doorway.
<u>Slowing down suddenly</u>, Deirdre signaled for a turn.
<u>Lifting the money high</u>, the crooks jubilantly ran out the door.
<u>Dropping the shot cleanly</u>, Junior raised his arm in triumph.
<u>Deadened by the noise</u>, the dog crept away.
<u>Calmed down for now</u>, Marnie and Luisa stopped worrying.

Apprentice writers have problems with the participial phrase only when they forget that the noun it modifies comes right after it, separated by a comma. If the noun it modifies is not immediately after it, the phrase is a dangling modifier. When the noun comes first that requirement is not so inflexible, as in: "As a boss, he was fun, excitable, and <u>amused by occasional practical jokes</u>." You can see how complex this can sometimes get by examining the previous examples. The past tense verbs: *hesitated, signaled,* and *raised* can all be visually confused with participles. They are, however, simple verbs. They state an action, and do not modify a noun or pronoun.

The Infinitive Phrase

The infinitive phrase begins with an infinitive and includes its object and any words modifying it. The infinitive phrase can function as a noun: the subject or object of a verb. It can also be an adjective, modifying a noun or pronoun, or an adverb, modifying a verb or adjective. Each example here is labeled according to its use and the infinitive phrases are underlined.

Noun (object of the verb) Margot wanted <u>to go home</u>.
Adjective (modifying *him*) She waited for him <u>to ignore her</u>.
Adverb (modifying *problematic*) It was problematic <u>to leave so early</u>.

The Gerund Phrase

The gerund phrase begins with a gerund and includes its object and any words that modify it. Like the gerund, the gerund phrase is used as a noun, which means it can be the subject or object of a verb and the object of a preposition. Each example here is labeled and the gerund phrases are underlined.

(Subject of a verb) <u>Buying a new winter coat</u> is not my idea of fun.
(Object of a verb) My friend from back home enjoys <u>shopping for all kinds of clothes</u>.
(Object of a preposition) He was surprised at my <u>being a reluctant shopper</u>.

The main problem writers have with gerunds is remembering that the subject of a gerund is always going to follow this form: possessive + gerund. You can always ask this question: "Whose buying is it?" "Whose shopping is it?" "Whose being is it?" The possible answers, *my, his, my,* are all in the possessive case. In the last example, *my* is the subject of the gerund *being*. The subject of the gerund is possessive. It would be incorrect to say *at me being,* because *me* is the objective form. *My* is possessive.

The Absolute Phrase

Certain phrases are impossible to categorize by the means described earlier. They do not modify other elements of the sentence, but seem to stand apart, or in addition to what is being said. They have an absolute relationship to the sentence and are therefore called absolute phrases. They always contain a noun or pronoun that acts as the subject of a participle, and any words that modify those words.

The fact that the participle has its own subject distinguishes the absolute phrase from the participial phrase. The absolute phrase modifies the rest of the sentence by introducing specific details or explanations. Here are some examples, showing the different positions absolute phrases can enjoy in the sentence.

> <u>Their flowers having just started to bloom</u>, the Zapporas insisted on holding a lawn concert.
> The entire performance, <u>the rains having just begun</u>, was put off for another evening.
> It was finally agreed that it was a fine concert, but the audience was a bit uncomfortable, <u>their lawn chairs still being somewhat wet from the storm</u>.

Absolute phrases are separated from the rest of the sentence with either one comma, when it comes at the beginning or end of the sentence, or with two, when it comes in the middle.

Writer's Workshop: Grammar for the Writer

1. Underline the noun phrases and circle the verb phrases in the following sentences:
   a. Michael would have been upset by the losing team's blunders.
   b. The pleasant looking people near the bleachers could have told us what was going on if we had thought to ask.
   c. We met the tall, dark-haired centerfielder later and I could have sworn that he was the fellow who turned his back on us earlier.
   d. Michael would not let me say a word about it, although I might have been quick to say something if he were not with me.
   e. What everyone else knew was that the centerfielder was a sore loser.
2. Underline the nouns and circle the verbs in the following sentences:
   a. Felix had understood the question, but decided not to answer.

b. When Sister Evita approached the limousine to see what kind of problem the reporters were having, Felix stepped out and smiled.

c. The reporters did not realize that Sister Evita was part of the consortium until that minute.

3. Underline the adjectives and circle the adverbs in the following sentences:

a. Suddenly, the sky darkened. The clouds were threatening and grim looking. People gasped loudly and pointed up at the single-engine plane overhead.

b. Slowly, the crowd parted and made an abrupt turn to their left. The open space was just enough for the small plane to land.

c. The pilot stepped forward, took off her dark cap, and shook her hair free. Her smile was magnetic, and the frightened crowd cheered.

4. Decide whether the underlined clauses in the following sentences are independent [I], or dependent [D]:

a. While the agents searched the rear of the truck, Simpson and the driver held fast to their passports.

b. No one dared approach them directly, because they were American citizens traveling on government business.

c. However, the car itself was registered improperly, and none of the agents was confident about his next move.

d. When Simpson directed the first inspector to return to the office, there was a distinct coldness to their response.

e. Simpson restored order after he explained his status, and the inspector understood why the car was registered so oddly.

f. Until the directives were handed down from the central office, no one said a word.

g. Luckily, everyone was permitted to go soon after the inspector returned with the forms, and the tensions were instantly alleviated.

5. Underline the prepositional phrases and circle the infinitive phrases in the following sentences:

a. Elizabeth Cady Stanton was prominent in feminist politics in the nineteenth century, when she began a movement that made women aware of the extent to which they were deprived of their civil rights.

b. Her husband was interested enough to want to help her to achieve the awakening of the consciousness of thousands of women to whom she was an inspiring leader.

c. She was able to galvanize men as well as women and secured the attention of the national press at a time when women were unable to vote, unable to own property independent of their husbands, and unable to take part in the political life of the nation.

d. Her most famous speech was given at Seneca Falls, New York, when she referred to the Declaration of Independence in such a way as to reveal its limitations in regard to women.

e. Today we think of her as a leader among those who strove to protect the rights of all oppressed people in America.

6. Underline the participial phrases and circle the gerund phrases in the following sentences:

a. According to people who knew him, thinking about mathematical puzzles was one of Einstein's favorite hobbies.

b. Approaching middle age, he sometimes amused himself with puzzles that would have stumped experts.

c. Solving puzzles seems to appeal to different kinds of people, but creating the puzzles seems to be the province of only a few.

d. With lightning speed, he could sometimes solve puzzles that took others hours of close reckoning on computer screens.

e. Solving such extraordinary problems, Einstein was able to protect his reputation as a striking mathematical mind.

Common Grammar Problems

These days certain kinds of grammar problems seem common. They can cause confusion for a careful reader, and they can produce problems in expression for the writer. Some problems are a matter of usage, which has to do with logic and custom, not just grammar. We generally agree that there is a preferred form of grammar and a preferred usage for most formal pieces of writing. These include writing done for college courses, writing for magazines and newspapers, and writing for business and publication.

There is no absolute agreement on some grammatical issues because the language is always in a state of flux and change. Therefore under some circumstances, and to achieve certain effects, some rules of grammar or usage may be open to interpretation. However, we have a general agreement on most of what follows.

PROBLEMS WITH VERBS

verb

Active and Passive Verbs

act/pass

A forceful writing style depends on active, rather than passive verbs. The difference between them is that an active verb transmits action from its subject to its object, whereas the passive verb transmits action back upon its subject. In certain fields, such as the sciences and business, the passive verbs are sometimes preferred, especially when you wish to shift emphasis from the person doing the action to the action itself. (See the box entitled "Tips: Action Verbs.")

> *Tips: Action Verbs*
>   A forceful writing style is usually an interesting style. One clue to keeping your style interesting involves your choice of verbs: the verb *to be* in all its forms usually reduces the activity of your verbs. The difference between "The dog jumped on the chair" and "The dog is on the chair" is a difference in action. *Jumped* is more active than *is*. When you have a choice, choose *jumped*. Always choose a verb that states a specific action rather than a verb that implies a state of being. This tip alone will help you activate your thinking and intensify your writing style.

Here are some specific examples of each form:

Active Constructions
Direction of action →

Subject	Verb	Object
Margaret	fixed	the typewriter.
Nobody	saw	my accident.
Carlos	approved	Sonny's plan.
The United States	reduced	its arsenal.
Pontoons	support	seaplanes.

Passive Constructions
Direction of action ←

Subject	Verb	Adverbial Prep. phrase
The typewriter	was fixed	by Margaret.
My accident	was seen	by nobody.
Sonny's plan	was approved	by Carlos.
Its arsenal	was reduced	by the United States.
Seaplanes	are supported	by pontoons.

Although it is possible for sentences to shift the position of the subject, verb, and object or complement, the best pattern for you to use is the basic pattern that is common to English:

subject + verb + object/or/complement

The passive construction sometimes finds its way into your writing when you are uncertain about things. You do not have the assurance you need to make a definite statement, often because you do not know enough about your subject. In general writing, remember: an active construction will, by itself, give your writing extra energy.

There are a few cases in which the passive construction is your only choice. Usually, they are cases in which the agent or subject of a verb is unknown. Here are a few:

The game was called off because of rain.
The store was closed early.
My uncle was known as a dandy.
The exams were graded when I got here.
This expression was approved in the last century.

Shift of Tenses

tense

Some writers have problems keeping the tense of the verbs in a given paragraph or passage consistent. To some extent, the problem is really a problem in logic rather than grammar. Logically, if you have been talking about an action that happened in the past, you use the past tense. Logically, you would not begin a sentence using the past tense, then without notice switch to the present tense. However, people do exactly that, and in virtually all cases they are unaware of the switch. (See the box entitled "Tips: Tense Shifts.")

TIP

> *Tips: Tense Shifts*
>
> The errors in the previous examples are the result of two things: first, the effort to imitate a kind of speech sometimes heard in informal gatherings. It is acceptable in the right situations, when you let your reader know that it is colloquial. The second is the result of inattention. The most important advice I can give you is to study your own verb choices carefully, and make sure, as you edit your work, that you do not shift tenses without a reason.

Consequently, you should establish awareness of your choice of tense from the very beginning, and then maintain that awareness in your editing stages so as to catch any mistakes. Once you understand this principle, you will find it relatively simple to follow. Here are some examples of sentences in which the tense shifts from past to present. I have italicized the illogical shifts. A corrected version then follows.

Incorrect: Margot was walking on Independence Avenue when along *comes* this mean looking fellow who was in the coffee shop earlier. "Hey lady," he *says* to her as if she were deaf. "You forgot your purse!"

And Margot *gets* all flustered and *does* not know what to say. So she *says,* "Thank you."

Correct: Margot was walking on Independence Avenue when along came this mean looking fellow who was in the coffee shop earlier. "Hey lady," he said to her as if she were deaf. "You forgot your purse!" And Margot got all flustered and did not know what to say. So she said, "Thank you."

The incorrect example sounds acceptable to some people. In fact, if this were in a mystery novel and the record of a narrator's commentary, it might be fine. People do talk this way, and they do so for a reason: it's an amusing mannerism. However, it is not acceptable in a formal piece of prose. Here is another example:

Incorrect: Lincoln saw that McClellan was not getting the job done, and so he *sits* down and *writes* him a short note that became one of the most well-read letters of the war.

Correct: Lincoln saw that McClellan was not getting the job done, and so he sat down and wrote him a short note that became one of the most well-read letters of the war.

Incorrect: When Thoreau went out to Walden he was unhappy with the kind of life Emerson *is living,* so he *resolves* to do things differently. He left the bourgeois comforts behind and set out to build his own dwelling place. Which he *does,* much to Emerson's consternation.

Correct: When Thoreau went out to Walden he was unhappy with the kind of life Emerson was living, so he resolved to do things differently. He left the bourgeois comforts behind and set out to build his own dwelling place. Which he did, much to Emerson's consternation.

Moods: Subjunctives

In addition to being active or passive, verbs have differences both in tense and in mood. Today, we do not pay much attention to questions of mood, but you should know that the following are three moods used in contemporary English:

mood

Indicative: The verbs in this sentence are in the indicative mood and when you write, you use the indicative mood virtually all the time.

Imperative: Pay attention. Listen up and get this message straight. These sentences use the imperative mood: they give an order, and they omit their subject, which in all cases is *you* (because the subject is the same in all cases *you* can be omitted).

Subjunctive: Were you a world-famous writer, you would not be likely to read this book. *Were* is a verb in the subjunctive mood, which is used not for stating things directly, like the indicative mood, or for giving orders, like the imperative mood, but for stating conditions that are contrary to fact.

The problem with the subjunctive is that it is not recognized by the writers who misuse it. The subjunctive is used when you say something that is not yet a fact, something that you wish for, something that is a suggestion, or something that is a requirement. (See the box entitled "Tips: Subjunctive.")

TIP

> *Tips: Subjunctive*
> The problems seem to arise with the past tense forms of *to be* when you are writing about something that is contrary to fact. Remember that when you begin a clause with: "if Hilda," or "if other people," or any other construction that begins with *if* or a similar conditional adverb, then you almost certainly follow with the subjunctive *were*. You should write: "if Hilda were tall," "if people were only more thoughtful," and then complete your sentence normally.

The form of the subjunctive verb is always the basic dictionary form: *send; have; felt; spend.* The present tense subjunctive for the verb *to be* is *be;* the past tense is *were* no matter what the subject. Here are some specific examples, all used correctly. The subjunctive verb is italicized.

(Contrary to fact) If you *were* a prince, you could afford me.
(A wish) Margaret wished you soldiers *felt* more like your old selves.
(A suggestion) DeForrest recommended only that she *spend* her last vacation day on the beach.
(A requirement) New Jersey state laws demand that all seat belts *be* in operating condition all the time.

The following examples show the most common kinds of uses for the subjunctive form of the verb. Each subjunctive is italicized.

Sylvester would be happy if he *were* in a tropical climate.
Napoleon III would never have gotten in the balloon if he *were* afraid of heights.
Were I overly cautious, I would never have any fun at all.

Writer's Workshop: Problems with Verbs
1. Underline the active verbs and circle the passive verbs in the following sentences:

a. Despite his reputation, General Patton was said to be a gentle man when he wished to be.

b. He carried a famous pearl-handled revolver that was given to him by a friend.

c. His expertise was in tank fighting, a relatively new science studied only by a few fighting men.

d. One of the most expert tank commanders was Field Marshall Rommel, known as the "Desert Fox."

e. When they met at El Alamein, Rommel attempted some amazing maneuvers but was outsmarted by the even more brilliant Patton.

2. Circle each inappropriate tense shift in the following sentences:

a. Mary Shelley wrote *Frankenstein* more than a century ago, which she begins on a dare from the poet Byron, who is certain that one of his friends can write a thrilling novel.

b. In the 1830s, *Frankenstein* is a best seller, and Mary Shelley is known all over England, when she was asked to talk about her creation.

c. Although it is best known as a horror movie today, in its own day it is thought of as a serious book.

d. Its message is, for 1830, associated with the question of whether people, especially scientists, are able to control their own creations.

e. The metaphor of the creature who is given life by a "mad" scientist is a way Mary Shelley has of talking about whether people will be able to control science or not.

3. Circle each use of the subjunctive in the following sentences:

a. John Brown wished that the nation were more liberal in its attitude toward slavery.

b. Were Brown born a slaveowner he would have freed his slaves as soon as possible.

c. "Be free," he would have told them, were he only in a position to do so.

d. Alas, the law in the South commanded that slaveowners be disciplined for such actions.

e. If Brown had his way, there would be no slaves.

PROBLEMS WITH SENTENCES

Sentence Fragment

frag

A sentence fragment lacks one or both of the basic elements it needs to be complete: a subject or a verb. Or, if it contains both subject and verb, it begins with a subordinating conjunction or other linking word. It does not have all the ingredients of an independent clause. The following sentence fragments begin with a capital letter and end with a period as if they were complete sentences. In a sense, they are masquerading.

(A dependent clause beginning with a subordinate adverb) After I thought that you would help me out.
(Lacking both subject and verb) Doing it.
(Lacking a verb) Because of the Black Prince and the other crusaders at that time.
(Lacking a subject) As a result of the plague killed in incredible numbers all over France.

There can be good reasons for using sentence fragments: they can pace the rhythms of your prose, and they can sometimes be used for emphasis. I included several very good examples here by professional writers. What worries me is not the instance in which a writer knows full well that a sentence fragment is posing as a sentence; rather, I worry when the fragment goes unrecognized. That spells trouble. (See the box entitled "Tips: Sentence Fragments.")

Tips: Sentence Fragments
Be aware. Examine any sentence that starts with a subordinating adverb or conjunction for its subject and verb. In the process of revision and editing all your sentences, do the following:

• Find the subject
• Find the verb

CS

Comma Splice

The comma splice is the opposite of the fragment. Its fault is not that it is only part of a sentence, but rather that it includes too much material. It joins together two or more sentences joined only by a comma. (See the box entitled "Tips: Comma Splices.")
Here are some examples of comma splice:

Caesar feared his men might betray him, he marched all the way to the coast without a stop.
The string theory is just beginning to come of age, all matter is linked together in mysterious ways.
I have no hope of going home for Christmas, what are your plans?

Each of these can be corrected in a simple fashion. You have three choices. Instead of splicing with the comma, use:

> *Tips: Comma Splices*
> Be on the lookout for comma splices as you proofread your work in the editorial and revising stages of writing. Be especially careful to examine every unusually long sentence for a possible comma splice. If you have a sentence in which you have more than one independent clause, do the following:
>
> - Examine each comma to see if it is followed by an independent clause.
> - Test for whether the comma should be a conjunction, semicolon, or period.

TIP

1. a coordinating conjunction: *and, but, or, nor, for, yet, so*
2. a semicolon to link independent clauses
3. a period to end one sentence, and then begin the next with a capital letter

Here are the sample comma splices in corrected form:

Caesar feared his men might betray him, so he marched all the way to the coast without stop. (1. coordinating conjunction *so*)
The string theory is just beginning to come of age; all matter is linked together in mysterious ways. (2. use of the semicolon)
I have no hope of going home for Christmas. What are your plans? (3. splitting into two sentences)

Run-on Sentence

Unlike the comma splice, the run-on sentence fuses together two independent clauses with neither a conjunction nor a form of punctuation to join the two clauses. In other words, they are abutted together with no transition, no clarifying element to join them. Here is a sample:

Incorrect:
Napoleon was born in Corsica his mother had great hopes for him there.
Correct:
Napoleon was born in Corsica. His mother had great hopes for him there.

For most writers of run-on sentences, the solution of splitting the separate elements with a period and making them independent sentences does not always solve the whole problem. Their errors are often complex, involving more than just the question of running elements together. Nonetheless, relating the independent clauses to each other by use of proper punctuation or

run

conjunctions is the first step toward making the sentences acceptable and effective. (See the box entitled "Tips: Run-on Sentences.")

> *Tips: Run-on Sentences*
>   Make one of your chief proofreading jobs center on examining longer sentences for unconnected elements. Examine joined independent clauses to see that they have a clearly expressed relationship. This is a difficult error for some people to spot on their own because it is marked by *an omission* rather than by the inclusion of something that you can consistently search for.
>
> - Look for long sentences and check the relationship of each independent clause.
> - Test for whether the clauses need to be joined by a transition word, or separated by a period and made into two or more sentences.

Some more samples and their corrections follow:

Incorrect:
Come here, Matthew there is someone who wishes to see you.

Correct:
Come here, Matthew. There is someone who wishes to see you.

Incorrect:
Radium glows in the dark it is a useful, but dangerous element.

Correct:
Radium glows in the dark; it is a useful, but dangerous element.

Incorrect:
Elephants are pachyderms like hippopotamuses they do not belong to the same zoological classification.

Correct:
Elephants are pachyderms like hippopotamuses, although they do not belong to the same zoological classification.

Writer's Workshop: Problems with Sentences
1. Correct the sentence fragments in the following sentences by inserting the proper punctuation and adding the appropriate capitals. You may have to strike out words and rewrite passages. Circle each correction.

   a. Because the Wright Brothers were bicycle makers and not aeronautical engineers. It was hard for some people to think of them as the inventors of flight.

   b. Romantics thought flight should have been first experienced by a genius. Like Leonardo da Vinci, who certainly tried to make a workable flying machine.

   c. Recently another more likely candidate for the laurels of the first flying human being came to public notice. Because his credentials included a college degree.

   d. However, today we do not understand the function of the bicycle makers of the last century. Who were the engineers and inventors of their time.

   e. After all. Henry Ford, inventor of the assembly line approach to making automobiles. Ford was originally a bicycle maker and repairman.

2. Correct the comma splices in the following sentences. Use a period and a capital letter where appropriate and circle your corrections.

   a. Until a few years ago the United States manufactured most of its own automobiles, now half the automobiles sold in any given year come from abroad.

   b. Japan, our adversary in World War II, and something of a significant manufacturing power in the 1930s, seems to have learned how to make automobiles as well as any nation in the world, depending on a patriotic approach to buying automobiles is no longer possible for American automakers.

   c. Customers praise Japanese workmanship, quality, and attention to detail, American automakers could profit from, above all, paying attention to the complaints of customers about their products.

   d. Other important manufacturing industries are now dominated by Japan, which has made inroads in cameras, computers, high-tech, and other areas, recently, according to the newspapers, Japan has been buying entire American companies and hotel chains to make them run more efficiently.

   e. Apparently United States banks are the next industry to be targeted by Japan, which has been very successful in banking, the control of capital and the formation of new companies is dependent on the decisions of major banks in any capitalist nation.

3. Correct the run-on sentences that follow. Add the proper punctuation and capitalization, and circle your corrections.

   a. Russian modernization has been ongoing for forty years ever since the end of the war Russia has sought to increase mechanization.

   b. Mechanization has had its greatest impact in farming farmers have been using tractors and other heavy equipment still the problem of supplying such equipment to the people who need it is serious.

   c. In other areas the situation is serious for instance in the area of computers, the Soviet Union has decided to imitate Apple computers rather than to design its own from scratch.

   d. The result is that Soviet computer technology is left behind in the wake of new developments because the design of new computer technology is dependent on the design of older technology, the Soviet Union has failed to keep up.

   e. According to recent observations, one of the biggest problems the Soviet Union has is with the manufacture of floppy disks the process is too delicate for certain manufacturing facilities, and the joke in the Soviet Union is that the only country that can supply the Soviet needs is Bulgaria.

PROBLEMS WITH AGREEMENT

$\boxed{\textit{pron/agr}}$

Pronoun agreement presents problems because pronouns often refer back or forward to nouns with which they must agree. Agreement problems with pronouns usually surface as a failure to make a pronoun plural or singular in accordance with its preceding noun.

The other most common failure of agreement has to do with verbs and their subjects. Because the subject comes early and the verb comes late in some sentences, it is possible to forget to make sure they agree in number. This is usually an editorial problem. Most writers see their error the moment it is pointed out to them—the trick, for most of us, is to keep track of the connection between the subject and its following verb.

Pronoun Agreement

One of the best ways to avoid problems in pronoun agreement is to examine sample sentences that have gone wrong. In the examples that follow there are two patterns: the first is the wide separation of the pronoun from its referent. In such a case, there are plenty of chances of error. The second is the familiar situation in which the pronoun refers back to the subject of a prepositional phrase, and the writer thought it referred to the object of the phrase.

The *This* and *These* *Problem*

One common error involves a misunderstanding with the pronouns *this* or *these*. Such pronouns must refer back to a specific thing, something that has been exactly identified and isolated from the general group to which it belongs. Otherwise, the referent is unclear.

(Incorrect) Although a certain amount of health is necessary, this should not intimidate people from participating in sports.

The writer expects that *this* refers to the entire clause, but how can it? What is the specific thing that *this* alludes to? Actually, nothing. The sentence suffers from a simple problem: the writer never revised it for good sense. For one thing, health does not come in amounts, so that phrase has to be changed. For another, the problem centers on the fact that good health, not just health, is usually a prerequisite for sports. Here is one improved version (although I cannot completely improve the sentence because it comes from a paragraph that was hastily written and needs total overhaul):

> People should not be intimidated from participating in sports because good health is necessary.

Here is yet another version of the problem, even more common:

> Habits start early. As a person ages, these habits are reinforced.

What habits? Sucking one's thumb? Slurping over one's coffee? If *these* is to be used, then it has to refer to *specific* habits. *Habits* in the first sentence refers to the general class of habits. In the second sentence, "these habits" refers to some specific habits, like burping after dinner, wiping your shoes on the bedspread, or falling asleep in front of the television set. But, no such habits have been mentioned. Therefore, the use of *these* is wrong. Improving the sentence is easy, although it really does not help the writer much. The essay from which that example comes goes on to talk about a good habit: being on time. Here is a revision:

> Habits start early. As people age, their habits are reinforced.

(See the box entitled "Tips: Using *This* and *These*.")

this/these

Tips: Using **This** *and* **These**
The rule is simple: *this* and *these* refer to specific things.

- Check to see that *this* or *these* refers to an explicitly named thing.
- Be sure *this* or *these* does not refer to a general class, but to a specific member of a general class of things.
- If you have a problem revising a sentence that uses these pronouns inaccurately, try a version of the sentence that omits them entirely.

TIP

Problems with Distance Between Referent and Pronoun
The samples immediately following show errors that seem to result from losing track of the word to which the pronoun refers.

pron

1. When someone makes those kinds of a statements under their breath, then they deserve what they get.

agr

In this sentence the subject is *someone,* and the following pronouns: *their, they,* and *they* all refer to it. But *someone* is singular. The pronouns must agree in number with the word they refer to. Here is the sentence correctly written, and notice that the verbs that the plural pronouns control have to be made singular to agree with the pronouns' change to the singular. In this case I have assumed that the *someone* referred to is a real person, a woman.

When someone makes those kinds of a statements under her breath, then she deserves what she gets.

2. Paul and Jimmy were figuring out how to hit it big in the state lottery because the hope was that if he won it a lot of people could really benefit from being able to go to college and not have to worry about work.

Paul and Jimmy are plural, but *he* is singular. The writer explained that she knew Paul had eleven brothers and sisters who wanted to go to college. She did not remember that she mentioned there were two people who bought lottery tickets. Here is how the sentence should read:

Paul and Jimmy were figuring out how to hit it big in the state lottery because the hope was that if they won it some of Paul's family could really benefit from being able to go to college instead of having to go right to work.

The following subject and pronoun fail to agree in person. The pronoun should refer to a third person noun, *Napoleon,* and be third person singular. However, it is plural by mistake.

3. Napoleon, like many generals, planned so carefully that you do not have any latitude to make important changes.

You has no business being in that sentence. Instead, it should read as follows:

Napoleon, like many generals, planned so carefully that he did not have any latitude to make important changes.

Problems with the Subject of a Prepositional Phrase

The most common errors in agreement occur when there is a plural or singular word modified by a prepositional phrase whose object is opposite in number. If the word is singular, the object is plural, and vice versa. Here is an example of the construction:

the pack (singular) of hounds (plural)

Here is how this structure can lead to problems:

   4. Darth saw the pack of hounds when they turned the corner.

The pronoun *they* is plural, but its subject, *pack,* is singular. The sentence should read:

   Darth saw the pack of hounds when it turned the corner.

I know the correction will sound odd to your ear, and maybe even appear odd in terms of logic. But grammatically, *hounds* is already an object of a preposition, so it cannot qualify for being the subject of the verb *turned.* Logically and grammatically the *pack* is what turns the corner.

   5. Seneca gave aid to Lucillius, one of Rome's senators, when they needed help.

They is supposed to refer to *one,* which in turn refers to *Lucillius,* who needed the help. All pronoun references to Lucillius should be singular. Here is the sentence corrected:

agr

   Seneca gave aid to Lucillius, one of Rome's senators, when he needed help.

   A common problem with agreement involves certain singular pronouns: none, neither, each. Even when followed by a prepositional phrase with a plural object, the verb must be singular. Here is a typical error:

   6. None of us are superstars at everything.

Corrected, the sentence should read:

   None of us is a superstar at everything.

None is the subject; *is* is the verb, which is singular to agree with *none.*
   Another problem occurs when the writer knows that conceptually the subject is plural even if its form is singular. For example, in the next sentence, the writer knew that *myth* really refers to *myths,* and acted accordingly. Unfortunately, the relative pronoun, *they,* still must be made to agree with *myth* in its grammatically singular form.

   7. Myth is common to all societies for one major reason—they give security to a society.

The sentence ought to read as follows:

Myth is common to all societies for one major reason—it gives security to a society.

The original version, with a plural *they*, is confusing because the only plural antecedent is *societies*. Obviously, *they* cannot refer to *societies*, and the sentence is not only unclear, but almost meaningless.

Subject-Verb Agreement

$$\boxed{agr\ s/v}$$

When a subject is singular, its verb must be singular; when the subject is plural its verb must be plural. Here are examples of proper subject-verb agreement:

Singular Subject	Singular Verb
Mahatma Gandhi	protests
a riverboat	steams
butter	melts
Philadelphia	does seem
a deer	will sleep
the book	recommends

Plural Subject	Plural Verb
the helicopters	hover
people	shout
competitors	do not cry
oceans	rage and swell
the pianos	played
deer	sleep

To some extent the problems that beset pronouns operate with verbs and their subjects. Distance between them often permits errors to creep in. The problem of agreement in number is most crucial with third person singular verbs. Corrected versions follow common mistakes in the following examples:

1. Parker, one of my old friends from home, go to a different college.

Correct: Parker, one of my old friends from home, goes to a different college.

Unfortunately, there are many people who do not hear the *-s* sound on the end of third person singular verbs. It simply is not there for them, and when they say sentences like the following:

My friend Parker sits up very properly at the table.

they do not pronounce the last -s on *sits,* and will often write *sit.* They are spelling the word from their memory of hearing it rather than their memory of seeing it. Because this is a common problem, I list here a few typical sentences first in their incorrect version, then in their correct version.

1. Lord Stanley, in a remote part of the western forests, keep a journal recording daily events even today.

Correct: Lord Stanley, in a remote part of the western forests, keeps a journal recording daily events even today.

2. Luiz have a friend who keep him supplied with good books.

Correct: Luiz has a friend who keeps him supplied with good books.

3. Jamie see me. He keep his eyes open for the taxi, too.

Correct: Jamie sees me. He keeps his eyes open for the taxi, too.

4. Do not move the Savin copier from where it sit now, because it have to be ready for the big job Philippa set up each week at this time.

Correct: Do not move the Savin copier from where it sits now, because it has to be ready for the big job Philippa sets up each week at this time.

Another sound that sometimes does not get heard on the end of verbs is -d. Look at the final d on *supposed* and *used.* In the following constructions, remember that the d must be present:

He used to like me.
I am supposed to finish up.

Writer's Workshop: Problems with Agreement

1. Correct the agreement problems in the following sentences. Be sure to circle your corrections.
    a. Unemployment, which is a product of the planning of governments, keep moving upward even in times of economic improvement.
    b. The director of the ministry of unemployment agencies are meeting with the president.
    c. People who have had only one job is certain to want more information on the unemployment of others.
    d. The director feel there is not any excuse for people not working.
    e. More jobs, of a sort that usually guarantee employment, seems to be opening up now, when the economy of the states are improving.
    f. However, most of the jobs, according to the *Washington Post,* is in service industries.

g. The glut of jobs, according to the government sources, are surprising people who expect to collect unemployment the rest of their life.

h. Unemployment, a serious problem that you should not have to deal with in the 1990s, certainly loom large.

---

mm

Misplaced Modifiers

Distance is a problem with elements of a sentence that modify the meaning of something else. For instance, if you separate an adjective from the noun it refers to, you might run into trouble. Here is a sample:

> The problem was, because of a mistake that had somehow gotten into the computer program at a stage when the planning and first-branching concepts were not solved by the project director, but instead by the part-time consultant from New York, huge.

This is by no means a good sentence, but the separation of *huge* from *problem*, which it obviously refers to, makes it almost indecipherable.

Fortunately, most of us rarely produce such sentences. Generally we know that adjectives should be close to their nouns or pronouns, and adverbs should be close to their verbs. Keeping them close helps produce clarity.

Misplaced Prepositional Phrases

Like adjectives or adverbs, prepositional phrases also ought to be close to the sentence elements they refer to. When they are not, they can produce this kind of error:

1. John Brown saw his opportunity to lead his men away from the armory on his own horse.

Is he really going to put the men on his horse? No, John Brown was on his horse. The sentence should read as follows:

> John Brown, on his own horse, saw his opportunity to lead his men away from the armory.

The same kind of problem occurs here in this fashion:

2. From his men, even after they all realized there was probably no chance that any of them would come out of the adventure alive, John Brown got the reassurance he needed.

This sentence should read as follows:

> John Brown got the reassurance he needed from his men even after they
> all realized there was probably no chance that any of them would come
> out of the adventure alive.

Try to place the prepositional phrase next to the element it relates to. Fortunately, you will find yourself doing this naturally. The problems you run into
usually occur in very long sentences that you agonize over. You write them
four or five different ways, and in the process you lose track of some of the
elements. In this way, you sometimes separate the prepositional phrase from
its proper relative.

Misplaced Clauses

Another common problem is the misplacing of noun, adjective, and other
dependent clauses. The *who, which, that,* and similar clauses have a way of
coming unglued from their referent. The usual problem involves placing the
clause too far away from what it refers to. So, once you realize that problem,
the simplest way to avoid it in the first place is to put the clause next to what it
modifies.

Here are a few examples, showing how things can go wrong. All of these
are from unrevised pieces. Some of them would have been corrected if the
writer had taken the time to revise carefully.

> The director, after many attempts to make a film about the discovery of
> the Congo River, met a producer from Africa, where he had actually
> begun filming *Livingston, Meet Stanley.*

This is a difficult sentence to revise, but we finally developed a reasonable
version that was closer to the author's intent. The problem in the sample
sentence is that you do not know if the director began filming in Africa or if
the producer began filming.

> The director, after many attempts to make a film about the discovery of
> the Congo River, where he had actually begun filming *Livingston, Meet
> Stanley,* met a producer from Africa.

This version, although not altogether satisfactory, does make the point clear.
The director was doing the filming. What the producer is doing was reserved
for the next sentence. Here is a more common variety of error involving a
misplaced clause:

> After a long day's march, John Brown set guards at the compass points of
> the camp who knew a great deal about the habits of the U.S. Army
> scouts.

When I pointed out that the sentence ought to read *guards who,* not *camp who,* the writer saw the problem immediately and suggested this revision:

> After a long day's march, John Brown set guards who knew a great deal about the habits of the U. S. Army at the compass points of the camp.

Here is another sentence with a similar problem:

> A habit people often put up with for years that surprises me is picking their teeth in public.

This is a very common structure, and many writers have a hard time correcting it. The problem is that *habit* is modified by two clauses. Both start with *that,* but the first omits the word. It ought to read: "that people often put up with for years." It is very difficult to correct, but here is one revision:

> Picking their teeth in public, a habit that surprises me, is something people often put up with for years.

A common kind of error is apparent in this sentence:

> V. I. Lenin was a person, unlike many of the younger subalterns of the yet to be formed Red Guard under Bukharov, who could be ruthless.

The problem is typical of the misplaced modifier: which person is ruthless? Actually, both of them were, but that does not solve the problem. The sentence needs to be rewritten as follows:

> Unlike many of the younger subalterns of the yet to be formed Red Guard under Bukharov, V. I. Lenin could be ruthless.

I had been quick to point out to this writer that we already knew V. I. Lenin was a person, so it was not essential that we say it again.

Typically, problems involving misplaced clauses can be solved by writing two sentences. Often, difficulties arise simply because the writer is trying to say too much in one sentence. Consider these revisions of the sample sentences:

> After many attempts to make a film about the discovery of the Congo River, the director actually had begun filming *Livingston, Meet Stanley.* At that point he met a producer from Africa.
> After a long day's march, John Brown set guards at the compass points of the camp. They knew a great deal about the habits of the U. S. Army scouts.

Picking one's teeth in public is a habit that surprises me. People often put up with it for years.

V. I. Lenin could be ruthless. He was unlike many of the younger subalterns of the yet to be formed Red Guard under Bukharov.

All of these solutions are clear. They avoid the ambiguities and the clumsiness of the earlier versions.

Writer's Workshop: Misplaced Modifiers

1. Correct the following sentences by circling the misplaced modifier and drawing a line to indicate where it should go:
    a. The problem, which had never been solved in all the years of the water commission's activities, proved insoluble now, of flooding.
    b. The commission recommended flooding, at regular intervals, and according to the backup of waters upstream, of the fertile valleys.
    c. Somehow, from the agricultural experts, the commissioner and his officers, received an okay to carry out this plan.
    d. For reasons that never emerged in the hearing, the commissioners approved a plan who did not trust it completely and thought it would not work.
    e. The dam failed at the crucial moment because of the hesitation and the essential failure of the planners and engineers originally designing the project in the 1930s who disagreed with the government bureaucrats who, for once, were right.

Writer's Workshop

Punctuation

You need to keep track of relatively few punctuation marks. The problem is not usually in identifying them, so much as it is in handling them properly at the right time. For convenience, here are the punctuation marks we are concerned with in this section:

the period	.
the question mark	?
the exclamation mark	!
the colon	:
the semicolon	;
the comma	,
quotation marks	"
the apostrophe	'

parentheses	( )
brackets	[ ]
the dash	—
the ellipsis	. . .

.?!

PERIODS, QUESTION MARKS, AND EXCLAMATION MARKS

End punctuations tell us when a sentence is finished, and whether it is declarative, interrogative, or exclamatory. The convention in English is to begin every sentence with a capital letter, and to end it with one of three punctuation marks: . ? !

Remember: only one end-punctuation mark per sentence.

If a sentence ends with a quotation that includes a question mark or an exclamation point, do not add another period.

The period, however, is also used to mark abbreviations within a sentence. Were you to say, "Born in the U. S. A.," you naturally use a period after each abbreviation, U. for United, S. for States, and A. for America. Here are a few common abbreviations:

B.A.	n.d.	Mr.	Ms.	Mrs.	etc.
A.D.	C.P.A.	dept.	Acct.	p.m.	a.m.

Some abbreviations do not use periods. They are usually the names of organizations that are familiar to the public or to a professional group.

NBC	CBS	IBM	MLA	NBA	YMCA

Acronyms, the initials of organizations which spell a word, like MADD, Mothers Against Drunk Driving, do not use periods. VISTA, UNCLE, and ERA are among these.

The question mark indicates that a sentence asks for a response from the listener. It is a question. Here are some examples:

Do you want to speak with Margot?
Are you sure?
Margot? No, I am Amy.
Why?
Have you enough patience to hold on any longer?

Do not use the question mark after indirect questions, such as this:

They asked me if I could write a book.
I asked you whether or not you were coming to the party early.

The exclamation point indicates a high degree of emphasis. The problem for most nonprofessional writers is that it is tempting to use it often. But it loses its edge quickly. You only need to use it two or three times on a page for the reader to weary of it, especially if it is obvious that the only thing exclamatory about the sentence is the end punctuation. Here are some examples:

This was Chamberlain's most outrageous statement!
You expect us to surrender? Never!
Nuts!

USE OF QUOTATION MARKS

" "

One troubling detail in punctuation concerns the use of quotation marks at the end of a sentence. Remember that in America the final punctuation mark comes *inside* the quotation marks. Here are some samples:

I heard him ask, "Where am I?"
According to Thorstein Veblen, we "admire conspicuous consumption."

It may not seem logical. The punctuation mark ends the sense of the sentence. But the reason we do this is to satisfy printers, who prefer sentences to end with the eye sweeping upward, from the period to the quotation mark.
When a question is quoted in the middle of a sentence, you retain the question mark, but end the entire sentence with the appropriate punctuation:

Guillermo asked "Where am I?" when he woke up.
We heard her say "May I please come in?" but we did not hear what the answer was.

However, when the question mark is not in the original, use this form:

Did you understand what she meant when she said, "I'll never leave here"?

In this last case, the entire sentence is asking a question, but the original quotation did not have a question mark. Therefore, the quotation stays inside the quotation marks as it was, and the question mark is added. Even if the original statement had a period, you do not include it. Only one end-stop punctuation is needed.

Commas sometimes give writers problems when using quotation marks inside a sentence. Remember: like end punctuation, they come inside the quotation marks. Here are some examples:

Shall we sing "Blues in the Night," or should we just hum along together?
Machiavelli said, "a prince must be little concerned with conspiracies,"
but I think a prince should be largely concerned with them.
I agree with Shakespeare, that we can "see feelingly," even though I do
not fully understand what he meant.

There are two punctuation marks that come outside the quotation marks: the colon and semicolon. These sentences are properly punctuated as follows:

Felix had four "friends": Janice, Fred, Phyllis, and Lupe.
De Maupassant wrote "The String of Pearls"; O. Henry wrote "Gift of
the Magi."
I was irritated, so I said "Skat"; why should I feel embarrassed about
it now?

Special Uses for Quotation Marks

The use of quotation marks can help clarify meaning. Certain special uses are important conventions. Here are some frequent instances:
Titles: We use quotation marks for titles of songs, sections of books, poems, essays, short stories, and articles. Generally, quotation marks are used to identify anything that would appear as part of a book, rather than as the entire book (which is properly italicized). Some samples are as follows:

John Updike's story, "A & P." (short story)
We heard Van Morrison play, "Rave on, John Donne." (pop tune)
Did you read, "Ode on a Grecian Urn"? (poem)
George Orwell wrote, "Marrakech." (article)

Special References

When you refer to a word as a word—not what it refers to—then you use italics to set it off. For instance, if you wished to comment on *word* as a word, you use italics to establish your meaning. You might say that *word* is peculiar for having only four letters, while *verbal* has six. If you do so, then use italics to establish the way in which you mean to use *word*.

When quoting inside a quotation, single quotation marks are used. Here are two examples:

"No one wants to stand by while others are shouting, 'Fire!' but what
were Chamberlain's choices in 1938?"

According to the report by Felix Urquhart, "no one had the good sense to take Brown seriously when he said, 'I will not shun danger, nor will I permit myself to be ignored.' We should have listened to him while we could."

COLONS AND SEMICOLONS

:/;

The colon and the semicolon are very close in meaning to an end-stop punctuation. They function as a sign of a strong pause rather than a full stop. Each has a special use.

The colon is used for the following purposes:

to indicate that a series follows
to indicate that an explanation follows
to indicate that a long quotation follows

The colon should come at the end of an independent clause. Thus, everything that follows the colon is supplementary or explanatory.

Here are some typical uses of the colon:

Socrates, in one famous expression, established a model for the scholarly life: "An unexamined life is not worth living." (Note that when the quotation begins with a capital letter, you may use it after the colon.)
Nietzsche had a profound effect on numerous modern figures: Wagner, Barthes, Camus, and Sartre.
I have never had a fear of flying: I spent my twenty-first birthday in a Piper Cub, my twenty-second birthday in a Cherokee, and I hope to spend my next birthday in a Lear Jet.
My suggestions for how we should solve this problem are as follows: first isolate the cells that have succumbed to the disease, then make a sterile solution in which you place three drops of sulphuric acid, and, finally, swab the infected area twice a day to remove the sloughed-away cells.

The semicolon is used for the following purposes:

to separate independent clauses when no conjunction is used
to separate two independent clauses when a conjunctive adverb is used
to separate items in a series when they include a comma

The semicolon is an effective item of punctuation. There are many times when a full stop is unnecessary, but something more than a comma is needed. Essentially, the semicolon links elements in a sentence that, given some rewriting, might be separable. Here are some examples of the semicolon in action:

I had no premonition of trouble; it took a thunderstorm to make me afraid. (joining two independent clauses)

People said John Brown would not do anything rash; however, he had a history of violence long before Harper's Ferry. (used before the conjunctive adverb *however*)

Emerson's problems with Thoreau had been longstanding; his patience, given the way Thoreau sometimes tested it, seemed unlimited; his affection, in light of the abuse Thoreau sometimes heaped on him, remained unabated, even through the extraordinary experience of the Walden experiment. (used to link a series of long clauses with their own punctuation)

The semicolon, like many special punctuation marks, is best not overdone. A great many semicolons can give your writing a pedantic or academic quality. Therefore, if you find yourself likely to overuse the semicolon, consider shortening your sentences.

COMMA

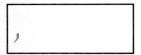

Unfortunately, of all the punctuation marks, the comma is the least understood. Some people use it as a pause equivalent to drawing a breath in speech. Others use it only at explicit grammatical moments, such as before and after a parenthetical clause. The tendency is to use it too often. But if it is omitted at critical moments, then the sense of a sentence can be lost. Therefore, it is essential that you know some of the most critical times when a comma is in demand.

What follows are some suggestions that should be taken as a guide. Your ultimate purposes in writing are to make sure that what you say is clear and not confusing. Here are some of the most important uses of the comma:

before a coordinate conjunction linking independent clauses
after transitional introductory phrases
before and after nonrestrictive phrases or clauses
before and after appositives
before and after parenthetical interruptors
before quotations
before items in a series
between adjectives modifying the same noun
between elements in a date or name of a place

Here are examples of each of these uses of the comma:

V. I. Lenin was released by the Germans, but no one expected that he would so quickly surface at the Finland Station. (before a coordinate conjunction linking independent clauses)

After a long ride in a sealed car, he found that much of his thinking had solidified regarding the revolution. (after transitional introductory phrases)

Bukharin, who approached the station after the appointed time, was disappointed not to meet him. (before and after nonrestrictive phrases or clauses)

> *Note:* A nonrestrictive phrase or clause could be applied to any of several people (in this case) and is not restricted to a specific person. Therefore, it is related to its subject by the commas. An example of a restrictive phrase is "The poet with one eye saw deep into the future." The phrase "with one eye" applies to one specific class of poets restricted to the class that has one eye.

The phrase, "with one eye," is limited to a small group of people. (before and after appositives)

> *Note:* An appositive is a group of words that means the same as the word or group of words before it. "With one eye" *is* the phrase referred to in the word just before it. Here is another example:

Your friend, Jonathan Edwards, was fascinated by spiders. ("friend" and "Jonathan Edwards" are one and the same, therefore the name is an appositive)

Lenin, it is reasonable to say, enjoyed the use of power.

Significance, not meaninglessness, will determine the future. (before and after parenthetical interruptors)

As Farley Stewart said, "Thoreau was not the kind of man who would suffer fools lightly." (before quotations)

Emerson was a poet, philosopher, citizen, and friend. (before items in a series) Note that there *is* a comma before *and.*

The astronauts were in a sleek, shiny starship. (between adjectives modifying the same noun)

Lynn was in Providence, Rhode Island, on June 5, 1982. (between elements in a date or name of a place)

APOSTROPHE

The apostrophe on the typewriter is the same as the single quotation mark. Fortunately, most writers have trouble with the apostrophe in only a few situations where there is confusion between whether a word is a possessive or whether it is two words joined together with a vowel left out: a contraction.

The apostrophe is used in the following situations:

1. to form the possessive case of nouns
2. to indicate that a letter or letters have been omitted in a contraction

Apostrophes can be tricky, so the following examples are worth examining in detail.

Here are examples using the possessive case:

A dog's bone (a singular noun)
the woman's computer (singular noun)
the boss's skirt (singular noun ending in -s)

The plural possessive usually adds the apostrophe without the -s:

the horses' stables (there are several horses, so this is plural)
the cats' home (plural word ending in -s)
the classes' meeting times (plural word ending in -s)
I used my brother-in-law's phone (the apostrophe -s comes at the *end* of hyphenated words)
Parker lived in Harry and John's garden house (Harry and John own the garden house together, therefore they share the possession, and the last item in the series gets the apostrophe)
Alphonse saw the same cat twice at Libby's and Martha's houses (Libby and Martha live in different houses, therefore each is identified in the possessive)

Contractions

The apostrophe indicates that a letter or letters are left out of contractions. Contractions are never used in formal writing, but they are useful in imitating conversation, because so much conversation contains them. (See the box entitled "Tips: Avoiding Confusion with Apostrophes.")

Here are some properly punctuated examples:

Complete expression	Contraction
She would help	She'd help
It is raining	It's raining
They are here	They're here
We have been home	We've been home
You are right	You're right
Lopez would cook	Lopez'd cook
I am stifled	I'm stifled
Parker cannot talk	Parker can't talk

Another form of contraction is the date:

1957	'57
1980	'80
1776	'76

Tips: Avoiding Confusion with Apostrophes

- *Its/it's*   This is the most common error I see in punctuation using the apostrophe. Remember, only the contraction *it is* has the form *it's*. Drill this with yourself and use a flashcard if it seems useful to you.
- *Their/they're*   This is the next most common error. It results from spelling according to the sound rather than the sense of the word. Again, the rule is that the apostrophe is used only when you are writing a contraction for *they are*.
- *Your/you're*   Again, the apostrophe is used only for the contraction of *you are*. Contractions should not be used in most formal writing. They are useful primarily when you are writing dialogue and trying to capture the feel of conversation. In such cases, use quotation marks to indicate that you are recording conversation.

Problems with the apostrophe often arise when it is used improperly. Here are some situations when you should not use the apostrophe.

Simple plural: Correct form is friends; animals; coats.
Possessive pronouns: Correct form is his, hers, ours, yours, theirs, its.
Dates: Correct form is 1940s; 1490s; 1100s.

PARENTHESES AND BRACKETS

The parenthesis (plural form is parentheses) and brackets are used to separate a clause or phrase within a sentence, or to provide special information in a separate sentence, which may be interpreted as an aside rather than as an essential part of the piece. Certain comments that might appropriately belong to a footnote can often be placed within parentheses. Often these comments are explanatory in nature.

Markov had three regiments (all in battle readiness) waiting at the border.
The Emperor Napoleon (without his Josephine) moved onto the altar at Ravenna before he was asked.
The novelist George Eliot (Mary Ann Evans) wrote a classic novel about the plight of women in the nineteenth century.
John Brown had sixteen men with him (not counting his sons).

Note that when the sentence ends with a parenthetical element, the end punctuation comes outside the parenthesis. However, when an entire sentence is included in parentheses, then the end punctuation comes *inside* the parenthesis. Here is an example:

Hazleton had four cannon and six Gatling guns. (Wilson, on the opposing hill, had only six outmoded 8-pound howitzers.)

Brackets serve a similar purpose in a very limited setting. They are used only in quotations when you are adding your own observations. When you quote another author, but wish to make a comment yourself, use brackets.

Marko told the government of Haiti, "Please be assured that nothing will happen to the prisoners while they are in my possession [they were killed the next day] because I hold their own interests uppermost."
"The General Staff had adequate evidence [Brown's confession] to proceed with the prosecution," said the inspector general.

THE DASH AND THE HYPHEN

The dash indicates a rapid shift in tone or tempo. It is not to be used interchangeably with the parenthesis, because it is not meant to signal a nonessential element or simple comment. It is designed to make an abrupt, but temporary switch from the subject at hand to an evaluative commentary.

President Wilson campaigned on a peace ticket—did he believe what he told the people?—even though the world was on the brink of war.
Napoleon snatched the crown from Pope Pius's hand—what arrogance —and crowned himself.

The dash is useful for setting apart introductory elements in a series and for setting apart ending elements in a series. The following sentences are properly punctuated:

Introductory series:
A good novel, a warm fire, soft music—these are the things that a serious woman can look forward to at the end of the day.

Ending series:
He had all the symptoms of flu—a racking headache, sore throat, vomiting, and pain in his stomach.

The hyphen, half the length of the dash, joins compound words: Chinese-American; last-minute; father-in-law. It is used for numbers: fifty-five; six-fifteen. Hyphens split words at the end of a line, but rely on the dictionary's syllable break. Always break before a consonant.

THE ELLIPSIS

The ellipsis is three spaced periods: . . . which indicate that something has been omitted in a quotation. Many writers forget to include a space between each period. (See the box entitled "Tips: Using the Ellipsis.")

Tips: Using the Ellipsis
- First, *always* place a space between each period in the ellipsis.
- Do *not* begin quotations with an ellipsis.
- If an ellipsis ends a quotation, use an extra period for the end punctuation.

Here are several simple things to remember about the ellipsis:

It always has a space between each period.
It is used in the middle of a sentence.
It is used at the end of a sentence (with an extra period) only when you break off in the middle of a quotation and omit a sentence, then continue your quotation.
It is *not* needed at the beginning of a sentence to indicate that you have omitted something from the beginning of that sentence.

Here is a quotation from Mary Wollstonecraft, and following are some examples of ellipses as they might be used when the passage is later quoted with omissions.

But, to have done with these episodical observations, let me return to the more specious slavery which chains the very soul of woman, keeping her forever under the bondage of ignorance.
Mary Wollstonecraft said that sexism keeps "woman . . . under the bondage of ignorance."

If you quote a long passage and wish to omit a sentence or even more, use the ellipsis at the end of the sentence that precedes the section you are omitting. Here is another quotation from Mary Wollstonecraft, omitting a group of sentences. The ellipsis follows the final period in the sentence which is itself broken off in the middle.

Mary Wollstonecraft said, "A truly benevolent legislator always endeavours to make it the interest of each individual to be virtuous. . . . Is one half of the human species, like the poor African slaves, to be subject to prejudices that brutalize them, when principles would be a surer guard, only to sweeten the cup of man?"

Writer's Workshop: Punctuation
Supply the proper punctuation for the following paragraphs:

1. After the French Revolution there was a period of disorder and anarchy that eventually came to an end during one of the provincial uprisings Napoleons troops acted especially vigorously and effectively his success was such that he was brought to the attention of the leaders of the revolution and eventually made commander of the army upon news of repeated successes domestically and abroad Napoleon was named First Consul then First Consul for life which is close to being named president for life but even this did not satisfy him soon he was declared Emperor of France in imitation of the grandeur of Imperial Rome the strangest turn was in his securing the succession of the emperorship on his own offspring because he had no children and was seen as possibly not having them in the future the succession was planned to continue through his nearest relatives what was the result of all this strange behavior indeed it was to create a family dynasty to rule a nation that had in effect had a revolution designed to put an end to the aristocratic policy of establishing dynastic families

2. the circle of stones that stands in Wessex England commanding a large open plain has been called stonehenge some 2700 years before Christ it was begun although no one has any idea why or by whom the circle of stones we see today is incomplete many have fallen and been destroyed but even in its ruined state it is commanding majestic and mysterious associated probably wrongly with the Druids it has been thought to be a form of solar or stellar calculator useful for predicting best times for planting and harvesting whatever its function it must have been of immediate practical use perhaps somewhat like the use of the cathedral in the twelfth century the seriousness of the project and its cultural significance to those who made it are underscored by the probability that its construction involved more man hours than did the construction of the pyramid of Giza one and a half million man days must have gone into the construction which involved moving huge stones over immense distances dressing them so they would fit properly and levering them into place without benefit of modern machinery or equipment

Common Misspellings

Spelling is a highly specialized problem for some writers. You may have heard of well-known writers who could not spell ordinary words. F. Scott

Fitzgerald was notorious for permitting his first novel to be published with over two hundred misspellings. The letters of William Butler Yeats, a Nobel prizewinner for literature, are sometimes comic in their approach to spelling. He even wrote a letter for a job at a university in which he referred to a "Perfessor." He did not get the job.

You must face the fact that people often judge your intelligence by how well you spell. It is unfair because spelling does not respect intelligence (Yeats was a genius). However, it is convenient, especially for people such as superiors in schools or businesses, when they themselves are excellent spellers. Therefore, if you know you have a spelling problem, you may wish to review the rules in this section.

For a really serious problem, you have several choices. One is to enroll in a course that reviews basic spelling rules. Another is to switch to a computer and use one of the excellent spell-checkers that will go over your work and even suggest the appropriate word for the error that you may have made.

You may hear older people complain that no one knows how to spell these days. Whether there is much of a change from a few generations ago is difficult to say. However, it is true that people read less than they did before the electronic age, and therefore they see words spelled in front of them less frequently. Furthermore, modern advertising often takes a perverse pleasure in purposely misspelling words (like *Finast*, which is a variant of the proper *Finest*) for effect. The result of the decline of reading is that people depend too heavily on their own pronunciation of a word. Therefore, *accept* and *except* get mixed up, and many other errors creep in, such as "I would of helped" for "I would have helped." Rule number one in spelling is Do not rely on your pronunciation of a word as a guide to its spelling.

SOME USEFUL SPELLING RULES

The *-ie* and *-ei* Words

The old rhyme usually works: "I before E except after C, and when the sound is like A in neighbor and weigh."

I before E: retrieve; thief; chief; grief; mischief; friend.
E before I right after C: conceive; receive; deceive; conceit; receipt.
E before I when it sounds like A: weight; neigh; sleigh; freight; eight; vein; veil; deign.

Exceptions: unfortunately there are a number, and these must be memorized because they do not follow any of the rules: sleight; neither; either; height; weird; leisure.

Suffixes

When you add an ending to a word, there are questions. Do you keep the *-y* on *worry* when you want to use the past tense? Most writers have very few problems with *worried,* but some words do give most people trouble. Following are a few samples.

When the ending you add begins with a vowel:

flurry, flurried
curry, curried
force, forcing
curse, cursing
condense, condensation

When the ending you add begins with a consonant:

manage, management
advertise, advertisement

Exceptions: again, there are a number of them, and some are designed to avoid odd pronunciation. Here are some: hoeing; courageous; argument; noticeable; changeable; judgment.

Vowels and Double Consonants

Doubled consonants usually follow a short vowel (pronounced *ah* if it is *a*). A single consonant follows a long vowel (pronounced *ay* if it is *a*). Examples: scrapping, scraping.

sloping, slopping   begin, begging   coping, copping
sale, sally   male, mall   hide, hidden   ripe, ripping

Forming Plurals

Some plurals are a problem for spellers. Most plural words are formed by adding *-s* to the singular. Here are some exceptions:

Words ending in *f* or *fe:* life, lives; knife, knives; leaf, leaves; loaf, loaves; self, selves.
Words ending in *-s* (or an *-s* sound): Miss, Misses; brass, brasses; grass, grasses; boss, bosses; box, boxes; tax, taxes; bunch, bunches; hunch, hunches; crutch, crutches.
Words ending in *-o* (preceded by a consonant): zero, zeroes; hero, heroes; curio, curioes; tomato, tomatoes; halo, haloes.

Compound words: here are the proper plurals of common compounds: fathers-in-law; mothers-in-law; brides-to-be; ladies-in-waiting; miles-per-hour.

Some Special Plurals

Because they are originally from other languages, such as Latin, some words definitely give modern writers a problem. Here is a brief list of words I have seen that are "spelling demons" for some writers:

Singular	Plural
datum	data
curriculum	curricula
medium	media
alumnus	alumni
alumna	alumnae
criterion	criteria

These rules should help you with many specific kinds of word problems. In the meantime, for a reference to some common errors, consult the following list of words frequently misspelled. They are spelled accurately here.

A BRIEF LIST OF SPELLING PROBLEMS

absence	annual	camouflage	conceit
absorb	ascend	category	condemn
academic	assassinate	cede	conquer
acceptable	associate	cemetery	conscience
accessible	athlete	census	conscientious
accidentally	auxiliary	certain	conscious
accommodate		chagrined	consensus
accumulate	balloon	changeable	continuous
accuracy	barbiturate	character	controlled
accustomed	basically	chief	convenience
achieve	beggar	choose	corollary
acknowledge	beginning	chose	corporate
acquaint	belief	cigarette	correlative
address	believe	climate	council
advice [n.]	benefited	climbed	counsel
advise [v.]	boundary	colonel	counselor
allot	breathe	column	courteous
all right	Britain	commitment	cruelty
a lot	bureaucracy	committed	curious
amateur	business	committee	
analysis	byte	competent	deceive
analyze		complement	definitely
angel	calculator	compliment	dependent
annihilate	calendar	concede	descendant

A BRIEF LIST OF SPELLING PROBLEMS (*cont.*)

desirable	friend	influential	moral
despair	fulfill	innocuous	morale
desperate		inoculate	mourn
develop	gauge	integrate	muscle
device	genealogy	intercede	mysterious
devise [v.]	generally	intercession	
disastrous	government	interpretation	necessary
disease	grammar	irrelevant	necessitate
disk drive	grief	irresistible	neighbor
dissatisfied	guarantee	island	neither
doubt	guard		noticeable
	guerrilla	jealous	nuclear
ecstasy	guidance	jewelry	nuisance
efficient		judgment	
eighth	harass		obedient
embarrass	height	knack	obstacle
eminent	hemorrhage	knife	occasion
enamor	heroes	know	occasionally
environment	hesitancy	knowledge	occurred
equipped	hoarse		occurrence
exaggerate	homicide	laboratory	omitted
exceed	hors d'oeuvres	laser	opportunity
excellent	humorous	leisure	opposite
exemplify	hurried	length	optimism
exhilarate	hurrying	lenient	originally
existence	hypocrisy	library	outrageous
extraterrestrial	hypocrite	license	overrun
exuberance		lieutenant	
	ideally	lightning	parallel
fallacy	idiosyncrasy	livelihood	particularly
familiar	illogically	loneliness	pastime
fascinate	imagine	loose	peaceable
fascist	imitation	lose [v.]	peculiar
February	immediate		pedal
fiery	immigrant	maintenance	perceive
forcibly	incidentally	manageable	permanent
foreign	incredible	maneuver	persevere
foresee	indict	marriage	persistence
forfeit	indiscriminately	minor	personnel
forty	indispensable	mischievous	persuade
forward	inevitably	misspelled	petal

A BRIEF LIST OF SPELLING PROBLEMS (*cont.*)

physical
playwright
playwriting
Plexiglas
poison
politician
possessive
practically
practice
prairie
precede
preference
prejudice
prescription
prevalent
primitive
principal
principle
privilege
probably
proceed
professor
proletariat
prominent
pronunciation
prophecy [n.]
prophesy [v.]
psychology
publicly
pursue
pursuit

quandary
questionnaire
quiet
quizzes

rebelled
recede
receipt
recession

recognize
recommend
referred
relief
relieved
religiosity
religious
remembrance
reminisce
rendezvous
renown
repetition
reservoir
resistance
restaurant
resurrect
rheumatism
rhythm
roommate

sacrifice
sacrilegious
safety
satellite
scarcity
scene
schedule
science
seize
separate
sergeant
several
sheik
siege
similar
sincere
skeptic
soliloquy
sophomore
source
souvenir

specifically
spontaneously
spreadsheet
strength
strenuous
strict
succeed
sufficient
suffrage
supersede
surely
susceptible
suspicious
synonymous

technical
technique
tendency
terrestrial
than
their
then
thorough
though
throughout
tomorrow
tourniquet
tragedy
transferred
troublesome
truly
twelfth
tyranny

unanimity
unanimous
unnecessary
until
usually

vacuum
vegetable

vegetarian
vengeance
verisimilitude
verses
versus
vessel
veto
vicious
vigilance
villain
virile
virtuosity
virtuoso
viscous
visibility
visible
vitiate

wastage
wearable
weather
Wednesday
weird
where
whether
whim
wholly
withhold
woman
women
writing

xenophobia
Xerox

yacht
yeoman
yield
you're

zealot
zodiac
zoology

Spelling is a problem for some writers, and not a problem for others. If you have a problem, then it is sensible to keep track of the words you sometimes misspell. Often, of course, the problem is simply a matter of proofreading your work. Make that your first strategy. If the problem goes deeper than this, make your own list of words—first as you often misspell them, then as they should be spelled. You may use the preceding list to help you. There is a small amount of space left for you to add words of your own.

Conventions of Modern Usage

us

Some writing problems stem not from grammar or spelling, but from accepted patterns and traditions of usage. Usage covers issues that are sometimes in flux, and what was unacceptable usage seventy years ago is often accepted usage today. Further, in certain social groups or regions of the English-speaking world, some forms of usage are acceptable that are unacceptable elsewhere. American usage, for example, differs in certain ways from English usage.

Controversy surrounds certain words. The idea that there is a standard form of the language is very bothersome to some people. James Baldwin wrote a famous essay, "If Black English Isn't English, Then Tell Me What Is," because of the controversy attending the standardization of the language. In fact, the English language is changing all the time. The changes do not come from those who are standardizing the language, and few changes seem to come from people who have advanced education—unless we account for the new vocabulary items introduced from technical areas. More often, changes seem to come from people whose communities demand active uses of language. Often these are ethnic communities, such as the Chinatowns, Little Italies, immigrant Jewish neighborhoods, Hispanic barrios, and black communities, including the ghettos, which stretch across the country.

In suggesting that there is an accepted usage for certain kinds of expressions in the language, I am not ignoring the fact that specific social groups conduct daily business quite nicely without reference to many of these observations about standard English. Nor do I want to place the language in chains. Personally, I am interested in development and growth. But I also realize that the realities of language usage, and the needs to communicate beyond the boundaries of ethnic or social groups, outweigh any nostalgia I may have for colorful speech.

Therefore, the suggestions that follow are to be taken in the spirit of developing a style for communicating in the largest community of readers. When your audience is limited to a specific social group—such as Mets or Celtics fans, truck drivers, jazz musicians, Islamic fundamentalists, break dancers, sailors, and so on, you can easily deviate from the suggestions. But when you want to speak to the broadest possible American public, then these suggestions will hold.

accept, except   These words sound alike but mean totally different things. When you wish to indicate someone is receiving something from another person, then use the verb *accept*. When you wish to refer to everyone in a group but one or two people, then use the preposition *except*. "Jamie did not *accept* the award, and the president spoke to everyone *except* Jamie."

advice, advise   The distinction here is that *advice* is a noun, the name of something; *advise* is a verb, an action. "Loring *advised* the president, but the president did not accept his *advice*."

affect, effect   Because they can act as verbs or nouns, this pair can be confusing. However, *affect* is usually a verb, and *effect* is usually a noun. "The radiation *affected* [verb] the laboratory animals minimally, but the *effect* [noun] on humans was lethal." When *affect* is used as a noun, it is a technical term used to refer to feeling states or emotions: "Poetry is a literature of *affect*." When *effect* is a verb, it means "to cause" and almost always is followed by "change": "The new regulations *effected* changes at all levels of government."

aggravate   This means to worsen. It does not mean to be irritated or annoyed, despite the fact that in conversation you use it that way all the time. This is one of those words whose usage may change under pressure of the masses who are using it. As of now, it is properly used in this way: "The covert Iranian arms deal may *aggravate* the already grim prospects for peace in that area." If you wish to use the word in its colloquial sense, I suggest you use "annoy," "irritate," or "bother."

ain't   This is still a colloquial expression. The proper form would be: am not, is not, or are not. If you wish to elide, use: isn't or aren't.

all right   The alternative spelling "alright" is not accepted usage. Simply avoid it.

all together, altogether   Again, these words mean totally different things: *all together* means "completely assembled"; *altogether* means "entirely" or "totally." "Mobutu was bored *altogether* by the parliament's wrangling. He eventually drew his ministers *all together* for a midnight session."

almost, most   are not interchangeable. *Almost* means "close, but not complete"; *most* means "the majority of something." "*Most* immigrants stayed and thrived in America. Some groups have lost *almost* all sense of their ethnicity."

a lot   This expression gives me the jitters. It is always improper to use the misspelling: "alot." I cannot understand why people use it, but they do. Simply remember: *a lot* is two words.

already, all ready   The first word means "by now," or "now"; *all ready* means "totally prepared." "The president knew that General MacAr-

us

thur was *already* out of the Philippines. Now the ships of the seventh fleet were *all ready* to steam back to hostile waters."

among, between　You choose *among* more than two things; you choose *between* only two things.

amount, number　When you are referring to something that we usually cannot count individually, such as sand, water, or fuel, use *amount*; when referring to something that we can count, such as automobiles, buildings, or people, use *number*. "Louis Sullivan designed a *number* of buildings for Chicago, and sometimes put up with an endless *amount* of abuse."

and/or　An evasive expression, which we sometimes use in conversation. Avoid it in your prose.

ante-, anti-　The first prefix means "before in time": "Dinosaurs *antedated* feathered birds." *Anti-* means "opposed to or against": "The stinger missile is a portable *antiaircraft* weapon." Common words using these prefixes are antedate; antediluvian (meaning, "before the flood"); antebellum (meaning, "before the war," and usually a reference to the period before the American Civil War). Anticommunist, antiterrorist, antidote, antibiotic, anti-American are all commonly used words.

anyways, anywheres　These words are conventional in spoken English in many regions; however, the final *-s* is never used in writing. The proper form is *anyway* and *anywhere*.

apt to, liable to, likely to　To keep them straight remember that *apt to* means "having a tendency to": "The baby is *apt* to put that toy in her mouth." *Liable to* means "in danger of": "Luther is *liable to* get into an accident if he drives in the condition he is in now." *Likely to* means "there is a high probability of": "Jeff is *likely to* get married tomorrow if the blood test is favorable."

as, like　Usually, *as* is a conjunction, and *like* is a preposition. So, when joining a clause (which needs a conjunction), always use *as*: "Fluther was *as* intense a teetotaler *as* I had ever seen." You will notice that the most accepted use of *as* is in sequence: *as . . . as*. *Like* is a preposition here: "*There were no people like* Fluther for telling stories."

as, than　The case of the pronouns following these words can be problematic. Ordinarily, they appear in sentences with verbs omitted before or after their following pronouns: "I have as much right to be here as Flipper." This sentence leaves out an understood verb: "I have as much right to be here as Flipper [does]." The problem arises between choosing a subjective case pronoun or objective case pronoun. With *than*, you can use either, depending on what verb is omitted: "I am taller than she" is correct, because the completed sentence would read: "I am taller than she [is tall]." "Denise gave Robin more syrup than him" is correct, because the completed sentence would read: "Denise gave Jill more syrup than [she gave] him."

assure, ensure, insure   These words are close to each other in meaning. However, there are differences: *assure* means "to reaffirm" or "to promise"; *ensure* and *insure* mean "to guarantee" or "make certain." *Ensure* is used in general senses, whereas *insure* is used in commercial, financial, or business senses. Some proper uses of these words are "Julio *assured* me that he would use the car only to go to the supermarket. The fact that I alone had the key *ensured* my control over how he was to use it. Apparently, the car is not *insured* against collision damages, so we did not want him out on the highway."

as to, as much as, as of today   These expressions signal a case of nerves. Edit them out of your prose. Instead of: "The distribution checks are in as of today," use: "The distribution checks came in today."

at, to   Using these words after "where" is usually superfluous and should be avoided. In conversation, some people say, "Where is he at?" But in formal writing, such a construction is never allowed. Simply say, "Where is he?" And avoid, "Where is he going to?" Just say, "Where is he going?"

awful, awfully   These words have become abused, like "terrific" and "terribly." They are intensives meaning the same thing as "very." Just avoid them unless you want them to mean "awe-inspiring," or, possibly, "very bad."

a while, awhile   The first item is an article and a noun referring to a nonspecific period of time. *Awhile* is an adverb and not the name of something; it modifies a verb. "The doctor examined me for *a while* during the interview. I waited *awhile* when my friend had his tooth extracted." Notice that in the first sentence *a while* is the object of a preposition, therefore identifying it explicitly as a noun.

bad, badly   It is not easy to remember that *bad* is an adjective and *badly* is an adverb. The first modifies a noun or pronoun, the second a verb. "Hortensio did *badly* on the music examination." (Here *badly* modifies the verb "did" and tells us how he did.) "Hortensio was angry because it was a *bad* examination, with material they had never discussed in class." (*Bad* modifies "examination" and gives us information about it.)

be   Avoid overusing the verb *to be* in all its forms. Choose action verbs instead, thereby giving your writing more power.

because, since   The use of *since* to mean *because* is ill-advised. *Since* refers to time—leave it that way. When you mean *because,* use it.

being as, being that   This is the same situation: when you mean "because" say so. *Being as* and *being that* are weak constructions and do not have the force of "because."

us

beside, besides   The first word is a preposition meaning "next to"; *besides* is an adverb meaning "in addition to" and sometimes "except." "Larry stood *beside* the president. And *besides* Larry, no one is as close to the seat of power."

between, among   See *among*. Use *between* for two things, *among* for more than two things.

bring, take   When you *bring* something, you come from a distance; when you *take* something, you go to a distant place. "*Take* this letter home to your mother, then *bring* me her reply."

bunch   In standard English, this word modifies grapes, coconuts, keys, and only such things that hang together. Do not use it to modify people, nonsense, or other such words.

burst, bust   The first word is the preferred form of this verb, meaning to break apart suddenly. *Bust* is used in this sense only in colloquial speech, never in writing. *Burst* is present tense, past tense, and past perfect. Use it.

but however, but yet, but still, but that, but what   These are not preferred to a simple "but." Avoid them. Use "but" alone.

can, may   These words imply different things: if you *can* do something, the implication is that you have the ability. If you *may* do something, the implication is that you have permission or approval. "The coach told me that I *may* now consider myself one of the starting five, but I do not think I *can* expect to make any three-point shots."

cannot, can not   The preferred form is one word: *cannot*. Some writers will use the two-word form for emphasis, but it is rarely effective.

can't hardly   In speech, in some regions, this is a common construction. It is used for intensification, but in formal writing it is a double negative, and not approved.

capital, capitol   The difference in spelling indicates the problem: *capitol* is used to refer to the seat of government of a region or nation—including the city or building in which the president or governor sits. *Capital* is used to refer to things of general importance: capital letters, capital appointments, capital punishment, capital gains, the capital that makes America a capitalist nation.

censor, censure   The first word means "to edit out on political or other grounds," as in *censoring* books or *censoring* information. *Censure* means "to punish or condemn someone," as in *censuring* an aide for lying to the press.

center around   Preferred usage is *center on*. The addition of "around" does not clarify the concept of "center," and it does not hold up logically.

compare, contrast   When you *compare* two things, you show their similarities and their differences; when you *contrast* two things, you only show their differences.

complement, compliment   When used as verbs, *complement* means "to complete or add to": "The new group of manuscripts will *complement* the university's existing Shakespeare resources." *Compliment* means "to praise someone" or "make someone a flattering comment": "The president *complimented* Colonel Savage on a job well done."

conscience, conscious   Because these words sound so much alike, they are sometimes confused. *Conscience* is one's internal moral censor, one's sense of what is right; *conscious* refers to one's awareness, one sense of being awake.

continual, continuous   The distinction between these words is slight, but important. An action that is *continual* occurs at generally regular intervals, but in between it stops. An action that is *continuous* keeps on going all the time. "Over the last eight years, we have gotten *continual* reports about missing persons in Southeast Asia, and we *continuously* monitor Chinese radio for corroborating evidence."

convince, persuade   You *convince* someone that you are right, but you *persuade* someone to do something for you. "First Luis *convinced* me that it was time to get a new car, but it took him another three months to *persuade* me to buy a Dodge."

could of, would of   These are misunderstandings of "could have" or "could've" and "would have" or "would've"; they should never be used in formal writing.

credible, creditable   Anything that is *credible* is believable; anything that is *creditable* is worthy. "Unusual as it was, Margot's explanation was *credible*. Her own experiences have demonstrated that the Red Cross is a *creditable* organization."

criteria, criterion   Remember: *criteria* is plural, whereas *criterion* is singular. The word is originally Greek, meaning standards of judgment. Today the plural form is sometimes used for both singular and plural, but in error. Use the appropriate singular and plural forms as shown here.

curricula, curriculum   This is the same situation as *criteria, criterion:* a Latin word that is currently often abused. *Curricula* is plural, *curriculum* is singular. The term refers to a program of study. Use the appropriate form for the singular or the plural.

data, datum   Remember: *data* is plural; *datum* is singular. The word refers to a body of information; we often use the plural form indiscriminately because data usually comes in numbers, not in individual items. But one number in a series would be a *datum*. The problem in general writing comes in using the noun with a verb. The proper form is: *Data* are convincing. However, this is one of the many areas in which the language is virtually changing usage. You will see the expression: *Data* is convincing, and it is accepted usage in all areas except those which are strictly scientific.

us

device, devise   The noun *device* is a machine or scheme by which things can get done. *Devise*, a verb, implies a means by which something can be accomplished. "Malatesta *devised* an interesting armor plate for the new machinery in the mill. However, the mill's owner thought the *device* was much too large and clumsy to be effective."

different from, different than   Because a distinction is implied, the force of "from" is greater and more explicit than "than." The proper expression is: *different from*. "Jasmine was *different* from Margot in her attitude toward sports."

differ from, differ with   People *differ from* each other in terms of their education, heritage, background, height, weight, age, and other such things. People *differ with* each other about opinions and viewpoints. "Eileen *differed from* Jasmine in that she never played basketball in college. She also *differed with* Jasmine about whether or not the Celtics had a decent club this year."

discreet, discrete   These are homonyms—words that sound alike but mean different things. The only way you can get these under control is to memorize them. *Discreet* means "cautious, confidential, thoughtful." *Discrete* means "distinct, separate, apart." "Felicity saw that Fritz and Jean were having a lover's quarrel, but she was *discreet* and pretended not to notice. Fritz later said that they had been together for so many months that it was going to be almost impossible to think of themselves as *discrete* from one another."

disinterested, uninterested   These words cause a massive confusion that needs careful thought and reflection. *Disinterested* means "not personally involved." "The three investors argued over the prospects of next year's market, and because Longo had no money invested, and was therefore a *disinterested* observer, they knew they could rely on him to decide who among them was correct." The word *uninterested* means something close to "bored." It means you are simply not interested in something. "I happen to love ballet, but Lydia, our vice president, is *uninterested* in dance in general." Frankly, the best advice I can give you is always to use *not interested*. It will clear up the problem entirely.

don't, haven't, won't, can't   Avoid all contractions in formal writing. Use the complete forms: "do not," "have not," "will not," "cannot."

due to   I have special problems with this expression used to mean "because." Technically, it is acceptable to use it as a subject complement: "The problems in the wing assembly were *due to* metal fatigue." But it is not acceptable to use the construction otherwise, as in this faulty sentence: "*Due to* unemployment, we are closing the plant." Use "because," or else be more inventive in establishing a causal analysis.

due to the fact that   This has all the inadequacy of *due to* and added to it is an assemblage of useless extra words. Avoid it entirely.

each and every one of us   Alas, this is so much a cliché that it is hard to get it out of our ears. But the proper form is to use "each" or "every," but not both.

effect, affect   See *affect, effect.*

elicit, illicit   Again, homonyms with quite different meanings. *Elicit* means "to learn from," "or draw out." *Illicit* means "illegal." (The double *lls* here might help your memory.) "Some careful questioning *elicited* the whereabouts of the still that Elliot Ness realized had produced *illicit* liquor for the entire neighborhood for years."

emigrate, immigrate   When you *emigrate* you leave a place. When you *immigrate* you arrive at a place. *Emigrate,* which has the *e,* means "leave." *Immigrate,* which has the *i,* means "arrive."

ensure   See *assure, ensure, insure.*

especially, specially   Both forms mean "particularly," but in slightly different senses. *Especially* means "preeminent," so that if I have been chosen *especially* for my talent for playing the piano, that talent is preeminent in the consideration. *Specially* usually means "specifically and particularly for a given person, place, or thing," as in: "Alonso made this purse *specially* for me." Usage has changed in the last two generations regarding these words, and the form, *specially,* is perfectly acceptable in all cases in which either may be considered.

et al., etc.   The first abbreviation means "and other people": "*et alia,*" and you should note that the second Latin word is abbreviated, and therefore must have a period after it. *Et* is Latin for "and," and is not an abbreviation. *Etc.* is also an abbreviation, for the Latin *et cetera.* It refers to things, not to people. It does not refer to actions, and it is therefore inappropriate to use it in this fashion: "I hit him, etc." Each of these expressions has a specific meaning and should be used in a specific way. The expression, "And *etc.*" is totally redundant. Avoid the construction entirely and use a more concrete description to explain what the following things are.

everyday, every day   The first word is an adjective meaning "ordinary." "Mario had on his *everyday* school outfit, and felt out of place." *Every day* is an adjective followed by a noun, and it means what it says: "I have lunch *every day* at the same time."

except   See *accept.*

farther, further   Today these words are being used more and more interchangeably. However, there is a difference: *farther* refers to distance: "I went two miles *farther* down the road." *Further* refers to additional degree of intensity, time, or anything that is measurable, but not specifically distance: "John Brown went *further* in his antagonism toward slavery than any other man of his day."

fewer, less   Use *fewer* when the things referred to are individual and

us

us

countable: "John Brown had *fewer* than thirty men with him." Use *less* when referring to quantities of uncountable things, such as sugar, sand, time, money, and anything that has general quantities. "John Brown had *less* tolerance for slavery than did Robert E. Lee."

field, in the field of   This word or expression is rarely accurate in its usage, and it is often redundant. A case in which it is badly used: "My sister is *in the field of* nursing." Simply avoid it. Say instead: "My sister is a nurse."

first off   This is sometimes used to mean "at first." Avoid it and use "first," or "at first."

fixing to   In some regions this is synonymous for "intending to." In standard English, the expression is not acceptable. Avoid it.

flunk   Alas, if you have to use this colloquialism, put quotation marks around it to indicate that you know its status.

formerly, formally   Close in sound, but very different in meaning. *Formerly* means "before," "a while ago." *Formally* means "officially," or according to an accepted pattern, "as prescribed by convention or tradition." "John Brown was *formally* charged with heinous crimes against the state by a man who was *formerly* an officer in the United States Army."

fun   In speech, this noun is sometimes used as an adjective: "We had a *fun* time." However, this is totally unacceptable usage. Simply say, "We had *fun.*"

gonna   Foreign speakers of English have trouble with this. It is a corruption of "going to." It never should appear in standard English. Use "going to."

good, well   This is a case of understanding the proper parts of speech: *good* is an adjective modifying a noun: "Fred wore his *good* shoes to the wedding." But *well* is an adverb, modifying a verb: "Fred threw the ball *well* that afternoon." Here are some acceptable usages: "Luiz was a *good* sport this afternoon, but he may have been sick because he did not look *well* to me."

good and   When used to mean "very": "Michelangelo was *good and* angry at the Pope," the expression is redundant and unnecessary. Instead simply say, "Michelangelo was very angry at the Pope."

got to   This is a colloquial expression meaning "have to." Use "have to," and avoid this entirely.

half, a half a   You may use "half a," or "a half." But *a half a* is redundant. Do not use it.

hanged, hung   The difference is important: when they are executed, people are *hanged.* Pictures and anything else are *hung.*

he, she   Currently, there is a shift away from using the general third person pronoun in order to avoid constant reference to "him, he, his"

us

when the gender of the referent is not known. Obviously, even if it is not intentional, this usage implies a sexist style. For a while, some writers were using a combination: "he/she," or even "s/he." This is regarded as awkward by many editors. Therefore, to avoid a sexist style, use the plural form "they," which has no gender constraints. Here are a few ways you can revise:

"No one likes to give someone his pink slip."
Revised: "No one likes to give people their pink slip."
"Does everyone have his work done?"
Revised: "Do all the people have their work done?"

hisself   A nonstandard form of "himself." Avoid it altogether.

hopefully   The problem arises when this is used to mean "it is to be hoped that." The proper meaning of the word is: "with hope." "My dog looked *hopefully* at my closed hand." It is improper to use it this way: "*Hopefully,* we will be done before dark." It would be better to say, "Let us hope we will be done before dark," or some such variant.

if, whether   When you mean *whether,* be sure to use it and not *if.* Although it is used colloquially, it is incorrect to write: "I will ask Professor Carnes *if* she is lecturing today." The appropriate form is: "I will ask Professor Carnes *whether* she is lecturing today."

illicit, elicit   See *elicit.*

illusion, allusion   These words sound alike, but are very different in meaning. *Illusion* is a false image or false understanding: "The magician created a striking *illusion* on our stage." But an *allusion* is a reference to something else, usually a piece of literature: "Geoffrey made an *allusion* to Shakespeare when he asked me to lend him an ear."

immigrate, emigrate   See *emigrate.*

imply, infer   This pair gives a good many writers a problem. Both words refer to developing an understanding. However, the difference is in who is developing it. When you develop it as the writer in your writing, then you *imply.* When you derive the meaning from someone else's writing (or speech), then you *infer.* Here is an example of the words used properly: "Isobel *implied* that she wanted to go to the church social that night, but I misunderstood her and *inferred* from her hesitation that she simply did not want to go out with me."

ingenious, ingenuous   These words are often confused. You must memorize their meanings. *Ingenious* means "brilliant, clever, remarkable." *Ingenuous* means "innocent, not cunning, open," and sometimes "naive." "Einstein's theories of relativity were *ingenious* in their application of mathematical formulas. And yet, he was virtually *ingenuous* in his response to some of the simplest human pleasures, such as watching goldfish swimming in a pond."

us

in regards to   This is nonstandard. Use: in regard to, or regarding.

inside of, outside of   The "of" is totally unnecessary. Avoid it. Use: inside or outside.

interested in, into   Popular slang has been at work on these words, so that people in everyday conversation say things such as: "Consuela is *into* computers these days." However, this is improper, and merely slang. Instead say, "Consuela is *interested in* computers these days."

interpretate   This is a nonstandard confusion for "interpret."

irregardless   This is a confusion for another word: "regardless."

is when, is where   These constructions are rarely used accurately. The best advice I can give you is to avoid them entirely. A common misusage would be "Pregnancy *is when* you are going to have a baby." This is wrong (on many counts) primarily because a noun, "pregnancy," cannot be equivalent to an adverb, "when." It is illogical. The same is true of the other construction in another misusage: "Confusion *is where* you get mixed up about what you are doing." Under no circumstances can "confusion" be "where." Again, this is illogical. If you must use these constructions, be sure that in the first you are talking about something that clarifies time and in the second something that clarifies a place.

its, it's   The problem is partly visual, partly aural. Remember that *its* is the possessive pronoun: "The dog wagged *its* tail." However, *it's* is a contraction for "it is": "President Roosevelt once said, '*It's* fear itself that produces fear.'"

-ize, -wise   There is a growing tendency to add these suffixes to words in an effort to sound more "high-tech." Instead, the words that are formed this way sound barbarous. Words such as: *finalize, sensitize, computerize, dollarwise, timewise, inputwise,* and others like them may be amusing in conversation, but they are jargon and should not appear in a standard piece of writing.

kind of   This expression, along with "sort of" and "type of," is vague and inaccurate. Again, in conversation, you will say, "I am *kind of* tired," but in writing use "somewhat," or "rather" instead.

later, latter   These words are pronounced differently and mean different things. *Later* refers to time, something which occurs after something else. *Latter* refers to something which is identified or mentioned second in a conversation or piece of writing. "Consuelo arrived at the news conference *later* than Benito did, and, as a result, the *latter* was much better informed about the political imperatives."

lay, lie   This is a bugaboo that needs to be memorized. The two verbs are different because one takes an object and the other does not. You can *lay* an object down on the table, but you cannot *lie* something on the floor. Here are some proper usages of these verbs, in their various forms.

us

lay: "Jefferson *laid* the pen aside and called Benjamin Franklin to him. Franklin pointed out that Jefferson would *lay* the pen aside only to take up the sword." ("Pen" is the object in both cases here.)

lie: "Aristotle would often *lie* down beneath the olive trees. Plato noted that where Aristotle *lies* knowledge resides. And where Plato *had lain* was the citadel of wisdom."

leave, let   The words are different: *leave* means to go away, to separate from. *Let* means to permit or allow something to happen or someone to commit an action.

less   See *fewer, less.*

literally, figuratively   Somehow these words have gotten mixed up. *Literally* means "absolutely, down to the letter, actually." So if you describe Nietzsche as *literally* dancing for joy, you mean he is really dancing. But most writers who would say something like that mean that he is *figuratively* dancing for joy. That is, he behaves as if he were dancing, but that he is not really dancing. *Figuratively* means "in a manner of speaking, not actually." It refers to figures of speech and the way writers use metaphor to intensify an expression. Therefore, this expression is correct: "Nietzsche was *figuratively* dancing for joy when he received news of Wagner's response to his book."

loan, lend   You *lend* people money; they go out to get a *loan. Lend* is a verb, whereas *loan* is a noun. If you can keep it that way, you will not go wrong in using these words.

lose, loose   The first word is a verb: "Van Gogh was afraid he would *lose* his ear if it were not immediately treated." *Loose* is an adjective: "There are 8000 prisoners *loose* on the island today." In order to give this word a verb force, use it in connection with "let": "The police *let loose* a brace of guard dogs who promptly fell asleep."

lots, lots of   These expressions are conversational and appropriate for dialogue. They should not substitute for "quantity" in a standard piece of writing. Instead, use approximate quantities or an expression such as "a great deal of."

mad, angry   Unfortunately, we tend to use these words as if they meant the same thing. They do not. *Mad* means insane. *Angry* means worked up, irritated, furious. Keep the distinction between these words in your writing.

-man   Our concern to avoid sexist language sometimes places you in a difficult position regarding words that usually refer to occupations, such as "salesman," "repairman," "postman." We have accepted some

us

forms, such as "salesperson," but rejected others, such as "repairperson," and "postperson." These latter two are simply too awkward for the language. Your approach to language should avoid sexism as much as possible by looking for alternatives to the collectives that end with *-man.* There are usually acceptable alternatives, such as "technician" for "repairman," "postal worker" for "postman."

media, medium   A *medium* is one instrument of communication; *media* are several instruments of communication. The newspapers, television, radio, and wire services are the *media.* A single newspaper, such as the *Los Angeles Times,* is not the media. A single newspaper is not a medium either: television is a *medium,* just as the press is a *medium.* "The *media* have reported extensively on the current scandals in city hall, but television is the *medium* that the mayor says has done the greatest damage to his party."

might of, must of   Corruptions for "might have" and "must have."

minority   Ordinarily this word is an adjective, but recently it has become a noun with a special meaning referring to ethnic groups who are not part of the majority ethnic groups in America. Generally, the major ethnic group is considered white and Anglo-Saxon. American Indians would then be a minority group. Blacks, Hispanics, Jews, and Orientals are all minority groups. Lately, I have heard people referring to themselves or others as "a *minority.*" This is illogical. The appropriate usage is to refer to someone as "a member of a *minority* group," or as "part of a *minority.*"

moral, morale   These are different words. *Moral* means virtuous or pertaining to virtue or proper behavior. *Morale* refers to the spirits of a person. A team's *morale* is its emotional mood.

most, almost   See *almost.*

Ms., Mr.   These terms do not indicate marital status and therefore are appropriate when addressing or identifying someone whom you do not know, or who has not requested a specific mode of address.

myself, himself, herself, yourself, ourselves   Because these are reflexive pronouns they must refer back to a previous noun or pronoun, such as: "Myra *herself* appealed to the president for aid." The use of the reflexive pronouns is usually to gain emphasis for someone who is doing something. However, it is unacceptable to use a reflexive pronoun without its proper antecedent or referent. Acceptable use is: "Peter and you [not *yourself*] have been chosen as leaders of the east face trek."

nothing like, nowhere near   These are colloquial expressions and should be avoided. Use "completely unlike" and "not nearly."

off of   This is a corruption. Use only *off,* as in: "President Garfield got *off* the train at Buffalo."

OK, O.K., Okay   No one knows the origin of this expression—which is now almost universal in most languages of the world. Each of these spellings is acceptable, and when you choose one, stay with it. However, you should know that in formal writing, it is better to use a standard form of approval.

	us

on account of   This is to be avoided. It is a fancy way of saying "because." Use because.

only   This word should be put right next to the word it modifies, otherwise confusions arise. "Metzger *only* saw the accident moments before the police arrived" is much more confusing than "Metzger saw the accident *only* moments before the police arrived."

owing to the fact that   This is wordy for "because." Use because.

passed, past   Because these words sound alike, they are often confused. *Passed* is a verb meaning "to have gone by, to have thrown, to have achieved a degree of facility [as in passing an exam], or to have been left behind." *Past* as a noun means "a time gone by," as a preposition it means "beyond, in another place or time." "V. I. Lenin *passed* the railroad station twice before entering. As he did so, he dwelt on the events of the recent *past* and their potential for a future success. By the time he purchased his ticket, the train had gone *past* the German border, and the fate of the world was sealed."

people, persons   The first word is a collective, used to refer to a mass of people the writer does not know. *Persons* is used to refer to individuals who are known either to the reader or writer. "The *people* who stormed the Winter Palace understood exactly what their success meant, and most of them left with a priceless piece of looted grandeur." "We have asked the *persons* who spoke with us earlier to return for a clarification."

per   In some technical writing, this expression is acceptable. In more generalized prose, however, it is not preferred. Instead of saying, "There are approximately 250 words *per* page," say, "There are approximately 250 words to a page."

percent, percentage   The first word must always be used with a specific number: "10 *percent*, 43 *percent*." *Percentage* is always used as a noun without a number: "a *percentage* of the population; a high *percentage* of the voters; an unknown *percentage*." When used as an adjective it may accompany a number: "4 *percentage* points; 16 *percentage* points; several *percentage* points."

phenomenon, phenomena   The first is singular, the second plural. "A solar eclipse at the equator is a *phenomenon* not easily forgotten." "Metzger asserted that *phenomena* known as star showers were elaborated dust clouds that sweep through the universe and sometimes come close to our planet."

plenty   A colloquial expression for "very." In conversation, in some parts of the country, people may say, "Marcos was *plenty* brutal when he had to be." However, in formal writing one would use: "Marcos was very brutal when he had to be."

plus   Never use this to mean "and" or "moreover." It means "in addition to," as in this example: "My brains *plus* his charm equal a winning combination."

precede, proceed   These are verbs which sound much alike, but that have slightly different meanings. *Precede* means "to go before," "to come ahead of something": "Ulysses S. Grant *preceded* Robert E. Lee into the railroad car office at the Appomattox siding." *Proceed* means "to continue," "to go on": "General Lee *proceeded* to study the instrument of surrender after he had formally turned over his saber."

pretty   Alas, this word is often overused to mean "very" or "rather." The following is typical, but inappropriate usage: "The doctor knew the situation was *pretty* serious the moment he looked at Lincoln's wound." In conversation, this would be acceptable, but in formal writing, use "very."

principal, principle   Because these words have several different meanings, they can be confusing. Here are their primary meanings and appropriate usages: *principal,* as a noun, means an amount of capital funds. "Dickens paid 10 percent interest on a loan whose *principal* was under eight thousand pounds." A second meaning as a noun includes the chief officer of an institution, as in a school: "Dickens's most famous teacher, Gradgrind, never stood in awe of the *principal* of his school." *principal,* as an adjective means "the foremost": "The *principal* ingredient of this dish is chicken, lightly curried." *Principle* is always a noun meaning a "rule, or precept." "Dickens became wealthy after a life of poverty, but he made certain that money did not distort the *principles* by which he lived."

question of whether   Usually this expression is meaningless, a form of padding. Use *whether* alone.

quote, quotation   Although the distinction is blurring, *quote* is a verb: "Joyce *quoted* several lines from Alexander Dumas." *Quotation* is a noun: "Joyce's *quotation* was from *The Count of Monte Cristo.*"

raise, rise   Each is a verb, but *raise* takes an object: "Turley *raised* the rent when he knew Jim could pay more." *Rise* does not take an object: "Each morning Louis the Fourteenth would *rise* exactly as the sun appeared, maintaining in himself the myth of the Sun-King."

real, really   The first word is an adjective: "Martin Chuzzlewit was a *real* man whom Dickens caricatured and renamed." *Really* is an adverb: "The public was *really* excited about the novel even before it was published in book form." The incorrect usage would be: "the public was *real* excited." Remember, use the adverbial form when you want to modify a verb.

us

reason is because, reason is that   The second form is accepted in formal writing, even though it may be wordy and unnecessary. But to say that a *reason is because* is illogical. The reason must be a causal event; "because" is not a causal event, it is a conjunctive adverb. If you are tempted to say *the reason is,* then by all means tell us the reason. Do not hedge by adding "because."

regardless, irregardless   See *irregardless.*

respectful, respective, respectable   The first word means "full of respect": "Lonny was *respectful* of the farmer's rights in this affair." *Respective* means "separate, apart, different": "In the battle of Gallipoli, Australians, Englishman, and Turks died almost willingly, marching to their *respective* graves."

round   Avoid this when you mean "around." Incorrect: "He came by *round* three o'clock." Correct: "He came by around three o'clock."

sensual, sensuous   The first word usually connotes sexuality or sexiness. *Sensuous* usually connotes a pleasant feeling involving the senses. "Margot's *sensual* expression aroused Flemington's interest." "The California hot tub was a surprisingly *sensuous* experience for the otherwise repressed McDew."

shall, will   Originally, *shall* was the future form for the first person: "I *shall* see; we *shall* see." Now, however, the distinction between the first person and the second and third persons has vanished. We generally use *will* for all forms of the future: "I *will* take the forms to the hidalgo, and he *will* sign them." "I *shall* return": General MacArthur's pledge as he surrendered the Philippines to the Japanese in World War II, has helped the form *shall* take on a degree of emphasis. Now we seem to use the form mainly for questions: "*Shall* we dance?"

sit, set   People *sit;* things are *set.* "The action of *Key Largo* is *set* in Florida." "My aunt *set* the origami bird close to the window. I was sitting next to it before I realized what it was."

the situation is that   This is almost always meaningless padding. Just state what the facts are and do not refer to them as a "situation."

so, so that   Avoid using *so* alone, without completing its sense. It is wrong to say: "You should have seen Mr. Lopez: he was *so* upset." You must complete the expression because it implies that something resulted from the upset: "You should have seen Mr. Lopez: he was *so* upset *that* he could not talk."

some   Colloquially, we often say: "They have to go *some* to beat us." However, this is a totally vague expression and has no place in writing. Avoid it entirely.

somewheres   Colloquial, but totally inadmissable in formal writing. Say "somewhere."

---
us
---

sort of, type of   See *kind of.*

specially   See *especially.*

such   See *so, so that.* Avoid using *such* in this fashion: "Shakespeare was *such* a good writer." Complete the meaning by adding "that" and explaining what comes next: "Shakespeare was *such* a good writer that his plays appeal to Africans, Asians, and many other people who know little or nothing about English literature."

supposed to, used to   The final *-d* is essential to make these expressions meaningful.

sure   Do not use this when you mean *surely.* "Stalin *surely* [not sure] approved of the genocide of the kulaks."

sure and, try and   The proper forms are *sure to* and *try to.* Correct: "Karen Horney was *sure to* upset the Freudians who would *try to* assert a masculine-based psychology as universal."

than, then   Many people use these irregularly because of their similar pronunciation. *Than* is a conjunction, usually used when making a comparison: "He was wiser *than* I." *Then* is an adverb of time: "Wagner stopped to listen to the distant melody, *then* moved on as if in a dream."

that, which   Certain stylists prefer *that* clauses to *which* clauses almost without question. The *New Yorker* magazine editors have complained about "whichy thickets." The difference is generally grammatical. When a clause provides information that identifies a specific noun, it is called restrictive. The clause is restricted in meaning only to that noun. Here is an example: "The three word message that Julius Caesar sent Pompey was: Veni, Vidi, Vici—I came, I saw, I conquered." The underlined clause is restricted to that "message" and that "message" only. When a nonrestrictive clause is used, you set it off with commas because it could be omitted without changing the meaning of the sentence: "Julius Caesar uttered his famous expression, which most Latin students remember, to specifically challenge the power of Rome."

their, they're, there   Use these accurately. Each word is different: *Their* is third person possessive: "We need *their* help." *They're* is a contraction for "they are." *There* is an adverb of place: "Put the aspidistra *there* by the front door."

theirself, theirselves   These are nonstandard forms for "themselves." Avoid them entirely in standard writing. Use themselves.

thusly   The proper form is "thus," which means "in this way," not "therefore."

till, until, 'til   The first two words are both accepted forms. *'Til* is an older form, usually avoided in contemporary writing.

time period, time frame, at this point in time   All these are redundant and pretentious. Use the simple form: "time." "At this time, the president is engaged in high-level discussions."

to, too, two   The first word is a preposition of place or action: "Give the water basin *to* the priest from Gandahara." *Too* is an adverb meaning also or overly: "The priest, *too*, had an acolyte who was *too* anxious about his trip to talk about it." *Two* is a number: "The priest and his acolyte were *two* holy men from one of the holiest places in India." *Too* is an intensifier like "so" or "such" and therefore needs to be completed in the same fashion. Avoid sentences such as "Gregory was too intelligent." Complete the implications by explaining why, or what the consequence is: "Gregory was *too* intelligent to be caught in a simple trap of the kind Captain DeForrest had set up."

type, type of   Both of these are to be avoided. See *kind of*. The worst usage of these is: "MacAullife was a flighty *type* commander." Also inappropriate is: "Macy's is a people's *type of* store." In each case the expression could be omitted entirely.

uninterested   See *disinterested*.

unique   This is another bugaboo. Remember, *unique* means "one of a kind." It is not a substitute for "unusual" or "remarkable." Therefore, it is illogical and meaningless to use expressions such as "very *unique*," "somewhat *unique*," "more *unique*," and "less *unique*." Something is *unique* or not. Period. Think of it as you do of "pregnant": a woman is either pregnant or not.

uptight   This is slang for being "nervous," "tense," or "upset." Use these standard words instead.

used to   See *supposed to*. Just remember that the final *-d* must appear in both expressions.

utilize   This is a word that many people prefer to "use." Frankly, it is pretentious and ordinarily a sign of someone who has to impress you. You choose: "use." It is direct, clear, simple, and not designed to impress an audience (who will not be impressed by *utilize*).

wait for, wait on   are not synonymous. To *wait for* someone means "to pause, stop, and expect someone's arrival." To *wait on* someone means "to serve that person," the way a waiter does in a restaurant.

way, ways   When used to mean "distance," the proper form is *way*. *Ways* is a colloquialism. "Chateaubriand's proposal had a *way* [not *ways*] to go to bring the combatants closer into agreement."

well, good   See *good, well*.

which, that   See *that, which*.

who   Clauses that refer to things usually begin with *that* or *which*. Clauses that refer to people begin with *who*. "Einstein eventually reexamined the thinking of Max Planck, *who* established a valued universal constant." For a reason that I have not discovered, some writers use

us

which in place of *who* in a situation much like the one here. Remember: *who* is a pronoun that refers only to people.

who's, whose   The first word is the contraction for *who is. Whose* is the possessive form of *who.* One way to avoid a problem with these words is to avoid using the contraction, which does not belong in most formal writing anyway. "Can you tell me *whose* book this is? I think she is someone *who's* a regular visitor to our laboratory."

-wise   See *-ize, -wise.*

woman, women   Some people pronounce both words the same way and therefore confuse them in writing. Remember that *woman* is singular and *women* is plural. It is very confusing to see *women* used in the singular.

would of, could of   See *could of, would of.*

your, you're   These are the form for the second person possessive, *your,* and the form for the contraction of *you are.* Again, to avoid problems, avoid using contractions. They are appropriate in formal writing only when you are quoting a conversation. "*Your* friends have told you about the ruins in Palenque. Now I hear *you're* planning to visit them and take part in the university's excavations."

yourself   See *myself.*

Writer's Workshop: Usage

Correct the usage errors in the following sentences. Circle your corrections.

1. Accept for the lucky timing of Margarita's advise to Luz, something could of gone wrong.
2. Luz was real aggravated at Hector alright, so's you knew something was up.
3. Hector had withheld a certain amount of money from her and she was mad.
4. Anyways, if this continues there's like to be some trouble round here.
5. Things was awful tense. I never seen Luz so uptight.
6. She looked at him badly when he came in since she wasn't going to give an inch on this one.
7. Being as how she was already behind in her own rent, she wasn't gonna stand for any of this.
8. Besides, this money he owed her was supposed to be the capitol for a new business, the beauty parlor on Main Street.
9. Hector was real disinterested in hearing about that. He thought it was a bunch of nonsense.
10. Nobody was especially happy about the end results.

11. First off, Luz thought he would pay up, but nothing could be farther from the truth.
12. Hector was fixing to tell her about the Camaro, but he knew she would be good and mad if he said anything about it.
13. Instead, he inferred that there might be a surprise waiting for her, since he knew she was into hot Chevies.
14. Luz once said that Camarowise she was an expert and don't have no allusions about that.
15. She shouldn't of loaned the money to him if she was afraid of loosing it.
16. When she saw the car, though, she knowed she would never get the money off of him on account of his obviously having spent it.
17. Things were pretty serious there for a while.
18. Margarita wanted to ease things and adviced Luz to take theirselves down to the coffee shop in Hector's new car.
19. Luz played coy and made them both wait on her while she went somewheres to fix her makeup.
20. Due to the fact that she really liked Hector under it all, Luz was really no where near as mad as she pretended. They all spend the rest of the day driving round town.

Avoiding Sexist Language

Today most writers make every effort to avoid language that assumes all indefinite pronouns refer to a *he*, or that titles that end in *-man* are appropriate only for men. In both cases the tradition in language looks back to a time when there was very little sensitivity on the part of society toward the feelings of those who were excluded. It also points back to a society that was dominated by males.

sexist

TITLES

Today terms such as *chairman* have been changed to *chair* or to *chairperson*. Other terms, such as *human, freshman, upperclassman,* and *patron,* which all have a male gender link built into them, are thought to be less associated with only one sex than they may appear. Those interested in promoting fairness in language have been willing to accept them (and *chairman*) as appropriate for both sexes.

However, terms such as *poetess, dramatess, stewardess, hostess, songstress, seamstress, authoress, clerkette,* and *majorette* sometimes have unpleasant connotations of inferiority. These are terms to avoid. A poet is a poet, a host a host, an author an author. A stewardess is more accurately described as a flight attendant, a term in wide use today.

Sometimes it is difficult to adapt to versions of titles that seem ingrained in the language, such as newspaperman, mailman, handyman, and even a more recent trademark for a plug-in tape recorder, the Walkman. For the most part such terms can be avoided. Newspaperman can be reporter or editor; mailman can be mail clerk or mail carrier. Handyman is difficult. Even the *New York Times* in February of 1988 used the following expression, referring to practices of school custodians: "Some auditors found outrageous abuses, including custodians who had hired their wives as 'handymen'." Perhaps this indicates that the term has lost its gender-linked qualities.

Titles such as Mr., Mrs., Miss, have certain problems, too. The *New York Times* has remained traditional on this point, but many publications now use Mr. and Ms. to indicate male and female. The *Mrs.* and *Miss* tell the reader the marital status of the female, as if that were the most important information one had about her. *Mr.* does not give that information. Fairness suggests that each sex be treated the same way in its generic title.

Then there are many words, also titles, that have a certain traditional gender linking. Professors, for instance, are often tacitly assumed to be male (some people say female professor, which is the giveaway). Nurses are assumed to be women, doctors male. Such assumptions are often so widely accepted that you have to be on your guard not to permit them to enter your writing.

Addressing letters can be a problem if you wish to avoid sexism in your language. "Dear sir" has obvious difficulties, which can be avoided by selecting "Dear colleague," "Dear friend," "To Whom It May Concern," or by omitting the salutation entirely by using the format of the memo. *Ms. Magazine* once pointed out the folly of the old style when it printed a letter it received beginning with "Dear sir." Other eras had more tolerance for this than we do. A 1916 edition of the works of Jane Austen, for instance, announces itself as part of the series titled "English Men of Letters."

PRONOUNS

Pronouns give us the most trouble with sexism in language. There are many ways to avoid using the generic *he* most of the time. One is to mix up the references so that the *he's* clearly refer to male figures and the *she's* clearly refer to female figures. By using some of each in a passage, you will be giving equal time.

The use of the double, *she/he, his or hers,* or *s/he* has proved to be clumsy enough so that no one is satisfied with it. The result is that the simplest solution—to make all such pronouns plural—has been adopted by most writers. The pronouns involved are *he, she, his, hers, her, him.* When these are not specifically related to a male or female who has been previously mentioned, they should be omitted and the plural used. The plurals are not gender linked: *they, their, them.*

Here are some samples with appropriate alternatives:

A writer knows how to control his imagery.
Writers know how to control their imagery.
Any doctor knows his vitamins from A to Zinc.
All doctors know their vitamins from A to Zinc.
When a person asks for help, he wants it immediately.
When people ask for help, they want it immediately.

Using the plural in these cases is an appropriate solution to the problem. However, you must be sure to avoid problems in agreement that may arise. For example, this kind of solution is not desirable: "When a person asks for help, they want it immediately." That would be an example of a failure in agreement, because *person* is singular and *they* is plural. Make the pronoun agree with its antecedent.

Writer's Workshop: Sexist Language
Correct the problems with sexist language in the following examples:

1. If you want a friend to look this over, why don't you ask him to stop by when I am here.
2. When someone pays his taxes too late, he will be required to pay a penalty.
3. Any professor worth his salt would stand up for the Freedom of Education amendment.
4. A nurse will always stand by her decision to administer a given drug.
5. Stewardesses are often annoyed because they are asked to retire young and take desk jobs.
6. During an election year, it is important for every citizen to exercise his right to vote.
7. Every candidate for president will arrive with his staff some time before the makeup call, which is at 6:30 P.M.
8. You will never see a truckdriver turn up his nose at a plate of Joe-Willie Brown's three-alarm chili.
9. The Little Leaguer will tell you that his coach knows just what kind of a game he should play.
10. Should you need a psychiatrist, choose one who knows his way around the Westside facilities, because that means he is on the best staff in the city.
11. Any student having trouble with this exercise should see his advisor before filling out the proper forms for graduation.

Writer's Workshop

12. A person with an extreme case of mellitus should be asked to keep to his bed unless a doctor gives him his okay to get up.

The Essay Exam

exam

Writing an essay exam is a specialized task. Certain college disciplines, such as history, sociology, English, art history, and anthropology rely on essay exams more than disciplines in the sciences and business. The process of responding to an essay exam is complicated by the fact that you spend a certain amount of time in advance studying and reviewing material that will provide the basis of the questions you face. In other words, you have a good deal of information in your possession before you begin to work, and you do not know in advance what is going to be of importance to you.

READING THE QUESTION

The first task is to calm yourself. Occasionally a question can seem very difficult at first glance and make you tense. Be assured that if you have studied, you will be able to work with the questions in front of you.

Your job, then, is to read the questions carefully, underlining those points that you know need careful attention. Here is a sample question with the key points underscored:

3. (30 minutes) Compare the Allies' approaches to rebuilding Europe and the defeated Germany after the first and second world wars. What were the differences in attitude toward Germany on the part of the Allies? What were the different results?

The question asks for two important things. First is a statement of how the Allies treated Germany after each of the world wars. This should be developed by means of comparison. The second thing is a question about what the different results were. This should be developed by the means of cause and effect.

PREWRITING

Your first step is probably best described as listing or brainstorming. What information do you have at your disposal that will be useful to the question? Here is a sample list of information:

World War I
Allies wanted to punish Germany
France wanted to humiliate Germany
France demanded Germany pay reparations in gold
Germany had demanded reparations after war of 1879
France took German-speaking territories
German economy collapsed
collapse caused worldwide depression
rise of Hitler

World War II
no reparation after the war
Allies divided Germany into East and West
Russia rebuilt East Germany
Allies through Marshall Plan rebuilt West Germany
Marshall Plan also rebuilt European economy
creation of European Common Market
no new wars in Europe

Using this list as a basis you can then construct an outline, such as the following, for your essay:

I. Allies after World War I
   A. France wanted to humiliate Germany
      1. France seizes German territory
      2. Allies demand reparations from Germany payable in gold
   B. Unreasonable demands for reparations cause collapse of German economy
      1. Worldwide economic depression
      2. Rise of Adolf Hitler in ruined German economy
II. Allies after World War II
   A. Germany divided into East and West
      1. Russia controls East Germany
      2. Allies rebuild West German economy
   B. Marshall Plan rebuilds war-torn Europe
   C. No new European wars
   D. Creation of stability through European Common Market

This is detailed enough to guide you. Now, you need a thesis to help focus your essay. Such a sample thesis might be as follows: The Allies learned from their mistakes after World War I that it is not wise in the long run to punish the losers. Instead, their strategy of rebuilding the destroyed European economies paid off after World War II in a stronger, more peaceful Europe.

Such a thesis is flexible, permits you to bring your information to bear as you need it, and also communicates a sense of your purpose in the essay. You have taken a stand, and you can defend it in thirty minutes. In the case of every item in your outline, you will want to decide how it should be developed. Remembering to cover all your points, and not to develop one in unreasonable detail, will help you keep to the thirty-minute limit.

ANSWERING THE QUESTION

It may sound obvious, but indeed it is not: your job in an essay question is to answer the question. Most people who fail essay questions do so not because they do not know enough, but because they choose to ignore the question. How this happens is difficult to say, but it may be the result of worrying over the question, avoiding outlining, not making lists of useful material. Losing the focus of the question is easy when you are nervous.

In the sample question, if you do not compare the behavior of the Allies in two different situations, then you are not answering the question. If you do not take into account the results of the different ways that the Allies behaved, then you are not answering the question. Therefore, it is essential to analyze the question carefully, establish its component parts, and then decide what material you have that applies to each part.

Unless you have an immense amount of time at your disposal, matters of style are not going to play a large part in your answer. Rather, you will be marked on the ideas and information you can come up with. In every case, you should be as detailed as possible. Being specific is what helps you establish your credentials and your authority over the subject of the question. When you have information, be as exact as possible. For instance, when mentioning that France took German territories, mention the names of those territories: the Saar and Alsace-Lorraine, and explain their significance and value (as coal-producing industrial areas). Such detail gives your reader a sense that you are prepared, observant, and in command of the material.

Here is a sample answer to the essay question posed earlier:

Question:

3. (30 minutes) Compare the Allies' approaches to rebuilding Europe and the defeated Germany after the First and Second World Wars. What were the differences in attitude toward Germany on the part of the Allies? What were the different results?

Answer:

The Allies learned from their mistakes after World War I that is is not wise in the long run to punish the losers. Instead, their strategy of rebuilding the destroyed European economies paid off after World War II in a stronger, more peaceful Europe. After the First World War, France especially wanted to humiliate Germany because Germany had demanded enormous reparations from France after the War of 1879. Now France saw its chance and decided to hurt Germany as much as it could by asking for enormous reparations for war damage. The reparations were to be paid in gold.

Further, France seized certain choice German territories on its borders. The industrial power of the Saar and coal-rich Alsace-Lorraine were long of interest to France, and when it had the power it took them. The inhabitants of those territories spoke German and thought of themselves as German, so there was some unrest in them. The Allies went along with France, although eventually England urged France to give up the idea of collecting reparations. Germany was showing signs of economic collapse. The German mark was so heavily inflated in 1922 that people had to take wheelbarrows full of paper money to the store just to buy bread.

The result of the Allies' punitive approach to Germany after World War I was the total economic collapse of Germany. What the Allies did not realize was that in the twentieth century, economies were essentially interrelated and that if Germany collapsed other nations would collapse as well. In 1929 the stock market crashed on Wall Street, Germany was already in collapse, and the rest of the European economies failed in rapid succession.

As a result of the worldwide collapse, fascist groups that promised to restore Germany to its original glory became very attractive. Hitler was able to play on the fact that the Allies had purposely humiliated Germany in order to gain power. He was able to ignore the Treaty of Versailles and rebuild German military might because the other European countries did not have the economic power to stop him.

By contrast, the approach of the Allies after World War II was not punitive. Rather than humiliate Germany and Italy, the Allies worked through the Marshall Plan to restore the European economies—including those of the losers—to a state that was actually better than it was before the war. Germany was divided into two nations, East and West, under the influence of Russia in the East and England, France, and the United States in the West.

The result of the different approach toward Germany is that there have been no wars in Europe, nor has there been a major economic collapse of the kind the world experienced in the 1930s. The establishment of the European Common Market in the West is yet another guarantee of the stability of Europe since World War II. The Common Market helps to keep the economies of the European nations on some standard of equality, thereby helping to prevent another war in Europe.

The difference in the approach the victors took after each of the World Wars is centered in their attitude. When they decided to punish the losers by harsh economic measures, they failed to win the peace. When, by contrast, they thought positively about how to guarantee economic recovery, peace became a reality.

The essay exam presents special problems to the writer for two reasons. The first is that most of the material that is to go into the exam must be studied beforehand, and therefore gathering your material before writing is best done by making lists of relevant items. The second reason is that because of time pressure, you do not have time to rewrite and revise; therefore your planning at first must be careful and accurate.

Using the methods described in the first five chapters of this book will help you. Listing, clustering and brainstorming, outlining and establishing your thesis—all these can be done quickly and efficiently. Then, using the means of development that are appropriate to the question will usually help you focus even more on what you wish to say. The time you spend in advance of writing the essay exam will be well rewarded in your superior organization and your focused answers.

Mechanics of Presentation

mechanics

When you hand your written work to someone for evaluation, you should do your best to make it as readable as possible. In an important sense this is more than a courtesy. It is a follow-through on one of the basic ingredients of the rhetorical situation: the concern you have for your audience. If your work is being evaluated for publication, then it is essential that you type your work and that you use good quality paper. Not only are the editors who will read your work concerned about its appearance, but so are the printers who might eventually use it to set up type. The editors will examine your work to see if it shows awareness of professional needs. Printers will want to make sure they can read your work easily and accurately.

When your work is handed to an instructor who will evaluate it for a course grade, you can be sure that a good, clear typed paper will help you earn a better grade. There is no question that a hastily prepared handwritten essay will prejudice a reader simply by its appearance. Of course not all instructors will require that you type your essays. I happen to be one who does, and the reason is simple: handwritten essays give me no place to provide editorial comments. They also force me to stop reading at times in order to make out obscure words.

HANDWRITTEN WORK

Choice of Paper

If you are permitted to present your work in handwritten form, use white paper 8½ by 11 inches, with faint blue lines. Never tear your paper from a notebook—it is impossible to work with. You may use paper from a pad, but if you do, write on each page only after it has been taken from the pad, otherwise the indentations from the previous page will be visible beneath your writing. Be certain to number all pages.

Choice of Pen

Use a dark blue or black pen, either ballpoint or fountain pen, and make every effort to keep your handwriting uniform in size and clean in appearance. Aim especially to make all circular letters well rounded and all vertical letters tall and straight. Maintain a left-hand margin of 1½ inches for the comment of your instructor. Do not crowd your page. Some instructors will want you to write on every other line. Ask before beginning your final draft.

pen

Correcting Mistakes

If you make a mistake, correct it with an ink eraser. If your mistake is not correctible in this fashion, then strike a single line through the passage you do not wish to have read. Do not make a large blot to indicate an error. Always write on only one side of the paper.

TYPEWRITTEN WORK

Choice of Paper

First, use white paper 8½ by 11 inches. Its weight should be sixteen or twenty pounds (the box will be labeled). It should not be an erasable paper because the ink smudges on such paper. The minute your instructor begins to write a comment on your work, some of the ink transfers to the instructor's hand, then smudges the rest of the page. Printers will not set up type from such paper for that reason. Never use a colored or toned paper; never use an oddsize paper, including legal size; never use more than one kind of paper in a given essay. Number all pages.

typewriter

Typewriter Ribbon

Your typewriter ribbon should be fresh and dark. This is very important. Some writers think a typewriter ribbon lasts forever, but the fact is that you should change yours to a new one on the first day you begin a course that asks you to write. Ribbons dry out when they are not used, and they wear out as they are used. Yours probably needs replacement right now. Your keys may need cleaning as well, especially if you have a typewriter that is more than a few years old. Use an old toothbrush to clean them.

Typeface

Your typewriter should use standard pica or elite typeface. Do not use a typewriter with script typeface. Those machines are designed for special uses, such as sympathy letters and society notes.

Making Mistakes

If you make a mistake you have several choices. You can use correction fluid—a white fluid that covers your mistake so you can retype over it. Or, you can use whiteout paper to type your mistake over in white, and then go back and type what you intended. Some typewriters are equipped with correction tapes and have a system that can erase errors. They all work well. You also have the option of using an ink eraser. But do not blot out large sections of a page, or strike out lines. Instead, retype the page. In the case of missing letters in a word, it is reasonable to caret-in your corrections without retyping.

COMPUTER-GENERATED WORK

Typeface

computer

You may have access to a personal or college computer. The printed draft you receive may be letter quality, which will look just like regular typewritten work, or it may be dot matrix, which is faster, but much less readable. If you are using a letter quality or laser printer, you simply follow the earlier directions: use a fresh ribbon or make sure the laser printer is crisp and dark. If you use a dot matrix printer, set it on letter quality printing. This is slower, but much more readable. Again, check the ribbon.

If you have a program that permits you to change font (size or style of letter) in the middle of a page or line, be sure not to introduce variety for no reason. Use one font style and size. You may use italics where they are appropriate. If your work needs subheadings, it may be appropriate to use boldface. But it is very important to avoid playing with the printer. The fact that you *can* create a variety of fonts does not mean that you must create them.

Continuous Feed Paper

Use the same kind of paper recommended for typing. Avoid the 132 column green and white paper sometimes available for computers. If you use continuous feed paper, be sure to carefully tear off the sprocket holes on the left and right (or top and bottom) of the paper, and be sure to carefully separate each page before handing it in. Be sure all pages are numbered.

Right Justification

Most computers are set up to justify the right margin. That means the right margin will end up straight (instead of ragged as it would on a typewriter). In other words, the finished product will look like a page in a printed book. I prefer the ragged right look because most computers do not proportionally space the text, and therefore there are many empty spaces in a line, and the line is harder to read. Check with your instructor on this. Depending on your software, I recommend you do not use right justification.

TYPING CONVENTIONS

Cover Sheets: Titles and Your Name

If you use a separate title page, follow the directions provided in the sample paper in Chapter 10, "The Research Paper." Center your title approximately one third down the page. Place your name, the course title and number, and your instructor's name in the lower right-hand corner. Include the date and any other information, such as the number of the particular draft or the assignment number. Your instructor's name should appear because if the paper is lost it will find its way to the instructor much more quickly than it will to you.

A separate title page may not be necessary for some essays. In that case use the uppermost left part of the first page for your name, your instructor's name, the course name, and the date. Begin one inch down from the top, and align this information with the left margin. Center your title below this by one inch.

Keeping a Copy

Always save all your notes, your early drafts, and a clean copy of your final version. Use carbon paper if you type, and run off an extra copy if you use a computer. If these methods are inappropriate, make a photocopy. Papers can be lost. Do not take a chance on that happening to you.

Margins

Your left margin should be one and a half inches wide to allow for commentary. You should leave a one-inch margin on the other three sides of the page. Remember, the margins are useful for comments, and they also open up the page and make it more inviting to read.

Double Spacing

Never hand in a single-spaced essay. You may use single spacing for early drafts if you must, but always hand in your final draft double spaced. The space between each line is useful first because it makes the copy easier to read, but second because it will permit you to make last-minute editorial changes. It also is useful to your reader for making observations or offering responses to what you have said.

Paragraphing

Every paragraph should begin with the first line indented five spaces. If you are using a computer program, your paragraph will be indented automatically and there will also be an extra space between paragraphs. Such a space is acceptable, but not necessary.

Spacing After Punctuation

After a period or other end punctuation, leave two spaces before beginning a new sentence. The new sentence always begins with a capital letter. After a comma, colon, semicolon, closing parenthesis, or bracket, leave one space. When you wish to use a hyphen, leave no space, unless you have reached the end of a line. A dash is two hyphens, with no space before or after it. If you need special symbols that are not on the typewriter or the computer, leave space and add them in ink on the final draft.

Indenting Quotations

If you have a quoted passage that is longer than four lines of prose or three lines of poetry, set them apart from the regular text by indenting them an extra five spaces on each side. Double-space these passages, as you would other copy. Years ago the recommendation was to single-space such passages, but we double-space them now because printers demand all their copy to be double spaced to avoid error. The passage quoted should definitely be double spaced from the main body of text. There should be no single-spaced lines in your final draft.

Pagination: Number Your Pages

Computer-generated work can be paginated automatically. Be sure to set up the pagination so that you can include your last name before the page number so that if pages become separated, your reader can reassemble them. In any event, *do not hand in any work that does not have page numbers clearly in evidence.* On the first page, the number one is centered at the bottom of the page. On subsequent pages, the number appears in the right-hand top corner, one half inch down, two lines above the first line of text. Satisfy yourself with using only a number; avoid adding decorative lines, asterisks, or other such devices.

Corrections After Final Proofreading

Sometimes you will have a final draft that you thought was perfect, but which you realize has a minor error or two. It is acceptable to make a small number of corrections, such as two or three, on a page. If you see letters that are inverted, you may use the editorial invert sign: ∿ in this fashion. If you have left out a letter, use a caret ∧: in this fashion. You may also caret-in short words if they have been omitted. Correct misspellings by writing in the word in ink above the error. Strike a line through the improperly spelled word.

FINAL PRESENTATION

Your paper should have its pages attached, either with a staple or a paper clip. If you wish, and your instructor agrees, you may use a transparent binder or other such device to keep the pages together.

Some instructors want their essays folded down the center lengthwise, with your name and other information on the outside. Check with your instructor on this.

Be sure to present your final draft in the neatest and most professional manner possible. A very important part of rhetoric is making sure that your presentation is the very best it can be. It is equivalent to presenting yourself to your audience. Do not undermine your work by not giving it the dignity it deserves.

INDEX

579